D0850638

**Building
Tomorrow:
The Mobile/
Manufactured
Housing
Industry**

The MIT Press
Cambridge,
Massachusetts,
and London,
England

Building Tomorrow: The Mobile/ Manufactured Housing Industry

Arthur D. Bernhardt

with the
assistance of
Susan A. Camardo
and
Herbert B. Zien

New material © 1980 by
The Massachusetts Institute of Technology

Research forming part of the basis for this
publication was conducted pursuant to a
contract with the Department of Housing
and Urban Development.

This book was set in Monotype Univers
and printed and bound by Halliday
Lithograph Corporation in the United States
of America.

Library of Congress Cataloging in
Publication Data

Bernhardt, Arthur D
Building tomorrow.

  Includes index.
  1. Mobile home industry—United States.
2. Construction industry—United States.
3. Housing—United States.
I. Title.
HD9715.7.U62B47   338.4′7′690810973
    79-19412
ISBN 0-262-02134-X

Contents

Preface

The world needs more, better, and lower-cost shelter. Yet the building industry here and abroad still is not equipped to respond adequately to what has long since grown into a building and housing crisis. The industry's performance is suboptimal: It produces shelter of higher cost and/or lower quality than it potentially can, and it does not supply enough. This problem is exacerbated (and, ironically, in no small part explained) by the fact that too many groups in too many countries have failed in attempts to create a more effective and efficient building industry, and very few people still believe that any significant improvement in performance can be attained.

This performance problem is alarming, for the social and economic significance of the shelter delivery process is great. Socially, shelter is a paramount part of two of our basic institutions, family and community, and an ineffective shelter delivery system can weaken our social structure. Economically, in most countries the building industry accounts for approximately 10 percent of gross national product (in the United States the industry's annual volume approaches $150 billion), and inefficiencies in such a key industry have direct ramifications for any national economy.

Low-cost, high-quality shelter, however, *can* be produced, and output can be increased at the same time. This is what this book demonstrates. It takes the case of one particular shelter industry, the mobile home industry in the United States, and shows that this industry can and does produce low-cost housing without impairing quality. More important, it demonstrates that this ability can be extended beyond generating that industry's current product: The mobile home industry, in collaboration with the traditional building industry, can produce low-cost shelter for high-density, medium- and even high-rise developments, and thus potentially meet most of the entire spectrum of shelter demand. Most significant, this book isolates the mobile home industry's know-how (much of which is still not consciously recognized by the industry) and shows that this know-how can be transferred to and applied by the building industries in any country. Thus, high-volume production of low-cost quality shelter *is* possible.

This conclusion is the exact opposite of what I had expected to find when I first looked at the mobile home industry years ago. Then, sharing with many others in this country a strong bias against the industry, I decided to write a negative case study on how *not* to develop the building industry. One of the first findings of my investigation, however, was startling: The mobile home industry is the most efficient building industry in the world. I then made the serendipitous discovery that many of the determinants of this outstanding efficiency can be

translated into actions that can aid other segments of the American building industry as well as its counterparts abroad to achieve quantum improvements in efficiency. For many years, I have worked in different countries, with corporations, government agencies, and international bodies to explore myriad avenues for improving the shelter delivery process, from devising new technology to shaping private and public policy; however, rarely had I come upon a concept with such dramatic potential for the future of the building sector as isolating and applying the mobile home industry's largely unrecognized know-how.

I thus became convinced of the importance of a thorough examination of this industry, and in 1969 Project Mobile Home Industry (PMHI) was born at the Massachusetts Institute of Technology as part of the Program in Industrialization of the Housing Sector (PIIHS), a national research group under my direction, which I founded to develop policy alternatives for improving the performance of the building and housing industries. In keeping with the broader scope of PIIHS, the major purpose of PMHI was to identify those factors that contributed to the mobile home industry's efficiency, and to determine to what extent its know-how could be transferred and applied to the operations of the other segments of the building industry here and abroad. The staff that I assembled to aid me in this investigation reflects the challenge, complexity, and national scope of PMHI: Members of the project were recruited from all of the various groups at work in or related to the building industry, from all over the country. The result was a team of more than one hundred professionals from industry, business, finance, government, and the military who brought to the project such relevant backgrounds as architecture, computer science, economics, engineering, law, finance, management, planning, political science, and sociology. The group proved not only equal to the task, but also motivated; most volunteered their time and expertise for years because they recognized the enormous potential of applying our findings to the mobile home industry and the larger building sector.

The major finding of PMHI can be summarized easily, although the ramifications are far-reaching. It is my basic philosophy, explained more fully in the introductory chapters of this book, that unless the building industry on its own initiative undertakes strategic restructuring of its own business organization as well as of its supporting, regulatory, and political environments, it will attain no major performance improvements. Since the 1920s, the mobile home industry's continual readjustment of its own organizational structure and its environments has resulted in an optimal business position; even though it has been largely unconscious, it is this expertise, more than any other know-how which we identified, that explains the outstanding economic performance and growth that the industry has achieved. Most important, my initial hypothesis was borne out: The know-how that accounts for the mobile home industry's evolution into the most efficient shelter industry in the world can be applied by any country's building sector with similar effect. We also realized that reliance on private enterprise alone has historically provided the impetus for the mobile home industry, and can continue to do so. Similary, the transfer of the industry's know-how to other building industries should and can be effectively accomplished by private initiative, which is significant at a time when increased government participation in business is beginning to enervate private enterprise in many countries.

PMHI has generated substantial interest over the years, with articles on our research appearing in publications around the world. This international recognition of PMHI as a leading effort in improving the performance of the building sector indicates that people here and abroad realize the impact of our work Our study therefore cannot be dismissed as a theoretical textbook with no relevance to the reality of the building industry. It is written to be *used*, as a practical illustration of how the building industry can attain the highest level of efficiency.

In the years I have spent studying the mobile home industry, many campaigns have been waged to create an image of the industry and its product that does justice to its performance achievements. Just as the industry worked for years to shed the outdated negative image of its product as the "trailer coach" of the 1930s, so has it recently striven to upgrade public perception of the also-maligned "mobile home": the industry now calls itself the "mobile/manufactured housing industry," and prefers to have its product known as "manufactured housing." Although these terms are already widely accepted within the industry proper, it takes time for such new phrases and attendant changes in attitude to filter down to other sectors of the economy as well as to the public at large. Until this new terminology is firmly established, the public and private sectors and the general public will continue to associate the industry and its product with the term "mobile home." Therefore, we use this still-prevalent term throughout this book for ease of identification.

This study was greatly facilitated by the sponsorship of the U.S. Department of Housing and Urban Development (HUD). In fact, the final project report to HUD was the seminal work from which this book, which is both a summary and an expansion of that report, developed. When I approached HUD in 1971 with my request for funding of PMHI, then Secretary George Romney and Assistant Secretary for Research and Technology Harold B. Finger were open-minded in approving an unsolicited proposal for which no specific funds had been allocated; HUD's sponsorship of an exploration of a concept that it had not generated itself reflects credit on the Department. Other research grants for PMHI were provided by M.I.T. and the Alfred P. Sloan Foundation.

This project could not have been completed without the participation of approximately ten thousand private and public firms and organizations that cooperated in our national surveys between 1969 and 1977. I am especially grateful for the mobile home industry's cooperation. My staff and I dealt with people in all segments and on every level of the mobile home industry in all parts of the country, from manufacturers to dealers to park operators, from chief executives to assembly line workers, and I have great regard for these people, who contributed much to this work. I also extend my thanks to many people from the on-site building industry, the manufactured building industry, and the supply and finance sectors; management in thousands of companies across the country gave generously of its time to help us better understand the complex interactions between the mobile home industry and its business environment. I also appreciate the participation of myriad public officials in our efforts to establish the impact of the regulatory environment on the mobile home industry; these people ranged from federal officials, to governors and commissioners in all fifty states, to local government people throughout the country.

The steady growth of PMHI owes much to several of my colleagues at M.I.T.: Professor Albert G. H. Dietz, who first sensed the promise of the endeavor and was instrumental in helping me to obtain major funding; Professor Charles L. Miller, Director of the then Urban Systems Laboratory, who also saw the potential of our approach from the beginning and gave us the seed grant from which the group was able to grow; and Boston's former mayor, Professor John F. Collins, who helped us in isolating the business and political implications of our work. These three men have been unstinting in offering wise advice and judgment as well as active support.

It would be impossible to list by name the many people at M.I.T., from my colleagues on the faculties of several departments to administration officers, who have helped me with this project. Similarly, I can thank only as a group the many students in my various courses on the building industry who over the years have contributed fresh ideas. However, special credit must go to three of my colleagues, all of them at M.I.T.'s School of Architecture and Planning: Dean Lawrence B. Anderson and Professors John T. Howard and Waclaw P. Zalewski. These men recognized the importance of conducting such a real-world investigation in academe, and their interest in and support of my work has never faltered over the years.

This book is not intended as a "how to" study. Rather, it must be used as a guide from which astute and imaginative members of the private and public sectors here and abroad can translate what has been done in the mobile home industry into viable actions that apply to the area of the building industry with which they are concerned. I have attempted to practice what I preach by moving PIIHS into the private sector as a consulting organization; I hope that this transition from research to practice will enable us to use the expertise of the PMHI staff to stimulate the application of this study, which was, after all, my primary objective in writing this book.

This book is a beginning, not a conclusion The housing crisis in this and other countries has been allowed to grow to such proportions that immediate action is imperative. In this book we prove that high-quality, low-cost shelter *can* be produced. It is up to you—the builders, the manufacturers, the government officials—to make sure that it *is* produced. Our responsibility to report the facts is concluded; your responsibility to use them is just beginning.

Arthur D. Bernhardt

Cambridge, Massachusetts
March 15, 1978

Acknowledgments

Susan A. Camardo more than any other person has helped me with this book. There is very little material that she has not been involved with: She wrote several chapters, and co-authored, edited, reviewed, or guided the work on many more. She also undertook the major task of coordinating the efforts of our large and far-flung staff of researchers, editors, and production people. I am also indebted to Herbert B. Zien. In particular, he directed the research on the various finance functions, wrote the chapter on finance as well as the major portion of one of the chapters on cost and price structures, and reviewed several other chapters. It is not possible to reflect adequately the time and talent that these two people have put into this book, and I can only offer them my sincere respect and thanks.

Major work on this project was done by Michael Burrill, Peter H. Greenwood, Jonathan Hale, Paul D. Jetter, Kenneth A. McPherson, Maria Wojtowicz, and Linda S. K. Zack.

The following people have made important contributions to the research and writing of this book: Joseph M. Aspray, Frank H. Benesh, Annette Cafarelli, Thomas R. DiBenedetto, Marc Ferranti, Sarah J. McCarthey, and Norman Y. Quon.

It is impossible to cite here all of the approximately 150 people on the staffs of PMHI and my consulting practice who have worked with me for many years on the research work summarized here. However, individual credit has been given to them in other publications of mine.

In addition to those already mentioned, I also thank the following people who contributed greatly: Susan M. Anderson, Gary A Bergquist, Winston Chiong, Kathleen B. Egan, Charles B. Goldfarb, Heidi M. Neumann, Phyllis Quigley, and John M. Wallach.

Finally, credit must also go to Beth Barnett, Robin C. Camardo, Sheila P. Ferguson, Nancy A. Irwin, and Debra Whitcomb, who helped to produce the manuscript.

Much of the research on which this book is based was conducted pursuant to a contract with the U.S. Department of Housing and Urban Development. The substance of this research is dedicated to the public. The Government Technical Representative to PMHI, Duane T. McGough, Director of the Division of Housing and Community Analysis in HUD's Office of Policy Development and Research, was most helpful, and I appreciate the time and expertise he has given to this project. I am grateful to HUD for its permission to base this book on the research that I conducted under its grant and to use selected material from our five-volume report to HUD (Bernhardt, Arthur D., et. al., *Structure, Operation, Performance and Development Trends of the Mobile Home Industry*, Volumes I through V, Report to HUD, Cambridge, Massachusetts: M.I.T., 1976). PMHI, of course, is responsible for the accuracy of statements in this book.

Only as a group can I thank the many concerns in the building industry and other sectors that have aided us in our research. However, special mention must be made of the following: *Automation in Housing/Systems Building News*; Automotive Credit Service, Inc.; Elrick and Lavidge, Inc.; Manufactured Housing Institute; *Manufactured Housing Dealer* (formerly *Mobile-Modular Housing Dealer*); *Mobile Home Merchandiser*; National Trailer Convoy, Inc.; and the Word Guild.

I am grateful for the help of Jeffrey R. Emig, who gave us information for several chapters, and Herbert W. Behrend, who provided data as well as reviewed copy on park construction.

Finally, I extend my appreciation to The Architects Collaborative Inc. Our projections of the architectural potential of the mobile home industry have been greatly aided by their cooperation.

Arthur D. Bernhardt

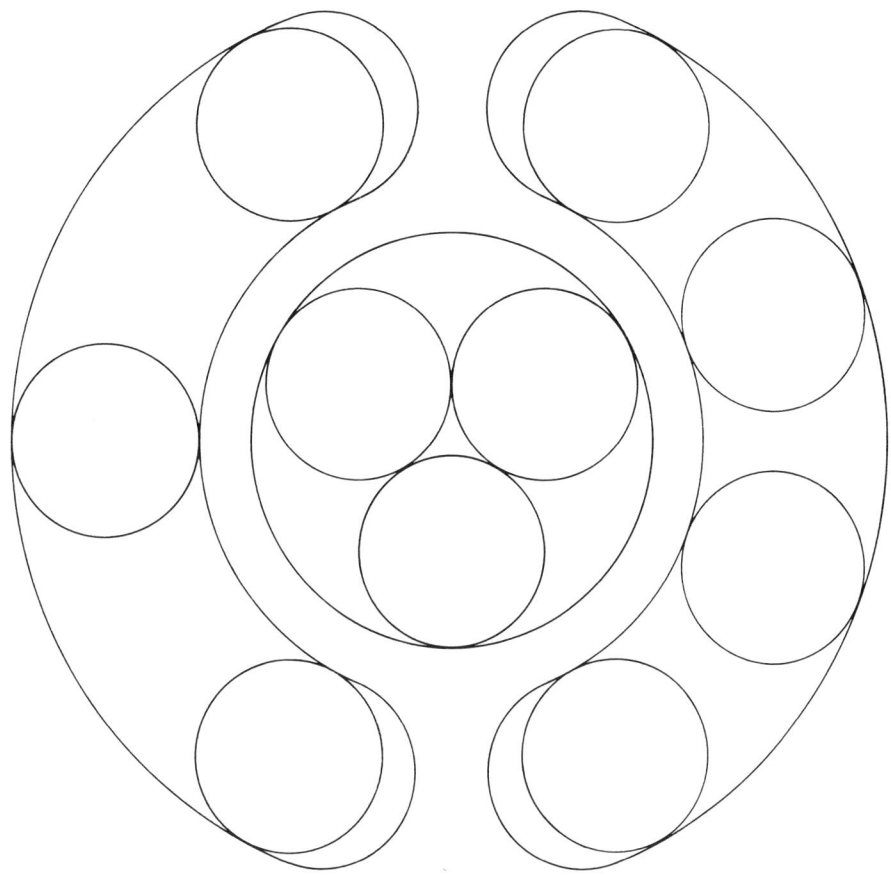

As the housing crisis continues to worsen, many people are asking whether mobile homes might become a viable housing alternative, not only for the United States but for other countries as well. My personal answer is "I hope not!" I have organized these introductory notes to make the case for rephrasing the question so that I will be able to answer in a more optimistic way. I will first discuss what I feel are the basic alternatives for building policy, for it was interest in general building policy that made me study the U.S. mobile home industry. I will then explain how I, with the help of the more than one hundred researchers I assembled at the Massachusetts Institute of Technology, looked at this industry; and I will sketch an overview of the mobile home industry today and tomorrow that reflects my group's perspective. Building upon this background, I will finally urge refocusing the question: mobile homes— a housing alternative? The question instead should be "Can the comprehensive restructuring of its total supporting and regulatory environment that the U.S. mobile home industry vigorously pursued for many decades be applied by this industry as it further matures, as well as by other building industry subsystems in the United States and abroad, to create the conducive business and political climate that is the prerequisite for producing shelter that not only responds to social needs but is truly low cost?"

Chapter 1

A General Strategy for the Development of the Building Sector

Policy Alternatives

We are asking the question "Are mobile homes a viable housing alternative?" because in the United States, as in most countries, the building sector at large is unable to meet the ever more pressing need for larger quantities of higher-quality, lower-cost shelter.

An easy and often politically convenient solution to this problem is a policy of subsidization of either the industry or the consumer. In many countries it has become a long-standing tradition to meet the need for adequate, affordable shelter by paying, through direct or indirect subsidization of the building sector, the difference between the true amount shelter costs to build and the lesser amount the consumer can afford to pay. This subsidization results in the diversion of resources from other chronically underfunded areas of high national priority—such as health, welfare, environmental quality, or education—and must continue as long as there is a need for increased production. Subsidization in this form fails to provide incentives for the sector to improve its responsiveness to the needs and desires of the consuming population or to reduce the cost of production of shelter.

The alternative policy is the much more difficult solution and thus has never been rigorously explored: to meet the need for adequate lower-cost shelter by decreasing the true cost of production. Decreased production costs, when reflected by price reductions, enable consumers to purchase more shelter and may provide a wider variety of forms of shelter within their price range. This second approach not only decreases the need for diversion of resources but also can and should encourage the sector to improve its social and economic performance.

I have long argued for reducing the need for subsidization by encouraging the building sector to increase its social effectiveness and economic efficiency. I firmly believe that in the long run this "more difficult" policy is the only avenue that can be justified in the public and private interest.

The Problem: Shortcomings of Previous Attempts to Improve Performance

Despite the overall merit of previous attempts to improve building sector performance, most initiatives have generally been characterized by one or more of the following six shortcomings:

Housing-oriented efforts have usually been based on a technocratically narrow definition of housing as the individual dwelling unit, as a product, as an isolated artifact, as a furniturelike object. However, the quality of housing is affected not only by the design or performance qualities of the unit itself, but much more by the physical, aesthetic, and social qualities of the larger urban context. Such factors as site design, density, functional and social neighborhood mix, availability and quality of services internal to the neighborhood or accessibility to other services, employment, and recreation are at least as decisive determinants of the quality of housing as those of the individual structure. The dwelling unit, the housing process, the neighborhood, and the community framework are inseparable systems.

The objectives of many efforts have differed substantially. For example, the emphasis in public policy, often designed in response to immediate needs, has frequently shifted abruptly from increasing the production and delivery capacity of the industry to improving cost performance. Within the industry itself, the range of corporate objectives has been more varied and has changed even more often. Because each new objective requires an initial adjustment period, these frequent shifts in emphasis have certainly canceled out any efficiencies that would have accrued had there been better synchronization of objectives at any one point and less frequent shifts over time.

Many initiatives have suffered from inadequate identification and definition of the problem and its complexity. There is no easily identifiable, limited set of obstacles barring the way to better performance. For example, the significance of constraints such as the erratically fluctuating impact of fiscal and monetary policies, the fragmentation of demand, zoning regulations, and alleged restrictive union practices has often been overestimated. The real problem is that the building sector represents a highly political system with tremendous vested interests, too complex and too intimately tied to other sectors for any one group of actors in it—industry, labor, or government—fully to understand or manipulate it.

In terms of problem definition, goal formulation, and policy development, most efforts have been designed on the basis of inadequate information. While our knowledge of even the existing structure, operation, and performance of the building sector is rather poor, our understanding of emerging and possible alternative trends in its development is absolutely inadequate. Almost nothing is known about the potential of and the prerequisite actions for improving present and future performance. This lack of understanding has contributed to the failure or relative ineffectiveness of many past and current efforts.

Most endeavors have not developed and substituted new concepts for old ones. Largely because of unfavorable environmental conditions, all attempts at innovation in the building production and delivery system have had to be confined merely to improvements of the dated concepts underlying the organization and operation of the building sector, without questioning these concepts. This approach leads to underestimation of the degree of potential improvements attainable through substitution of new, more effective concepts. A de-emphasis of positive analysis and a much greater accent on normative analysis is indicated.

Many efforts have been characterized by failure to identify the most appropriate method of attack. Since there is no single best strategy for improving the performance of the sector, a primary reliance and emphasis on only one or a limited number of strategies (be that vertical integration by private initiative or fiscal stimuli from the public sector) will result in only minor improvement. Simultaneous exploration of all opportunities, however, can be expected to result in substantial improvement.

The Solution: Development of the Entire Building Sector

Based on observations of the shortcomings of previous efforts to improve performance and on extensive personal field experience, I believe that the only way to expand the capability of the building industry is to develop the building sector as a whole. This strategy for improving performance extends radically beyond present efforts to manipulate selected functions of the established building process and has not yet been extensively investigated or considered for adoption as corporate or public policy. The strategy amounts to a comprehensive evolutionary development of the entire building sector, entailing essential structural and operational changes in the industry proper and its environment. While this may seem simplistic at first glance, it must be recognized that in most countries no development goals have been set, no reliable understanding of the available or necessary resources has been achieved, and no coherent strategy has ever been supported by the industry, the government, and the consuming public. The strategy I am proposing has four important aspects:

We must develop a reliable understanding of the present and probable future situation of the building sector and of the extent to which emerging trends could be manipulated.

We need a comprehensive and systematic normative analysis of the entire building sector to determine to what extent, at what rate, and in what ways performance could realistically be improved.

We must synthesize the actions necessary for improving performance into a comprehensive course of action for the industry and for government. Such a plan would comprise a large number of coordinated actions in the entire spectrum of promising areas, ranging from efforts to improve production management, financing, marketing, and distribution to increasing the effectiveness of taxation, building code regulation, land use planning, and housing, building, and economic policy. It would be designed to provide an atmosphere that would both stimulate needed new actions and encourage innovation in general. To create such a setting, industry and government must jointly restructure and synchronize the operations and organization of the building industry proper and the supporting and regulatory environments within which it operates.

We must develop and adopt enduring corporate and public policy aimed at long-range planning for and initiation, stimulation, and coordination of the transformation process.

This strategy is not a proposal for revolutionary change but rather for consistent, carefully planned, evolutionary development. The two basic components of this proposed strategy—the comprehensiveness and the national scale of attack—must be implemented in a graduated manner. Since any major restructuring of the industry by definition will significantly stress the response capacity of the various actors and interests within or affiliated with the building industry, only through evolutionary implementation will this strategy succeed.

Chapter 2

Implementing the General Strategy: Project Mobile Home Industry

The strategy I have proposed has been designed to maximize the performance of the entire building sector. The ultimate test will be whether the performance of the sector can be significantly improved through the formulation and implementation of a comprehensive strategy for its development. However, the large size and highly complex nature of the building sector made it necessary to identify a smaller, more manageable, representative segment for an initial implementation of the strategy. The criterion I devised for defining representative segments for analysis is that they be relatively independent (both structurally and operationally) national scale subsystems of the larger building production and delivery system. If the application of the strategy to one such subsystem succeeds and the strategy is refined based on the results of implementation, then a viable model of an approach to the development of other subsystems and the building sector at large will be available.

The three basic subsystems within the U.S. building sector—the on-site building industry, the manufactured building industry, and the mobile home industry—meet this criterion and operate autonomously enough for separate analysis (see chapter 4, note 1, for a detailed discussion of the three subsystems). Since each is an integral component of the total building sector, a separate analysis of any one subsystem must cover interactions and interrelationships with the other two as well as with the supporting and regulatory environments within which it operates.

Of the three subsystems identified, I chose the mobile home industry for three reasons. First, the mobile home industry has the potential to expand significantly its capability to produce low-cost, high-quality shelter, especially in high-density areas. Second, the mobile home industry is presently the most efficient of the three subsystems in terms of economic performance, and a detailed analysis of this exceptional efficiency can have significant implications for improving the performance of both the mobile home industry and other building industries here or abroad. Finally, the mobile home industry is the youngest and least understood of the three subsystems in terms of its structure, operation, performance, and role within the building sector; as such, it deserves priority over the other subsystems for study at this time.

In 1969, I established Project Mobile Home Industry (PMHI) at the Massachusetts Institute of Technology to develop a model approach for the implementation of the general strategy for the mobile home industry. PMHI has since expanded into a national organization with a professional staff of over one hundred persons strategically located in industry, business, finance, government, and academia, across the United States, representing backgrounds including architecture, computer science, economics, engineering, finance, management, law, planning, and political science. Our endeavor first involved comprehensive research that would lay the foundation for action-oriented work—the formulation of policy alternatives for industry and government.

The initial stages of the project, based on new national fieldwork, entailed a comprehensive analysis and evaluation of the present state and emerging trends of the mobile home industry as well as its environments. To build a viable basis for the research stages, we devoted several years to assembling a broad body of primary data by surveying approximately ten thousand private and public entities and to developing firsthand experience by working in the field as well as recruiting people directly from industry, business, and government. Our methodology, although outlined here in terms of PMHI, is relevant to the application of the general strategy to any building industry. It represents a radical departure from existing studies, which generally concentrate on specific, limited areas of consideration within the industry. We emphasized the discovery of fundamental interrelationships within the industry and its environment and their impact on performance. Our research design was intended to make as broad as possible the identification of areas that potentially influence performance. Rather than assuming that some areas have marginal effects, we included all. Only when analysis indicated that areas of possible importance were merely peripheral were they discarded. If additional areas of importance were uncovered in the course of data analysis, the project scope was expanded. Thus the study was not limited by initial working assumptions about either the scope of the industry or the areas that influence performance but rather remained flexible in terms of investigation of new areas.

Within our study of the mobile home industry, we used our data base and our staff's aggregate experience to conduct a national analysis of the following three areas:

1. The mobile home industry: We examined the present state and developing trends in the structure and operation of the industry, including its role within the building sector and the economy. This focused on existing and emerging structural and operational factors that are decisive in determining the present and probable future performance of the industry at large as well as of the individual firm.

2. The industry's supporting environment: We looked at the present state and developing changes in the supporting environment of the industry and identified the influence of materials supply, labor supply, land supply, and finance on the social-economic performance of the industry.

3. The industry's regulatory environment: We analyzed the present state and emerging trends in the regulatory and institutional environment of the industry, concentrating on factors likely to influence the industry's production and delivery performance such as land use controls, taxation, and building code regulation.

We confined the examination of the mobile home industry to analysis of the production and delivery of shelter and excluded study of demand characteristics. Improving industry performance implies developing industry capability to respond to a wide range of demand for shelter that may arise rather than to one specific form of demand as predictable at a given point in time. Whatever data on demand may be needed can more efficiently be obtained from groups specializing in the study of demand.

This book represents both the results of analysis of the industry and the critical point of transition from research to the formulation of policy alternatives. As such, it has several important implications. The comprehensive scope of our project as a model approach can indicate the breadth and detail of analysis that we believe necessary for any application of my strategy to improve the performance of any building industry. Furthermore, the comprehensive industry study summarized in this book, which is based on extensive new field research, can provide an important information base for the public and private sectors. The industry's efficiency should serve to redirect the thinking and efforts regarding the mobile home industry's potential. Also, the efficiency the industry presently achieves in many phases of the production and delivery process is in great part transferable to other subsystems of building industries here or in other countries.

Since this analysis was primarily designed to be the initial step toward the formulation of alternative development strategies for improving industry performance, we used our results to identify specific and realistic key potentials for the industry so that viable policy alternatives for achieving them could be devised. This required and led to increased participation by industry and government. The later stages of our project involved normative analysis of the industry to determine in what ways, to what extent, and at what rate the industry could improve its performance. The actions found necessary for improving performance are suggested as policy alternatives for the industry's long-range development.

PMHI moved toward encouraging change in an entire national industry as much as I felt justifiable for a group based in academe. We have suggested alternative futures for the mobile home industry. The next step must be undertaken by the industry itself. It is the industry that must decide for one specific development alternative and then must initiate and sustain the move toward the future it will select. We can offer only an outline of how the industry could adopt the general strategy in pursuit of its further development. Once one of the basic policy alternatives has been selected by the major interests involved, the policy must be translated into a viable, long-range national strategy.

Specific outcomes of a development effort spearheaded by the mobile home industry as based upon the strategy might include the following:

1. A national plan of action would provide a climate in which the mobile home industry could initiate and undertake broad-based innovations in its structure and operations in collaboration with, as well as producing benefits for, the other subsystems of the building industry.

Figure 2.1.
Potential product
capabilities of
the mobile home
industry: An example.

2. Individual plans of action would modify the national plan and be designed with and for consumer organizations, labor, individual firms, trade associations, and local, state, and federal agencies. These individual plans would also include provisions for incentives and suggestions for forming effective coalitions. The plans would be developed with and for other segments of the building industry as well as the mobile home industry.

3. Pilot project plans would field test the policy recommendations and be implemented jointly by the private and public sectors. These projects might be oriented toward either new products or new processes and should feature significant innovations that would enable them to serve as demonstration projects with substantial impact.

Our work provides a model of an application of my strategy. Many of the individual measures developed to improve the mobile home industry's performance are applicable to other building industries. Most important, the basic methodology designed and tested here is transferable to other programs to improve the performance of building industries in other countries as well as other subsystems of the building sector in this country.

When compared to other systems of the building sector, the most notable feature of the mobile home industry is the separation of its three functional systems: manufacturing, distribution, and park development and operation. While most firms in the mobile home industry specialize in only one of these tasks, these functional systems are clearly interdependent: The success of one relates directly to the success of the others. For example, the availability of park space determines the number of mobile home units produced and sold, which in turn affects the overall growth and performance of the industry. That common goals exist for all three systems is also evidenced by the industry's approach to the development of supporting industries and the restructuring of its regulatory environment. On the basis of the industry's common goals and its pattern of development, we define the mobile home industry to include the entire complex of functional systems for manufacturing, distribution, and site location.

Although the industry's product must meet the full range of human expectations, officially the industry rather dryly defines a mobile home as a structure, transportable in one or more sections. A singlewide, or single-section mobile home (figure 3.1), usually is 14 feet or more in width and up to 70 or 85 feet in length, built on a permanent chassis and designed to be used as a dwelling with or without a permanent foundation when connected to the required utilities. It includes plumbing, heating, air conditioning, and electrical systems. A doublewide or triplewide (also called multi-section) mobile home (figure 3.2) consists of two or more sections combined horizontally at the site. A modular home is almost identical to the doublewide except that it is designed to be situated on a permanent foundation.

Mobile homes are built to the Federal Mobile Home Construction and Safety Standards, while modular units are engineered to conform to state factory-built housing codes. Most new mobile homes are sold fully equipped; major appliances, furniture, draperies, lamps, and carpeting are all included in the purchase price. Such optional features as air conditioning, automatic dishwashers, automatic garbage disposals, trash compactors, and central vacuuming systems are also available. The home is centrally heated by gas, oil, or electric furnace.

The "product" of the mobile home industry is housing, which is not just a physical artifact. Housing includes not only the dwelling unit as produced by the production system but also its service and maintenance as provided by the distribution system and the physical and community framework and the services provided by the mobile home park system. In this overview of the mobile home industry, we will discuss the organization and operation of its three functional systems and the interactions between the industry and its supporting and regulatory environments.

**A. An Overview
of the Mobile
Home Industry,
Its Supporting
Environment and
Its Regulatory
Environment**

The Industry

The structure of an industry can be determined by gauging the control that individual participating firms exercise over the industry's product market. If industry cost schedules permit, firms can increase their control over or their independence from market forces in three ways: by controlling a large proportion of the industry activities in which they are presently participating (concentration); by expanding into other phases of the production and delivery process (integration); and by establishing interests in areas outside the industry, thus increasing total resources while decreasing dependence on the industry (diversification). By measuring these factors, it is possible to identify areas in which several firms exercise extensive market control and areas where competition is more intensive.

Figure 3.3 depicts some important elements of the structure of the mobile home industry. Concentration is indicated by circle size, integration, by connector size, and diversification, by the size of the shaded circle extensions. The

Figure 3.1.
A singlewide (or single-section) home.

Figure 3.2.
A doublewide (or multi-section) home.

Figure 3.3.
Relative degrees of concentration, integration, and diversification in the mobile home industry.

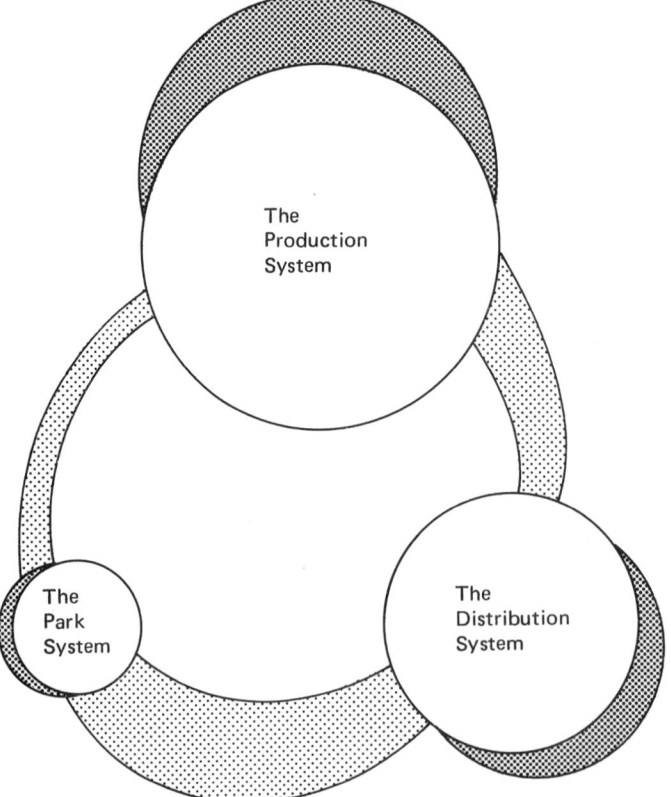

The Production System

The Park System

The Distribution System

five largest mobile home manufacturers (out of approximately two hundred fifty) account for approximately one-third of the total unit shipments, the ten largest, for almost one-half of unit shipments, and the top twenty-five, for close to two-thirds. Thus the production system is quite concentrated. Although entry into the system is still easy, signs point to more concentration in the future. The level of concentration in the distribution system is much lower. Less than 30 percent of the more than ten thousand dealerships are controlled by chains, although single-lot dealerships have considerable control in some markets. Concentration in the park system is slight; few park owners control more than one of the twenty-four thousand mobile home parks.

Most industry manufacturers have not integrated extensively. About 25 percent of all manufacturers have interests in park developments, dealerships, or both; 12 percent have interests in the production of mobile home components. About 30 percent of all dealers are involved in park development, about 60 percent in park operation, and roughly 15 percent in consumer financing. Similarly, about 30 percent of all park owners are involved in dealer operation or park development. About one-third of all mobile home manufacturers have diversified into other building-related industries, and dealers have also moved into this area. However, the most popular area of diversification is the sale of recreational vehicles (about 25 percent of all dealers). Park owners have not diversified into any particular field to a large extent. On-site construction firms have found the mobile home industry an attractive area for diversification and have interests in all phases of the production and delivery process.

The Production System

The first agent in the mobile home production and delivery process is the mobile home manufacturer, who converts the basic real resource inputs of materials and labor into the mobile home unit. The manufacturer's function includes procurement of raw materials and components, the production of the mobile home unit, and its sale to the mobile home dealer. The manufacturer purchases raw materials and components from suppliers who produce products tailored to the specific needs of the mobile home industry. In recent years, as manufacturers have begun to rely increasingly on suppliers for their components, the supply sector has become a still more important element of the mobile home industry's supporting environment.

Mobile home components are brought together on an assembly line, where the major subassemblies—chassis, floor, walls, roof, and internal fixtures—are joined together. Subassemblies are produced at stations off the main assembly line, where mechanized equipment, which would interfere with assembly line operations, can be employed. In general, the production process is not highly mechanized. Manufacturers rely upon unskilled or semiskilled labor to adjust production rates to seasonal fluctuations in demand. Production efficiency is optimized by careful production flow planning and sophisticated material-handling techniques. The finished mobile home unit, delivered by the manufacturer to the dealer, is the first and basic element of the total housing service provided by the mobile home industry.

The Distribution System

The mobile home dealer is the coordinating agent in the production and delivery process, handling those functions associated with unit distribution, marketing, and sale. This distribution system separates and protects the highly centralized production function from the fragmented, localized functions of marketing, consumer financing, and land development; it allows the manufacturer to emphasize production while the dealer copes with the complex tangle of local markets, regulations, and politics. Mobile home dealers usually purchase their units from several producers, considering the working arrangements that can be established, the quality of the units offered, and the variety of models available. Although franchise agreements between manufacturers and dealers are increasingly more popular, most dealers establish such agreements with several manufacturers.

A mobile home dealer's lot, commonly located on a "trailer row" near several other dealerships, displays a wide variety of units. In addition to selling new and used mobile homes, most dealers offer accessories and some dealers sell recreational vehicles or modular housing on the same lot.

Dealers must be aware of the supporting and regulatory environments that affect their operations. As the primary source of information for most buyers, the dealer must be familiar with park space availability, credit terms, land use controls, and taxation policies. The dealer customarily arranges to transport the purchased unit to its site and handles on-site setup and installation, during which the unit is set in place, blocked, leveled, and connected to the utilities. The mobile home dealer provides a second critical element of the total housing service produced by the mobile home industry in the role of coordinating agent.

The Park System

Nearly half of all mobile home units are located in mobile home parks and this percentage is growing. Thus the park developer or operator is the important final agent in the production and delivery process. The park operator provides the owner with site, foundation, needed facilities, community framework, and services. In most cases the park operator rents the site to a mobile home owner; in some cases the consumer will buy the entire park site-mobile home package from a subdivision developer.

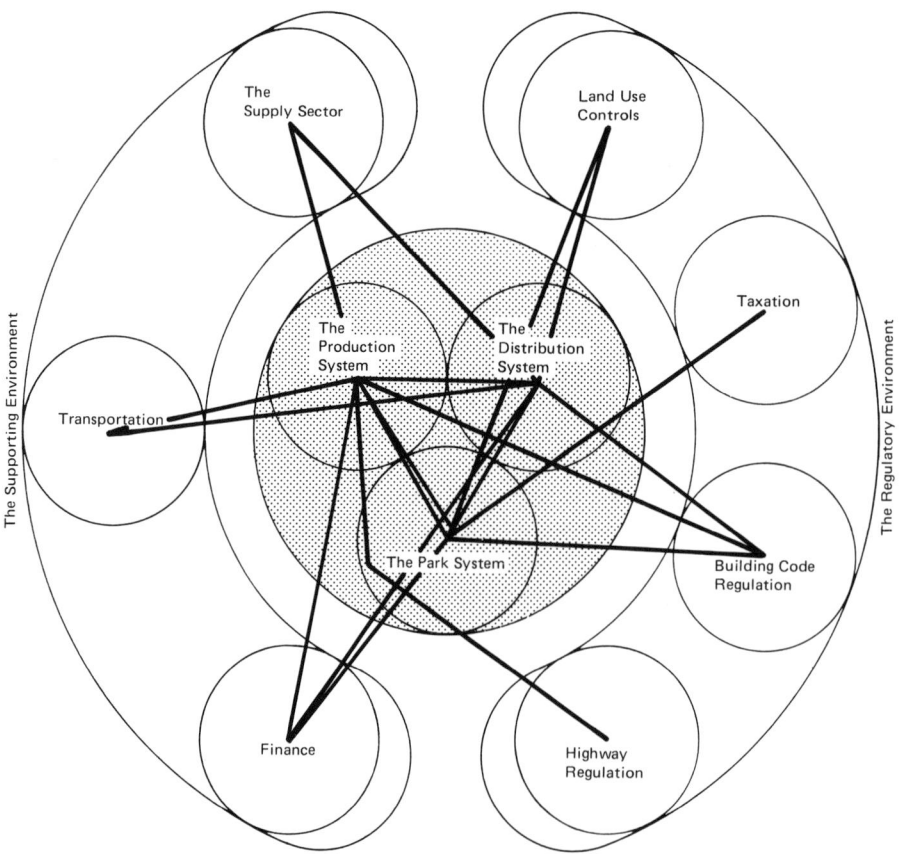

Figure 3.4.
Interactions within and among the mobile home industry and its environments from the standpoint of the industry and its subsystems.

The number and capacity of mobile home parks have historically been grossly inadequate to provide a market of sufficient size for the rapidly expanding production system. Recognizing this problem, the Manufactured Housing Institute (MHI) started a major drive in the late 1940s to create the indispensable market—the park system—to serve as an adequate companion to the production and distribution systems. The association worked vigorously to promote investments in park development and to revise discriminatory zoning practices. Without this sustained effort at building its own market, the mobile home industry would probably not exist. Today the mobile home park system is growing rapidly, having evolved into a nationwide system of significant economic proportions.

Two basic patterns of mobile home park management accompany the most common park types. The owner-manager, who runs the park as a livelihood, is usually associated with older, smaller parks. Such parks are often managed by a husband-wife team with no prior experience in park management. A full-time manager usually runs the newer parks for an absentee owner. Managers of smaller parks are often park residents with no prior experience who receive payment for their services in the form of rent on a space; large parks are usually managed by salaried professional managers.

The park developer must make sure that local building codes and land use regulations, including zoning, are not violated. The manager screens prospective tenants, ensures compliance with park regulations, and maintains public areas and community facilities as well as the overall appearance of the park. The physical, social, and community framework, as well as the continuous maintenance services offered by the park developer and manager, are the final elements of the total housing service provided by the mobile home industry.

The Supporting Environment

Because many mobile home manufacturers have entered the industry from mass production-oriented industries, the mobile home industry has always recognized the importance of synchronizing its operations with those of its supporting industries. Thus in the 1940s the mobile home industry embarked on a long-range systematic effort to restructure or further develop its larger supporting environment. Important areas of such development have been the industry's supply sector, the transportation system, and the financial sector.

The Supply Sector

The mobile home industry and its suppliers form a functional partnership in which responsibilities are well coordinated. It is important to note the degree to which responsibilities are delegated to the supply sector and the superior coordination that makes this possible. Suppliers, for example, perform much of the research and development, provide the bulk of warehousing and inventory maintenance, provide technical training and support, and even perform some advertising. Another essential support function of the supply sector is the widespread extension of trade credit to manufacturers. Suppliers generally allow manufacturers credit for several months, while manufacturers demand cash on delivery from dealers. The efficiency of the mobile home production system is due in large part to the willingness of suppliers to undertake these responsibilities and their ability to execute them.

Manufacturers turn over their inventories very rapidly; they hold little inventory and rely on suppliers to perform the primary inventory function. Each manufacturer will have many suppliers and many of these will have inventory responsibility. The manufacturers' strategy is viable only if each supplier is dependable and offers frequent delivery. Specialized firms have developed to perform these functions for those suppliers who cannot do so themselves.

Through the efforts of suppliers, manufacturers have been able to concentrate their energies and resources on the production of mobile homes.

The accomplishmenls of the mobile home industry should be attributed in large measure to the early recognition by suppliers of the industry's potential. It would be equally fair to criticize suppliers for contributing to the inadequacies of the industry. The responsibility is joint. Slightly more than half of the suppliers' products are tailored to the specific requirements of the mobile home industry. Suppliers and manufacturers have worked jointly to coordinate dimensions. Moreover, almost half of the suppliers have research and development programs oriented to the mobile home industry. The fruits of these efforts are better-quality and lower-cost housing.

The Transportation System

The transportation system serves as the vital link connecting the mobile home manufacturer with the dealer and the dealer with the consumer. The network of dealerships associated with a manufacturing plant may reach a radius of one thousand miles. Because long-distance transportation of bulky products like entire dwelling units is both difficult and expensive for an individual firm to accomplish, the mobile home industry has stimulated the development of a separate national industry specializing in such transportation, which has become an integral component of the larger production and delivery system.

The availability of a national system of commercial carriers is an important option for manufacturers and makes entry and operation easier, especially for smaller firms. Uneconomical empty back hauls are also eliminated because a new load can be picked up by the carrier near the destination of the first haul. Unlike the mobile home industry, the modular housing industry has not yet developed an equivalent commercial carrier capability and the diseconomies of

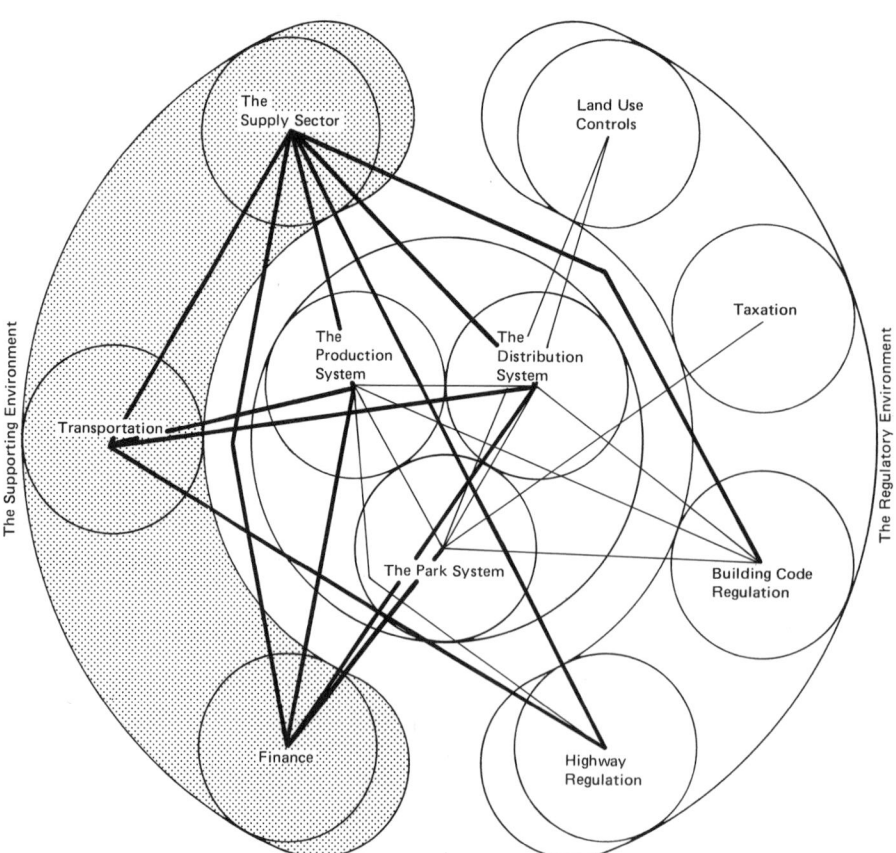

Figure 3.5.
Interactions within and among the mobile home industry and its environments from the standpoint of the supporting environment.

the return trip pose a substantial problem. Comsumers who want to relocate their homes also turn to commercial carriers (although, once moved from factory to home site, less than 3 percent of all units are ever moved again).

The Financial Sector

Because the "new" mobile home industry was orginally perceived as an unreasonable risk by the financial community, financing was hard to obtain. It took many years to convince the financial sector that investment in the industry was not only a sound but often an attractive move. The supply sector has traditionally been the key financier for the manufacturer, with financing usually taking the form of trade credit. Combined with the manufacturer's policies of production-to-order and cash-on-delivery to the dealer, trade credit gives the mobile home manufacturer relatively high liquid and working capital ratios.

The mobile home industry has had to develop new sources and instruments for dealer and consumer financing. In the late 1940s and the 1950s, the MHI waged a successful campaign to persuade the financial sector to provide low-interest floor plan financing to dealerships. Financial institutions often offer relatively low-yield floor plan loans to gain access to the lucrative mobile home consumer finance market. Retail purchases of mobile homes are still financed primarily with short maturity, high-interest, add-on loans. In the 1960s, another effort by the MHI successfully stimulated federal government agencies to ensure or guarantee loans for retail purchases.

Mobile home parks have some financial advantages over conventional real estate developments: They require less capital; a larger percentage of the mobile home park investment is dedicated to the purchase of land that will appreciate over time; a mobile home park can be removed after ten or fifteen years if the land becomes valuable enough to support a conventional development.

Despite these advantages, mobile home park developers have been slow to attract funds. This is due in part to the "trailer camp" image of most parks. The combination of this poor image and the belief that mobile home park occupants do not carry a fair share of the local tax burden have led to stringent local zoning ordinances against such developments. Financial institutions, not wishing to arouse the ire of local citizenry, have avoided mobile home park loans. This has resulted in an undercapitalization of many parks that have been built, thereby creating a condition that supports the trailer camp image. However, this chain of events leading from undercapitalization to low-quality parks has recently begun to weaken. There is evidence that the financial community is changing its attitude toward mobile home parks. As mobile homes continue to have an increasing impact on the housing market and lenders become more familiar with the advantages of mobile home park financing, sophisticated approaches to financing are becoming more common. Consumer demand for low-cost housing combined with lender desire for efficient utilization of funds will lead to a nationwide expansion of the favorable lending climate that is now available for park development in such states as California, Arizona, and Florida.

The Regulatory Environment

The mobile home industry has been significantly influenced by government regulation. The industry was able to develop only through concerted efforts to integrate its production, distribution, and park systems with its regulatory environment on a national scale. As early as the 1940s, the industry had begun to take strategic actions related to public regulation; it has worked continuously since then to identify regulatory patterns conducive to its growth, to adapt its organization and operation accordingly, and to achieve structural changes in its regulatory environment by tactical lobbying at the state and federal levels whenever legal obstacles to growth became evident.

By identifying supportive patterns of public regulation, the mobile home industry has tactically exploited the vehicular definition of its product, which "exempted" the industry's product from real property taxation or, more importantly, protected the industry from many restrictive controls operative in the housing market. For example, because operating in this legal vacuum enabled the industry to avoid traditional building codes and labor opposition, it could standardize production nationwide as well as employ mass production techniques and semi- or unskilled factory labor. This tactic of operating outside the traditional control system could only succeed because the industry designed its entire production and delivery system, including the mobile home unit itself, to support this approach. On the other hand, the industry attempted strategic restructuring of public regulation whenever it could not beneficially adapt its own system. Prime areas of such restructuring have been land use controls, building code regulation, and highway regulation.

Land Use Controls

The initial reaction of most communities to mobile homes was negative: The homes were either prohibited or forced into undesirable areas through zoning regulations. Although the industry's product has changed dramatically over the years, most land use controls have similar effects today. Some communities completely exclude mobile homes; most others place severe restrictions on their location. Complete exclusion of mobile homes is nonexistent in some states but a common practice in others, with up to 95 percent of the municipalities being off limits. States with a higher population density generally have a greater amount of exclusion. States with a fee or license system of taxation restrict mobile homes to nonresidential areas in 8 percent to 18 percent

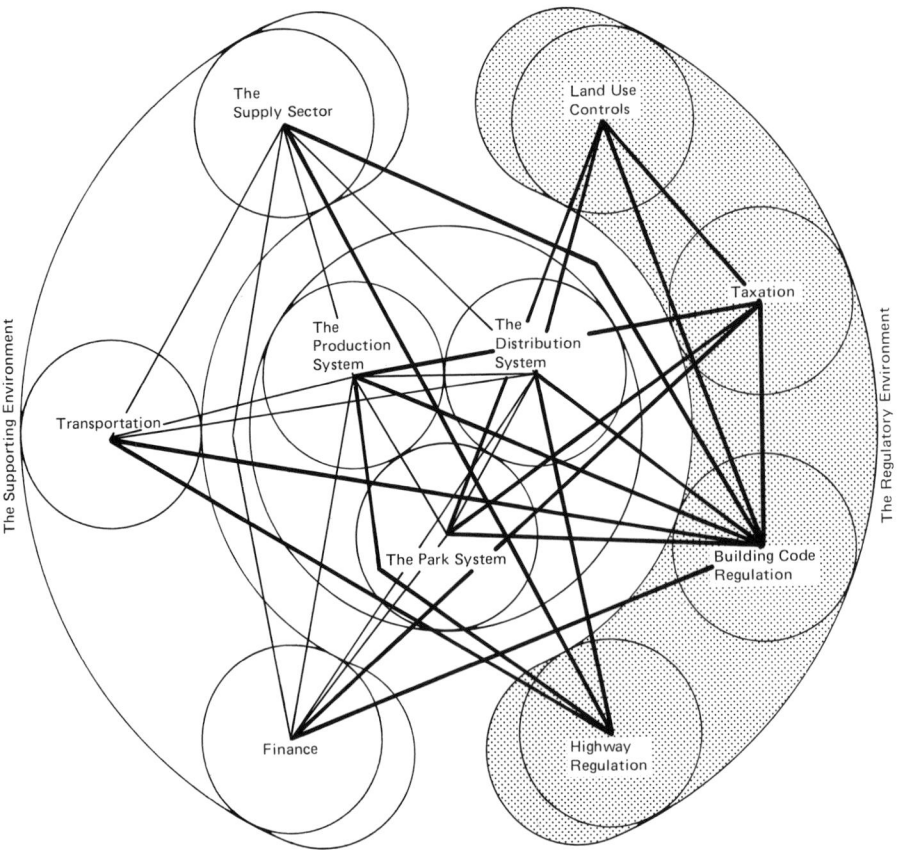

Figure 3.6.
Interactions within and among the mobile home industry and its environments from the standpoint of the regulatory environment.

more of their municipalities than states with a real estate or personal property system. Suburban areas are more restrictive than urban or rural areas.

Restrictive zoning limits the supply of land available for the placement of mobile homes, which has posed a major problem for the industry. Now, however, zoning is becoming much less discriminatory and restrictive in most states, partly as a result of the industry's effort over the last three decades to encourage more liberal patterns of land use control. The process of change has been slow because every municipality in the country has its own land use regulations, and the efforts must therefore extend to every local planning official in the country.

Taxation

By viewing mobile homes as personalty rather than realty, the industry has avoided the imposition of local building codes. On the other hand, the mobile home owner has thereby been denied tax exemptions and deductions associated with the realty tax. The personalty characterization has usually led to lower direct taxes on mobile homes, but it has made the homes subject to attachment and forced sales. How mobile homes are taxed helps determine a community's overall view of them. In this light, differential tax treatment reinforces negative attitudes toward mobile homes, which leads to discrimination and community exclusion. Even if taxes play a minor role in the decision to exclude mobile homes, local officials are likely to defend exclusionary policies by arguing that mobile home owners do not pay their fair share of taxes.

In recent years, as mobile homes have become less distinguishable from conventional housing, there has been a movement toward realty taxation. Approximately 60 percent of the entire mobile home unit inventory in the United States is already subject to real property taxation. The restriction of mobile homes to nonresidential areas is directly linked to a particular state's method of taxation. States with a fee system more frequently restrict homes to parks and nonresidential areas than do states with a property tax. Though the realty tax will in the long run benefit both the mobile home owner and the industry at large, the mobile home industry has not pushed its adoption. The industry must encourage this trend, for when mobile homes are taxed like other housing, restrictive zoning attitudes will ease. If the regulatory environment is fully to integrate with and support the development of the mobile home industry, taxation must undergo careful restructuring on a national scale.

Building Code Regulation

The development and ultimate federal government adoption of a national performance-type building code was an important advancement for the mobile home industry. Building code restrictions had previously been used to exclude mobile homes from many areas. The centralization of operations and quality control systems, hitherto site-oriented operations, automatically makes obsolete established local control systems. This is particularly true in the case of complex assemblies like mobile homes, which conceal most of their components and subassemblies from local inspection. In response to this problem, the MHI initiated a long-term program of self-regulation during the 1950s to develop a national performance-type building code. The basic tactic was to enlist the cooperation of respected, impartial national institutions, such as the American National Standards Institute (ANSI).

In 1969, "ANSI Standard A 119.1 for Mobile Homes—Body and Frame Design and Construction: Installation of Plumbing, Heating and Electrical Systems" was published. By the mid-1970s this nationwide performance-type building code for the mobile home industry was already adopted by forty-six states and preempted thousands of different local codes. This code now forms the basis of the new Federal Mobile Home Construction and Safety

Standards, which at last provide the industry with a uniform national performance code, an advantage that no other subsystem of the building industry enjoys.

Highway Regulation

One of the early obstacles confronting the mobile home industry was highway regulation, which originally limited the width of the mobile home to 8 feet. Because this limitation made it impossible to design housing competitive with the products of the traditional housing industry, the mobile home industry's national and state associations lobbied continuously to change highway safety laws to permit wider loads. Through the years legislation has been passed to allow transport by permit of first 10-foot-wide units, then 12-foot, 14-foot, and in a few states 16-foot-wide units. In addition to dimension limitations, state regulation on mobile home highway movement takes two major forms: permit requirements and traffic regulations specific to oversized vehicles. Problems still exist in both areas, and the industry's efforts are now focused on their resolution.

Since nearly all mobile homes exceed the maximum width dimensions (ranging from 8 to $8\frac{1}{2}$ feet in all but one state), transporters must obtain permits to move these "oversized" loads. Single-trip permits, which usually cost $5 to $10, are available from every state. Each permit may be used only once and large manufacturers must obtain many of them each year. A more feasible practice is the extended permit, available in twenty-four states, which allows movement of all mobile homes under a single permit for periods of up to one year.

In addition to the usual traffic regulations, mobile home transporters must comply with specific rules for oversized loads, which differ from state to state. These regulations include requirements governing extra equipment, safety equipment, travel time, and escorts. Some routes may be restricted or prohibited altogether. Clearly, the mobile home industry must stimulate significant further restructuring of highway regulation to attain greater interstate uniformity as well as more cost-effective highway safety laws.

B. The Industry Tomorrow

The Performance Record of the Industry

The mobile home industry has grown considerably. Its production, distribution, and park systems have come to provide a comprehensive housing service at a higher level of efficiency than those achieved by other subsystems of the building sector (the on-site building industry and the manufactured building industry). During the last fifteen years the mobile home production system's annual output in terms of unit shipments has increased by approximately 500 percent, reaching a peak level of about six hundred thousand units in 1972. This large production volume has been achieved with total labor costs of often less than 8 percent of the FOB factory price, approximately one-third of the equivalent labor costs required in traditional home building. That efficiency is reflected in total FOB factory costs of $8 to $10 per square foot. Equally significant is the fact that, compared with the 1950s, per-square-foot costs have declined slightly while the product has been much improved. The equivalent per-square-foot costs for on-site home building are often two or even three times as high. It is understandable, then, that the industry is the only producer of low-cost housing on a first-cost basis, having virtually captured the under-$30,000 new single-family house market. The mobile home inventory as a share of total housing stock continues to grow.

The mobile home distribution system has experienced a comparable rate of growth; its annual retail sales volume is approaching $5 billion, up from only $500 million in the mid-1950s.

The finished mobile home unit, once in place on a park site and exclusive of foundation, represents a labor consumption of only one hundred fifty to two hundred fifty man-hours per 1000 square feet of net floor area, as opposed to at least three hundred fifty man-hours for the manufactured building industry and from seven hundred to one thousand or more man-hours for the on-site building industry. The high level of efficiency that extends throughout the mobile home industry is reflected in the continuing expansion of its park system, which today supports over 1.6 million mobile homes nationwide.

The outstanding performance achievements of the mobile home industry have been the result of continuous industry efforts to develop a fully coordinated national network of production, distribution, and land development systems that is integrated with its supporting and regulatory environments. The consistency, comprehensiveness, and logic of these efforts and the resulting performance achievements of the industry lend significant support to my general strategy—a comprehensive, evolutionary development of the entire building sector and its social-economic-political environment.

Barriers to Further Development

Although the record of industry achievements is impressive in absolute terms, the industry's present performance appears to reflect only a fraction of its potential. Substantial problems still inhibit its growth and development. The structure of the industry is still immature, research and development intensity is very low, and many firms are seriously undercapitalized. Marketing is relatively undeveloped, the effectiveness of the distribution system needs substantial improvement, and the interest costs of the present system of retail financing are excessively high. Public regulation of mobile homes still represents a significant obstacle. The system of taxing the mobile home as personalty is obsolete, and mobile home park zoning is still highly discriminatory, if not exclusionary.

Future Potentials

The challenge for the industry is greater than merely working toward elimination of growth barriers. The industry can evolve into an entirely different and more effective new industry.

The present product of the mobile home industry does not reflect the basic and inherent product capabilities of the industry. Rather, it is the accidental result of the industry's historical evolution and of the influence of public regulation. The nature of the industry's present product provides no indication of what the product of tomorrow will or can be. This summarizes one of our first findings, which is of overriding importance and has far-reaching ramifications: Since today's mobile home provides few clues to the nature of the industry's future product, it can be implied that the industry's present situation indicates little about its future organization and markets.

What product, then, can the industry produce tomorrow? There are clues in three of our findings. First, the industry can effectively utilize materials other than wood—steel, aluminum, plastics, and even concrete. With these substitutions the industry can produce high-rise shelter that requires greater strength and fire resistance. Second, the industry can substitute alternative materials without jeopardizing its production efficiency and cost performance. Thus the industry can produce the full range of housing types available today in conventional markets, equaling or excelling them in design quality, function, and especially cost performance. Third, the mobile home industry shows an outstanding record of continual innovation and flexibility in its operation. This means that not only does the industry have the technological capacity for new products, but it also has the resourcefulness and vigor to exploit these latent alternative product capabilities.

What product will the industry offer tomorrow? The three observations above suggest that the industry can easily develop into a resource for low-cost shelter serving the entire spectrum of needs—from low-density, single-family detached housing and nonresidential structures to high-density, multi-family residential and nonresidential environments.

The results of our work clearly indicate that the industry can achieve the objectives of producing more and much better shelter at a lower unit cost, especially for the urban market. However, to accomplish these goals, the industry must overcome barriers to development through further changes in its industrial organization and social-economic-political environment. Such future development would have to be at least as comprehensive as that exhibited in the industry's past; this observation lends further support to the general strategy I have been advocating for so long.

I am moving back full circle to the question implied all along: "mobile homes—a housing alternative?" Based on the preceding discussion, I suggest changing this question. I propose to ask "Can the general strategy I proposed be implemented with benefit by the mobile home industry as well as other building industries here and abroad? Can higher-quality, lower-cost shelter be produced in adequate volume?" And to that question I respond with an enthusiastic "Yes!"

Let me, however, repeat my warning. The building sector tomorrow will only reach the potentials I have alluded to if industry and government join in "rebuilding" the building industry as well as the industry's supporting and regulatory environments.

Figure 3.7.
Potential product capabilities of the mobile home industry, example: Low-cost, low- to medium-density urban housing environment.

Figure 3.8.
Potential product capabilities of the mobile home industry, example: Low-cost, medium- to high-density urban housing environment.

Figure 3.9.
Potential product capabilities of the mobile home industry, example: Low-cost, high-density urban housing environment.

Part 1

The Mobile Home Production System

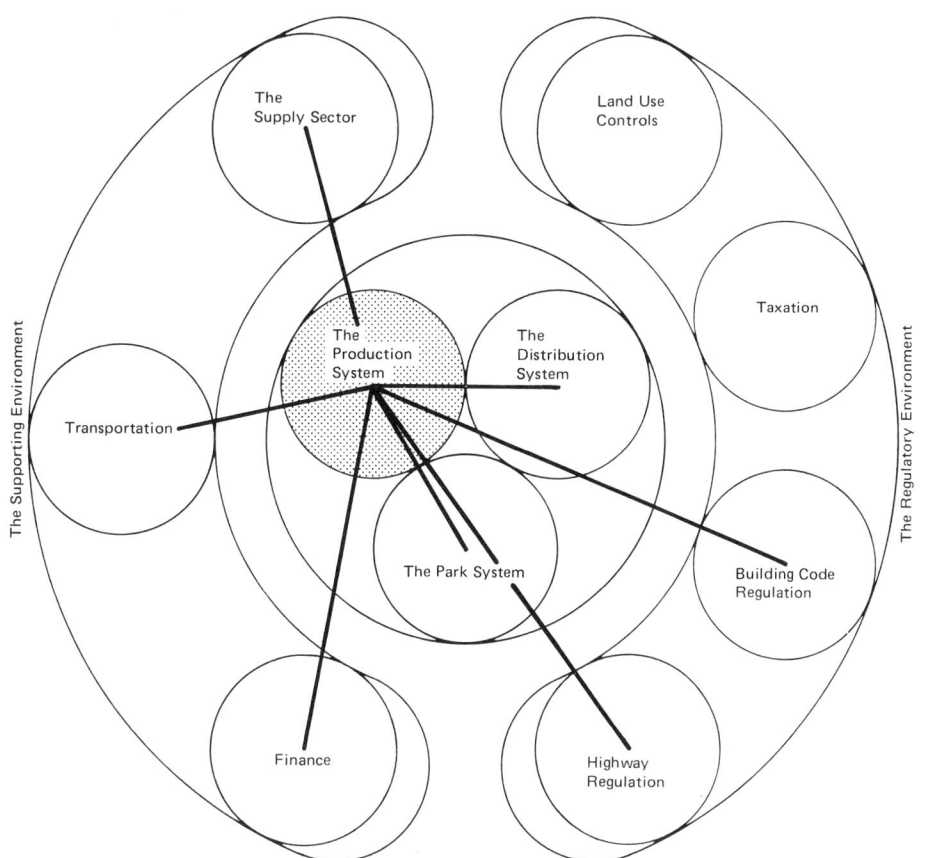

The Supply Sector

Land Use Controls

Taxation

The Production System

The Distribution System

Transportation

Building Code Regulation

The Park System

Finance

Highway Regulation

The Supporting Environment

The Regulatory Environment

Chapter 4

Industrial Organization of the Production System

As an industry grows and matures, it begins to assume a particular form of organization with respect to its internal relationships and to its patterns of interaction with other elements of the environment within which it operates. The nature of the organization is the result of a continuing process in which individual firms attempt to modify the existing organization in order to gain advantage in relation to other firms in the industry. If the modifications are successful, they will presumably be adopted by the remainder of the firms in a similar position in the industry. If the modifications are not successful, they will be dropped. The form that evolves is therefore the result of a continuous series of experiments on the part of individual firms undertaken with the objective of improving their performance.

Analysis of the evolution and current status of the organization of an industry is therefore a valuable source of information about two areas with important implications concerning the potentials for performance improvement by the industry. The pattern of evolution indicates the nature of the major constraints the industry has faced during its development and provides insight into the feasibility of various policy alternatives of circumventing these constraints. It is not uncommon to discover that some firms have been successful in adapting to certain constraints while other firms have found similar efforts unrewarding. In such circumstances, the most valuable form of investigation focuses upon characteristics of individual firms to attempt to isolate specific characteristics of firms that have led to either success or failure.

The current status of an industry's organizational development provides information about the level of performance that may be expected from an industry as it develops and about limitations to policy alternatives designed to alter the normal course of development. There are two elements of organization that normally affect industrial performance. The structure of an industry determines the institutional framework within which the firms must operate. Some industries exhibit a very simple structure with low levels of concentration, diversification, integration, and entry barriers, and with few complications such as seasonality, significant economies of scale, or complex labor problems. Other industries are far more complex. Because complexity arises from reactions to environmental factors, it does not necessarily imply poor performance by an industry and may be a necessary condition for improved performance. A highly complex industry, however, requires thorough investigation of the ramifications of policy proposals for improved performance.

The second element that affects performance is the operation of the industry. While the structure of an industry provides a basic framework within which firms operate, individual firms' reactions to specific structures may generate significant interfirm differences in operation. The effect of operational factors on industry performance is reflected in the pattern of entry and exit from the industry. High rates of entry of new firms into the industry indicate that existing firms have not been able to develop policies that would make entry either undesirable or impossible. Decreases in the rate of entry may indicate that existing firms are in the process of establishing barriers to entry or that the degree of market control by existing firms makes successful participation in the industry doubtful. Increases in the rate of exit by existing firms may indicate that the remaining firms are effectively increasing the degree of control they can exert on the market performance of the industry or it may indicate that marginal firms are taking advantage of low barriers to entry and attempting to develop their own positions with varying success.

In this chapter, experiences and data garnered from seven years of nationwide field research on the mobile home manufacturing system are used to investigate the nature of the evolution and current status of factors determining structure, operation, and performance in the mobile home industry, as well as evolving policy alternatives. The approach in this chapter is transferable to other subsystems of the building industry here as well as to building industries in other countries.

A. Evolution

History

The mobile home of today is a far cry from the simple trailers of the 1920s. The desire of the early automobile owners to make full use of their vehicles resulted in two-wheeled carts attached to the back of automobiles. In 1929 a Detroit manufacturer of vaccines built, for his own vacation use, a small structure consisting of a canvas-covered wooden frame placed on a chassis with wheels. Pleased with the utility of his "house trailer," he reasoned that there were many other travel vacation enthusiasts like himself who could make use of such a vehicle-shelter. Convinced of their marketability, he began to manufacture house trailers designed after his own. Demand for the product grew steadily, and they became commonly called "trailer coaches." Large-scale production of the house trailer soon began as hundreds of manufacturers entered the trailer coach market. By 1936 more than four hundred manufacturers were producing forty thousand house trailers per year; trailer coach manufacturing was reported to be the fastest growing industry in the United States. It was predicted that by 1956 more than half of the total population of the nation would be living in trailers. The remarkably rapid development of the trailer coach market aroused the interest of the large automobile companies. The

Ford Motor Company and General Motors Corporation seriously considered entering the young industry, and some automobile and truck companies actually did.

At first, virtually all trailers were bought for recreational use. But with the onset of the Great Depression, more and more people began to live permanently in their trailers. By 1937 only half of all trailers sold were used for vacation purposes. At this time half of all trailers produced were used as year-round homes by retirees and migratory workers. A total of two hundred thousand families were now living permanently in trailers.

At the onset of World War II serious housing problems arose as a result of the huge defense buildup. Federal government officials recognized the potential of mobile dwellings as an adjunct to the defense housing program. Private sales of trailer houses were prohibited by executive order. Throughout the United States and Europe trailers were utilized as communications headquarters, first aid stations, kitchens, and, most important, housing for military personnel and defense workers. Government purchases of trailers, however, were drastically curtailed in the last few years of the war. The number of manufacturers then declined to fewer than fifty.

Despite the tremendous cutback in government purchases during the later war years, the war had positive effects on the mobile dwelling industry. The war brought about a change in perspective toward trailers. During the war large numbers of servicemen and workers became used to the idea of trailers as primary housing. Veterans and defense workers, together with the retirees and migratory laborers who had lived in trailers during the depression, formed a large percentage of the national population. Postwar America, then, was well prepared for the emergence of the mobile dwelling industry as a supplier in the housing market.

In the immediate postwar period, during the reconversion to a peacetime economy, the demography of the United States shifted. A migrant army of workers was needed for long overdue heavy construction projects in remote areas of the country. This, associated with a severe housing shortage, created an abnormal mobile dwelling market. The federal government requested manufacturers to increase the production of trailers. The number of manufacturers doubled. By 1950 only a minor portion of all trailer coaches produced were sold as vacation vehicles. Up to 90 percent of all owners used their trailers as year-round homes. Migrant laborers, especially, found that their mobile homes combined comfort with practicality.

The outbreak of hostilities in Korea resulted in yet another upsurge in the use of trailers as primary housing. Mobile homes were needed to house the vast numbers of workers streaming into isolated parts of the country for the construction of huge atomic energy plants. Previously unheard-of numbers of trailers were being transported to these construction sites. More than ten thousand trailers each were shipped into several single-project sites. The reactivation of the armed forces caused the establishment of trailer parks on more than one hundred ten military bases. Most sales in 1951 were attributed to defense workers and military personnel. At this stage in their development mobile units began to serve a variety of special purposes. They were used as offices, banks, or chapels. There was, however, a spillover into other sectors of society. The use of mobile homes by married workers increased on private construction jobs as well as on foreign construction jobs undertaken by American firms.

The transformation of mobile housing from recreational travel trailers to permanent homes was dramatized in 1952 when the trailer coach industry split into two distinctly separate industries. The Trailer Coach Manufacturers Association split into the Mobile Home Manufacturers Association and the Recreational Vehicle Institute. The "mobile home" industry began to concentrate exclusively on the production of primary housing; the "travel trailer" industry specialized in the production of vehicles for recreational use. In terms of structure, operation, and markets both industries are separate and independent to such a degree that this book can concentrate exclusively on the mobile home industry. By 1953 the transformation to primary housing was complete: Almost two million Americans lived permanently in more than seven hundred thousand mobile homes. The growth record of the industry since 1950 warrants a more detailed analysis.

After the mobile home boom of 1947 and 1948, aided by the postwar housing crisis, the conventional home builders dramatically built up their production capacity and could effectively respond to the demand for housing. The mobile home market diminished. During the boom, the advantages of mobile homes became evident; they were seen as a very serviceable form of low-cost housing that could be manufactured quickly and efficiently in response to public demand. Although stationary houses could not be built as quickly as mobile homes, the conventional housing industry finally caught up with the general demand for housing, and certain disadvantages of mobile homes became apparent: Mobile homes were relatively small and they lacked bathroom facilities.

Alarmed at the popularity of conventional houses, mobile home manufacturers introduced homes with bathroom facilities in 1950. Although these facilities contained only a shower and a washbasin, the market responded immediately. Finally, in 1951, toilets and length were added. With the further design improvements of walk-through bedrooms and bathrooms, the industry continued its growth. Not much more could be done at this time, given an 8-foot width limitation due to highway safety regulations. Marketing tactics led to a name change from "trailer coach" to "mobile home," but nothing was done practically to provide the public with additional floor space. Mobile home producers were finally stimulated into manufacturing the first 10-foot units in 1953 when the market once again indicated public dissatisfaction with the small size of mobile homes. The size of the new units provided space for the addition of private bedrooms and bathrooms that opened into a hall. By 1955, a prosperous year for all housing, the 10-wide became accepted by the public and the industry passed the one hundred thousand unit mark. The following year the 10-wide was manufactured in large production runs. The 10-wide was now a sensational success. Manufacturers' enthusiasm, however, led to over-production and dealers overstocked the product. The industry then saw a general decline in sales in 1957 and 1958.

Because public demand for more space continued unabated, the industry introduced a 12-foot-wide model in 1959. Permits for the transportation of 12-wides, though, were not forthcoming—highway regulations remained constricting. The 10-wides were then made longer, causing a mass market upsurge in 55-foot-long 10-wides. Similarly, expandable units were introduced—homes with one or more room sections that fold or telescope into the unit when being transported and which can be expanded at the site providing additional space. After the initial enthusiasm for the longer or expandable 10-wides the mobile home market sought wider units with further design innovations, but 12-wide permits were still rare. Sales declined until 1963, when many states finally yielded their highway regulations to 12-wides.

With the relaxation of highway regulations, mobile home sales skyrocketed. The 12-wides became standard and the industry experienced astonishing growth, increasing production volume by 500 percent in the years 1962–1972. By 1965 industry shipments passed the 200,000 mark. The industry experienced a minute drop in 1966. Money was tight. Finance companies limited wholesale financing. Because of the Vietnam war and the draft, young marrieds were reluctant to purchase homes. Nevertheless, shipments went up sharply in 1967, passed the three hundred thousand mark in 1968, and the four hundred thousand mark in 1969. The peak came in 1972 with almost six hundred thousand shipments.

A review of the boom of the late 1960s and early 1970s indicates several significant reasons for the popularity of mobile homes. The industry grew in response to the demand for low-cost housing. The inflationary spiral of the 1960s pushed conventional housing costs up as the rise in construction materials and the cost of labor priced the conventional home out of the moderate income bracket. In addition, 14-wides, doublewides, and expandables became available during the boom, providing the consumer with more options within the low-cost housing range than ever before. Accompanying the increased size of mobile homes were improved quality, design innovations, and greater availability of mobile home parks. Mobile homes then became an attractive, increasingly available low-cost alternative to conventional housing.

In 1974 the effect of the recessionary conditions of tight money and increased unemployment had a severe impact on the mobile home industry. Blue-collar workers, the major occupants of mobile homes, were most affected by the high rate of unemployment and many did not have the income either to purchase or to maintain loan payments on homes. Repossession rates rose and lenders became overly cautious and further reduced effective demand. Yet even with the drastic fall in shipments, the mobile home industry has maintained its viability as a low-cost housing alternative.

Today, in the late 1970s, the industry has adopted the name, "manufactured housing industry." The "manufactured homes" produced today are larger than ever. More than half of the total output is comprised of 14-wides, which provide up to 1000 square feet of floor space, and doublewides, which supply up to 1900 square feet per unit. In comparison, these are housing standards to which Europeans of middle and upper income levels aspire. The trend toward larger, "immobile" homes and the development of higher construction standards signify the permanence of mobile homes in the low-cost housing market and the potential for further development of the entire industry. Figures 4.1 through 4.5 attempt to recap the evolution of the trailer coach of the early half of this century into the im-mobile home of the latter part of the twentieth century.

Origin

The structure of an industry, particularly in the early stages of its development, is often determined by the history of firms that enter it. The relationship is reciprocal. Market conditions that permit the emergence of a new industry may dictate the nature of firms entering, and the strengths and limitations of the entering firms may influence the pattern of industry development for a significant period of time.

The mobile home industry evolved independent of the on-site building industry. Today the mobile home industry exhibits

Figure 4.1.
Evolution of the mobile home: An 8-wide of the early 1940s.

Figure 4.2.
Evolution of the mobile home: An 8-wide of the early 1950s.

Figure 4.3.
Evolution of the mobile home: An expandable 10-wide of the early 1960s.

Figure 4.4.
Evolution of the mobile home: A 12-wide of the early 1970s

Figure 4.5.
Evolution of the mobile home: A doublewide of the late 1970s.

structural and operational characteristics very different from those of the traditional building industry. Performance, similarly, is different: Production efficiency in general and labor productivity in particular are much higher in the mobile home industry than in the on-site building industry.

The mobile home industry's higher performance level can be attributed to a great extent to the sectors of origin from which mobile home manufacturers came. Most producers do not have a background related to the on-site building industry; they either went straight into mobile home manufacturing or came from sectors such as the automotive industry or aircraft production. The difference of origin is significant. It accounts for the "industrial" mentality intrinsic to the mobile home industry, whose operation relies on technological and managerial know-how drawn from manufacturing- or mass production–oriented industries—an intellectual and philosophical makeup radically different from that of the traditional building industry.

Contrary to what one might expect, the lack of building industry expertise in the mobile home industry has proven to be one of its greatest strengths. In the late 1940s the industry discovered, very much to its surprise, that it was in the business of producing primary housing. The trailer coach, always perceived, intended, and designed by the industry as secondary housing, had begun to be used by the consumer as year-round, primary housing. Suddenly faced with this realization and with the need to produce "permanent housing," the absence of building industry know-how forced manufacturers to find their own way of producing shelter. The industry unconsciously developed a systems analysis approach to housing production and delivery, designing and producing housing with the most efficient utilization of the basic resource inputs of materials, labor, money, and time. This approach, logical if one considers the background of the firms, led to a highly efficient product and process that is radically different from the on-site built house and the traditional construction process.

The fresh approach to building production, reinforced by the sophisticated managerial know-how drawn from other, nonbuilding sectors, explains a great deal about the industry's organization and outstanding performance. Because mobile home manufacturers entered the industry unbiased by century-old building traditions, they were able to establish an organizational structure new to the building sector. Thus mobile home manufacturers avoided inefficiencies that had become entrenched in the traditional housing industry.

Our extensive fieldwork establishing the significance of origin is corroborated quantitatively by this project's national survey of all mobile home manufacturers (PMHI/MS). As can be seen from table 4.1, only three of the responding firms originated either in the on-site building industry or in the related fields of building supplies and building manufacturing.[1] On the other hand, forty-three respondents (approximately 85 percent of these who specified their background) had their origin in fields not related to the traditional building industry but relevant to the mobile home industry—mobile home and recreational vehicle production. The dominating frequency of mobile home industry origins does not contradict the earlier statements about the origins of the early manufacturers. Heavy activity in mergers and acquisitions involving the mobile home industry has resulted in many firms changing hands more than once. Thus many officers of the large multioperation firms who completed the PMHI/MS questionnaires may have been unaware of the "real" origin of their mobile home divisions or subsidiaries. For example, for one specific mobile home producer who originated in the early fifties from aircraft production the returned questionnaire gave "mobile home production" as origin.

In many cases "mobile home industry background" corroborates yet another field-work-generated insight. Corporate officers in the industry, once they have acquired the necessary competence and built the necessary connections with lending institutions and suppliers, often tend to start their own firm. This phenomenon suggests that over the decades the industry has developed mobile home industry-specific know-how that makes entry easier for insiders and more difficult for outsiders.

As stated above, one significant aspect of the origin of firms in the mobile home production system is that the firms possessed a comparative know-how advantage over the on-site building industry. As is shown in table 4.1, thirty-four of fifty-nine firms responding to the PMHI/MS reported initial activity in the area of mobile home production; an additional six reported initial activity in the production of mobile homes and another area. Table 4.2 indicates that twenty-two of the twenty-five responding firms active in the industry prior to 1968 originated in the mobile home industry. This lack of market penetration by outside industry provides some indication of the existence of either disincentives to entry or barriers to entry.

During the pre-1968 period there were no major disincentives to entry. Effective demand in the low- and middle-income housing markets was great, and for those firms in the industry able to produce low-cost housing, real or potential profits were high. Furthermore, the industry was characterized by small firm size, geographically limited marketing ability, and low technology. Thus neither significant market power nor technological entry barriers existed. Because entry incentives did exist, an explanation for the lack of penetration lies in the fact that firms were unfamiliar with the production and delivery process and did not possess industry-specific soft know-how. Such firms were incapable of producing and effectively distributing products that would be competitive in the market.

The rapid entry of firms with more diversified backgrounds in the period after 1968 not only reflects Wall Street's increasing attention to the industry at that time but also indicates that know-how could be acquired, usually by "pirating" top management personnel from the mobile home industry. We have met several executives who in 1969 were plant managers with salaries in the $15,000 range. After being "pirated" several times, they are now executive officers of mobile home divisions of corporations that entered the industry in the late 1960s and early 1970s and enjoy compensation packages in the $50,000 to $150,000 range. The ratio of compensation for key executive talent to research and development expenditures is much higher in the mobile housing industry than in manufacturing industries in general. Funds are normally allocated to areas that promise the highest return; the expenditure pattern found here, then, indicates that advancing or acquiring the know-how for effectively and profitably marketing mobile homes represents an important method of either overcoming an existing market disadvantage or, conversely, maintaining an existing market advantage. Also signified is the importance of mobile home industry-specific knowledge and the relative unimportance of manufacturing technology per se.

An analysis of general size characteristics of firms by sector of origin (table 4.3) initially seems to indicate that firms evolving from other sectors compare unfavorably with firms originating in the mobile home industry. In all measures of size, firms originating outside the mobile home sector, especially those that entered from the on-site building industry, were clustered around the lower levels. Although the small size of those firms originating in the on-site building sector can be attributed partially to their relatively young age, their origin and lack of industry-specific know-how are undoubtably contributing factors.

The mobile home industry of the late 1970s shows structural, operational, and performance characteristics very different from those of the industry in the late 1960s. It is understandable, then, that the patterns of origin are also changing. This chapter will prepare the reader for a discussion of the forces that will direct the future evolution of the industry.

Table 4.1.
Sector of Origin of Mobile Home Manufacturing Firms

Sector of Origin	Number of Firms
Aircraft production	0
Recreational vehicle production only	3
Building supplies only	1
Mobile homes only	34
Building manufacture only	1
On-site construction only	1
Other single activities	3
Mobile homes and another area	6
Multiple sectors of origin (except mobile homes)	1
No sector indicated	9
Total firms	59

Source: PMHI/MS

Table 4.2.
Year of Entry into Mobile Home Production by Sector of Origin

	Number of Firms by Sector of Origin	
Year of Entry	Mobile Home Production[a]	Other Than Mobile Home Production[b]
Prior to 1950	4	1
1950–1955	3	0
1956–1960	5	0
1961–1965	7	2
1966	1	0
1967	2	0
1968	1	2
1969	7	4
1870	4	6
1971	4	0
1972	2	3
1973	0	1

a. Includes firms originating in both mobile home production and additional activity.
b. Includes seven firms not indicating sector of origin.

Source: PMHI/MS.

Table 4.3.
Size Characteristics of
Firms by Sector of
Origin

Size Characteristics	Number of Firms by Sector of Origin				
	Recreational Vehicles	Building Supplies	Mobile Homes	Building Manufacturing	On-Site Construction
Sales (× $1000)					
0–2500	1	1	10	—	2
2500–10,000	2	—	10	2	—
10,000–40,000	—	—	15	1	—
40,000–500,000	—	—	6	—	—
Number of plants					
1	3	1	19	1	1
2–5	—	—	12	2	—
6–20	—	—	10	—	—
20+	—	—	1	—	—
Total employment					
0–100	3	1	13	—	1
101–400	—	—	13	3	—
401–1000	—	—	11	—	—
1001+	—	—	5	—	—

Note: Totals of characteristic blocks may not correspond because of nonresponse.

Source: PMHI/MS.

Production Trends

Mobile home production has grown steadily since 1946, when industry sources began maintaining accurate records of annual industry production. The remarkable aspect of this growth appears in the period 1962–1972, when mobile home unit production rose dramatically by 500 percent, from a little more than one hundred thousand to about six hundred thousand units per year. This extraordinary increase in mobile home production is rendered all the more notable when one considers that doublewide units, though twice the size of singlewides and capable of accommodating twice as many people, are counted as single units. Doublewides comprised 15 percent of total mobile home production in 1972, so counting them as two units each brings the total units produced in that year close to seven hundred thousand. In comparison, this figure exceeds by more than two hundred thousand units the entire annual national housing production volume of such major European countries as the United Kingdom and West Germany.

The rapid increase of mobile housing production is evidence of the industry's potential to meet demands for low-cost housing. The industry's growth rate has demonstrated that the mobile housing subsystem can respond quickly and effectively to such phenomena as the "baby boom" of post–World War II years and the economic prosperity of the 1960s. The baby boom resulted in the growing families of the late 1960s, many of which desired low-cost housing. The business boom of the 1960s enabled young families to secure incomes sufficient to obtain modest single-family homes. Since the early 1960s mobile homes have increasingly accounted for a greater percentage of new single-family housing production. Mobile home unit output rose from an equivalent of 11.9 percent of single-family housing starts in 1961 to a peak of 50.8 percent in 1972 (table 4.4). As the economic and demographic trends of the 1960s affected the mobile housing industry, however, so too did the national recessionary trend of the 1970s have consequences for mobile home production. In 1974 the mobile home industry output fell drastically and bottomed out a year later at a level below that of 1966 unit production (see table 4.4).

One aspect of the national recession of 1974 was a decline in the demand for single-family housing—mobile as well as conventional. Unlike the labor intensive traditional housing system, the capital intensive mobile home production system is more vulnerable to changes in demand. A sudden demand drop can drastically reduce the capacity utilization rate; correspondingly, the fixed cost per unit of output increases, leading to a reduction and, ultimately, to the elimination of profit. When even minimal profits were eliminated in the recession, many mobile home producers filed for bankruptcy. The traditional on-site builder, on the other hand, not having to absorb the

Table 4.4.
Comparison of Annual
Mobile Home Ship-
ments with Single-Unit
Housing Starts, 1947–
1977

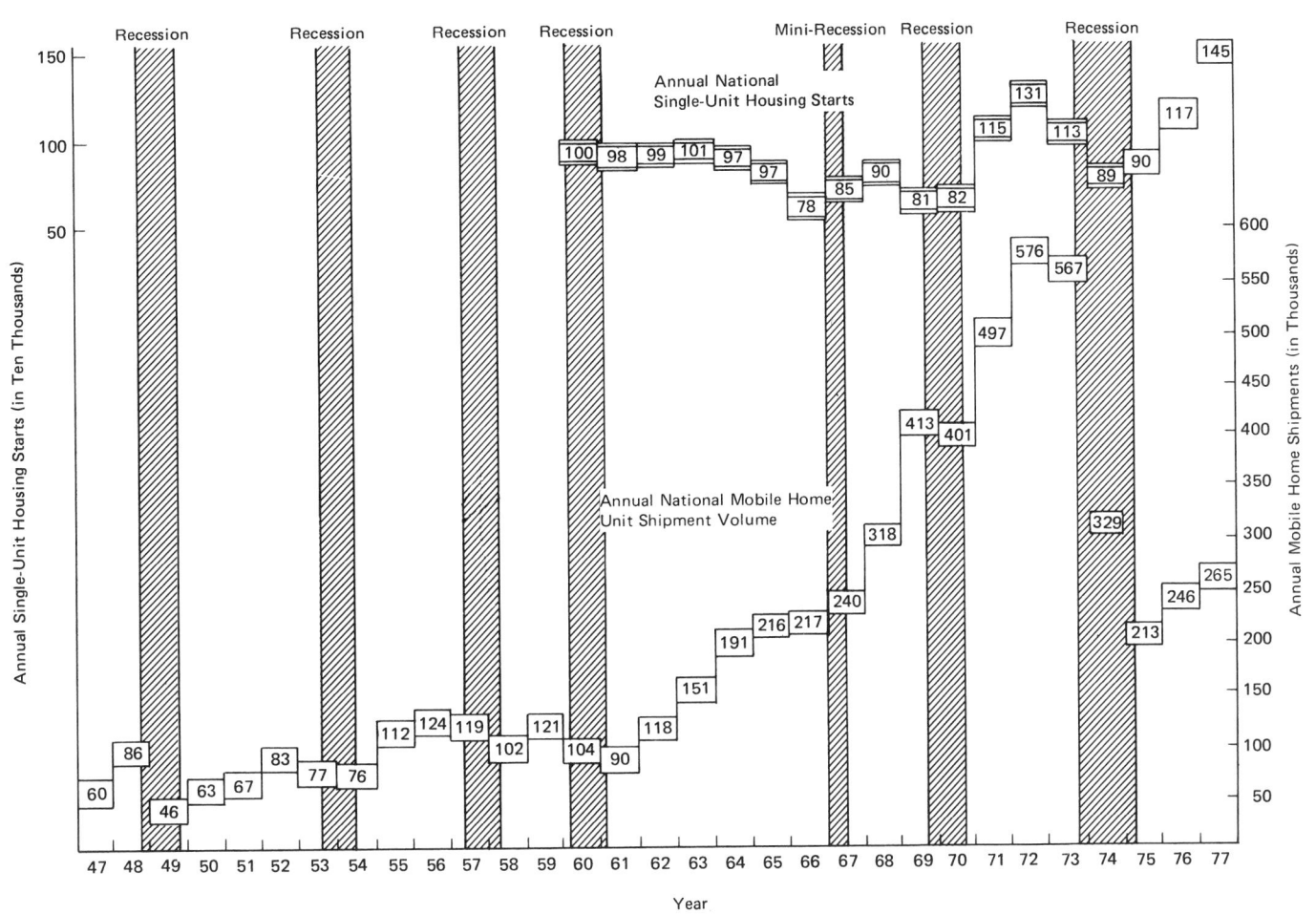

Source: Elrick and Lavidge, Inc.; U.S. Dept. of Commerce, *Construction Review.*

fixed costs of maintaining a factory, needed only to adjust work force size as demand slowdown dictated. The traditional on-site builder, then, can adapt to sudden demand drops more easily than a mobile home manufacturer.

The mobile home industry was recovering from the 1974 recession more slowly than the conventional housing industry. The high rate of business failures in the mobile home industry during the recession had important consequences for future recovery. Many surviving companies became overly cautious in capital appropriation decisions regarding the addition of production capacity. Business failures of mobile home producers have also caused financial institutions and entrepreneurs outside the industry to be apprehensive about entering the mobile home production field. Mobile home business bankruptcies caused mobile housing producers to lose credibility with many banks. Thus many banks are now hesitant to lend money to such ventures. Finally, new legal and know-how barriers make entry into the field difficult even for seasoned entrepreneurs. Such barriers include public regulatory burdens imposed upon the industry, which have significantly raised the absolute cost of entry. Other entry obstacles include the increasing complexity of technical and managerial know-how specific to the mobile home industry.

In accordance with the drop in mobile home unit production, the total wholesale dollar volume for the industry leveled off at $3.75 billion in 1973. This nevertheless represents significant growth from the 1968 total wholesale dollar volume of $1.5 billion. Table 4.5 highlights this dramatic increase of $2.25 billion over a six-year period. It is evident, however, that the wholesale dollar trend does not exhibit as serious a downswing in the postrecession years as does the trend for national unit production volume. This is at least partly due to the inflationary trend of the dollar, which accelerated in this period. Of more significance to the mobile home industry, however, was the rapidly increasing dominance of larger units (doublewides and 14-wides) in the product mix. These large units are more expensive than the 12-foot-wide singlewides of the early 1970s. As unit sizes and production costs increased, then, average unit prices rose significantly. Therefore, although fewer units were actually sold in this period, the industry dollar revenue recorded only slight decreases.

It is now clear that the industry has come out of the trauma caused by the 1973–1975 recession. It is also evident that the industry's production volume was curtailed not by endogenous factors but by exogenous conditions, and the industry should once again attain its former levels of production in the early 1980s (assuming that the recession expected within the next few years will not be as severe as that of 1973–1975).

Table 4.6 details regional distribution of production over the seventeen-year period, 1960–1977. Although every region exhibits strong upward trend in unit production through 1972, it is obvious that the industry has grown much faster in some regions than in others, causing a shift in the relative market shares for these regions. For example, early production was concentrated in the East North Central region of the country, especially in Indiana, Michigan, and Ohio. Several explanations can be offered for this concentration. First, the mobile home industry was heavily dependent upon automotive suppliers and therefore took root in the same area as the big automotive plants. Second, much of the labor force was drawn from the local automotive and related industries, and these workers wanted to remain in the East North Central region. Third, because early mobile homes were much smaller, transportation costs were a minor consideration in terms of overall expenses. Thus there was little impetus at that time to decentralize.

However, since the 1960s, as shown in table 4.7, there has been a trend toward greater production in the South Atlantic and South Central regions of the country.[2] This is due not only to the recent economic growth in the South but also to beneficial climate conditions, lower land costs, and sympathetic zoning regulations. These conditions, coupled with low population densities in parts of these regions, favor the mobile home as compared with alternate forms of low-cost housing. The trend toward greater production in the South Atlantic and South Central regions as opposed to the North will continue. However, increasing industry maturity, the larger production levels that now exist in these regions as compared to earlier years, as well as the general trend of the economy indicate that the growth rate in the future will not be as high as that recorded between 1961 and 1972. The regions' shares of national wholesale dollar volume as given in table 4.8 of course reflect the same trend over time, but do so less markedly; the two southern regions' dollar volume shares (18 percent and 21 percent) are lower than their unit volume market shares (20 percent and 25 percent) because wholesale unit prices are below the national average in the South and above-average in the North Central area (the Pacific region's high dollar volume share similarly is caused by the generally higher-priced unit typical especially in California).

Tables 4.9 and 4.10 present data on the five states with the greatest annual unit production and wholesale dollar volume. Ever since the early 1960s there has been a clear trend in the decline in state concentration of

Table 4.5.
Comparison of Annual
National Mobile Home
Unit Shipment Vol-
ume with Annual Na-
tional Wholesale Dollar
Volume, 1947–1977

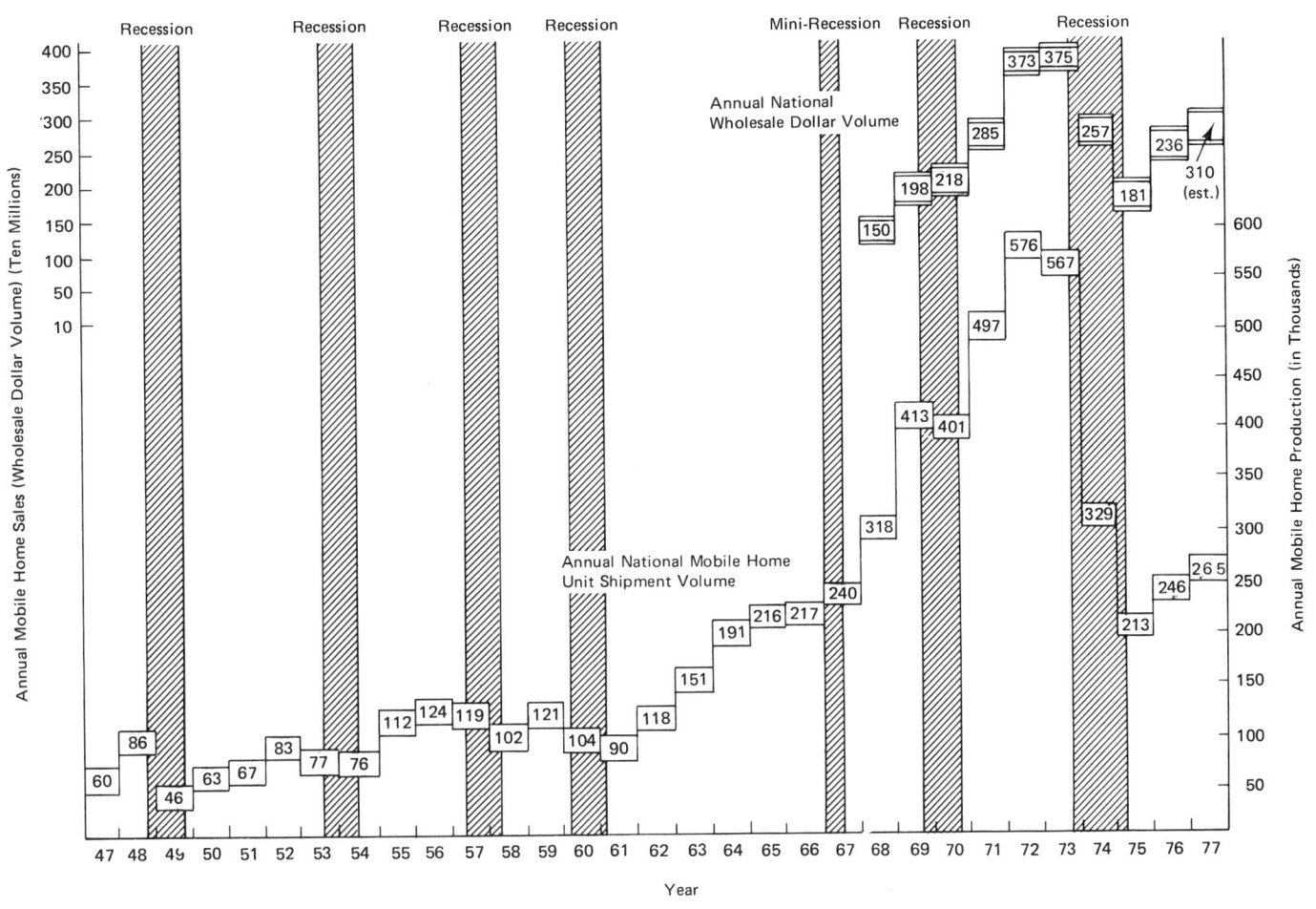

Source: Compiled from several years of back issues of "The Monthly Market Letter of Mobile Home Shipments" published by *Mobile–Modular Housing Dealer Magazine;* Elrick and Lavidge, Inc.

Table 4.6.
Regional Shares of Annual National Mobile Home Production (Unit Production Volume) and Mobile Home Sales (Wholesale Dollar Volume), 1960–1977

Pacific

Year	1	2
1960	13	N/A
1961	13	N/A
1962	12	N/A
1963	12	N/A
1964	11	N/A
1965	9	N/A
1966	9	N/A
1967	8	N/A
1968	10	12
1969	11	13
1970	11	12
1971	11	13
1972	10	14
1973	9	13
1974	11	16
1975	15	20
1976	15	20
1977	19	23

Mountain

Year	1	2
1960	4	N/A
1961	5	N/A
1962	4	N/A
1963	3	N/A
1964	3	N/A
1965	3	N/A
1966	3	N/A
1967	3	N/A
1968	4	4
1969	3	4
1970	3	4
1971	4	4
1972	5	5
1973	5	6
1974	7	7
1975	8	9
1976	7	8
1977	7	8

West North Central

Year	1	2
1960	12	N/A
1961	11	N/A
1962	11	N/A
1963	10	N/A
1964	9	N/A
1965	8	N/A
1966	9	N/A
1967	9	N/A
1968	9	10
1969	9	9
1970	9	10
1971	9	9
1972	9	10
1973	8	9
1974	9	9
1975	9	9
1976	9	10
1977	7	9

South Central

Year	1	2
1960	14	N/A
1961	13	N/A
1962	11	N/A
1963	12	N/A
1964	13	N/A
1965	16	N/A
1966	16	N/A
1967	16	N/A
1968	17	15
1969	21	19
1970	22	21
1971	24	22
1972	25	22
1973	26	22
1974	23	20
1975	24	10
1976	25	9
1977	26	8

East North Central

Year	1	2
1960	41	N/A
1961	40	N/A
1962	40	N/A
1963	39	N/A
1964	36	N/A
1965	31	N/A
1966	28	N/A
1967	27	N/A
1968	25	27
1969	21	24
1970	20	22
1971	19	20
1972	17	17
1973	15	16
1974	16	17
1975	17	16
1976	16	15
1977	16	15

South Atlantic

Year	1	2
1960	11	N/A
1961	13	N/A
1962	16	N/A
1963	19	N/A
1964	20	N/A
1965	24	N/A
1966	26	N/A
1967	27	N/A
1968	27	24
1969	28	24
1970	27	22
1971	26	23
1972	27	23
1973	29	26
1974	26	22
1975	20	18
1976	21	19
1977	20	18

Northeast

Year	1	2
1960	5	N/A
1961	5	N/A
1962	6	N/A
1963	5	N/A
1964	8	N/A
1965	9	N/A
1966	9	N/A
1967	10	N/A
1968	8	8
1969	7	7
1970	8	9
1971	6	8
1972	8	9
1973	8	8
1974	7	8
1975	7	7
1976	7	8
1977	6	7

1. Regional share as percent of annual national mobile home production
2. Regional share as percent of annual national mobile home wholesale dollar volume

Source: Compiled by PMHI from data prepared by Elrick and Lavidge, Inc., for the Manufactured Housing Institute, from back issues of "Annual Production Survey" published by *Mobile-Modular Housing Dealer Magazine*, and from data provided by the National Conference of States Building Codes and Standards, Inc.

Table 4.7.
Regional Shares[a] of
National Annual Mobile
Home Production
(Unit Production
Volume[b] 1960–1977

	1960		1961		1962		1963		1964		1965		1966		1967		1968	
Region	Units	%	Units	%	Units	%	Units	%	Units	%	Units	%	Units	%	Units	%	Units	%
Northeast	5,400	5	4,350	5	7,250	6	8,010	5	16,470	8	20,090	9	20,012	9	24,531	10	27,553	8
East North Central	43,190	41	36,630	40	47,530	40	59,850	39	70,130	36	68,170	31	62,912	28	67,307	27	82,270	25
West North Central	12,170	12	10,280	11	13,250	11	15,410	10	18,100	9	18,920	8	19,488	9	21,363	9	29,574	9
South Atlantic	12,060	11	12,270	13	19,320	16	29,130	19	39,840	20	52,530	24	56,843	26	65,755	27	87,103	27
South Central	15,010	14	12,330	13	13,750	11	18,600	12	24,360	13	34,570	16	36,618	16	38,246	16	54,595	17
Mountain	4,310	4	4,530	5	4,830	4	5,200	3	6,300	3	7,000	3	7,550	3	7,453	3	12,269	4
Pacific	13,560	13	11,810	13	14,540	12	17,740	12	20,720	11	20,760	9	19,277	9	20,458	8	31,076	10
Total U.S. Production	105,700	100	92,200	100	120,470	100	153,940	100	195,920	100	222,040	100	222,700	100	245,110	100	324,440	100

	1969		1970		1971		1972		1973		1974		1975		1976		1977	
Region	Units	%	Units	%	Units	%	Units	%	Units	%	Units	%	Units	%	Units	%	Units	%
Northeast	30,350	7	32,300	8	32,975	6	46,771	8	45,601	8	23,922	7	14,915	7	17,582	7	16,379	6
East North Central	85,520	21	81,760	20	98,207	19	101,153	17	87,914	15	54,127	16	35,423	17	40,601	16	40,337	16
West North Central	38,210	9	37,710	9	44,328	9	52,087	9	43,514	8	28,951	9	19,458	9	22,007	9	19,413	7
South Atlantic	115,510	28	108,510	27	133,567	26	164,961	27	163,635	29	86,458	26	42,617	20	50,865	21	52,538	20
South Central	88,230	21	90,140	22	119,257	24	149,575	25	144,946	26	77,514	24	52,032	24	61,353	25	64,378	25
Mountain	14,460	3	14,130	3	23,350	5	28,223	4	29,123	5	22,325	7	16,040	8	17,533	7	18,635	7
Pacific	44,900	11	43,800	11	55,536	11	58,480	10	53,685	9	37,503	11	32,485	15	38,079	15	48,177	19
Total U.S. Production	417,270	100	408,350	100	507,220	100	601,250	100	568,020	100	330,800	100	212,970	100	248,020	100	265,640	100

a. Percentage figures rounded to nearest whole %
b. Includes exports, government, and factory sales
c. In order to protect proprietary information, 1977 volumes of states with less than three manufacturers are included only in the U.S. total and not in the regional totals.

Source: Compiled by PMHI from data prepared by Elrick and Lavidge, Inc., for the Manufactured Housing Institute, and from data provided by the National Conference of States on Building Codes and Standards, Inc.

production. In 1963, almost two-thirds of national production was concentrated in the top five states, whereas in 1977 the five leading states accounted for less than one-half. A closer examination of the data in these tables rein forces what the regional data indicate: that the mobile home industry has grown from a few production centers into a large number of regional production clusters spread across every part of the country. Originally, in the 1930s and 1940s, there were only two production centers: the Indian-Michigan-Ohio area and California: there is now an almost homogeneous network of plants throughout the country complementing the nationwide on-site home building industry. Today, in virtually every part of the country, mobile homes as a low-cost housing form augment the supply of higher-priced traditional shelter.

Product Mix Trends

By the early 1950s the mobile home industry had developed a recreation-oriented vehicle into a widely accepted form of primary housing. With this change the demand for larger, traditional housing dimensioned homes was inevitable. The public was only briefly satisfied by the introduction of 10-foot-wide homes, and mobile home manufacturers and dealers soon realized the importance of size to its status as a serious competitor with the conventional housing industry. Size restrictions of highway regulations, however, constricted further development of mobile home dimensions. The industry has since been involved in an ongoing struggle with those who contend that the transportation of homes is a highway safety hazard.

The development of the product mix is a reflection of the successful efforts for more flexible highway regulations permitting the transportation of larger homes (table 4.12). In the early 1960s, when 12-wides were finally allowed on the highways of many states, the production of 12-wides began in earnest. By 1970 12-wides comprised 78 percent of the market. Demand for yet more floor space led to the development of the 14-foot and doublewide homes (table 4.11). Lobbying continues into the late 1970s in an effort to persuade the last two states still limiting the transportation of 14-wide mobile homes to relax their restrictions.

It should be noted that a study of product mix based solely on a national view can be misleading. Regional and state situations can be radically different from that of the nation. This is exemplified by a comparison of Florida, where doublewide homes comprise more than 70 percent of the state's production, with Wisconsin, where 6 percent is doublewides (see table 4.12).

The product mix reflects not only highway transportation regulations but also the availability of park spaces and taste preferences for homes. Past and present trends indicate

that the product mix will increasingly be dominated by 14-foot and doublewide homes, with 12-wides rapidly losing significance and in time, disappearing. The use of mobile homes as primary housing in competition with the conventional housing industry necessitates the production of homes of greater size and permanence. The struggle against size restrictions continues. Many state legislatures as well as state highway departments, however, are unlikely to yield easily to the increasing industry requests for 16-foot or even 18-foot width permits—not last because ever more energy-conscious administrations are unlikely to continue the past rapid expansion of lane width and density of the highway network. The product mix, then, of the 1980s is likely to consist of 14-foot-wide (and to a minor extent 16-foot-wide) singlewides, expandables as the next space-increase option, and, finally, doublewides—with either extreme dominating the mix. However, although 16-foot- and 18-foot-wide units are being produced, they are unlikely to come into widespread use in more than a few states with low population densities as well as low highway traffic loads. We have found that the 14-wide with on-site added storage sheds can meet the floor space requirements of basic housing codes—except for large families. Expandable 14-wides, as well as doublewides, provide readily available means of increasing floor space up to almost 2000 square feet.

During the growth period of the late 1960s and early 1970s the number of both mobile home manufacturing firms and plants increased rapidly. The general tendencies of the establishment of both firm headquarters and plants indicate the regional nature of the industry as well as the relationship between the industry and trends in demography and economic growth.

The 165 firms in 1968 swelled by over 100 percent to close to 400 firms in 1971 (table 4.13). Given the general history of the industry and the production volume trends discussed above, one would expect that the majority of mobile home manufacturers are headquartered in the East North Central, South Atlantic, and South Central regions. Table 4.15 shows that in 1977 the firms in these regions indeed made up 68 percent of all mobile home producers and the remaining 32 percent were spread throughout the other four regions. Together with Indiana, leading the list with 39 firms or 15 percent of the nation's mobile home manufacturers, California, Texas, Alabama, Georgia, and Florida are the headquarters for 143 of 262 firms in the entire country, or approximately 55 percent of all manufacturers (table 4.14). Table 4.15 compares firm distribution in 1973 with 1977. The shakeout is dramatically reflected, but no interregional shifts have occurred. There has also

B. Structure

Location of Firms and Plants

Table 4.8.
Regional Shares*ᵃ* of
Annual National Mobile
Home Sales (Wholesale
Dollar Volume*ᵇ*),1968–
1977

	1968		1969		1970		1971		1972	
Region	Wholesale $	%	Wholesale $	%	Wholesale $	%	Wholesale $	%	Wholesale $	%
Northeast	124,543,250	8	142,422,083	7	188,601,275	9	225,132,103	8	325,322,522	9
East North Central	398,416,602	27	473,212,937	24	484,273,840	22	565,365,635	20	624,392,151	17
West North Central	145,340,275	10	187,425,232	9	212,042,982	10	265,297,802	9	342,527,630	10
South Atlantic	361,295,736	24	470,576,368	24	402,460,742	22	662,691,736	23	875,576,431	23
South Central	219,845,899	15	381,220,106	19	472,278,838	21	621,266,375	22	836,534,297	22
Mountain	63,025,907	4	73,212,921	4	85,147,610	4	127,850,753	4	194,471,296	5
Pacific	188,659,948	12	253,328,408	13	280,653,083	12	380,838,521	13	532,797,509	14
Total	1,501,127,617		1,981,388,060		2,184,638,900		2,848,442,925		3,731,621,836	

	1973		1974		1975		1976		1977(est.)	
Region	Wholesale $	%	Wholesale $	%	Wholesale $	%	Wholesale $	%	Wholesale $	%
Northeast	275,274,379	8	215,535,127	8	131,000,350	7	187,158,163	8	NA	7
East North Central	610,826,478	16	429,551,902	17	291,050,851	16	346,674,261	15	NA	15
West North Central	340,731,593	9	223,495,935	9	171,184,601	10	208,900,438	9	NA	8
South Atlantic	977,396,299	26	571,689,233	22	317,038,214	18	453,907,729	19	NA	18
South Central	825,970,940	22	545,583,921	21	376,803,342	20	506,349,529	21	NA	21
Mountain	220,376,708	6	167,002,313	7	152,803,074	9	187,274,471	8	NA	8
Pacific	500,553,111	13	409,736,630	16	368,002,006	20	468,691,695	20	NA	23
Total	3,751,029,308		2,566,656,061		1,807,882,438		2,358,956,286		3,100,000,000	

a. Percentage figures rounded to nearest whole %.
b. Includes exports, government, and factory sales.

Source: Compiled by PMHI from back issues of "Annual Production Survey" published by *Mobile-Modular Housing Dealer Magazine*; publication discontinued in 1977; 1977 data are industry estimates.

Table 4.9.
Share of Annual National Mobile Home Production Volume (Unit Production Volume) Accounted for by the Top Five Mobile Home Producing States, 1963–1977

Year	Top Five States	Unit Production per State[a]	National Unit Production[a]	Total of Five-State Unit Production as Percent of National Production[b]
1963	Indiana	32,290		
	Michigan	22,220		
	California	16,810		
	Georgia	15,750		
	Kansas	8,550		
		95,620	153,940	62%
1967	Indiana	40,249		
	Georgia	32,960		
	Pennsylvania	24,363		
	Michigan	18,601		
	California	16,621		
		133,794	245,110	54%
1970	Indiana	49,500		
	Georgia	48,160		
	Texas	35,860		
	California	33,550		
	Pennsylvania	32,090		
		199,160	408,350	49%
1971	Indiana	61,527		
	Georgia	56,711		
	Texas	45,894		
	California	42,622		
	Florida	35,432		
		242,186	507,220	48%
1972	Georgia	69,334		
	Indiana	61,638		
	Texas	49,096		
	California	46,948		
	Alabama	43,980		
		270,996	601,250	45%
1973	Georgia	67,794		
	Indiana	50,767		
	Texas	46,085		
	Florida	44,724		
	Alabama	42,066		
		251,436	568,420	44%
1974	Georgia	30,925		
	Indiana	29,620		
	Texas	27,595		
	California	25,382		
	Florida	24,038		
		137,560	330,800	42%
1975	California	21,543		
	Indiana	20,324		
	Texas	19,641		
	Georgia	14,315		
	Alabama	12,496		
		88,319	212,970	41%
1976	California	24,951		
	Indiana	23,140		
	Texas	23,134		
	Georgia	18,562		
	Alabama	15,716		
		105,503	248,020	43%
1977	California	31,399		
	Texas	28,294		
	Indiana	25,371		
	Georgia	18,157		
	Alabama	15,667		
		118,888	265,640	45%

a. Includes exports, government and factory sales.
b. Rounded to nearest whole percent.

Source: Compiled by PMHI from data prepared by Elrick and Lavidge, Inc., for the Manufactured Housing Institute and from data provided by the National Conference of States on Building Codes and Standards, Inc.

| | | | | Total of Five-State Wholesale Dollar |
| | | Wholesale $ | National | Volume as % of National |
Year	Top Five States	per State[a]	Wholesale $	Wholesale Dollar Volume[b]
1968	Indiana	260,578,884		
	Georgia	175,571,084		
	California	156,705,479		
	Pennsylvania	123,557,250		
	Florida	100,044,349		
		816,457,046	1,501,127,617	54%
1969	Indiana	305,883,469		
	Georgia	227,433,708		
	California	192,237,792		
	Texas	141,464,581		
	Pennsylvania	141,026,088		
		1,008,045,638	1,981,388,060	51%
1970	Indiana	325,823,430		
	California	215,577,998		
	Georgia	205,145,751		
	Pennsylvania	186,398,823		
	Texas	170,251,616		
		1,103,197,618	2,184,638,900	50%
1971	Indiana	348,490,219		
	California	293,298,096		
	Georgia	255,941,704		
	Pennsylvania	220,416,190		
	Texas	208,417,155		
		1,326,563,364	2,848,442,925	47%
1972	California	424,064,737		
	Georgia	379,463,847		
	Indiana	355,969,219		
	Pennsylvania	302,919,500		
	Texas	281,944,000		
		1,744,361,303	3,731,621,836	47%
1973	Georgia	417,192,472		
	California	389,964,146		
	Indiana	355,037,710		
	Texas	316,949,361		
	Florida	264,088,649		
		1,743,232,338	3,751,029,308	46%
1974	California	295,235,262		
	Indiana	232,729,325		
	Texas	209,396,639		
	Georgia	185,608,976		
	Florida	168,131,315		
		1,091,101,517	2,566,656,061	43%
1975	California	254,519,561		
	Indiana	167,130,141		
	Texas	153,676,048		
	Georgia	101,010,720		
	Florida	95,915,944		
		772,252,414	1,807,882,438	43%
1976	California	330,009,987		
	Texas	204,159,695		
	Indiana	191,134,111		
	North Carolina	161,236,397		
	Pennsylvania	138,238,929		
		1,024,779,119	2,358,956,286	43%
1977 (est.)	California	NA		
	Texas	NA		
	Indiana	NA		
	Georgia	NA		
	North Carolina	NA		
		1,400,000,000	3,100,000,000	45%

Table 4.10.
Share of Annual National Mobile Home Sales (Wholesale Dollar Volume) Accounted for by the Top Five Mobile Home Producing States, 1968–1977

a. Includes exports, government and factory sales.
b. Rounded to nearest whole percent.

Source: Compiled by PMHI from back issues of "Annual Production Survey" published by *Mobile-Modular Housing Dealer Magazine*. Publication discontinued in 1977; 1977 data are industry estimates.

Table 4.11.
1977 Product Mix by
Regions and States, %
Total Production in
State, Singlewides
versus Doublewides

Northeast

	% SW	% DW
Connecticut	0	0
Maine	100	0
Massachusetts	0	0
New Hampshire	N/A	0
New Jersey	0	0
New York	83	17
Pennsylvania	90	10
Rhode Island	0	0
Vermont	N/A	0

West North Central

	% SW	% DW
Iowa	8	92
Kansas	87	13
Minnesota	86	12
Missouri	67	31
Nebraska	81	18
North Dakota	0	0
South Dakota	94	6

East North Central

	% SW	% DW
Illinois	N/A	N/A
Indiana	81	13
Michigan	N/A	N/A
Ohio	77	23
Wisconsin	90	10

Pacific

	% SW	% DW
California	21	71
Oregon	52	46
Washington	66	34

Mountain

	% SW	% DW
Arizona	70	3
Colorado	66	34
Idaho	69	31
Montana	99	0
Nevada	0	0
New Mexico	N/A	N/A
Utah	N/A	N/A
Wyoming	0	0

South Central

	% SW	% DW
Alabama	84	16
Arkansas	84	13
Kentucky	82	18
Louisiana	89	11
Mississippi	64	36
Oklahoma	86	14
Tennessee	76	22
Texas	93	7

South Atlantic

	% SW	% DW
Delaware	0	0
Florida	12	82
Georgia	55	44
Maryland	N/A	N/A
North Carolina	78	21
South Carolina	N/A	N/A
Virginia	86	14
West Virginia	0	0

SW=singlewides.
DW=doublewides and triplewides.

Source: Computed by PMHI from raw data provided by the National Conference of States on Building Codes and Standards, Inc.

Table 4.12.
Trends in Product Mix,
Product-Category[a]
Shares of Annual National
Mobile Home Production
Volume (Unit Production
Volume), 1950–1977

Size	1950	1955	1960	1965	1970	1975	1976	1977
Sectionals, expandables and others[b]	—	—	—	14%	4%	1%	2%[b]	1%[b]
Doublewides[c]	—	—	—	—	10%	26%	27%	31%
14-wides	—	—	—	—	8%	41%	47%	53%
12-wides	—	—	—	45%	78%	32%	24%	15%
10-wides[d]	—	—	90%	41%	—	—	—	—
8-wides[e]	100%	100%	10%	—	—	—	—	—

a. Percentage figures rounded to nearest whole percent.
b. Included 8-wides for 1965–1977, 10-wides for 1970–1977, and 16-wides for 1975–1977.
c. All widths, including 20-wide, 24-wide, 26-wide, and 28-wide doublewides.
d. 1970–1977 included in first line.
e. 1965–1977 included in first line.
f. Estimates.

Source: Mobile home data prepared by Elrick and Lavidge, Inc., for the Manufactured Housing Institute.

been rapid growth in the number of manufacturing plants in the mobile home industry, increasing from 366 in 1967 to 888 in 1973 (see table 4.16). The reason for the increase in the number of plants rather than the expansion of existing production facilities was due in large part to manufacturers' desire to decrease transportation costs; this was accomplished by geographic decentralization of production and marketing.

Preferred plant locations were originally close to automotive suppliers. As manufacturers and suppliers concentrated in the so-called "prefab belt" of the Detroit, Chicago, and northern Indiana and Ohio areas, a large labor pool with specific skills developed and the general external economies became significant. In the early 1950s the increasing unit dimensions and corresponding rise in transportation costs stimulated the decentralization process in which company size expanded more than plant size. Producers expanded their operations either through acquisition of other companies or construction of branch plants in key market areas. This continued trend toward plant, and thus production, decentralization is exhibited by the fact that in 1963 the top five states accounted for 62 percent of total national unit production, in 1967, for 54 percent, in 1970, for 49 percent, and in 1977, for only 45 percent.

In the last 20 years, the mobile home industry has experienced a marked shift in the location of mobile home production from the North Central region to the South Central and South Atlantic regions (table 4.16). This is a response to higher rates of sales growth in these areas.

A comparison of the distribution of plants with regional production figures shows the close correlation between the geographical distribution of mobile home sales and plant locations. By establishing plants as close as possible to the actual market, transportation costs are minimized and regional rather than national market strategy becomes the mode of operation for the multiplant firm. Production is further decentralized by new firms entering the industry. New firms, hoping to capture a share of sales in booming markets, tend to follow expanding multiplant firms into the expanding southern regional markets.

Concentration ratios viewed over a long period of time often serve as indicators of scale economies. In an industry where substantial scale economies do not exist, the typical firm remains small relative to the size of the total market, and therefore the concentration ratios are low. The higher the concentration ratio, the greater the impact size has upon production costs. This also serves to some extent as an indicator of an industry's stage of development, for as a rule concentration tends to increase with the age of an industry.

The national concentration ratios suggest that the mobile home industry is rather concentrated. The industry saw a steady rise in concentration as it developed throughout the 1950s and 1960s, such that by the 1970s a pattern for market shares has evidently been set. The single largest firm, with a sales volume of roughly $500 million in 1977, continues to control about 10 percent of the market.[3] The

Concentration

Table 4.13.
National Totals, Number
of Firms and Number of
Plants in the Mobile
Home Industry, 1968–
1977 (Including Average
Output per Plant)

Year	Number of Firms[a]	Number of Plants	National Production (in Units)	Average Output per Plant
1968	165	501	324,440	648
1969	165	642	417,270	650
1970	334	593	408,350	689
1971	380	691	507,220	734
1972	334	672	601,250	895
1973	334	888	568,420	640
1974	368	800	330,800	414
1975	225	596	212,970	357
1976	229	499	248,020	569
1977	220	479	265,640	555

a. Excludes firms not primarily in the business of producing mobile homes.

Source: Data taken from several sources.

Table 4.14.
State and Regional
Mobile Home Firm
Distribution, 1977

State	Number of Firms	% of U.S. Total[a]
Indiana	39	15
California	35	13
Texas	14	7
Alabama	18	7
Florida	18	7
Georgia	19	5
Total	143	55

a. Percentage figures rounded to nearest whole percent.

Source: List of firms compiled by PMHI from various industry and government sources.

Table 4.15.
Mobile Home Firm Distribution, Top Six States, 1977

Region	No. of Firms 1973	% of Totals 1973[a]	No. of Firms 1977	% of Totals 1977[a]
Northeast	42	7	22	8
Connecticut	2		0	
Maine	0		3	
Massachusetts	3		0	
New Hampshire	2		1	
New Jersey	1		0	
New York	9		3	
Pennsylvania	25		15	
Rhode Island	0		0	
Vermont	0		0	
East North Central	126	21	63	24
Illinois	10		1	
Indiana	77		39	
Michigan	13		10	
Ohio	15		4	
Wisconsin	11		9	
West North Central	50	8	13	5
Iowa	7		0	
Kansas	5		2	
Minnesota	11		3	
Missouri	14		4	
Nebraska	10		4	
North Dakota	2		0	
South Dakota	1		0	
South Atlantic	130	22	53	20
Delaware	0		0	
District of Columbia	0		0	
Florida	35		18	
Georgia	38		14	
Maryland	4		1	
North Carolina	20		11	
South Carolina	22		5	
Virginia	9		4	
West Virginia	2		0	
South Central	146	25	62	24
Alabama	38		18	
Arkansas	14		4	
Kentucky	8		3	
Louisiana	7		3	
Mississippi	5		1	
Oklahoma	10		4	
Tennessee	12		10	
Texas	52		19	
Mountain	31	5	11	4
Arizona	11		4	
Colorado	6		4	
Idaho	3		1	
Montana	2		2	
Nevada	0		0	
New Mexico	6		0	
Utah	3		0	
Wyoming	0		0	
Pacific	71	12	38	15
California	61		35	
Oregon	4		0	
Washington	6		3	
Alaska	0		0	
Hawaii	0		0	
United States	596	100	262	100

a. Percentage figures rounded to nearest whole percent.

Note: Figures include firms not primarily in the business of producing mobile homes.
Source: List of all firms (including marginally mobile home-oriented companies) compiled by PMHI from several sources.

Table 4.16.
Regional Distribution of Mobile Home Industry Plants, 1967–1969, 1972–1977

Region	Plant Distribution[a]																	
	1967	%	1968	%	1969	%	1972	%	1973	%	1974	%	1975	%	1976	%	1977	%
Northeast	32	9	46	9	47	8	45	7	61	7	55	7	42	7	36	7	32	7
East North Central	82	23	102	20	117	18	118	18	129	15	120	15	94	16	79	16	79	16
West North Central	37	10	47	9	56	9	61	9	76	9	74	9	57	10	49	10	39	8
South Atlantic	88	24	130	28	177	28	157	23	220	25	205	26	146	25	116	23	104	22
South Central	67	18	84	18	146	23	151	22	233	26	198	25	133	22	108	22	105	22
Mountain	18	5	28	4	30	4	38	6	55	6	54	7	44	7	39	8	37	8
Pacific	42	11	64	12	69	10	102	15	114	13	94	12	80	13	72	14	83	17
Total	366	100	501	100	642	100	672	100	888	100	800	100	596	100	499	100	479	100

a. Percentage figures rounded to nearest whole percent.

Source: 1967–1969, Mobile-Modular Housing Dealer Magazine annual "Market Studies"; 1972: Census of Manufacturers, U.S. Department of Commerce; 1973–1976, data prepared by Elrick and Lavidge, Inc., for the Manufactured Housing Institute; 1977, industry estimates.

top twenty-five companies' combined production continues to account for approximately two-thirds of total national output (table 4.17).

Although the concentration ratios per se might seem to suggest that the industry is concentrated, this concentration pertains only to the nonexisting "national" market. Despite the existence of many national producers, the industry in reality competes in regional markets. Thus state-by-state concentration ratios, though volatile, are much more meaningful than national ratios. One random example serves to emphasize the difference between national and state concentration ratios: In 1976, when the nation's top firm accounted for 10 percent of the total national production, it controlled 15.4 percent of California production. A manufacturer, moreover, may switch production from one state to another, strongly affecting state concentrations without affecting national concentration. The national ratios, then, explain certain "national" activities, but they do not necessarily permit any generalizations regarding the competitive behavior of the industry on either a regional or state level.

Since the last recession, concentration ratios have risen slightly, not least as a result of the high rate of business failure among the smaller, younger firms. With the economic recovery after the 1974 recession and the revived incidence of entry of new firms into the industry, the trend toward stabilization should continue. As discussed later in this chapter, entry barriers are rapidly increasing—largely due to ever-increasing public intervention. If government, however unintentionally, continues to raise barriers to new competition, concentration will rise and may ultimately approach an oligopolistic market structure. The industry leaders that have survived the recession with strong balance sheets can be expected to grow in strength

Integration

Integration is the process of increasing the production of intermediate goods that are direct inputs to a firm's major production process or of expanding the activities related directly to the distribution and sale of the final output. Integration is a measure of a firm's desire to control more than one or all phases of the production and delivery process. It offers significant advantages to a firm. First, integration assures the firm of a stable supply of inputs as well as a consistent market for its output. Integration eliminates the dependence on independent sources of supply that can result in shortages and resultant price changes. These variations require constant readaptation of production techniques, possible reduction of output because of unavailable inputs and absorption of supply price increases in order to maintain some price stability in the output market. In addition, integration can minimize costly inventory maintenance by the close coordination of production scheduling and input receipt.

The second advantage of integration is the opportunity for expansion into other, more profitable areas of operation within the same industry. If the firm is successful in increasing its size and profitability through integration, it will also accrue additional market power associated with the dominant firms within an industry. Finally, integration provides an established route of expansion for firms that have reached an optimum size within their existing geographical markets. Firms constrained geographically may be able to maintain growth patterns without the establishment of expensive national management structures.

Although integration offers several significant advantages to a mobile home producing firm, the production system exhibits only a low level of integration, both upward and downward.[4] One-fourth of the respondents to the PMHI/MS have integrated downstream into park development and mobile home dealerships. Within this group, four firms have integrated into both areas, while thirteen have entered only one field. Of another sample that we took of twenty-five leading firms, nine have integrated downward, three indicating that they have begun to integrate upstream and two have either abandoned previous efforts at integration or have adopted a policy of not integrating.

Two factors contribute to the low level of integration into the supply sector. First, the high absolute costs of entry and, second, perceived low profit margins act as deterrents to movement into this area. This may be indicative of significant economies of scale in the supply sector. Because mobile home industry demand represents only a limited portion of some suppliers' total sales, they are able to take advantage of scale economies unavailable to mobile home producers, who, even had they integrated upward, would still produce at much smaller volume. Strong corroboration of the limited extent of upward integration by manufacturers is provided by our national supplier survey (PMHI/SS). Of 188 responding suppliers only nineteen felt any erosion of sales due to integration by manufacturers.

Downward integration into the distribution and park systems is hampered by a variety of obstacles. The operation of dealerships and parks requires certain forms of expertise that are not necessarily associated with successful operation in the production system. Some producers find it more profitable to use what market power they possess to pass sales costs to dealers, and this advantage would be lost if the firms integrated into the distribution system.

The "specialized-expertise" barrier was dramatized in the early 1970s when several large manufacturers failed in their attempts to integrate into park development and operation. These moves were strongly motivated by an objective much more important than merely to add an additional profit point. The main objective was rather to increase and stabilize demand for homes by increasing available park spaces—a crucial objective for manufacturers facing demand volumes that are both curtailed by restrictive land use controls and highly volatile due to highly seasonal demand fluctuations. Thus, if integration moves powered by such crucial needs had to be abandoned, the difficulties encountered must have been substantial; and, in fact, they were. Park development (not unlike distribution) is simply a business totally different from manufacturing, requiring a totally different expertise—real estate development. Similarly, suppliers rarely integrate downward, although they have the financial resources to do so. The production of mobile homes requires specialized know-how that often is not readily "piratable" by suppliers attempting to enter the system. Finally, an important disincentive for downward integration is fear of retaliation by dealers and park operators who, feeling that their "suppliers" are competing with them, might stop transacting business with them.

The most significant trend concerning integration is the continued low level of interest in integration among producers, suggesting that most firms are aware of the disincentives mentioned earlier. Firms that have integrated tend to be smaller, indicating a decision to dominate one particular market rather than to expand production facilities into other geographical markets. Integration,

Table 4.17.
Cumulative Market Share (%) of the 1, 3, 5, 10, 25 Largest Mobile Home Producers by Units Shipped, 1969–1977

Largest	1969	1970	1971	1972	1973	1974	1975	1976	1977
1	9.7	11.2	11.1	10.0	10.4	NA	NA	NA	NA
3	21.6	23.6	24.0	23.1	26.9	NA	NA	NA	NA
5	31.0	33.0	34.5	33.7	37.8	34.0	31.0	31.0	32.0
10	47.3	47.6	49.4	46.0	53.8	43.0	43.0	44.0	45.0
25	69.3	68.6	69.8	66.4	81.2	61.0	60.0	63.0	64.0
1	9.7	11.2	11.1	10.0	10.4	NA	NA	NA	NA
2–3	11.9	12.4	12.9	13.1	16.5	NA	NA	NA	NA
4–5	9.4	9.4	10.5	10.6	10.8	NA	NA	NA	NA
6–10	16.3	14.6	14.9	12.3	16.0	9.0	12.0	13.0	13.0
11–25	22.0	21.0	20.4	20.4	27.4	18.0	17.0	19.0	19.0

NA = Not available.

Source: Data estimated by PMHI from various sources including *Automation in Housing, Professional Builder,* 1973 through 1977 *Bluebooks of Major Home Builders,* MHI *Annual Industry Surveys.*

when it does occur, is more prevalent among new firms, reflecting the inclination toward greater integration activity by the more broadly based firms that entered the industry before the 1974 recession. Table 4.18 gives more specific information on individual characteristics of integrating firms. These data were revised to indicate the average number of integration activities per responding firm and are presented with the integration coefficients. After revision, the limited trends are evident.

Before the 1974 recession, of the firms responding to the PMHI/MS, 11 percent planned downward integration. Four firms indicated plans to integrate into park development, two stated intentions to enter the dealer market, and six planned to enter both. The characteristics of firms planning to integrate were transformed into planned integration coefficients (see table 4.19) comparable to the integration coefficients of table 4.18. The comparison of the planned integration coefficient and the existing integration coefficients indicate that planned activity would, if accomplished, have tended to make integration patterns more homogenous; but

again, it was the younger and smaller firms that seemed inclined toward integration. Whether the manufacturers' plans to integrate were realized is questionable; most likely they were not. The responses to more recent PMHI industry interviews indicated that integration was decreasing. Only 10 percent of the respondents stated that the number of manufacturers integrating into dealerships was constant. The remaining respondents stated that manufacturers were integrating less than before or not at all. At the height of the boom, firms that did plan to integrate were small and young—those most likely to have been forced out of the industry during the last recession. Thus it appears that the specialization of each system has been maintained and integration will continue to be low.

Diversification (movement of firms into areas not directly related to their present business) may be accomplished either through acquisition or internal development, with advantages present in both. The acquisition of a firm involves not only the absorption of assets

Diversification

Table 4.18.
Characteristics of
Integrated Firms and
Integration Coefficients

Characteristic	Park Development		Dealerships		All Responding Firms	
	Number of Firms	Integration Coefficients	Number of Firms	Integration Coefficients	Number of Firms	Integration Coefficients
Year of entry						
1900–1950	1	0.16	0	0.00	6	0.16
1951–1960	1	0.14	2	0.29	7	0.43
1961–1970	7	0.25	7	0.25	28	0.50
1971–	1	0.11	2	0.22	9	0.33
Not stated					1	
Total company sales, 1972						
0–2.5M	4	1.00	3	0.27	11	0.63
2.5–10M	3	0.36	2	0.13	15	0.33
10–40M	1	0.20	3	0.21	14	0.28
40M–500M	1	0.07	2	0.22	9	0.33
Not stated	1	0.11	0	0.00	1	1.00
Number of plants, 1972						
1	7	0.30	6	0.26	23	0.59
2–5	1	0.07	2	0.13	15	0.20
61–0	0	0.00	2	0.25	8	0.25
11–20	1	1.00	0	0.00	1	1.00
21–	0	0.00	0	0.00	3	0.00
Sector of origin						
Recreational vehicles	1	0.25	2	0.50	4	0.75
Mobile homes	6	0.17	7	0.19	36	0.36
Building manufacturing	0	0.00	1	0.25	4	0.25
On-site construction	0	0.00	0	0.00	0	0.00
Not specified	3	0.50	1	0.17	6	0.67
Percent unionized						
0–10	9	0.23	6	0.15	39	0.38
11–50	0	0.00	1	0.20	5	0.20
51–100	1	0.17	4	0.67	6	0.84

Source: PMHI/MS.

but also of personnel. When there are administrative intricacies peculiar to the business of the acquired firm, problems of transition can be avoided by allowing direct management to stay on. Although a negotiating time lag must be considered between the intent to acquire a given firm and its acquisition, production can physically begin immediately upon acquisition. Diversification is more easily accomplished internally if the production process of the new good is related to that of the original good. In this case the firm can benefit economically from the similar assembly procedures, labor requirements, and raw materials needed for the production of the new good.

Motivations for diversification are signified by a firm's efforts to maximize both its profitability and stability. A firm may see greater potential for profits in an activity in which it is not currently engaged and is therefore prompted to diversify to ensure future profitability. To achieve stability, a firm may diversify in order to decrease the risk that the market demand for its good will fall. By operating in two or more different markets through the production of two or more goods, a firm achieves stability by minimizing the likelihood that their markets will collapse simultaneously.

A last inducement to diversify is related to the possible existence of optimal firm size and stability. If a firm should reach its optimal size, it may first attempt to ensure its supply and distribution structure through vertical integration and then attempt to achieve power in more than one product market by diversifying. In this case the diversification is prompted less by desire for stability than by exhaustion of expansion possibilities within a single-product market.

Diversification may have far-reaching effects on other elements of market behavior. For example, a firm operating in several markets can better afford to use pricing policy as a tool to gain more market power. Because the competitive conditions in the market for any one good are entirely unrelated to the other goods a firm produces, the firm may be able to accept a short-term loss while pursuing policies with the goal of increasing its market share. The burden of this loss can be somewhat lightened by the profits gained from other products. Thus diversification may

Table 4.19.
Characteristics of Firms
Planning to Integrate
and Planned Integration
Coefficients

Characteristic	Park Development		Dealerships		All Responding Firms	
	Number of Firms	Integration Coefficients	Number of Firms	Integration Coefficients	Number of Firms	Integration Coefficients
Year of entry						
1900–1950	1	0.17	1	0.17	6	0.34
1951–1960	0	0.00	0	0.00	7	0.00
1961–1970	2	0.07	3	0.11	28	0.18
1971–	3	0.33	1	0.11	9	0.44
Not stated	1	0.00	0	0.00	6	0.00
Total company sales						
0–2.5M	2	0.18	1	0.09	11	0.27
2.5–10M	2	0.13	3	0.20	15	0.33
10–40M	1	0.07	0	0.00	14	0.07
40M–500M	1	0.11	1	0.11	9	0.22
Not stated	1	1.00	0	0.00	1	0.00
Number of plants						
1	5	0.22	4	0.17	23	0.39
2–5	1	0.07	0	0.00	15	0.07
6–10	1	0.12	1	0.12	8	0.25
11–20	0	0.00	0	0.00	1	0.00
21–	0	0.00	0	0.00	3	0.00
Sector of origin						
Recreational vehicles	0	0.00	0	0.00	41	0.00
Mobile homes	5	0.14	3	0.08	36	0.22
Building manufacturing	0	0.00	0	0.00	4	0.00
On-site construction	0	0.00	0	0.00	11	0.00
Not specified	2	0.33	1	0.16	6	0.49
Percent unionized						
0–10	6	0.15	5	0.13	39	0.28
11–50	0	0.00	0	0.00	5	0.00
51–100	1	0.17	0	0.00	6	0.17

Source: PMHI/MS.

provide a pricing advantage that could lead to increased market power as smaller, single-good competitors unable to lower the price of their product may be driven from the market. To the extent that diversification increases a firm's size, it may result in easier access to capital because the firm can obtain lower interest rates on any necessary debt. This, however, tends to be dependent on size more than on diversification. Other benefits related to size and therefore indirectly to diversification include a large firm's ability to conduct research and development, to spend more on product promotion, and to deal more effectively with another large firm with regard to such aspects as purchase contracts.

Regarding movement of mobile home manufacturers into unrelated fields, we found a trend toward greater cross-ownership among the mobile home, manufactured building, and on-site residential building industries. Firms that previously performed only one activity are now diversifying into alternate methods of housing production. This trend is most prevalent among larger firms with sufficient resources to enter new markets, but it is also characteristic of smaller firms in the industry.

The incidence and patterns of cross-ownership were examined for the entire housing industry and for the mobile home industry in particular.[5] During the period 1970 through 1977 the pattern changed little. The average pattern during this seven-year period shows that of the hundred largest housing firms, one-half specialize. One-third specialize in on-site construction only, one-sixth, in mobile home production, and one-twelfth, in manufactured building. Another half are active in more than one sector of the housing industry. Roughly one-twelfth of the firms produce both mobile homes and manu-factured units, one-fifth produce on-site and manufactured residential shelter, and one-tenth operate in three or more areas.

A look at the extent to which these firms operate in major subsectors of the industry conveys again the impression of extensive cross-ownership as well as the existence of many multioperation producers. Two-thirds of the firms are active in on-site residential construction, one-third, in mobile home production, and one-half, in building manu-facturing. Only one-fifth are involved in non-residential construction. To the extent that such diversification takes the form of acqui-sition, this cross-ownership activity does not increase the total capacity of the mobile home industry. However, it has a profound effect on industry structure because large on-site builders are likely to acquire a number of small mobile home companies. The original mobile home management usually continues to run these operations as independent sub-sidiaries of the parent company, thus yielding very decentralized housing giants.

The PMHI survey indicates that 36 percent of its respondents are also operating in fields unrelated to mobile home production (table 4.20). The three predominant areas of diver-sification are factory-produced nonmobile housing, recreational vehicles, and building supply production. Most diversified firms are involved in only one field other than mobile home production. However, as shown in table 4.21, in addition to mobile home pro-duction, a single firm may participate in as many as four of the areas listed above.

Diversification into each of the areas shown in tables 4.20 and 4.22 were cross-tabulated with demographic variables such as size, age, and region to determine any correlation. We had anticipated, prior to the running of the cross-tabs, that the larger the firm, the greater the tendency would be to diversify. This was confirmed only in the area of recreational vehicles, where the firms do tend to be large. With regard to age, recrea-tional vehicles was again the only area of

Table 4.20.
Number of Responding Firms Indicating Diversi-fication by Sector of Diversification

Area of Diversification	Firms Now In	Firms Planning to Enter
Mobile home consumer financing	2	1
Factory-produced nonmobile housing	11	3
Factory-produced nonresidential shelter	4	1
On-site residential construction	8	2
On-site nonresidential construction	5	0
Production of building supplies	7	0
Distribution of building supplies	3	0
Production of recreational vehicles	7	0

Source: PMHI/MS.

Table 4.21.
Number of Reported Diversifications per Firm

Number of Diversifications	Number of Firms
Greater than 4	2
4	1
3	3
2	4
1	15
0	43

Source: PMHI/MS.

Table 4.22.
Number of Diversified Firms by Type of Diversification and Company Characteristics

Characteristic	Consumer Financing	Factory-Produced Nonmobile Housing	Factory-Produced Nonresidential Shelter	On-Site Residential Construction	On-Site Nonresidential Construction	Production of Building Supplies	Distribution of Building Supplies	Recreational Vehicles	Number of Firms
Sector of origin									
Aircraft									0
Recreational vehicle									1
Building supplies									0
Mobile home	1	9	2	5	2	5	1	5	36
Building manufacturing		1	2	1	1			1	2
On-site construction				1	1				1
Other						2	2		4
Year first production									
<1950		3	1	2	1	2	2	2	6
1951–55						1		2	3
1956–60	1	2	1	3	1			1	4
1961–65	1	3						1	9
1966–70		3	2	2	2	3	1	1	19
1971–				1	1	1			9
1972 Company sales (×1,000)									
0–500				1	1				4
500–1,000									2
1,000–5,000		1			1	2	1		13
5,000–10,000		2	1	2		1		1	7
10,000–50,000	2	4	2	1	2	1		2	17
50,000–100,000		2	1	1	1	2	1	1	3
100,000+		1		2		1	1	3	3
Not Listed									1
1967 Total company sales (×1,000)									
0–500		1							1
500–1,000		1							1
1,000–5,000	1	3	1	3	1				8
5,000–10,000		1		1				1	2
10,000–50,000	1	2	1		1	2	1	3	8
50,000–100,000		1		2		1	1	1	2
1963 Total company sales (×1,000)									
0–500									0
500–1,000									0
1,000–5,000	1	1	1	2	1				4
5,000–10,000		1							2
10,000–50,000		2		2		2	1	4	6
Number of plants, 1972									
1–5	1	5	2	3	3	4	1	1	38
6–10	1	2	2	2		2	1	2	8
>10		2		2	2	1	1	4	4
Number of plants, 1967									
1–5	2	7	2	4	2	1	1	2	19
6–10				1		2		1	2
>10		1					1	2	2
Number of plants, 1963									
1–5	1	3	2	3	2	3	2	2	11
6–10								2	2
>10									0
Percent unionized									
0–20	1	6	2	5	3	5	2	5	41
21–50		2	1	1	1	1	1		3
51–100	1	3	1	2	1	1		1	6

Source: PMHI/MS.

Table 4.23.
Diversification Quo-
tients and Planned
Diversification
Quotients by Firm
Characteristics

Characteristic	Number of Responding Firms by Category	Diversification Quotient[a]	Planned Diversification Quotient[a]
Year of first mobile home production			
Prior to 1950	6	2.00	0.00
1951–1955	3	1.00	0.00
1956–1960	4	2.25	0.00
1960–1965	9	0.55	0.00
1966–1970	19	0.74	0.11
1971–	9	0.33	0.33
1972 company sales			
0–500,000	4	0.50	0.25
500,000–1,000,000	2	0.00	0.50
1,000,000–5,000,000	13	0.38	0.15
5,000,000–10,000,000	7	1.00	0.29
10,000,000–50,000,000	17	0.82	0.00
50,000,000–100,000,000	3	3.00	0.00
Over 100,000,000	3	2.67	0.00
1967 company sales			
0–500,000	1	1.00	N.A.
500,000–1,000,000	1	1.00	N.A.
1,000,000–5,000,000	8	1.13	N.A.
5,000,000–10,000,000	2	1.50	N.A.
10,000,000–50,000,000	8	1.38	N.A.
50,000,000–100,000,000	2	3.00	N.A.
1962 company sales			
0–500,000	0	0.00	N.A.
500,000–1,000,000	0	0.00	N.A.
1,000,000–5,000,000	4	1.50	N.A.
5,000,000–10,000,000	2	0.50	N.A.
10,000,000–50,000,000	6	1.83	N.A.
Number of plants, 1972			
1–5	38	0.55	0.21
6–10	8	1.50	0.00
Greater than 10	4	3.00	0.00
Number of plants, 1967			
1–5	19	1.10	N.A.
6–10	2	2.00	N.A.
Greater than 10	2	2 00	N.A.
Number of plants, 1963			
1–5	11	1.63	N.A.
6–10	2	1.00	N.A.
Greater than 10	0	0.00	N.A.
Percent of labor force unionized			
0–20	41	0.70	0.20
21–50	3	2.33	0.00
51–100	6	1.67	0.00
Census region			
Not ascertainable	4	0.75	0.75
New England	1	1.00	0.00
Mid-Atlantic	8	0.50	0.25
South Atlantic	17	0.94	0.00
East North Central	4	0.75	0.50
East South Central	3	1.67	0.00
West South Central	6	1.17	0.16
West Mountain	4	1.00	0.00
West Pacific	4	1.00	0.00
Sector of origin			
Recreational vehicles	1	0.00	0.00
Mobile home industry	36	0.83	0.20
Building manufacturing	2	3.00	0.00
On-site constuction	1	2.00	0.00
Other	4	1.00	0.00

a. Quotients are total number of diversifications (Planned Diversifications) by firms with characteristic indicated divided by number of firms with that characteristic.

Source: PMHI/MS,

diversification in which there seemed to be a prevailing trend. As expected overall, those firms that diversified into recreational vehicle production were old as well as large. During the early development of the mobile home industry, there existed considerable overlap in the markets for mobile homes and for recreational vehicles. The primary distinction between the two goods was one of size. Because both could be legally trailered with minimum legal restriction, it was natural for dealers to maintain a product mix that included the entire size range. The technology required for the production of mobile homes and of recreational vehicles is quite similar, so this demand at the distributional level provided an attractive area for diversification. The percentage of unionized labor the firm employed was examined under the expectation that firms in mechanized industries with unskilled labor, such as factory-produced shelter, would have fewer unionized employees than those firms that also operate in on-site construction. This did not prove to be the case; all areas of diversification showed the low unionization levels characteristic of the mobile home industry in general. The origins of the diversified firms proved to be mobile home and building manufacturing (see table 4.22).

The data in table 4.22 tends to overstate the behavior of certain classes of firms because of the increased representation of responding firms in those classes. Table 4.23 presents the data in the form of diversification quotients that demonstrate additional patterns. These quotients indicate that size is an important determinant of diversification activity. Firms moving into other fields tended to have higher sales in 1972, 1967, and 1963. The pattern is equally pronounced with respect to the number of plants in operation. Firms with more than ten plants for the production of mobile homes averaged three diversifications per firm; firms with fewer than five plants had approximately one-half diversification per firm. The apparent correlation between age and diversification is also strengthened.

One relationship that appeared in the untransformed data disappears after the adjustment. Firms originating in the mobile home production system, which dominated activity as measured by raw data, yield a quotient lower than three of the four other groups of firms. One other revealing measure of diversification activity is an analysis of the 1970–1977 "average" pattern of the twenty-five leading firms in the mobile home production system.[6] Of these firms, close to three-quarters have diversified. One-third of the firms report production of recreational vehicles, which was the most popular form of diversification. One-quarter of the firms were part of large firms with broad patterns of diversification into fields not related to housing,

and one-sixth were associated with firms having large numbers of subsidiary firms within the general housing field. In general the findings corroborate the earlier conclusion that size is a major determinant of diversification: Almost 75 percent of the major industry leaders are diversified, as opposed to approximately 33 percent of all mobile home producers.

Firms responding to the PMHI Producers Survey indicate that even before the 1974 recession only a limited amount of diversification was planned. Planned activity was restricted to four areas: consumer financing, factory production of nonmobile housing, factory production of nonresidential shelter, and on-site residential construction. Characteristics of firms planning diversification do not indicate any readily observable patterns. Planned diversification was converted to planned diversification quotients in table 4.23. Comparison of these quotients with the diversification quotients also in this table provides further explanation of the patterns of planned diversification. If all planned activity were accomplished, diversification would be evenly distributed among the various characteristics. This, of course, is not unlikely considering the high rate of business failure induced by the 1974 recession.

Economies of scale are changes in the real per-unit cost of producing a good as quantities change, assuming that complete advantage of existing technology is taken at each production level. The typical firm will first experience increasing or positive economies of scale as production increases, with the magnitude of economies decreasing until an area of production is reached in which no further positive economies are realized and per-unit costs remain constant. In fact, a level of production often exists beyond which the firm finds that per-unit costs increase as production levels increase, which is known as the area of negative economies of scale. The range of output levels through which per-unit costs remain constant is the subject of debate in a number of empirical studies of various industries, varying from short to long ranges, depending on the nature of the production process.

Factors generating positive economies of scale may be grouped into three categories. First there are organizational efficiencies arising from higher levels of production. In small operations it is necessary for one individual to fill more than one position in the production process so that the worker cannot gain the increased proficiency associated with constant repetition of a specific task. As the scale of production increases, greater specialization is possible and workers may concentrate on one task. Recent experience seems to indicate that the apparent benefit of increased specialization may have upper limits imposed by worker boredom or other

Economies of Scale

personnel problems, and several manufacturers have returned to group assembly after increased usage of assembly line technique resulted in decreased efficiency.

The second area in which economies of scale may arise is in the application of technology to the production process. As scale of production increases, the firm is able to utilize more efficient equipment and is able to organize its use more efficiently. Cost per unit of output for capital equipment tends to decrease as the degree of mechanization and the size of equipment increase, and as the quantity of production increases, it is possible for equipment of different capacities to be more efficiently scheduled.

The third area is the firm's ability to exert its power in financial dealings. As the quantity of goods purchased increases, it may be possible to obtain volume discounts or to integrate vertically to ensure sources of supply.

Negative economies of scale are generally attributed to decreased managerial efficiency; as the level of production increases, management contact with the actual production process decreases and organizational hierarchies are established. Economies of scale are a major determinant of plant and firm size and therefore of industrial structure. If the nature of the productive process is such that negative economies of scale become important at attainable levels of production, firm growth will be limited and, in the absence of other countervailing factors, a competitive industry with few dominant firms should develop. However, if economies of scale continue to increase over the feasible range of production or at least do not become negative, there is no limit to firm size and a tendency for industry domination exists. This tendency again may be ameliorated by other factors in the market structure, such as general patterns of integration or product differentiation.

The range over which economies of scale remain positive or neutral is particularly significant in an industry such as the mobile home industry, in which transportation costs limit the accessible market area. A firm enjoying lower average costs because of positive economies of scale will be able either to underprice competitors and obtain larger market shares by absorbing some transportation costs or to maintain the existing price scale and enjoy higher profits. Equally important, expansion of geographical markets may allow firms to isolate themselves from local cyclical economic fluctuations and therefore achieve more stable production scheduling.

Since 1955 the average capacity of a mobile home plant initially increased, reaching a maximum of twelve floors per day, and then gradually decreased to the present level of four per day. This leads to two hypotheses concerning the possibility of economies of scale in the mobile home industry. First, the attempts to expand productive capacity would indicate that manufacturers recognized the existence of potentially sizable economies of scale but that significant external barriers to expansion outweighed the benefits accruing to larger plants. Second, the retrenchment could show that the industry's estimates of potential economies of scale were in error. Because realization of potential economies of scale would have a major impact on the cost of housing production as well as upon the competitive advantage of manufactured housing relative to other sectors of the housing industry, we devoted a major effort to testing the validity of these hypotheses.

Considering the factors generating positive economies of scale, three scale economy categories can be defined: organizational economies, technological economies, and "financial" economies (for example, as the quantity of supplies purchased increases, it may be possible to obtain volume discounts or to integrate vertically to ensure sources of supply). Two of these categories are technical; they refer to relationships between physical quantities of inputs and outputs. Organizational economies of scale imply that proportionately less indirect labor is necessary as levels of output increase; technological economies of scale imply that proportionately less direct input is necessary as production increases. Investigation of the relationships between these inputs and their associated levels of output for the purpose of estimating economies of scale requires the determination of the technical production functions of the plants and firms in the industry. Our Manufacturer Survey was not designed to collect data that would make such estimation possible.

The third category of factors is related to maket financial structure. If technical economies of scale could be held constant, the cost data available from our Manufacturer Survey would be sufficient to estimate these economies. However, because these other economies cannot be held constant, the investigation is restricted to net economies of scale with all three categories combined.

Respondents to PMHI's national Manufacturer Survey provided information on eight components of their costs as reflected in both firm operating expenses and model expenses. Model expense data were based upon an industry-typical average priced model, fully finished and with furnishings. This model was specified by PMHI as a standardized unit to ensure general comparability of data among firms' responses. The eight cost components were material costs, indirect labor costs, direct labor costs, selling expenses, general and administrative expenses, overhead costs, profit before taxes, and taxes. Because taxes are predetermined, no attempt was made to analyze their behavior. The remaining seven cost components were further divided into costs for single-plant firms and costs for all responding firms in order to isolate the effects associated with plant characteristics from more general characteristics. The range of the seven costs other than taxes, reported as percentages of total model costs for firms in four size categories, is shown in tables 4.24 and 4.25. Data in table 4.24 refer specifically to one-plant firms and data in table 4.25 refer to all responding firms. The seven costs reported as percentages of total company operating expenses are shown in tables 4.26 and 4.27. Table 4.26 refers to single-plant firms and table 4.27 refers to all responding firms.

Economies of scale would be shown in this data if those cost components generally assumed to be fixed decreased as a percentage of total costs as firm size increased, while those costs considered variable increased in percentage terms. Of the seven costs other than taxes, material costs, direct labor, and selling expenses were assumed to be variable costs, while the other four components were assumed to be fixed costs.

For all responding firms there is some tendency for material costs to increase as a percentage of total costs as production rises. Direct labor costs, however, appear to decrease slightly as production increases. This may indicate the existence of organizational economies of scale or it may reflect either increasing material costs or increased labor market power for larger firms. There is some evidence of decreases in indirect costs as firm size increases; however, because some larger firms show higher costs in this area, generalizations are not possible.

In order to develop quantitatively the relationship between size and cost structures, the data were used to estimate several cost parameters. Two classes of relationships were analyzed. First, regression analysis was used to investigate in greater detail the behavior of percentage cost components as firm size increases. Second, the available data were modified to obtain estimates of average total model costs, which were then associated with various characteristics of the relevant plants in a multiple-regression format. We hoped that such analysis would produce more precise estimates of the orders of magnitude of possible economies of scale. Although consideration of tables 4.24 through 4.27 did not reveal substantial evidence of expected trends, regression analysis would make it possible to account for variations in additional factors that might mask trends in more naive forms of analysis. A wide range of such additional factors, including the geographical region of operation, product line composition, and degrees of integration and diversification, were included at various stages of the analysis. In general, the results did not support the initial presumptions concerning cost behavior. The lack of significant results may be attributed

Table 4.24.
Model Costs, Single-
Plant Firms

% Model Costs	Total Company Sales ($\times$ $1,000)			
	0–2,500	2,501–10,000	10,001–40,000	40,001 +
Materials				
0–60	2	0	0	NR
62	1	0	0	NR
64	0	0	1	NR
65	2	0	0	NR
67	1	2	0	NR
68	2	1	0	NR
69	0	2	0	NR
70	2	5	0	NR
71 or more	3	3	0	NR
Direct labor				
0–8	1	4	0	NR
9	2	3	0	NR
10	2	3	0	NR
12	1	1	1	NR
13	2	2	0	NR
14 and more	5	0	0	NR
Indirect labor				
0	2	0	1	NR
1	1	2	0	NR
2	4	1	0	NR
3	2	1	0	NR
4	1	3	0	NR
5	1	0	0	NR
6	1	0	0	NR
10	1	0	0	NR
Selling expenses				
1	7	1	NR	NR
2	0	4	NR	NR
3	1	5	NR	NR
4	1	1	NR	NR
5	4	2	NR	NR
General and administration				
1	1	0	NR	NR
2	1	2	NR	NR
3	5	6	NR	NR
4	2	4	NR	NR
5	1	0	NR	NR
6	1	1	NR	NR
7	1	0	NR	NR
8	1	0	NR	NR
Plant overhead				
2	1	2	NR	NR
3	4	1	NR	NR
4	1	4	NR	NR
5	4	2	NR	NR
6	2	1	NR	NR
7	0	3	NR	NR
8	1	0	NR	NR
Profit				
3	2	0	NR	NR
4	1	1	NR	NR
5	2	2	NR	NR
6	2	3	NR	NR
7	1	3	NR	NR
8	1	1	NR	NR
9	0	1	NR	NR
10	1	1	NR	NR
11	0	1	NR	NR
13	2	0	NR	NR

NR = no responding firms.

Source: PMHI/MS.

Table 4.25.
Model Costs, All
Responding Firms

% Model Costs	Total Company Sales ($\times$ \$1,000)			
	0–2,500	2,501–10,000	10,001–40,000	40,001 +
Materials				
0–60	2	0	0	1
62	1	0	0	0
64	0	0	2	0
65	2	0	0	2
66	0	0	2	0
67	1	2	3	2
68	2	1	2	0
69	1	2	2	1
70	2	5	0	3
71 and greater	3	4	2	0
Direct labor				
0–8	1	4	3	0
9	2	3	2	1
10	3	4	5	1
11	0	0	1	4
12	1	1	2	2
13	2	2	0	0
14 and more	5	0	0	1
Indirect labor				
0	2	0	3	3
1	1	2	2	1
2	5	8	6	1
3	2	1	0	1
4	1	3	1	2
5	1	0	1	0
6	1	0	0	0
7	0	0	0	1
10	1	0	0	0
Selling expenses				
0	0	0	0	0
1	7	1	1	0
2	0	4	2	6
3	1	5	4	2
4	1	1	1	1
5	5	2	2	0
6	0	0	2	0
General and administration				
0	0	0	0	0
1	1	0	1	1
2	1	2	0	2
3	5	6	3	2
4	3	4	5	1
5	1	0	1	1
6	1	1	2	0
7	1	0	0	0
8	1	0	0	0
Plant overhead				
2	1	2	0	2
3	4	1	2	0
4	1	4	2	1
5	4	2	1	2
6	2	1	4	1
7	0	3	0	0
8	2	0	3	2
Profit				
0–3	3	0	2	0
4	1	1	0	0
5	2	2	0	1
6	2	3	1	1
7	1	3	2	1
8	1	1	2	2
9	0	1	2	1
10	1	1	0	0
11	0	1	3	0
12 or more	2	0	0	2

Source: PMHI/MS.

Table 4.26.
Operating Characteristics, Single-Plant Firms

Characteristic	Total Company Sales (× \$1,000)			
	0–2,500	2,501–10,000	10,001–40,000	40,001
Planned investment new plants				
0–200	5	4	1	N.R.
201–700	5	3	0	
701–3500	2	2	0	
>3501	2	2	0	
Planned investment existing plants				
0–30	5	3	NR	N.R.
31–100	4	4	NR	
101–500	2	2	NR	
>501	1	0	NR	
Company expenses				
% operating expenses in materials				
<65%	4	0	2	N.R.
65%–67%	3	0	0	
68%–70%	5	10	0	
>70%	2	3	0	
% operating expenses in direct labor				
7%–9%	2	4	0	N.R.
10%–11%	1	6	1	
12%–13%	5	3	0	
>14%	6	0	1	
% operating expenses in indirect labor				
0%–1%	4	2	0	N.R.
2%–3%	6	8	2	
4%–5%	2	3	0	
6%–10%	2	0	0	
% operating expenses in selling expenses				
0%–1%	6	1	0	N.R.
2%–3%	2	8	1	
4%–5%	5	4	1	
6%–7%	1	0	0	
% operating expenses in general and administration				
0%–1%	1	0	0	N.R.
2%–3%	5	8	1	
4%–5%	4	4	1	
6%–10%	4	1	0	
% operating expenses in plant overhead				
0%–2%	1	2	0	N.R.
3%–4%	5	5	0	
5%–7%	7	5	1	
>8%	1	1	1	
% operating expenses in profit before taxes				
0%–2%	0	2	0	N.R.
3%–4%	3	3	0	
5%–7%	6	6	1	
>8%	4	2	1	
% cost decrease if production 100% efficient				
0%–4%	2	5	1	N.R.
5%	3	3	1	
6%–10%	5	1	0	
>11%	4	2	0	

Table 4.26. (cont.)

Characteristic	Total Company Sales ($ × 1,000)			
	0–2,500	2,501–10,000	10,001–40,000	140,00
Ratio of lowest to highest monthly production				
0–0.40	10	2	0	N.R.
0.41–0.55	1	3	1	
0.56–0.61	0	4	1	
>0.62	3	3	1	
Number of product lines used				
1	6	1	0	N.R.
2	5	10	0	
3	4	1	1	
4–6	0	2	1	

NR = no responding firms.

Source: PMHI/MS.

Table 4.27.
Operating Characteristics, All Responding Firms

Characteristic	Total Company Sales (× $1,000)			
	0–2,500	2,501–10,000	10,001–40,000	40,001
Number of plants in operation				
0–1	17	14	3	0
2–5	1	3	13	0
6–10	0	0	5,	5
>11	0	0	0	4
Planned investment new plants				
0–200	6	5	2	0
201–700	5	3	3	0
701–3500	2	3	6	1
>3501	2	2	4	5
Planned investment existing plants				
0–30	6	4	1	0
31–100	4	5	3	0
101–500	2	2	7	1
>501	1	0	2	5
Operating expenses				
% operating expenses in materials				
<65%	5	1	2	1
65%–67%	3	1	6	4
68%–70%	5	11	6	4
>70%	2	3	2	0
% operating expenses in direct labor				
7%–9%	2	5	3	1
10%–11%	1	7	11	6
12%–13%	5	4	1	2
>14%	7	0	1	0
% operating expenses in indirect labor				
0%–1%	4	2	5	2
2%–3%	7	9	7	3
4%–5%	2	6	4	3
6%–10%	2	0	0	1

Table 4.27. (cont.)

Characteristic	Total Company Sales ($\times$ \$1,000)			
	0–2,500	2,501–10,000	10,001–40,000	40,001
% operating expenses				
in selling expense				
0%–1%	6	1	1	0
2%–3%	2	8	6	6
4%–5%	5	5	6	3
6%–10%	2	1	3	0
% operating expenses in				
general and administration				
0%–1%	1	0	0	1
2%–3%	5	8	6	2
4%–5%	5	6	7	4
6%–10%	4	1	3	1
% operating expenses in				
plant overhead				
0%–2%	1	2	0	2
3%–4%	5	5	4	1
5%–7%	7	7	6	2
>8%	2	1	6	4
% operating costs in				
profit before taxes				
0%–2%	0	2	3	0
3%–4%	4	4	5	2
5%–7%	6	7	6	3
>8%	4	3	2	3
Cost decrease if 100% efficient				
0%–4%	3	6	10	3
5%	3	3	2	3
6%–10%	5	1	3	0
>11%	4	3	1	1
Ratio of lowest to highest				
monthly production				
0–.40	11	3	6	2
.41–.55	1	3	4	2
.56–.61	0	4	4	2
>.62	3	3	3	1
Number of product lines used				
1	7	1	0	1
2	5	11	2	0
3–6	4	5	10	2
>7	0	0	7	5

Source: PMHI/MS.

to some combination of two factors. First, the large number of variables included in the estimated equations caused severe reductions in the number of observations for any equation. Because it was necessary to eliminate any firm's response if it had not provided information for all included variables, the sixty-eight responses resulted in only ten to twenty available observations. Application of regression analysis to samples of this size yields questionable results. Second, because it was not possible to hold constant technical production variations, some economies may have remained masked. Thus, although general consideration of the data in tables 4.24 through 4.27 gives some indication of the existence of trends, the evidence for the existence of scale economies is weak, at times contradicted, and not supported by the results of regression analysis. These tables are included nevertheless because the data are drawn from a uniquely comprehensive primary data base.

Additional data in tables 4.26 and 4.27 support the hypothesis of the existence of scale economies. First, planned investment in both new and existing plants appears proportional to firm size. Because profits, which are one indicator of ability to invest, do not increase with size, this increase in planned investment for larger firms is strong evidence that these firms have not yet reached a position close to the optimal size and are still interested in growth.

Second, larger firms have been able to reach more efficient levels of production as measured by two variables. Firms were asked to estimate the amount by which their per-unit costs would decrease if they could produce at 100 percent capacity rather than at fluctuating seasonal rates. Smaller firms said that substantial decreases in costs were possible; larger firms indicated smaller reductions. In a related question, firms were asked to estimate their highest and lowest monthly production. Larger firms produced higher ratios of lowest to highest monthly production, suggesting better adjustment to fluctuations.

Third, larger firms offer a greater number of product lines, which represents a significant marketing advantage. An increase in the number of product lines increases variable as well as fixed costs. Because these cost increases cannot simply be passed on in the form of higher FOB factory prices (the industry is highly price competitive), one can speculate that larger firms can offset these added costs by exploiting scale economies accruing to them.

Fourth, in several national field surveys, PMHI staff members asked top management personnel of mobile home firms to indicate the optimal size of a single mobile home plant, the optimal size of a firm, and the necessary expenditures to establish a plant and a firm. There was general agreement that the optimal plant should have a capacity of one to two thousand floors per year, with a majority of responses suggesting around fifteen hundred floors per year. Estimates of the cost of establishing such a plant varied from $500,000 to $1,500,000. There was no agreement on optimal firm size; estimates ranged from three thousand to one hundred fifty thousand floors per firm per year. Estimates of cost of establishing optimal firms also varied to a similar degree. This ability to agree upon the optimal plant size, although not approaching consensus on firm size, may indicate that benefits of size are more evident at the plant level than at the firm level.

Optimal plant and firm size in this context were defined with the assumption that there would be no modification in existing constraints to expansion. In order to obtain information on optimal firm size under conditions of reasonable relaxation of these constraints, we prepared detailed cost estimates in field interviews with the presidents of three of the largest mobile home firms. They estimated that under such modified conditions the optimal plant size would approach fifty thousand to sixty thousand floors per year.

In order more reliably to develop the relationship between size and cost structures, PMHI Manufacturer Survey data were used to estimate several cost-scale relationships. Estimates of firms' average total costs were derived by eliminating profits from the price of the average cost model produced by the firm. Presumably, if some firms are operating at lower average total costs than other firms in the market, the reduced costs will yield higher profits rather than lower prices; therefore elimination of profits yields reasonably accurate measurements of average total cost. To ensure comparability of data, the average total unit costs were expressed as average costs per square foot of the model. In the interest of making the comparison of models between firms as accurate as possible, further adjustments due to variations in the number of bathrooms and bedrooms were made using average marginal cost estimates for these variations as derived from a detailed FOB factory price analysis undertaken by PMHI. Costs per square foot prior to adjustment ranged from $3.34 to $11.46; after adjustment the costs ranged from $3.36 to $11.46 per square foot. Before adjustment the average cost per square foot for all firms was $6.93; adjustment raised this average to $6.98. Although these gross numbers do not indicate significant modifications, the adjustments process was more important for certain firm responses.

The first estimated equation related unadjusted average total costs to the capacity of the plant producing the model. If it is assumed that each plant is operating in the area of its short-run minimum average total cost, the relationship between observed average total costs and capacity would be interpreted as the long-run average total cost curve.

The estimated relationship was

$$ATC = 7.64 - 0.09 \text{ CPLMO} \quad R^2 = .17,$$
$$(23.57)(3.38) \qquad F = 11.43,$$

where

ATC   = unadjusted average total cost
CPLMO = capacity of plant producing the model, in floors per day
t   = values in parentheses.

This equation indicates that as capacity increases by one floor per day, average cost per square foot decreases by $0.09. Both the equation and the estimated coefficients are significantly different from 0.00 at the 95 percent confidence level.

The unadjusted data may not adequately measure the average total cost, so the same equation was reestimated using adjusted data. The resulting form was

$$ADATC = 7.71 - 0.10 \text{ CPLMO},$$
$$(16.42)(1.97)$$

where

ADATC = adjusted average total cost, and all other variables remain the same.

This equation indicates that adjusted average total costs may decrease as much as $0.10 per square foot as capacity is increased by one floor per day. The coefficient of the capacity variable, however, is no longer significant at the 95 percent confidence level. The decrease in statistical significance of the regression coefficient after data adjustment may be ascribed in part to reductions in the number of usable observations incurred during the adjustment process.

In order to isolate more fully the nature of the potential economies of scale indicated by the average cost analysis, we investigated several other operating characteristics of the responding firms. The relationship between plant capacity and output per man-hour is of particular interest. The estimated relationship is

$$XMH = 5.4428 + 0.0984 \text{ CPLMO}$$
$$(0.0348)$$
$$- 0.2621 \text{ VRTIN}$$
$$(0.1199)$$
$$+ 0.4366 \text{ A1}$$
$$(0.4318)$$
$$+ 0.0001 \text{ POMO}$$
$$(0.0001)$$
$$- 0.0033 \text{ PCTUN}$$
$$(0.0066)$$
$$- 0.2389 \text{ XLXH}$$
$$(0.9317)$$
$$(R^2 = 0.5202, F = 4.8786, \text{ standard errors in parentheses}),$$

where

XMH   = output per man-hour
CPLMO = plant capacity
A1   = dummy variable for regional variation
POMO = price deviation from popular model
VRTIN = plant square footage per unit of capacity, a proxy for vertical integration
PCTUN = percentage of labor force unionized
XLXH = lowest to highest monthly production ratio.

The coefficient of plant capacity is significant and indicates that output per man-hour increases by $0.0984 for every unit increase in plant capacity. This relationship provides additional strong support for the existence of potential economies of scale; it further indicates that the most likely source of these economies within the range of plant sizes included in the survey is more efficient utilization of the direct labor force.

The linear cost functions derived from the survey data are not applicable for plant sizes in excess of approximately two thousand five hundred floors per plant per year (the upper plant size range of the sample). In order to obtain estimates of the magnitude of potential economies of scale beyond this range, we asked presidents of three of the largest manufactured housing firms to develop detailed estimates of the cost reductions that would be associated with sustained production in ranges up to one hundred thousand floors per plant per year. Their estimates, in conjunction with further analysis by PMHI staff, indicate the following: Increasing capacities from approximately two thousand five hundred to five thousand floors per year would yield additional cost reductions of 10 percent to 15 percent; increases to fifty thousand floors per year would reduce costs by 20 percent to 25 percent; increases beyond this level would result in savings in excess of 25 percent. These estimates are based upon existing technologies; it was generally agreed that such large increases in production levels would constitute a major incentive for the development of new materials and production methods that could yield even greater cost reductions.

The evidence developed supports the first hypothesis: The potential cost reductions are large both for increases in size within the range of existing plants and for plants with capacities up to one hundred thousand floors per year. However, under present conditions firms are not anticipating use of larger plants and the average size plant in the industry has actually decreased.

In view of the pressing need for low-cost housing that represents a viable alternative to conventionally built housing, this inability to take full advantage of cost reductions necessitates consideration of the constraints to larger capacities as well as investigation of policy actions that could encourage larger capacity and therefore lower costs.

There are three major categories of constraints that have discouraged increases in plant capacities: fluctuations in demand due to seasonality and the business cycle; high economic concentration, high costs, and restrictive regulations in the transport sector; and the negative impacts of restrictive land use controls on demand volume and stability. First, the mobile home industry, like most other subsectors of the housing industry, is subject to demand that fluctuates seasonally as well as in longer cycles induced by the general business cycle. Mobile home manufacturers tend to require continuous cash flows and have developed an industry structure that facilitates these flows. Producers are reluctant to invest in large quantities of capital equipment that may lie idle for several months per year and may be underutilized for prolonged periods during downturns in the business cycle. The industry, although relatively capital intensive within the context of the general building industry, places strong 'reliance upon its ability to expand or contract its labor force as economic conditions dictate. In order to encourage larger plant and firm capacities, magnitude of fluctuations in demand must be reduced. The available alternatives for dealing with seasonality can and should be explored. A massive study should be focused on isolating the determinants of seasonality and, if possible, dealing with causal factors. At the same time, viable approaches must be devised for accommodating seasonality; there are many possibilities in this area.

Basically, the problem in a future, more capital-intensive mobile home industry is to develop a capability to maintain inventories of housing that increase as normal demand decreases and that provide an additional source of housing during periods of high demand. One possible way to smooth demand is to create an intermediary institution that could buy and sell housing on a countercyclical basis. This approach has proven successful in other sectors of the economy in which either demand or production is cyclical; for example, in agricultural production the commodities market provides both producers and consumers with the possibility of hedging against unfavorable market developments. Another approach would be increased financial strength in the distribution and land development systems, which might make it feasible for dealers and community developers to purchase inventories during periods of slack demand. This would be most attractive if price concessions were made by manufacturers during these periods. Such concessions could be balanced against the benefits from lower cost production in larger plants with more regular production sched-

ules. Because it is unlikely that dealers or community managers would be willing to build inventories during prolonged downturns in the business cycle, an institution with the necessary capital available for such long-term inventory accumulation should be found. One alternative may be legislation that would permit savings and loan associations to purchase under carefully controlled circumstances stocks of housing for use as transient rental housing during the duration of the downturn of the business cycle and that could be sold as demand increases. Yet another possibility is the strategic scheduling of large-scale housing purchases for production during the off-season; manufacturers indicated to us that they would respond by bidding at cost or would even be prepared to incur losses of up to 20 percent. Clearly, such proposals would require intensive investigation before becoming fully effective policy recommendations. We simply wish to describe possible areas of consideration for reducing seasonal and cyclical fluctuations.

A second major category of constraints arises in the area of the costs of and restrictions on the transportation of manufactured housing units. The oligopoly structure of the transport industry and the regulatory methods of the Interstate Commerce Commission have served almost to double the cost per floor mile for producers that do not maintain their own fleets of transports. The rate structure problem is compounded by restrictive highway regulation. Dimension limitations, permit requirements, and special traffic regulations differ unnecessarily from state to state, raising transportation costs and effectively hindering interstate marketing. Most serious are the restrictions upon the maximum size of manufactured housing units that may be transported. California, for example, restricts widths to 12 feet, effectively eliminating producers from other states from competing in the California market for 14-foot-wide units. The problem of transportation could be significantly reduced through more effective regulation (or deregulation) of transportation companies and through the development of a coordinated system of highway regulation of greater interstate uniformity.

The third category of constraint comes from the complex, if not chaotic, system of land use controls promulgated largely by local government. Because most mobile home plants produce for markets in more than one state, the industry finds itself in the dilemma of producing for a wide array of locations with different and often unpredictable land use control practices. The widespread employment of land use controls to restrict the location of manufactured housing units in Standard Metropolitan Statistical Areas (SMSAs) eliminates a large and possibly more stable market for manufacturers. Restrictive zoning practices must be eased as a third and crucial requirement for expansion of plant capacities and the realization of lower-cost housing.

For the building industries in other countries, the major implications of this project are threefold. First, low-cost housing can be built without need for public subsidization—the average 1977 FOB price for a fully finished and furnished mobile housing unit was only $8.95 per square foot, or $8270 for a typical 14-foot by 66-foot, 924-square-foot home. Second, substantial potential scale economies, yet to be realized, indicate that these prices can be reduced. Last, there is no reason why similarly low-cost housing could not be produced in most countries.

Product Differentiation

Product differentiation is one of several methods used to create demand conditions in a market for a specific narrowly defined good. A good, in this sense, may be defined by a vector of characteristics defining its physical and functional nature. Two units differing in only one such characteristic are defined as two goods, and the strength of the "monopoly" position is determined by the significance of the difference between one good and its closest substitute good.

An industry or subindustry grouping is a collection of firms producing goods that are more similar to each other than any good produced by any other industrial group. Therefore the "monopoly" position considered here is an intraindustry "monopoly" in the production of a good with many close substitutes, as opposed to the more traditional concept of "monopoly," which is the production by one firm of a good with no close substitutes. Because "monopoly" position generates a return to the seller in proportion to its strength, firms may attempt to maximize this return by pursuing policy aimed at maximizing the difference between their goods and the goods of other firms. Such policy is defined for the purposes of this book as "product policy."

Alternatively, firms may attempt to create a similar distinction between their goods and those of others by changing buyers' perceptions of the characteristics of their goods rather than actually changing those characteristics. These actions by the seller are defined as product differentiation. And, as with real characteristic variation, the return to perceived variation is proportional to the buyers' estimate of real cost of choosing the next best alternative good. Firms that can increase the perception of this cost will realize increased returns.

In the mobile home industry firms produce a relatively homogeneous mixture of goods. Legal and technological restrictions limit the variation that is possible in the physical "exterior" nature of the product. It is, then, reasonable to expect that product differentiation policy in the form of brand name advertising would be an important method of generating increased demand for an individual firm's output. Because franchising arrangements similar to those found in the automobile industry are largely absent, such policy may be directed to either of two separate markets that determine demand for the mobile home producer. The producer may either advertise to the final consumer market, which ultimately determines demand, or to the dealer in order to increase the number of outlets for the product and the degree of market exposure. Considering the restrictions on physical exterior form, one expects emphasis on interior design. Finally, manufacturers differ in quality and service intensity of their products—whether voluntarily achieved or regulatorily demanded—and it can be expected that "total package" difference will be stressed.

It is possible to consider product differentiation between subindustries within the same industrial category. A subindustry is a clustering of firms producing similar products within a more general industry group. The on-site and factory-produced housing subindustries offer goods that provide a significant quantity of similar characteristics such as shelter from the elements, cooking facilities, and sleeping accommodations. The on-site industry, however, benefits from positive buyer perceptions, which have tended to minimize incursion by the mobile home industry as well as the manufactured building industry into the medium- and upper-income housing market.

Product differentiation is a significant determinant of two areas of firm and industry behavior. First, it helps establish the magnitude of returns to either the firm or subindustry resulting from market position. Second, it is a partial determinant of relative firm and industry power in nonrevenue areas.

High profits can occur if a firm or small group of firms are able to establish a strong position relative to all other firms. They will be able to obtain high returns at the expense of other firms within the industry or subindustry so that the other firms will either accept lower profit rates or be forced out of business. However, if the industry achieves product differentiation, a substantial barrier to entry will exist and all the firms in the subindustry will enjoy higher returns.

In addition to the direct revenue-generating possibilities, there are other ways in which product differentiation may increase the profitability of a firm. A limited number of firms may become leaders within the industry and determine nonprice aspects of industry behavior. It may become difficult for smaller firms without the benefits of differentiation to introduce innovations within the product line or expand into new territories. The range of such possible difficulties is great and offers significant advantage to the leading firms.

Product differentiation may have significant benefits at the secondary level. Firms may expand and be in a position to undertake expanded research and development within the field. However, if product differentiation (again, defined here as perceptual rather than real differences) is indeed effective in creating perceptions of difference, then a firm may not be inclined to invest in research and development aimed at generating "real difference."

Finally, in an industry characterized by high transportation costs, product differentiation may be restricted to limited market areas. This makes it feasible for firms to achieve market power in one specific area while remaining undifferentiated in others. Returns to such limited geographical area power are restricted by the possible movement of additional firms into the market if the return is high enough to justify the cost of the movement.

Mobile home manufacturers attempt to achieve product differentiation in three ways. First, advertising is used in an effort to increase brand name loyalty. Interior styling of the unit is then employed to increase the perception of different products. Last, the extent to which manufacturers are able to cope with the ever-increasing burden of government regulation is cleverly used to enhance the appeal of the total product package.

As stated previously, product differentiation is a condition of demand; and, due to the supply orientation of this study, information is limited. Some data are available for gauging advertising intensity and brand name identification from PMHI's surveys of producers and dealers. In our Manufacturer Survey, producers were asked to state their selling expenses in terms of percentages of

model costs and total company operating expenses. These measurements provide some concept of the relative importance producers place upon advertising as a means of accomplishing product differentiation. Second, we obtained information on both dealers' use of brand names in advertising and consumers' brand name identification and loyalty.

Table 4.28 shows the distribution of selling expenses as a percentage of total operating costs and as a percentage of model costs listed by firm size. Selling expenses represented between 1 percent and 10 percent of total operating expenses, with the mean percentage being 3.6 percent. Selling expenses as a percentage of model costs ranged from 0 percent to 6 percent, with a mean value of 2.9 percent. Although these values appear low, dealers absorb a major portion of selling expenses. The PMHI Dealer Survey requested information concerning brand name loyalty in several areas. Most of the dealers who responded replied that they did have evidence of the development of brand name loyalty with respect to at least one of the lines of mobile homes they carried and further indicated that loyalty was associated with lines produced by nationally known companies. This dominance by nationally known companies may be a result of significant economies of scale in advertising and may represent a major advantage available only to larger producers.

Closer examination of the data reveals that, in general, the level of brand name loyalty is much lower. Most of the responding dealers indicated the use of manufacturer brand names in their consumer advertising,

Table 4.28.
Selling Expenses

	Total Company Sales (× $1,000)			
	0–2,500	2,501–10,000	10,001–40,000	40,001 +
Selling Expense as Percentage of Operating Costs				
1	6	1	1	0
2	1	4	2	4
3	1	4	4	2
4	1	1	5	2
5	4	4	1	1
6	0	0	3	0
7	1	0	0	0
10	1	1	0	0
Selling Expense as Percent of Model Costs				
0	0	0	0	0
1	7	1	1	0
2	0	4	2	6
3	1	5	4	2
4	1	1	1	1
5	5	2	2	0
6	0	0	2	0

Source: PMHI/MS.

but the results of such advertising are questionable because a majority of firms indicated that less than 20 percent of their customers requested products by specific brand names. These dealer estimates, of course, may be subject to error because dealer selection may represent the prior selection of one or several particular brand names handled by that dealer. An additional indication of low levels of brand name loyalty is the low number of repeat customers purchasing the same brand of mobile home; a majority of dealers reported requests for the same brand of mobile home by less than 25 percent of their customers. Because there is an upward bias to this number due to the limited number of lines a dealer may carry, the low estimate is likely to be indicative of generally low loyalty. Further information on dealer product differentiation is given in Part II on the mobile home distribution system.

The 1969 through 1977 editions of Mobile/Modular Housing Dealer Annual Directory are another gauge of the extent of product differentiation attained by producers. This directory indicates that broad patterns of multiple usage of model names are present in the industry, and there is no evidence that multiple usage has decreased during the 1969–1977 period. Because product differentiation requires that consumers or dealers associate certain characteristics with both producer and model names, this multiple usage indicates that producers have not been able to achieve high levels of product differentiation.

Part V on the regulatory environment deals with many legal and regulatory reasons that have historically forced manufacturers to foster the tin-can appearance of their mobile homes. Yet even in the late seventies a mobile home whose exterior design too closely resembles that of traditional housing might be inviting organized labor's resentment or the local building inspector's attempt to "interpret" the federal mobile home construction safety standards as not covering such homes. It still carries less risk for the manufacturer to focus "styling" efforts on the home's interior, where they have historically been concentrated. An added stimulus to the emphasis on interior design is that highway regulation severely constrains exterior design. It is much more difficult for any designer to create "architecture" by working with the elongated "box" dictated by highway regulations than it is to "style" the interior. Most manufacturers therefore offer at least basic options such as "early American," "contemporary," and "modern" for a given line. Many producers offer more options and strain their imagination to create highly romantic interior style names in their marketing efforts. Additionally, they carefully adjust "style" mix to regional taste preferences. One plant of a national producer may find that "early Mediterranean" and "early Spanish" sell best in its region while

another plant has success with "manor de luxe" and the "duke crown royal" designs. Figures 4.6 through 4.11 indicate the extent to which manufacturers use interior styling in their attempts to differentiate their products. And it "works." Women, in general, remain intrigued by interior design and usually decide on the housing purchase.

Whenever infringement on the private business sector's independence looms, the industry fights the threat. If the government prevails, however, firms are quick to turn the inevitable to advantage. In the mid-seventies the federal building code was imposed upon the mobile home industry. Manufacturers quickly exploited the marketing potential by advertising that their model mobile home either met or exceeded the Federal Construction and Safety Standards. Similarly, when the U.S. Federal Trade Commission persuaded four industry leaders to consent to stringent warranty performance regulation, these four companies attempted to recover the imposed cost burden by exploiting their "advantage" over the rest of the industry, stressing their one-year full warranty and implying that their homes were serviced by especially well-trained dealers.

The FTC's Trade Regulation Rule (TRR), some form of which may well be imposed upon the industry at large by 1980, already increases product differentiation. Manufacturers of doublewides and traditional code-conforming sectional units, fearing consequences if the TRR is actually implemented, are stressing in dealer training and advertising the competence of their dealers in on-site setup, hookup, and "responsible immediate warranty service."

It seems clear that government intervention will soon shift the strong product differentiation emphasis away from interior styling and that, in general, compliance with new regulations will stimulate an increase in product differentiation. Policy alternatives seem apparent. Ever-more stringent regulatory requirements may improve the product-service package, but they will also increase costs to the extent that smaller firms will become less competitive. This situation will increasingly close off this least-cost housing option to lower income groups.

What types of entry barriers exist in the mobile home production system? This question is limited here to the following four categories: barriers to entry from vertical integration, scale economy barriers, product differentiation barriers, and absolute cost barriers. The findings of the preceding subsections on integration and scale economies clearly indicate that entry barriers in the first two categories are low and that although barriers from vertical integration may gain significance, scale economy barriers will remain insignificant in the near future. Product differentiation barriers, however, promise to become sizable in the future,

Barriers to Entry

Figure 4.6.
Product differentiation
by interior design: living
room.

Figure 4.7.
Product differentiation
by interior design: living
room.

Figure 4.8.
Product differentiation
by interior design:
living room.

Figure 4.9.
Product differentiation
by interior design:
kitchen.

Figure 4.10.
Product differentiation
by interior design:
bedroom.

Figure 4.11.
Product differentiation
by interior design:
bathroom.

as the preceding information makes clear.

Historically, there were hardly any absolute cost barriers. Newly entering mobile home firms were not confronted with absolute cost disadvantages that would make their production cost curves lie above those of going firms. Although established firms possessed valuable know-how, management could be bought and there were, for example, hardly any exclusive patent rights. Mobile home production required relatively small amounts of equity capital. In the early fifties, for example, it took only about $10,000 to $20,000 in equity capital to start a manufacturing plant. The manufacturing process is largely assembly, which has contributed to making mobile home manufacturing a good "small business." As the industry matured, however, more capital was required; and a minimum of close to $200,000 was necessary in the early 1970s provided one had good credit and supplier connections. This amount was still very low compared with most manufacturing fields. However, during the mid- and late 1970s absolute cost barriers were growing.

The dramatic shakeout of the 1973–1975 recession resulted in an industry where the "surviving" firms are financially sophisticated. Increasing government intervention has forced these "survivors" to develop new staff and expertise in dealing with the new regulatory red tape. This has resulted in industry-specific know-how more advanced than ever before. The Federal Construction and Safety Standards and the FTC's looming imposition of some form of its TRR on warranty performance have added significantly to the demands faced by personnel and equipment. The absolute cost necessary for a major entry into the industry today, in the late 1970s, is at least $2 million. The costs for pirating know-how, meeting payrolls of swollen white-collar employment necessitated by increased governmental red tape, and for capital equipment have all risen.

In summary, entry has become difficult. This is one explanation for the decline over the last few years in the number of newly entering firms. Section C below, on operation of the production system, gives a detailed analysis of the dynamics of entries and exits.

The irony seems to be that consumerism and government have raised entry barriers to the point that new competition is discouraged from entry and production costs are significantly higher. The policy implication for consumer and government alike is simple. Further interference with the only industry still capable of producing least-cost housing will deny low-income consumers the chance to own a home. By decreasing competition in the system, the industry could be crippled and finally killed. It would be a major American tragedy. The most efficient building industry in the world, which has grown and been nurtured by private enterprise alone,

would be destroyed by the very government that is supposed to defend liberal capitalism—the United States' uniquely efficient economic system.

When we started this study in 1969, we met with chief executive officers of major mobile home manufacturing companies who were running their companies single-handedly out of humble offices. Today, in the late 1970s, this is not the case. Monstrous corporate headquarters with swarms of sophisticated corporate legal and other personnel have replaced the lean, simple offices of the sixties. It is ironic that consumers are paying for this "fat" that they have invited.

A major problem that has plagued traditional home building is seasonality, which adds to housing costs through higher industry wage rates, material costs, and operating overhead. Wage rates in the housing industry are higher per hour than those of industry in general, in large part because building tradespersons are not able to work twelve months, and material costs tend to be higher because prices rise during periods of active construction because of competition among builders for a limited supply of materials. In addition, overhead costs incurred by builders during the winter months, when little or no building takes place, adversely affect costs. *Seasonality*

The drop in home-building activity during the winter months does not indicate that seasonality in the housing industry is primarily caused by adverse weather. The precise determinants of seasonality in on-site residential construction are not yet known and it is clear that many factors act as determinants. It is not clear what many of these factors are and to what extent they contribute to seasonality. Thus it is not surprising that the mobile home industry faces a degree of seasonality similar to that experienced by the housing industry. The answer may or may not be the same for both industries; it is possible, for example, that the influence of weather fluctuations on seasonality may be very different for both industries. The existence of seasonality in the mobile home industry serves to increase costs and adversely affects industry performance. Additionally, mobile home manufacturing takes place within a factory, greatly increasing the fixed overhead charges. The traditional home-building industry has overcome many of its seasonality problems in this area by relying on the use of very little equipment or fewer physical facilities or both.

Although one might intuitively expect relatively little seasonality in the mobile home industry, production comparisons between the mobile home industry and the traditional on-site building industry indicate strikingly similar problems. Because one operates off-site and the other operates on-site, the similarity seems to suggest that weather is not a main determinant.

At the outset it is useful to examine over-all yearly production cycles to determine whether there are basic seasonal problems. PMHI compared mobile home production to two widely referred to statistical series on housing production. Table 4.29 charts monthly mobile home shipments from 1958 to 1977; table 4.30 charts monthly one-family housing starts from 1960 to 1977; and table 4.31 charts monthly one-family housing completions from 1968 to 1977 (this data series only became available in 1968).

An examination of table 4.29 indicates that the peak in mobile home shipments each year generally occurs in August, September, or October. Those years that depart from the norm, 1959 to 1961 and 1972 to 1976, coincide with recessionary periods. The regular seasonal fluctuations during these periods may have been offset by seasonal economic fluctuations. The month of lowest mobile home production is usually December or January. A comparison to table 4.30 indicates that the peak in housing starts each year generally precedes the peak in mobile home shipments and occurs in April, May, or June. The month of lowest production is usually January or February. Obviously, mobile home shipments and housing starts are both subject to variations in production.

It is evident that the seasonality of mobile home production differs from the seasonality of the on-site construction industry as expressed by housing starts. We can reconcile this difference by remembering that the two groups are not strictly comparable. Table 4.27 represents a finished product whereas table 4.30 represents an unfinished one. A more useful examination may be made by comparing mobile home shipments to data on another finished product, housing completions. An examination of table 4.31 indicates that housing completions generally peak in September or October. The month of lowest production is usually January or February. The production of completed housing, then, whether on-site or mobile homes, seems to peak in late summer and early autumn. The lowest production occurs in the dead of winter. We may explain the dissimilarity to housing starts as follows: Large-scale production builders and sepculative builders are free to begin building at any time, but they try to have the product ready when the demand is greatest. Because the demand for completed housing is strongly affected by the schedules of institutions, such as schools, the end of summer finds the greatest demand for completed housing. Demand does not as strongly dictate housing starts, and the peak production occurs in spring and early summer.

It is clear that seasonality is present in the mobile home industry as well as in the traditional housing industry, whether we use data from housing starts or housing completions. There is a problem, however, in identifying the extent and cause of these seasonal production shifts.

At this point it is useful to make month-by-month calculations to determine the severity of seasonality in the mobile home industry as compared to the on-site building industry. Table 4.32 shows the increase from low month to high month each year in percentages. These figures indicate that the mobile home industry and the on-site building industry suffer from extreme seasonality. Because the mobile home requires relatively little on-site work, its production pattern may be greatly attributed to the seasonality of demand rather than to the effects of weather on production. The slight drop in average production that usually occurs in July can be explained by the fact that many firms in the industry close their plants for one or two weeks during the month for employee vacations.

Direct comparison to the available data on the finished on-site product, housing completions, shows the mobile home industry plagued by greater fluctuations and by less predictable trends in fluctuations. Comparison to housing starts again suggests that seasonality in the mobile home industry is at least as severe as in the traditional housing industry. Although the housing starts appear consistently more vulnerable to seasonal fluctuations, the mobile home industry may, in fact, be more unpredictable. Despite the presence of consistently wide fluctuations between low and high months each year in the on-site housing industry, it must be remembered that regular seasonality may be somewhat planned for and compensated for by the industry. The mobile home industry, in contrast, shows irregular fluctuations, some relatively low, some quite high, indicating uniform production output in some years, severe seasonality in others. This makes it difficult for the mobile home industry to forecast production reliably.

Looking at the number of months each year in which peak production is achieved gives us a general impression of how the industries cope with seasonality. A somewhat accurate figure for capacity utilization in the mobile home industry can be obtained by beginning with the assumption that the month of highest production each year approximates full capacity output. In the on-site building industry, however, with its subcontracting and vacillating work force, the term "full capacity" becomes rather vague. Regardless of these obstacles, a comparison between full capacity utilization in the mobile home industry and the on-site building industry indicates the mobile home industry's relative problems in coping with seasonality.

During the ten-year period from 1968 to 1977, mobile home manufacturers attain more than 90 percent capacity utilization an average of 4.2 months per year. For the same period, housing completions show more than

Table 4.29.
Monthly Mobile Home
Shipments, 1958–1977

Month	1977	1976	1975	1974	1973	1972	1971	1970	1969	1968
January	14,730[b]	15,070	11,490[b]	26,050	39,790	33,470[b]	24,710[b]	23,900[b]	27,140[b]	19,040[b]
February	18,020	18,610	14,450	27,130	41,940	39,960	28,720	24,090	29,360	21,170
March	23,450	21,230	16,030	33,340	55,760	49,130	36,000	29,520	32,480	23,960
April	24,170	23,260	18,870	37,990[a]	60,170[a]	53,710	43,260	39,920	36,010	27,080
May	24,920	24,070[a]	19,960	37,100	56,000	51,820	41,310	32,860	34,600	27,560
June	26,830	23,360	20,030	35,600	56,010	55,030[a]	47,800	35,650	36,420	26,460
July	22,280	20,040	19,730	31,050	49,170	48,470	45,650	37,120	35,210	27,150
August	27,300	23,390	20,850[a]	29,180	52,470	52,060	49,990	38,400	38,070	30,540
September	26,800	22,360	20,100	24,100	43,770	49,130	54,000[a]	41,370[a]	40,090	29,920
October	27,400[a]	21,880	20,840	20,700	44,970	54,450	50,850	40,840	43,440[a]	33,480[a]
November	22,600	17,810	16,520	15,310	38,980	50,730	39,900	30,480	32,710	27,620
December	18,300	15,040[b]	13,820	11,750[b]	27,890[b]	37,980	34,380	27,040	27,160	23,970
Total	276,800	246,120	212,690	329,300	566,920	575,940	496,570	401,190	412,690	317,950

Month	1967	1966	1965	1964	1963	1962	1961	1960	1959	1958
January	12,220[b]	11,610[b]	12,860[b]	10,990[b]	8,530[b]	6,850[b]	5,620[b]	6,750	6,790[b]	7,760[b]
Febuary	14,410	14,250	14,230	12,800	10,230	8,130	6,430	9,060	8,450	8,630
March	18,390	20,050	18,790	16,120	11,700	9,740	8,010	9,270	10,990	10,270
April	19,400	19,580	17,950	16,710	13,610	10,540	7,730	8,520	10,200	11,250
May	21,910	20,150	18,940	17,820	14,660	11,700	9,090[a]	11,170[a]	11,770	11,520
June	22,640	21,740	21,060	18,920	13,730	11,390	8,340	10,350	12,120[a]	13,520
July	19,450	18,000	17,710	16,900	13,050	9,320	6,690	7,660	10,510	10,900
August	24,690[a]	22,420[a]	21,110	17,920	13,680	10,690	8,030	10,190	9,650	11,850
September	24,210	19,980	21,430[a]	19,040[a]	14,210	10,900	8,180	9,960	11,760	13,350
October	24,290	19,250	20,580	18,210	15,620[a]	12,300[a]	8,990	8,730	11,510	14,120[a]
November	20,900	17,400	17,920	14,250	11,810	9,060	7,090	6,360	8,630	10,680
December	17,850	12,870	13,890	11,640	10,010	7,380	6,000	5,680[b]	8,120	9,900
Total	240,360	217,300	216,470	191,320	150,840	118,000	90,200	103,700	120,500	133,750

a. Highest shipments.
b. Lowest shipments.

Source: U.S. Department of Commerce, Bureau of the Census, including latest Bureau of the Census data released as of April 1978.

Table 4.30.
Monthly Single-Unit
Housing Starts (in
1,000s), 1960–1977

Month	1977	1976	1975	1974	1973	1972	1971	1970	1969
January	55.8[b]	54.0[b]	40.0[b]	43.3	77.2	76.4	54.9[b]	33.5[b]	51.3
February	87.2[a]	72.9	40.2	57.6	73.6	76.4	58.4	41.4	48.0
March	125.9	92.5	62.6	77.3	105.1	111.5	91.6	62.1	72.0
April	138.9	107.9	77.9	102.3[a]	120.5	120.1	116.3	73.8	85.0
May	152.2	112.4	92.8	96.4	131.6[a]	135.4[a]	115.9	74.9	91.4[a]
June	149.2	119.7[a]	90.4	99.6	114.8	131.9	117.2[a]	83.9[a]	82.9
July	138.2	113.3	92.9	90.9	114.8	119.1	108.0	75.8	73.6
August	140.6	113.6	91.7	79.8	107.2	131.4	111.7	77.8	69.5
September	131.6	108.2	84.8	73.4	84.5	120.6	102.2	76.0	71.6
October	135.5	110.2	94.7[a]	69.5	86.0	117.2	103.2	79.4	68.1
November	109.9	89.9	71.8	57.9	70.9	97.4	93.0	67.4	55.1
December	87.0	72.4	55.7	41.0[b]	46.8[b]	73.3[b]	80.5	69.1	42.8[b]
Total	1,451.9	1,166.4	895.5	889.1	1,133.2	1,310.7	1,152.9	815.1	811.2

Month	1968	1967	1966	1965	1964	1963	1962	1961	1960
January	45.3[b]	40.6	46.6	52.3	55.4[b]	47.4[b]	54.4	51.8[b]	69.8
February	55.4	40.4[b]	50.4	47.2[b]	63.9	52.4	53.8[b]	56.5	70.9
March	79.4	66.6	83.3	82.2	82.1	80.6	79.8	80.1	74.0
April	98.0[a]	79.9	94.5[a]	101.3[a]	89.2	105.7	101.7	85.4	102.3
May	87.0	87.4	84.8	98.5	98.8	107.1[a]	107.7[a]	97.9	101.6
June	81.6	87.7[a]	79.9	97.6	102.2[a]	100.4	96.9	100.6[a]	101.5
July	86.5	82.4	69.1	96.6	91.9	98.2	96.0	97.6	90.6
August	82.6	83.8	69.4	89.0	90.2	95.8	101.7	96.1	102.9[a]
September	80.3	78.2	59.7	80.9	79.2	92.9	76.4	91.5	79.9
October	85.6	81.8	53.6	85.8	92.0	102.7	91.0	94.1	85.1
November	65.1	69.1	50.2	72.4	69.5	71.9	78.4	74.1	71.4
December	53.9	47.1	38.1[b]	61.2	58.8	51.5	56.1	54.4	49.0[b]
Total	900.7	844.9	779.5	965.0	973.0	1,006.6	993.9	980.1	999.0

a. Highest starts.
b. Lowest starts.

Source: U.S. Department of Commerce, Bureau of the Census, including latest Bureau of the Census data released as of April 1978.

Table 4.31.
Monthly Single-Unit
Housing Completions
(in 1000s), 1968–1977

Month	1977	1976	1975	1974	1973	1972	1971	1970	1969	1968
January	77.1[b]	65.9	67.0	70.0	89.4	78.3	56.5[b]	56.1	56.4	59.4
February	82.6	64.8[b]	53.2[b]	68.8	84.9[b]	77.0[b]	59.1	51.7	59.2	54.3[b]
March	85.3	71.9	53.7	66.4[b]	89.9	79.8	64.2	49.3[b]	62.2	59.7
April	86.1	70.8	55.4	68.5	92.7	85.5	76.1	56.0	55.1[b]	67.3
May	92.0	78.4	69.1	73.1	100.9	91.8	81.3	61.2	66.8	73.0
June	108.1	92.0	72.1	93.8[a]	110.6	99.8	84.2	69.0	76.6	69.7
July	109.2	91.5	76.0	80.9	90.6	96.4	89.7	69.1	69.9	79.7
August	121.3	98.3	79.3	84.1	104.5	111.8	95.2	80.3[a]	73.3	78.1
September	135.7[a]	94.5	88.8	83.2	104.5	102.7	100.3	80.3[a]	72.3	83.3[a]
October	122.5	98.9	74.9	89.6	112.8[a]	115.4[a]	106.3[a]	79.5	78.6[a]	78.9
November	116.5	99.5[a]	86.8	76.7	97.1	99.0	96.4	74.0	65.5	75.1
December	116.9	99.4	90.1[a]	76.4	96.4	105.9	104.7	75.4	71.7	80.1
Total	1,253.9	1,026.0	866.5	931.5	1,174.1	1,143.3	1,014.0	801.8	807.5	858.6

a. Highest completions.
b. Lowest completions.

Source: U.S. Department of Commerce, Bureau of the Census, including latest Bureau of the Census data released as of April 1978.

Table 4.32.
Percentage Increases in
Mobile Home
Shipments, Housing
Starts, and Housing
Completions from Low
Month to High Month,
1958–1977

	1977	1976	1975	1974	1973	1972	1971	1970	1969	1968
Mobile home shipments	86%	60	81	222	116	64	119	73	60	76
Housing starts[a]	173%	122	136	150	181	84	113	150	114	116
Housing completions[b]	76%	54	69	41	33	50	88	63	43	53

	1967	1966	1965	1964	1963	1962	1961	1960	1959	1958
Mobile home shipments	102	93	66	73	84	78	63	96	78	81
Housing starts[a]	117	148	115	84	126	100	94	110		
Housing completions[b]										

a. Data series begins in 1960.
b. Data series begins in 1968.

90 percent capacity utilization an average of 4.3 months per year, and housing starts show more than 90 percent capacity utilization an average of 4.0 months per year. The three sets of data indicate similar capacity utilization. The mobile home firms' fixed costs are much higher than fixed costs in on-site construction, so it follows that the mobile home industry is handicapped by below capacity utilization far more than is the on-site housing industry. Although all industries benefit from high capacity utilization, the mobile home industry in particular suffers from its low capacity utilization and acute seasonality because of its unchangingly high fixed costs.

The point is that seasonality is present in the mobile home industry as well as in the on-site housing industry, though we might not expect it, and that it poses a severe problem. Aggregate industry data, however, can cloud differences in seasonality among firms, states, and regions. It is helpful to go beneath the aggregate data for all manufacturers and look at the impact of seasonality on individual firms. The responses obtained in the PMHI surveys of manufacturers and suppliers give us this closer look at the problem of seasonality in the mobile home industry.

Individual differences among manufacturers are highlighted in the PMHI index of production fluctuation, calculated by taking the ratio of lowest monthly production to highest monthly production. Frequency distribution of this index is shown in table 4.33; the mean of this index is 0.46. Because mobile home manufacturers, as a matter of policy, carry no finished unit inventories, these monthly production indexes closely approximate monthly factory sale indexes and thus are similar to the monthly sales indexes for suppliers shown on the same table.

Monthly industry statistics on suppliers' sales of mobile home parts are not available on the national, regional, or state level. Consequently, analysis of suppliers' seasonality relies solely on responses to the PMHI Supplier Survey. Table 4.34 shows the distribution of the month of suppliers' highest and lowest sales. For 20.6 percent of the suppliers, the month of highest sales is August, and May and March are highest sale months for 15.1 percent and 13.5 percent of the suppliers, respectively. For 42.6 percent of the suppliers, however, lowest sales occur in December. Combining both January and December totals suggests that lowest sales are concentrated in these two months for approximately 65 percent of the suppliers.

Suppliers' seasonal fluctuation index, defined as the ratio of lowest to highest monthly sales, is given in table 4.33. The mean of this index is computed to be 0.37. In contrast, the manufacturers' seasonal fluctuation index has a mean of 0.46. This

suggests that seasonal fluctuations in suppliers' sales to mobile home manufacturers are more severe. As mentioned, these two indexes, while similar, are not strictly comparable because one deals with dollar sales volume and the other with unit production. Consequently, the ratio of manufacturers' lowest monthly shipment value to manufacturers' highest monthly shipment value was computed. This ratio has a mean of 0.41, which still suggests that suppliers' sales are more seasonal than manufacturers' shipment values.

In order to test whether climate has any bearing on production fluctuation, PMHI divided the continental United States into six climatic regions. Among the numerous criteria suggested in meteorological literature for classifying climatic conditions, only three were used alternately by PMHI in constructing climatic regions: regions based on seasons, regions based on frequency of frost, and regions based on annual normal total of hot degree days.[7] Since the PMHI/MS production fluctuation data are firm and not plant data, multiplant firms whose plants are located in different climatic regions were omitted from the sample. The production fluctuation index of the remaining firms was cross-tabulated alternately against regions based on season, on frost frequency, and on hot-day frequency. The resulting Chi-square values, however, were not significant. Nonetheless, these tests by no means demonstrate conclusively that climate has no effect on the seasonality of production. The failure of these tests to detect the influence of the climate may stem from the omission of large multiplant manufacturers from the sample.

It is clear that seasonality is a disruptive problem. It remains, however, an unexplained one. The exact determinants of variable seasonal demand are unclear, and so far the mobile home industry has not been able to pinpoint the solutions. To find out whether the severity of seasonality in mobile home shipments has decreased over time, the ratio of lowest monthly mobile home shipments to highest monthly shipments (XLHM) was regressed on time (T).

The result was as follows:

$$XLHM = 55.563 - 0.1838\,T \quad R^2 = 0.0299,$$
$$(0.2803) \quad F = 0.4299,$$

Origin: 1/1/66
T: 1/2 year unit.

The standard error is directly below the coefficient of T. It can be seen that the estimated coefficient of T is insignificant. In addition, both the R^2 and F values of the regression are extremely low. A trend in the ratio of lowest to highest monthly shipments of mobile homes is not observed. This failure to observe a trend from year to year in the severity of seasonality is unlikely to stem from the aggregative nature of the data; our data do not establish whether regional differences do exist. It would appear that manufacturers

Table 4.33.
Range of Values, Manufacturers' and Suppliers' Seasonal Fluctuation Indexes

Index	Mobile Home Manufacturers[a]	Mobile Home Suppliers[b]
0–0.09	1	11
0.10–0.19	3	8
0.20–0.29	8	15
0.30–0.39	7	21
0.40–0.49	8	20
0.50–0.59	10	29
0.60–0.69	11	15
0.70–0.79	3	1
0.80 and over	1	4
Missing values	7	64

a. Production Fluctuation Index = ratio of lowest monthly unit production to highest monthly unit production.

Source: PMHI Manufacturer Survey.

b. Sales Fluctuation Index = ratio of lowest monthly dollar sales volume of mobile home supplies to highest monthly sales volume of mobile home supplies.

Source: PMHI Supplier Survey.

Table 4.34.
Highest and Lowest Monthly Suppliers' Sales to Mobile Home Manufacturers

Month	Highest Number of Firms	Highest % of Total	Lowest Number of Firms	Lowest % of Total
January	1	0.8	27	22.1
February	3	2.4	11	9.0
March	17	13.5	2	1.6
April	10	7.9	3	2.5
May	19	15.1	1	0.8
June	15	11.9	3	2.5
July	3	2.4	5	4.1
August	26	20.6	0	0
September	12	9.5	2	1.6
October	12	9.5	2	1.6
November	4	3.2	14	11.5
December	3	2.4	52	42.6
Missing values	62		66	

Source: PMHI/SS.

have not succeeded in reducing the seasonality of production.

There are potential means by which manufacturers could alleviate seasonality in production. First, production could theoretically be kept at a steadier rate throughout the year with excess of production over sales inventoried. However, stockpiling of the finished product would incur extraordinary costs for financing such inventories and therefore is hardly feasible. Detailed field interviews conducted by the PMHI staff in January 1975 with top management of eighteen leading manufacturers confirmed this: Fourteen of the seventeen respondents to the question on stockpiling were opposed to this method as an alternative to seasonal production and the main reason for their opposition is the high cost of carrying inventory. Second, shipment to dealers on consignment rather than directly in response to dealer orders could reduce seasonality. All but one respondent were opposed to this solution, citing risks as the principal reason. Third, measures could be undertaken to reduce seasonality of demand, for example, staggering the introduction of new models or more intensive advertising. Many manufacturers are carrying on advertising campaigns during the off-season. Fifteen of those interviewed individuals agreed with this approach but in general did not feel that a substantial reduction of seasonal fluctuations could be achieved. When asked what, in their opinion, could or should be undertaken to alleviate seasonality, the range of responses was as follows: four stated that seasonality is not a problem; seven prescribed various measures, not necessarily viable, to reduce seasonality of demand; one advocated proper state laws, such as the removal of state inventory tax; four were resigned to the fact that nothing could be done to alleviate seasonality; and two had no opinion or offered no specific suggestions or comments.

Between 1976 and 1977 we again interviewed key executives of fourteen large companies and a surprising consensus emerged. Most agreed that seasonality is a serious problem but no one offered any alternative. We recommend that the industry undertake a massive project to isolate determinants of seasonality and to devise and test viable actions for reducing seasonality or making it less painful.

Industry Labor Structure

We examined the structure of the mobile home industry's labor force to understand better how this force influences the entire industry. Further, we compared it wherever possible to the conventional on-site housing industry because of the significance of the labor function in conventional residential construction.

In 1977 there were approximately 44,000 people engaged in the manufacture of mobile homes nationally. Of these, an estimated 35,000 were in production; the other 9,000 worked in administrative, technical, clerical, maintenance, and other nonproduction capacities. The figures for the "boom production year" 1972 were 71,000, 60,000, and 12,000, respectively. National annual labor statistics for the entire 1972–1977 period are given in table 4.35. A regional breakdown for the same period is given in table 4.36. In 1974/1975 the mobile home industry experienced a traumatic recessionary drop in employment; production workers were down to nearly 33,000 from a 1973 level of 63,000. Management decreased proportionally. Only in the late 1970s has there been a gradual recovery from this catastrophic plunge in the mobile home labor force.

Throughout the early 1970s, even when employment in general fell, the breakdown of types of employment within an average plant has remained relatively the same, with the ratio of management to production workers shifting gradually in favor of increased management in the latter part of the decade. In 1972 an average plant had 90 production workers and 15 nonproduction workers, at a ratio of about six to one. The lowering of this ratio from 5.2 in 1972 to 3.9 in 1977, brought on by an increase in management in the late 1970s has been largely due to increased government regulation. Regionally, this same trend is evident—with the exception of the West, where the ratio has increased, probably because of the West's much less restrictive regulatory climate (see table 4.36). The ratio's decline is especially dramatic in the Northeast and the North Central regions; this clearly reflects the increased costs of doing business in these regions with restrictive public regulation and with land use control practices hostile to mobile homes. (The reader will see these correlations in reading part V, "The Regulatory Environment.") Whereas a typical mobile home company in 1972 required only a small staff without a particularly high level of training or expertise at the middle management level, today's larger mobile home firms often have, of necessity, corporate headquarters swarming with managerial and in-house legal staff occupied all too often primarily with interpreting the new and increasingly complex regulations being imposed on the industry. Thus, although the ratio of production workers to management is still weighted on the side of production labor, an increase in management in the late 1970s has affected mobile home industry labor costs.

In general, mobile home producing firms tend to be relatively small operations. Most mobile home manufacturing companies have a production worker range of 50 to 150 and a managerial administrative and clerical staff of fewer than 30. Approximately one-quarter of all mobile home manufacturers have a production work force of fewer than 50, but the five largest firms each employ thousands of production workers in their nationwide networks of plants. The single largest plant we encountered had a one-shift work force of slightly more than 550. At the opposite extreme is the very small "shop" with one or two employees doing custom work.

Nationwide the average yearly pay for a production worker in the mobile home industry in 1972 was $6764; in 1977 it was $9200. The average yearly pay by region is shown in table 4.37. As can be clearly seen, the pay in the South is far less than elsewhere. Because the South employs the largest number of production workers of these four regions, this accounts for the low national yearly average. The average white-collar worker in the manufacturing end of the mobile home industry made approximately $20,000 a year in 1977. This is twice what the average blue-collar worker received. The range for the white-collar salary is from an estimated average of $14,000 for an assistant purchasing agent to $17,000 for a phone- and $20,000 for a road salesperson, to $45,000 and up for an owner-manager. Yet, because there will continue to be many more blue-collar than white-collar workers, the largest labor expense will remain the cost of production labor, even though through the early 1980s white-collar salaries in this industry are likely to rise faster than blue-collar wages and the ratio of blue- to white-collar employment is likely to decline further.

The most significant factor concerning the structure of the mobile home industry labor force is the use of relatively unskilled workers. The only trade areas in a mobile home plant where skilled workers are likely to be found are in chassis welding (if fabricated in-plant), plumbing, and electrical wiring; and then a typical plant will have only one skilled worker in each of the trade areas supervising the work of other unskilled factory-trained workers. The intentionally low degree of automation and mechanization in the industry also contributes to the use of unskilled and semiskilled labor. Tasks are kept relatively simple by the absence of complicated machinery and equipment, thereby reducing the need for skilled workers.

Manufacturing facilities are typically located in small rural communities within major product market areas, drawing from a labor force that is largely agricultural in origin and unskilled. However, manufacturers locate plants away from metropolitan areas essentially for two non—labor-oriented reasons: Finished unit shipment is easier from rural areas and demand within urban markets for mobile homes is relatively small due to high land costs and regulatory restrictions placed on the siting of mobile homes. The large unskilled labor pool in nonmetropolitan areas contributes to the high percentage of unskilled labor in the mobile home industry, but unskilled labor itself is only one of several

Table 4.35.
Estimated National Labor Statistics. Mobile Home Industry, 1972–1977

Year	All Employees (1,000s)	Production Workers (1,000s)	Ratio of Production Workers to Non-Production Workers
1972	71.3	59.8	5.2
1973	76.0	63.0	4.8
1974	57.0	45.0	3.8
1975	42.0	33.0	3.7
1976	43.0	34.0	3.8
1977	44.0	35.0	3.9

Source: U.S. Bureau of the Census, 1972 data; estimations made for PMHI by Elrick and Lavidge, Inc., from data compiled for the Manufactured Housing Institute, 1973–1977.

Table 4.36.
Regional Labor Statistics, Mobile Home Industry, 1972–1977

Region	Year 1972	1973	1974	1975	1976	1977
All Employees (1,000s)						
Northeast	5	6	4	3	3	3
North Central	18	18	14	11	11	11
South	35	41	29	19	19	20
West	14	11	10	9	10	10
Total U.S.	71	76	57	42	43	44
Production Workers (1,000s)						
Northeast	4	5	3	2	2	2
North Central	15	15	11	8	8	8
South	29	34	23	15	15	16
West	12	9	8	8	9	9
Total U.S.	60	63	45	33	34	35
Ratio of Production Workers to Non-Production Workers						
Northeast	4	5	3	2	2	2
North Central	5	5	3.7	2.7	2.7	2.7
South	4.8	4.9	3.8	3.8	3.8	4.0
West	6	4.5	4	8	9	9

Source: U.S. Bureau of the Census, 1972 data. Estimations made for PMHI by Elrick and Lavidge, Inc., from data compiled for MHI, 1973–1977.

Table 4.37.
Average Yearly Pay by Region, 1972 and 1977

Region	1972	1977
Northeast	$7125	$9100
North Central	$7732	$10,447
South	$6117	$8147
West	$6983	$9140

goals in deciding plant location. Table 4.38 shows the percentage of the work force employed year-round.

Normally, because of the rural location of mobile home manufacturing plants, alternate forms of employment for the work force are limited. Where there is only one mobile home manufacturer in an area, the core work force in the plant tends to be relatively stable and immobile. In areas where there are a number of mobile home manufacturers, there is typically a moderate movement of core workers from firm to firm. Compared to these core workers, the remainder of the work force in the plant is always relatively unstable and highly mobile. This portion of the plant work force is hired when production is up and laid off when production is down. The people who make up this secondary work force are often farmers, hunters, or fishermen who prefer seasonal to full-time employment.

On the whole, the mobile home industry turnover rate is much higher than that of the average manufacturing firm; but because of the nature of mobile home production with its intentionally low automation and mechanization, the low training requirements, and the low labor content of the product, this labor instability and mobility has little adverse effect on the performance of typical firms.

Since the industry has traditionally located manufacturing facilities in smaller communities or rural areas and relied on unskilled and semiskilled workers, manufacturers have had little trouble in the past in securing adequate labor. The reduced competition for available labor from other firms and the larger number of workers in these areas who are willing to work on a seasonal basis has enabled the average mobile home manufacturer to secure adequate labor at wage rates appreciably below the national average. In the past the adequacy and availability of cheap, unskilled labor has contributed greatly to the cost performance of the industry. However, there is clear evidence that this will not be the case in the future. As the industry grows, manufacturers are rapidly building new facilities in major market regions. As a result, manufacturing facilities are being located closer together, oftentimes developing competition between plants seeking to hire labor from an area's labor force not large enough to supply adequately the new facilities. Yet it is relatively certain that the industry will not have the problems locating adequate labor that industry in general experiences because mobile home manufacturers can employ almost entirely unskilled workers in their plants.

Although the mobile home industry uses assembly lines, tasks are structured in such a way as to avoid many of the problems workers encounter on typical assembly lines. Instead of assigning workers independent tasks with limited scope, mobile home assembly lines are organized on a crew/team

Table 4.38.
Size of Core Work Force in Mobile Home Plants

Percent of Plant Work Force Employed Year-Round	Percent of all Firms Reporting
0–10	0
10–20	2
20–30	9
30–40	5.5
40–50	3.5
50–60	9
60–70	18
70–80	23
80–90	25
90–100	5.5

Source: PMHI/MS.

basis. Workers are assigned to crew/teams and given the responsibility for a certain portion of the assembly or fabrication process, such as exterior wall and cabinet installation. In this manner manufacturers avoid the high degree of operation standardization that dampens worker morale and causes other labor problems in industries such as the automotive industry. Although it has not been proven true for all manufacturing situations, it is claimed that the crew/team approach results in greater worker commitment and job satisfaction in a great many areas. Although the crew/team approach will likely be adopted as the assembly line of the future for most manufacturing firms, this factor is certainly a major strength of the mobile home production process and presently exerts a strong positive influence on the productivity of the labor force used in the mobile home industry.

Few formal training programs are found in the industry because it has been so successful in tailoring its manufacturing process to the utilization of unskilled laborers who require little or no training. Manufacturers tend to hire the best workers available and then give them two to four weeks of on-the-job training. At the conclusion of this period, the worker is considered fully trained and can be expected to achieve the average production rate in his or her area. Because most production tasks require a very low skill level, even relatively "unemployable" individuals can often be trained for mobile home work. However, with an adequate supply of qualified workers normally available, manufacturers have shown little interest on their own in training programs that utilize workers who would not otherwise be employed. When subsidized government training programs were used within the industry, they had much success; but manufacturers will probably continue to shun this type of government-financed training as long as adequate labor supplies exist elsewhere. Still, if adequate sources of unskilled or semiskilled

labor should become scarce, the mobile home industry is plainly in a better position than most other industries to increase its labor supply through the use of training programs for previously unemployed workers. Another advantage is that the ease with which workers can be trained at very little cost and with little loss of productivity has helped the mobile home industry cope with production seasonality and prevent much of its adverse influence on labor costs.

Wage Structure
Several wage patterns are evident. The cost per man-hour for labor in the mobile home industry is lower than the cost per man-hour for labor on conventional home-building sites because the mobile home industry can hire relatively unskilled laborers as factory workers as opposed to the conventional housing industry's need for, as an example, construction tradespersons. Also, because most of the labor is relatively unskilled and plants are usually located in small communities or rural areas, mobile home labor costs average less than labor costs in the typical manufacturing plant. Figures showing the average wage trend for mobile home workers, all U.S. factory workers, and construction workers over the past several years show that factory workers have always been paid less for their labor than construction craftspersons. Of course, the seasonal nature of the conventional construction industry causes many of its workers to be unemployed for part of the year. Therefore total yearly average construction wages are not as much higher than those of factory workers as hourly wage comparisons suggest. But the rise of construction wages has been much more rapid than the rise of factory wages, and mobile home wages have always followed the trend of average factory wages rather than construction wages. In early 1977 average hourly union wage rates plus employer payments to health, welfare, pension, and vacation plans for bricklayers was $11.90 per hour; electricians received $12.57—some skilled union workers were making $20.00 an hour. The average hourly union wage rate without employer payments was for all trades $9.59. When compared to the average mobile home production worker's wage of $4.40 per hour, it is obvious that production labor costs are significantly lower in the mobile home industry.[8] The average wage paid direct labor is listed by region in table 4.39. As can be seen, nationally the average hourly wage went up approximately 11 percent between 1970 and 1972 and 30 percent between 1972 and 1977.

Table 4.40 shows the wide distribution of wages.

In Table 4.41 labor is shown as a percentage of total operating cost for plants of varying sizes in three different years. The table clearly shows that as the sales volume of the

The Mobile Home Production System

Table 4.39.
Average Wage on
Direct Labor by Region,
1970, 1972, and 1977

Region and Subregion	1970		1972		1977	
	Hourly	Weekly	Hourly	Weekly	Hourly	Weekly
National	2.76	116	3.06	133	4.40	176
Northeast	3.06	124	3.03	138	4.32	175
New England	3.08	100	2.90	—	3.98	159
Middle Atlantic	3.03	147	3.16	138	4.68	191
North Central	2.78	127	3.49	153	4.37	182
East North Central	3.09	146	4.04	181	5.05	205
West North Central	2.47	108	2.93	125	3.96	168
South	2.38	100	2.63	110	3.82	157
South Atlantic	2.49	111	2.76	117	4.12	165
East South Central	2.40	96	2.58	108	3.40	149
West South Central	2.26	93	2.54	106	3.41	151
West	2.80	114	3.08	130	4.19	177
Mountain	2.41	101	3.05	134	3.78	155
Pacific	3.19	128	3.10	127	4.60	200

Source: "Cost and Profit Survey," *Mobile-Modular Housing Dealer Magazine*, 1970, 1973, and 1977.

Table 4.40.
Average Gross Pay
of Direct Labor

Year	Percentage of Companies	Hourly Wage	Percentage of Companies	Weekly Wage
1970	41	$1.90 to $2.50	27	Up to $100
	35	$2.52 to $3.00	41	$101 to $125
	23	Over $3.00	15	$126 to $175
			16	Over $175
1972	3	$1.20 to $2.00	3	$ 76 to $ 80
	21	$2.01 to $2.50	14	$ 81 to $100
	39	$2.53 to $3.00	40	$103 to $125
	21	$3.05 to $3.50	28	$128 to $150
	9	$3.56 to $4.00	7	$153 to $190
	4	$4.30 to $6.00	7	$220 to $330
	3	$7.00 to $8.15		
1977	3	$2.80 to $3.00	5	$110 to $125
	15	$3.10 to $3.50	25	$126 to $150
	28	$3.59 to $4.00	22	$151 to $175
	14	$4.12 to $4.50	29	$176 to $200
	23	$4.60 to $5.00	11	$205 to $250
	9	$5.10 to $6.00	6	$254 to $300
	8	$6.10 to $7.25	2	$301 to $400

Source: "Cost and Profit Survey," *Mobile-Modular Housing Dealer Magazine*, 1970, 1973, and 1977

Table 4.41.
Labor as Percentage of
Total Operating Cost,
1970, 1972, and 1977

Year	Volume of Company (Millions)	Labor as Percentage of Total Operating Cost
1970	1–3	12.82
	3–4	11.22
	4–6	9.30
	6–15 and up	9.68
1972	1–2	14.29
	2–4	11.77
	4–6	10.79
	6–8	10.20
	8–10	10.41
	10–15 and up	11.92
1977	1–2	12.00
	2–4	10.43
	4–6	10.26
	6–8	11.53
	8–10	9.00
	10–12	11.60
	15–20	11.00
	20–30	13.20

Source: "Cost and Profit Survey," *Mobile-Modular Housing Dealer Magazine*, 1970, 1973, and 1977.

Table 4.42.
Average Weekly Bonus,
1970, 1972, and 1977

Amount of Bonus	% of Firms			
	1970	1972	1977	
			Departmental	Plantwide
$2–$11	42	31		
$12–$25	29	45	27	} 86
$26–$50	29	13	35	11
$51–$100	—	2	11	3
Over $100	—	2	27	—

Source: "Cost and Profit Survey," *Mobile-Modular Housing Dealer Magazine*, 1970, 1973, and 1977.

company rises to eight to ten million, labor as a percentage of total operating cost decreases. But at the ten to twelve million mark it turns around and increases slightly. A possible explanation for this is that the volume of a single plant is usually below ten million. Thus, companies with a volume under ten million would most likely be single plant operations; a company with a total volume exceeding ten million would very likely be a multi-plant company. A company with a volume up to ten million would be better able to manage its labor force efficiently. Once it is over ten million, multi-plant operations are considered, and plant multiplicity puts restrictions on labor management, thus introducing diseconomies and raising labor as a percentage of total operating cost.

In contrast to conventional home building, mobile home building's similarity to typical factory work makes it possible for mobile home manufacturers to make extensive use of labor incentives, and two-thirds of them do. Manufacturers employing some form of labor incentive system have significantly lower production costs than manufacturers who do not. The most frequently used type of direct labor incentive is the bonus system. In 1977 of the firms that use bonuses, 95 percent pay them on a weekly basis, but others use monthly (5 percent) plans. Other manufacturers use a piecework plan or some variation of it. The piecework and bonus systems are typically broken down on either a departmental (used in 1972 by 36 percent of all firms, in 1977 by 51 percent), or plantwide basis (1972: 62 percent, 1977: 46 percent). Table 4.42 shows average weekly bonuses.

Profit sharing plans for direct labor seem to be used increasingly. While only 6 percent reported such plans in 1972, 19 percent had this system in 1977.

Seasonality as a key problem for the industry has been discussed previously in this chapter. When asked which single factor would be most responsible for a cost reduction if seasonality were eliminated, half of all firms surveyed by our Manufacturer Survey responded that the prime factor would be the institution of a permanent rather than seasonal labor force. Short of this ideal, a seasonal work force will continue to be used by the mobile home industry. Between the peak summer sales period and the early winter slack period, sales drop considerably. Because of manufacturers' reluctance to inventory finished mobile homes, production is cut and layoffs result when there are seasonal sales drops. When increased production is required, layoffs cease and workers are rehired.

The effect of seasonality on labor costs, however, is less serious in the on-site building industry because of responses that can be made within the mobile home industry but are not possible in conventional on-site building. Mobile home manufacturing seasonality is attributed to the reduced consumer purchasing interest during the winter season rather than to the adverse effects of weather factors on construction itself. Even in the North, unlike on-site conventional home building, mobile home construction is seldom, if ever, completely shut down. Mobile home manufacturers utilize some labor during slack periods to perform plant maintenance, carry out model changeovers, modify jigs and fixtures, and complete other needed tasks within the plant. When sales begin to increase, production can be increased rapidly by utilizing the core of experienced workers maintained during the slack period. Therefore, although seasonality has overall negative effects on performance in the mobile home industry, it has only limited adverse effects on labor costs. In fact, manufacturers' ability rapidly to adjust production on short notice continues to be used by the mobile home industry as a primary strength.

Unionization

Unionization of the mobile home industry has lagged behind unionization of manufacturing as a whole, and in recent years the role of unionization in the mobile home industry has hardly increased and the gap has not narrowed significantly. Fluctuating from year to year, between 15 percent and 25 percent of the manufacturing plants in the industry are now unionized. This low rate can be attributed to the small initial beginning of the industry; the small size of the average plant (about sixty to one hundred and twenty workers; more than 10 percent of mobile home plants in the United States have fewer than twenty workers); the rural setting of most plants (many manufacturing facilities are located in rural areas; 45 percent of all plants are located in the South, where unionization is less prevalent than in other parts of the nation); and the development of the mobile home industry after the era of great union organizing in this country. The foremost reasons for the lag in industry unionization seem to be plant location and size.

The same factors that contributed to the lag in industry unionization also fostered union fragmentation and local union autonomy. Industry fragmentation and the small size of individual plants have discouraged large unions from attempting to organize the industry or even major firms within it. These factors have also discouraged the formation of an industrywide trade union. Instead, unionization has taken place on a plant-by-plant basis either as a result of organizing efforts of national unions strong in the local area and solicited by members of the local labor force or by the labor force organizing itself alone as an independent union. This unionization pattern has resulted in many different industrial and trade unions representing plants within the industry and within individual firms. The range of unionization is surprisingly mixed: Roughly 25 percent of unionized plants have Carpenters Union representation; approximately 10 percent each are unionized by the Joiners & Carpenters, the United Auto Workers, the Teamsters, the Steelworkers, and the Woodworkers. The Firemen and Oilers and the International Association of Machinists and Aerospace Workers are represented in perhaps 5 percent of unionized plants, and for some of the mobile home firms who have vertically integrated upstream to include their own furniture production, the United Textile Workers are at hand. Unionization of the mobile home industry, fragmented though it may be, is primarily along industrial lines, a factor that is significant in labor costs when considering union trends, by comparison, in the conventional building trade unions.

The managements of some firms with more than one manufacturing facility have made deliberate efforts to ensure that their plants, if unionized, are unionized by different unions. Both unions that have been organized locally (without affiliation to national or regional unions) and unions that have been organized as part of a national or regional union have considerable autonomy in contract negotiations and other dealings with management. Faced with these smaller, fragmented, locally autonomous unions, management seems to have more bargaining strength than the unions. Because some of the organized plants belong to industrial unions, for example, the United Auto Workers, almost all production workers may be classified as assemblers rather than on a job or craft basis, as is the case with the construction trade unions of the conventional home-building industry. This allows mobile home plant management to rearrange tasks and manpower as necessary to increase productivity, a major reason that labor in the mobile home industry shows higher productivity than conventional home-building labor. To date, the unions in the mobile home industry have imposed few restrictions on industry management with regard to items such as work rules and employment guarantees, yet another reason for the high labor productivity of the mobile home work force.

Industry management has been able to extract greater productivity from the work force in the past because of union weakness, but this is decreasingly the case today. As can be seen in table 4.43, up through 1972 unions had little effect on wages but after 1972 unionization increased wages. The growing strength of the unions in the industry is resulting in greater restrictions being placed on industry management with regard to labor. This trend, however slow, to greater unionization is also increasing labor bargaining power, which is resulting in wages and work rules less favorable to management. The cost advantages that the mobile home industry has had over the construction industry as a result of managements' favorable bargaining position with the unions have been notably reduced.

Although this trend is increasing labor costs more rapidly now than in the past, it is expected that the industry will continue to realize an increasing labor cost advantage over conventional construction because there is little likelihood that the unions in the industry will develop the same degree of power that the construction unions have. The unions are too fragmented in relation to the manufacturing firms to exert the same bargaining pressures within the mobile home industry as construction unions exert in the construction industry, where unions are strongly organized and industry management is greatly fragmented. In the late 1970s unionization of the American labor force in general is declining. Thirty years ago almost 40 percent of American labor was unionized; today it is at most 25 percent. This trend is especially strong in the mass production industries, such as the mobile home industry; relatively new industries, such as mobile home manufacturing, have not been strongly unionized also because they originated after the big unionization wave of the 1930s.[9] Furthermore, the success of major companies, including IBM and Eastman Kodak, which are operating without unions, is hardly encouraging management in the industry to soften its resistance. The mobile home industry can no longer look with great assurance to a lack of unionization to realize cost advantages; but relative to the construction industry and industry at large, it will continue to show superior performance with regard to labor cost management.

Table 4.43.
Average Gross Wages,
1970, 1972, 1977

	1970		1972		1977	
	Hourly	Weekly	Hourly	Weekly	Hourly	Weekly
Union	$2.68	$111.81	$2.98	$130.00	$4.71	$193.16
Nonunion	$2.80	$128.10	$3.18	$135.78	$4.35	$130.31

Source: "Cost and Profit Survey," *Mobile-Modular Housing Dealer Magazine*, 1970, 1973, and 1977.

C. Operation

Expectations Based on Structure

We have shown that the mobile home production system possesses the characteristics of a highly competitive industry, even though the industry probably cannot be characterized as perfectly competitive. The structural features of the industry show substantial regional differences. The extent of regional orientation is indicated by the distribution radii of production facilities; PMHI's field interviews with leading manufacturers revealed that the mean of the average radius served by the respondents' plants is 349 miles. The intensity of competition varies from one region to another. Although most regional markets seem to be largely competitive, perfect competition may exist in several market areas. Two of the three operational industry characteristics we examined—price policy and product policy—are extremely sensitive to even slight variations in competitiveness and therefore cannot be predicated for the industry at large. Less sensitive to such variations and therefore more predictable is the third operational characteristic examined—entries and exits; the turnover of firms must be expected to be substantial.

Dynamics of System Growth: Entry and Exit

The terms "entry" and "exit," or "termination," are not unequivocally defined. Firms may be newly formed, legally independent entities or may be legally terminated; but these options cover a broad range of circumstances. For example, firms may terminate independent operation as a result of failure, merger, or acquisition. Industry structure is affected regardless of the cause of termination: Failure indicates poor performance; the merged or acquired firm, on the other hand, is frequently sought for its superior performance and special assets (for example, access to a particular market, special product line, well-developed dealership network, and so forth). Similarly, entry is not a simple categorization. It might signify the building by an entirely new firm of new facilities or the purchase of already existing facilites. It might also indicate the legal independence of a firm that was previously a division of an existing mobile home manufacturer. Even affiliated or owned subsidiaries or divisions may be legally distinct organizations under independent management. If a company were to expand via acquisition, the new facility would likely become a wholly owned subsidiary but treated legally as a distinct operation.

Because a rigid definition of terms is difficult to arrive at, statistics on entry and termination vary from source to source and must be treated accordingly. This is especially true in the mobile home industry, where many marginal firms continue to operate and where mergers and acquisitions are still frequent occurrences. Aggregate figures can be compiled (that is, for mobile home firms as well as those that produce sectional units), but accurate disaggregation is difficult.[10]

Tables 4.44 and 4.45 give a state-by-state breakdown of firms entering and exiting the mobile home industry over the seven-year period from 1970 to 1977 with regional and national totals. Tables 4.46 and 4.47 draw our attention to the trends in the national totals over this seven-year period, the former plotting entry figures against exits and the latter showing the ratio of entries to exits for each year as well as over the entire period. Table 4.46 indicates the steady decline in both entries and exits since 1972, with the number of firms leaving the industry continuing to outnumber those that enter. This means that there was a corresponding decline in the total number of firms in the mobile home industry, as is borne out by the statistics on industry firm totals previously noted in this chapter.

The entry/exit ratios given in table 4.47 show that of the last seven years, only one year shows a balance in favor of entering firms: 1970, when 12.9 firms entered the mobile home industry for every 10 that left. Since then, exits have consistently outnumbered entries at the national level; and over the seven-year period, only 5.8 new firms entered the industry for every 10 that went out of business. The trend of greater number of firms exiting versus entering the industry is in part explained by increasing entry barriers and by the fact that of those firms that entered, most were marginal operations that took advantage of the relatively easy entry requirements at the time but were unable to develop viable operations and so exited the industry because of failure. In some cases their facilities were eventually taken over by other manufacturers; but because of the relatively small capital requirements of the industry, there exists no great incentive to acquire the physical capital of a liquidating firm unless its other assets—location, product line, and so forth—have special appeal. Furthermore, many of these small companies had facilities with insufficient capacity to interest large concerns.

An analysis of regional entry and exit patterns provides a more revealing picture of current trends and uncovers previously hidden factors in firm growth trends. From tables 4.44 and 4.45 it is apparent which regions are most involved in the dynamics of system growth (the South Atlantic, South Central, and East North Central regions). Because unsuccessful fledgling firms result in most terminations, it is not surprising that the regions with the largest number of recent entries—the South Atlantic and South Central regions—are also the regions with the largest number of terminations. The newly developing or growing markets—South Atlantic, South Central, and Pacific—are attracting many new firms, some quite marginal, and therefore are also the regions of heaviest business failure. The more well

Table 4.44.
New Mobile Home
Manufacturing Firms
by Region and State,
1970–1977 (with
National Totals)

Region	1970	1971	1972	1973	1974	1975	1976	1977	State and Regional Totals
Northeast									
Connecticut	—	—	—	—	—	—	—	—	—
Maine	—	—	1	—	1	1	—	1	4
Massachusetts	—	—	—	—	—	—	—	—	—
New Hampshire	—	1	—	—	—	—	—	—	1
New Jersey	—	—	—	—	—	—	—	—	—
New York	1	—	1	—	—	—	1	—	3
Pennsylvania	3	1	1	1	2	—	1	—	9
Rhode Island	—	—	—	—	—	—	—	—	—
Vermont	—	—	—	—	—	—	—	—	—
Total	4	2	3	1	3	1	2	1	17
South Atlantic									
Delaware	—	—	—	—	—	—	—	—	—
Florida	3	2	2	5	3	1	—	—	16
Georgia	8	3	2	2	4	1	—	—	20
Maryland	—	—	—	—	—	—	—	—	—
North Caroline	3	4	1	1	1	1	2	—	13
South Carolina	1	4	—	2	2	1	1	—	11
Virginia	1	—	—	1	—	—	—	—	2
West Virginia	—	1	—	—	—	—	—	—	1
Total	16	14	5	11	10	4	3	—	63
South Central									
Alabama	6	4	5	8	4	—	2	2	31
Arkansas	6	4	3	2	1	2	—	—	18
Kentucky	1	—	—	—	1	—	1	—	3
Louisiana	—	3	2	9	1	—	—	—	15
Mississippi	2	2	2	—	—	—	—	—	6
Oklahoma	1	2	1	1	—	—	—	—	5
Tennessee	3	2	2	3	1	1	2	—	14
Texas	4	6	7	3	1	1	1	—	23
Total	23	23	22	26	9	4	6	2	115
East North Central									
Illinois	1	—	—	—	—	—	—	—	1
Indiana	6	4	8	—	—	—	2	1	21
Michigan	—	—	1	3	—	—	2	—	6
Ohio	4	1	—	—	—	—	—	—	5
Wisconsin	2	—	—	1	1	—	—	—	4
Total	13	5	9	4	1	—	4	1	37
West North Central									
Iowa	2	—	—	1	—	—	—	—	3
Kansas	—	1	—	1	—	—	1	1	4
Minnesota	5	—	2	1	—	—	—	1	9
Missouri	1	1	—	—	—	—	—	—	2
Nebraska	2	—	2	—	—	—	—	1	5
North Dakota	1	—	—	—	—	—	—	—	1
South Dakota	—	—	—	—	—	—	—	—	—
Total	11	2	4	3	—	—	1	3	24
Mountain									
Arizona	3	2	1	—	—	—	—	—	6
Colorado	—	—	3	—	—	—	—	—	3
Idaho	1	—	—	—	—	—	—	—	1
Montana	1	—	—	—	—	—	—	—	1
Nevada	—	—	—	—	—	—	—	—	—
New Mexico	2	—	1	—	—	—	—	—	3
Utah	—	1	—	—	—	—	—	—	1
Wyoming	—	—	—	—	—	—	—	—	—
Total	1	3	5	—	—	—	—	—	15
Pacific									
Alaska	—	—	—	—	—	—	—	—	—
California	6	6	9	4	1	1	3	3	33
Hawaii	—	—	—	—	—	—	—	—	—
Oregon	—	—	—	—	—	1	—	—	1
Washington	—	—	1	—	—	—	—	1	2
Total	6	6	10	4	1	2	3	4	36
Grand Total	80	55	58	49	24	11	19	11	307

Source: Compiled by PMHI from monthly raw data obtained from *Mobile-Modular Housing Dealer Magazine.*

Table 4.45.
Mobile Home Firms Out of Business by Region and State, 1970–1977 (with National Totals)

Region	1970	1971	1972	1973	1974	1975	1976	1977	State and Regional Totals
Northeast									
Connecticut	—	—	—	—	—	—	—	—	—
Maine	—	—	—	—	1	—	1	—	2
Massachusetts	—	—	—	—	—	1	—	—	1
New Hampshire	—	1	—	1	—	—	3	—	5
New Jersey	—	—	—	—	—	—	—	—	—
New York	—	—	2	2	—	—	3	3	10
Pennsylvania	—	2	2	1	2	7	1	—	15
Rhode Island	—	—	—	—	—	—	—	—	—
Vermont	—	—	—	—	—	—	—	—	—
Total	—	3	4	4	3	8	8	3	33
South Atlantic									
Delaware	—	—	—	—	—	1	—	—	1
Florida	6	9	8	7	4	3	2	2	41
Georgia	8	9	3	2	4	9	1	1	37
Maryland	—	—	1	—	—	—	—	—	1
North Carolina	2	4	1	1	3	5	2	—	18
South Carolina	1	4	6	2	2	4	2	1	22
Virginia	—	—	1	—	—	—	—	—	1
West Virginia	—	2	2	—	1	1	—	—	6
Total	17	28	22	12	14	23	7	4	127
South Central									
Alabama	9	5	8	7	7	5	2	1	44
Arkansas	6	2	1	5	5	2	1	—	22
Kentucky	1	1	1	—	—	—	1	—	4
Louisiana	1	2	1	2	3	7	—	—	16
Mississippi	1	1	1	—	1	1	2	—	7
Oklahoma	—	1	1	2	1	1	—	—	6
Tennessee	3	2	1	1	2	7	3	1	20
Texas	3	10	7	3	9	10	—	2	44
Total	24	24	21	20	28	33	9	4	163
East North Central									
Illinois	—	—	1	2	—	—	—	—	3
Indiana	3	9	6	7	2	4	4	3	38
Michigan	5	6	4	5	2	4	1	—	27
Ohio	1	3	2	—	1	4	—	3	14
Wisconsin	1	—	2	1	—	2	—	—	6
Total	10	18	15	15	5	14	5	6	88
West North Central									
Iowa	2	1	—	—	1	2	1	—	7
Kansas	—	1	1	2	1	3	—	—	8
Minnesota	1	3	—	2	—	1	—	—	7
Missouri	1	1	1	2	1	—	1	—	7
Nebraska	1	—	—	—	1	—	1	—	3
North Dakota	—	—	1	—	—	1	—	—	2
South Dakota	—	1	—	—	—	—	—	—	1
Total	5	7	3	6	4	7	3	—	35
Mountain									
Arizona	—	1	3	—	1	—	2	—	7
Colorado	1	2	1	—	1	2	1	—	8
Idaho	—	1	—	—	1	1	1	—	4
Montana	—	—	1	—	—	—	—	—	1
Nevada	—	—	—	—	—	—	—	—	—
New Mexico	1	—	1	1	1	1	1	—	6
Utah	—	—	1	—	—	1	—	—	2
Wyoming	—	1	—	—	—	—	—	—	1
Total	2	5	7	1	4	5	5	—	29
Pacific									
Alaska	—	—	—	—	—	—	—	—	—
California	4	12	9	8	4	4	5	—	46
Hawaii	—	—	—	—	—	—	—	—	—
Oregon	—	2	—	—	—	—	1	—	3
Washington	—	2	2	—	—	—	—	—	4
Total	4	16	11	8	4	4	6	—	53
Grand Total	62	101	83	66	62	94	43	17	528

Source: Compiled by PMHI from monthly raw data obtained from *Mobile-Modular Housing Dealer Magazine.*

The Mobile Home Production System

Table 4.46.
Entry and Exit Trends
at the National Level,
1970–1977

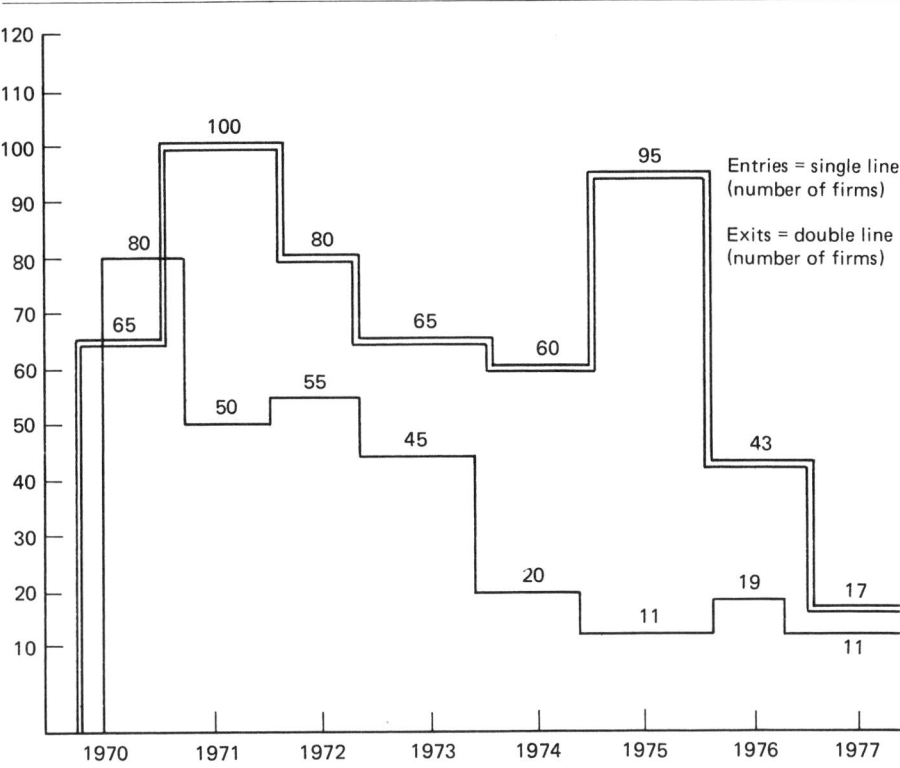

Source: Compiled by PMHI from monthly raw data obtained from *Mobile-Modular Housing Dealer Magazine*.

Table 4.47.
National Entry/Exit
Ratio, 1970–1977

Year	Entry/Exit[a]
1970	12. 9/10
1971	5. 4/10
1972	6.9/10
1973	7.4/10
1974	3.8/10
1975	1.2/10
1976	4.4/10
1977	6.5/10
Total	5.8/10

a. Figures are rounded to one decimal place.

Source: Compiled by PMHI from monthly raw data obtained from *Mobile-Modular Housing Dealer Magazine*.

established market—in the East North Central, for instance—is undergoing less expansion, as it is already fully penetrated by stable, existing firms. Thus terminations in this region are relatively infrequent. However, the last recession of the economy has not been without its effect, as some of the older, established firms have not been able to withstand the external stress and have gone under in the last few years.

Within an active region, two or three states generally account for the majority of firms entering and exiting the mobile home industry. In the South Atlantic region, Florida and Georgia accounted for 36 of 63 entries from 1970 to 1977, as well as 78 of 127 terminations over the same seven years. In the South Central region three out of eight states—Alabama, Arkansas, and Texas—accounted for 72 of 115 entries and 110 of 163 terminations. California is the single active state in the otherwise slack Pacific region, accounting for 33 of 36 entries and 46 of 53 exits over the seven-year period. The most active states in terms of firms entering and exiting the mobile home industry from 1970 to 1977 are California, with 33 entries and 46 terminations; Alabama, with 31 and 44, respectively; Texas, 23 and 44; Florida, 16 and 41; Indiana, 21 and 38; and Georgia, 20 and 37. Significantly, there is no state among these leaders that experienced a growth in the number of mobile home firms in this period.

Table 4.48 represents a detailed breakdown based upon number of years in business of the lifetimes of mobile home companies exiting in the seven-year period from 1970 to 1977.[11] A discernible pattern in the figures is that the majority of firms left the industry within two to three years of joining it. The companies that terminated after three years or more were more likely involved in a merger or acquisition. These firms had more to offer the acquiring company than just physical plant facilities. They also had established distribution networks, brand names, product lines, and so forth. The figures may also point to increasing industry maturity. That is, as the larger, more established firms have already "staked out" their share of the market, it becomes relatively more difficult for an entering firm to garner its portion of the market. Beyond this, market growth is severely stunted in times of recession, and the overall economic trend in 1973 and 1974 would suggest that the alternative to capturing a share of the existing mobile home market, that is, to add to effective demand through stepped-up marketing was likewise difficult for entering firms to accomplish, and they were forced to terminate operations. Only efficient and knowledgeable management can keep a company afloat after the 1973–1975 recession, a challenge that may be compounded by the fact that top-level industry management and know-how is already concentrated in the established

firms. The case for age being correlated with security is strengthened when we see that from 1970 to 1972, 91 percent of the firms that went out of business had been in business for ten years or less; those firms that had a longevity of at least eleven years seemed to fare better, making up only 8 percent (ten firms) of industry failures. By 1974 this figure had advanced to only 9 percent (twenty-one firms) and by 1977, to 8.6 percent (twenty-seven firms) of the total number of failures over the seven-year period. This percentage, though small (less than 10 percent of the total), suggests that even age and industry experience are no sure haven from the effects of a national recession.

Of 307 listed entries from 1970 to 1977, 255, or 83 percent of all entering firms, listed their initial plant size. A breakdown of the number of firms and percentage of total in that year according to size (in increments of 10,000 square feet) is given in table 4.49. In a comparison of medians and averages, we found that the averages are indicative of the general trend. An increase in average plant size is registered from 1970 to 1971 and from 1972 to 1973, with the numbers of firms entering clustered around the higher "rungs" on the incremental ladder. More significantly, over the seven-year period, 125 of 255 firms (50 percent) entered with a plant size somewhere between 21,000 and 50,000 square feet. The average size of production facilities for the 255 firms entering from 1970 to 1977 was 45,026.4 square feet, or just slightly higher than the median would suggest. As for the remaining firms, only 18 percent entered with facilities covering less than 21,000 square feet, while 33 percent began production with plant facilities covering 51,000 square feet or more.

Out of this comparative analysis of firms entering and leaving the mobile home industry over the past seven years, some trends emerge. As in all economic analyses of the last few years, what is difficult is the task of distinguishing between pure industry trends and those induced by the poor state of the national economy. During the 1973–1975 recession, considering the entire economy, business failures reached their high in 1975 —the same recession year in which business failures in mobile home manufacture peaked.[12] Thus, the mobile home industry did not escape the effects of the 1974/1975 downswing; rather, it was part of the statistics. Bearing in mind the overall economic climate, we many conclude that certain trends exhibited in the last few years will continue. Exits will continue to outnumber entries but then will level off as the fledgling firms are gradually eliminated (we can expect no significant rush of newly entering firms). In the early 1980s management must face up to a demanding test, and we expect the older, established firms, which have proven

Table 4.48.
Lifetimes of Mobile Home Companies That Went Out of Business, 1970–1977

Firms That Entered Industry and Went Out of Business	1970 No.	%[a]	1971 No.	%[a]	1972 No.	%[a]	1973 No.	%[a]	1974 No.	%[a]	1975 No.	%[a]	1976 No.	%[a]	1977 No.	%[a]	Totals Through 1972 No.	%[a]	Through 1974 No.	%[a]	Through 1977 No.	%[a]
Same calendar year	3	8	3	7	—	—	—	—	—	—	—	—	—	—	—	—	6	4	6	3	6	2
One calendar year later	22	56	9	21	7	13	3	7	10	20	2	4	—	—	—	—	38	28	51	22	53	17
Two calendar years later	4	10	11	26	18	33	8	18	6	12	6	12	—	—	—	—	33	24	47	20	53	17
Three calendar years later	4	10	5	12	13	24	12	27	4	8	11	20	2	8	—	—	22	16	38	17	51	16
Four calendar years later	—	—	3	7	4	7	8	18	9	18	1	2	2	8	—	—	7	5	24	11	27	8
Five calendar years later	3	8	2	5	1	2	3	7	7	14	6	12	2	8	1	11	6	4	16	7	25	7
Six to ten calendar years later	1	3	5	12	7	13	7	16	5	10	18	30	8	39	5	56	13	10	25	11	56	18
Eleven to twenty calendar years later	2	5	3	7	4	7	1	2	6	12	6	12	5	20	—	—	9	7	16	7	27	8
Over twenty calendar years later	—	—	1	2	—	—	2	5	2	4	3	6	4	17	3	33	1	1	5	2	15	5
Total	39	100	42	99	54	99	44	100	49	98	53	98	23	100	9	100	135	99	228	100	313	98

a. Percentage figures rounded to nearest whole percent.

Source: Compiled by PMHI from monthly raw data obtained from *Mobile-Modular Housing Dealer Magazine.*

Table 4.49.
Size (in Square Feet) of Production Facilities of Firms Entering the Mobile Home Industry, 1970–1977

Size of Production Facilities (in Square Feet)	1970 No.	%[a]	1971 No.	%[a]	1972 No.	%[a]	1973 No.	%[a]	1974 No.	%[a]	1975 No.	%[a]	1976 No.	%[a]	1977 No.	%[a]	Totals No.	%[a]
1–10,000	9	14	1	2	4	7	—	—	1	5	—	—	—	—	—	—	15	6
11–20,000	8	13	6	14	6	11	4	10	3	15	2	25	1	6	1	9	31	12
21–30,000	15	24	8	19	6	11	8	20	3	15	1	12	4	25	—	—	45	18
31–40,000	8	13	7	17	11	20	5	12	6	30	2	25	2	12	4	36	45	18
41–50,000	7	11	7	17	9	17	7	17	2	10	—	—	2	12	1	9	35	14
51–60,000	7	11	3	7	10	19	8	20	1	5	1	12	4	25	1	9	35	14
61–70,000	3	5	4	10	5	9	4	10	3	15	1	12	—	—	4	36	24	9
71–80,000	5	8	2	5	—	—	—	—	—	—	—	—	2	12	—	—	9	3
81–90,000	1	1	1	2	1	2	1	2	—	—	—	—	—	—	—	—	4	2
91–100,000	—	—	1	2	1	2	1	2	—	—	—	—	—	—	—	—	3	1
101,000 and above	—	—	2	5	1	2	3	7	1	5	1	12	1	6	—	—	9	3
Total	63	100	42	100	54	100	41	100	20	100	8	98	16	98	11	99	255	100
Average size	36155.5		45761.9		42529.6		49231.7		41350.0		47750.0		48568.8		48863.6		45026.4	

a. Percentage figures rounded to nearest whole percent.

Source: Compiled by PMHI from monthly raw data obtained from *Mobile-Modular Housing Dealer Magazine.*

themselves and carved out their definite market shares, to maintain production and perhaps force a further concentration of the industry.

D. Performance Indexes

Measures of Firm Efficiency

The performance of individual firms in the mobile home manufacturing sector can best be measured by various economic "noncost" criteria of efficiency—profitability, output per man-hour, and so forth. (Cost structure and related measures of performance are covered in chapter 6.) Some measures of mobile home firm efficiency can be isolated from data collected on individual firms in order to discuss the significance of several efficiency criteria, show in aggregate how the individual firms responding to the PMHI Manufacturer Survey fared according to these measures, and investigate the determinants of these efficiency measures.

The simplest market measure of efficiency is profitability. Two such measures have been investigated: company profits before taxes as a percentage of overall company operating expenses and profits before taxes as a percentage of FOB factory price for the selected standardized model. In each case the profit margin represents a markup over costs. If all firm strategies were consistent, these profit rates would have an unambiguous measure of efficiency. However, firms try to maximize total dollar profits or even market share rather than rate of profit, and therefore some adhere to a low markup/high volume strategy in order to maximize total profits. Firms following such strategy would appear to be low-efficiency producers according to the rate of profit criteria. In fact, any attempt to attribute economies of scale to higher profit rates would fail if large firms purposely accept low profit margins in order to maintain high volumes. In addition, profit rates are likely to be unreliably reported by companies, even when assurances of confidentiality are made. Companies in either extreme position —very high or very low profit rates—are likely to modify their replies. Therefore the data may well be biased away from either extreme. Nevertheless, profit rate is a reasonable measure of market efficiency and worth investigation. Table 4.50 gives the range of company profits and model profits reported by the survey respondents.

Labor productivity, for which there are many measures, is another criterion of efficiency. We have limited the data used to the standardized model and to the one specific plant at which it is produced. Using these model data, we constructed two measures of labor productivity: value added per man-hour and output (square footage) per hour. Table 4.51 gives the ranges reported by the respondents. An additional measure of firm performance is capacity utilization (the total number of floors produced divided by annual productive capacity). Table 4.52 gives the range of capacity utilization for the reporting companies.

Table 4.50.
Range of Values, Profits Before Taxes

Rate of Profit	Number of Firms	% of Respondents
Percentage of Overall Company Operating Expenses		
Less than 1	1	1.7
1	3	5.0
2	3	5.0
3	9	15.0
4	5	8.3
5	6	10.0
6	5	8.3
7	8	13.3
8	4	6.7
9	1	1.7
10	4	6.7
11	1	1.7
Missing values	10	16.0
Percentage of standardized model F.O.B. factory price		
1	1	1.7
2	3	5.0
3	2	3.3
4	1	1.7
5	4	6.7
6	7	11.7
7	8	13.3
8	5	8.3
9	4	6.7
10	4	6.7
11	2	3.3
12	1	1.7
Missing values	18	30.0

Source: PMHI/MS.

Determinants of Firm Efficiency

Factors relevant to firm efficiency will vary with the particular measure of efficiency being used. For example, as previously indicated, even if scale economies exist, they would have little effect on the rate of profit if a firm purposely accepts low profit margins in order to gain high sales volume. We investigated the determinants of firm efficiency by regressing measures of efficiency against likely explanatory variables.

Company profit rate should vary with a number of structural and behavioral firm attributes. A scale factor could be one such attribute. More important might be the effect on profit rates of number of plants, which is a proxy of sorts for firm size but which also roughly indicates the number of markets in which the firm operates. Several other marketing and product-related variables are potential determinants of profitability: the number of dealer outlets, relative both to firm scale and to number of firm plants; the number of product lines (brand names) offered, relative both to total firm scale and to number of plants; the breadth of product line offered; the composition of output, particularly the percentage represented by double-wide units; the extent of firm production

Table 4.51.
Range of Values: Value
Added per Man-hour
and Output (Square
Footage) per Man-hour,
Both for Standardized
Model

Range of Values	Number of Firms	% of Respondents
Value Added (in dollars)		
0.01–2.99	2	2.9
3.00–3.99	9	13.2
4.00–4.99	9	13.2
5.00–5.99	8	11.8
6.00–6.99	7	10.3
7.00–7.99	6	8.8
8.00–8.99	3	4.4
Greater than $9.00	7	10.3
Missing values	17	25.0
Output (in square feet) per man-hour		
0.01–2.00	3	4.4
2.01–3.00	13	19.1
3.01–4.00	12	17.6
4.01–5.00	13	19.1
5.01–6.00	7	10.3
6.01–7 00	2	2.9
Greater than 7.01	6	8.8
Missing values	12	17.6

Source: PMHI/MS.

Table 4.52.
Range of Values,
Company Capacity
Utilization

Capacity Utilization	Number of Firms	% of Respondents
0.01–0.25	5	7.5
0.26–0.40	11	16.5
0.41–0.50	2	3.0
0.51–0.60	7	10.5
0.61–0.70	9	13.5
0.71–0.80	2	3.0
0.81–0.90	2	3.0
0.91–0.99	2	3.0
Greater than 1.00	1	1.5
Missing values	27	39.5

Source: PMHI/MS.

of its own components; integration into activities such as mobile home park development, dealerships, and so forth; the percentage of equipment leased rather than owned; the age of the company as a potential proxy for managerial efficiency; capacity utilization; and the degree of seasonal production fluctuation.

Such structural and behavioral firm attributes should be indicators of profit rates. However, when all the explanatory variables mentioned above were included in our company profit rate equation, none of the coefficients was significant. This is to be expected because the number of explanatory variables was large and the likelihood of collinearity would be high. We reran the regression and omitted variables one at a time. The F value of the regression became insignificant whenever one or more variables were added to the following estimated equation:

$$COPBT = -0.2493 + 10.0959 \, XLXH$$
$$(4.2533)$$
$$+ 1.3175 \, DIV1$$
$$(0.8743)$$

($R^2 = 0.3154$, F = 3.9163, standard errors in parentheses),

where COPBT is the company profit rate; XLXH is the ratio of lowest to highest monthly production; and DIV1 is the dummy variable for integration into park development. Although the coeffficient of DIV1 is insignificant, its t-value is relatively high. Moreover, when more variables were added to the above equation, the only variable to remain significant was DIV1, the dummy variable for integration into park development.

Using the profit margin of the standardized model (instead of overall company profit rate) as the dependent variable, we investigated plant-related variables that might be significant. Once again there is some ambiguity with respect to either plant scale or company scale. However, by limiting the analysis to a single plant, it is possible to include regional variables. Also, two proxies for extent of firm production of its own components—percentage model costs in materials divided by percentage model costs in labor and plant square footage per unit of capacity—can be tried. In addition, two measures of labor productivity—value added per work hour and output per work hour—can be introduced. Because the standardized model need not be typical for the firm, a variable relating the standardized model price to the price of the firm's most popular model had to be included. A proxy to adjust for quality differences (for example, price per square foot) was also tried.

All explanatory variables were included in the same equation at the initial state of experimentation and none of the coefficients was significant. Further experimentations consisted of dropping variables one at a time.

The only equation with a significant F value was the following:

$$CMPBT = 0.4340 + 0.71594 \, VAMH$$
$$(0.3110)$$
$$- 0.1648 \, CPLMO$$
$$(0.0787)$$
$$+ 0.6306 \, VRTIM$$
$$(0.3117)$$

($R^2 = 0.2564$, F = 3.3326, standard errors in parentheses),

where CMPBT is the standard model profit rate; VAMH is the value added per worker; CPLMO is the plant design capacity; and VRTIM is the material to labor cost ratio of the model. Although the seasonal production index had significant coefficients in company profit rate regressions, it did not have a significant sign in any of the equations involving the standard model profit rate. This may not be hard to explain because the seasonal production index pertains to the entire company and may be totally irrelevant to the plant producing the standard model.

Both measures of labor productivity—value added per man-hour and output per man-hour—relate to the standardized model. Fortunately, for each firm there are data on one specific plant in which the model is produced. The potentially most important relationship is between scale of plant and labor productivity. Does a positive relationship exist? Also of interest are any regional variations. Either of the two proxies for vertical integration can be used to investigate the impact of firm production of its own components on labor productivity. Once again allowance must be made for differentials between the standardized model and the firm's typical model and a proxy for quality (for example, price per square foot) should be included. Finally, unionization might help to explain labor productivity.

In investigating value added per manhour, we again found that the initial regression included all the explanatory variables, and the F value of the equation was found insignificant. The F value of the equation did not become significant until the number of variables was reduced to the following:

$$VAMH = 11.844 - 0.0912 \, AGECO$$
$$(0.0347)$$
$$- 0.0002 \, VRTIN$$
$$(0.0001)$$
$$- 0.0154 \, PCTUN$$
$$(0.0108)$$

($R^2 = 0.3157$, F = 3.6904, standard errors in parentheses),

where AGECO is the age of the company; VRTIN is the plant square footage per unit of capacity; and PCTUN is percentage of plants unionized. The sign of the AGECO coefficient was significant and ran counter to prior expectation because time is presumably required before an efficient work force can be organized. The two remaining variables likewise were negative in sign, although the coefficient of VRTIN was significant at the 0.10 level only. Based on the correctness of the signs and significance of the coefficients, the regression on VAMH was generally poor. Part of the problem could very well lie in the fact that profit rate was involved in the construction of VAMH. If the profit rate were unreliably reported, it would affect the reliability of the proportion of the selling price in labor costs. Since both profit rate and labor costs were involved in the computation of VAMH, so VAMH would be doubly unreliably constructed.

Regression results were much more satisfactory when output per man-hour became the dependent variable. More independent variables can be included in the same equation before its F value turned insignificant. The last equation before the F value turned insignificant was detailed under "Economies of Scale" in section B above.

The capacity utilization measure employs companywide data. There are many structural and behavioral variables that might be of significance here. Potential scale effects— the effect of total company capacity and of capacity per plant on capacity utilization— should be investigated. The influence of number of plants also is relevant, though here the significance may relate more to the number of markets in which the firm produces than to firm size. Number of plants is but one of many marketing and product-related variables that might influence capacity utilization. The number of dealer outlets relative to scale and to number of plants (that is, number of markets) is likely to be positively related to capacity utilization. So are the number and breadth of product lines offered, provided they do not add more to costs than to demand. Seasonality will have a strong impact on capacity utilization. A production fluctuation index (lowest monthly production divided by highest monthly production) has been devised to measure such seasonality. There are also certain behavioral characteristics—offering special incentives to dealers during the off-peak period, shipping on consignment—that might lessen seasonal fluctuations and hence increase capacity utilization.

Of all the performance measures, capacity utilization has the most satisfactory sets of regression results. The R^2 and F values were generally very high, and even when the number of explanatory variables was large, the respective t values of the coefficients were still high. Consequently, only the equation with t values of the coefficients in excess of 1 is presented below:

$$JCAP = -0.1944 + 106.792 \; QUABAR$$
$$(16.7623)$$
$$+ \quad 2.9771 \; NCCAP$$
$$(1.3108)$$
$$+ \quad 0.0102 \; NPL$$
$$(0.0052)$$
$$+ \quad 0.4571 \; XLXH$$
$$(0.2069)$$
$$+ \quad 0.0919 \; SINC$$
$$(0.0741)$$
$$+ \quad 0.0027 \; PEQL$$
$$(0.0018)$$
$$+ \quad 0.0301 \; VRTIM$$
$$(0.0258)$$

($R^2 = 0.8245$, F = 11.408, standard errors in parentheses),

where

JCAP	= capacity utilization
QUABAR	= breadth of product line
NCCAP	= dealer outlets per company capacity
NPL	= number of plants in operation
XLXH	= lowest to highest monthly production
SINC	= special incentives offered to dealers
PEQL	= percentage of equipment leased
VRTIM	= ratio of material to labor costs

All of the coefficients appear to have reasonable signs. The three coefficients that were significant at the 5 percent level are QUABAR, OUTCAP, and XLXH. First, it would mean that an increase in the breadth of the product line will enhance capacity utilization. Second, a large dealership network will reduce underutilization of plants. Third, large seasonal fluctuation in production will create underutilization of capacity. The coefficient of the number of plants variable was significant at the 10 percent level. This would seem to indicate that a large number of markets can increase utilization of plants to the extent that seasonality of production can be decreased when different markets have different seasonal peaks and troughs. Finally, the three remaining variables were not significant. Overall, the estimated equation is highly satisfactory judging from the R^2, F, and the number of significant coefficients.

Conclusion

We found several factors to be important in explaining a firm's performance. Based on the results presented earlier, seasonality is an important factor whenever company data (company profit rates and capacity utilization) were used. Seasonality, however, played no role in the regressions involving the standard model. This apparent inconsistency of seasonality stems from the fact that the seasonal fluctuation index was computed on the companywide basis and hence may be irrelevant to the particular plant producing the standard model. Monthly productive capacity of the plant and vertical integration variables were important in explaining performance measures based on the standard model. We found monthly capacity is negatively related to the standard model profit rate. This seemingly contradictory relationship between plant capacity and standard model profit rate can very well reflect the fact that firms with typically large plants tend to pursue a low markup/high volume strategy for profit maximization. We used two measures of vertical integration: plant square footage per unit of capacity and the ratio of material to total labor costs. The former measure was inexplicably affecting performance adversely. Finally, when capacity utilization was used as a measure of performance, marketing variables such as breadth of the product line and the number of dealer outlets were also important factors affecting utilization of plants.

E. Policy Implications

The evolution and current structure of the mobile home production system indicate several conclusions about the nature of the constraints that have led to its present form and about the prospects for industry performance improvement through modifications in industry organization. Historically, three major trends have determined the structure of the system. First, by default, the industry arose in response to demand for low-cost housing that could best be produced by using highly centralized, off-site production techniques. Those companies that dominated the industry in its early stages were highly sophisticated in the management of production facilities but were less familiar with the nuances of market strategies and not at all familiar with the peculiar characteristics of the housing market. The general maturation of the industry and the entry of more diversified firms during the later 1960s attracted or brought to the industry managerial talent with experience in areas other than production and the system's behavior began to lose its bias toward technical considerations. While safeguarding its proprietary, mobile-home-industry-specific expertise, the industry must now shift emphasis radically toward marketing and toward reliably understanding the housing market as a whole.

Second, the system has faced major constraints due to the problem of high transportation costs and the resultant regional focus of production facilities. The limited distribution areas that result constrain the firm in the use of plants sufficiently large to capture potential economies of scale. Plants are less than optimally sized for minimum costs and this leads to prices that are higher than necessary. The regional focus must be maintained as the only viable response to the competitive regional market structures. As more firms grow to operate nationally, however, they must learn, from the precedents set by the industry leaders, to find the most effective balance between centralizing non—region-specific functions and decentralize all other functions that require regional focus for effectiveness.

Third, the system has been characterized by the same problems of seasonality that are associated with the conventional housing industry. Unlike the conventional builders, however, the use of unskilled labor has not forced the mobile home production system to provide high wages to compensate its workers for layoffs during slack seasons. The seasonality does, however, generate serious problems associated with unstable production, including underutilization of capital equipment. The industry must move toward both alleviation of seasonality and development of more viable responses to living with it.

The current structure of the industry can best be described as indeterminant. As the industry matures, firms are attempting to determine if increased integration and diversification are desirable. Diversification could be desirable for firms that are limited to specific geographic areas with limited expansion possibilities. It may also enable some firms to minimize the effects of seasonal and cyclical instability. However, some of the most successful firms shun diversification (except for recreational vehicle production) and we feel there is great business wisdom in concentrating on one specialty, especially in a relatively immature industry. As will be stated in a later chapter, under "Supply Sector Influence," the relationship between producers and their suppliers currently results in a number of benefits for the producer, including decreased inventory costs and decreased need for in-house research and development; but it also tends to hinder in some ways innovation on an individual firm basis. Although some producers, notably larger and newer firms, have reported successful integration into the production of inputs, more have found the costs of integration too high and have withdrawn. Likewise, firms are not unanimous about the relative merits of forward integration into the areas of retail dealerships and park development, management, or both. Some firms have been successful and others have retreated. Because the strength of the dealer structure and the form of future land development— the "real" market for the industry's product— have serious implications for the future of the industry, it is desirable for producers to explore these areas. However, we feel that increased control will be more efficiently gained through means other than integration because successful operation in these areas requires managerial skills significantly different from those producers inherently possess. Again, we believe that for a maturing business to concentrate on its specialty is imperative, and the most successful companies do just that. However, the industry cannot reach a blanket solution to the issues of integration and diversification. Individual firm characteristics may dictate differing arrangements depending on the nature of firms' relationships with their dealers and suppliers and on individual firms' perceptions of the need for diversification. Any policy that affects firms' actions in these areas should aim toward maximizing the ability of the firm to adapt to its own set of circumstance rather than attempting to establish industrywide norms. The innovative nature of the system is threatened by rapidly increasing barriers to entry as well as increasing degrees of product differentiation. A more definitive industrial form and consolidation are imperative.

The past structure of the mobile home production system led to patterns of operation characterized by high entry and exit levels. The lack of entry barriers in the past made it relatively easy for entrepreneurs to begin production. The lack of a determinant industrial form both encouraged entry and prompted exits. But the past structure is becoming actual history, and systems operation cannot be targeted any longer by relying on history.

Production system performance reflects the influence of the structure and operation of the entire system. As would be expected in a growing industry with few established structural norms, some firms are able to attain high profit levels while the industry average is considerably lower. But as structure evolves and competition formalizes, firms must prepare to live with more predictable and often more frugal rewards while having to aim for consistent, more efficient firm performance.

Notes to Chapter 4

1. In addition to the mobile home industry, the U.S. building sector consists of two other basic subsystems: the on-site building (or construction) industry and the manufactured building industry. The mobile home industry evolved and operates independently from either of these.

The on-site building industry can be further broken down into on-site residential construction and on-site nonresidential construction. Major factors operating within the on-site subsystem are stick builders, general contractors, and production builders. (Production builders, large-scale track builders who specialize in home and apartment construction, use industrial production set-ups at their construction locations. Most build their structures at job sites using various components made for them by component manufacturers, and most use subcontractors to finish their buildings on-site. Production builders always sell their housing units directly to the consumer.)

The other subsystem, the manufactured building industry, consists of packaged home manufacturers and modular home producers, which both produce nonresidential shelter as well. (Both are also referred to as "factory-built housing/shelter producers" or simply as "factory builders" or "factory producers.") Packaged home manufacturers (also known as "prefabricated," "panelized," or "componentized" home manufacturers, or simply as "home manufacturers") produce the components for their home or apartment packages in off-site factories and then transport them to the site for assembly; these manufacturers sell their packages through a network of builder-dealers who handle on-site erection and final marketing to

the consumer. Modular home manufacturers (also referred to as "sectional home manufacturers") produce completely finished three-dimensional sections of one or more rooms in off-site factories, usually on an assembly-line basis quite similar to that used by mobile home manufacturers; they then ship these sections to the job site, where they are joined with one or more such sections to form single-family homes similar to doublewide mobile homes. Modular homes are also sold primarily through builder-dealers. (The primary difference between mordular and mobile homes is that modulars are placed on permanent foundations and are usually built to state-wide factory-built housing codes, not to the Federal Mobile Home Construction and Safety Standards.)

A more substantive discussion of the other two subsystems can be found in chapter 21. But this brief description should serve to show, among other points, why we chose to retain the term "mobile home" in this book: not only is there a confusing similarity among the terms used in the various subsystems ("manufactured housing industry," "manufactured building industry," "home manufacturer"), but this terminology is also in a state of flux, and is likely to be so for some time to come.

2. The data given in the different tables are inconsistent because the data bases are not compatible. For instance, the *Mobile-Modular housing Dealer Magazine* production data are higher than those prepared by Elrick & Lavidge, Inc. (e.g., 621,804 vs. 576,000 units in 1972) due to different sampling and projection methods used. Since some indicators are only projected by one and not the other sources, however, PMHI had to use both sources. As another example, the MHI data supplied by Elrick & Lavidge through 1977) used for plant and firm totals in table 4.11 do not include firms that produce fewer that ten units a year. So in 1973, for example, the MHI estimated 334 firms in existence, but PMHI tabulated 596 firms.

3. The main sources of data used for calculating concentration ratios were *Automation in Housing* (AIH), *Professional Builder*, the 1973 through 1977 issues of *Bluebook of Major Homebuilders*, several MHI *Annual Industry Surveys*, as well as annual reports, 10Ks, and prospectuses of leading companies. This array of data bases, none intended for detailed statistical analysis, suggests that the computed concentration ratios can be taken only as estimates. The ratios, furthermore, have a slight upward bias: For some companies the non–mobile home percentage of total unit volume, even though small, could not be isolated. In addition, the MHI data series chosen for national annual unit production volume excludes estimates of export, federal government, and factory sales. (For 1973 this series covered more than 99 percent of total production: The unit shipment figure used was 566,920, excluding the estimated 1500 units for exports and so forth.)

4. Information on movement into the ownership of mobile home dealerships and into park development was available from the PMHI/MS. Backward integration into the production of supplies was determined to be subject to more variation in interpretation about the significance of differing patterns and levels of such activity and therefore was not included on the PMHI/ MS questionnaire. Information on this form

of integration was taken from a collection of annual reports, 10Ks, and prospect uses of the leading twenty-five firms in the industry. This list of the twenty-five top firms was compiled by PMHI from the 1974 *Automation in Housing* listing of the leading firms, the 1977 *Blue Book of Major Home Builders*, and annual reports and 10Ks from 1968 to 1977. This latter data base was also utilized to supplement information on forward integration available from the PMHI survey. Information on integration by suppliers was taken from the PMHI Suppliers Survey (PMHI/SS).

5. The fieldwork and the major data bases used in analyzing diversification patterns within the mobile home industry are similar to the ones used to examine integration. The data have been tabulated by PMHI from the *Automation in Housing* compilations of the leading firms in the industry, the 1977 *Blue Book of Major Home Builders*, as well as annual reports, 10Ks, and prospectuses of leading companies covering the 1970–1977 period.

6. This list has been constructed by PMHI by drawing on a large number of industry publications, including the listings of the leading firms in the housing industry in the magazines *Automation in Housing* and *Professional Building*, the *Blue Book of Major Home Builders*, as well as annual reports, 10Ks, and prospectuses of leading companies.

7. Stephen Visher, *Climatic Atlas of the U.S.* (Cambridge, Mass.: Harvard University Press, 1954).

8. "Wages in Unionized Building Trades Rising at Slower Pace," National Association of Home Builders' *Journal-Scope*, February 21, 1977, p.1.

9. "The Decline in Unionization," *Wall Street Journal*, October 5, 1977.

10. "The Monthly Market Letter on Mobile Home Shipments," published by *Mobile-Modular Housing Dealer*, provides the most complete compilation of entries, terminations, mergers, acquisitions, and so forth. The primary source of their information is a credit service that gives credit reports on every mobile home and modular housing manufacturer. Any company purchasing on credit (all but the very smallest) is covered by the report. Relatively complete listings of entries and terminations can be tabulated in this way, but the exact circumstances surrounding entry or termination for the individual firms are not reported by the market letter.

11. Listings of terminations were taken from "The Monthly Market Letter"; ages were computed by cross-checking the date of founding of the firms in several annual dealer directories published by the same company. Not all the terminations of firms listed in the market letter were listed in the annual dealer directories. The data in table 4.48, although not complete, are still significant. If there is an exclusionary bias, it is in favor of the younger firms, which may have entered and exited the industry without ever being listed in the annual dealer directory, which is published as a guide to manufacturers and as a link between suppliers and manufacturers in the industry; it is not intended to serve as a census of manufacturers.

12. "Business Failures," *Wall Sheet Journal*, May 10, 1977.

Chapter 5

Manufacturing

The following description of the mobile home manufacturing process consists of three sections. The first evaluates the product itself, its architectural design and functional problems, its unique structural principles, and the problems that arise during transportation and on-site use. The second section describes the facilities, materials, and stages of production; assembly techniques and the various sorts of mechanization involved are considered. Finally, in the third section, the organization of plant and firm management is set forth; decision-making procedures upon which all operations depend are identified and their interrelationships are explored.

A. The Product

The Product: Rationale

The design of the mobile home is governed by one objective: to provide a fully furnished primary housing unit that can be transported from the factory to its eventual home site. The design criteria of the mobile home are essentially the same as those of the conventional home, aside from the requirement of transportability. It must effectively respond to the user's physical, psychological, and social needs. It must be able to accommodate facilities for lighting and electricity, waste and water transport, and heating or full air conditioning. It must be adequately insulated from the outside. It must be structurally sound, able to withstand effectively the loading it will encounter when in use.

It is important to remember that the design objectives of the mobile home did not always resemble those of the traditional home. Mobile homes were originally designed exclusively as temporary living units with a heavy emphasis on transportability. During and after World War II, the mobile home industry discovered that its product was increasingly being used as primary housing and that it could compete effectively in the low-cost housing market. Recognizing a new market potential and knowing that it could efficiently produce a highly marketable product, the industry changed its design objectives: Rather than producing a secondary housing unit, the industry evolved a primary housing unit equipped with all of the services necessary for a permanent home.

Today, although the design criteria of mobile homes are similar to those of conventional homes, the physical details of

mobile home design are radically different for two reasons. First, the architectural design of the unit has always been constrained by highway regulation. This has imposed a severe limitation on the designer that does not confront the architect designing the traditional home. Second, there is a difference in approach to engineering design. While conventional home construction has continuously refined traditional techniques, the mobile home industry has developed a new and unorthodox approach to product design. This can be characterized as a "systems analysis" approach by which the industry aims to maximize its utilization of basic resources—material, labor, and money—in achieving its given design objectives. The resulting efficiency in product design has contributed significantly to the industry's success.

The product analysis in this discussion examines data collected by PMHI through comprehensive national field surveys in five target years: 1969, 1971, 1973, 1975, and 1977. This extensive survey, referred to as the PMHI 3000 Survey, involved more than one hundred fifty manufacturers, both large and small, and yielded detailed information on product lines as well as complete plans and specifications for approximately three thousand models of all varieties. Tables 5.1 and 5.2 provide an overview of the survey sample distribution.

The sample distribution for PMHI 3000 is fairly representative of overall industry distribution figures. Table 5.3 details production of the three types of units for five target years. Analysis of this table reveals a definite trend toward the larger/wider units. Single-wide manufacture has shifted from almost exclusively 12-wides to predominantly 14-wides. Doublewides, introduced in 1969, have captured a substantial share of the market, while the smaller units, 12-wides and expandables, have steadily become less popular. There are many reasons for this shift. Because mobile homes are now almost universally accepted as permanent rather than transient housing, people want larger homes. In addition, only in the 1970s have

The Product: Architectural Design

Table 5.1.
Average Number of
Models per Manufacturer

Year	12-foot Singlewides	14-foot Singlewides	Expandables	Doublewides	Sample (Number of Models)
1969	14.7	—	2.2	3.2	331
1971	17.3	3.2	1.4	3.6	696
1973	15.6	9.4	4.9	4.2	778
1975	17.8	17.9	6.5	7.9	1114
1977	12.1	21.3	0.2	7.6	819

Source: PMHI 3000 Survey.

Table 5.2.
PMHI 3000 Survey
Sample Distribution

Year	12-foot Singlewides	14-foot Singlewides	Expandables	Doublewides	Others	Total
1969	90.0%	0%	3.2%	6.7%	0.1%	100%
1971	72.1%	9.8%	4.6%	9.2%	4.3%	100%
1973	64.0%	21.7%	6.9%	7.0%	0.4%	100%
1975	40.0%	35.3%	8.7%	16.0%	0%	100%
1977	24.2%	47.3%	1.2%	27.3%	0%	100%

Source: PMHI 3000 Survey.

Table 5.3.
National Product Mix

Year	12-foot Singlewides	14-foot Singlewides	Expandables	Doublewides	Others	Total
1969	87.24%	1.14%	0.86%	9.28%	1.48%	100%
1971	71.77%	15.51%	1.33%	10.29%	1.10%	100%
1973	58.06%	24.46%	0.44%	15.65%	1.39%	100%
1975	31.90%	41.40%	0.40%	25.90%	0.40%	100%
1977	15.20%	52.60%	0.30%	31.10%	0.80%	100%

Source: Compiled by PMHI from "Market Review.," *Mobile-Modular Housing Dealer Magazine*, 1969, 1971, and 1973, 1975 and 1977 data prepared by Elrick and Lavidge, Inc., for the Manufactured Housing Institute.

mobile home manufacturers been allowed to transport 14-wides to the site on the highway; relaxation of this restriction has made production of these units feasible.

The following product analysis is limited to an examination of spatial qualities and interior planning. Activity zoning, circulation and access patterns, and space distribution are analyzed in detail in order to evaluate the degree to which mobile home design responds to consumer desire and functional need.

Activity Zoning
Privacy was the primary criterion for analyzing activity zones within the mobile home unit. Three distinct activity areas were distinguished: public areas (living rooms), semiprivate areas (kitchens and dining rooms), and private areas (bedrooms and bathrooms).

Analysis of the PMHI 3000 data base identified three types of activity zoning for singlewides and expandables:

The shape of an expandable will differ from the basic shape shown, but the zoning will not. Activity zoning in doublewides is not analyzed here because it closely approximates the zoning in traditional homes.

Type A1 provides maximum privacy by separating the private areas and the public areas from the semiprivate areas. Visual privacy is quite good and noise penetration is minimized. The indoor-outdoor relationship is especially appropriate for a site perpendicular to the street (as with most parks) because private zones can easily be placed away from the noise and bustle of the street.

Private areas are adjacent to public areas in type A2. This relationship does not provide the privacy afforded by type A1: A noise/privacy conflict exists between the public area and at least one bedroom. In all layouts in PMHI 3000 the affected bedroom is the secondary (children's) bedroom.

Two private activities areas are separated by semiprivate and public areas in type A3.

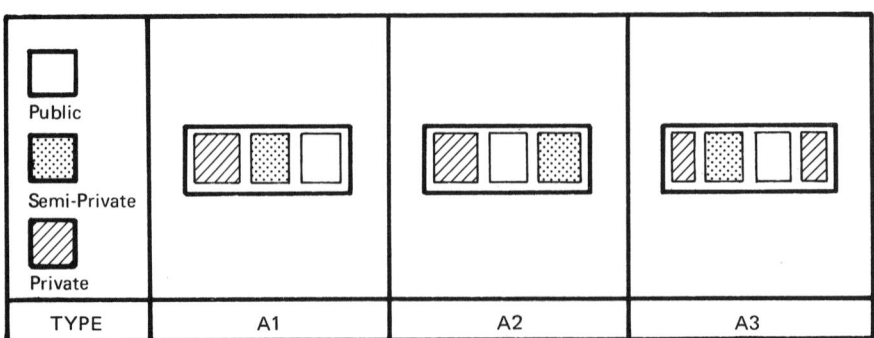

This arrangement seems least desirable in terms of privacy; in particular the bedroom adjacent to the public area suffers from both noise penetration and lack of visual privacy. To provide more visual privacy for occupants of this area, a second bath is often added. The area required for this bath is usually carved out of either the bedroom itself or the public area. This configuration is particularly unsuitable for sites perpendicular to the street: One bedroom is always subjected to street noises. The preceding evaluation, however, seems to have little bearing on industry planning. Since 1969, industry planners seem to have cut back on the models available for type A1 and increased those for A2 and A3 (table 5.4). This may not be the trend in actual sales, but it is the trend in planning, and as such may be an issue that the mobile home industry should address.

Circulation and Access

The PMHI 3000 Survey identified three basic patterns of access and circulation for single-wides and expandables and one for double-wides. These patterns are examined in terms of both practical considerations (waste space, site utilization, and so forth) and aesthetic considerations (design flexibility, privacy, and so forth).

For the singlewide and expandable, type B1 provides single-side access and a single-loaded corridor. This configuration minimizes

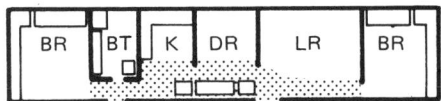

Type B1

area lost to circulation but provides limited response to both practical and aesthetic considerations. Outside, single-side access renders use of the rear areas of the site difficult. Inside, variety of view and exposure to natural light is restricted to the side opposite the corridor.

The second type of singlewide/expandable circulation and access, B2, provides two-sided access, a single-loaded corridor, and a diagonal circulation path. The diagonal circu-

Type B2

lation path promotes better activity zoning by placing public and private circulation on opposite sides of the unit. However, it is longer than the B1 path and thus increases the area devoted to circulation. In addition, the area cut by the path is adversely affected by heavy traffic. On the positive side, two-sided access is a definite improvement over single-sided. It facilitates full utilization of

outdoor space and provides options for outdoor activity zoning, such as recreational area in the rear and parking and service area at the front.

Increased flexibility in living space arrangement is afforded the singlewide by type B3.

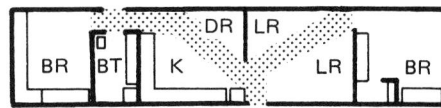

Type B3

Although this arrangement offers some of the advantages of type B2, it compounds the disadvantages. Two areas (in the example above, the living area and the cooking/dining area) lose space to circulation and are subject to heavy traffic.

Distribution of total model mix by circulation type agrees with PMHI's evaluation for both singlewides and expandables (tables 5.5a and 5.5b). Type B1, the primary design in 1969 and earlier, has largely been replaced by models with two-sided access. Type B2, by our evaluation the most desirable, now dominates the market with over half of all models.

The PMHI 3000 Survey revealed only one pattern of circulation and access for the doublewide home, as shown in the accompanying diagram. Two-sided access is provided: the main entry in a public zone, a secondary entry in a private zone on the far side of the home. Circulation depends upon a central spine, double-loaded. This pattern minimizes circulation area and provides two-sided access without the adverse effect of the diagonal path. The overall pattern is close to that of typical single-family homes.

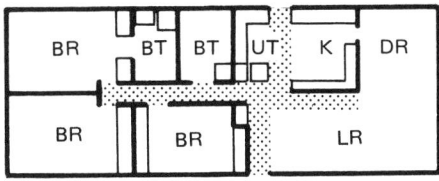

Space Distribution

Data from the PMHI 3000 Survey was also analyzed with respect to space distribution. The analysis was performed in two steps. First, ten activities with different space needs were identified: sleeping, entertainment, circulation, built-in storage, cooking, dining, sanitation, utilities, entrance, and storage. Then space distribution by activity and unit type (singlewide, expandable, doublewide) was computed by using the gross square footage of each home as "100 percent space."

Singlewides

In order to remove the bias resulting from the change of product mix (from smaller units to

Table 5.4.
Distribution by Type of Activity Zone

Year	A1	A2	A3	Total
1969	48.0%	36.0%	16.0%	100%
1971	41.0%	38.0%	21.0%	100%
1973	24.0%	50.0%	26.0%	100%
1975	16.3%	48.5%	35.2%	100%
1977	14.0%	48.0%	38.0%	100%

Source: PMHI 3000 Survey.

Table 5.5a.
Singlewide Distribution by Circulation Type

Year	B1	B2	B3	Total
1969	59%	36%	6%	100%
1971	32%	60%	8%	100%
1973	27%	62%	11%	100%
1975	27%	53%	20%	100%
1977	19%	58%	23%	100%

Source: PMHI 3000 Survey.

Table 5.5b.
Expandable Distribution by Circulation Type

Year	B1	B2	B3	Total
1969	84%	16%	—	100%
1971	58%	38%	4%	100%
1973	53%	42%	5%	100%
1975	33%	49%	18%	100%
1977	30%	54%	16%	100%

Source: PMHI 3000 Survey.

14-wides) over the target years, table 5.6 has been computed using only a standard-sized unit (12 feet × 65 feet). In this way a percentage change in distribution can be taken as a true indicator of change. Almost half the gross area of the singlewide mobile home is devoted to sleeping and entertainment functions. The area distribution among the ten activity functions has changed only slightly over the eight years of the PMHI survey. Sleeping facilities have shown the greatest increase in size (2.3 percent), while dining and cooking areas have decreased. Area required for circulation decreased between 1969 and 1973 but rose again in 1975, probably as a result of the increased use of circulation patterns with diagonal paths (see "Circulation and Access" above).

Expandables
Space distribution, as we defined it for singlewides and doublewides, is not a meaningful measure for the expandable unit. Consumers may alter a wide variety of function spaces. They may increase the area by a few square feet or by an entire room. Under such circumstances we felt that computation of space distribution figures for expandables would be misleading and thus counterproductive. Instead, using the total number of expandable models each year as "100 percent expandables," PMHI has calculated the frequency with which each functional area is expanded.

The percentage totals indicate that expansion often affects more than one function space. In 1969, two basic pullout configurations were offered. One package offered expansion of sleeping and sanitary spaces (usually with a third bedroom); the second offered expansion of the dining and entertainment spaces. In 1973 the first package was almost completely phased out. The dining/entertainment package predominated in 1977, although the sleeping/sanitation package appears again. Pullouts affected an average of 1.56 function spaces in 1969, 1.37 in 1973, and 1.42 in 1977, while add-ons affected 2.78 in 1969, 3.10 in 1973, and 2.00 in 1977 (table 5.7).

Doublewides
Analysis of space distribution in doublewides is based upon all doublewides in the PMHI 3000 Survey. As with singlewides, the trend in doublewide design is toward larger sleeping and entertainment spaces. Comparison of the 1973 and 1977 space distribution figures illustrates the flexibility of doublewide design. Space within each activity zone can be redistributed for various activities. Although total space available in the semiprivate/public zones (cooking-dining/entertainment) is identical for the two years, there is a noticeable difference in its distribution (table 5.8).

Every builder will have noticed that the space distribution of singlewides is roughly equivalent to that of average-sized apartments and that the doublewide's distribution closely resembles that of comparably sized single-family homes. With this realization in mind, this overview of the product's architectural design sets the stage for comparing the mobile home's engineering with that of the conventional home.

The Basic Design Principle: The Structural Box Beam
Mobile home design theory views the unit as a structural box. A mobile home is designed and constructed as a completely integrated structure capable of sustaining its design load requirements and capable of transmitting these loads to stabilizing devices without causing an unsafe deformation or abnormal internal movement of the structure or its parts.

Theoretically, the mobile home can be compared to a box beam supported by a semielastic steel chassis foundation. This structural box design is advantageous for several reasons. The skin can provide longitudinal rigidity. The continuity of horizontal and vertical surfaces minimizes side-to-side motion. With its large cross-sectional dimensions, the box beam design is especially resistant both to twisting or lateral buckling induced by over-the-road transportation and to wind or roof forces while on concrete blocks at the owner's site.

The structural box design of a mobile home is also more efficient than conventional home design. In the conventional home the main load is carried exclusively by the frame, whose members must be very large. The surface carries loads only minimally and acts mainly as an enclosure element. In the box structure the surface serves as both an enclosure element and a load-bearing element. Because the box structure can distribute loads throughout the entire unit, thinner walls and smaller member sizes can be used.

The mobile home is subject to three kinds of loading conditions: in-transit, erection, and on-site. In-transit loading includes all loads encountered by the mobile home while it is awaiting shipment to the dealer, during its trip from the manufacturer to the dealer, while it is waiting to be sold or delivered by the dealer, and during its final journey from the dealer's lot to the owner's site. Although less than 3 percent of all mobile homes are ever moved from original sites, the unit must be able to withstand shipment from the manufacturer to the dealer and from the dealer to the owner. In-transit support conditions add to the need for greater strength. No intermediate supports exist, as is the case in on-site loading, and the unit must independently span a substantial distance between the rear wheel and hitch. In contrast,

The Product:
Engineering Design

Table 5.6.
Average Space Distri-
bution: Singlewides

Function Space	1969	1971	1973	1975	1977
Sleeping	23.7%	22.9%	23.6%	26.0%	26.1%
Entertainment	19.3%	20.1%	21.3%	20.3%	21.2%
Circulation	20.2%	18.1%	17.9%	18.6%	18.2%
Built-in storage	10.0%	9.8%	10.3%	10.3%	10.8%
Cooking	11.4%	11.1%	10.3%	9.6%	9.5%
Dining	7.2%	7.0%	7.0%	6.1%	6.0%
Sanitation	7.7%	7.8%	7.3%	7.6%	7.3%
Utilities	1.4%	1.3%	1.4%	1.4%	0.9%
Entrance	—	0.4%	0.3%	0.1%	—
Storage	—	1.5%	0.4%	—	—
Total	100%	100%	100%	100%	100%

Source: PMHI 3000 Survey.

Table 5.7.
Average Expansion
Frequency

Function Space	Pullout Expandable					Add-on Expandable				
	1969	1971	1973	1975	1977	1969	1971	1973	1975	1977
Sleeping	16%	22%	—	10%	6%	53%	60%	70%	40%	20%
Entertainment	83%	80%	100%	50%	90%	94%	90%	60%	60%	80%
Circulation	—	—	—	—	—	24%	—	—	—	—
Built-in storage	—	—	—	—	—	30%	—	—	7%	10%
Cooking	8%	—	—	—	—	—	—	—	—	—
Dining	33%	20%	37%	45%	40%	12%	10%	40%	13%	20%
Sanitation	16%	—	—	—	6%	18%	—	30%	10%	—
Utilities	—	—	—	—	—	12%	10%	30%	30%	10%
Entrance	—	—	—	—	—	35%	60%	80%	93%	50%
Storage	—	—	—	—	—	—	—	30%	35%	10%
Total	156%	122%	137%	105%	142%	278%	230%	310%	288%	200%

Source: PMHI 3000 Survey.

Table 5.8.
Average Space
Distribution:
Doublewides

Function Space	1969[a]	1971	1973	1975	1977
Sleeping		31.4%	29.0%	30.5%	33.1%
Entertainment		17.2%	17.0%	20.3%	22.1%
Circulation		14.9%	12.4%	13.6%	11.4%
Built-in storage		2.1%	10.7%	9.5%	8.7%
Cooking		10.0%	8.5%	7.3%	6.5%
Dining		8.6%	9.2%	6.9%	6.1%
Sanitation		10.8%	9.2%	9.3%	8.9%
Utilities		4.0%	3.8%	1.7%	2.1%
Entrance		1.0%	—	0.9%	1.1%
Storage		—	—	—	—
Total		100%	100%	100%	100%

a. 1969 doublewide sample is too small to support statistical conclusions.
Source: PMHI 3000 Survey.

once installed at its final site, the unit is supported at least every 12 feet along its entire length.

Erection loading conditions include all the loads incurred during setup, lifting, and securing, both at the dealer's lot and on the owner's site. Erection loading conditions are increasing in importance because the mobile home is placed on permanent foundations with increasing frequency and thus is subject to high tensile stresses during positioning with special equipment. Normally, however, only small erection stresses are incurred because of the very simple procedure. To erect a mobile home, the unit is jacked up, concrete blocks are set in place, and the unit is lowered into position. The stresses induced by jacking are distributed along the chassis I beam rather than throughout the whole unit as in crane lifting of a sectional (a traditional code-conforming doublewide).

Finally, on-site loading conditions constitute all loads sustained by the unit while blocked and occupied on the owner's site. On-site loading conditions include both dead loads and live loads. The dead load portion of on-site loading includes the weight of the mobile home plus its contents. Live loads constitute the more complex factor in on-site loading; three live loading conditions are defined: floor loads, roof loads, and wind and hurricane loads.

Although most traditional housing is constructed on-site and consequently is not subject to erection or in-transit loading conditions, it is, of course, subject to all the on-site loading conditions that the mobile home experiences including hurricane and earthquake loads. Wind load requirements are similar for both housing types except for those pertaining to vertical uplift forces. In the building codes for traditional housing, uplift force requirements are stipulated to prevent the shearing off of eaves, cornices, and other roof projections from the main structure. The code governing mobile home construction establishes vertical uplift force standards to prevent the whole unit from overturning or sliding. The differences are easily understood if one compares the weight of a typical mobile home to that of a conventional modular home. A traditional site-built house weighs at least 25,000–35,000 pounds, including the weight of appliances and excluding the foundation. A typical similarly furnished 14 foot × 70 foot mobile home weighs approximately 15,000–20,000 pounds. Because the mobile home is lighter in weight, built on a chassis which is off the ground, and not attached to a permanent foundation, it is especially susceptible to overturning and sliding.

With respect to earthquake resistance, the lightweight construction of the mobile home becomes an advantage. The optimal structure in an earthquake is one that is light and flexible enough to move with the shock waves. In addition, the chassis and running gear will absorb some of these horizontal stresses. On the other hand, the structure most vulnerable to damage has heavy, inflexible, shear walls that will absorb the shock waves. Although the conventional stud-frame home is not as vulnerable as a concrete or brick building, it still lacks the flexibility of a mobile home and will absorb some of the loads, which can result in damage. This is why earthquake loads are specified for conventional homes in areas where earthquakes are likely to occur.

The building code governing mobile home construction is discussed in greater detail in Chapter 18 of this book.

Mobile Home Construction
Apart from the box beam concept, the design of the mobile home in general seeks to exploit fully the structural capabilities of materials used in construction. Furthermore, to maximize assembly efficiency the mobile home is specifically designed to meet the requirements of assembly line production. The components of the mobile home are standardized and interchangeable, thus permitting fast assembly and mass purchasing to achieve economies of scale. The product can be constructed in a controlled environment, which permits the use of techniques and machinery that cannot be used in traditional home building, thereby allowing for finer tolerances and better quality control. The structural properties of materials are consequently exploited to an extent that could not be achieved otherwise. The importance of this is overriding: Material costs account for 65 percent to 70 percent of total unit cost, so the industry's savings in material consumption contribute much to its outstanding cost performance.

The unibody design relies on four major subassemblies (the chassis, floor system, wall system, and roof system), which are firmly bonded together to act as an integrated structural unit. Nonstructural subassemblies include cabinets, windows, and doors. Mechanical service systems are housed within and integrated with the structural subassemblies. Figure 5.1, an exploded view of a mobile home structure, shows these major subassemblies as described in detail below. Although the following discussion is limited to singlewides, doublewides have essentially the same structural parts. Some of the detailed differences that do exist in the construction of singlewides and doublewides are mentioned in the Technology part which follows.

The Chassis
The chassis frame (figure 5.2) is the structural base of the mobile home, receiv-

ing all vertical loads directly from the walls and floor and transferring them either to the wheel assembly when the unit is in transit or to the foundation at the home site.

The floor area of today's mobile home is much greater than it was in the past. The standard size today is 14 feet × 70 feet. Because the area of the chassis is much greater than before, it must be built to sustain much greater loads. Two main beams running along the length of the chassis provide the primary structural strength for the unit. The beams have built-in cambers to ensure that the mobile home will be level when the weight of cabinets, walls, and other assemblies are added at points not supported by the axle assembly. Steel cross-members are used to provide additional strength. The cross-bracing members are 6- or 8-inch-high Z, I, on open web joists spaced 48 inches apart and spanning the distance between the beams.

Preformed outriggers are cantilevered from the sides of the two beams, allowing for more floor area while making more efficient use of the loading capabilities of the chassis. The outriggers may either be open web steel joists or steel beams. Starting from a depth of 6 or 8 inches where they join the main beams, the outriggers taper toward the outside. Additional 6- to 12-inch longitudinal beams reinforce the axle assembly, an area of load concentration. In front of the chassis frame is the hitch assembly, an A-frame comprised of two tongue members and the coupling mechanism, a socket that joins the mobile home to the towing vehicle.

The running gear assembly includes springs, spring hanger, axles, bearings, wheels, brakes, rims, and tires. The size of this assembly is commensurate with the load of the unit; in most cases either tandem or triple axles are required. The wheel assembly area serves as the main support for the mobile home when in transit. As noted above, parts of the chassis are cantilevered beyond the wheel assembly to achieve a more balanced load.

The Floor System
The floor assembly (figure 5.3) encloses and insulates the home from beneath and provides a level floor surface. Structurally, like the roof, it serves as a sidewall positioner. The floor system is designed to be wholly dependent upon its foundation, the chassis, which assists the floor in load bearing as well as in providing rigidity. A wooden floor frame structural design is used.

Structural Components. As a result of the integration of floor systems and chassis, smaller structural components can be used in the floor system of the mobile home than

in a conventional building. No girders are used in mobile homes; the floor joists are placed directly on the chassis frame. Instead of the conventional 2 × 8 floor joists, steel spliced 2 × 6 joists can be used, spaced 16 inches on center. Variations in the size of floor joists correspond to the width of the floor sections: 12-wides use 2 × 6s; 14-wides generally use 2 × 8s. Dadoed 1 × 4 cross-members spaced 48 inches on center provide cross-bracing for the floor joists and serve as nailers for the subfloor on top and the undersiding below. As in conventional homes, standard decking material is 5/8-inch plywood or particle board; these are nailed and glued firmly to the floor joists, spanning the full width of the floor.

Ductwork and piping can be easily installed lengthwise. Openings in the floor joists must be made for horizontal distribution. Careful attention must be paid to the size and location of the openings to avoid any decrease in structural strength. Openings in the decking must also be cut to accommodate heat ducts, vents, plumbing fixtures, and the furnace connections.

Insulation. For insulation, 1 1/2-inch fiberglass blankets with a polyethylene vapor barrier are placed between the joists and the heat ducts. Often an aluminum foil vapor barrier is placed on the inside floor structure to protect the fiberglass from condensation resulting from contact between cold exterior air and warm, moist interior air. A 3/8-inch asphalt impregnated insulation board seals the bottom of the floor from moisture and rodents. This latter precaution is unnecessary in conventional home construction because the floor bottom generally opens to a crawl space fully enclosed by foundation walls.

Floor finish. The industry prefers a one-piece floor covering such as nylon carpeting or linoleum because of the ease and speed of installation. The floor can be completely covered in one simple operation without custom fitting. Carpeting is installed in one piece over a pad. When linoleum is used, a 1/4-inch underlayment is glued on the subflooring to prolong wear and to act as a cushion. Block tiles are also used for floor covering. The variety of floor finishes is generally very limited in mobile homes compared to the wide selection in conventional homes.

The Wall System
The sidewalls are vertical enclosing elements that must be sufficiently weatherproof to resist rain and snow. The walls must be structurally able to withstand the roof loads and transfer them to the floor system (figure 5.4).

Structural Components. The mobile home wall consists of an interior skin of plywood paneling, glue-nailed to 2 × 4 wall studs spaced 16 inches on center, and an exterior skin of aluminum siding. The structural behavior of the wall can be explained in terms of the "stressed-skin" principle. Stressed-skin construction maximizes material efficiency by integrating framed components to create a continuous skin; the structure acts as a unit and a considerable portion of the load is carried diagonally by the covering material. Both strength and rigidity are increased substantially. The stressed-skin principle also permits use of smaller structural components than those demanded by conventional construction. Instead of 2 × 4 studs which are now typically being used, 2 × 3 studs can be used and 1/4-inch rather than 1/2-inch plywood can be used for sheathing.

Mobile home manufacturers employ stressed-skin construction for several reasons: Under controlled assembly line conditions the covering material can be attached securely and continuously to the framing members; dadoed horizontal belt rails are used to form a structural matrix that resists twisting and buckling; plywood paneling is used for interior walls in the mobile home rather than the mineral or mineral fiber board commonly found in conventional homes. Whereas mineral fiber has very little structural strength, wood provides the strength needed to carry diagonal loads; and the aluminum used for exterior siding contributes sustantially to strength.

Unlike the traditional home, where the sheathing is applied to the exterior, the sheathing in mobile homes is applied to the interior side of the walls and serves additionally as a finished wall surface. The result is a wall that is much thinner and uses less material than can be produced under on-site building conditions. Attempts have been made to approach this condition in conventional construction through the use of interior plywood sheathing. However, the mere use of plywood sheathing is not enough; a secure glue bond between the covering material and the framing members must be formed. On-site conditions make this difficult to achieve—nailing simply does not produce a sufficient bond.

To avoid sliding caused by loading and potential overturning caused by wind forces, wall and floor assemblies are joined to form a continuous unit. The bottom plate is glue-nailed or bolted to the floor. Steel tie plates reinforce the connection between the wall and the floor systems. Three-quarter-inch diagonal steel strapping binds the floor, walls, and roof into one complete unit. To ensure complete continuity between the

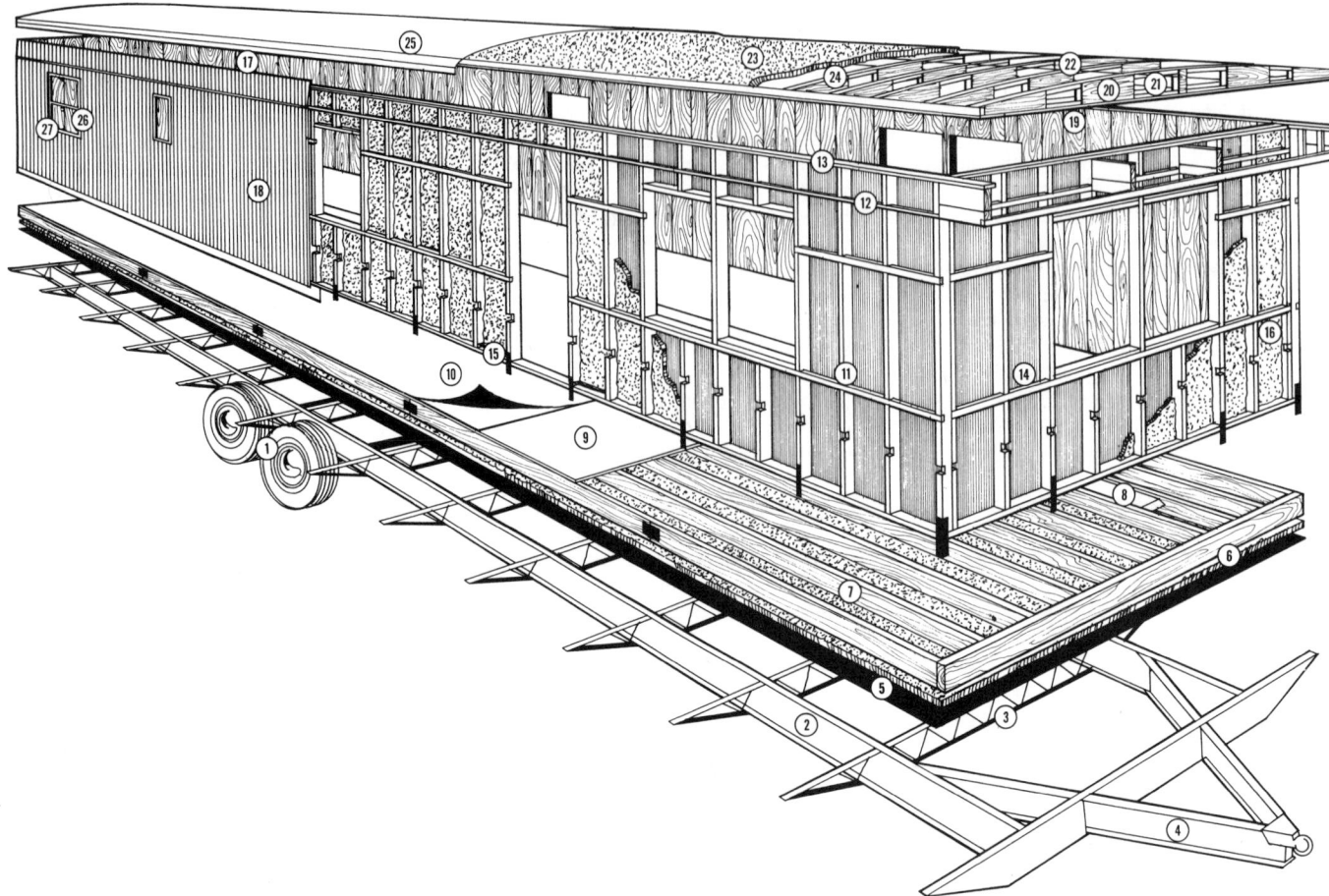

Figure 5.1.
Exploded view of
a mobile home.

The Chassis

1. Chassis—heavy-duty axles, leaf springs, and tires comprise the running gear.
2. Frame—"I" beam—heavy-duty steel welded frames. 8″, 10″, or 12″ "I" beams depending on length of frame.
3. Rigid steel outriggers and center cross members.
4. Hitch—sturdy "I" beam hitch members—optionally removable for cleaner appearance.

The Floor System

5. Bottom board—tightly sealed on bottom of floor.
6. Floor insulation—all-weather insulation for temperature control, blanket fiberglass installed under entire floor for complete weatherproofing.
7. Floor joists.
8. Heat duct—aluminum-framed duct.
9. 5/8″ decking particle board glued and fastened to floor joists.
10. Roll goods—cushioned vinyl floor in non-carpeted areas.

The Wall System

11. 2″ × 4″ studs.
12. Dadoed belt rails for unitized sidewall construction.
13. 1″ × 4″ top and bottom plate.
14. Interior paneling—prefinished fire rated interior paneling glued and staped to sidewall studs for unitized construction.
15. Rugged metal anchor bonding ties sidewalls to floor for additional strength.

16. Sidewall insulation—heavy-density fiberglass insulation.
17. Trim to harmonize with exterior decor.
18. Rigid exterior metal is prefinished aluminum with baked-on enamel finish.

The Roof/Ceiling System

19. Decorative ceiling board.
20. Gusseted truss-type rafters for extra roof strength.
21. Blanket fiberglass insulation between rafters.
22. Steel straps full length of roof over rafters support insulation and galvanized roof between rafters.
23. Thick fiberglass roll insulation over rafters.
24. Vapor barrier on warm side of roof to prevent condensation buildup.
25. Galvanized steel one-piece roof.

Windows and Doors

26. Large aluminum-framed windows with screens and optional storm windows.
27. Egress windows for emergency exit from every sleeping room.

Mechanical Service Systems

28. Electrical, plumbing, heating, and construction conform to or exceed the Federal Mobile Home Construction and Safety Standards.

Figure 5.2.
The chassis frame.

Figure 5.3.
The floor system.

Figure 5.4.
The wall system.

floor system and exterior walls, some manufacturers design their exterior walls to tie into the floor system; their wall studs are extended past the bottom plate to meet the floor side members. The stud extensions are then nailed to the floor side members.

Insulation. Standard fiberglass insulation thicknesses vary from 1 1/8- to 2-inch blanket types to 2 5/8-inch batt types. The batt types are 16 inches wide and fit tightly between the studs of the wall sections.

Exterior Finish. The standard exterior finish is prefinished aluminum siding, although shingles, shakes, battens, and exterior plywood are now available for mobile homes. In contrast to the exterior finish of conventional homes, the aluminum siding of the mobile home contributes to the structural rigidity of the sidewalls while weatherproofing the home against snow and rain. The siding may have a painted or baked acrylic finish. For protection against leakage, all joints except the siding joints are sealed with a nonhardening rubberized vulcanizing material. A drip rail is installed along the the entire length of the unit on both sides.

Interior Finish. As previously noted, the interior walls are finished with prefinished 1/4-inch plywood that also contributes to the structural rigidity of the wall assembly. Most prefinished plywood is grooved to simulate random-plank paneling and fastened to the wall studs with glue and nails. To ensure a good appearance, all nails used to fasten the plywood to the wall studs are set and the holes are filled with matching putty. In 1975 several manufacturers started using drywall for interior finish and by the late 1970s this had become an industry-wide trend. Use of this material, although largely sacrificing the stressed-skin principle, has major advantages, including traditional homelike interior appearance and vastly improved fire protection characteristitcs.

The Roof/Ceiling System
The roof/ceiling assembly (figure 5.5) must weatherproof and insulate the unit from above. It structurally transfers roof loads to the walls and also serves as a sidewall positioner contributing to the shear strength of the exterior walls.

Structural Components. The roof design is one of the unique features of the mobile home. It is a lightweight assembly using a minimum of building materials. There are two general types of roofs that resemble those used in traditional homes: One employs a rafter system of $2 \times 8s$ to support the roof and a separate joist system of $2 \times 8s$ for the ceiling; another (typical of double-wides) uses triangular trusses for the roof

structural system. Most prevalent, however, is the bow string truss system developed by the mobile home industry. This truss is jig-fabricated using small structural members. It consists of a 2×2 bottom chord and a 1×2 cambered top chord. The truss is 2 inches high at its ends and increases gradually in height to 6 or 8 inches at the center. Plywood plates 1/4 inch thick are glued and nailed at each side for reinforcement. The result is an efficient, prestressed, curved form that meets roof loading requirements and provides proper water drainage. From a structural standpoint this system is highly efficient and contrasts with the components used in traditional home construction, which are considerably heavier but structurally redundant.

The subroof is installed directly on top of the trusses. Instead of the 1/2-inch plywood used in conventional homes, a 3/8-inch rigid insulation board is used. The board is sufficiently water-resistant to eliminate the need for any felt underlayment; the exterior roof can be placed directly on top of the subroof. Manufacturers usually specify that all joints of the exterior subroof occur at the centerline of the roof truss.

The exterior roofing is of galvanized steel or aluminum decking and is attached to the subroof material. For weather protection, the roof decking is covered with a rubberized and fibered coating which will last longer than one that is simply painted because of the thickness of the coat and the water resistance of rubber. The ceiling usually consists of acoustical planks or drywall and is fastened directly to the underside of the roof trusses enclosing the the entire roof system.

The total structural roof system possesses unusual strength. When interviewed, many manufacturers expressed the opinion that the roof will separate from the wall before it fails structurally because of shear, local buckling, or bending. No roof structural failures were reported by the manufacturers; additionally, none were reported in any investigations of consumer complaints conducted by consumer protection agencies that we have seen.

Insulation. In the roof, where the most heat would generally be lost, insulation is a very crucial issue. Fiberglass blanket types are most commonly used in mobile home roofs and extend the full width of the roof. Thicknesses range from 1/2 to 3 7/8 inches. Often the blanket itself has an aluminum foil vapor barrier; otherwise, single or double vapor barriers are placed below the trusses, over the trusses, or both. Some manufacturers use an insulation board above the finished ceiling in addition to the insulation board used for the exterior sub-

roof. Heat generated by the furnace in the winter is retained longer; less heat is allowed to penetrate to the living area in the summer. This double insulation also serves as an effective sound barrier.

Interior Finish. Ceiling finishing material is attached to the 1/4-inch ceiling board. A large variety of ceiling finishes is employed by manufacturers. Custom textured acoustical ceilings or acoustical planks with a 1/4-inch plywood backup are found in more expensive models. Less expensive models substitute 1/4-inch upson board or insulation board for the 1/4-inch plywood ceiling.

Windows and Doors
The most frequently used window is an all-aluminum awning type. Whenever possible, manufacturers try to position their windows to provide cross-ventilation; in many cases, a bay window is placed at the front of the unit. The screen unit provided is usually removable. The interior garnish of the window is anodized. Strip caulking is applied to window and door frames and to wall openings to prevent leaking.

Exterior doors are prehung in extruded aluminum frames. The common size is 32 inches in width and 72 inches in height. The doors are usually all-aluminum and fully insulated with fiberglass or styrofoam in the core. A jalousie-type ventilating sash with a crank-type operator is generally found at the bottom of the door. Interior doors are usually 1 3/8 inches thick and finished with 1/4-inch plywood to match the interior paneling. Most closet and cabinet doors are also built and finished to match the decor. Closet doors are louvered to provide ventilation.

In the latter part of the 1970s house-type windows and doors are being used increasingly (figure 5.6).

Mechanical Service Systems
Mobile home mechanical service systems (figure 5.7) are the same as those in traditional buildings: plumbing, electrical, and heating systems. The various components of these service systems have been standardized to a high degree and innovative engineering has reduced cost by using less expensive and more easily installed details. For example, water lines are generally made of plastic tubing, which has the advantage of being lightweight and easier to fabricate and install than metal tubing. As in traditional homes, water, gas, and oil feed directly through plumbing lines into the mobile home from underground pipes. Forced air ducts for central heating and air conditioning systems (the latter is optional) are made of lightweight aluminum that can be easily cut and formed. The electric service of

Figure 5.5.
The roof/ceiling
system.

Figure 5.6.
Windows and doors.

Figure 5.7.
Mechanical service
systems.

mobile homes is comparable to that of traditional homes; a standard 120/240 volt source is typical.

The mechanical service systems of the mobile home have been developed to accommodate all the conveniences of traditional housing such as gas range ovens, televisions, air conditioners (for units with no central air conditioning system), and refrigerators. The appliances and the bathroom, kitchen, and utility equipment used in mobile homes are essentially identical to those of conventional housing.

Mobile Home versus Conventional Home

Like the conventionally built home, the mobile home uses four walls in combination with a floor and roof to form a rigid structure. However, the principles embodied in mobile home construction differ significantly enough to result in a substantial cost savings. Three basic differences are:

1. Whereas main loads are carried by a stud-frame system in the conventional home, the mobile home uses a stressed-skin system.
2. The mobile home employs unibody construction.
3. The mobile home is dependent on the chassis to carry a portion of the floor loads.

Stud-Frame Wall versus Stressed-Skin Wall. A firm bond between the studs and exterior wall sheathing cannot be achieved using traditional construction techniques because glue-nailing cannot be done extensively at the site. The conventional home therefore relies principally on the stud-wall to carry the load to the foundation. The studs and other bracing or framing members are 2 × 4s. Because mobile home manufacturers are able to utilize a stressed-skin system, framing members in the past were 2 × 3. Aluminum siding and interior wood paneling act together to resist shear forces and form an inner and outer skin diaphragm with the studs. Some diaphragm action is possible with conventional home wall sheathing, but substantially larger sizes are necessary. The conventional home uses 3/8- to 1/2-inch plywood sheathing compared to the 3/16- to 1/4-inch plywood interior wall sheathing and the 24-gauge exterior aluminum siding found in most mobile homes. In spite of these advantages, however, since 1972 state code officials and third-party inspection agencies have been exerting pressure upon mobile home manufacturers to use 2 × 4 framing members; it was already a clear trend by 1977. The 2 × 4 is structurally not necessary but pleases code officials and "2 × 4-obsessed" consumers who believe that

2 × 4s are structurally more sound than 2 × 3s.

Mobile Home Unibody Construction. The conventional home relies primarily on the sucessive action of structural components transmitting their loads from one to another; the mobile home is constructed to absorb stress as a unit. Although the mobile home is formed by a number of subassemblies, the connections are designed to ensure structural continuity.

Chassis Support for Structural Box and Floor. The floor spans of a conventional home are usually greater than those of a mobile home because the floor joists must independently carry all loads. As indicated earlier, the mobile home chassis carries a substantial portion of the load and prevents floor sag. Thus, although 2 × 8 floor joists must be used in a conventional home, mobile home manufacturers can use 2 × 6 members.

Shortcomings. The theoretical principle is not always respected by actual construction practices in the structural design of conventional housing; the same holds true for mobile home design. Our analyses of mobile home design spanned many years, and we discovered many shortcomings. If this book were written only for engineers, we could suggest improvements covering hundreds of pages; here we can only give some entirely random examples. For instance, it is extremely difficult to design a completely integrated structure and to ensure that the joints between the horizontal and vertical surfaces are tight enough to transfer stresses completely from one surface to another. Ideally, to achieve complete structural integration, only a minimum number of openings should be introduced because the box derives its strength from the continuity of the surface. This requirement contrasts sharply with the preferences of the mobile home owner, who desires more and larger windows and at least two entrances. Under repeated loading, resistance to shearing might be dangerously reduced at these openings. Large shear deflections might ultimately occur, causing the paneling to buckle.

Similarly, because the mobile home is constructed of structural subassemblies, joints between the horizontal and vertical surfaces (at the wall-floor or wall-roof junctions) must be secure if the transfer of stresses is to be complete. A joint breaks up the continuity of the structure, completely disrupting the flow of stresses or making them follow other paths. The bonding must be extremely tight because the joints are internally weaker than any other part of the structure. Any high stress concentration may cause subassemblies to separate.

Other special construction problems result from in-tranist conditions. Over-the-road movement causes dynamic impact stresses. The majority of these stresses is absorbed by the running gear assembly; stresses not absorbed by the running gear are distributed throughout the frame as secondary stresses. Critical areas, where stresses are likely to be extreme, are points of structural discontinuity, particularly the bottom junction points between the floor-chassis and wall-floor. To absorb these stresses successfully, the mobile home must act as a complete unit.

When interviewed, all manufacturers claimed that no serious structural failures occur during transportation if trained drivers are used. Otherwise, however, they did mention a number of problems that may arise during shipment. The junction formed by the wall and roof members is especially vulnerable; a sharp load may cause a break in the weatherseal and result in a roof leak. Dynamic or handling loads may cause exterior studs to fail; screw connections may shear off or screw holes may enlarge during transportation and eventually exterior siding panels may blow off. Upward movements of the transverse chassis members may cause cracks in the floor materials and floor seams may come apart. The highest concentration of stress in the chassis occurs at the area over the axles or between the axles and hitch; any large jar that cannot be absorbed by the springs may twist one of the crossmembers, which are particularly vulnerable.

These problems occur very rarely; in fact, during hundreds of factory and dealer lot inspections we have never seen any one of these defects. The point, rather, is that the theoretical design principle is difficult to apply and that designing a mobile home is not "easy."

Conclusion. At this point it should be evident that it is absurd to compare mobile home and conventional home construction on a one-to-one basis because different structural principles are employed. The mobile home, from an engineering point of view, is a more sophisticated structure than the conventional home. It is engineered to satisfy the same loading conditions (on-site) as a conventional home while selling at a fraction of the cost. At the same time it must withstand the greater, sharper, and unpredictable dynamic conditions caused by over-the-road movement. A few minor problems exist but these could be corrected without a substantial change in materials or techniques. The claim that mobile homes are poorly constructed is not justified. Indeed, it has been shown that mobile home design principles are more efficient than those guiding the structural design of the conventional home.

This section will focus upon aspects of the production process explicitly related to the physical assemblage of mobile home units. Various types of plant facilities, assembly operations, and machineries utilized in production will be discussed.

The production process is a crucial determinant of the production efficiencies achieved by the mobile home industry. Production resources are utilized rationally and rigorously, and the industry has achieved this high degree of efficiency by integrating all aspects of the production process. Therefore, in addition to describing what the production process is, it is also important to explain why it has been organized to function as it does. This section has been divided into two parts: The first covers the general principles and problems of mobile home production; the second describes the specific features and activities of the process.

The Objective

The objective of any production system is to produce a particular marketable product at specified rates in a manner that will most efficiently untilize the given resources. General methods that can be applied to production systems range from labor-intensive custom handiwork to capital-intensive automated manufacturing. The mobile home unit, a highly standardized product produced at moderately high annual volumes (most plants produce between 500 and 1,000 units annually), can be manufactured most efficiently when mass production techniques are applied to the production process.

The advantages of mass production are numerous. In-plant construction work can proceed without concern for the inconstancies of weather. A controlled working environment permits strict work planning and close quality control monitoring; through carefully organized material handling and processing, waste is minimized and, to a significant extent, reused. By means of work standardization and labor specialization, operations can be completed quickly and with consistent results; labor specialization allows for constant repetition of tasks that can be quickly learned. Consequently, a low-skilled labor force can be used. Through the utilization of mechanized equipment, processing times can be further shortened. However, the efficiencies of mass production have a price: Investment costs are higher than those required for on-site construction. Therefore production process planning becomes a particularly critical issue in the manufacturing of mobile homes.

The Production Mode

One basic issue of a production system is the "production mode" or the general manner

The Rationale of the Production Process

in which materials are brought together with machinery and human resources to be processed into the final product. There are two basic modes of production for the mass production of housing: the assembly point and the assembly line.

In the assembly point arrangement, the product does not move. Materials, equipment, and labor are brought to the construction point. Tasks cannot all be performed simultaneously, so sets of tasks are scheduled in sequence. One set of tasks must be completed and the necessary equipment removed before another set of tasks can begin. Generally, a number of assembly points will be distributed throughout the factory floor, each operating independently of the others. This arrangement is most successful when products with many model variations, such as certain modular housing units, are produced in small quantities because in this mode custom features can easily be added to individual units. One disadvantage of the assembly point mode is that a high degree of labor specialization cannot be achieved. The cost of transporting materials, labor, and equipment makes it desirable to have a skilled labor force capable of completing many operations before the work crew is moved to another assembly point. Only small and portable equipment can be used because all tools must be removed periodically from the construction site. This method makes it difficult to schedule operations because of the variations in time taken to complete different tasks, and idle men and machinery may wait for a previous group to finish their tasks. Inventory is difficult to manage because material handling is sometimes awkward when large building components are involved.

In the assembly line arrangement, labor and equipment are stationary and located at work stations. The product passes through a programmed sequence of work stations at which the successive stages of construction occur, and the finished unit eventually emerges at the end of the sequence. Materials are transported from storage to the work stations as needed for assembly operations. Timing is critical in this mode because operations are sequentially interdependent and delays in one station can affect the entire production line. The assembly line is best suited for highly standardized products produced in large quantities, such as automobiles. Capital costs are higher than for assembly point systems, but the sequential interdependency of activities permits better work organization and control. Idle and processing time fluctuations can be minimized, and inventories and material handling can be managed more efficiently. When labor remains stationary, tasks can be standardized and specialized and shorter processing times can be achieved. Fewer skills are required of the individual worker, so labor costs can be reduced and heavier

machinery can be utilized to a higher degree of efficiency when equipment remains at one work station.

Thus a very efficient utilization of labor, equipment, and material can be achieved. It is logical, then, that the mobile home industry has adopted the assembly line mode of production in order to achieve maximum efficiency. The mobile home unit is a highly standardized product produced in large quantities with interchangeable components. Special design variations are usually minor and can be accomplished within the constraints imposed by the assembly line arrangement. And, because an average plant produces only two model lines, evidence shows that specialization is intensifying. Plants are increasingly limiting production to either singlewide or doublewide mobile homes.

The Planning of Production Process Operations
A production process consists of a set of interrelated tasks that must be carefully coordinated so that product units can be completed and specified production quotas filled. Mobile home assembly line production activities must be especially well planned to ensure efficient and continuous production runs. Three basic activities are involved in any production system: assembly activities or the actual construction of the product units, material storage (storing supplies, components, or product units until they are used in the production process or shipped from the plant), and material handling (the transportation of materials for storage, shipping, or use in assembly activities).

Assembly activities are determined by and arranged according to the nature of the product, materials used, structural details, and manner in which the components are to be connected. There are two types of assembly activities: main assembly activities and subassembly activities. Main assembly or "on-line" activities bring about the completely assembled product unit and include such tasks as the joining of a wall section and a floor section. Subassembly or "off-line" activities are those tasks that involve the processing of raw materials and the fabrication of product components that will later be installed or joined to other components and subassemblies on the main assembly line. For example, the construction of separate wall sections is a subassembly activity.

Production activities are assigned to either on- or off-line stations, depending upon which would be most operationally efficient. Wall sections could be constructed stud by stud on the main assembly line; but by constructing the sections separately off-line, more efficient construction techniques, such as those requiring the use of heavy machinery, can be utilized.

Subassembly stations must produce the particular components of the final product at rates that ensure maintenance of an adequate supply of components for use in main line assembly or in other subassembly operations. It is usually desirable to utilize subassembly construction as much as possible because a greater degree of labor specialization and shorter processing times can be achieved by reducing the number of operations that must be performed at main assembly stations. In this way, main assembly operations can be simplified and interference between labor and machinery resources can be minimized. Labor-saving devices such as jigs, fixtures, and automated machinery, which could not be used in main assembly operations because of the great bulk of the housing unit, can be used at off-line assembly stations.

The organization of main assembly activities is governed by the design throughput rate, which is based on plant production rates and the number of assembly lines in use. The number of work stations and the distribution of tasks among them are determined on the basis of the desired throughput rate. Clearly, as more work stations are established, a higher throughput rate is possible because fewer operations need to be completed at each station.

An efficient main assembly line is possible only if idle station time is minimized. Interference between worker and machinery performing operations in one station, variations in processing time among on-line stations, or overloading one work station with too many sequentially dependent tasks can lead to idle station time. To avoid such interference, conflicting operations must be assigned to separate stations and tasks must be distributed in a manner that will result in roughly equal processing times. Whenever possible, tasks requiring long processing times should span several stations so that each can complete a segment of the task.

Mobile home plants generally use a fully coupled main assembly line, with subassembly stations feeding in from either side at various points on the line. Throughput rates for individual production lines vary from one unit every eight hours in small plants to more than fifty units every eight hours in the largest plants. A unit may spend from eight hours in small plants to twenty minutes in larger plants at a given station. So, depending on the throughput rates, the number of main line stations may range from five to twenty or more. Manufacturers usually supplement in-plant subassembly production by purchasing prefabricated components, but all seek to utilize off-line construction for as many components as is feasible. Components such as wall sections, floors, roofs, cabinets, and plumbing are generally produced off-line (see figure 5.8).

The role of material storage is important to the manufacturing function because capital and operating expenses are incurred when extensive inventory and storage facilities are maintained. Storage facilities must be kept to a minimum and materials processed through the plant as quickly as possible. The inventory turnover ratio (the number of times inventory is completely replenished each year) must be kept as high as the plant's production rate and the frequency of deliveries will permit. Two types of storage, inventories and buffers, are used. These two terms are often used interchangeably but are, in fact, distinct: Inventories are the stored supplies of those raw materials and components that are delivered to the plant; buffers are used for the storage of components and processed materials made in the plant.

Since costs can be reduced when materials are purchased in large quantities, and since it is impossible to synchronize material deliveries with the plant production schedule, inventories of supplies must be maintained in order to ensure the continual availability of materials for use in the production process. Nevertheless, large inventory turnover ratios are most desirable, particularly when oversized components are involved; ratios as high as fifteen or twenty are frequent, and ratios of more than fifty have been achieved.

Buffers make it possible to correct variations in subassembly processing times and maintain a constant overall production rate. Operational planning cannot ensure that processing times are exactly the same for all work stations, allowing production to run continuously from one station to the next, because the nature of the work done at a particular station may necessitate that processing times deviate from other stations. In this case a buffer is used as a "cushion" between the station and the rest of the line. The components, processed materials, or partially completed product units coming from the one station can be fed into a buffer area while the rest of the line draws upon materials from the stockpile maintained in the buffer as they are needed. For instance, fluctuations in the processing time required to produce cabinets could seriously delay operations throughout the production line. However, the finished cabinets are fed into a buffer area instead of being moved directly to a main assembly station so that the main assembly station can still draw on stockpiled buffer supply even though cabinet manufacturing is temporarily halted. Hence, the result of placing a buffer between two stations is to "decouple" one station from the other, allowing each to operate continuously and independently of the other. The capacity of a buffer will vary according to the anticipated degree of variation in processing times between the two

Figure 5.8.
Schematic diagram of
the mobile home
production process.

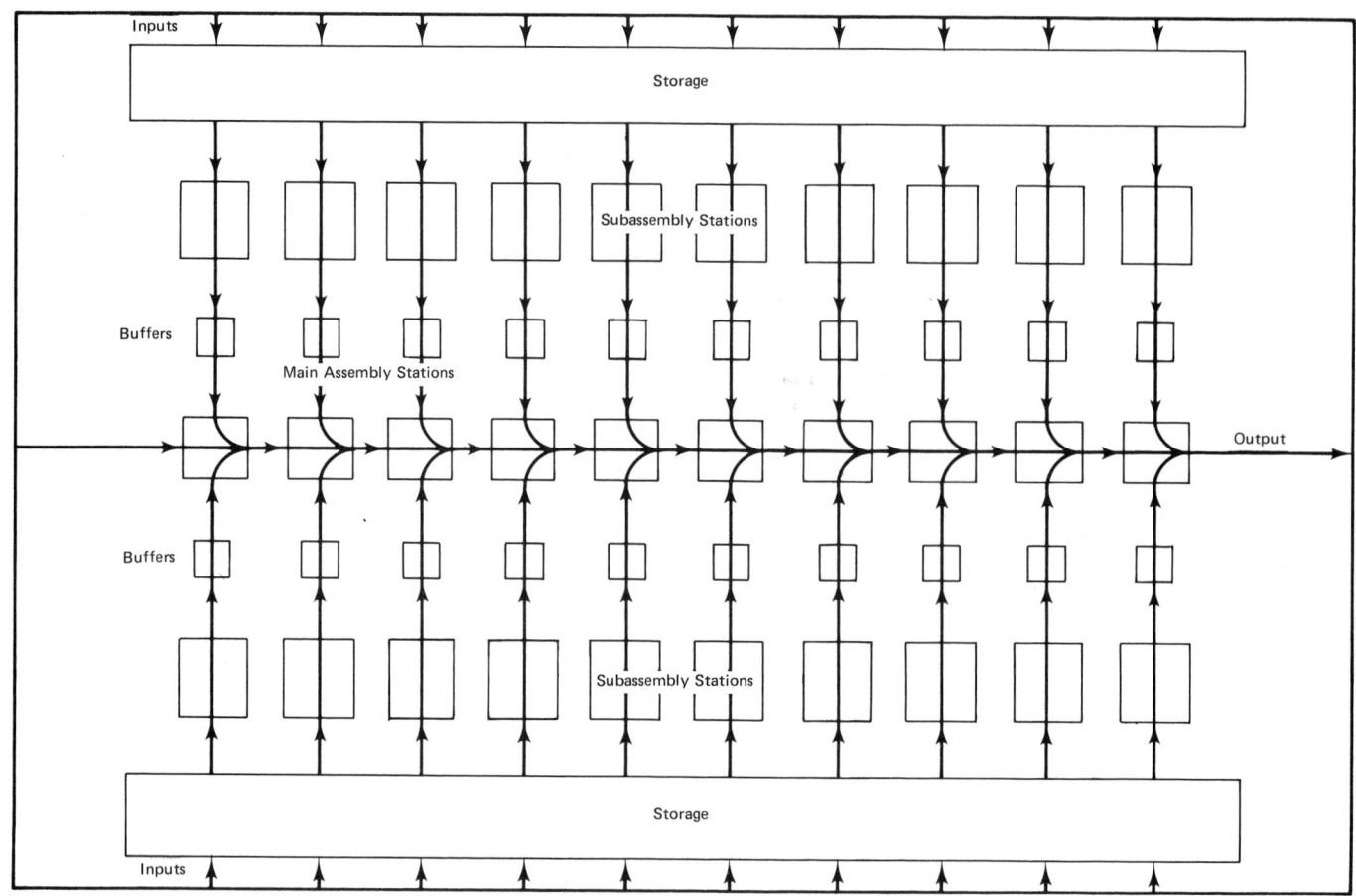

stations being decoupled; the greater the variation, the greater the capacity required.

Because of the strict scheduling of operations in the assembly line production mode, material handling has become especially intensive. Supplies must be unloaded on time and brought to storage; materials must be distributed to the work stations as they are needed; and finished product units must be stored until they are required on the main line. To avoid wasteful inefficiencies in material handling, the right amount of material must be moved to the right place at the right time. Moving an item as little as possible maximizes efficiency. Work stations and storage are laid out in a manner that permits direct routes for material flow that do not interfere with the ongoing assembly operations. Sometimes storage facilities are centrally located to minimize the distances for material transport, and buffers are generally designed so that material may be conveniently loaded on one side while the components may be withdrawn for main assembly on the other side. Materials are most likely to be damaged when moved frequently and farther than necessary. Finally, the scheduling of material flow must be carefully coordinated with assembly operations so that components produced in one area will be available in time for subsequent operations in another.

The Allocation of Human and Machinery Resources

To deal with the highly seasonal nature of sales, the industry has relied on the availability of unskilled or semiskilled labor, which allows the industry to adjust production rates by hiring and layoffs. As a consequence, the level of mechanization is not high, but important labor-saving devices have significantly streamlined operations in many areas.

In main assembly stations the equipment used is very much the same as that used in conventional home construction, and mechanization has been utilized where economically justifiable. Therefore pneumatic hammers and staplers, power screwdrivers, spray painters, and mechanical glue applicators are used often; but operations such as gluing and fastening components, wiring, and installing insulation are not mechanized because the high degree of seasonality in the mobile home business would not permit the expense. By contrast, production at subassembly stations can be mechanized more economically and has been mechanized more extensively. In-plant conditions make possible the utilization of heavy machinery in material processing operations such as wood cutting or metal siding fabrication. Subassembly operations are largely standardized, so jigs and fixtures have been introduced to streamline construction and much of the print reading and measuring necessary in conventional home building has been eliminated.

The mobile home production process has appropriated the technology of material handling to deal with the unwieldy bulk of items that must be moved during production operations. It is in these operations that mechanization has advanced furthest and, because of the significant impact on labor productivity, mechanization of this function is justified.

There are three general types of material-handling equipment used extensively in the production process: hand-propelled conveyors (carts and dollies); self-powered conveyors (fork lifts); and overhead equipment (overhead hoists and monorails). Carts and dollies are used primarily to move raw materials and small components such as wood studs and windows, and dollies can serve as vehicular bases for mobile home units in production. Forklifts are the most popular and versatile material conveyors because they can be used to transport and store all materials except the very largest subassemblies. Overhead hoists are used to move and position bulky items. This particular equipment demonstrates clearly the indispensability of mechanized material handling; without this equipment, bulky items such as wall units could not be moved and would have to be constructed on-line. With hoists, however, even a 70-foot-long wall can be efficiently constructed off-line with the use of jigs and then transported by only one person to the appropriate on-line station.

Automation is almost nonexistent in the industry because production volumes are not high enough to merit the high capital investment required for expensive automated machinery. Manufacturers have relied on a highly elastic labor supply in lieu of automation. Large fixed investments in automated and mechanized processing equipment would eliminate much of the flexibility that is so vital to success in a seasonal industry.

Automation and mechanization are extensively used by industry suppliers of components and subassemblies because suppliers are often able to maintain production volumes that enable them to handle the necessary fixed costs and to offset seasonal demand fluctuations. If automation were increased to improve mobile home production in the near future, it would most likely increase in the supply sector.

We all know how many months it takes for one on-site-built home to be completed. In comparison, the mobile home production process is dramatic; approximately every twenty minutes one completely finished and furnished home is leaving the assembly line. This description cannot substitute for a factory visit so readers must continuously compare their experience with traditional building in order to witness a dramatic experience.

Description of the Production Process

Table 5.9
Average Factory Area:
1963, 1967, and 1972

Year	Average Factory Area (in 1,000s of sq. ft.)								
	0–20	20–40	40–60	60–80	80–100	100–120	120–140	140–200	200–300
1963									
% of all plants	12.5%	18.8%	25.0%	6.2%	18.8%	12.5%	0.0%	6.2%	0.0%
Mean: 66.8									
Median: 57.8									
Mode: 100.0									
1967	0–20	20–40	40–60	60–80	8–100	100–120	120–140	140–200	200–300
% of all plants	14.3%	21.4%	28.6%	10.7%	14.3%	3.6%	0.0%	3.6%	3.6%
Mean: 63.9									
Median: 48.8									
Mode: 40.00									
1972	0–20	20–40	40–60	60–80	80–100	100–120	120–140	140–200	200–300
% of all plants	9.1%	21.6%	30.7%	20.0%	12.3%	3.1%	1.6%	0.0%	1.5%
Mean: 59.6									
Median: 55.0									
Mode: 60.0									

Source: PMHI/MS.

Plant Facilities

Although individual mobile home plants employ an average of 114 people, larger plants may employ more than 500. Typical plants produce between 500 and 1,000 units annually and the average plant has a production capacity of four units per eight-hour day. The PMHI Manufacturer Survey revealed that the average plant floor area has dropped from 67,000 square feet in 1963 to 64,000 square feet in 1967 and to 60,000 square feet in 1972 (table 5.9). Smaller plants are, in fact, the trend; a decentralized approach to production has been adopted by many mobile home firms who are developing new facilities. At least 92 percent of the industry's plants occupy an area of less than 120,000 square feet, and 30 percent to 40 percent of the plants fall between 40,000 and 60,000 square feet for the three years examined. During a given year, typical individual plant output peaks at a high of one hundred thirty units in the month of August and falls to a low of sixty-five units in January.

Today's mobile home plants are most commonly single-story, slab foundation, pre-engineered metal buildings. New mobile home production facilities generally cost much less to construct than plants for other manufacturing operations: A mobile home facility producing ten units or more per day can be constructed with an initial capital investment of less than $2 million. The essential requirement for a mobile home production facility is ample floor area for the production system, overhead clearance to accommodate cranes and monorails, 100 to 120 psi service, and 440 volt power sources for special equipment. Modern plants are usually designed in accordance with the needs of a specific production process. Lay-out is worked out prior to construction and basic considerations include the number and size of storage facilities, work stations, and material flow paths. The typical layouts used are straight, U-shaped, and L-shaped; sub-assembly and storage areas are located along the assembly line. Older facilities must compensate for physical restrictions by altering plant layout.

Generally, plants place units on the assembly line either end-to-end or side-by-side (see figures 5.9–5.12). When arranged end to end, the units move longitudinally through the assembly line on their own wheel assemblies; when arranged side by side, the units are placed on dollies and moved laterally through the stations. In some instances, the end-to-end and side-by-side methods are used for different parts of the assembly line. The end-to-end method was originally used by early mobile home manufacturers because all subassembly stations are within a short distance of the on-line stations and older warehouses had column spacings that dictated an end-to-end arrangement. In addition, early mobile home units were generally 20 feet shorter than today's models, which are usually 70 feet long.

The current trend among larger manufacturers is to establish side-by-side assembly lines, which permit more efficient use of floor

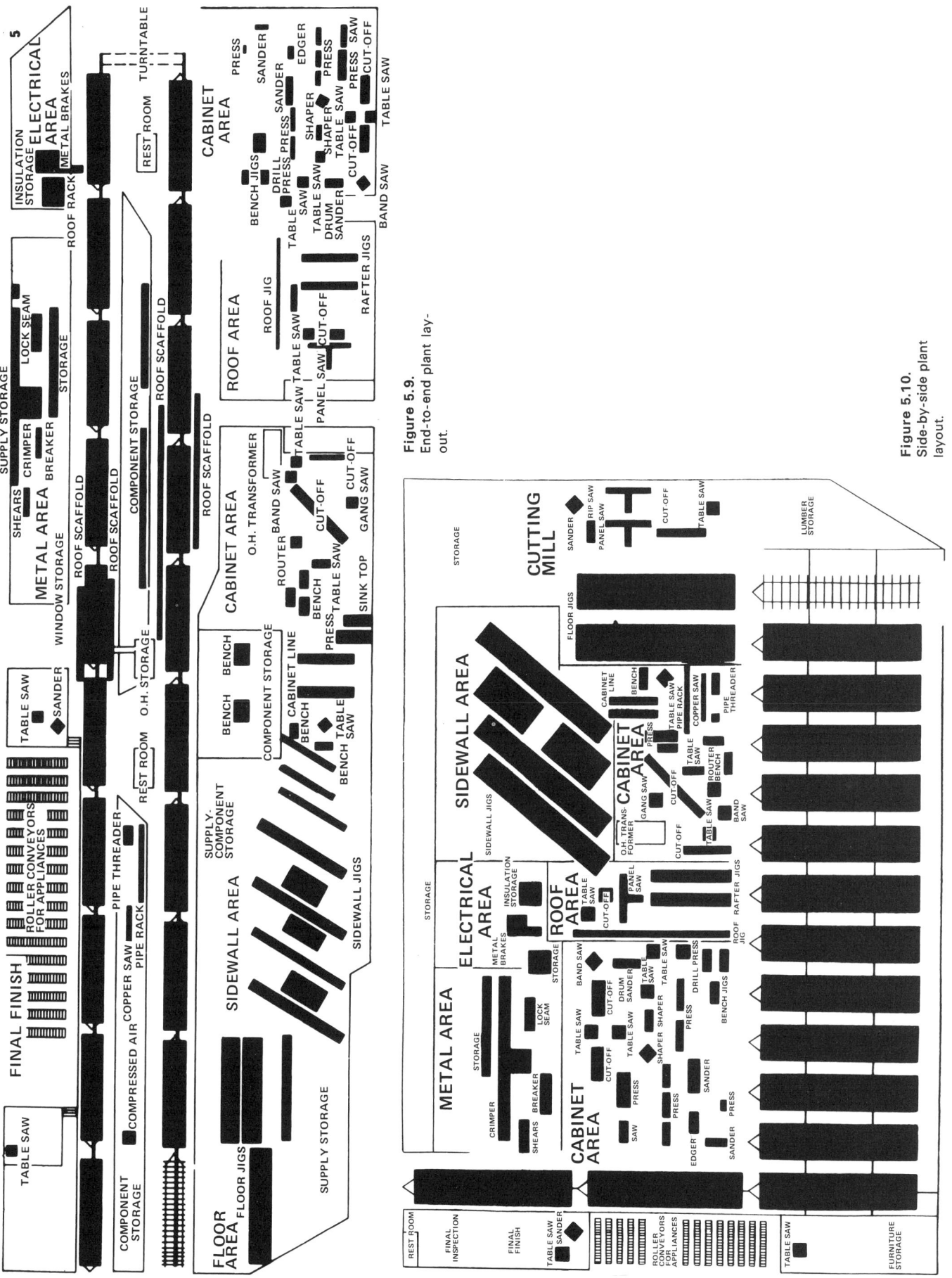

Figure 5.9.
End-to-end plant layout.

Figure 5.10.
Side-by-side plant layout.

Figure 5.11.
End-to-end assembly line.

Figure 5.12.
Side-by-side assembly line.

space than end-to-end lines. The side-by-side assembly line is broader and shorter and therefore better wall/floor area ratios can be achieved, reducing construction costs. With the advent of doublewides in recent years, the side-by-side arrangement has become even more desirable, for it permits the two units mated on-site to be assembled side by side, permitting better alignments and closer tolerances.

The Main Assembly Operations
Because the mobile home unit is designed and produced in the same fashion by different manufacturers, a sequence of basic main assembly operations is followed in most plants. Manufacturers generally construct the mobile home from the bottom up and the inside out, starting with the chassis frame and moving to the floor assembly, wall system, and finally the roof. To discuss main assembly operations station by station would be meaningless because the number of main line stations varies from plant to plant. However, the major assembly operations will be treated as a sequence of task sets because each set of operations requires one or more work stations (figures 5.13 through 5.25).

The chassis is first obtained from the plant storage or assembly area, then moved to the chassis-floor station by an overhead hoist and mounted onto a finished floor frame that contains heat ducts and insulation. The chassis is mounted upside down onto the floor frame because the floor frame is often assembled most efficiently upside down. Lag bolts are power driven through the outriggers and wood members to join the chassis and floor frame and the complete unit is then turned upright and pulled to the next station, where floor plumbing and flooring are installed. In some plants the floor assembly is assembled off-line and stored in buffers so that, when needed, the subassemblies are removed from storage by an overhead hoist and mounted on an upright chassis.

Finished flooring is installed next. The seams between the decking panels are first filled with a patching compound and, when the compound dries, are mechanically sanded until they are flush with the decking. Next, adhesive is hand troweled or mechanically sprayed onto the appropriate areas and linoleum or tile flooring is unrolled and installed. This surface is pressed with a heavy roller to eliminate trapped air bubbles, and cutouts for plenums, registers, and plumbing are made as required. Finally, the carpeting is unrolled from a rack, positioned, and stapled in place and additional cutouts are made for mechanical equipment and carpet trim.

Contrary to traditional home-building techniques, interior components such as partitions and cabinets are installed before all the external walls are erected. The order in which interior and exterior walls are installed varies greatly. One or more exterior walls may

Figure 5.13.
Main assembly line
(end-to-end): Chassis
on first station.

Figure 5.14.
Main assembly line
(end-to-end): Floor
section installation.

Figure 5.15.
Main assembly line
(end-to-end): Installa-
tion of flooring and
beginning of wall sec-
tion placement.

Figure 5.16.
Main assembly line (end-to-end): Plumbing fixture installation.

Figure 5.17.
Main assembly line (end-to-end): Cabinetry installation.

Figure 5.18.
Main assembly line (end-to-end): Wall section installation.

The Mobile Home Production System

Figure 5.19.
Main assembly line (end-to-end): Completion of wall section installation.

Figure 5.20.
Main assembly line (end-to-end): Roof section installation.

Figure 5.21.
Main assembly line (end-to-end): Siding installation.

Figure 5.22.
Main assembly line (end-to-end): Window/door installation.

Figure 5.23.
Main assembly line
(end-to-end): Appli-
ance feeding.

Figure 5.24.
Main assembly line
(end-to-end): Appli-
ance feeding.

Figure 5.25.
Main assembly line
(end-to-end): Finished
units leaving assembly
line.

The Mobile Home Production System

be installed prior to interior wall installation. Some manufacturers install all the exterior walls first and then move the interior walls into position with an overhead crane. Otherwise, pneumatic nailers or screwdrivers, framing squares, and assorted hand tools are needed to install flooring, mechanical components, and exterior walls. The remaining exterior walls are obtained from storage and joined to the unit. Clamps are used to ensure a tight joint between the wall and the floor and steel straps are attached to tie the floor and wall together when the walls have been secured to the floor and to each other.

Electrical wiring runs through holes or dadoes cut into the studs of the exterior walls. Metal sleeves are inserted to protect the wire from puncture during the subsequent siding operation. In most plants, the wiring in exterior walls may be installed before the wall sections are brought to the main assembly line, where the wiring of several wall sections is joined together and to the wiring in the roof.

At this point, interior work on the unit begins, and these operations span roughly half of the main assembly work stations. Although assignments to particular work stations may differ, this basic order of operations is generally followed throughout the industry. First, overhead cabinets are obtained from storage and installed. Interior electrical work, such as wall switches, electrical service panels, circuit breakers, furnace wiring, and water heater wiring is completed. This work is continued up to the wall siding station. Overhead fixtures are installed after the roof/ceiling assembly is in place. Special groups may be assigned specific interior electrical work because of the particular skill these operations require. It is during this phase that interior prehung doors and cabinet drawers are installed and joints between the individual prefinished interior panels are covered with prefinished molding. Finally, sliding closet rods and other miscellaneous items are installed.

The next major task is the installation of the ceiling and roof. The ceiling assembly is obtained from storage and positioned on top of the exterior walls. All the time, while the internal walls were joined to the floor subassembly and while the exterior sidewalls were fastened to the interior walls, the unit on the mainline looked unstable. But now, as the roof-ceiling subassembly is lowered into place, the interior and exterior walls suddenly become positioned and secured. Only when the roof is in place does a totally rigid one-piece structure emerge—the integrated unibody structure in which each component stabilizes and is stabilized by the others. The structural instability of the unit until roof placement suggests that no structural redundancies exist and that superb, material efficiency-maximizing engineering has been at work. Then metal tie straps may be used to secure the ceiling. Any electrical wiring in

the ceiling area is unrolled, cut to length, and installed. When wiring is complete, rolls or batts of insulation are put in place. In some plants ceiling wiring and insulation are installed off-line at the ceiling subassembly work station.

Weatherproof wall siding may be installed at one or more work stations. It is brought from the metal shop and installed with power-driven rustproof screws, usually Pittsburgh-type joints. The metal panels are designed to form watertight joints when fitted together and openings for windows are made with a router or tin shears. Metal framed windows and exterior doors are then installed and secured with power-driven screws.

Workers on scaffolds cover the roof/ceiling assembly with a sheet of polyethylene. A roll of galvanized 26- or 30-gauge steel roofing metal is hoisted by overhead crane or monorail to the unit. The sheet is unrolled, bent over the top edge of the sidewalls, and secured with staples. This procedure yields a durable one-piece roof. The metal roof may also be assembled in sections and the joints sealed with a waterproof aluminized roof coating. Strips of caulking are applied over the staples on the outer edge of the wall and fabricated gutters are added. Roof vents and stacks are installed and joints sealed. The unit is then moved to the final finishing station.

Exterior trim work must now be completed. Name plates, code compliance seals, and running lights are installed. Screens, curtain rods, and drapes are added to the interior. The unit is cleaned thoroughly and furniture and appliances are moved out of storage and into the unit. Mirrors, shower rods, curtain and towel racks, medicine cabinets, and other fragile interior items are installed. Warranty kits and checkout kits are stored in the unit and the completed mobile home is moved to the inspection and test station. In some plants inspection tasks are performed at the final finishing station.

The mobile home is ready for inspection at the last on-line station or in the plant yard. Utilities are checked by qualified inspectors and all electrical circuits are tested to ensure continuity and detect faults in the insulation of wiring. Plumbing fixtures are pressure tested for leaks. The inspection sheet is given to rework personnel, who make any necessary repairs or adjustments. The unit is given a final cleaning, prepared for shipment, and then either moved to a temporary storage facility or shipped immediately.

The Subassembly Stations
There are two types of subassembly operations: the processing of raw materials into components that will eventually be used in construction and the fabrication of major subassemblies from either processed or purchased components. Some mobile home

plants manufacture most of their own subassemblies and components and are called Michigan-type plants; others purchase most of their subassemblies and components and are called Indiana-type plants. The extent to which subassemblies are fabricated in the plant is based upon the availability of labor and material, local shipping costs, and the proximity of suppliers.

The principal raw materials used in mobile home construction are wood, metal, and plastic. Wood is used for framing, sheathing, and finishing; metal is needed for siding, roofing, and duct work; and plastic is used primarily for plumbing. All major and minor subassemblies, including floors, walls, roofs, cabinets, windows, and doors are fabricated from these materials. In 1975 PMHI conducted industry interviews in which manufacturers were asked to estimate what percentage of mobile home plants in the nation manufacture rather than purchase certain standard components. The range of estimates for many of the items was quite wide, indicating little agreement (table 5.10).

In the description that follows, all the major subassembly operations used by mobile home facilities will be covered. (The text is accompanied by figures 5.26–5.33.) Where the option to purchase prefabricated materials exists, it will be noted.

The chassis assembly station fabricates the chassis frame. Generally, the shop purchases steel parts cut to length so that no additional cutting is required. It is usually constructed upside down on a jig that can be used to construct chassis frames of several sizes. Two I beams, preformed outriggers, and purchased A-frame parts are positioned and welded together on the jig. The I beams are then cambered with a bead weld and the running gear assembly is joined to the frame, which is then spray painted. In an average plant, the assembly of the chassis takes about eight man-hours. When needed, the chassis is moved by overhead hoist to the chassis-floor assembly station. Some plants utilizing this assembly operation may purchase complete running gear assemblies instead of producing them in the plant. Indiana-type manufacturers bypass this shop by purchasing preassembled chassis frames.

In the wood mill, wall studs, cross-braces, paneling, and all wood items are cut to specified dimensions. The shop utilizes a wide variety of lumber, including studs, plywood, and particle board. Cut-off saws, panel saws, rip-saws, or highly automated machinery are used to cut studs and sheets to length. The cut wood is delivered by means of carts or pallets to the appropriate subassembly stations, where it will be used for wall, floor, roof, or cabinet fabrication. This shop is used almost exclusively only by advanced Michigan-type plants. Most plants purchase all or most of their wood precut and sized.

Table 5.10.
In-Plant Integration:
1974 and 1979
Estimates

Item	Range of Estimates of In-Plant Fabrication in 1974 (%)	Range of Estimate Predictions of In-Plant Fabrication in 1979 (%)	Evaluation of Estimates
Chassis	10–87.5	10–87.5	No consensus
Heating ducts	20–87.5	40–100	Some consensus
Cabinets	20–95	30–90	Some consensus
Cabinet doors	5–90	10–90	No consensus
Cabinet fronts	25–95	10–95	No consensus
Cabinet drawers	25–100	15–95	No consensus
Doors, exterior	0–30	0–70	Some consensus
Doors, interior	5–30	5–50	Some consensus
Precut framing members	25–100	10–100	No consensus
Roof/bow trusses	25–90	10–90	No consensus
Metal siding	5–75	0–62.5	Some consensus
Window units	0–37.5	0–12.5	Consensus
Rolls of roofing	0–5	0–5	Consensus
Draperies	1–50	0–50	Some consensus
Furniture	0–37.5	0–37.5	Consensus

Source: From 1975 field interviews of management personnel of leading mobile home manufacturers, conducted by PMHI staff.

The metal shop produces exterior siding, exterior metal trim, gutters, roofing metal, and other metal panel components. The basic material used is baked enamel-finished or precoated light-gauge aluminum sheeting. Coiled rolls of sheeting are unrolled with a decoiling reel and then fed continuously into a roll former, where creases are made to create the structural sections desired. It is then fed through an automatic cutter, which produces sheets of the required lengths. Fabricated components are placed on carts and pallets and moved to the exterior siding station, where most of the formed sheeting components are used. Coiled steel stock that has been formed into duct sections is transferred to the ductwork subassembly station. Most Michigan-type plants have a metal shop. Some manufacturers purchase all their sheeting components ready-made, although most purchase some and manufacture others.

The ductwork, plumbing, and electrical component fabrication shop manufactures all heat ducts, plumbing pipes, plumbing trees, and electrical harnesses used in floor framing and covering operations. The main in-floor heat duct is fabricated in one piece from panels of aluminum sheeting. Plumbing pipes are cut to length and used in plumbing trees, which are assembled on standard jig equipment. Various electrical subassemblies, such as floor wiring made into a harness, are precut, stripped, and assembled. Furnaces and water heaters are unpacked here and prepared prior to on-line installation. Most of the completed in-floor subassemblies

(ducts, wiring harnesses, and plumbing components) are moved to the floor subassembly station. The other subassemblies are fed into the cabinet shop and cabinet installation stations, where plumbing is completed.

The floor subassembly station fabricates floor subassemblies complete with insulation and main heat duct. For construction efficiency, the floor is often constructed upside down, facilitating installation of the floor insulation board last. Fabrication begins with the construction of joists. Because of the length required, joists are made by gang-nailing 2 × 6s together end to end on a buildup table, which is done with a hydraulic press. A radial saw at the end of the buildup table is used to cut the joists to the exact length. The joists are assembled on a jig that permits construction of several lengths of floors. After the main heat duct is positioned between the joists and strapped in place, front and rear precut end boards are positioned and nailed to the joists. Insulation is installed between the joists and secured with staples. Finally, the entire floor bottom is covered with an insulation board, which is stapled to the floor frame along its entire perimeter. Next, in-floor plumbing and flooring operations are completed. First, mechanical components such as water lines, plumbing drains, and clothes drier vents are positioned and secured to the floor. Templates are used to position the mechanical components. When all wiring and mechanical components have been installed, floor decking begins. Cross-braces (1 × 4s) are positioned between joists 16 inches on center and nailed. Adhesive is manually or

mechanically applied to the joists and cross-braces, and the floor decking is positioned and pneumatically screwed or stapled to the wooden members. Openings in the floor decking for, ducts furnaces, and plumbing may be routed or cut into the decking panels before they are brought on-line or after they have been installed on the floor frame. Templates are used to locate the areas where the openings are to be made. The floor is now ready to be attached to the chassis.

The wall subassembly station fabricates exterior and interior wall subassemblies complete with insulation, wiring, and paneling. The subassembly is constructed on a jig from studs. Assembly details may be painted on the jig or small wooden blocks may be nailed to the jig to facilitate the positioning of studs. The positioned studs are nailed together pneumatically and adhesive is applied to the wall members by pressure or hand applicators. Prefinished and precut paneling is then positioned on the walls and secured with staples. Openings for windows, outlets, and switches are routed. Fiberglass insulation may then be installed between the studs and holes drilled for electrical wiring. This entire operation for a 70-foot-long wall section may only take from four to eight man-hours of direct labor. Many types of jigs are used including vertical, A-frame, and horizontal. When horizontal framing jigs are used, the partially completed wall unit must be lifted to an upright position before the insulation can be installed. This is not required for A-frame or vertical jigs. Separate jigs are generally used for end walls and sidewalls. In some plants that run models in blocks, a wall frame is assembled at the start of the run according to the production drawings and used as a pattern for subsequent walls in the run. Eventually, the original wall is used as the last wall unit required in the run. Completed wall units are then brought by overhead hoists to buffers near the wall installation stations.

The cabinet shop manufactures kitchen and bathroom cabinets, built-in furniture, and interior partitions. These are constructed primarily from wood, which is either processed through the wood mill or purchased. Many simple jigs and fixtures are used to speed fabrication. Standardized design has minimized the number of jigs required, although the individual cabinet units, furniture, and partitions can be utilized in a variety of design schemes without affecting on-line work. Pneumatic nailers and staplers facilitate quick assembly and finished units are placed in buffers near the interior finishing stations. Some plants purchase all their cabinets; others make their own cabinets or elect to purchase finished cabinet doors, fronts, drawers, or prepainted trimwork.

The roof/ceiling subassembly station fabricates the roof/ceiling assembly or assemblies to be used at the roof installation

Figure 5.26.
Subassembly station:
Running gears.

Figure 5.27.
Subassembly station:
Chassis.

Figure 5.28.
Subassembly station:
Wood mill.

Figure 5.29.
Subassembly station:
Metal shop.

Figure 5.30.
Floor subassembly
station.

Figure 5.31.
Wall subassembly
station.

Figure 5.32.
Subassembly station:
Cabinet shop.

Figure 5.33.
Roof/ceiling subas-
sembly station.

station on the main line. Specific designs vary from plant to plant. Roof subassembly operations begin with the construction of roof trusses from wood members, often on an automated bowstring truss machine. Some plants prefer to purchase trusses prefabricated. The roof/ceiling subassembly is constructed on a jig. First the trusses are positioned; then wooden side plates are applied and the subassembly is completely covered with polyethylene. Glue is applied to the trusses and sheets of ceiling material are positioned and secured with staples, which are power driven along the seams. Finally, openings are cut for electrical outlets and vents. The entire subassembly operation for a 14 foot × 70 foot roof section may take only from three to four total man-hours of direct labor. Vertical, slanted, or horizontal assembly jigs are used in this construction. When the roof is completed, it is lifted by overhead cranes to a buffer area near the roof installation station. This subassembly operation is carried out in all plants.

The window and door subassembly station produces door and window units that may be assembled from raw or half-finished materials. For instance, interior doors may be completely fabricated in the plant or assembled from precut frames and doors.

The drapery and furnishing shop provides the small hardware needed in final finishing operations. Many plants utilize this facility to make their own draperies and furniture.

Labor Consumption

Table 5.11 details the labor consumption for a particular mobile home model, a typical 14 foot × 70 foot singlewide unit made in an average-sized factory. Most manufacturers do not detail labor consumption in this manner. The three factories that served as the sources of this information conformed to the norms of the average plant and therefore may be considered representative. Obviously, if a plant buys many of its materials in a nearly completed form, fewer man-hours will be necessary to build a mobile home. Table 5.12 indicates that these plants represent an average degree of in-plant integration.

C. Management of Production

Plant Location and Design

The establishment of a new mobile home plant involves three fundamental interrelated considerations. First is plant location. Second, given the regional market characteristics, firm management must determine the optimal output capacity. The last consideration is the desired degree of in-plant fabrication of subassemblies and components, commonly called the degree of in-plant integration, which, together with plant capacity, is reflected in the determination of square footage needs.

Industry interviews conducted by PMHI between 1975 and 1977 give an indication of the relative importance of various factors in plant location decisions. A consensus was reached when respondents identified what they perceived to be the four most important factors: labor availability, proximity to suppliers, transportation technology limitations, and land use control attitudes prevailing in the new plant's market area. The interviews covered a national sample of manufacturers, so the importance of these four factors appears to be independent of specific regional conditions. A mixture of responses was given to most of the other category choices, however, indicating that their significance varies from region to region. The other three factors are highway regulation, building code regulation, and mobile home taxation.

Availability of labor is often the key determinant of plant location. The technology of mobile home production requires little skilled labor and the overall cost structure of a mobile home manufacturer necessitates a low labor cost factor.

The plant's proximity to suppliers has an impact on both operations and management policies. For example, if a plant is built in Elkhart, Indiana, which is already densely populated with mobile home manufacturers, it may benefit from external economies that have arisen because of the concentration of component suppliers in the area. Conversely, if western Montana is the prospective location for a new plant, management policy is likely to include plans for in-plant integration in plant design.

On the other hand, the generally high transportation costs dictate that a plant be located close to the market. This objective is often incompatible with and overrides the goal of proximity to production and warehousing centers of suppliers.

Community attitudes, zoning restrictions, and tax advantages play an important role in plant design and location decisions. In some densely populated areas, no effective demand can evolve because of exclusionary land use controls. Conversely, mobile home manufacturers are given tax advantages and incentives to establish production facilities in some depressed rural areas. Such tax advantages add to other cost advantages that prevail in rural areas, such as low wage rates and a high level of labor availability.

Firm decisions about the nature of optimal plant size place important constraints on the degree to which individual plant behavior can be modified by policy measures. Three groups of factors most affect the optimal size of a plant. First, the possible existence of significant economies of scale tends to generate an upward bias in the size of plants. Because mobile homes represent a relatively homogeneous product grouping, any cost reductions made possible by more efficient production present the firm with a significant advantage. This upward bias is countered by the second and third factors. The second factor, limitations on market area due to high transportation costs, imposes an upper limit on the possible size of the plant. Although cost reductions through increased plant size could offset some increased transportation costs, industry behavior indicates that this factor is not sufficient to make plants larger than those producing about two thousand units per year economically feasible except in unusual circumstances. The third factor affecting plant size arises from the risk-averting behavior of some mobile home manufacturers. The low capital requirements necessary for entry into the industry, coupled with favorable financial arrangements afforded manufacturers by their dealers and suppliers, tend to encourage entry by firms with limited supplies of liquid assets. Because larger plants with higher fixed costs could, in periods of receding demand, impose cash flow requirements smaller manufacturers would be unable to meet, some producers have traded the possible benefits of reduced costs from larger plants for the possibility of more financial security from smaller plants.

Determining the degree of in-plant integration is an important aspect of plant design and establishment. The choice between in-plant component manufacturing and dependence upon component suppliers is based upon the combined effects of several factors. Overall firm policy for multiplant firms is of decisive importance. In some cases, lack of managerial expertise may restrict in-plant integration to a less than optimal degree. Many new single-plant firms wish to keep capital investment and fixed costs to a minimum before their market positions are established. Of course, the impact of these factors may be modified by plant location or size. For example, the management policy of a new single-plant firm in western Montana that could benefit from extensive in-plant integration may be inclined toward a low degree of integration if the managerial expertise available is minimal. On the other hand, the lack of local suppliers or the hope of becoming a major regional mobile home producer may cause management to implement a high degree of in-plant integration even in light of possible risks to plant performance.

Regional variations in the sizes of new plants suggest a pattern of in-plant integration that supports the deductions made above. During the 1971–1977 period, the average size of new plants established per year in the East North Central region was consistently well below the national average for all new plants. Because the concentration of manufacturing facilities in this region is very high per square mile, there is support for the hypothesis that as the number of mobile home manufacturers in a given area increases, manufacturers are able to support local component suppliers and that as local suppliers become more numerous, the average

Table.5.11.
Labor Consumption by Component for a Typical 14′ × 70′ Singlewide Unit from Plant Described in Table 5.12.

Component	Man-hours	Item
Chassis/wheels	8.20	Chassis, wheel/axle assembly (excluded: heating, plumbing, electrical)
Floor	10.20	Framing members, subfloor, underflooring insulation, vapor barrier (excluded: floor finish, heating, plumbing, electrical)
Exterior wall	12.30	Framing members, exterior siding, interior paneling, insulation, vapor barrier (excluded: wall finish, heating, plumbing, electrical)
Roof	13.60	Framing members, trusses, exterior roof & subroof, ceiling insulation & vapor barrier (excluded: ceiling finish, ventilation fans, electrical)
Interior partitions	5.40	Framing members, paneling (excluded: wall finish, heating, plumbing, electrical)
Doors & windows	3.40	Fixed & operable window units, exterior & interior door units
Exterior finish	.40	Exterior painting, shutters, gutters & downspouts, other exterior trim & ornamentation
Interior wall finish	6.10	Interior painting, wallpaper, vinyl wall covering, baseboard, other wall trim
Floor finish	2.30	Linoleum & vinyl flooring, carpeting & pad
Ceiling finish	.90	Ceiling tile, planks, panels, plaster or painted ceiling
Heating & ventilating	3.80	Furnace, exhaust fans, heating ducts, grilles & registers (excluded: air conditioner)
Plumbing	7.90	Hot water heater, water supply system, drainage/vent system, bath & kitchen fixtures, gas system
Electrical	10.10	Distribution panel, circuit breaker, wiring, switches & outlets
Kitchen equipment	24.80	Range, range hood, refrigerator, kitchen sink, cabinets, other storage, counter tops (excluded: disposal, dishwasher)
Bathroom equipment	1.10	Bathtub & shower, watercloset, lavatory, medicine cabinet, lavinette
Furnishings	11.90	Furniture, beds, lamps, drapes
Delivery	6.00	Assume 100 miles delivery distance
Total	128.40	

Table 5.12.
Degree of In-plant Fabrication for an Average Mobile Home Plant as a Determinant of Labor Consumption Given in Table 5.11.

Component	Item	Precut	Supplied in Rolls	Preassembled	Prefinished	Prepainted
Chassis/wheels	Chassis	☒		☐	☐	☐
	Wheel-axle assembly			☒	☐	☐
	Chassis with wheel-axle assembly			☐	☐	☐
Floor	Framing members	☒		☐		
	Subfloor	☐			☒	
	Underflooring	☐	☒		☐	☐
	Insulation & vapor barrier	☐	☒			
Exterior wall	Framing members	☒		☐		
	Exterior siding	☐	☐		☐	☒
	Interior wall paneling	☐			☒	☐
	Insulation & vapor barrier	☒	☐			
Roof	Framing members	☐		☐		
	Exterior roof	☒			☐	☐
	Exterior subroof	☐	☐			
	Ceiling insulation & vapor barrier	☐	☒			
	Preassembled roofing			☐	☐	☐
Interior partitions	Framing members	☐		☐		
	Paneling	☐			☒	
Windows & doors	Window units			☒	☐	☐
	Exterior door units			☐	☒	☐
	Interior door units			☐	☒	☐
Exterior finish	Exterior painting					☐
	Gutters & downspouts			☐	☒	☐
	Shutters	☐		☒	☐	☐
	Other exterior trim & ornamentation	☐	☐	☐	☐	☐
Interior wall finish	Interior painting or plastering					☐
	Wallpaper, vinyl wall covering	☐	☐		☐	
	Paneling	☐			☒	
	Other trim (baseboard, etc.)	☐		☐	☒	☐
Floor finish	Carpeting & pad	☐	☒			
	Linoleum, vinyl, asphalt flooring	☐	☒		☐	
Ceiling finish	Ceiling tile, planks, panels	☐			☒	☐
	Plaster or painted ceiling					☐
Heating & ventilating	Heating ducts	☐	☐	☐	☐	☐
Plumbing	Water supply system	☐		☐		
	Drainage system	☐		☐		
Electrical	Distribution panel			☒		
	Circuit breaker			☐		
	Wiring	☐		☐		
	Wiring harness	☐		☐		
Kitchen equipment	Range hood	☐		☐	☒	☐
	Kitchen sink & equipment			☐	☒	
	Kitchen cabinets	☐		☐	☐	☐
	Counter tops	☐	☐	☐	☒	☐
	Other kitchen storage	☐		☐		☐
Bathroom equipment	Bathroom & shower			☒	☐	☐
	Medicine cabinets	☐		☐	☐	☐
	Lavinette	☐		☐	☐	☐
	Other bathroom storage	☐		☐	☐	☐

degree of in-plant integration and mobile home plant size tend to decrease.

Product development is a significant determinant of marketing success for two reasons. First, in the mobile home industry, a highly competitive industry that devotes relatively little effort to advertising, product development significantly affects marketing performance. Second, regional tastes vary to the extent that, even for national firms, each plant's product lines must be designed (or design-modified) to meet local needs.

Factors Important to Product Development

A major factor affecting product development is the number of product lines and options that the manufacturer intends to market. It is common to find single plants that distribute two or three different product lines in the same area, although the majority of firms report only one to five product lines.

The number of product lines is determined by another factor that indirectly affects product development: the effect of location and regional demand. Such a relationship between number of product lines and regional location does exist. Data obtained from PMHI/MS indicate that a plant in the East North Central or the South Atlantic region will offer relatively higher numbers of product lines than a plant in other regions. These findings make sense: Mobile home production in these regions is high and competition is fierce.

The average mobile home price is also an important determinant of product development policy. Buyers of higher-priced mobile home models are often willing to pay for experimental innovations. Thus a plant located in a region where popular model prices are high enough to permit product research and development, as in the California market, is likely to adopt a policy that emphasizes experimentation and innovation.

Company age is related to product development. PMHI/MS reveals that a relationship exists between the number of product lines a firm develops and the firm's age. For example, firms established between 1935 and 1950 are likely to have fifteen to thirty product lines, but companies less than ten years old average fewer than five lines. There is a direct correlation between company age and number of product lines, for one reason because older companies are likely to operate several plants in different regions but new companies are often single-plant firms operating in one region with no funds available yet for product development.

Plant-Level Organization in Product Line Development

In large multiplant firms product engineering and design are either confined to the central staff or relegated to the plant level. Product design is distinct from product

engineering in many organizations. In such organizations exterior drawings and floor plans as well as additional design materials are prepared by the design group in conjunction with marketing departments and are then transmitted to product engineering, where all research and development is conducted. Product development is integrated with other plant functions for another reason: The mobile home industry follows the common automotive practice of changing product design yearly, and, because yearly design change is often determined by product marketability, product engineering must work closely with the marketing department to develop new designs and floor plans. This communication facilitates a two-way feedback channel. The product engineering staff sends new ideas to the marketing staff, who then measure the market potential of innovations. It became industry policy in the 1960s, however, to avoid displaying the model year in any easily visible manner. Therefore mobile homes do not have a built-in obsolescence; only "experts" can identify model years.

The following discussion is limited to functions that directly relate to the "manufacturing" process. Therefore the focus is on the plant rather than on the corporate level, on operations rather than on corporate functions. For example, marketing, corporate planning, and capital appropriation decisions are not mentioned here. It must be stressed that this focus in no way suggests any overriding importance of "manufacturing" over other firm activities. In fact, the sales function, which is the single most critical determinant of firm or plant performance, is barely touched upon here.

Importance of the Plant to the Firm: Management at the Plant Level

There are two primary determinants of plant performance: efficient and effective organization and synchronization of all production and distribution tasks and clear communication channels. In multiplant firms, overall firm performance is determined by the performance of each plant within the context of overall firm organization. A centralized approach may be implemented, in which case the plant is very dependent on the central staff for guidance and authorization, or a decentralized approach, which allows the plant almost complete autonomy over its own operations, may be adopted. Firm organization is rarely an "either-or" proposition; achieving a balance of autonomy and responsibility between firm and plant is a complex matter.

Each plant is normally managed by a plant manager or general manager, depending on the functions for which he or she is responsible. In some cases, the plant manager may only be in charge of production, whereas a general manager may be assigned responsibility for sales as well as production. However, because the plant manager is assigned some responsibility for nearly all production tasks, this individual's role in plant performance is important. Plant managers act as both liaison between plant and firm and as coordinator of intraplant communication, often helping organize and direct such plant functions as marketing, sales, purchasing, inventory, production, and distribution. They may also be able to aid in industrial engineering, facilities engineering, product design, and accounting, even though these are normally organized as firm functions. The plant manager or general manager applies important knowledge of the operational functions in order to expedite daily operations.

Manufacturing and Facilities Engineering

Once the product mix is determined, the production process is geared to operate effectively. Problems pertaining to the technology of production must be solved by the manufacturing and facilities engineering staffs. Manufacturing engineering includes matters of methods improvement, work place layouts, production labor standards, and other related tasks of plant production such as make-versus-buy analysis. Facilities engineering is of much less importance to daily plant-level operations and involves nonroutine, basic tasks such as the installation and replacement of plant facilities, equipment, and tooling. The importance of these engineering functions is greater when firm resources are extensive and a large number of plants is involved. As production volume increases, firms can devote more funds to improve production methods and facilities; as the number of plants increases, firms may realize some economies by increasing the utilization of more sophisticated production technology. Smaller or single-plant firms generally draw on the expertise of other firms or contract for these services.

A second factor determining the importance of manufacturing engineering is the utilization of incentive plans. In plants with incentive plans, manufacturing engineering normally assumes a more active role because labor standards, productivity, and quality control assume a much more significant role in the production process.

Sales

The sales department serves two functions that are vitally related to production: generation of sales and preparation of a sales order or work order for each unit to be produced. There is a great deal of variation in the organization of sales activities among mobile home plants. Plants that operate under centralized sales departments generally retain only a telephone coordinator in their sales offices; most of the sales managerial personnel and sales representatives are members of the central staff. In such cases most design, pricing, and marketing decisions originate at this center because most relevant information is gathered and evaluated in one place. On the other hand, in decentralized sales operations each plant undertakes responsibility for these matters. The plant sales manager must supervise all aspects of the sales effort, including any postsale details. Consequently, in decentralized firms intraplant organizational coordination (among sales, production, and distribution functions) is necessary to facilitate plant operations.

Purchasing and Inventory Control

Because 65 percent to 70 percent of operating expenses are allocated to materials, purchasing and inventory control are important and must be carefully managed to maximize plant performance. Most mobile home manufacturers prefer to work with minimal inventories, but inventory turnovers may occur as few as three or as many as sixty times a year. Some manufacturers are able to arrange for one or more precisely scheduled daily deliveries from supply sources, in effect realizing a no-inventory policy. To achieve high inventory turnover ratios, purchasing and inventory personnel must be especially aware of the supply flow and alert and responsive to any delays or mistakes that may arise so that manufacturing' operations and unit output are not hindered.

For small plants the interrelationship between plant size, inventory, and purchasing presents complex problems. Large plants can withstand the cost of storage facilities and of financing inventory when demand slackens unexpectedly, but smaller plants with limited capital cannot afford either supplementary storage facilities or sizable inventories. In addition, the small plant cannot generate enough purchasing volume to warrant special supplier services such as daily scheduled deliveries.

The degree of in-plant integration will also affect the organization of a plant's purchasing and inventory function. A less complex purchasing and inventory function will usually accompany a high degree of in-plant integration where stocks of materials that can be used for more than one purpose in subassembly fabrication are maintained. These materials will generally be less expensive than prefabricated components; because a plant with a high degree of integration has greater plants square footage, it will have a greater percentage of assets invested in plant equipment, tooling, and facilities. As a result, the proportion of plant assets tied up in supplies is not as great as in a nonintegrated plant.

Organization and management of the purchasing and inventory function is not simply dependent upon the centralized or decentralized nature of firm organization. In some cases where purchasing is centralized, the supplier receives orders from the plant and then ships specified items to the plant, placing much of the responsibility for material acquisition on plant management.

Inventory management policies also vary. Many firms determine the inventory levels that must be maintained and establish order points for all items; others do so only for certain higher-cost items and use open stocks and lines for lower-cost items. Automated data processing has recently been introduced to deal with the complexities of inventory forecasting, procurement, and warehousing.

Firms offering a variety of models can keep their inventories at a level similar to firms producing a much more limited product line by applying "requirements planning" to inventory management. Future production schedules and model bills that outline the materials necessary for each unit to be produced are used in requirements planning to facilitate precise production scheduling.

Purchasing is normally the responsibility of an individual in each plant known as the purchasing agent. In a multiplant firm that operates this function on a completely decentralized basis, the purchasing agent is responsible for all aspects of material procurement. However, even in somewhat centralized firms, the agent will locate materials, negotiate prices, place material orders, and ensure timely delivery. Purchasing agents must be able to place orders on short notice and react to changes in production schedules. It is their responsibility to ensure that correct production materials at the most competitive price are stocked at the right time and in the right quantity. They may also be responsible for material receiving functions, incoming material inspection, and the coordination of all in-plant component fabrication. Thus the purchasing agent often becomes responsible for inventory control and is involved in make-versus-buy analysis.

Production Scheduling

The role of production scheduling is to ensure the prompt filling of dealer orders. Dealers insist upon precisely timed deliveries. Production scheduling also reflects the number of models and options offered by the manufacturer. The greater the number of unique models produced, the more difficult it is for the manufacturer to operate an uninterrupted production line. Hence, such a plant relies heavily on efficient scheduling. Inventory policies also directly influence production scheduling. Although manufacturers try to minimize their inventory problems by maintaining high inventory turnover ratios and ordering their supplies at frequent intervals, they must be responsive to consumer tastes and needs. Materials that cannot be acquired quickly must be on hand to maintain production scheduling flexibility. Because nearly all aspects of production are coordinated to follow an exacting output schedule, production scheduling plays a determinant role in the integration of plant activities and performance.

The production department prepares the production schedule in one of two ways. One approach is called the "block run" method and the other is called the "mixed line" method. With the "block run" method unit production is scheduled according to model type; models of similar type are produced in groups or blocks so that setup time and expense are reduced. This method may be implemented by producing a predetermined number of a given model and then switching to another or by manufacturing a given model for a predetermined number of days before changing to another. Dealers are notified of the dates a given model will be run and encouraged to place orders as far as sixty days in advance. During peak selling months, when dealer orders exceed plant capacity, the manufacturer may build the same model until dealer pressure forces a change to another model. In addition to reducing the number of assembly setups and setup labor in subassembly fabrication, block run scheduling also ensures greater efficiency. Workers become more familiar with specific processes as tasks are repeated. Furthermore, block run scheduling allows the plant purchasing agent to acquire large quantities of special materials, thereby reducing both material and overall inventory expenses. There are certain disadvantages of block run scheduling, however, that affect company sales volume. This method is incompatible with producing units to individual dealer specifications and often delays the filling of dealer orders because such an order must be held until that model is being run on the assembly line. Some manufacturers respond to changing dealer demands by operating more than one assembly line, each on a block-run basis yet for a different model, in order to reduce the required number of model changeovers. Not a realistic solution for manufacturers operating small plants, this increases the cost of entry into the business and raises fixed expenses in a seasonal and highly competitive industry. With the "mixed line" method orders are scheduled as they are received without regard for the model type or floor plan. This approach is basically the opposite of the block run method, with the opposite advantages and disadvantages. The greatest production flexibility may be achieved, but more setup time is required and worker efficiency is reduced because the production tasks are no longer as regularized and repeatable.

Production

Organization of the production function includes coordination of the sales, purchasing, and distribution functions of the plant.

This is the responsibility of a production manager or superintendent, who supervises the efforts of the foremen or group leaders in assembly areas of the plant and carries out production-related tasks. With respect to daily plant operations, production managers are probably the second most important persons because, like the plant managers, they must be constantly aware of all stages of production in order to ensure smooth plant operation.

Once the production schedule is finalized, the production manager receives a work order from the sales department. The work order is of particular significance because of its simplicity. It contains all the information necessary to produce each unit, such as model type, exterior color scheme, interior decor, appliances, special features, and options. This simple form can be easily understood by all employees and substituted for the myriad of complex working drawings used in conventional construction, which only a few people on the job site can interpret. It is simply one of hundreds of timesaving efficiencies peculiar to the mobile home industry. Copies of the work order are sent in production sequence to production areas (frame shop, cabinet shop, and metal shop).

Before the actual assembly of a unit begins, those components or subassemblies required by the work order must be fabricated or purchased so they are ready for assembly at the proper point in the assembly process. As each chassis is placed on the assembly line, a copy of the work order is attached to the frame for identification purposes. This work order remains on the unit through the assembly line stations and is removed only when the unit is completed. Production change orders are handled in much the same manner as the original work order. Throughout the phases of the production process, all cooperating organizational elements must function in a wholly integrated fashion.

Quality Control

The role of quality control is especially important in mobile home production for four reasons. First, tolerances must be fine. In contrast to on-site housing construction, where each task is built on the work of the previous one, mobile homes are assembled from a large number of subassemblies that are fabricated independently and then brought together on a main assembly line. Subassemblies, therefore, are interchangeable and tolerances must be finer than those adequate for on-site construction. Double-wide mobile homes must be built with particular precision so that the two fabricated halves will fit together securely once they are joined on-site. Considering that each half is 10 feet high and as much as 80 feet long, it is not hard to see why maintaining satisfactory tolerances is so crucial; a variance of

1 inch in length amounts to only .1 percent variance but would make joining difficult, if not impossible.

Second, when an assembly line production method is employed, errors and quality problems are likely to be costly. When the production schedule is close, a flaw in one unit can adversely affect production throughout the entire plant because of the continuous and repetitive nature of mass production.

Quality control deserves attention for a third reason: Many plants use some form of incentive system to stimulate labor productivity. The "go home plan" is an especially influential determinant of plant performance because it permits workers to leave the plant when they complete their set objective. Consequently, workers may pay less attention to quality because the incentive is based on output/time; thus manufacturers must develop an effective quality control function to ensure workmanship and quality. Examples of the success of incentive systems among leading mobile home manufacturers can be quite impressive. Leading national manufacturers are telling us that their incentive systems allow workers to earn as much as $8 or $10 per working hour, calculated on a base rate of approximately $4 per hour.

Quality control improves overall plant performance in a fourth way: by facilitating the promotion of sales and the development of good customer relations. Effective quality control measures will ensure the manufacturer a competitive position in the market. Although the industry as a whole has a history of high quality control standards, some manufacturers have had difficulty (and a very few simply did not care to) meet consumer expectations, especially since damages can be incurred as a result of extreme in-transit conditions. The reputation of an individual manufacturer, whose overall record of quality performance has been excellent, could be seriously marred by one or two defective units; a few bad experiences with inferior quality units may seriously hinder the sales performance of an individual firm or even the entire industry. The U.S. Federal Trade Commission's intent to impose upon the industry a most demanding trade regulation rule regarding warranty performance is an example of an unexpected backlash in response to occasional laxity. Quality control does merit special attention in plant organization.

Organization of the quality control function is difficult to characterize. Generally, there are two basic approaches. Quality control may be handled by inspectors who report to the production manager, the sales manager, the plant manager, or to the firm's central staff. Otherwise, quality control may be organized as a separate management function similar to the organizations of production, sales, accounting, and purchasing functions and similarly report to the plant manager or to the central staff. Now, in the late

1970s, with the Federal Mobile Home Construction and Safety Standards already in effect nationally since 1976, the quality control function has become organizationally more standardized in mobile home plants. Most plants utilize quality control inspectors who check raw materials upon delivery and monitor subassemblies and final assemblies at various points throughout the manufacturing process. If a quality problem is discovered, the flaw is noted on an inspection form and the workers responsible for the problem or a specialized rework crew corrects the flaw and notes the repairs on the inspection form. At the end of the main assembly line, the unit is completely reinspected along with the utility systems and any quality problems are rectified in a similar fashion. Chapter 18 on building code regulation details the inspection procedure mandated by the federal code.

Distribution and Dealer Service

Distribution and dealer service can have a substantial impact upon plant performance and sales volume. Large multiplant firms that distribute to many dealers may adversely affect performance in all their plants by failing to establish an adequate distribution system. According to PMHI's national survey of mobile home dealers, sales competition among manufacturers who distribute through the same dealer outlet is very strong: Approximately half of all respondents reported representing between three and four manufacturers; 41 percent claimed to represent over five manufacturers. In an industry that does very little nationwide advertising, sales competition must include a great deal of attention to the effectiveness of distribution and dealer service practices.

The organization and management of the distribution and dealer service functions is important. Generally, the plant administers distribution and dealer service policies that orginate at the firm level. At the same time, however, performance bonuses to plant management are often based upon plant profit and loss records. Consequently, the precise strategies developed by plant managers or general managers are unique. The manager of each plant is likely to get the best production results only after modifying general firm policies to meet the competitive conditions in the regional market.

Distribution and service are frequently organized as part of the sales function. In these cases nearly all sales aspects are managed by a sales coordinator, who also assume responsibility for transportation and service management. Other interdepartmental functions are performed by a plant sales staff, which usually consists of "outside" and "inside" sales representatives who maintain telephone contact. This integrated approach to sales and distribution facilitates responsive cooperation between the distribution and production functions, promoting overall efficiency among all plant operations.

Integration among Plant Operations

Because of their extensively integrated nature, plant operations and therefore management functions and relationships are less than distinct. The technological requirements as well as the economic factors favor integration of operations. Mobile home production requires little capital investment. Sufficient facilities may in fact be established by adapting an existing building, such as an airplane hangar. As a result, the ratio of variable costs to fixed costs is unusually high. Consequently, operating expenses that form the bulk of variable costs must be carefully managed. Because unskilled labor is used extensively, the proportion of operating costs allocated to labor, in contrast to conventional construction labor costs, is not significant. Furthermore, most labor is not unionized, so the chances that management is obliged to form long-term contractual agreements is slim. This indicates that one of the greatest threats to plant survival is poor management of material costs. No-inventory policies further increase a manufacturer's vulnerability to fluctuating material costs. Thus, because the prevailing technology creates a strong pressure on material costs and other variable expenses, efficient plant operations are dependent upon efficient management, in-plant communication, and coordination throughout the production process. Fully integrated plants are more competitive and profitable and can best capitalize on technology.

In its present product, the mobile home industry does not fulfill its potential. What is presently manufactured reflects the history of an industry that grew out of trailer manufacture and only by accident became a major producer of primary housing. The mobile home of today is still regulated as a vehicle, not a dwelling, and still largely exists in a legal vacuum. Its styling, its whole rationale for existence still derives greatly from the automobile. These factors have militated against imaginative designs and product innovations and have locked the mobile home product into a very few basic designs. Thus many socially desirable and practical uses are never attained.

The present technology employed by the mobile home industry represents a response to the needs of its present markets. A new view of the mobile home would open up new markets. Rather than being doomed never to be more than a single-family unit in a trailer park, the product of the mobile home industry could be a component in a housing cluster, a structural member in a low-rise building, a unit fitted into a high-rise structural frame. The existing product has barely scratched

D. Potentials

Innovative Materials

the surface of potential uses. Many potential markets could be tapped with new products created by some well thought out innovation. Innovations in design will require major changes in the industry. Future products will not only have to meet more exacting standards of strength, fireproofing, and design quality (without sacrificing product efficiency or cost performance) but can only succeed if the industry first works to achieve strategic changes in its supporting and regulatory environments. Assuming a restructured environment, we have concluded that the use of alternative materials of construction is one of the most promising innovations to meet the demands of the future. Replacing the currently employed wood-frame-on-steel chassis may be designs calling for aluminum-frame-on-steel chassis or all-steel construction; even plastics and lightweight concrete can be used. It should be noted that lumber prices have risen 90 percent from 1975 to 1977, and a full 20 percent from July to August 1977. It seems, then, that an industry change from wood to other construction materials would make good economic sense.

The degree of production process adaptation required by the use of these materials will vary widely. The fabrication and assembling technology exists for the metals, but it must be transferred to or rediscovered by mobile home manufacturers. This will mean extensive change of production facilities by companies already producing mobile homes.

Plastics hold some promise as structural materials in mobile home construction, but considerable research and development on them will be needed. New production facilities will also be required. However, no matter how effective plastics ultimately become as a structural material, the oil shortage makes large-scale dependence on their use questionable. The capability to use reinforced, lightweight concrete has long existed and has already been proven by one major mobile home manufacturer; but much more research and development is necessary for cost-efficient application to mobile construction.

Overall, metals show the most immediate promise as alternative mobile home construction materials. We suggest that steel and aluminum may become more important in the future as structural members, and, in the case of aluminum, for walls, roofs, and floors. More detailed analysis of these two materials follows. This is not meant as a recommendation that the industry in fact use these two materials. Rather, it is meant to provide a concluding perspective to this chapter on manufacturing: that the mobile home industry tomorrow may well produce shelter for markets not considered possible for it today.

Use of Aluminum and Steel in Mobile Homes

Aluminum and steel have long been used in industry. A material used in the mobile home industry should maximize strength; flexibility (for structural as well as nonstruc-

tural applications); fire protection; and workability while minimizing weight (for ease of transport); susceptibility to corrosion, thermal conductivity, and thermal expansion; and price. Because both steel and aluminum come in a wide variety of alloys of varying composition, physical properties, and price, only the qualities of "average" steel and "average" aluminum are addressed. Since this treatment does not include quantitative measurements of the material properties, all qualitative descriptions (such as "strong" or "light") are relative to wood.

There are many advantages to the use of aluminum. Its light weight makes for easier shipping and handling and may serve to reduce the weight of the product. An aluminum oxide layer on the surface of the metal protects against corrosion. Contact with cement, masonry, or wood may initiate corrosion by shielding the metal from oxygen and contact with other metals may cause corrosive galvanic action, but there are ways to protect against this. A protective coating of aluminum can be used on those nonaluminum parts in contact with aluminum. Because the strength to weight ratio in aluminum is high, this will be of benefit in building units for high-rise construction, where light weight will mean that less supporting structure is necessary and less expensive cranes can be used. Great strength can be achieved by using alloying elements and metallurgical hardening processes. Aluminum is one of the most workable of all common metals and can be fabricated easily and precisely to provide a great variety of forms, shapes, colors, and textures by using most of the conventional methods. Aluminum fabricating technology is not at all unknown among mobile home manufacturers; many have relied extensively on this metal in the past. But because mobile home firms going into aluminum must make a high capital investment for new equipment and possibly new plant facilities, the real problem is not technological capability but whether there is marketing potential to justify the investment.

There are problems associated with the use of aluminum in mobile home production. Despite the metal's strength, its elastic qualities cause difficulties in structural design. Aluminum also has low impact strength, which poses, for example, the problem of dents on panel walls. Heat is an enemy of this metal; its high thermal conductivity causes condensation and insulation problems. When there is a great difference between the indoor and outdoor temperature, condensation, which can cause corrosion of adjacent materials, is likely to occur on an aluminum wall member such as a window sash. Aluminum has a high coefficient of thermal expansion, necessitating the use of expansion joints between adjacent panels to avoid breakage and distortion. Finally, the strength of the metal continually declines with heat, posing fire-resistance problems. The last and perhaps greatest disadvantage is that aluminum's unit cost is higher than that of wood. But this may be compensated for by saving in other areas: less quantity used in construction (due to greater strength), lower assembling cost (due to greater precision and scrap saving), and lower shipping cost (due to lower weight).

Steel presents another situation. Although heavier per unit volume than wood, its high strength to weight ratio means that much less steel is needed to provide the same support as a wooden post or beam; thus a steel structural member is 20 percent to 30 percent lighter per linear foot than its wooden counterpart. Although steel is liable to corrode into ferrous oxide (rust), it can be made corrosion-resistant by galvanizing or painting. Alloying will also remove the danger of rusting, but the resulting stainless steel is presently too expensive to be used in the mobile home industry.

One of steel's advantages is the reduction of work when compared to wood construction because of a simple component assembly system. Even for on-site construction, some estimates place the amount of time necessary to build a steel structure at only 75 percent of the time needed for an equivalent wood wall-stud structure. Steel members can be sized to standard wood dimensions to be compatible with existing systems, and unconventional shapes are also easily fabricated. Steel products exhibit a high degree of uniformity and quality control. Beams are straight, will not warp or shrink as wood does, possess a good surface finish, and show great resistance to local damage (nicks, scratches, and so forth). Steel panels, sized to fit each other, are light enough for a few workers without handling equipment. Prepunching of holes makes for easy assembly, and several assembly systems other than bolting are available. In addition, steel responds well to heat treatment. Because it has high strength and a high strength to weight ratio, a well-made steel unit could serve as a structural member in a high building. The plethora of different alloys assures choice of material with the properties for particular use.

Since steel is already used in the construction of mobile home underframes, steel fabrication technology is well known to manufacturers. Extending the use of this material to the product's whole structural frame will not present major technical difficulties to the typical mobile home manufacturer. Rather, the main problem in following this course will be justifying investment in more machinery and working the greatly increased amount of steel. A firm would have to be reasonably assured of a stable demand of sufficient volume for its new steel-frame product before taking this step. The fact that some firms have done just that seems to indicate that such a demand can be cultivated.

However, steel, like aluminum, has its disadvantages. First, it is liable to fail unless adequately fire-protected. As mentioned above, it is very susceptible to corrosion (rust), but this can be overcome economically by coating. Although the unit price of steel is higher than that of wood, this may be balanced out by other factors: since less steel will be used, it will be lighter and cheaper to transport, and timesaving production processes will cut labor costs and allow increased production. In addition, steel prices do not fluctuate as dramatically as wood prices, although steel shortages have occurred in the past.

Case Studies

The marketing possibilities of mobile homes produced with other than conventional materials have not been totally ignored by the mobile home industry. There have been and are companies that produce aluminum- or steel-frame mobile homes. Two cases are referred to as examples to emphasize the fact that such material and design innovations are technically feasible.

The Spartan Aircraft Company in Tulsa, Oklahoma, was one of several mobile home manufacturers using aluminum in the 1950s. Starting around 1956, using mass production techniques, it produced an average of twenty mobile homes per day. Capitalization ran $2.5 million for tooling, machinery, and equipment plus $2 million for buildings and other facilities (expressed in 1956 dollars).

Spartan mobile homes consisted of an all-aluminum shell resting on a steel underframe. This aluminum shell was made up of two end panels, two side panels, and a roof joined into a light-skin-stressed structure, as is common in aircraft construction. They stocked 3804 different items to equip the final product. The aluminum shell was constructed in the following way: Processing of aluminum stock began with a Wean Shear leveling line. After leveling, aluminum panels dropped onto a conveyorized inspection table. Stiffeners for curved panels of the front- and rear-end subassemblies were formed on a Hufford stretch press. An aircraft fixture was used to assemble front and rear ends. Once the basic framing was assembled, it was placed upright on a wheeled jig for assembly of the skin panels. Only rivets were used in the stressed-skin construction. Skin panels with deep forms were produced in a Cecostamp fitted with Kirksite dies. Front- and rear-end assembly jigs rolled along floor tracks as in many straight-line-flow assembly systems. Side-panel assembly began on aircraft-type jigs of welded tubular construction. After the main members and skins were in place, the partially completed subassembly was transferred to a conveyor line. Ribs and stringers were riveted at various stations. Roof panels were assembled on roll-over jigs, which were heavily braced to avoid distortion of the assembly. Final assembly was supported by modern metal shearing, forming, and assembly practices. The finished product's exterior design was functional and clearly reflected aircraft technology.

In the mid-1970s the DMH Company, a division of National Gypsum, began serial production of a steel-frame unit in two converted plants in Alma and St. Louis, Michigan; production began at four units a day and was expected to rise to fifteen a day. The units were introduced after eighteen months of research and design and field and laboratory testing. They were produced by a new off-line assembly method in converted conventional mobile home plants, which DMH says will allow improved production and quality control. In the first half year of production, approximately four hundred major manufacturing problems had been solved. Everyone from assembly line worker to dealer encountered unfamiliar problems related to the new product that had to be resolved. However, according to DMH, the steel bond construction showed itself not only structurally superior but also greatly surpassed the fireproof qualities of conventional mobile home construction.

The Steel Bond frame unit differs from the conventional mobile home in many aspects. It consists of 2×4-inch steel wall studs, 2×8-inch steel floor joists, and rigid 2×6 inch steel roof rafters that act together to prevent warping, shrinking, and sagging. Interior walls are gypboard panels. Thermal and noise insulation is provided by foamed-in-place urethane, which also acts as a structural bonding agent, eliminating the need for nails and staples on interior walls and ceilings. Figure 5.34 shows the application of sprayed-on foam to a perimeter wall assembly consisting of gypsum wall panel and steel studs. The perimeter wall, with interior partitions and windows in place, is shown hoisted alongside a mobile home's main frame in figure 5.35. A one-piece, permanent, weathertight roof of fiberglass provides a quieter topping than the conventional galvanized roof, with a dead air space between roof and foam providing additional insulation. The Steel Bond unit was manufactured in three sizes: two singlewide units, dimensioned 14 feet × 66 feet and 14 feet × 70 feet and a doublewide unit, 24 feet × 60 feet.

In 1974, the price of the steel bond units was at least comparable to the luxury class conventionally built mobile home, but DMH feels that the price could go down. The 1973–1975 recession forced DMH to halt production of this line. However, DMH may resume production around 1980.

Figure 5.34.
Foam is applied to perimeter wall assembly.

Figure 5.35.
Perimeter wall is hoisted alongside mobile home's main frame.

E. Policy Alternatives

We have found the mobile home industry to be by far the most efficient building industry in the United States and probably in the world. Our research has shown that the advantages over traditional housing need not be limited to the standard mobile home, as the industry is capable of mass-producing shelter utilizing materials other than wood without a loss of production efficiency. This means that the mobile home industry could potentially produce low-cost, high-quality shelter units designed for integration into medium- and high-rise structures that could be built for all density ranges. And its management systems can easily be modified to cope with different products and a new technology tomorrow. The mobile home industry, then, is the world's most promising resource for providing low-cost, quality shelter.

This conclusion, however, must be taken with extreme caution. The industry should not exploit any one of its technological potentials without first making its supporting and regulatory environments conducive to innovation. Without investment in corporate planning and in the implementation of viable plans, the industry would be inviting "suicide" because it would be seeking to exploit technological potentials, having forgotten the overriding importance of creating a strong and safe market first.

Policy alternatives, then, seem clear. Manufacturing possibilities can only be realized if the mobile home industry mounts an effort to use all of its major resources to create a business and political climate supportive of innovation and an increase in demand that would justify new investment.

Should the industry decide not to aim for a significant share of the traditional housing market or if it cannot reorganize its own organization or business environment, then the product, the technology, and its management should remain unchanged. Given the present economic and regulatory climate, the present product and technology make good business sense—returns on equity in mobile home manufacture are currently higher than in most other businesses.

Chapter 6

Cost and Price Structures in the Production System

As real per-capita income in the United States has risen to ever-higher levels, the percentage of families able to meet monthly payments on the average new single-family home has decreased substantially. It is generally agreed that fewer than 30 percent of American families can presently meet the minimum financial requirements to buy a median-priced new home. This significant increase in housing costs has created a market for lower-cost single-family housing produced by methods different from those of conventional construction. The mobile home industry has become the dominant force in this market, producing homes at an average factory price of $8.95 per square foot in 1977. The equivalent per-square-foot prices for site-built homes are roughly twice as high. This performance is a function of both the ability of manufacturers to maintain highly efficient production technologies and the capacity of the other elements of the industry and its supporting environment to facilitate such performance.

Analysis of mobile home manufacturers' cost and price performance can provide information on two aspects of this performance. In section A data from PMHI/MS and other PMHI surveys are evaluated to estimate general industry cost patterns and to explain variations among firms. Three specific questions with implications for improvement in the performance of both the mobile home industry and the conventional housing industry are covered: What are the elements of mobile home production costs? What conditions or events affect these elements? Is it possible to influence these cost elements in the interest of further reducing manufacturing costs and FOB factory prices?

In section B primary industry data are analyzed to compare FOB factory prices for specific model lines. First we evaluate variations in FOB factory prices associated with variations in quality while holding constant unit size. Then we hold quality constant to evaluate variation in FOB factory prices associated with changes in unit size. These analyses not only provide explanations of present price variations, but they also permit extrapolation of price estimates to units that may emerge as the mobile home industry expands its market in the direction of conventional housing markets.

Section C summarizes our findings and suggests several policy alternatives for the mobile home industry and the conventional housing industry.

A. Manufacturing Cost Analysis

Elements of Manufacturing Costs

The FOB factory price of $8.95 per square foot represents the national mean value of the 1977 FOB prices reported by a national sample of mobile home manufacturers (table 6.1). Regional variations in mean 1977 FOB factory price per square foot range from a low of $8.03 in the mountain states to a high of 10.51 in New England and the Mid-Atlantic

Table 6.1.
Range of Values, Total FOB Factory Price per Square Foot, 1977

FOB Factory Price/Sq. Ft.	Number of Firms	% of Respondents to Question
0–$5.00	1	1.6
$5.01–$6.00	1	1.6
$6.01–$7.00	6	9.8
$7.01–$8.00	14	23.0
$8.01–$9.00	15	24.6
$9.01–$10.00	11	18.0
$10.01–$11.00	6	9.8
Above $11.00	7	11.6
Missing	7	—
Mean: $8.95		

Source: PMHI/MS and 1977 follow-up survey.

states. The four main census regions show mean FOB prices per square foot as follows, expressed as a percentage of the national mean value:

Northeast	117.4%
North Central	107.9%
South	94.3%
West	92.1%

Such price performance invites an analysis of the contributing factors. The principal source of data for this analysis is Project Mobile Home Industry's Manufacturer Survey (PMHI/MS), to which, unless otherwise indicated, all survey references are made.

Table 6.2 gives a breakdown of the overall cost and profit structure of companies to show average values and range of values for five categories of fixed and variable costs. It is important that the reader compare this data with cost breakdowns for on-site building. For example, the fact that many mobile home manufacturers operate with a direct labor content of less than 10 percent of FOB factory price becomes more meaningful if one realizes that labor costs account for as much as 25 percent of on-site conventional construction costs.

Expressed as a percentage of total revenue, 81 percent of manufacturing costs are variable costs, which include material costs, direct labor, and selling expense. Eleven percent are fixed costs: general and administrative expense, and plant overhead. The remainder is miscellaneous expenses, profit and taxes. The single largest component of manufacturing cost is material cost, which represents 67 percent of the FOB factory price per square foot.

Table 6.3, based on the same survey as table 6.2, compares the cost structures of profitable (table 6.2) and unprofitable companies. For people in industry and business, the implications of the data in table 6.3 are obvious. For the layperson, the most important observation is that control of all

Table 6.2.
Companies' Overall
Cost and Profit
Structures 1977

Materials

Average of all companies reporting 67.31%
22% show materials cost 61.2% to 64.2%; average: 63.07%
54% show materials cost 64.8% to 69.4%; average: 66.81%
22% show materials cost 70.4% to 74.0%; average: 72.05%
 2% show materials cost 75%;   average: 75.00%

Direct Labor

Average of all companies reporting: 10.84%
 4% show direct labor cost   8% or less;   average: 8.00%
55% show direct labor cost 9.03% to 10.03%; average: 9.49%
21% show direct labor cost 10.50% to 12.00%; average: 11.50%
16% show direct labor cost 13.90% to 14.20%; average: 13.91%
 4% show direct labor cost   over to 16.30%; average: 16.15%

Manufacturing or Plant Overhead

Average of all companies reporting: 6.58%
29% show overhead cost 4% or less; average: 2.86%
29% show overhead cost 5% to 7%; average: 5.56%
30% show overhead cost 8% to 10%; average: 8.89%
12% show overhead cost 11% to 13%; average: 11.83%

Selling Expense

Average of all companies reporting: 3.04%
33% show selling expense 0.5% to 2%;   average: 1.62%
51% show selling expense 3.0% to 4%;   average: 3.22%
16% show selling expense 5.0% to 6.6%; average: 5.35%

General and Administrative Expense

Average of all companies reporting: 3.96%
19% show general expense 0.4% to 2%; average: 1.68%
50% show general expense 2.5% to 4%; average: 3.38%
19% show general expense 4.5% to 5%; average: 4.90%
12% show general expense 5.5% to 11%; average: 8.30%

Other and Miscellaneous Expense

Average of all companies reporting: 2.77%
46% show miscellaneous expense 0.5% to 1%; average: .86%
34% show miscellaneous expense 1.8% to 4%; average: 2.32%
17% show miscellaneous expense 4.7% to 10%; average: 7.42%
 3% show miscellaneous expense 11%;   average: 11.00%

Net Income Before Federal and State Tax

Average of all companies reporting: 5.50%
48% show before tax 0.5% to 4%; average: 2.91%
36% show before tax 5.0% to 8%; average: 6.80%
10% show before tax 9.0% to 10%; average: 9.66%
 6% show before tax 10.9% to 13%; average: 11.63%

Source: "Cost and Profit Survey," *Mobile-Modular Housing Dealer Magazine*, December 1977.

Table 6.3.
Comparison of Profit
and Loss Companies

Materials

Companies Profit (%)	Cost of Materials (%)	Companies Loss (%)
35	up to 65%	
45	68 to 70%	18.75
20	71 to 75%	68.75
—	76 to 82.7%	12.50

Average of companies reporting a loss 72.52%
Average of companies reporting a profit 67.31%

General and Administrative Expense

Companies Profit (%)	General and Administrative (%)	Companies Loss (%)
19	up to 2	13
50	3 to 4	31
21	5 to 6	25
10	7 to 15	31

Average of companies reporting a loss 5.65%
Average of companies reporting a profit 3.96%

Direct Labor

Companies Profit (%)	Cost of Direct Labor (%)	Companies Loss (%)
4	up to 8	12
55	9.2 to 10	26
21	11 to 12	38
16	13 to 14	12
4	15 to 16	6
—	17 to 18	6

Average of companies reporting a loss 11.48%
Average of companies reporting a profit 10.84%

Miscellaneous Expenses

Companies Profit (%)	Miscellaneous Expense (%)	Companies Loss (%)
46	up to 1	27
34	2 to 4	53
9	5 to 7	20
—	8 to 11	11

Average of companies reporting a loss 2.69%
Average of companies reporting a profit 2.77%

Plant Overhead

Companies Profit (%)	Overhead (%)	Companies Loss (%)
29	up to 4	13
29	5 to 7	34
30	8 to 10	27
12	11 to 13	13
—	14 to 20	13

Average of companies reporting a loss 8.46%
Average of companies reporting a profit 6.58%

Summary: Average for Companies Reporting
a Profit (%)

Materials	67.31	
Direct Labor	10.84	
Manufacturing Overhead	6.58	
Total Cost		84.73
Gross Profit		15.27
Operating Expense		9.77
Net Profit before Taxes		5.50

Summary: Average for Companies Reporting
a Loss (%)

Materials	72.52	
Direct Labor	11.48	
Manufacturing Overhead	8.46	
Total Cost		92.46
Gross Profit		7.54
Operating Expense		12.47
Net Loss before Taxes		−4.93

Selling Expense

Companies Profit (%)	Selling Expense (%)	Companies Loss (%)
33	up to 2	19
51	3 to 4	57
16	5 to 6	12
—	7 to 8	12

Average of companies reporting a loss 4.13%
Average of companies reporting a profit 3.04%

Source: "Cost and Profit Survey," *Mobile-Modular Housing Dealer Magazine*, December 1977.

costs is of overriding importance. Not always will a firm be able to significantly influence variable costs, but good management controls and usually can reduce fixed costs substantially.

We attempted to obtain even finer cost breakdowns in many field interviews. Although most companies were unable to divert the necessary time for computing these detailed values, three companies went to considerable trouble to supply the information. The composite experience of these companies, believed to be fairly typical, is shown in table 6.4.

The importance of variable costs is illustrated in table 6.5, which gives the range of variable and fixed costs per square foot. PMHI/MS obtained from manufacturers information on indirect labor costs in addition to direct labor data; thus, a third cost element is added to the fixed cost category.

(Categorizing indirect labor as variable or fixed is difficult. Some firms include any labor not performed directly on the main assembly line as indirect labor, for example, cabinet makers in a vertically integrated plant. Thus there is a mixture of both variable and fixed costs in the indirect labor figures sampled. For this analysis it is assumed that variable costs included in indirect labor are insignificant and indirect labor is defined as a fixed cost. In any case, indirect labor costs are a fairly small percentage of total costs.) Table 6.5 shows the average 1977 variable costs to be $7.17, with 82 percent of the respondents between $5 and $9. The table indicates a mean of $0.98 for 1977 fixed costs, with 86 percent of the respondents between $0.71 and $1.30.

We then used data generated by the PMHI/MS questionnaire to investigate the determinants of cost variations. In the fol-

Table 6.4.
Material and Labor Costs, Breakdown for a Typical Mobile Home Manufacturer (Only Materials, Direct and Indirect Labor Are Included)

Component	% of Total Cost	Item
Chassis/wheels	12	Chassis, wheel/axle assembly (excluded heating, plumbing, electrical)
Floor	10	Framing members, subfloor, underflooring, insulation, vapor barrier (excluded floor finish, heating, plumbing, electrical)
Exterior wall	15	Framing members, exterior siding, interior paneling, insulation, vapor barrier (excluded wall finish, heating, plumbing, electrical)
Roof	8	Framing members, trusses, exterior roof & subroof, ceiling insulation & vapor barrier (excluded ceiling finish ventilation fans, electrical)
Interior partitions	5	Framing members, paneling (excluded wall finish, heating, plumbing, electrical)
Doors & windows	7	Fixed & operable window units, exterior & interior door units
Exterior finish	0	Exterior painting, shutters, gutters & downspouts, other exterior trim & ornamentation
Interior wall finish	2	Interior painting, wallpaper, vinyl wall covering, baseboard, other wall trim
Floor finish	3	Linoleum & vinyl flooring, carpeting & pad
Ceiling finish	2	Ceiling tile, planks, panels, plaster or painted ceiling
Heating & ventilating	3	Furnace, exhaust fans, heating ducts, grilles & registers (excluded air conditioner)
Plumbing	3	Hot water heater, water supply system, drainage/vent system, bath & kitchen fixtures, gas system
Electrical	5	Distribution panel, circuit breaker, wiring, switches & outlets
Kitchen equipment	15	Range, range hood, refrigerator, kitchen sink, cabinets, other storage, counter tops (excluded disposal, dishwasher)
Bathroom equipment	2	Bathtub & shower, watercloset, lavatory, medicine cabinet, lavinette
Furnishings	8	Furniture, beds, lamps, drapes
Total	100	

Source: PMHI field interviews.

Table 6.5.
Range of Values,
Average Variable and
Fixed Costs per Square
Foot, 1977

Average Costs per Square Foot	Number of Firms	% of Respondents to Question
Variable costs		
$1.01–$4.00	1	2.0
$4.01–$5.00	4	8.2
$5.01–$6.00	8	16.3
$6.01–$7.00	11	22.4
$7.01–$8.00	12	24.5
$8.01–$9.00	9	18.4
$9.01–$10.00	4	8.2
Missing values	19	—
Mean: $7.17		
Fixed costs		
$0.01–$0.50	1	2.3
$0.51–$0.70	3	6.8
$0.71–$0.90	16	36.4
$0.91–$1.10	15	34.1
$1.11–$1.30	7	15.9
$1.31–$1.50	2	4.6
Missing values	24	—
Mean: $0.98		

Source: PMHI/MS and 1977 follow-up survey.

lowing discussion we summarize the results of analysis of differences in these characteristics and explore some implications.

Factors Influencing Variations in Cost

We devoted extensive resources to computer analyses of the cost data generated by PMHI/MS and other relevant surveys undertaken between 1969 and 1977. Patterns of price and cost behavior were sought in PMHI/MS data by cross-tabulating nine categories of price and cost data with six company and production related measures.

Price and Cost Categories	Company and Production Measures
Adjusted FBO price	Total annual sales
Total variable costs	Company structure
Material costs	Company age
Direct labor costs	Plant capacity
Selling expenses	Output composition
Total fixed costs	Seasonality
Indirect labor costs	
General administrative costs	
Plant overhead	

The 54 resulting series of cross-tabulations do not reveal major influences on FOB factory price or on costs. Because the mobile home industry is a highly complex system, it is not surprising that simplistic analysis of one

measure relative to a second does not indicate significant relationships. In contrast, multivariate regression analysis permits the effect of several variables to be considered independently.

Data generated by the PMHI/MS questionnaire were subjected to regression analysis in order to seek determinants of four categories of costs, including variable and fixed costs for the company and for the standardized model. (The PMHI questionnaire was designed for analysis of both company and standardized model costs. For the purposes of this questionnaire, "Company" was defined to include only those subsidiaries or divisions involved in the production of mobile homes. The "physically" standardized model was specified by PMHI to ensure comparability of data.) Costs are broken down into the following four categories:

1. Total variable costs per square foot for the company.
2. Total fixed costs per unit for the company.
3. Average variable costs per square foot for the standardized model.
4. Average fixed costs per square foot for the standardized model.

It would go beyond this book's scope to deal with our reasons for the selection of factors included in the regression analyses. Even the results of our analyses must be summarized because of the great number of regressions that we ran. This summarizing sketch is shown in the following two items: Determinants of Company Cost Variations and Determinants of Model Cost Variations.

Determinants of Company Cost Variations

A regression was run separately with every company cost category as a dependent variable: material costs, direct labor, selling expense, indirect labor, general and administrative expense, and plant overhead. Only the material costs, selling expense, and overhead regressions showed significance. Regressions for the company cost categories are shown in table 6.6. A compressed tabulation of the significant results is included in table 6.7.

The following were significant determinants in at least one equation:

Economies of scale: Economies of scale were influenced by the variables SA (total sales) and UFCTAR (units per day divided by the square footage of the company's average plant).

Number of product lines per plant: Product lines (brand names) per plant were measured by the variable PRONPL.

Output composition: The fraction of non-singlewide units as a measure of output composition was measured by the variable ZZ.

Seasonality: Seasonality was measured by the variable XHXL, the ratio of highest

Table 6.6.
Company Cost Regression Table

	Variable Costs			Fixed Costs		
	Materials	Direct Labor	Selling Expense	Indirect Labor	General and Administrative	Plant Overhead
XHXL		.19855 (.21710)	−.06548 (.10746)	.28924 (.20870)	−.31650 (.24119)	−.28680[a] (.07890)
ZZ	−14.20853[a] (2.94553)	4.53762 (5.37451)		−4.16899 (2.32395)	5.64137 (2.68566)	1.11421 (.87862)
CDMIL				−1.59681 (.70325)	−.76756 (.81270)	1.89794[a] (.26588)
X				−1.28200 (6.98482)	−26.53773 (8.07196)	19.93857[a] (2.64076)
SA	.00002 (.00007)	−.00004 (.00010)	−.00002[a] (.00001)	.00017 (.00009)	.00033 (.00010)	.00009 (.00003)[a]
UFCTAR				29.55678 (20.36431)	31.55367 (23.53388)	−58.89401[a] (7.69915)
UNPL				−.23009 (.19662)	.41770 (.22722)	−.12780 (.07434)
YRST				.17213 (.12640)	−.53189 (.14608)	.14979[a] (.04779)
UCAP	.01881 (.05773)	.02048 (.06586)		−.07884 (.05177)	.13823 (.05983)	.01626 (.01957)
WAGER	−2.95983[a] (1.50255)	.54160 (1.64432)	1.02168[a] (.55245)	1.21324 (1.37203)	−.49992 (1.58558)	−1.41920 (.51873)
PRONPL	2.28410 (1.05830)	−.25545 (.70743)	−.25580 (.45736)	.12076 (.61358)	−1.32392 (.70908)	1.47301[a] (.23198)
XHUCAP	−1.04403 (3.41640)	−2.16453 (2.84457)	2.64680[a] (1.03176)			
R²	.61552	.72119	.40987	.96191	.91703	.99586
F	5.06962[b]	1.10857	2.77821[b]	4.59213	2.00957	43.73719[b]
t − k	19	3	20	2	2	2

a. t significant at 0.05
b. F significant at 0.05
Source: PMHI/MS.

monthly sales to lowest monthly sales, and by XHUCAP, the ratio of highest monthly sales to monthly production.

Vertical integration: Vertical integration, or the degree of in-plant integration, was approximated by variable CDMIL, the ratio of material cost to total labor costs.

Company age: Company age was measured by the variable YRST, the first year of production.

Regional variations: Regional variations were approximated by the dummy variable WAGER, the mean of wages for the states in a region and thus the regional wage value. WAGER reflects variations in material resources, capital, and labor markets, and was used to analyze differences in cost structure by regions.

Company activities: Company activities was described as the number of fields into which the parent company or subsidiaries have integrated or diversified (e.g., park development, consumer financing, building supplies, on-site construction, etc.). This was measured by the variable X.

Company Variable Costs
Regressions were run with material costs, direct labor, and selling expense as dependent variables. Of these, only the material costs and selling expense regressions were significant.

The significant determinants of material costs were:

Output composition: The regression showed that an increase in non-singlewide units will decrease material costs. Since, in the PMHI/MS sample, 75% of the units other than singlewides are doublewide, the variable reflects the savings in material costs gained by producing one doublewide rather than two singlewides. The variable ZZ had a t = 4.82.

Vertical integration: By definition the variable CDMIL was significant in the material and labor cost regressions. A vertically integrated company must increase capital and labor investment to produce components in-plant; thus vertical integration decreases material costs.

Regional variations: The variable WAGER (t = 1.97) shows that the Northeast, East

North Central, and Pacific regions have decreased material costs. The cause is difficult to explain since we cannot determine the frequency of vertically integrated plants in each region.

The significant determinants of selling expense were:

Economies of scale: The variable SA (t = 2.00) showed that an increase in sales will decrease selling expense.

Seasonality: Variable XHUCAP (t = 2.57) showed that seasonality increases selling expense. During slack periods, much more sales effort per unit of sale is required, in terms of both manpower and special incentives to dealers.

Regional variations: WAGER (t = 1.85) indicated that the Northeast, East North Central, and Pacific regions have increased selling expenses compared to the rest of the country. The decrease in material costs was greater than the selling expense increase.

In conclusion, the significant determinants of company variable costs are economies of scale, output composition, seasonality, vertical integration, and regional variations.

Company Fixed Costs
Regressions were run with the fixed cost elements of indirect labor, general and administrative expense, and overhead expense as dependent variables. Only the overhead expense regression was significant.

The significant determinants of overhead costs are:

Economies of scale: Variable SA (t = 3.00) shows that an increase in total sales will increase costs. On *a priori* grounds one would expect that since overhead is a fixed cost, it would decrease as sales increase. Therefore, this unexpected finding might be caused by low levels of capacity utilization. The variable UFCTAR (t = 7.59), "units per day divided by square footage," is basically a measure of the firm's efficiency and is directly related to the plant's technology and management methods.

Number of product lines per plant: Variable PRONPL (t = 6.35) shows that an increase in product lines per plant increases overhead costs. This could be caused by an increase in the variety of materials and equipment, larger and more diverse inventories, and hence, increase in capital needed to cope with more product lines.

Seasonality: XHXL (t = 3.63) is only questionably significant. It shows that an increase in seasonal fluctuations decreases costs. This result is questionable, even though the t statistic is significant, because there are no *a priori* grounds to justify seasonality decreasing overhead costs. For this reason, seasonality is rejected as a determinant of overhead variations.

Vertical integration: CDMIL (t = 7.14) shows vertical integration to cause increased overhead costs.

Company age: YRST (t = 3.13) shows newer companies incurring increased overhead expense. This could occur for many reasons. Newer companies may be paying higher prices for their capital and land than older companies. Newer companies also more frequently start out with newly constructed plants rather than converted facilities. Older companies can draw on their experience to minimize costs while newer companies must still obtain this experience.

Company activities: Variable X (t = 7.55) shows that an increase in company activities will increase costs. This is expected since integration and diversification require additional capital. Although the number of company activities is significant in itself, together with the number of product lines per plant they comprise 37 percent of the residual variation.

In summary, the determinants of company fixed costs are economies of scale, number of product lines per plant, vertical integration, company age, and company activities.

Determinants of Model Cost Variations

Since 62 percent of the companies provided data for a standard model differing slightly from the precise PMHI specifications, the FOB factory price and retail selling price were adjusted by complex calculations that consumed several man-months. Regressions for the model cost categories are shown in table 6.8. A separate regression was run with every model cost category as a dependent variable: materials, direct labor, selling expense, indirect labor, general and administrative expense, and plant overhead. Only the indirect labor regression is significant. This regression has one significant determinant:

Seasonality: Seasonality is influenced by XHLPH, which is the ratio of highest monthly production to lowest monthly production divided by highest monthly employment to lowest monthly employment. This is a measure of the relationship between employment and seasonal output.

Model Variable Costs

The regressions with material costs, direct labor, and selling expenses as dependent variables are not significant.

Model Fixed Costs

Of the regressions run with indirect labor, general and administrative expense, and plant overhead as dependent variables, only the indirect labor regression is significant. The significant determinant of indirect labor cost is:

Seasonality: Variable XHLPH (t = 3.40) is significant with a positive coefficient. This indicates that an increase in seasonal production relative to seasonal employment increases indirect labor costs. This could be caused by overtime and inefficient use of labor.

Implications

Which characteristics of the mobile home industry are primarily responsible for its outstanding cost performance? To what extent are these characteristics transferable to other home builders? Two observations from the cost analysis may have the greatest implications: First, the mobile home industry has historically maintained low fixed costs, presently 11 percent of revenue. The largest component of fixed costs is plant overhead. Because production is essentially a manufacturing assembly operation, relatively low-cost plants suffice. They are frequently leased and require very little specialized equipment. Overhead costs are further reduced by maintaining low inventory of supplies and manufactured units. Increasing numbers of product lines per plant and increasing areas of company activities might tend to increase overhead costs; but because overhead costs represent only 5.6 percent of total operating expenses, these increases would be insignificant.

Second, variable costs represent 81 percent of total revenue. Of this, by far the largest proportion (67 percent of total revenue) is for material costs. Direct labor accounts for only 11 percent. Material costs represent two-thirds of the production cost of a mobile home, so particular attention should be given in further studies to factors influencing material costs even in a minor way. The cost analysis indicates that a company producing a high proportion of doublewide units reduces its material costs. This is important, particularly in view of the trend toward more conventional construction standards. As mobile homes compete with traditional housing as a lower-cost alternative, the industry will continue to produce a steadily increasing proportion of doublewide units.

The analyses indicate that structural and production differences among firms result in only minor variations within the nine cost categories. This suggests that the successful cost performance of the industry is the result not of single factors but of the integration of many factors, including maintenance of low fixed costs, acceptance of technology and standardization, and, most important, a general integration of industry operation and functions in the supporting and regulatory environments.

In view of the present low price, however, we feel that it would be futile to consider significant general cost reductions in the manufacture of mobile homes. It would appear that greater benefit would result from a similar analysis of other housing alternatives —traditional on-site as well as factory-built shelter—to determine which of the approaches developed by the mobile home industry are applicable to other subsectors of the building industry to reduce costs in all forms of housing.

Table 6.7.
Significant Manufacturer Cost Regressions

Determinant	Variable	Materials	Selling Expense
Economies of Scale	SA	.00002 (.00007)	−.00002[a] (.00001)
	UFCTAR	—	—
	UCAP	.01881 (.05773)	—
	UNPL	—	—
Composition of output	ZZ	−14.20853[a] (2.94553)	—
	PRONPL	2.28410 (1.05830)	−.25580 (.45736)
Seasonality	XHXL	—	−.06548 (.10746)
	XHUCAP	−1.04403 (3.41640)	2.64680[a] (1.03176)
	XHLPH	—	—
Vertical integration	CDMIL	—	—
Age	YRST	—	—
Regional variations	WAGER	−2.95983[a] (1.50255)	1.02168[a] (.55245)
Company Activities	X	—	—
Dealer outlets	OUTNC	—	—
Unionization	PCTUN	—	—
	R²	.61552	.40987
	F	5.06962	2.77821
	t−k	19	20

a. t significant at 0.05.
Source: PMHI/MS.

Table 6.8.
Standardized Model
Cost Regression Table

	Variable Costs			Fixed Costs		
	Materials	Direct Labor	Selling Expense	Indirect Labor	General and Administrative	Plant Overhead
XHXL	.28901 (.26355)		−.20793 (.10845)		−.06275 (.09947)	−.05557 (.17660)
X	−5.57829 (7.62886)	4.65619 (3.97866)		−3.44151 (3.47967)	.49038 (2.56519)	
WAGER	−3.45341 (1.78613)	1.14236 (.95329)	.76417 (.73292)	.75742 (.87612)	−.36759 (.57944)	2.27543 (1.04385)
PRONPL	.49380 (.92774)				−.33685 (.31287)	.48121 (.52985)
Y	.00058 (.00044)	.00039 (.00055)	−.00053 (.00041)			
OUTNC	−.00052 (.00145)			.00080 (.00062)	.00006 (.00046)	
PCTUN	.01595 (.02673)	.02070 (.01211)	−.02036 (.01000)	−.00352 (.01253)	−.01317 (.00946)	.02165 (.01748)
CAPLMO	−1.87831 (2.88620)	1.58803 (1.62075)			.36872 (.94974)	−.70325 (1.58674)
XHLPH		1.27008 (.54441)		1.91752 (.49181)[a]		
CPLMO8		−1.61768 (2.03392)	1.35134 (1.35443)			
O17					−.05216 (.24110)	.40192 (.42871)
R²	.44305	.58487	.39821	.58933	.36651	.52385
F	.79549	1.81450	1.45577	3.15704[b]	.57855	1.83359
t−k	8	9	11	11	8	10

a. t significant at 0.05.
b. F significant at 0.05.

Source: PMHI/MS.

Trends of Manufacturing Costs and Profits over Time

During the 1970s, FOB factory prices for mobile homes have risen much less than prices for traditional homes. Of course, there is no such thing as an FOB factory price for an on-site-built home. Thus, for the comparison in figure 6.1 we used U.S. Department of Commerce data for the average price per square foot of site-built single-family housing excluding the price of land. Figure 6.1 shows that the price gap is not only substantial, but ever widening. (In the chapter on cost and price structures in the distribution system, the Department of Commerce data will again be compared against retail price per square foot for mobile homes, which is, of course, a more directly comparable value.)

How have mobile home manufacturers' cost breakdowns changed over the years? Has any cost category shown a stronger influence on total costs with time? This brief analysis is intended to search out developing trends, using cost breakdown figures for 1965, 1968, 1970, 1973, and 1977. Total costs, broken down in the five categories of material costs, direct labor, overhead, operating expenses, and net profit are tabulated

for comparison in table 6.9. No dramatic change is evident in any cost category during the ten years. There is some indication that the percentage of costs for plant overhead is continually increasing. For an industry that places such great emphasis on maintaining low fixed costs, this trend is alarming. The regression analyses discussed above suggest that it may be related to increased sales, greater number of product lines per plant, or increased company diversification and integration. Other reasons may include increases in the cost of replacement capital and differences in access to capital markets because of changes in the industry's financial position. Experience suggests that this trend also reflects the burden imposed upon the mobile home industry by ever-increasing government regulation.

Company size may influence trends in cost breakdown. For example, a small, growing company may be developing economies of scale already experienced by larger companies; larger companies may be entering new areas requiring more specialized equipment and higher skills. To search out any

Figure 6.1.
Cost comparison of
mobile homes and site-
built homes.

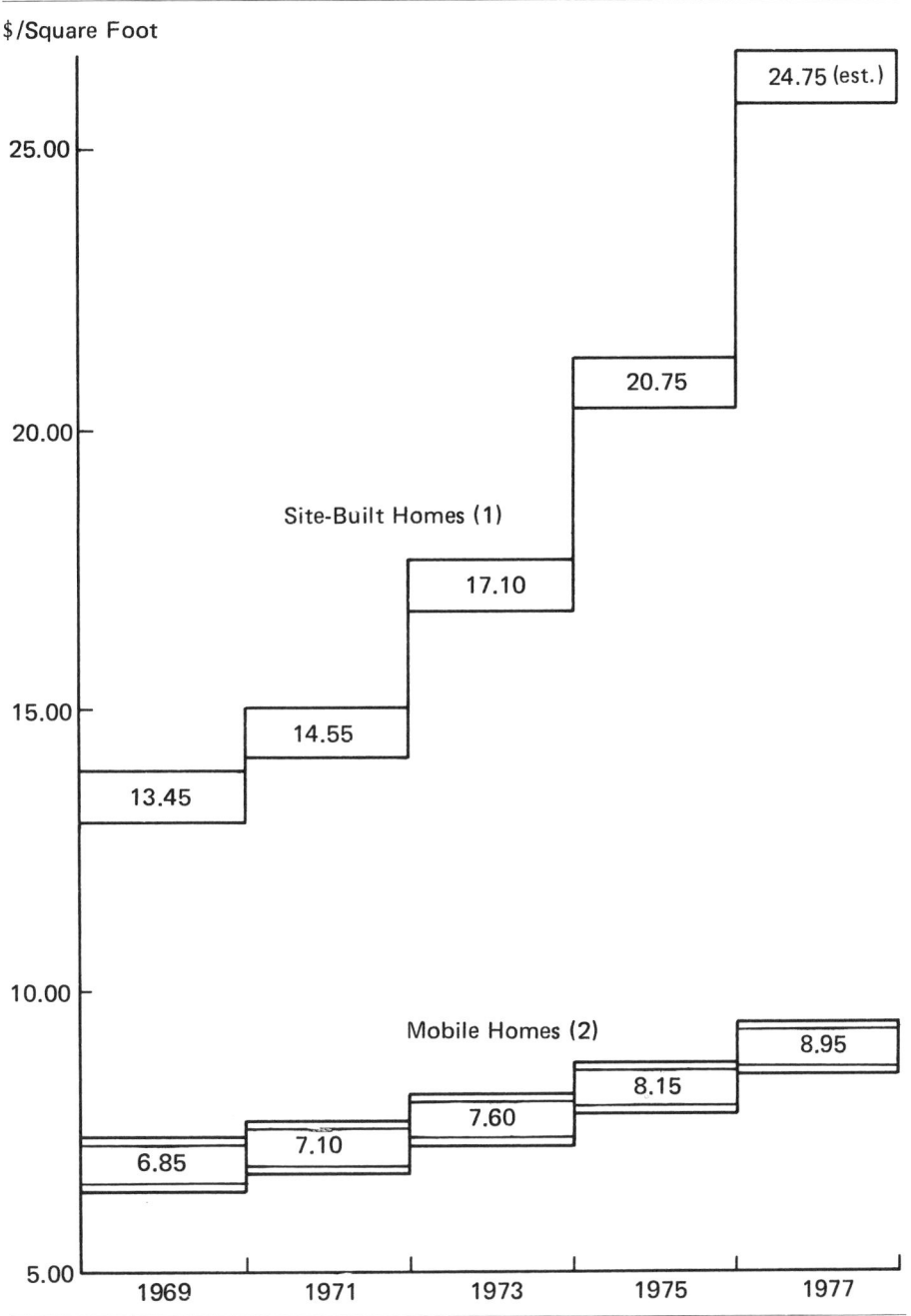

$/Square Foot

Site-Built Homes (1)

24.75 (est.)

20.75

17.10

14.55

13.45

Mobile Homes (2)

8.95

8.15

7.60

7.10

6.85

25.00

20.00

15.00

10.00

5.00

1969   1971   1973   1975   1977

Sources: 1. Price per square foot, site-built homes; excluding land, furnishings, and appliances (U.S. Department of Commerce, Bureau of the Census, Construction Reports Series C25).
2. F.O.B. factory price per square foot, mobile homes; excluding land, including furnishings and appliances (PMHI National Surveys 1969, 1971, 1973, 1975, and 1977).

Table 6.9.
Average Cost (in dollars)
of Goods Sold and
Operating Expenses,
1965–1977

	1965	1968	1970	1973	1977
Cost of goods sold					
Materials	68.31	64.55	66.27	65.75	67.31
Direct labor	12.40	11.66	10.60	11.62	10.84
Manufacturing or plant overhead	5.47	6.04	6.39	6.75	6.58
Total cost of good sold[a]	86.18	82.25	83.29	84.09	84.73
Gross profit on sales	13.82	15.32	16.83	15.91	15.27
Cost of goods and gross profit[a]	100.00	97.57	100.12	100.03	100.00
Expenses					
Selling	3.55	3.50	3.57	3.51	3.04
General and administrative	5.01	4.70	3.77	3.62	3.96
Other and miscellaneous	N.A.	1.52	2.25	2.31	2.77
Total expenses	N.A.	8.53	9.28	8.72	9.77
Net income before tax	5.64	6.76	7.47	7.48	5.50

a. All values represent mean values.

Source: "Cost and Profit Survey," *Mobile-Modular Housing Dealer Magazine*, 1966, 1968, 1970, 1973, and 1977.

such influence, table 6.10 tabulates the cost breakdown in 1968, 1970, 1973, and 1977 for materials, labor and overhead costs, and gross and net profit for companies reporting $1 to $2 million, $2 to $4 million, $4 to $6 million, and $6 to $15 million in annual sales.

Material costs decreased for all company sizes except $2 to $6 million annual sales. Because for most of the target years this is the largest sample group, the material costs results are ambiguous. Overhead expense is the only cost category to show an increase for all sales sizes, reinforcing the steady increase indicated in the aggregate cost tabulation.

Trends in labor costs are divided between small and large companies. Those with annual sales of less than $4 million reported decreased labor costs; companies with sales above that figure experienced increased labor costs with time. This might suggest that expanding companies can take better advantage of new technology and labor-saving devices or that larger companies demand personnel with more experience and must pay a higher wage. If we exclude the 1977 results because of probable recession-induced distortions, then profit tends to mirror the labor cost trends, increasing over time for companies smaller than $4 million annual volume and decreasing for the larger companies. It may be that smaller companies gain more from greater economies of scale than larger companies, experience lower labor costs, or receive a larger share of new markets.

In summary, three observations are made:

1. No dramatic change in cost breakdown is observed from 1968 to 1977.
2. Overhead costs are increasing over time,

regardless of company size.
3. Profit and labor cost trends mirror each other and are affected by company size. Companies with annual sales of $4 million or less have somewhat lower labor costs and greater profits than those with higher sales.

Mobile homes are offered in a wide range of prices, shapes, and qualities. In 1969 we started a very detailed analysis to determine pricing patterns for these varying products. Two basic issues are addressed: price variation with product quality and price variation with product size. First we compare units of varying qualities but identical sizes. Then we turn the approach around and compare units of varying size but otherwise identical quality. It should be noted here that manufacturers' prices are usually carefully kept secrets. However, for this project we were able to obtain from a national sample of forty-two firms the confidential dealer price lists that detail the manufacturers' FOB prices for three target years: 1969, 1973, and 1977. These lists form the primary source for nearly all the prices and thus lead to the conclusions made in this section. Although this detailed study spanned the entire period from 1969 through 1977, only the most important findings can be summarized here.

This analysis initially was performed to compare individual mobile home units from one product line to another, from one region of the United States to another, and from one year to another. For purposes of our discussion, the scope of analysis is somewhat restricted. The area considered is limited primarily to the Midwest; most statistics apply only to the Ohio-Michigan-Indiana region. For methodological reasons, doublewides

B. FOB Factory Price Analysis: Quality and Size Variations

Price and Quality

are not considered. Data sources include promotional brochures, dealer magazines, and dealer price lists giving FOB factory prices, along with floor plans and construction specifications.

This analysis has three objectives: to provide mobile home consumers with standards by which to evaluate sales price according to the type of product offered, to identify quality standards in construction, and to indicate the direction of price trends over time.

Patterns of discrete price and quality groupings were identified from the dealer price lists. Typical models for each grouping were isolated for purposes of in-depth investigation. First we defined a typical single-wide unit: a 12 foot × 60 foot, front kitchen, two-bedroom, one-bath, reverse-aisle unit. This is the unit that appeared most frequently during the years 1969 and 1973 and therefore was chosen also for 1977 (even though, of course, in the late 1970s 14-wides greatly outnumbered 12-wides in the industry's product mix). Second, manufacturers producing lines of similar quality construction were assembled and a set of construction standards for each grouping was synthesized. Price ranges were established for each standard construction model by noting the price of each unit and construction deviations (extras or substandard items).

Three distinct product categories were represented: low-line, medium-line, and high-line. Both the low-line and medium-line models were subdivided between standard and deluxe models. The deluxe models often featured raised ceilings, many windows and door accessories, or better and more carpeting—added interior furnishing "frills" rather than a real difference in construction quality. We measured quality of construction variables by increases to higher category levels (for example, low-line to medium-line). In total, this study isolated five models representing the whole spectrum of models available within the mobile home industry: standard low-line model, deluxe low-line model, standard medium-line model, deluxe medium-line model, and high-line model.

The standards for these models changed over the years. A detailed listing of the features incorporated in each model type yearly is beyond the scope of this book. Prices are the FOB dealer's factory price and include only the listed items under the standard specification sheet developed for the respective model types; additional features are included as cost options.

Price Structure

Table 6.11 shows the cost structures for 1969, 1973, and 1977. Between 1969 and 1973, we see an increase of approximately $200 in the two medium-line models. The standard low-line model has virtually the same price and the deluxe low-line model shows a price decrease. These changes are 5 percent or less and one can conclude that

Table 6.10.
Breakdown of Costs and Profit by Company Size, 1968–1977

Category/Year	Company Size (Total Sales in $Millions)			
	1–2	2–4	4–6	6–15
Materials (%)				
1968	68.60	66.66	66.74	69.10
1970			65.95	68.20
1973	64.01	65.46	67.56	66.00[a]
1977	63.50	68.01	67.36	66.45
Labor (%)				
1968	14.69	12.40	9.64	9.74
1970			9.30	9.68
1973	14.29	11.77	10.79	10.84[a]
1977	12.00	10.43	10.26	11.27
Overhead (%)				
1968	5.89	6.16	5.82	4.62
1970			7.77	4.91
1973	7.60	6.76	6.24	6.39[a]
1977	10.50	7.62	7.29	NA
Gross Profit (%)				
1968	10.86	14.78	17.80	16.54
1970			16.98	17.21
1973	14.10	16.01	15.41	16.59[a]
1977	14.00	13.94	15.09	17.26
Net Profit before Taxes (%)				
1968	3.38	5.88	8.12	9.33
1970			7.93	8.03
1973	7.07	6.29	7.27	8.03[a]
1977	7.00	3.58	5.51	6.86

a. In later years companies are broken down into smaller groups of $6–8 million, $8–10 million and $10–over $15 million. This number is the average of the three groups.

Note: All values represent mean values.

Source: "Cost and Profit Survey," *Mobile-Modular Housiug Dealer Magazine*, 1968, 1970, 1973, and 1977 (1965 survey not comparably categorized).

Table 6.11.
Price Structure, 1969, 1973, 1977

Model	Average Range		
	1969	1973	1977
Standard low-line	$3350–4050 ($3800)	$3550–3900 ($3800)	$4900–5300 ($5160)
Deluxe low-line	$3950–4300 ($4140)	$3800–4100 ($3950)	$5200–5300 ($5280)
Standard medium-line	$4600–4900 ($4720)	$4700–5250 ($4930)	$5650–6200 ($6040)
Deluxe medium-line	$5300–6500 ($5710)	$5650–6150 ($5880)	$6650–7300 ($6980)
High-line		$6400–7300 ($6730)	$7550–10600 ($7970)

FOB prices have undergone no significant changes in the 1969–1973 period. The larger price increases from 1973 to 1977 reflect not only the costs of increased government regulation but also the 12-wide's declining importance in the product mix, which leads to sporadic production accompanied by higher unit costs.

Product Comparisons

The quality of the product has moved noticeably closer to conventional housing standards. Some of this is just in surface treatment and furnishings, but there have been important changes in the framing construction and quality of insulation and paneling. Furnaces and water heaters have also increased in size and quality. The number of pieces of furniture offered in each line has decreased somewhat, but the size and quality of what is offered seems higher. The 1977 model comes with warranties and certification that it meets the federal mobile home construction and safety standards.

The clearest upgrading from 1969 and 1977 is in the sizes of the wall studs and other framing members. In 1969 all models had 2×3s as studs and plates in exterior walls and 2×2s for interior partitions. In the 1977 models the exterior walls are made with 2×4s and the interior partitions with 2×3s. In 1969 one had to buy a medium-line model to get 2×6 floor joists; in 1977 all lines use 2×6 members. Window and door framing has been similarly improved. Paneling, subflooring, and insulation also show slight improvements from 1969 to 1977.

There has been no significant increase in the number of windows with model lines. Sliding or house-type windows might now be used in place of awning windows and bay windows appear more often as a standard feature. Jalousie metal doors were not included in the 1969 low-line models but are standard in 1977.

Carpeting is much more prevalent in 1977. A 1969 medium-line home had carpeting in the living room only, with roll vinyl or linoleum elsewhere. The 1977 medium-line model has a carpeted hall and master bedroom as well as the living room. The 1977 high-line often has high-shag carpeting throughout the entire unit except for bathrooms and kitchen. Furnishings have also improved with time. Sofas in 1977 are larger. Beds are longer and more likely to have a headboard. However, the 1969 model offered more pieces of furniture—an extra chair or end table and a coffee table.

The 1969 models had oil-burning furnaces; the 1977 models offer gas, oil, or electric. In 1977, hot water heater capacities range from typically thirty gallons in the lowest lines to forty gallons in the highest lines. The difference between 1977 and 1969 is that in 1969 one had to purchase a high-line model to get a thirty-gallon hot water heater.

Figure 6.2 shows a typical sales form for a mobile home. The form gives an example of the range and kind of options available as well as the associated FOB prices. The reader will note that the particular model ordered is a doublewide home of 1344 square feet selling with optional equipment for $15,822.00 ($11.77 per square foot). This form shows how easy it is for a dealer to order with just one form (often over the phone) a totally furnished, ready-for-occupancy home.

Summary

The mobile home has undergone many quality improvements in the eight years between 1969 and 1977. Although a number of the improvements are in appliances, finishings, and furnishings, several are important structural and mechanical improvements. One sees ample evidence of a consistent trend toward more conventional construction standards. And at a time of soaring construction costs in conventional building, one cannot fail to be impressed with the mobile home industry's ability to hold the line on prices. There was actually a price decrease for some models.

Price and Size

Mobile homes are offered in many lengths, widths, and shapes with added-on configurations of various types: add-ons, tip-outs, pullouts, and so forth. In 1969 the 60-foot model was often the longest a manufacturer offered. In 1977 the 60-foot length is sometimes the shortest model offered; it is generally exceeded by 65- or 75-foot lengths. The following discussion is limited to the most common units: rectangular shapes with lengths between 50 and 75 feet and widths of 12 and 14 feet. It examines price increments as units are lengthened, widened, or doubled up.

All figures in this discussion are manufacturers' 1977 FOB prices. Comparisons are made within a single product line. Units with the same brand name and quality designation that are differentiated on dealer price lists only by size, room arrangement, and price are considered otherwise identical. Price differences are taken between two units of different sizes but identical floor plans. For instance, a 70×14 two-bedroom front kitchen model is compared to a 75×14 two-bedroom front kitchen model. If the price difference found is the same as the price difference between all 70×14 and 75×14 units when other floor plans are considered, then this is the cost of adding 5 feet of length to a 70×14 for the product line considered. Differences are calculated for all sizes available in the product line. The cost of extra rooms is calculated in a similar fashion.

Doublewide mobile homes are less susceptible to this manner of study. Instead, a rough approximation of the costs of doublewides

Figure 6.2.
Sample order form.

INDIANA HOME SYSTEMS	Series SKYLARK	
ELKHART, INDIANA	Plan No. PD-404	Date: 1/11/77
	Sales Order No. P-76-180	Salesman:

Dealer   Jane Doe
Address   303 Liberty Road
City Evanston   State Illinois
Phone 666-6490   Zip 60201
Finance Co. Evanston First Bank
Date Required A.S.A.P.   Ship By Owens Trading Co.
Retail Customer John Morgan

Serial No: 5624 P3B2   COPD-2611-126
Tag _____ To _____ So _____
Decor   Gold Contemporary
Exterior Color: Shutters   Black
Top Trim   White   Bottom Trim   White
Verticals   White Lap

Detachable Hitch: A ☒ B ☒ Special	STD	
Axles: A 2 Brake 1 Non Brake 1	STD	
B 3 Brake 2 Non Brake 1	STD	
Floor Coverings:		
Den MF-001 CBR #2 Summer Gold	56	
Hall MF-001 RBR #3 Summer Gold	44	
Bath Summer Gold FBR #1 Summer Gold	32	
L/RM #1628-17 Gold Kitchen MF-001	STD	
Dining #1628-17 Gold Other Slate Foyer	STD	
Appliance Color:		
Avocado ☐ Gold ☒ White ☐		
Stainless Steel Sink		
Refrigerator No. GE 14' 2 Door	STD	
Range: Gas ☒ Electric No. ☐ 30" Deluxe	STD	
Dishwasher No. _____		
Disposal No: _____		
Mini ☐ Stack ☐ Side by Side ☐		
Wiring for Dryer ☒ Washer Plumbing ☒	STD	
Total Electric Package		
Double Insulation ☐ Roof Only ☒ Full/House Type	65	
Fome-Cor Sidewalls ☐		
Furnace No. AGC 80		
Gas ☒ Oil ☐ Electric ☐	STD	
Water Heater No. 30 Gallon Electric		
Gas 30 ☐ Electric 30 ☒ 40 ☐	STD	
Air Conditioner No. _____		
Wire Thermostat ☐		
Bath Fixtures:		
Avocado ☐ Gold ☐ Blue ☐ White ☒		
Fiberglass Wall Tub ☒ Baths #1 & #2	STD	
Fiberglass Corner Tub ☐		
Fiberglass Shower ☐		
Double Lavs ☐		
Folding Tub Enclosure ☐		
Exhaust Fan Master Bath ☒	STD	
2nd Bath ☒ Color ☐ White/Brown Barkley Square	STD	
Exhaust Fan 2nd Bath ☒	STD	
100 AMP Service	STD	

Paneling 1/4" Natural Black Birch	STD
Kitchen Paneling Yellow Rosebud	STD
Bath Paneling Brown Barkley Square	STD
Rear Bedroom Feature	
Center Bedroom Feature	
Front Bedroom Feature	
Radio/intercom ☐	
Speaker Locations	
Bay or Bow Window No: Front ☐ Rear ☐	
Lights: Front ☐ Rear ☐ Porch ☒ 1-Std. Two	STD
Patio Door ☐	
Shutters all Around ☐ Front & Doorside	STD
Decor Kit ☐	
Special Features:	
House Type Door with Colonial Storm Door	STD
Aluminum Lap Siding/Shingle Roof/Hinged	
Overhangs	STD
STANDARD FURNISHINGS: Gold Contemporary	
(1) Sofa	245
(1) Chairs	140
( ) Loveseat	
( ) Den Chair	
(2) End Tables	90
(2) Coffee Tables	110
(2) Lamp _____ ( ) Floor Lamp	60
(1) Dinette Set w/4 Chairs Wooden	140
(1) Buffet & Hutch	STD
(3) Bar Stools 24" Gold	60
(1) 39" Beds ( ) Headboards 39" (1) Sprd	112
(2) 54" Beds ( ) Headboard 54" (2) Sprds	244
( ) Chests Loose	
( ) Chests Built In	
( ) Nightstands	
1-Bedroom Vanity Lamp	18
2-Vanity Stools	36
1-Living Room Accent Chair	75
Smoke Detectors (2)	STD
Indiana Seal H.U.D.	STD
Options:	1527
Omissions:	( )
Tag, Tip Out, Slide Out:	
Base Price: F.O.B. Elkhart, Indiana	14,295
TOTAL PRICE: $15,822.00	

relative to singlewides is presented, based on an examination of manufacturers who produced both doublewides and singlewides of the same product lines.

Price Structure

We found considerable variation in price structure among manufacturers. However, a typical price structure can be described. To the extent that higher-priced lines do not fit this scheme, the conclusions can only be applied to the lower-priced lines.

The price increments charged by a manufacturer are generally independent of the quality of his product line. Manufacturers who offer only the higher-priced lines often charge more for extra length than do manufacturers of lower-priced lines. In fact, the proportional increase for extra length roughly corresponds to the proportional increase in the price of the 14×65 unit for the higher-priced line. But the higher- and lower-priced lines of a single manufacturer almost always show identical increments for length additions; there is no correlation between the cost of added length and the quality of the product line. So, with the exception of some higher line units that cost more for added length, the generalization holds.

The price of adding length to a mobile home unit is generally constant over the spectrum of lengths and widths, provided no extra bedrooms or bathrooms are added in the process. Again the price may be greater for higher lines of other manufacturers. One might expect that adding a foot of length to a 12-wide unit would cost less than the same addition to a 14-wide because in the former case one is adding fewer square feet of area. But manufacturers charge the same in both cases—in fact, the average cost of a length addition to a 14-wide is actually less than for a 12-wide. Similarly, one might expect prices to vary for lengthening units of different initial lengths but manufacturers charge the same increments for the entire range between 60 and 75 feet, typically about $120 per foot of length. Thus a 65-foot unit costs $600 more than a 60-foot unit and a 68-foot unit costs $360 more than the 65-foot home. (Charges for lengthening 50-foot or 52-foot units do not fit the pattern. There the price is $30 to $60 per foot of length.)

The price charged for widening a 12-foot unit to 14 feet is likewise constant over the spectrum of lengths—again, provided no additional rooms are added. The generalization in this case holds true over all quality lines among almost all manufacturers. A 14-wide typically costs $750 more than the corresponding 12-wide. One might expect the price difference between a 60×12 and a 60×14 to be less than the difference between the 70×12 and 70×14 units; in the former case one is adding 112 square feet, versus 132 square feet in the latter. But

the $750 figure is roughly the same in both cases and it applies to all lengths between 60 and 70 feet.

Per-Square-Foot Comparisons

Price per square foot can serve as a measure of price versus size efficiency. Starting with a typical low-priced product line with the 65×14 unit priced at $6,400, the prices of other size units can be reconstructed using the typical incremental prices from the previous analysis. (It must be noted here that the manufacturer's designation of a length includes a 4-foot trailer hitch. Thus all lengths must be reduced by 4 when areas are calculated. A 70×14 unit is actually 66×14 and has an area of 924 square feet.) Prices for 14×65, 14×70, and 14×75 units are $6,400, $7,000, and $7,600, respectively. Their respective costs per square foot are $7,49, $7.58, and $7.65. Costs for 50×12 or 52×12 units are about $4,590. Thus per-square-foot costs rise continuously as length increases in the 60- to 70-foot range and also rise as length decreases at the 50-foot end of the spectrum. The 14×65 unit has the lowest price per square foot. Thus we can designate this model as the most economical. The most efficient way to get a unit larger than the 14×65 is to look for width rather than length. The 12×70 and 14×60 units might illustrate this point. They both provide roughly the same area (792 versus 784 square feet), but the 14-wide unit costs $7.52 versus $7.56 per square foot for the 12-wide.

Utilities, bathrooms, and kitchens are the most expensive components of a home. Thus one might reasonably expect square foot costs to decrease if floor area increases because these high-cost items become a smaller percentage of the total floor area. Our findings indicate that this may be true for units smaller than the 14×65 unit, but larger sizes tend to cost more per square foot.

As a final point, one would expect a 60×24 doublewide home to cost less per square foot than a 60×12 singlewide home. This is not true. In three out of four cases the price for a doublewide was actually higher than the price for two corresponding singlewides.

Summary

Five generalizations can be made about mobile home prices:

1. The 65×14 is the most economical unit. Larger units cost more per square foot.
2. Additional space in a high-line unit costs little more than additional space in a low-line unit, that is, incremental charges are independent of the product's base price.
3. One gets more space for less money by widening rather than lengthening the unit.
4. Price differences are not proportional to the amount of area added; rather they are

based on the amount of added dimension in each direction independently—typically $120 for 1 foot of added length and $750 for 2 feet of added width.

5. Doublewides cost as much per square foot as singlewides.

C. Policy Alternatives

Three characteristics of the mobile home industry are important determinants of the industry's cost and price performance. First, analysis of production costs indicates an emphasis on maintaining low fixed costs. The industry's strength relative to other elements of the total housing production system is partly based upon its increased use of capital-intensive means of production, so this emphasis on low fixed costs would appear to be a contradiction. However, several considerations explain this strategy.

In part, the industry is able to operate with low fixed costs by indirectly "renting" capital equipment from its suppliers. As detailed in chapter 13, on "Supply Sector Influence" manufacturers tend to rely upon suppliers for research and for production of more capital-intensive subassemblies. The mobile home manufacturer therefore "rents" capital equipment to produce these sub-assemblies, and a portion of their price represents the "rent" payments for the equipment. In this way the manufacturer can maintain flexibility in cash flow and reasonably high rates of capital usage without incurring a heavy debt burden. The total cost of production is presumably higher under this arrangement because the supplier will be compensated for maintaining capital equipment during slack periods, but manufacturers apparently find this additional cost justifiable as an alternative to the carrying cost of idle capital stocks.

Strong cyclical fluctuations in demand also dictate low fixed cost operations. Although the process of "renting" capital equipment permits some adjustment, it is likely that the level of capitalization, and therefore of fixed costs including "rented" equipment, is lower than would be expected if manufacturers were able to produce at reasonably constant levels. In comparison with conventional building producers, the mobile home manufacturer has a higher fixed cost exposure during cyclic downswings, but the extent of this exposure is minimized.

Second, there is no major explanatory factor associated with variations in cost structure among firms. This finding supports a hypothesis that the industry is competitive at the regional market level and that individual manufacturers in these markets are effective in altering the production and delivery process in response to local conditions. Such adaptation is highly efficient from a social welfare viewpoint and should be encouraged.

Finally, it is possible to conclude that the industry tends to adapt its product mix toward units that compete directly with conventional housing units. There is some evidence that as units increase in size, the cost of production decreases and FOB price increases. This is expected because manufacturers will presumably move toward more profitable areas of operation. There is some danger that as mobile home manufacturers continue to approach direct competition with conventional builders, some of their natural advantage may be diminished. However, the increased competition for both mobile home manufacturers and conventional builders will not only have favorable social benefits but will also stimulate greater efficiency in the building sector at large.

A caveat is important. The overriding observation is that the production system's cost performance is in large part explained by the effective interaction between the production function and forces operating in the industry's supporting and regulatory environments. The industry will not be able to compete successfully against conventional builders on their turf unless this important interaction with the entire industry environment is further developed.

Part II

**The Mobile
Home
Distribution
System**

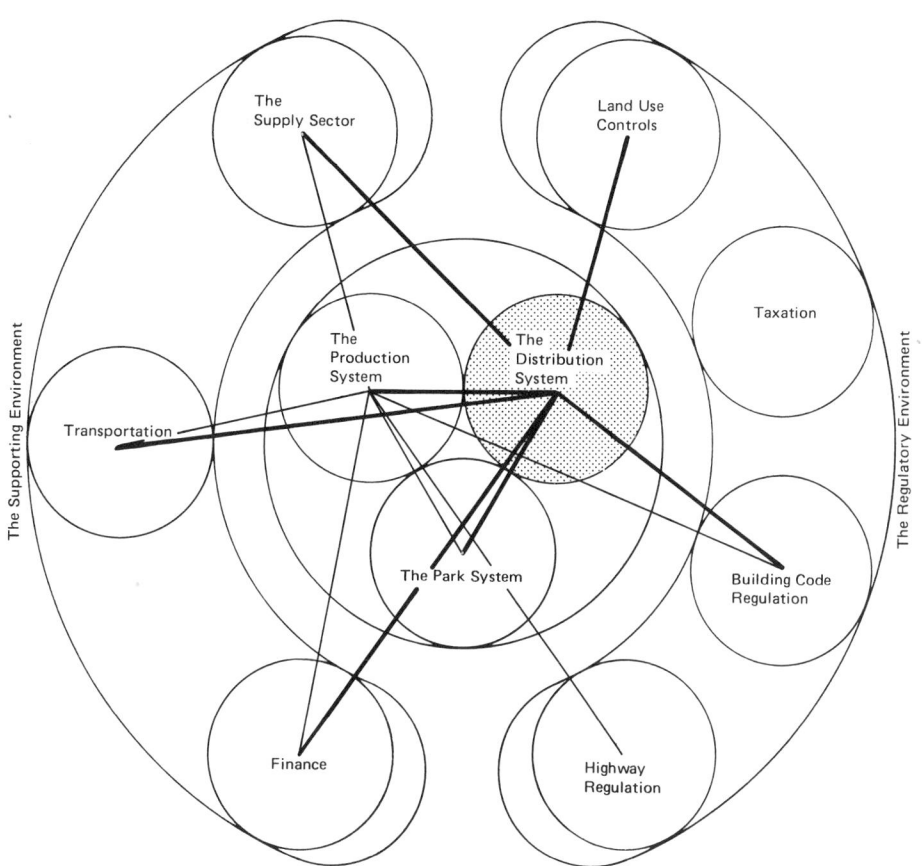

Chapter 7

Industrial Organization of the Distribution System

A. Evolution
Origins of the Mobile Home Distribution System

The ancestor of the contemporary mobile home, the "trailer" (or "trailer coach") of the 1920s and 1930s, was distributed by automobile dealers. By the early 1950s trailers had developed into two distinct products, mobile homes and recreational vehicles, and their distribution system had become distinct from that of the auto industry. In the late 1950s both mobile homes and recreational vehicles generally were still sold through the same dealer network. However, specialization soon developed between mobile home and recreational vehicle dealers. Today the two distribution systems have become independent networks, although still overlapping to a certain extent, with more than a quarter of all dealers selling both products.

Historically, the mobile home distribution system developed independently from the distribution systems of other forms of manufactured shelter (such as packaged and modular housing). These were introduced as improvements on the traditional methods of on-site residential construction, whereas mobile homes emerged as alternatives to on-site construction. The distribution of "nonmobile," factory-built housing relies largely on local builder-dealers who are involved in both on-site erection and "retail" sale of the finished product.

Background of Owners and Managers

The entrepreneurial talent in the mobile home distribution system comes from various fields, most of which are related to the system through both functional and historical development patterns. This can be observed from the results of the PMHI Dealer Survey (PMHI/DS), which dealt with the background of dealers. Roughly one-third (32.9 percent) of all dealers who responded to the questionnaire came from either the recreational vehicle or auto dealer industry. This is largely the result of three factors. First, the structures of these sectors of origin are similar to the mobile home distribution system's present-day organization. Second, both product and sales techniques in the three industries are similar. Third, the organizations distributing mobile homes and recreational vehicles overlap. These factors make it possible for managerial talent to move among the industries in response to public demand and subsequent industrial need.

Another 41.4 percent of all respondents to the PMHI/DS came from other subsystems of the mobile home industry: 7.1 percent from mobile home manufacturing and 34.3 percent from the park system. The know-how requirements of these systems, although different from those of mobile home dealerships, are nevertheless relevant to the distribution system. We found that 18.5 percent of the dealers were in either real estate or land development before entering the mobile home distribution system, which represents a movement of managerial talent from the broadly

defined housing sector to mobile home distribution. Again, a functional affinity can be detected here.

In total, almost three-fourths (74.3 percent) of all dealers began in either the mobile home industry or in one of the industries closely related to it; 59.9 percent of the dealer population had their origins in or related to the housing sector. Thus we found that the mobile home distribution system largely draws its managerial talent either from the housing industry itself or from closely related fields, leading to a more efficient distribution system composed primarily of dealers with relevant experience.

The following statistical overview of the retail sales volume of the mobile home industry on a national and regional basis will be complemented later in this chapter by a detailed analysis and explanation of these figures dealing with particular aspects of the industrial organization of the mobile home distribution network.

National Distribution Volume
Table 7.1 lists mobile home retail sales and the number of units shipped for the period from 1947 to 1977. Although the shipments and retail sales have shown a strong overall growth trend, the record has not been consistent. Factors exogenous to the industry, such as the decline in general economic activity in 1969 and in 1973–1975, as well as endogenous factors, such as product design changes, have played an important role in the fluctuations in shipments and retail sales.

Table 7.2 shows that between 1947 and 1977 the general direction of fluctuations in both sales and quantity of shipments was the same. A deviation from these concomitant trends occurred between 1952 and 1954, when units shipped decreased substantially while retail sales increased slightly. At that time the postwar housing shortage was alleviated to the extent that consumers began to shy away from the mobile homes, which then were still largely produced without bathrooms. Manufacturers responded to the decline in shipments by adding bathrooms as standard equipment and by adding floor space; this caused a rise in unit price and the overall slight increase in retail sales. A similar deviation occurred between 1972 and 1973. However, the number of units shipped is biased downward because it includes double-wides, which had captured a significant share of the market. The tables also exclude the number of units shipped to the government and for export, which had also been increasing.

Regional Distribution Volume
The regional distribution of shipments to dealers is shown in tables 7.3 and 7.4, which give the volume of shipments received by dealers and the relative regional growth

Distribution Volume

Table 7.1.
Annual U.S. Mobile
Home Shipments to
Dealers and Retail
Sales, 1947–1977

Year	Units Shipped	Retail Sales (Thousands $)
1947	60,000	146,000
1948	85,500	204,000
1949	46,200	122,000
1950	63,100	216,000
1951	67,300	248,000
1952	83,000	320,000
1953	76,900	322,000
1954	76,000	325,000
1955	111,900	462,000
1956	124,330	622,000
1957	119,300	596,000
1958	102,000	510,000
1959	120,500	602,000
1960	103,700	518,000
1961	90,200	505,000
1962	118,000	661,000
1963	150,840	862,064
1964	191,320	1,071,392
1965	216,470	1,212,232
1966	217,300	1,238,610
1967	240,360	1,370,052
1968	317,950	1,907,700
1969	412,690	2,496,775
1970	401,190	2,451,271
1971	496,570	3,297,225
1972	575,940	4,002,783
1973	566,920	4,406,382
1974	329,300	3,213,681
1975	212,690	2,432,661
1976	246,120	3,136,616
1977	265,145	4,030,000

Source: Compiled from data supplied by the
Manufactured Housing Institute.

Table 7.2.
Change in Mobile
Home Shipments
Received by Dealers,
1947–1977

Year	% Change Units Received	% Change Retail Sales
1948 change from 1947	+42.5%	+39.7%
1949 change from 1948	−46.0%	−40.2%
1950 change from 1949	+36.6%	+77.0%
1951 change from 1950	+ 6.7%	+14.8%
1952 change from 1951	+23.3%	+29.0%
1953 change from 1952	− 7.3%	+ 0.6%
1954 change from 1953	− 1.2%	+ 0.9%
1955 change from 1954	+47.2%	+42.2%
1956 change from 1955	+11.1%	+34.6%
1957 change from 1956	− 4.0%	− 4.2%
1958 change from 1957	−14.5%	−14.4%
1959 change from 1958	+18.1%	+18.0%
1960 change from 1959	−13.9%	−14.0%
1961 change from 1960	−13.0%	− 2.5%
1962 change from 1961	+30.8%	+30.9%
1963 change from 1962	+27.8%	+30.4%
1964 change from 1963	+26.8%	+24.3%
1965 change from 1964	+13.1%	+13.1%
1966 change from 1965	+ 0.4%	+ 2.2%
1967 change from 1966	+10.6%	+10.6%
1968 change from 1967	+32.3%	+39.2%
1969 change from 1968	+29.8%	+30.9%
1970 change from 1969	− 2.8%	− 1.8%
1971 change from 1970	+23.8%	+34.5%
1972 change from 1971	+16.0%	+21.4%
1973 change from 1972	− 1.6%	+10.1%
1974 change from 1973	−41.9%	−27.1%
1975 change from 1974	−35.4%	−24.3%
1976 change from 1975	+15.7%	+28.9%
1977 change from 1976	+ 7.7%	+28.5%

Source: Compiled from data supplied by the
Manufactured Housing Institute.

Table 7.3.
Shipments to Dealers,
1967–1977, by Region

New England

	Shipments Received	Total % of Shipments
1967	7,839	3
1968	9,600	3
1969	11,814	3
1970	11,148	3
1971	10,915	2
1972	10,954	2
1973	10,669	2
1974	6,385	2
1975	1,882	2
1976	2,438	2
1977	2,383	2

Middle Atlantic

	Shipments Received	Total % of Shipments
1967	22,890	10
1968	28,926	9
1969	36,080	9
1970	32,783	8
1971	36,368	7
1972	46,152	7
1973	45,889	7
1974	24,402	6
1975	7,827	7
1976	8,932	7
1977	7,902	6

South Atlantic

	Shipments Received	Total % of Shipments
1967	58,929	25
1968	90,740	28
1969	111,003	27
1970	114,443	28
1971	138,590	28
1972	175,720	28
1973	176,624	29
1974	110,476	28
1975	23,507	21
1976	28,300	22
1977	29,970	21

West North Central

	Shipments Received	Total % of Shipments
1967	22,677	10
1968	27,910	9
1969	34,157	8
1970	33,135	8
1971	40,492	8
1972	50,881	8
1973	48,398	8
1974	37,338	9
1975	11,760	11
1976	14,380	11
1977	13,638	10

East North Central

	Shipments Received	Total % of Shipments
1967	38,275	16
1968	48,093	15
1969	65,669	16
1970	65,012	16
1971	69,926	14
1972	74,021	12
1973	80,436	13
1974	47,971	12
1975	12,004	11
1976	13,946	11
1977	15,487	11

West South Central

	Shipments Received	Total % of Shipments
1967	24,494	11
1968	33,164	10
1969	44,103	11
1970	50,228	12
1971	61,678	12
1972	87,205	14
1973	76,563	12
1974	45,976	12
1975	16,274	15
1976	20,337	16
1977	22,220	16

East South Central

	Shipments Received	Total % of Shipments
1967	20,548	9
1968	27,854	9
1969	33,701	8
1970	33,163	8
1971	51,403	10
1972	68,430	11
1973	70,574	11
1974	43,957	11
1975	9,283	8
1976	10,331	8
1977	10,609	7

Pacific

	Shipments Received	Total % of Shipments
1967	21,324	9
1968	39,289	12
1969	45,601	11
1970	38,807	9
1971	50,971	10
1972	54,938	9
1973	56,828	9
1974	44,177	11
1975	17,673	16
1976	18,669	14
1977	23,560	17

Mountain

	Shipments Received	Total % of Shipments
1967	15,261	7
1968	21,883	7
1969	29,041	7
1970	32,632	8
1971	43,564	9
1972	53,181	9
1973	52,721	9
1974	35,127	9
1975	10,566	10
1976	12,092	9
1977	16,220	11

Source: Computed by PMHI from ten years of back issues of "A Marketing Review of Monthly Mobile Home Shipments,"
published by *Mobile-Modular Housing Dealer Magazine*, Chicago, Illinois, 1967–1977.

Table 7.4.
Regional Distribution
of Shipments to Dealers,
1967/1977 Averages,
Ranked in Decreasing
Order of Importance

Region	Shipments Received as % of Total Shipments	Cumulative %
South Atlantic	27.11	27.11
East North Central	13.60	40.71
West South Central	12.35	53.06
Pacific	10.55	63.61
East South Central	9.73	73.34
West North Central	8.57	81.91
Mountain	8.25	90.16
Mid-Atlantic	7.64	97.80
New England	2.20	100.00
Total	100.00	

Source: Table 7.3.

patterns. These figures show that half the shipments to dealers are concentrated in three regions: South Atlantic, East North Central, and West South Central. During the last ten years the shares of shipment distribution in the South Atlantic, West South Central, East South Central, and Mountain regions have slightly risen while the shares in the other regions have fallen. This trend could be fostered by population shifts to areas of economic growth and favorable climate as well as by public regulatory attitude toward mobile homes and availability of land for use as park space.

Emerging Trends
In 1974 the recession had a severe impact on the mobile home industry as the national volume of unit shipments was curtailed by nearly 60 percent from its 1972 mark. However, pre- and post-1974 conditions indicate that no substantial endogenous problems (on a national or regional basis) limited either the production capabilities of the industry or the establishment of new dealerships. Demand for mobile homes will increase as the quality of the unit improves, attitudes toward mobile homes change, and prices of alternative forms of housing increase. This demand will be met by a distribution system well located throughout the nation and operated by dealers who have had previous experience within this or related industries' distribution systems. Present trends indicate that national shipment volume will increase but that interregional differences will become more accentuated. The population move to the sunbelt and western states, as well as the greater amount of available space for parks, should result in continued expansion of both the production and distribution systems in these areas.

Outlet Distribution
As of 1977, there were 12,815 distribution outlets for mobile homes and recreational vehicles in the United States. PMHI estimates the following breakdown of the dealerships: 6886 sell only mobile homes, 2436 sell only recreational vehicles, and 3493 sell both products. Table 7.5 shows the structural breakdown of the dealerships among these three categories between 1970, the earliest year for which such information is available, and 1977.

From 1970 to 1974 the number of dealerships selling only mobile homes as well as the number of dealers selling both products had increased and the number of dealers selling only recreational vehicles had decreased. After 1974 all categories show a severe cut in the number of distribution outlets. The number of outlets selling mobile homes only and selling both mobile homes and recreational vehicles declined about 23 percent between 1974 and 1977. The overall decline in the number of new dealerships selling both mobile homes and recreational vehicles after the dramatic rise between 1971 and 1972 may be due to the fact that joint outlets became relatively unprofitable. This could be caused by two factors: an increase in various services required by each product, which can best be supplied by specialized outlets, and, more important, the decline in the demand for recreational vehicles with the onset of the fuel shortage in late 1973 and the higher fuel prices that followed. The regional breakdown of dealerships according to category (table 7.6) brings to light change patterns that are lost in the national figures.

Table 7.7 highlights the same kind of interregional differentials in mobile home distribution outlets as we had found in shipments. The demand and supply forces that determine shifts in the regional shipment volumes also affect the regional distribution of outlets. The southern regions are clearly increasing their share of the national number of outlets, which parallels the South's increasing share of national volume of shipments.

Specialization Patterns
Throughout the late 1960s and 1970s there has been a continued separation of the distribution networks for mobile homes and recreational vehicles. Table 7.8 shows the trend in specialization patterns by expressing the number of mobile home-only outlets as a percentage of all outlets selling either mobile homes or both mobile homes and recreational vehicles. On a national level the sharp decrease in specialization from 1970 to 1973 corresponds to the increase in dealerships selling both mobile homes and recreational vehicles during this period. However, with the decrease in joint outlets after 1973, specialization increased and has remained at roughly the same level since 1974. This same trend has been evident across all regions.

Table 7.5.
National Distribution of Outlets Selling Mobile Homes Only, Recreational Vehicles Only, and Both Mobile Homes and Recreational Vehicles, 1970–1977

Year	Total Number of Outlets	Mobile Homes Only	Recreational Vehicles Only	Both Mobile Homes and Rec. Vehicles
1970	12,743	6,253	4,401	2,089
1971	14,204	6,915	4,963	2,326
1972	14,808	7,505	3,034	4,269
1973	15,961	8,376	3,063	4,522
1974	16,511	9,122	2,997	4,392
1975	14,394	7,919	2,669	3,806
1976	13,441	7,306	2,545	3,590
1977	12,815	6,886	2,436	3,493

Source: Compiled by PMHI from *The Directory of Mobile Home and Recreational Vehicle Dealers in the United States and Canada*, published by Automotive Credit Service, New York, 1970–1977 issues.

Table 7.6.
Regional Distribution of Mobile Home and Recreational Vehicle Dealers in the United States, 1970–1977

Region	Total Number of Dealers								Mobile Home Dealers Only							
	1970	1971	1972	1973	1974	1975	1976	1977	1970	1971	1972	1973	1974	1975	1976	1977
New England	548	604	595	610	606	550	529	510	254	269	245	249	262	236	231	225
Middle Atlantic	1559	1680	1688	1768	1833	1691	1659	1624	687	699	843	911	995	917	894	864
East North Central	2995	3262	3284	3377	3394	3032	2865	2812	1409	1510	1591	1691	1768	1598	1489	1458
West North Central	1202	1411	1404	1499	1550	1357	1278	1243	622	723	669	768	824	732	696	666
South Atlantic	2427	2714	2835	3183	3283	2851	2606	2404	1246	1380	1800	2049	2182	1875	1690	1544
East South Central	945	1057	1080	1188	1396	1208	1124	1035	460	530	646	740	939	819	751	692
West South Central	1055	1252	1395	1418	1572	1299	1181	1109	533	626	759	782	925	731	670	618
Mountain	750	796	946	1137	1147	969	905	849	411	437	345	468	501	427	381	342
Pacific	1262	1428	1581	1781	1730	1437	1294	1229	631	741	607	718	726	584	504	477
Total	12743	14204	14808	15961	16511	14394	13441	12815	6253	6915	7505	8376	9122	7919	7306	6886

Region	Recreational Vehicle Dealers Only								Mobile Home and Recreational Dealers							
	1970	1971	1972	1973	1974	1975	1976	1977	1970	1971	1972	1973	1974	1975	1976	1977
New England	181	200	183	187	176	161	157	148	113	135	167	174	168	153	141	137
Middle Atlantic	568	632	457	454	447	412	404	402	304	349	388	403	391	362	361	358
East North Central	968	1095	828	798	780	700	654	627	618	657	865	888	846	734	722	727
West North Central	416	498	230	232	233	204	200	193	164	190	505	499	493	421	382	384
South Atlantic	958	1072	362	375	370	339	333	309	223	262	673	759	731	637	583	551
East South Central	399	430	139	153	151	133	117	107	86	97	295	295	306	256	256	236
West South Central	374	440	255	252	256	213	202	182	148	186	381	384	391	355	309	309
Mountain	200	219	158	158	153	133	129	126	139	140	443	511	493	409	395	381
Pacific	337	377	422	454	431	374	349	342	294	310	552	609	573	479	441	410
Total	4401	4963	3034	3063	2997	2669	2545	2436	2089	2326	4269	4522	4392	3806	3590	3493

Source: Compiled by PMHI from *The Directory of Mobile Home and Recreational Vehicles in the United States and Canada*, published by Automotive Credit Service, New York, 1970–1977 issues.

Table 7.7.
Percentage Distribution of Dealerships Selling Mobile Homes Only and Dealerships Selling Both Mobile Homes and Recreational Vehicles, on a Regional Basis, 1970–1977

Region	Mobile Home Dealers Only							
	1970	1971	1972	1973	1974	1975	1976	1977
New England	4.1%	3.9%	3.3%	3.0%	2.9%	3.0%	3.2%	3.3%
Middle Atlantic	11.0	10.1	11.2	10.9	10.9	11.6	12.2	12.5
East North Central	22.5	21.8	21.2	20.2	19.4	20.2	20.4	21.2
West North Central	9.9	10.5	8.9	9.2	9.0	9.2	9.5	9.7
South Atlantic	19.9	20.0	24.0	24.5	24.0	23.7	23.1	22.4
East South Central	7.4	7.7	8.6	8.8	10.3	10.3	10.3	10.0
West South Central	8.5	9.1	10.1	9.3	10.1	9.2	9.2	9.0
Mountain	6.6	6.3	4.6	5.6	5.5	5.4	5.2	5.0
Pacific	10.1	10.7	8.1	8.6	8.0	7.4	6.9	6.9

Region	Recreational Vehicle Dealers Only								Mobile Home and Recreational Vehicles Dealers							
	1970	1971	1972	1973	1974	1975	1976	1977	1970	1971	1972	1973	1974	1975	1976	1977
New England	4.1%	4.0%	6.0%	6.1%	5.9%	6.0%	6.2%	6.1%	5.4%	5.8%	3.9%	3.8%	3.8%	4.0%	3.9%	3.9%
Middle Atlantic	12.9	12.7	15.1	14.8	14.9	15.4	15.9	16.5	14.6	15.0	9.1	8.9	8.9	9.5	10.1	10.2
East North Central	22.0	22.1	27.3	26.0	26.0	26.2	25.7	25.7	29.6	28.2	20.3	19.6	19.3	19.3	20.1	20.8
West North Central	9.5	10.0	7.6	7.6	7.8	7.6	7.9	7.9	7.9	8.2	11.8	11.0	11.2	11.1	10.6	11.0
South Atlantic	21.8	21.6	11.9	12.2	12.3	12.7	13.1	12.7	10.7	11.3	15.8	16.8	16.6	16.7	16.2	15.8
East South Central	9.1	8.7	4.6	5.0	5.0	5.0	4.6	4.4	4.1	4.2	6.9	6.5	7.0	6.7	7.1	6.8
West South Central	8.5	8.9	8.4	8.2	8.5	8.0	7.9	7.5	7.1	8.0	8.9	8.5	8.9	9.3	8.6	8.8
Mountain	4.5	4.4	5.2	5.2	5.1	5.0	5.1	5.2	6.7	6.0	10.4	11.3	11.2	10.7	11.0	10.9
Pacific	7.7	7.6	13.9	14.8	14.4	14.0	13.7	14.0	14.1	13.3	12.9	13.5	13.0	12.6	12.3	11.7

Source: Compiled by PMHI from *The Directory of Mobile Homes and Recreational Vehicles in the United States and Canada,* published by Automotive Credit Service, New York, New York, 1970–1977 issues.

Table 7.8.
Specialization Patterns:
Mobile-Home-Only
Outlets as a Percentage
of All Outlets Selling
Either Mobile Homes
Only or Selling Mobile
Homes and Recrea-
tional Vehicles

Region	1970	1971	1972	1973	1974	1975	1976	1977
New England	69.2	66.6	59.5	58.9	60.9	60.7	62.1	62.2
Mid-Atlantic	69.3	66.7	68.5	69.3	71.8	71.7	71.2	70.7
East North Central	69.5	69.7	64.8	65.6	67.6	68.5	67.3	66.7
West North Central	79.1	79.2	60.0	60.6	62.6	63.5	64.6	63.4
South Atlantic	84.8	84.0	72.8	73.0	74.9	74.6	74.4	73.7
East South Central	84.2	84.5	68.7	71.5	75.4	76.2	74.6	74.6
West South Central	78.3	77.1	66.6	67.1	70.3	67.3	68.4	66.7
Mountain	74.7	75.7	43.8	47.8	50.4	51.1	49.1	47.3
Pacific	68.2	70.5	52.4	54.1	55.9	54.9	53.3	53.8
Total	75.0	74.8	63.7	64.9	67.5	67.5	67.1	66.3

Source: Table 7.6.

It is significant that the mobile home distribution system has maintained a relatively high degree of specialization throughout the past decade. This trend is indicative of the specialization in both marketing and maintenance required to operate a mobile home dealership profitably; with the increased sophistication of the product, we expect this trend to increase.

Concentration

The distribution system exhibits virtually no national economic concentration. In the late 1970s the distribution system's structure is characterized by single-outlet firms: 90 percent of all firms operate one lot only. Approximately 5 percent are largely two- and some three-lot operations. One percent of all firms control between four and ten establishments and a handful of firms operate between eleven and twenty-five lots each. At most, five to ten firms control up to fifty lots each. The largest chain has fewer than one hundred outlets.

Of course, national data are misleading: Mobile home distribution is typically a local business and even the very largest retailer's operations do not extend beyond a regional scale. Table 7.9 gauges economic concentration by giving the share of total regional sales volume as well as retail outlets captured by some of the largest firms in their respective areas of operation. The table clearly indicates that concentration is very low, with the percentage of sales in the region covered by the largest firm only 6.5 percent and the percentage of outlets in most states operated by that firm well below 10 percent. Significantly, the table also reveals the operational scope of the largest firms in the business—the South East. These firms have been operating in this region since the late 1960s; compared to the northern markets, the mobile home business in this region is young and rapid growth has made it a business environment conducive to retail chain formations.

Low concentration is shown even when the three companies profiled in table 7.9 are viewed in aggregate. Table 7.10 gives the share of all mobile home-only outlets accounted for by these three firms in the states in which at least two of them operate. With the exception of North and South Carolina, the concentration ratios remain low.

Most of the giants in the distribution system have been affected by the 1974 recession. The number of outlets controlled by the largest retail chain dropped from nearly 300 in 1973 to 83 in 1977. In addition, the average number of homes sold per lot has declined significantly during this four-year period. The second firm profiled in table 7.9 experienced a similar fate: Its number of outlets dropped from 136 (unit retail sales volume of 8101) to 47 in 1977 (unit retail sales volume of 2695). The decline rates of the largest retailers roughly correspond to the overall decline of the national number of mobile home retail outlets as well as national retail sales volume; thus, from the boom days through the subsequent recession, the low degree of economic concentration in the distribution system has persisted.

Integration

In the mobile home distribution system, integration typically takes one of the following three forms:
1. Integration between the agents in the distribution and production systems (dealers and manufacturers)
2. Integration between the agents in the distribution and park systems (dealers and park owners)
3. Integration between agents in the distribution system and in its supporting environment (dealers and lenders)

Table 7.9.
Indications of Economic Concentration in the Mobile Home Distribution System

States in Which Firm Operates	Total Number of MH-Only Outlets in State	Number of MH Outlets Operated by Firm	% of MH Outlets in State Operated by Firm	Total Unit Shipment Volume to All States	Total Unit Sales in All States by Firm	% of All Unit Sales in All States Accounted for by Firms
The Largest Retailer of Mobile Homes in the U.S., 1977:						
Alabama	126	7	5.6			
Florida	335	18	5.4			
Georgia	150	8	5.3			
Louisiana	77	6	7.8			
Mississippi	65	2	3.1	50162	3240	6.5%
North Carolina	202	20	9.9			
South Carolina	101	12	11.9			
Tennessee	137	2	1.5			
Texas	206	8	3.9			
Virginia	108	4	3.7			
West Virginia	89	4	4.5			
One of the Largest Retailers of Mobile Homes in the U.S., 1977:						
Alabama	335	7	2.1			
Georgia	150	16	10.7			
Louisiana	77	1	1.3			
Mississippi	65	3	4.6	37512	2695	7.2%
North Carolina	202	9	4.5			
South Carolina	101	9	8.9			
Tennessee	137	1	.7			
Texas	206	1	.5			
One of the Largest Retailers of Mobile Homes in the U.S., 1977:						
North Carolina	202	13	6.4			
South Carolina	101	3	3.0			
Tennessee	137	3	2.2	17494	1317	7.5%
Virginia	108	9	8.3			
West Virginia	89	6	6.7			

Source: Compiled by PMHI from various sources.

Table 7.10.
Indications of Impact of Three Large Retailers in One Region

States in Which at Least Two of the Three Firms from Table 7.9 Operate	Total Number of MH-Only Outlets in State	Total Number of Outlets Operated by the Three Firms	% of MH-Only Outlets Accounted for by the Three Firms
Alabama	126	14	11.0%
Georgia	150	24	16.0%
Louisiana	77	7	9.1%
Mississippi	65	5	7.7%
North Carolina	202	42	20.1%
South Carolina	101	24	23.8%
Tennessee	137	6	4.4%
Texas	206	9	4.4%
Virginia	108	13	12.0%
West Virginia	89	10	11.0%

Source: Compiled by PMHI from various sources.

Integration of Dealers into the Production System

In the PMHI Dealer Survey (PMHI/DS), 6 percent of the respondents stated that they were involved in manufacturing. The small figure can be explained by the different requirements of the two sectors, especially in terms of capital needs, technology, and know-how. A main drawback is that dealers' financial capabilities are limited, but there are other problems as well. It is difficult for a single dealer or a small-sized chain to absorb all of the output from its manufacturing operation without losing sales to dealers with a more diversified product line. The alternative of supplying other dealers as well gives the integrating dealership the opportunity to maintain a diversified brand mix itself; this alternative, however, has often proven an illusion because competing dealers are quick to boycott the integrating rival's plant.

Integration of Dealers into the Park System

Of the respondents to the PMHI/DS, 62.7 percent stated that they were involved in park operations and another 5.9 percent planned to enter the field; 34 percent were involved in park development and another 12 percent planned to enter that field. This implies that a high percentage of dealers start from scratch when entering park operations rather than buy their way into the system. Although there are differences in know-how required for sales and park operations, these are not enough to be prohibitive. In localities where park space is scarce, integration of this type gives dealers the often all-important additional leverage with respect to the consumer because of their ability to supply the "other part" of the product, the park site. In addition, a small dealer obtains a useful income supplement from parks that, unlike sales revenue, is not subject to seasonal fluctuations.

Integration of Dealers into Consumer Financing

Only 14 percent of the PMHI/DS respondents stated that they were also involved in consumer financing. The reason for this relatively low degree of integration may be that the degree of financial acumen required in consumer financing is not available to most dealers. There are also critical differences in skill requirements. Integrating into consumer financing may be advantageous only to the larger dealer with a high sales volume because the small dealer does not have access to sufficient capital to bear the risk of consumer finance. A small dealer may find it more profitable, in terms of cost and effort required, to work out an informal relationship with an independent lender.

Emerging Trends

No respondents to PMHI/DS indicated plans to move into manufacturing, which is not surprising considering the factors we discussed above. Slightly less than 6 percent of the responding dealers indicated plans to move into park operations. Again not surprisingly, none of the dealers indicated plans to integrate into consumer financing. The relatively small percentage of planned integration moves may indicate that integration initiated from the distribution system may be slowing down.

The decline in shipments to dealers partially resulting from the 1974 recession may have led to a short-term retrenchment in the industry. Because of the changes in the economy in 1973–1974, it is likely that most of the plans for integration have not yet been realized. However, given the gradual growth of the industry since 1975, integration of the distribution and park systems can be expected to continue. The growth in competition and product differentiation will lead dealers to increase the number and kinds of services provided; provision of park space will remain a crucial competitive advantage.

Diversification

In the PMHI/DS, diversification indirectly related and unrelated to the mobile home industry covers 96 percent of all responses concerning diversification. The remaining 4 percent indicated that their diversification activities were in other directions.

Diversification into Activities Indirectly Related to the Mobile Home Industry

Of the respondents to PMHI/DS, 16 percent indicated that they were diversified into recreational vehicle dealerships; 2 percent indicated that they planned to move in this direction. Diversification into recreational vehicles may be due either to industry origin of the dealer (relevant know-how) or to factors related to sales performance.

Table 7.11 gives the industry origins of dealers presently working with both mobile

Table 7.11.
Diversification from the Mobile Home Distribution System into Recreational Vehicle Dealerships, According to Industry Origins of Dealer

Industry Origins	Not in, No Plans to Enter	Now in	Plan to Enter	Total
Recreational vehicle dealers	60% (6%[a])	40% (4%)	0 –	100%
Industry related to mobile home industry	80.8% (42%)	15.4% (8%)	3.8% (2%)	100%
Other	89.5% (34%)	10.5% (4%)	0 –	100%
Total[a]	82%	16%	2%	

a Figures in parentheses represent percentages of all PMHI/DS repondents.

Source: PMHI/DS.

homes and recreational vehicles and shows their present relationship to the recreational vehicle industry. This table reveals that the industry background of the owner-manager does not play a part in the present relationship of the dealer to the recreational vehicle industry: Only 40 percent of all dealers who started in recreational vehicles are still involved in this area, and they make up only one-quarter of the dealers who are presently involved in recreational vehicles. Half of the dealers who diversified into recreational vehicles originated within the mobile home distribution system itself; another quarter of the dealers began in other areas. Know-how requirements do not seem to present a barrier for diversification from mobile home into recreational vehicle dealerships.

Financial success in mobile home distribution could also lead dealers to diversify into recreational vehicles. Sales volume is taken here as a crude indicator of probable financially successful performance. The responses to PMHI/DS indicate that 31.3 percent of the dealers who have annual sales of more than $1 million are in recreational vehicles. This group also comprises 71.4 percent of all respondents who are presently involved with recreational vehicles. The only dealers planning to diversify into recreational vehicles had annual sales above $1 million (table 7.12). The PMHI/DS responses lead us to believe that diversification into the recreational vehicle industry seems to be more a function of sales factors and size than of know-how.

Diversification into Activities Unrelated to the Mobile Home Industry

Diversification into activities unrelated to the mobile home industry includes movements into distribution of building supplies, distribution of factory-produced nonmobile housing and shelter, and on-site construction. Although all three of these areas are related to the building industry, they have no direct functional connection with the mobile home dealership organization. Of the respondents to the PMHI/DS, 15 percent indicated involvement in one or more of these areas. Only one responding firm is presently involved in the distribution of building supplies, and its origins lie in the mobile home distribution system itself. Eight percent are presently involved in the distribution of factory-produced, nonmobile housing and shelter, with 6 percent having originated in the mobile home distribution system itself and 2 percent in fields unrelated to the mobile home industry. The sample results show that the main direction of diversification is from the mobile home industry rather than to it. Ten percent of the respondents are presently involved in on-site residential construction; 40 percent of these originated in the mobile home industry itself, and the remainder came from sectors outside of the mobile home industry. A number of firms are

Table 7.12.
Diversification from the Mobile Home Distribution System into Recreational Vehicle Dealerships According to Total Annual Sales

Total Annual Sales	Not in, No Plans to Enter	Now in	Plan to Enter	Total
$0–$75K	100% (14.9%[a])	0 —	0 —	100%
$75K–$1M	91.7% (48.8%)	8.3% (4.3%)	0 —	100%
Greater than $1M	62.5% (21.3%)	31.3% (10.6%)	6.3% (2.1%)	100%
Total[a]	83.0%	14.9%	2.1%	

Note: Figures in parentheses represent percentages of all PMHI/DS respondents.

Source: PMHI/DS.

diversified into both distribution of factory-produced nonmobile housing and shelter and on-site residential construction. This may be a case of diversification into the mobile home industry by larger builder-dealers representing building manufacturers. No correlation was found between diversification into any one of these three areas and dealership size.

Emerging Trends

Only 2 percent of the respondents to the PMHI/DS planned to diversify into recreational vehicle dealerships. This corroborates the trend noted above in tracing specialization patterns that the increased specialization needed profitably and effectively to operate a distribution outlet has reduced the number of dealerships selling both mobile homes and recreational vehicles. Thus diversification from the mobile home distribution system into recreational vehicle distribution most likely will be reduced to an insignificant level in the future. It is important to note the incidence of diversification into both factory-built and conventional shelter. The implied horizontal transfer of know-how can result in increased complementarity between the mobile home industry and the other subsectors of the building sector. In this respect it is especially important that more than half of all dealerships active in on-site building did not originate from the mobile home industry; many, in fact, are builders who have diversified. As long as diversification of this type continues to foster a better mutual understanding between the mobile home industry and the other building subsectors and as long as there is no danger of economic merger of the industries, this trend is in perfect accord with our thinking regarding the future of the building sector. We believe that the mobile home industry and the rest of the building sector must come to interact effectively without, however, losing their respective identities.

Economies of Scale

The primary question regarding economies of scale concerns the behavior of dealers' cost structures as the size of the outlet or firm increases. The chapter on cost and price structures at the end of this part provides a detailed statistical examination of the impact of scale on the various cost elements of dealers' operating expenses. The focus here is on the relationship between scale and the primary input cost, the FOB factory price. In a service sector, finished goods can be treated as inputs. Do large firms exert a degree of leverage vis-à-vis the manufacturer and realize some savings in input costs as their size increases? We have already noted the existence of a small number of larger chains. Is it probable that firms belonging to chains exercise such leverage? These questions will be pursued first by examining single outlets and then, chains.

Mobile home distribution has been and still largely is a grass-roots business. If a particular market is characterized by specific local traits, a small-scale operation is often the most effective. A small town with a stagnant economy and little in-migration may generate only ten or twenty new mobile home sales per year. In spite of a quasi-exclusionary zoning ordinance and resultant park shortage, these sales may be made only because the single dealership in town has for some time rented several "empty" spaces in the area's only two mobile home parks (in addition to offering other financial incentives) to enable the customer to place the unit. And the buyer may have purchased the unit only because of the long-standing good reputation of the dealership, which may have been founded in the 1930s. This type of business in this kind of environment is best operated as a "Mom and Pop" or small family business. A minor increase in business would lead to strong diseconomies of scale: The hiring of only one or two persons suddenly means a payroll, with two employees having at best half the motivation and hence productivity of the owner-operators. Only when the next threshold in business volume is reached can increased scale begin to yield economies. But diseconomies will enter as well; analysis of our surveys found that increasing sales per lot yield higher general and administrative costs as well as overhead per unit. More seriously, increasing sales mean an enlarged marketing and hence transportation radius. In particular, the rapidly mounting costs of transporting units to distant locations and providing ongoing service to these units keep the individual distribution outlet from growing beyond its present typical size.

The production function of the single outlet in the distribution system shows some characteristics of constant returns to scale. The size of an individual outlet is rather limited: The largest units probably sell no more than two hundred fifty homes per year (less than four per week), and most sell far fewer. Larger outlets would be established

if substantial economies were present. As noted, the constraints imposed by the size of the market for a single outlet are a major factor in determining outlet size. Given this constraint, large outlets could exist only if the reduction in costs associated with scale would more than compensate for the limitations imposed by transport costs. However, this is not the case.

But there is one strong factor tempting dealers to move beyond the small-scale, one-lot operation: The major cost element of the retail price of mobile homes is the FOB factory price of the unit, usually ranging from at least 60 percent to more than 80 percent of the retail selling price. With often less than 20 percent of retail price left to cover the dealer's costs and profit, the vital question is whether scale economies can permit dealers to exert any leverage with respect to the price at which they receive the units. Such leverage does not exist to any significant degree for large dealers who represent many manufacturers—in their case the purchasing power with regard to each individual manufacturer is small. Yet this leverage is significant for large dealerships that concentrate on working with very few or even one single manufacturer, in which case the ability to buy in large volume puts the dealer into a position of strength in negotiating volume purchase contracts. Most dealers who indicated to us that they planned to reduce the number of manufacturers represented gave as their major reason consolidation in order to increase buying volume discounts. Several dealerships with annual sales of more than $1 million made this point, and even a twenty-one-lot dealership chain grossing more than $3 million per year said it planned to concentrate on developing more volume purchasing power by decreasing the number of manufacturers. It should be stressed that such leverage did not arrive with the cutthroat competition in the industry's production system induced by the last recession; it already existed in the 1960s and early 1970s.

To demonstrate the influence of scale on FOB price as well as pretax profit, we compared a national sample of dealerships of different sizes and held several variables constant. First, we included only dealers that sold singlewides of comparable quality at roughly the same dollar-per-square-foot price. Second, we included only firms whose unit product mix consisted of less than 50 percent doublewides (a doublewide-oriented operation shows different cost structures). Third, we included only dealerships that had no interest in any mobile home park (dealers even channeling only 5 percent to 10 percent of their sales into parks they control again have different cost structures). Table 7.13 shows the results of this analysis.

The FOB factory price savings indicated in table 7.13 primarily reflect the influence of volume. There are other leverage factors that

Table 7.13.
Dealership Size Versus
FOB Factory Price and
Pretax Profit

	Dealership Size Categories (Annual Retail Sales Volumes)		
	Less than $500,000	$501,000–$1,000,000	$1,001,000–$1,500,000
Average FOB factory price as % of unit retail selling price	80.2%	77.2%	64.1%
Average profit before state and federal taxes as % of unit retail selling price	5.0%	10.4%	19.1%

Source: PMHI/DS.

dealers could use. For example, PMHI obtained quotations with significant price concessions from manufacturers if larger-scale purchases could be scheduled for production during off-peak. (See the discussion of scale economies in chapter 4.)

Exploitation of scale economies yields indirect business benefits as well. The second reason given by most dealers planning to decrease the number of represented manufacturers was their hope to develop more clout and get better and faster service from manufacturers, both with regard to delivery of homes as well as prompt response to warranty claims and other repairs that dealers cannot handle alone.

The benefits mentioned do not necessarily result from size. These scale economies can be attained if a given manufacturer can benefit from a larger order and if a dealer with astute business sense realizes the advantage and shrewdly exploits it. But scale economies per se do not promise these benefits. In fact, our regression analyses did not show scale economies to be a determinant of FOB factory price (see chapter 9, "Cost and Price Structures").

We anticipate that scale economies will influence the distribution system in distinctly different ways in two types of basically different markets. In parts of the country with stagnant economies, little migration, and restrictive land use controls, scale economies will at most tempt individual dealers to cut down on the number of manufacturers they represent; but the necessary grass-roots nature of businesses in such markets will militate against the emergence of large outlets or of chains. On the other hand, in areas of rapid economic growth where population in-migration is heavy and land use controls are lenient and hence sites are abundant, large outlets in densely populated areas as well as chains linking outlets in less dense areas are likely to emerge. In these markets there will be a need for quickly provided least-cost housing demanded by geographically or upwardly mobile households for limited-period use. Because land for home placement is readily available, referrals of park sites and other services become unimportant and price becomes all-important. This is the business climate in which scale

economies can be exploited and service-type costs of generating business are not essential and hence will not inject diseconomies. This scenario of large chains oriented toward high turnover coexisting with Mom and Pop single-lot operations parallels the probable future industrial organization of the production system, where we expect only a few large, national multiplant corporations to coexist with small shops specializing in custom work.

As we noted earlier, transportation costs effectively limit the market radii of dealerships to between two hundred and three hundred miles. Hence, in purely economic terms, the dealerships in a given location operate under conditions of imperfect competition with other dealers who are within a given distance from the market. These dealers then rarely compete with dealers beyond this radius. This has implications for the price and the product policies of an individual dealer.

Dealers set prices by adding a markup to the FOB prices of the units. The dealer's fixed and variable costs plus conception of a "fair return" are the basic factors in determining this markup. In a given location, a situation of imperfect competition prevails. If the number of dealers serving a given market is small, the situation theoretically approximates an oligopolistic formation. Because any single firm's resources are limited, in the boom years of the early 1970s few firms were willing to take the consequences of a price war. Thus there was relatively little price competition between dealers in many localities. The 1973–1975 recession radically changed this.

In the mid- and late 1970s competition in the distribution system has become fierce and in many areas has reached cutthroat dimensions. This has quickly exhausted most dealers' resources, to the extent that they cannot continue to rely on price competition as a major competitive weapon. When actual net income drops to a level at which exit from the business begins to be considered, even invasion by shoestring operators or well-capitalized chains that try to build profits by volume sales based on unrealistically low margins will not induce established

Product Differentiation

dealers to engage in all-out price war. Instead, dealers soon begin to resort to product differentiation as a complementary or primary competitive weapon. It is within this framework that product differentiation emerges to play an ever more important role as a main tool within the competitive structure of the distribution system.

As we noted in the chapter on the industrial organization of the production system, national field interviews we conducted between 1969 and 1977 indicated that producers have not yet been able to achieve any high levels of product differentiation. The distribution system, however, has been able to increase the level of product differentiation. The dealer's basic aim is twofold: getting the consumer to the lot and making the sale. The first objective is largely being pursued by advertising and lot decoration, but this yields little product differentiation. In attempting to achieve the second objective, dealers use an approach that greatly increases product differentiation: adding a variety of services to the product received from the manufacturer. Essentially, all of the service functions described in chapter 8 on distribution are used in completing the product package, but they are employed in different combinations by various dealers.

Typical product "additions" include referral to or provision of park sites, attractive financing packages, competence in reliable on-site setup, and superior warranty and general repair performance.

In markets with shortages of park space and difficulty in placing units on isolated property, the most powerful competitive weapon is provision of park space. Dealers accomplish this in two ways. They may refer customers to parks whose operators' co-operation has been secured by financial incentives from the dealers; these often involve regular cash payments that may reach $2000 to $3000 per year, even for a small dealership selling only a few units per year. Alternatively, dealers either provide spaces in one or several parks they directly control or, in anticipation of future sales, they keep a small "open" site inventory by renting sites in nonowned parks; rentals in the latter can reach up to $1000 per year for small dealerships selling only 20 units per year.

Equally important in closing the sale is the extent to which the dealer can offer favorable financing arrangements. Chapter 15 on finance sector influence provides details on the various arrangements. Closely related is a dealer's willingness to accept trade-in items; for many consumers this is the only possible way of making the down payment.

Another aspect of product differentiation is a dealer's demonstrable capability in setup and hookup, especially of larger doublewides, Skills and equipment for reliable placement upon the foundation become especially important for sectionals. In rural areas where

many units are placed on isolated lots and many buyers have done at least some owner-building, a dealer's skills as a "builder" can make or break a sale.

The most crucial product differentiation aspect for repeat sales or word-of-mouth advertising is a dealer's record in warranty performance, handling repairs, and providing general service. Most respondents to the PMHI/DS who complained about tardy manufacturer response to warranty problems handled such problems themselves; although not legally obliged to do this, these dealers realize that blame for nonresponse in any event would fall upon them. Similarly, dealers usually go beyond their own warranty terms and give practically lifetime service. If an elderly person got trapped for several days in winter in a park-sited home without getting help in restoring heat, the entire park population would form an opinion of the dealer in question without regard for formal obligations.

Most PMHI/DS respondents are "adding" all of the above services to their product (except park space referral if spaces are abundant) and are often aggressively advertising; this is as good evidence as any for a highly competitive situation. Because competition occurs in local markets, product differentiation can, in fact, be very high in areas with few distribution outlets in which one or two outlets clearly lead the others in terms of quality, scope, and intensity of the services offered.

Emerging trends indicate that product differentiation will become an increasingly important element of the distribution system's structure. If the government continues to intervene, it is possible that dealers will stress conformance as part of their product package whenever compliance with some new regulation will have become inevitable. For example, just as the new Federal Mobile Home Construction and Safety Standards have been used by manufacturers and to a lesser extent by dealers to emphasize product differentiation in the late 1970s, we expect that manufacturers and dealers will begin to use warranty performance differences in the early 1980s—especially if the FTC succeeds in imposing its warranty performance regulations on the entire industry.

Related developments in the on-site housing market will have some impact on product differentiation. As doublewides and sectionals gain more dominance in the product mix, the mobile home industry will increasingly come into competition with the residential on-site industry. Because product differentiation, especially brand name recognition, is more developed in the housing industry, we expect this to act as a stimulant to mobile home dealers, who will increase competition among themselves by developing and accentuating product differentiation.

In fact, product differentiation is one of the major means by which a dealer can carve out a market share in markets yet untapped by the present mobile home distribution system: markets totally controlled by the on-site builder. By stressing lifetime service and providing park and financial arrangements, dealers can make inroads into the traditional housing market while at the same time creating a good reputation for their outlets.

In the 1960s and through the early 1970s entry barriers resulting from scale economies or product differentiation did not play any substantive part in the organization of the distribution system. The only barrier that had some influence on system structure was entry costs. In the late 1950s and early 1960s estimated entry costs were approximately $15,000 and were in the range of $25,000–$50,000 in the early 1970s. The rise in the cost level during this period indicates that in real terms entry costs have risen about three-fold in one decade. Most of this increase could be attributed to factors endogenous to the system, such as the growth in the starting size of the average dealership. Before the 1973–1975 recession, entry costs into the system consisted primarily of the costs of establishing the physical business and the necessary business connections. Costs to be incurred before the outlet can physically start operations include land, buildings, vehicles, and other equipment; the purchase or lease price of these items was the basic element in entry cost. The search for a location, manufacturers, lenders, park locations for prospective consumers, and so forth represented the major costs of establishing necessary business connections.

The net entry/exit figures in table 7.14 show that during the 1970–1974 period the total number of dealers selling only mobile homes increased. This increase more than offset the decline in the number of dealers selling both mobile homes and recreational vehicles in the 1973–1974 period. Because the total numbers of entries outweighed exits, it appears that entry costs did not act as a prohibitive factor and that the barriers to entry were low. Table 7.14 also shows another indicator of the low barriers to entry, the percentage change in the shipments per outlet. The negative changes during this period clearly indicate the increased addition of new outlets in the distribution system given the continued increase in shipments.

However, after 1974 factors both endogenous and exogenous to the industry caused entry barriers to increase: the markedly growing product differentiation, the greater concentration of market power among the firms that survived the recessionary shakeout, the higher costs of administration brought about by the extra responsibilities required of dealers under the Federal Construction and

Safety Standards, the substantially increased difficulty in obtaining wholesale as well as retail financing due to great lender caution triggered by the high recession-caused repossession rates, and stiffer bonding requirements. All of these developments combined to raise absolute entry costs to an estimated level between $50,000 and $100,000 in the late 1970s. As table 7.14 shows, net exit figures continue through the late 1970s. This is paralleled by the reversal of the declining trend in the percentage change of shipments per outlet because the exit of dealers caused the shipments per outlet to increase. Even with the revival of the industry and the increase in demand for mobile homes, a net entry figure is unlikely to be reached before 1980 and for years to come will remain at a relatively low level. Thus the distribution system, which had almost no entry barriers as recently as 1970, is entering the 1980s with sizable absolute cost barriers to entry.

What used to be an almost ideal small business may soon have to be written off by the U.S. Small Business Administration as one of its pet industries. Entry costs as well as the costs of doing business have risen, not last due to consumerism-induced regulatory overreaction by government. The direct added costs are being passed on to the consumer, who will also bear the costs resulting from the fact that higher entry barriers will not enhance competition.

At the National Level

Chapter 4 on the industrial organization of the production system explained that seasonality adversely affects manufacturers' performance measured in terms of both company profit rate and capacity utilization. Seasonality also produces similar results for dealers. The extent to which the harshness of seasonality in the production and distribution systems differ is one main question with which this analysis is concerned.

Table 7.15 was constructed from the PMHI/DS to identify the months of highest and lowest sales at the dealership level. The dealers' highest sales were not overly concentrated in any given month. In contrast, approximately one-third of the dealers had their lowest monthly sales in January and half in December and January. The ratio of dealers' lowest to highest monthly sales is given in table 7.16. The mean of this ratio is 0.222 for dealers as compared with 0.37 and 0.46 (based on similar PMHI surveys) for suppliers and manufacturers, respectively. This would indicate that seasonal fluctuations at the dealership level are more severe than at the production level. This reveals that the distribution system is playing a vitally important role in protecting the production system from direct exposure to seasonal variations in demand.

At the Regional Level

The average monthly shipments to dealers are given in table 7.17, which shows that shipments were generally lowest during the winter months of December and January.[1] In contrast, the month of seasonal peak shipments was somewhat diverse for different regions. Shipments to the South Atlantic region, by far the largest recipient of mobile homes, on the average peaked in August. The peak in shipments occurred in June for the West North Central region and in July for the Pacific regions. For the remaining regions, highest monthly shipments were in April, August, September, or October. What factors account for regional differences in the ratio of lowest to highest monthly shipments to dealers? Table 7.17 would seem to indicate that regions such as New England, which are characterized by cold winter months, tend to be associated with a low ratio. But states within a census region may not have the same climatic conditions. For instance, on a 1 to 5 rating given to seasonal conditions in each state (where "1" indicates a long hot summer and "5" means no summer, long winter), Florida would have a rating of 1 and West Virginia a rating of 3; yet both states belong to the South Atlantic region.[2] In an effort to find out whether climatic conditions influence seasonality, we assigned each state within a region a seasonal rating of 1 to 5. Then the ratio of lowest to highest monthly shipments was regressed on the average seasonal rating of the states within a region. The estimated relationship is as follows:

$$LSMS = 0.7944 - 0.0686\ S$$
$$(0.0666)$$
$$(R^2 = 0.1326),$$

where LSMS is the ratio of lowest to highest shipments to dealers and S, the regional seasonal rating (constructed by averaging the seasonal ratings of states within a region). Note that the standard error is located directly below the estimated coefficient of S. The coefficient of S is negative in sign, indicating that warmer climate (low seasonal rating) is associated with high LSMS. Nevertheless, the coefficient of S is not significant and the R^2 value is also very low. Thus the relationship between climatic conditions and seasonality is tenuous. This conclusion is compatible with the results of our similar analyses on seasonality in the production system, where climatic conditions also were not shown to be determinants of seasonality.

In order to determine whether dealers in these regions have succeeded in reducing the seasonality of demand, we regressed on time the yearly ratio of lowest to highest monthly shipments to dealers. Over the ten-year period of 1968–1977, no trend in seasonality was established in any of the nine census regions; seasonal variations neither diminished nor worsened. Again, this finding cor-

Table 7.14.
National Net Entry/Exit Figures and Annual Percentage Change of Shipments per Outlet for the Mobile Home Distribution System, 1970–1977

| Year | Change from Previous Year | | | Shipments per Outlet (% Change) |
	Dealers Selling Mobile Homes Only	Dealers Selling Mobile Homes and Recreational Vehicles	Total Dealers	
1970/1971	662	237	899	11.9
1971/1972	590	1943	2533	− 8.9
1972/1973	871	253	1124	−10.1
1973/1974	746	−130	616	−44.6
1974/1975	−1203	−586	−1789	−25.6
1975/1976	− 613	−216	− 829	24.5
1976/1977	− 420	− 97	− 517	18.1

Source: Compiled by PMHI from tables 7.1 and 7.5.

Table 7.15.
Dealers' Months of Highest and Lowest Sales

| | Highest | Lowest |
Month	% of Firms	% of Firms
January	1.7	32.7
February	3.4	15.4
March	10.3	1.9
April	3.4	3.8
May	20.7	3.8
June	10.7	7.7
July	6.9	3.8
August	15.5	0
September	10.3	1.9
October	5.2	0
November	1.7	5.8
December	6.9	17.3

Source: PMHI/DS.

Table 7.16.
Dealers' Ratios of Lowest to Highest Monthly Sales

Ratio	% of Firms
0 −0.09	23.9
0.10–0.19	21.8
0.20–0.29	19.6
0.30–0.39	17.5
0.40–0.49	6.6
0.50–0.59	4.4
0.60 or above	4.4

Source: PMHI/DS.

Table 7.17.
Monthly Shipments to
Dealers by Census
Regions, 1968–1977

Month	New England	Mid-Atlantic	East North Central	West North Central	South Atlantic	East South Central	West South Central	Mountain	Pacific
January	686[b]	2,627[b]	4,744[b]	3,781[b]	14,937	4,515[b]	7,437[b]	4,938[b]	7,007[b]
February	808	3,375	7,021	4,984	16,333	5,757	8,633	5,274	7,945
March	1,199	4,072	8,672	7,650	17,809	6,574	10,456	6,585	8,660
April	1,682	5,506	9,431	7,391	19,416	7,395[a]	11,010[a]	6,907	10,152
May	1,766	5,940	10,264	7,726	19,346	7,181	10,291	6,746	8,981
June	1,943	6,625	10,343	8,099[a]	18,787	7,373	10,490	6,789	9,088
July	1,722	6,812	9,693	6,921	17,437	6,320	9,193	7,110	10,190[a]
August	2,022[a]	6,996[a]	10,060	7,831	19,465[a]	6,738	10,292	6,933	9,505
September	1,758	6,128	11,159[a]	7,572	18,283	7,152	10,311	7,052	9,406
October	1,608	5,617	10,338	7,194	19,203	7,142	10,990	7,169[a]	9,934
November	1,043	3,886	7,083	5,399	16,998	6,263	8,982	6,014	7,325
December	737	2,721	5,942	4,536	14,413[b]	4,701	7,863	5,963	7,500
L/H[c]	0.339	0.376	0.425	0.467	0.741	0.611	0.676	0.695	0.688

a. Highest shipments. b. Lowest shipment s. c. L/H = ratio of lowest to highest monthly shipments.

Source: Computed by PMHI from ten years of back issues of "The Monthly Market Letter on Mobile Home Shipments," published by *Mobile-Modular Housing Dealer Magazine*.

responds with the conclusions reached in part I that seasonality in the production system has not declined either.

Observations

There are two important implications regarding seasonality. First, although seasonality has a negative impact on dealer performance, it does not diminish nor are its causes clear. Thus, unless and until manufacturers and dealers decide to attack this business problem and to isolate its causes, they will have to continue living with the consequences. Second, the examination of seasonality in the distribution system determined that seasonal variations are more severe in the distribution system than in the production system. This means that the distribution system has served and is serving the important function of shielding the production system from direct exposure to seasonality on the demand side.[3]

C. Policy Alternatives

The fact that at most 25 percent of all dealerships generate at least 75 percent of the mobile home distribution system's total sales volume seriously inhibits the growth and efficiency of the system. Efforts must be made to stimulate the dormant effectiveness and productivity of the remaining 75 percent of dealers; effective demand potentially could increase significantly, as could overall system efficiency. Many constraints confronting smaller dealerships can be alleviated and many incentives for more effective business operation can be activated.

There are external considerations that constrain dealers. For instance, although there are scale economies in the distribution system, these are most likely to be exploited by chains and are not readily available to small Mom and Pop outlets. In order to help smaller dealers enjoy scale economies, manufacturers could offer volume discounts to small outfits that may join together in cooperative or pooling arrangements. Not only might this help small outlets compete more effectively with traditional builders, but it would also allow manufacturers to increase their sales.

Another artifical restraint on dealer effectiveness is the fact that governmental intervention has led to a plethora of regulations that make it difficult especially for smaller dealers to do business. The mobile home industry at large through association efforts and individual suppliers, manufacturers, or both through intensified training programs should offer guidance (perhaps in the form of seminars or handbooks) to educate dealers on how to deal effectively with the red tape as well as how to turn new regulations to their advantage. In a similar vein, the industry could also try to persuade the government to provide the same kind of help to the distribution system. For example, the U.S. Small Business Administration in years past has made efforts toward preparing training material for dealers. It might be appropriate for the MHI to lobby that funding be provided for the SBA or another logical agency to devise rigorous instructions for dealers on how to cope efficiently with government regulations.

Not all of the distribution system's problems, however, stem from external factors. A major shortcoming within the system itself is the lack of business expertise of many dealers. The distribution system might call upon the production system and the supply sector to help it to build better business skills. Manufacturers (and suppliers as well) who are interested in increasing "pipeline volume" could screen the 75 percent of the less active dealers to identify those ambitious ones with the greatest potential. The manufacturers could help these dealers enhance their business acumen by training them in business administration and marketing. With their increased business knowledge, these dealers could in turn work with park operators and developers to stimulate new park development in areas of scarcity.

Many of these goals for increasing the efficiency of the distribution system can best be accomplished by the cooperation and interaction of all of the interlocking components of the mobile home industry working together for their mutual benefit. Since the 75 percent of the less effective dealers have already committed themselves to the mobile home industry, they now only need a catalyst to help them to fulfill their potential. Whether this push comes from manufacturers, suppliers, or park operators, it will be to the ultimate advantage of the entire mobile home system.

Enhancement of the efficiency and professionalism of dealers should help to improve manufacturers' perception of the distribution system. In our interviews with key personnel of many mobile home manufacturing firms, we discovered that the producer's assessment of the dealer tends to be quite negative; many manufacturers assert that the distribution system is not only inefficient but is also detrimental to overall industry image and performance. Dealers counter that manufacturers display immature distribution and marketing practices. This pointless infighting benefits neither group and obscures what should be the main objective: all components of the mobile home system working together for their mutual benefit. Increased display of professional behavior on the part of dealers may be a helpful step in setting both groups on a course of cooperation and interaction so that energy previously wasted in internal wrangling can be channeled into solving such larger industry concerns as the industry's image and seasonality.

A rich and growing segment of business for mobile home dealers has recently emerged in the preowned home market. In the late 1970s over eight hundred fifty thousand existing mobile home units changed ownership per year; this represents about three times the number of annual new unit shipments. The preowned market, however, is actually a mixed blessing, simultaneously providing both a business opportunity and a threat.

The opportunity of this market is obvious: substantial enhancement of sales volume. The threat it represents is more intangible and thus potentially more dangerous. Because many of these used units are older, and often unsightly, deteriorated, or both, their presence on a dealer's lot could harm the image not only of the individual dealer but also of the mobile home industry in general. Prospective buyers who see an old, dilapidated unit next to a new doublewide or sectional may wonder if their shiny new unit will eventually deteriorate to that state.

In order to take advantage of the business promise of the preowned market while at the same time minimizing the potential risk, a dealer has several alternatives. Dealers could screen used units, keeping the sound and attractive ones for display on their lots and channeling those in poor condition through any one of the following alternative distribution methods:

1. Export less desirable used units to underdeveloped countries in sore need of low-cost housing. For example, lenders with large inventories of repossessed units could make a nice profit by selling them (directly or through a middleman) to such less developed areas as Latin America, which has a tremendous housing need and yet is close enough to allow shipping to remain economically viable. (Some lenders have already taken this step.)

2. Refurbish basically sound units. This could be done either by the dealer or in specialized shops. Such plants would be ideal training grounds for the service crews of the manufacturer or dealer who owned them; this would also help to make maximum use of the crews' time. They could work on the unscheduled refurbishing work when they were not needed to handle service calls. Such refurbishing plants would have several advantages: since they would be in-factory, work would not suffer from weather-related problems; there would be significant scale economies in purchasing of supplies; repair crews would become highly skilled and versatile, able to work in the field efficiently on various models of different years; and the crews would be working constantly, thus obviating slack time problems that field-only service work implies. Although on the surface the idea of refurbishing shops may sound somewhat naive, it does have enough potential benefits to merit further consideration.

3. Establish a system analogous to a used car lot. For image purposes, such a lot could ostensibly sell units for special uses (such as construction offices); yet at the same time, the dealer could make it clear to very low income (for example, rural poor) potential buyers that these inexpensive units were available to them.

4. Deploy unsightly used units to fairly inaccessible locations where little image damage can be done by their display. There are many isolated regions that badly need temporary or low-cost housing, such as Wyoming's Powder River Basin and other new natural resource extraction areas. Until these regions develop high-quality permanent or mobile housing, dealers could sell used units wholesale to the companies undertaking these projects for clearly temporary use.

An indirect, although potentially important, benefit of the establishment of refurbishing plants for preowned units would be the use of such plants to help combat the seasonality that constantly plagues the mobile home industry and its distribution system. Seasonality is more pronounced at the distribution than at the production level, which indicates that the dealer shields the producer from direct exposure to seasonality on the demand side. The counterseasonal use of refurbishing shops could help to smooth seasonal variations by allowing maintenance of a full complement of personnel to handle the constant work. Even salespeople could be kept on the payroll while at the same time learning firsthand concrete information about the product.

A very basic, but vitally significant, step toward reducing the harsh impact of seasonality on dealers would be to undertake research and development efforts to understand better the causes of seasonality. Because all segments of the mobile home industry are affected by the seasonality problem, all would benefit from any breakthrough in coping with it. Thus members of all components of the system—from suppliers and manufacturers to dealers to park operators and developers—should help to underwrite such a research effort.

Another method by which the distribution system might counteract seasonality would be to increase the level and composition of demand for the product. Growth of effective demand, which would obviously affect the level of sales, could stem from a change in the demand composition. The latter could be effected by enlarging the pool of prospective buyers, especially by attracting consumers who are in the market for new housing but refuse to consider mobile housing as a viable alternative. More aggressive and sophisticated advertising and sales promotion to further the idea of mobile home living as a viable permanent housing alternative could be concentrated during slack periods. The costs for such promotion could be borne jointly by dealers, manufacturers, suppliers, and park operators, for all would prosper from the enhanced image and sales and reduced seasonality that might result.

A major obstacle to the growth and maturation of the distribution system as well as of the entire industry is the large number of dealerships still selling both mobile homes and recreational vehicles. In the past, the combination made sense: Both products were mobile and required similar sales techniques, service, and maintenance; this pairing even yielded scale economies, for the same servicing facilities could handle both products. As the two products have become increasingly different, however, the gap between them has widened: Mobile homes now more frequently require on-site service and maintenance and necessitate skills resembling those of on-site home building. Mobile homes have thus come to have more of a kinship with traditional housing than with recreational vehicles. Given this development, displaying both mobile homes and recreational vehicles on the same lot tends to perpetuate the negative image of mobile homes as glorified trailers. Unnecessarily reinforcing this fallacy in the consumer's mind represents a major marketing mistake on the part of dealers.

In order to avoid this problem, dealers, if they decide for diversification, should direct their diversification efforts toward traditional housing industry-related activities (currently the rare exception) and away from the usual route of moving into recreational vehicles. Dealers could expand into such areas as distribution of factory-built housing or perhaps even land development and on-site building. It is in these traditional housing areas where the most important skills that will be needed in the future can be acquired. We would caution, however, that dealers should first concentrate on developing expertise in their own product before branching out into these related fields.

In some situations, of course, simultaneous activity in mobile homes and recreational vehicles is desirable, especially for a firm that has a solid reputation in both fields. However, these dealers should display the different units on separate lots so that a clear differentiation will be made between mobile homes (housing) and recreational vehicles.

This distinction between the mobile home and the recreational vehicle industries was recognized some time ago by the industry's national association and the trade press. For some time, the MHI has advocated the interests of the first industry, the Recreational Vehicle Institute, those of the latter. Similarly, the *Mobile-Modular Housing Dealer* magazine, which used to cover both the mobile home industry and the recreational vehicle industry, has for many years issued a separate publication for each industry; in addition, it slants the content of its mobile home-oriented journal toward not only mobile homes but also toward sectionals and other forms of factory-built housing. More members of the industry's press, associations, and public relations staffs should stress this difference between both industries, which could in turn foster more awareness on the part of dealers of the need to solidify the image of mobile housing as a home in the eyes of consumers.

Notes to Chapter 7

1. Two data sources were used in the analysis of seasonality at the dealership level. The first source, the PMHI Dealer Survey, was used principally in the discussion of seasonality at the national level. The second source, ten years of back issues of "The Monthly Market Letter on Mobile Home Shipments" published by *Mobile-Modular Housing Dealer*, was used primarily for the analysis of seasonality at the regional level. It should be noted, however, that the two data sources are not strictly comparable because the PMHI figures concern dealers' sales to customers, whereas those from the second data source concern shipments to dealers. Because shipments precede final sales, it is to be expected that the peak and trough of the shipments will precede those of the sales series.

2. For a complete seasonal rating of each state, see Steven Visher, *Climatic Atlas of the U.S.* (Cambridge, Mass.: Harvard University Press, 1954), p.362.

3. PMHI/DS and 1977 follow-up survey.

Chapter 8

Distribution

A. Operations

Profile of Dealership Operations

Economic Performance and Growth

The entry rate into the mobile home distribution system has paralleled industry growth patterns, particularly during the 1968–1972 period. Nearly two-thirds of all respondents to the PMHI Dealer Survey (PMHI/DS) began their companies between 1963 and 1972; most respondents (40 percent) began their dealerships during the period of dramatic industrial growth between 1968 and 1972. Thus it appears that the mobile home industry's market expansion has induced a proportional acceleration in the entry rate of new dealerships. The distribution system's highly flexible response to increased product demand has not been paralled by a similar response in the park system: While the distribution system has grown with rising demand, the park system's growth has been artificially constrained by regulatory barriers.

The entry rate increase during the 1968–1972 period, however, led to rising excess capacity within the distribution system. This contributed to the abnormally high frequency of firm exits in 1974 and 1975; during one recession year alone, 40 percent of the total number of mobile home dealerships folded. There are now approximately ten thousand mobile home dealerships, down from a pre-recession high of about thirteen thousand in 1973. The postrecession recovery rate in the distribution system has been slow because entry barriers are higher and lenders are more cautious.

Naturally, the growth of the mobile home industry and its distribution system has been reflected in a similar pattern of retail sales growth. Mobile home sales climbed steadily from $146 million in 1947 to $596 million in 1957 to $1,370,052,000 in 1967. Sales jumped to a boom year high of $4,406,382,-000 in 1973, then slid to a recession low of $2,432,661,000 in 1975. The slow recovery in sales parallels the industry comeback: By 1977, sales had only returned to the $4 billion level.

In response to the escalating demand for mobile homes, average annual mobile home dealership volume per outlet has risen sharply: from about $120,000 in 1957 to $200,000 in 1967 to approximately $390,000 by 1977. Although sales dipped in the mid-1970 recession years, in the mid-1980s the average volume per dealership should break the $1 million mark, in large part because of the growth in the sale of doublewides and increased marketing of used units.

Backgrounds of Dealers

In general it appears that the largest portion of mobile home dealers had formerly been involved in a business activity either within or closely related to the industry. Before becoming mobile home dealers, about one-third of all PMHI/DS respondents had previously been engaged in recreational

vehicle (12.9 percent) or automobile dealerships (20.0 percent). Our survey found that 41.4 percent of the dealers had originally been involved in activities of other subsectors of the mobile home industry: 7.1 percent in manufacturing and 34.3 percent in park development and operations. Real estate or land development were the origins of 18.5 percent. Other respondents had formerly been involved in work related to the mobile home or housing industries: mobile home sales, servicing, and supplies sales; modular housing sales; home building; and the sales of furniture and appliances. A small number of respondents came from fields with no connection to the mobile home or related industries (such as teaching and electrical engineering).

Of the 24 percent of the PMHI/DS respondents who came into the business between 1938 and 1957, most had formerly been involved in mobile home park development/operations, recreational vehicle dealerships, or automobile dealerships. Most of the 16.5 percent of the dealers who had started in 1958–1962 had formerly been engaged in automobile dealerships or mobile home park development/operations. Of the 19.5 percent of the dealerships founded during the 1963–1967 period, the majority of owners had been in mobile home manufacturing or park development/operations. The greatest number of the 40.3 percent of dealers who began their business in 1968–1972 had come from park development/operations, with others entering from automobile dealerships or other types of land development. Thus it appears that over time the field of mobile home park development/operations has served as the most frequent springboard into the distribution system. This does not necessarily indicate a movement of individuals away from the park system into distribution but rather suggests the establishment of small dealerships to complement existing parks.

Responses to PMHI/DS seem to indicate that many recent dealerships have been started by relatively young people not formerly engaged in operating a business of their own. For example, many were once employed by other dealers, usually as a salesperson. A few founders had been college students before entering the mobile home distribution business. Most of those whose initial business venture was a mobile home dealership began these operations within the boom years of 1968–1972.

The type of company or legal form of business enterprise formed by the owners of mobile home dealerships depends on the operation's capital requirements and intended business volume. In the past, typical mobile home dealerships were usually small Mom and Pop family-owned operations. Today, however, small dealerships that sell only a few

Legal Form of Business Enterprise

mobile homes per year and have access to limited working capital are usually not profitable enough for owners to maintain. Most dealers obtain working capital through the sale of securities to a few individuals instead of to the public at large. Of all PMHI/DS respondents, only one company was publicly owned. A significant 26 percent were not incorporated. The majority (69 percent) of the companies were incorporated but privately held; our data indicate that this represents a trend that has developed in recent years: We would expect that as dealer operations become more sophisticated, the distribution of mobile homes will be largely dominated by privately held, incorporated dealership companies, although we also foresee the slow evolution of more publicly held firms. Information from a PMHI computer cross-tabulation (table 8.1) indicates that unincorporated dealerships are more likely to be involved in both park operation and park development activities. This probably reflects the many small dealerships established by park developers/operators primarily to sell units to be located in their own parks. This upstream integration usually occurs on a minor scale. Because downstream integration by dealers into park development/operations requires extensive resources, it is more likely to be undertaken by larger, incorporated companies. The data in table 8.1 support this hypothesis: None of the unincorporated companies (with little working capital) plan to enter park development/operation, but 8.1 percent of the incorporated dealerships plan to integrate into park operation and 16.7 percent plan to enter park development.

Multilot Chains

The dealer's desire to cover more than one market area and the expanded sales of mobile home dealerships during the 1960s and early 1970s have led to the formation of multilot chain operations. These include a number of sales lots in several states owned and operated by one dealership company. Table 8.2 shows the number of sales lots managed by a dealership in 1963, 1967, 1972, and 1977. Although the majority of respondents have one sales lot, a trend toward two-lot operations seems to be emerging; this might indicate the optimal number for lots that dealers can maintain effectively.

Nearly two-thirds of the manufacturers interviewed by PMHI in 1975 cited problems related to financial considerations as the major factor retarding the future development of dealership chain operations. Other problems included lack of well-qualified personnel and a lack of sophistication in the management of many lots spread out over a large area. Manufacturers polled by PMHI in 1974 and 1975 expressed varying opinions concerning the emergence of multilot chains.

Although 1974 respondents unanimously predicted that both national and regional chains would play a major role in the distribution system in the ensuing five years, in 1975 half of the manufacturers believed that the number of dealership chains was decreasing and one-fourth stated that the number was remaining constant. We believe that these differences of opinion can be traced to the discouraging changes in economic conditions between early 1974 and 1975. Follow-up interviews conducted in 1977, reflecting the guarded optimism of the postrecession recovery phase, support our conclusion that eventually a trend toward dealership expansion into large interstate chains will emerge.

Lot Organization

Before deciding on the location for a mobile home sales lot, a dealer examines the factors related to the overall market demand for mobile homes in the area being considered. It is important to investigate the general environment by determining such aspects as the number of other mobile home dealerships in the vicinity, the availability of park space, zoning laws pertaining to the site location of the units, taxation methods, and the financial terms offered by lenders in the area.

The prime location for a mobile home sales lot is an area bordering a main thoroughfare that will be accessible and recognizable to prospective customers. Lots are often located on "trailer rows" of several dealerships that allow consumers to compare the price and quality of several product lines. It is particularly advantageous for new dealers to be located near the lots of well-established dealerships with whom the public has become familiar. Some lots are located next to mobile home parks or in sales malls that are designed to recreate a mobile home park atmosphere. The importance of the accessibility of a particular lot as well as its exposure is pointed out in the responses to a question asked in a periodic survey of the distribution system conducted by Owens-Corning Fiberglas: in 1975, 51 percent of all mobile home owner-respondents revealed that they had learned about the dealer from whom they purchased their home by "driving around"; 27% of the respondents had heard about their dealer from a friend or relative. Various techniques used to attract potential buyers to sales lots include prominent display of the company sign and the practice of stacking small mobile units on top of each other and utilizing the bottom unit for an office.

The physical layout and design of most mobile home lots do not vary significantly. In addition to the office in which the final sales transactions are conducted, there may be other structures to store materials (parts and supplies, accessories, and so forth) or to accommodate service and maintenance facilities. Because of the high costs of providing covered exhibition space, almost all dealers display mobile homes outdoors on gravel or macadam surfaces. Aware of the need to offer the consumer a choice, a dealer usually displays several models. As can be seen in table 8.3, the number of mobile home units displayed on an individual lot ranges from fewer than ten to sixty.

In order to maximize sales, a dealer usually attempts to display units in an attractive manner that affords customers maximum inspection ability. Most units are shown complete with interior furnishings and accessories such as dishwashers and garbage disposals. Many dealers show at least one model in a landscaped setting with add-on features such as awnings to show the buyer what the unit will look like at a park site. Used mobile homes are usually arranged in a special area separate from the main display location.

Many dealerships are open seven days a week; in fact, several dealers find that Sunday is their best selling day. Where state and local laws prohibit commercial operations to be open on Sundays, dealers feel that their sales volume is greatly reduced. Market risks related to physical deterioration and destruction of units affect all mobile home dealerships. Since units are stored outside, dealers often experience potential sales losses from units that develop a weathered appearance. The open nature of sales lots leaves them prone to vandalism and theft, even though the lots are usually fenced in and provided with automatic lighting.

Because a large number of consumers purchase a mobile home from a dealer discovered by "driving around," the location and the appearance of a sales lot are essential marketing tools for the distribution system. An attractive, highly visible, and organized lot provides the consumer with much nonverbal information about the dealership and the mobile homes for sale.

Dealership Personnel

A mobile home dealership may be staffed with a number of employees or may be operated by only one or two individuals, in which case the owner of the dealership ("dealer" or "operator") usually serves as both sales manager and lot salesperson. Large dealership operations, particularly those involved in multilot operation, are typically staffed with several persons performing specialized functions. The sales manager and the staff of sales representatives are usually responsible for developing prospects and following up on potential buyers. The sales representatives often assist the owner or sales manager in selecting new product models from those displayed at mobile home shows sponsored by industry associations. Owners usually offer bonuses, trips, and awards as incentives for their salespeople. (One company offers a bonus

Table 8.1.
Breakdown of Dealerships Involved in Park Operation and Development According to Legal Form of Company Ownership

	% of Respondents		
Legal Form of Ownership	Not in; Entry Not Planned	Now in	Plan to Enter
	Park Operation		
Unincorporated	14.3	85.7	0
Incorporated but privately held	37.8	54.1	8.1
	Park Development		
Unincorporated	50.0	50.0	0
Incorporated but privately held	55.6	27.8	16.7

Source: Computer cross-tabulation from PMHI/DS.

Table 8.2.
Number of Lots per Dealership

	% of Respondents			
Numbers of Lots	1963	1967	1972	1977
1	81.1	72.8	70.7	57.6
2	6.4	13.0	13.8	23.1
3	12.5	4.6	6.2	7.9
4	0.0	0.0	3.1	2.1
5 or more	0.0	9.0	6.2	9.3

Source: PMHI/DS and follow-up survey.

Table 8.3.
Number of New Mobile Homes Displayed at One Lot Location

Number of New Homes Displayed at One Lot Location	% of Respondents	
	1969	1974
10 or less	31	40
11–20	38	40
21–30	17	11
31–40	10	6
41–50	1	1
51–60	3	—
Mean	18.7	13.8

Source: Owens-Corning Fiberglas, Inc., *A Research Study: Focus on the Mobile Home Market* (1970, 1975).

to the sales representative who sells the oldest or least attractive unit on the lot.)

A dealer's staff also includes "set crews," who place the mobile homes on buyers' sites, "after set crews," who exclusively perform postsale service work and repairs, warehouse managers, maintenance workers, decorators, tow truck operators, and employees for parts and accessories stores. A large dealership often has a home installation and consumer service manager in charge of delivering a unit to a customer's park site or individual lot location and placing the unit on the site ready for hookup to utilities. This person installs such accessories as awnings, skirting, carpets, or steps and handles service calls to ensure proper functioning of the unit once it is established on a site. Many large operations also employ an advertsising and marketing or public relations manager to collect information affecting dealership's sales level and to chart the company's public relations course.

Dealer-Manufacturer Relations

Although some small mobile home manufacturing companies sell their products directly to consumers (usually in the form of custom orders), the majority utilize independent dealers to distribute their units. The structural as well as dynamic relationship between the mobile home manufacturer and dealer can have a significant impact on the organization and efficiency of the distribution process.

A small percentage of manufacturers controls the distribution of their products by managing their own dealerships. However, 84.8 percent of the respondents to the PMHI Manufacturer Survey indicated that they did not own dealerships. Most of the manufacturers interviewed by PMHI did not foresee any increased integration of manufacturers into mobile home distribution. In general, manufacturers seem content to market their products through independent dealers. There are several reasons why manufacturers do not extend their activities to include distribution: They are satisfied with present producer-dealer relationships in terms of maintaining separate entities to handle mobile home manufacturing and distribution activities; quite a few have tried but failed to do so profitably; and many manufacturers either consider integration into dealership operations as a conflict of interests or they fear possible retaliatory boycotts by other dealers.

Very few dealers are engaged in mobile home production activities. Only 6 percent of the respondents to the PMHI/DS indicated that their companies were involved in manufacturing, and no dealer intended to expand into production. Most dealers appear satisfied with operating their businesses separately from the control or ownership of a manufacturer. Because of the large amount of capital demanded for investment, dealers are less

inclined than manufacturers to integrate production and distribution operations.

In recent years manufacturers have adopted more rigorous screening and evaluation schemes in selecting dealers. They consider the most important requirement in the selection process to be an individual dealer's possession of the working capital and credit necessary to purchase the product from the manufacturer. Many manufacturers review the dealer's credit reports or information concerning the lot(s). Some select only those dealers who are willing or able to request immediately a minimum order for a certain number of units. An increasing number of manufacturers select dealers on the basis of a proven track record in mobile home distribution or another business. Manufacturers are interested in acquiring dealers who are professionally and socially well established in the community. Not only does this ensure the manufacturer that its representative is respected in the community, but it also implies that because of connections the dealer will generate a certain amount of obligatory sales from friends and associates.

However, three factors often compromise the rigor of the dealer evaluation and selection process. First, the large number of dealerships that any one manufacturer employs puts a practical limit on the amount of attention that can be economically devoted to the examination of an individual dealer. According to the PMHI Manufacturer Survey, most of the respondents (49.2 percent) use between 6 and 99 non-company-owned outlets; some (9.2 percent) used more than 1000, which necessitates a complex network of communications for distribution. The average number of non-company-owned outlets used was 405. Although some respondents keep close rein on the dealers distributing their mobile homes, at least one manufacturer was uncertain of the number of dealerships representing his company. Second, the dramatic growth of many producers in the late 1960s and early 1970s as well as the more recent cutthroat competition induced by the last recession has often tempted manufacturers to overlook a weak or discredited dealer if a potential sale was at stake. Third, dealers generally exhibit little loyalty toward manufacturers. Many dealerships can terminate a business relationship unilaterally with short or no advanced notice. This factor alone forces manufacturers to seek new dealers continually, a fluctuating need not conducive to the careful structuring of a sound business relationship.

Another problem arises from an often vaguely defined contract between dealer and manufacturer. For example, aside from franchises, many manufacturers establish agreements with one or more dealers to delineate certain marketing areas in which the manufacturer will not sell to other dealers. These agreements, however, are usually oral and do not provide a concrete business base for either party. The absence of formal agreements of responsibility often causes difficulties that may be manifested in manufacturers' delays in delivery or failure to perform servicing.

Difficulties may also occur in routine relations. Although some manufacturers seek to establish good relations with dealers through direct mail programs, personal calls by sales representatives, and trade advertising, other manufacturers may avoid contact with dealers. After making the initial contact with a dealer, many manufacturers carry through with the actual selling of the units only by telephone; by not periodically sending representatives to dealerships, some manufacturers may seek to avoid being pressured to attend to difficulties that later may develop into major problems.

Maintaining a separation of the economic control of production and distribution within the mobile home industry provides a competitive and efficient marketing process. However, problems can arise in the relationships between manufacturers and dealers primarily because of lack of communication between the two parties. Industry trade journals have helped to bridge the communication gap between manufacturer and dealer by serving as a source of industry information and as a forum for discussion of common concerns. Manufacturers further assist dealers by sponsoring training programs, advising dealers on business problems, and offering informative literature concerning manufacturing operations and marketing programs. Greater communication and cooperation should foster the improvement in the manufacturer-dealer relationship that we believe can substantially increase the efficiency and effectiveness of both operations.

Dealership Representation of Manufacturers

In order to offer consumers a broad range of unit types and prices, most mobile home dealers represent a number of manufacturers. Most dealers feel that maximizing the array of brand names, sizes, prices, and floor plans on the sales lots will allow the consumer a choice and therefore increase profits. The number of manufacturers represented by dealers in 1970, 1972, and 1974 is shown in table 8.4. Between 1970 and 1974 there was a substantial decline in the percentage of dealers representing two manufacturers and a notable increase in representation of three and four producers. By 1974, 85 percent of the dealers represented three or more manufacturers and 41 percent represented over five manufacturers. Large dealerships are more inclined to represent numerous manufacturers than are small ones.

Table 8.4.
Number of Manufacturers Represented by Dealerships

Number of Manufacturers Represented	% of Respondents		
	Owens-Corning (1969–1970)	PMHI (1972)	Owens-Corning (1974)
1	9	2.9	8
2	30	8.6	8
3	11	21.4	24
4	12	24.3	20
5+	53	41.3	41

Source: Owens-Corning Fiberglas, Inc., *A Research Study: Focus on the Mobile Home Market* (1970, 1975); PMHI.

In response to a PMHI/DS query as to why they plan to increase, decrease, or maintain the number of manufacturers, about 10 percent of the respondents stated that they intended to expand representation beyond four or five manufacturers in order to provide customers with a greater selection. This strategy enables the dealer to discover which models or brands tend to have the greatest consumer acceptance and to obtain a greater variety of units from other manufacturers. Some dealers mentioned that greater representation tended to decrease the likelihood of brand name loyalty.

The 21 percent of the respondents who planned to decrease the number of manufacturers wanted to stay only with the best lines in order to reduce consumer confusion and to concentrate upon volume purchases from a few companies. These dealers considered consolidation in terms of buying volume discounts and also felt that working with only a small number of manufacturers eliminated duplication of supplies in their inventories. They also thought it better to represent fewer manufacturers because the distant locations of some producers' plants hampered the dealer's ability to obtain fast delivery of service and parts. The majority (57.7 percent) of the respondents, who wished to remain with their present representation arrangement, had an average of 4.7 manufacturers' brands on their sales lots; they felt that this allowed them to maintain a sufficient variety in price, size, and floor plans. These dealers noted that although they did not intend to change the number involved, they were always looking for new manufacturers.

Franchise Agreements

Though franchise agreements, mobile home manufacturers delegate to individual dealers exclusive rights to market their mobile homes in a particular area or within a given radius of the dealers' lots. The majority of PMHI/DS respondents (56.5 percent) did not have any franchise agreements with manufacturers. About 36 percent had between one and six franchises, and approximately 7 percent had between seven and twelve. The mean number of manufacturers with whom dealers had franchise agreements was two. There has been a trend in recent years toward increased dealer willingness to enter into franchise agreements with manufacturers. The manufacturer provides the contract for agreements with dealers, and a franchise agreement usually becomes effective for a period of one year if not canceled by either party within thirty days after it is signed. The Dealer Relations Committee of the MHI has devised a twenty-six-point model "standard franchise" code in order to designate the features necessary for a workable contract in manufacturer-dealer agreements.

Dealers with franchise agreements do not necessarily refrain from representing other manufacturers on a nonfranchise basis. Although most manufacturers produce several brand name products, many dealers feel that they can obtain a greater product line differentiation by not limiting the selection of manufacturers represented on their lots. In order to appeal to the broadest audience and to expand their potential markets, many dealers do not enter into franchise agreements.

Manufacturers interviewed by PMHI felt that the industry's use of franchise agreements as a marketing tool is somewhat premature. The presence of so many manufacturers in the industry makes it difficult for any one firm to interest dealers in marketing only its products, and many manufacturers are competing for good dealers. Franchise agreements are not very useful to dealers, particularly because brand name identification is not yet strong in the mobile home market. In order to induce dealers to accept franchise agreements, many of the larger manufacturers are offering special considerations.

Despite the difficulties of securing franchise agreements with dealers, many manufacturers have indicated that they are attempting to enter into franchise agreements on a more frequent basis. Nearly one-third of the manufacturers interviewed by PMHI mentioned that they would favor contractual agreements, such as franchises, with dealers. A few preferred the formation of exclusive dealerships, and others focused on the importance of the overall need to secure closer and more formal dealer-manufacturer relationships. Thus it appears that some manufacturers may consider franchise agreements a way to assure the marketing of their mobile home products by a competent dealer in a particular area as well as to secure closer relations with their dealers.

Figure 8.1.
A dealership carrying singlewides as well as doublewides.

Figure 8.2.
A dealership specializing in doublewides.

Figure 8.3.
A dealership stressing doublewides and sectional homes.

B. Sales
Annual Volume

The PMHI/DS found that the total annual sales volumes of mobile home dealerships vary widely. Respondents' total sales ranged from $16,000 to $5,811,000 for a ratio of 363:1. This tremendous range in annual sales volume is due to the fact that these dealerships include both multilot operations and small, one-lot businesses. Of the dealership operations, 41.6 percent had a total annual sales volume of up to $500,000 and 52.8 percent ranged between $500,000 and $2 million, with very few (5.7 percent) exceeding the latter figure. The average figure per dealership was approximately $895,000 for the entire PMHI/DS sample.

Table 8.5 shows the average total sales volumes per dealership reported by PMHI/DS respondents. Singlewide and expandable units represented the greatest share of the total sales volume, followed by doublewide and triplewide units. In 1963 and 1967, sales of doublewides and triplewides were comparatively small because of low demand and production at that time; the hefty jump in sales volume by 1972 gives an indication of the rapid increase in the marketability of these units that is continuing into the late 1970s. Until the early 1970s, sales of used mobile homes showed minimal variation compared to the figures for new units; average sales volume for used units approximately doubled in the mid-1970s, indicating more trade-ins and increased demand for used units. By the late 1970s this trend has become even more pronounced because of the effects of the recession: The number of repossessed units in dealers' stocks has increased, and economic conditions have forced many buyers to consider a used rather than a new unit.

The rising sales of accessories reflect the growing permanence of mobile homes and the resulting increased desire of mobile home buyers to have add-on features for their units. Sales of special (nonresidential) units have been minimal and several dealer-respondents did not report any sales in this category; special units are now most often ordered directly from the manufacturer. Table 8.5 does not reflect the heady expectations in the early 1970s for a growing market and increased profitability in the sales of mobile homes, nor does it show the retrenchment that followed the 1974 recession. Unfortunately, many dealers were overly optimistic in the early 1970s; they were headed not for the million dollar mark but rather for Chapter XI.

Several external factors influence the ability of individual dealerships to make mobile home sales. These include the availability of park space, constraints placed on consumer financing, the competitiveness of the market, and government-imposed regulations that govern the sale and location of mobile homes. In the 1970 Owens-Corning Survey, 59 percent of dealers cited major problems related to park space, 55 percent had difficulty with local zoning ordinances, and 25 percent found consumer financing to be a problem (table 8.6).

The PMHI/DS found that by 1973 consumer financing had superseded park space as the major obstacle to potential sales. About two-thirds of the respondents attributed their inability to sell mobile homes at the time of the survey to factors associated with either the consumer's difficulty in financing the purchase of a mobile home or price competition. The economic factors also mentioned by dealers included general market conditions and price cutting and discounts on units offered by other dealers. Almost one-third of the respondents thought they forfeited sales because they did not stock the particular model a customer desired and thus lost

Table 8.5.
Breakdown of Dealership Annual Sales Volume by Unit Type

Unit Type	Average Sales Volume			
	1963	1967	1972	1977[a]
Singlewides & expandables	$114,550	$185,600	$619,700	Declining importance in product mix
Doublewides & triplewides	$13,320	$19,200	$168,530	Many firms specializing in multiple-section units
Used units	$56,530	$53,630	$58,150	Increased importance in product mix
Recreational vehicles	$4,100	$6,920	$33,180	No clear trend
Accessories	$3,140	$3,560	$14,620	Increased importance in product mix
Special units	$180	—	$770	No clear trend
Total annual sales	$191,820	$268,910	$895,050	

a. Since the 1974 recession there has been no such thing as a "typical" dealership; rather, there is a clear trend toward dealer specialization.

Source: PMHI/DS.

Table 8.6.
Problems Affecting
Dealership Business

Problem	1974	1969
Consumer financing	63%	25%
Local zoninig	43%	55%
Industry image	26%	14%
Park space	21%	59%
No national advertising	19%	7%
Poor-quality products	15%	17%
Long delivery time	1%	5%
None	1%	2%

Source: Owens-Corning Fiberglas, Inc., *A Research Study: Focus on the Mobile Home Market* (1970, 1975).

business to rival dealers. One-fifth of the dealers specified that their failure to make a sale often stemmed from poor sales techniques or a lack of follow-up on prospective customers. Many respondents regarded the lack of available park space or site locations and laws regulating the sale and taxation of mobile homes as factors hindering their total sales.

The 1975 Owens-Corning Survey confirmed PMHI's major finding that in recent years difficulties in obtaining financing have overtaken the lack of space as the major barrier to mobile home sales (table 8.6). In 1969, 59 percent of the dealers considered park space the major problem, but only 21 percent felt so in 1974; by 1974 the most frequently cited problem was consumer financial restraints (63 percent versus 25 percent in 1969). There was a marked decrease in mobile homes sold during the recession years of 1974 and 1975, which was a period of tight credit supply and increasing finance rates; the financing problem was compounded by the fact that the recession-induced increase in the rate of repossession of units caused lenders to be more cautious.

Product Mix

The product mix maintained within the inventory of a mobile home dealer's lot depends on a number of variables, including consumer preferences for unit types, access to manufacturers' plants, franchise agreements with manufacturers, and the sizes, brands, and prices of products available through local competitors. In order to provide consumers with a wide choice of units, most mobile home dealers will stock models with the largest possible range in size, price, and style. Because the number of different models has greatly increased over time, it is virtually impossible for any one dealer to market all available models. Dealers have indicated to us that consumers who want a larger unit tend to prefer doublewide models over the intermediary expandables. As more middle-income groups come to regard mobile homes as an acceptable substitute for other forms

of housing, the product mix has shifted toward an increased share of doublewides. In the late 1970s this trend has accelerated to the extent that in some areas almost all units sold may be doublewides. (An analysis of the national mobile home product mix over time can be found in chapter 4.)

In the last few years the average sales price of a mobile home unit has risen from $6060 in 1969 to about $13,000 for a single-wide and $20,350 for a doublewide in 1977; dimensions have increased from an average of 684 square feet in 1969 to over 950 square feet for a singlewide and 1500 for a doublewide in 1977. Manufacturers questioned by PMHI projected that this trend toward larger units will continue through the 1980s. Although medium- and lower-priced units will continue to be popular, singlewide units will become longer and more conventional materials will be used in the interiors and exteriors of mobile units. We expect that changes in product design that provide an increasingly homelike atmosphere at least cost will further attract persons in the middle-income market who would otherwise choose a condominium or apartment. There is now an emerging trend toward use of sectional units (doublewides conforming to factory-built housing codes) in urban areas and doublewides conforming to the federal mobile home construction and safety standards in rural areas. Any discussion of "average" price, however, is somewhat misleading in that it fails to reflect pronounced regional variations. In California, for instance, high-quality, high-priced products predominate, but substantially lower-priced units are most common in Appalachia.

Although doublewides will increasingly occupy a major portion of the mobile home market, higher-quality units will have a marked effect on dealer operations. Lot size may increase or the number of units displayed may decrease in order to accommodate the demand for larger models. Dealers with small lot areas may have to rely more on sales from custom orders than display and inventory stock. The sale of sectional units implies greater dealer familiarity with local regulations and more sophisticated setup procedures. Finally, in anticipation of the sale of more expensive units increasingly designed for urban situations, dealer marketing orientation and servicing procedures may expand in response to a more diversified and demanding customer population.

Renting and Leasing of Units

Dealers usually do not rent or lease mobile homes. According to the PMHI/DS, 68 percent of the respondents indicated that none of the units they distributed to consumers were rented or leased. The respondents who did engage in renting or leasing activities (32 percent) noted that 87 percent of those units were utilized for residential purposes and 13 percent were used for non-residential purposes. We would infer from this sampling that dealers are interested in obtaining the immediate benefits of direct sales as opposed to the deferred cash benefits derived from short-term rental and leasing activities that might cultivate buyers.

Although renting and leasing activities may detract from potential sales, more rentals of units could bring about positive results over the long term. Mobile home rentals allow dealers and the industry at large to tap new housing markets, reaching those who otherwise would usually rent apartments. In areas in which the existing rental housing stock is scarce, rental mobile homes may provide a viable housing alternative. Mobile home rental would appeal to consumers who want to live in a mobile home but cannot finance the purchase of a unit. More emphasis on the renting and leasing of units might help dealers to cope with the seasonality that plagues the mobile home industry and thus its distribution system by providing a source of income during slow selling seasons. Increased renting activities would also acquaint more people with this form of housing and thus create a new market of potential buyers.

The Used Mobile Home Market

According to the PMHI/DS, only 6.7 percent of respondents' total sales revenue was derived from the sale of used mobile homes. This figure may be a misleading indicator of the importance of used mobile homes in dealership operations because one-third to two-thirds of all dealership sales transactions involve trade-ins. A survey conducted during the 1968–1972 period by *Mobile Home and Recreational Vehicle Magazine* indicated that 74 percent of the sample population of dealers resold used units. There is a growing market for used mobile homes: One industry source estimates that the sale of used mobile homes will occupy 50 percent of dealers' future business operations.

The sale of used mobile homes is profitable for both dealer and consumer. The low price and predominantly low down payment appeal to buyers seeking the least costly yet most comfortable housing possible. Many dealers sell used units for as little as $1500, with a down payment of $500 or less. The mobile home owner who can trade in an old unit for a new model also benefits from the increasing marketing for used units. Some dealers claim up to 100 percent profit on the sales of used units. The dealer profits twice on such sales: from the sale of the used unit and of the new unit generated by the trade-in. Furthermore, a satisfied customer might eventually return to the dealer's lot for the purchase of a new unit.

Dealers sell used units either "as is" or considerably refurbished. Although dealers who do recondition units invest considerable time and money, the returns on such investments are generally high. Some large dealerships have an area specifically designed for renovating used mobile homes; this process includes interior and exterior cleaning and replacement of worn furniture, draperies, carpeting, or flooring. The item most carefully selected for a refurbished unit is the furniture because dealers feel that if the furniture is attractive, the entire unit will be appealing to the prospective buyer. The cost of completely refurbishing a used unit can range from a few hundred dollars to $2000, depending on the type and quality of the furnishings.

According to the PMHI/DS, the largest number of dealers pay $1501–$2500 (44 percent) or $2001–$3000 (22 percent) for used units. The most frequently reported resale prices are $2801–$2500 (26.1 percent) or $3001–$3500 (24.2 percent). The markup rate for pricing a used unit is determined by the age and condition of the unit, the extent of refurbishing, and the amount of warranty coverage. (Many dealers offer a thirty-day warranty on used mobile homes.) The average markup on a used unit is 20–25 percent. Dealers surveyed by *Mobile Home and Recreational Vehicle Magazine* in 1969–1972 set markup rates that varied from 6 percent to 25 percent of the price they had paid; in 1973 these dealers' markup rates were between 10 percent and 33 percent. The increased rate probably reflects dealers' recognition of the growing demand for used mobile homes as well as more extensive and costly refurbishing. Some dealers used fixed markup rates that ranged from $150 to $900. Although it provides a small share of dealers' total sales revenue, the sale of used mobile homes has a substantial impact on dealer profits for both new and used mobile homes. There will probably be increased marketing of the new, larger, and more expensive units whill will stimulate trade-ins and the sale of used mobile homes.

Retail Pricing Policies
To satisfy the various tastes of mobile home buyers, manufacturers produce a wide assortment of units. In the late 1970s the prevalent retail price range for new single-wides is $7000–$19,000 and for double-wides, $11,000–$30,000; this is at a time when the average sales price of a new single-family home is exceeding $50,000. The primary factors influencing dealer pricing policies include overall supply and demand conditions, the costs incurred for operational expenses, and the desired rate of return on investment. In order to determine how a dealer arrives at final retail prices, the PMHI/DS asked dealers to indicate, by percentage breakdown, all costs and expenses incurred in selling a typical, average-priced model. A detailed examination of this information on the fixed and variable costs, as well as company and plant characteristics and other

factors that determine variations in dealership distribution costs, can be found in chapter 9.

Most manufacturers offer dealers a suggested retail price for the units they produce. After ascertaining the acceptable local price levels, dealers most often set prices by a percentage markup from the wholesale price of the unit. The resulting price may or may not correspond to the retail price suggested by manufacturers. Of the dealers queried by PMHI, 77.4 percent did not follow the suggested retail prices of their manufacturers, either because the manufacturers did not suggest any retail prices or because dealers chose to set their own retail price; 42.6 percent lowered their retail prices and 34 percent increased retail prices above those set by the manufacturer. Retail prices were changed by a margin of 1 percent–25 percent by 90.2 percent of these dealers; 7.3 percent adjusted prices by a margin of 26 percent–50 percent. Thus, for these dealers the adjusted selling price usually did not vary more than 25 percent from the suggested retail selling price.

According to manufacturers interviewed by PMHI, dealer markups from wholesale prices normally range from 10 percent to 40 percent. The manufacturers noted two major conditions conducive to high markup rates: The markup percentage for doublewides and more expensive models is considerably greater than those for standard 12-wides and 14-wides and markups are usually higher in states with either strict zoning regulation or closed park situations. When land is scarce, as in areas with strict zoning regulations or park space shortages, sales are often inhibited and dealers raise prices in order to achieve an adequate profit. Dealers associated with closed parks can often exert price leverage because they enjoy a somewhat monopolistic position. However, we expect that as zoning regulations become more favorable for mobile home developments and the number of closed parks decreases, local dealer competition will regulate price policy.

When asked by PMHI to state factors that influence their pricing policies, most dealers cited the status of the local market. In areas where competition is low, dealers are able to employ high markup rates. However, the recent tight economic conditions have resulted in greater competition, especially in the Southern and Western regions. This has forced dealers to lower prices, often offering substantial discounts to local consumers. Selling at low markup rates and at prices lower than manufacturers' suggested retail prices allows such dealers to maximize total sales volume and consequently increase total sales revenue and total profits. Respondents also noted that manufacturers often cannot accurately account for added expenses or circumstances that are assumed by dealers. Added costs include overhead and sales commissions, hauling and delivering the mobile home, setting up the unit, installing additional furnishings, and providing the services specified by the terms of the dealer's warranty. In addition, for those units with less attractive outward appearances or with suggested retail prices set too high for a particular market area, the actual selling price may be reduced.

Both manufacturers and dealers mentioned seasonality as a condition that influences dealership pricing policies. In the slow winter months, some manufacturers offer bonuses, promotions, rebates, or lower prices on units to those dealers who can reach a specified quota during this time. According to the manufacturers interviewed by PMHI, some dealers buy these low-priced units from producers but do not pass on the price reductions to consumers. On the other hand, in trying to fulfill manufacturers' quotas, some dealers are left with too many units in their inventories and have to lower profit margins by cutting retail prices in order to sell these excess units. If manufacturers do not offer off-season bonuses, dealers may have to lower retail prices to match the competitive prices of those dealers who do receive such reductions.

Dealer Organization of Retail Sales

Depending on the size and location of dealerships and the markets available, mobile home sales are either directly from inventory or from custom orders. Most buyers will purchase what is available in a dealer's inventory stock. However, because most dealerships are unlikely to maintain an inventory large and diverse enough to please all customers, direct factory custom orders can satisfy individual buyer preferences as well as provide additional sales for the dealer.

A mean of 68 percent of units sold by PMHI/DS respondents came directly from lot inventory. Most dealers (34.3 percent) sold 81 percent–100 percent of their units from inventory; a small 8.6 percent sold only 0–20 percent of units from inventory. The variation in consumer preference for size and price of units is the major factor that controls the inventory level maintained by dealerships. Other key influences include the availability of wholesale financing, the credit terms available from manufacturers, the past rates of inventory turnover, local demand conditions, seasonal variations in demand, the extent of local competition, the size of the dealer's lot, and the delivery time of units from a manufacturer. For 43.3 percent of the PMHI/DS respondents, the dollar value of their average inventory level was $101,000–$500,000; 33.4 percent had average inventories of $21,000–$100,000.

Dealers generally keep up to four months of potential sales in their stock. The average turnover of merchandise for most dealerships ranges from once every two months to ten times a year.

Dealers order homes from manufacturers after becoming aware of the selection through several sources: mobile home shows, advertisements in national dealer or consumer magazines, or manufacturers' sales representatives. The manufacturer usually delivers the mobile homes directly to the dealer's lot. Over 75 percent of the PMHI/DS respondents stated that the length of time from order to delivery was between sixteen and fifty days; the mean figure is thirty days. However, a relatively long delivery time for orders does not appear to present a significant disadvantage to dealers.

Although some dealers attempt to keep custom orders to a minimum, others profit primarily from retailing custom-built units or special orders. Those who engage in the sale of custom orders either offer manufacturers' products that are custom built or add various options to a basic model. Customizing and rearranging may involve various structural changes, such as moving the interior walls of a unit. The added cost of custom work done by the dealer is figured into the total purchase price of the product. One manufacturer interviewed by PMHI allows customers to design their own units through special "design aids" obtainable from dealers. These materials include floor plan diagrams for designing interior space and information concerning available decors and colors.

Custom orders do not affect length of delivery time from the manufacturer for 49.2 percent of respondents to the PMHI/DS; 35.6 percent stated that delivery of custom orders takes up to ten days longer than standard orders. The delivery time for customized units rarely exceeds thirty additional days. Variations in the length of delivery time for customized units depend primarily on the degree of the manufacturers' capacity utilization at the time the order is placed. The extent of customization needed, replacement of parts, and major structural changes are also taken into account.

Sales of Accessories

Almost all dealerships sell accessories and many maintain accessory stores on their lots. Mobile home buyers often want extra features that, if not ordered in the initial sales transaction, can be purchased from a dealer at a later time. Features that mobile home owners most often order with their initial purchase are central air conditioning, full skirting, automatic clothes washer and dryer, carpeting throughout, extra insulation, and a patio or carport. Although most of these items represent factory-installed standard options, many of them can be supplied and installed by the dealer. The major items purchased by many owners after the sale of the home include automatic clothes washer and dryer, steps, full skirting, patio or carport, awnings, and a window air conditioner (table 8.7). Some items added to a unit by the dealer, such as central air conditioning,

Table 8.7.
Demand for Special-Order Features

Feature	% Respondents				
	Came with Home	Special Ordered	Purchased Later	Owned Previously	Do Not Have
Automatic clothes washer	10	12	33	3	42
Clothes dryer	10	11	29	2	48
Full skirting	18	13	25	a	44
Steps	51	6	27	a	16
Central air conditioning	13	16	11	a	60
Patio or carport cover	8	8	15	–	69
Awnings	5	7	15	a	73
Window air conditioner	1	2	15	a	82
Deluxe furniture pack	29	7	9	2	53
Carpet throughout	58	9	2	–	31
Extra insulation	29	9	1	–	60
Deluxe grade carpet	32	8	2	–	58
Double-door refrigerator	37	6	3	1	53
Dishwasher	15	5	4	a	76
Garbage disposal	23	6	1	–	70
Extra-large hot water heater	30	6	1	–	63
Deluxe electric range	16	4	1	a	79
All-electric home	24	7	–	–	69

a. Less than 1/2%.

Source: Owens-Corning Fiberglas, Inc., *The New Mobile Home Market* (1975).

carpeting, extra-sized water heaters, and plumbing for wash'ng machines, are difficult to install.

Table 8.8 illustrates mobile home owners' preferences for particular items, many of which can be supplied by dealers. Given the broad range of extra features that mobile home owners desire, dealers consider it an advantage to maintain as wide a stock of accessories as possible. Dealers who provide a wide variety of accessories not only serve the consumers by offering them the convenience of one-stop shopping but also substantially contribute to the retailing of the mobile homes by making the units look more attractive. PMHI/DS respondents indicated that an average of only 1.6 percent of their total revenues was derived from the sale of accessories. Thus dealers do not provide the time-consuming and difficult accessory installation services solely for profit. By responding to users' wants a dealer generates sales and aids the consumer who may later prove to be a repeat customer or who may recommend the dealer to friends.

Trade-in Policies

Many mobile home owners who want a larger and newer unit offer their present unit in trade to a dealer. The average age of trade-in units accepted by most (36 percent) of the respondents to the PMHI/DS was five to six years old. Although the sale of used units from trade-ins represents only a small portion of the total sales revenue for most dealers, these sales are indirectly very profitable. The percentage markup on trade-ins is generally lower than that on new units, yet dealers are able to save on expenditures by avoiding some of the costs inherent in the sale of a new unit (such as warranty servicing). As a result, a dealer's profit margin on used units often parallels the profits on new units. If, as is usually the case, a dealer buys a used unit from a customer in the form of credit toward the purchase of a new unit, the dealer often nets a profit on the sales of both new and used units. However, when competition for new unit sales is strong, a dealer may forego any profit on the traded unit in order to sustain the level of new unit sales. There was a marked rise in the number of trade-ins during the last recession as a result of the increased competition as well as the generally poor economic conditions.

A PMHI cross-tabulation indicates that more newer dealerships tend to make sales involving trade-ins than do older ones (table 8.9). Newer dealers trying to get established seem more willing to chance the risks inherent in accepting trade-ins. Those dealers who do not readily accept trade-ins are usually concerned with the future marketability of a used product.

When asked what items other than mobile homes they accepted as trade-ins, about 20 percent of PMHI/DS respondents indicated that they accepted no other items as trade-ins, and several dealers accepted almost anything. As listed in table 8.10, dealers accept a varied array of trade-in items ranging from automobiles and furniture to horses and pigs. Some dealers who did not specify particular items remarked that they accepted anything with a cash value, that can be resold, or that can be brought to their lots. One dealer noted he will accept anything "that doesn't eat"; another indicated he will accept anything "that doesn't have to be fenced in or fed." In accepting trade-in items other than mobile homes, dealers enable people who do not have access to cash resources to afford to purchase a mobile home by trading in durable goods of value. These wide-ranging trade-in policies are particularly important to the two major populations of mobile home buyers: young married couples who have few cash assets and the elderly who over time may have acquired several durable items of cash value. The general flexibility of present trade-in policies illustrates the highly significant service function dealers perform.

Market Profile

In order to make advertising an effective marketing tool, dealers must ascertain which consumers are most likely to be interested in mobile home living and what may influence their decision to buy a unit. Various marketing techniques, including professional marketing research, are available to dealers to give an overview of the local buyer potentials and particular consumer preferences. A market profile will not only suggest advertising themes and the best type of media to be used but may also provide information concerning selling approaches and techniques to be used once the consumer is at the sales lot.

Our mobile home occupant profiles, drawn largely from data from the U.S. Bureau of the Census, indicate that the mobile home dweller differs significantly from the rest of the population in such aspects as income, ownership, occupation, age, and family size. Income is the most important variable: The average income of mobile home families is much lower than that of families in conventional housing, who are, however, less likely to own their homes. The primary demand for mobile homes comes from such moderate-income groups as blue-collar working families and retirees. There are more young families in mobile homes than in conventional housing, and the mobile home families tend to have more children under six. (A detailed description of the characteristics of mobile home versus conventional housing dwellers can be found in chapter 11, section A.)

After accounting for demographic and economic characteristics of the local potential

Table 8.8.
Purchase Probability of
Accessories for a New
Mobile Home

Accessory/Extra Cost	% Consumers Who Definitely or Probably Would Buy
Frost-free refrigerator ($127–175)	74
Full-sized tub ($15–25)	70
More insulation ($75–125)	67
Better-quality interior paneling ($75–100)	63
Better-grade carpet ($100–150)	62
Large-capacity water heater ($70–80)	61
Deluxe draperies and curtains ($100–125)	60
House–type windows ($150–200)	58
Central air conditioning ($700–800)	58
Carpet throughout home ($125–175)	55
Fiberglass tub/shower ($125–150)	55
Foam sheathing insulation ($150–200)	52
Storm windows ($175–200)	52
Better-quality furniture ($400–600)	46
Better ceiling material ($40–60)	46
Washer ($180–220)	41
Disposal ($40–60)	41
More attractive kitchen cabinets ($75–125)	41
House-type lap siding ($500–625)	39
Dryer ($150–175)	39
All-electric home ($400–500)	38
Dishwasher ($175–200)	37
Deluxe electric range ($125–175)	37
Shingle roof ($100–150)	33
Sliding glass door ($75–125)	33
AM/FM system ($200–250)	25
Central vacuum system ($125–175)	20
Trash compactor ($175–225)	15

Source: Owens-Corning Fiberglas, Inc., *The New Mobile Home Market* (1975).

Table 8.9.
Percent age of Retail
Sales Involving Trade-
ins Compared with Age
of Dealership Operations

% Retail Sales Involving Trade-ins	Age of Dealership Operations (Years)				
	0–5	6–10	11–15	16–25	>25
0–5	21.2	3.0	1.5	4.5	1.5
6–10	6.1	7.6	1.5	4.5	0.0
11–20	10.6	4.5	1.5	6.1	1.5
21–30	3.0	1.5	6.1	1.5	0.0
31–50	3.0	1.5	3.0	3.0	0.0
>50	0.0	0.0	1.5	0.0	0.0

Source: Cross-tabulation from PMHI/DS.

Table 8.10.
Items Accepted as
Trade-ins by Dealers

Item	Number of Dealers
Automobile	23
Furniture	10
Travel trailer	8
Boat	8
Motorcycle	6
Real estate	5
Camper	4
Truck	3
Vehicles	2
Recreational vehicles	2
Appliances	2
Livestock	2
Pickups	2
Airplanes	1
Real property	1
Motor homes	1
Tools	1
Farm machinery	1
Houses (conventional)	1
Snowmobiles	1
Automotive vehicles	1
Horses	1
Pigs	1

Source: PMHI/DS.

mobile home buyer, a market profile often determines a consumer's needs and desires. Using this information, a dealer may direct advertising and sales promotion toward the particular assets in the mobile homes on his lot. The Owens-Corning Survey found that in purchasing a particular brand 73 percent of the mobile home owners were influenced by the floor plan of a particular unit. A majority indicated that price was a major factor in considering a purchase; interior design, construction, and exterior appearance were also important consumer preferences (table 8.11).

Advertising

Marketing any product involves the use of mass media to attract public attention to the product and to the particular retailer. Advertising in the mobile home industry assumes two forms: Manufacturers and suppliers advertise in national trade magazines, and dealers advertise in their local markets. We consider manufacturer advertising methods in our discussion because they influence dealer purchasing decisions and inform dealers of new products available for retail.

Manufacturer advertising in general tends to be competitive rather than cooperative. Competitive advertising is found in most trade journals and is geared toward readers who are already familiar with mobile homes, specifically, dealers and park developers. Such advertising stresses the selling points and features of a particular product and introduces product innovation. Manufacturer advertising in trade journals is one of the few areas in mobile home marketing in which brand names are considered important. Two major mobile home manufacturers have recently implemented marketing methods rather innovative in the industry. In 1977 Champion Home Builders launched an unprecedented national network television campaign, sponsoring commercials on such widely viewed programs as the "Tonight Show," "Today Show," and all three network news shows. The company complemented the national effort with local advertising by supplying its retailers with merchandising materials designed to be used in the dealer's individual market. Skyline joined the growing ranks of companies sponsoring entertainment at industry trade shows in order to enhance corporate image when it mounted a musical revue focusing on the mobile home industry at a recent Annual National Mobile Home Industry Convention.

In relation to their size and the limited geographic boundaries of their market, dealers tend to pursue local competitive advertising. Ads are directed for the most part toward those population sectors most likely to be attracted to mobile home living (most often young couples and retired people).

The size of the dealer's advertising budget may fluctuate. When retail sales fail to produce a desired profit margin, dealers may

Table 8.11.
Reasons Consumers
Buy a Particular
Mobile Home

Reason	%
Floor plan layout	73
Price	51
Interior design and decor	46
Construction	36
Exterior appearance	22
Approved by U/L or other test agency	13
Dealer's warranty	9
Manufacturer's warranty	7
Other	4

Source: Owens-Corning Fiberglas, Inc., *The New Mobile Home Market* (1975).

invest large sums of money in extensive promotion campaigns in order to increase sales volume quickly. Although sales volume may fall off during seasonal periods of slower sales and decreased competition, dealers usually maintain normal advertising budgets in anticipation of attracting at least some sales during slow selling periods.

A dealer may make use of all advertising media or choose to concentrate in one. PMHI/DS found that most respondents (86 percent) advertised in local newspapers, usually running classified ads in the real estate section of the weekday issues. The Yellow Pages were used by 82 percent, 73 percent bought radio time, 50 percent advertised on television, and 27 percent relied on mobile home shows. Only a few use television and/or radio advertising exclusively. Mobile home dealers prefer to run TV advertising in April, May, June, September, and October. Since most of the dealers who use television or radio advertising or both have sales lots distributed over several counties, they therefore maximize the geographic coverage of a broadcast signal. The obvious advantage of TV advertising is that it offers a greater number of people a more complete visual and audio presentation of the mobile home product than do "stationary" ads. Because a large and diverse population is exposed to such advertising, it also creates a consumer consciousness and product orientation to those unfamiliar with mobile home living. Ads in the Yellow Pages, mail campaigns, billboards, handbills, and displays in shopping centers are relatively inexpensive yet often highly effective advertising methods, especially when a dealer wishes to reach a specific type of consumer.

Dealers feel that it is advantageous to pursue general themes in advertising. They may be identified by a particular printed logo or an unusual song or voice. Dealers often hire advertising agencies to prepare ad presentations. In the 1975 Owens-Corning Survey dealers indicated the dominant themes used in their presentations: 76 percent used the dealer's name, 17 percent mentioned the manufacturer's name, and 12 percent indicated the name of a park. Because of the lack of public familiarity with individual firms in the mobile home industry, brand names are seldom stressed. In order to attract buyers to the sales lot, dealers often advertise the most popular or the most attractive unit even though it may not be the most profitable selling item for the retailer. Dealers also use advertising to inform the public of new product design and innovation. Emphasis is placed on the product's similarity yet cost savings compared to conventional housing. This attracts old as well as new mobile home consumers. "Image" advertising may further sell the mobile home concept as convenient, comfortable, and economical.

Public Relations

A major obstacle to the growth and improvement of the mobile home industry today is its poor public image. Dealers can be instrumental in improving the image and reputation of the mobile home industry, for they have the greatest public access and exposure and stand as the communication link between consumers and manufacturers.

Dealers may undertake public relations programs on their own or carry out programs funded by manufacturers or suppliers. Some large dealerships hire their own public relations person to maintain full-time community relations. An informative and substantive public relations program is a profitable investment; it not only presents an attractive mobile home image to the community but also may directly increase sales. The 1975 Owens-Corning Survey found that 15 percent of mobile home owners bought from a particular dealer because of his or her reputation. Mobile home consumers have become more critical and demanding, looking for quality and good construction in homes. The "fast sell" is being replaced by consumer awareness and assistance programs conducted by dealers with the help of state and regional trade associations. Thus dealers are not only responsible for selling the mobile home product, but they have also assumed more of a role in selling the concept of mobile home living in general.

In order to maintain a good reputation within their communities, dealers often stress the importance of continued communication with former customers by employing such follow-up methods as periodic telephone calls, personal visits, informative mailings, and Christmas cards. Dealers contact new customers through direct mailings slanted toward such prime mobile home prospective buyers as newlyweds, retired people, young professionals, and military personnel.

Public relations programs can successfully communicate product improvement. These programs are often initiated by manufacturers and implemented at the retail level. Many dealers send out literature prepared by their manufacturers concerning various models of mobile homes as well as association-prepared pamphlets that describe mobile home living. Consumer response to this type of material is often passed on to manufacturers or suppliers for production and marketing information. Most members of the general public, industry, and government are unfamiliar with the mobile home product of today and its potentials in the housing industry of the future. Several steps have been taken to remedy this: Associations are offering dealers packages of multimedia material to be used in schools, shopping centers, and sales lots; manufacturers and suppliers produce films to be shown at dealer "open houses"; and, recognizing the "trailer park" image of mobile homes, associations are launching series of nationwide seminars intended for the media, government, and housing officials. That not nearly enough is done in the public relations area, however, is clear from the fact that the word "trailer" is not yet a word of the past.

Conditioning of Units

Before being sent to a dealer, mobile homes are outfitted with interior furnishings at the last main assembly line stations of a manufacturer's factory. Unit interiors are designed to recreate a variety of the design patterns used in middle- to upper-income conventional housing (for example, early American, French provincial, or Mediterranean). Most units are equipped with furniture, carpeting, draperies, curtains, bedspreads, mirrors, and, occasionally, reproductions of paintings. Refrigerators and ranges are the basic appliances placed in all units. Higher-priced models often include luxury items such as dishwashers, laundry units, air conditioners, special partitioning, and garbage disposals. The dealer receiving the unit decides if the interior furnishings or the general decor should be improved. Because the unit is totally factory finished, there is little a dealer can do to change the overall appearance; however, dealers can change the more minute particulars of the interior by adding or substituting accessories from their own stocks. A customer may request additional furnishings that the dealer can install. The cost of redecorating a new unit can range from a few dollars to a few hundred dollars.

Dealers who carefully inspect a mobile home before it is sold encounter fewer service problems once the home is occupied. When units are received from manufacturers, dealers clean the homes and check for any possible defects, such as the operations of all appliances as well as plumbing, electrical, and heating/cooling systems. In the 1970 Owens-Corning Survey, 84 percent of dealers questioned conducted an electrical test, 78

C. Services

Presale Operations

percent tested the water-plumbing mechanisms, and 67 percent tested the heating system; by the late 1970s these tests had become fairly common practice. There are also several presale service problems that usually require the dealer's immediate attention; the most common of these include malfunctioning of the heating system, plumbing and gas leaks, roof and window leaks, loose electrical connections, or minor damage to the interior of the home. Presale inspections alert dealers to malfunctions that may be costly later under warranty provisions.

Aid to Consumers
The purchase of their mobile home is often the most costly investment ever made by many buyers. In fact, in most cases, it is their first owned home. (According to the Owens-Corning Survey, 73 percent of the mobile home owner-respondents had not owned a primary residence before buying a mobile home.) Therefore, before deciding on a particular unit, prospective buyers take time to view homes and to discuss with salespeople all of the possible products and special features available within their budget. The 1975 Owens-Corning Survey found that people visited an average of 4.21 dealerships and considered an average of 2.61 brands before reaching a final decision. Floor plan layout, price, interior design and decor, and construction heavily influenced the buyer's decision.

When a consumer decides to buy, a reliable dealer will explain all of the particulars related to mobile home ownership and any special aspects of the home selected. The explanation of the financing plans offered by the dealership is perhaps the single most important factor involved in transacting a sale. The Consumer Protection Act (Truth-in-Lending) requires that the mobile home dealer specify the cost of financing the home to the consumer. If a mobile home sale involves financing (many consumers pay the full amount in cash), a specific percentage of the sales price has to be paid immediately as a down payment. The size of the down payment varies from a minimum of 5 percent under VA and FHA regulations to 10 percent–15 percent of the selling price. The dealer should explain the insurance plans offered and should also know how to assist those eligible to obtain VA or FHA loans. In addition, most dealers explain the methods and types of taxation levied on mobile home owners by state and local governments. Financing plans are described in detail in the discussion of consumer financing in chapter 15.

If the mobile home is to be located on a park site and the buyer has not already located one, some dealers give information on park sites in the area. A dealer should alert buyers to the regulations pertaining to parks as well as to the laws governing mobile home use and occupancy. Most dealers are familiar with these regulations because many are involved in park ownership/operations. Dealers also explain the services offered by the dealership or by local specialists for setting up the mobile home, for maintenance and repairs, and for replacement of parts. Before the sales contract is signed, it is the dealer's responsibility to discuss the details of the contract and the warranty agreements with the buyers.

Referral to Parks
About 86 percent of the PMHI/DS respondents did not help prospective buyers find park sites other than in parks they owned. We thus surmise that most dealers believe it is the buyer's responsibility to locate a mobile home park site. The 10 percent who did provide the service of park referral did so primarily because they thought it was a good sales policy and that it helped to finalize a sale. Different methods are used in referring customers to park sites. Some dealers locate park sites by contacting local park managers or owners; others rent lots in mobile home parks in anticipation of potentian sales. Dealers rely on listings of park operators and "good parks," listings of parks with vacancies, and updated maps distributed by dealer and park associations. Although the severe lack of park space has been alleviated somewhat in recent years, this continues to be a major problem in the mobile home distribution system and often thwarts sales. Dealers responding to the PMHI/DS claimed that they could have sold an average of 49 percent more homes had more park space been available.

Integration into park ownership or other park activities can be a profitable investment when coupled with the retailing of mobile homes. The continuing shortage of park space enables those dealers who have an ownership interest in mobile home parks to locate sites for more customers than dealers who do not maintain any park interests. According to the PMHI/DS, it appears that integration into park ownership or park activities (having greater access to park space) could enhance dealer sales. However, the greatest obstacle limiting dealer location of park sites is unfavorable zoning regulations, which are further discussed in chapter 16. Park development activities also provide dealers with a year-round income that subsequently allows them to sustain the sharp sales declines during the slow winter months. It is therefore not surprising that 62.7 percent of the PMHI/DS respondents were involved in park operations and 34 percent were involved in park development. There is a growing interest on the part of many dealers to become active in park management, especially with the slower sales activity of recent years.

Only 1 percent of the PMHI/DS respondents who had an ownership interest in mobile home parks generally accepted as tenants only those who purchased units directly from them, but this does not mean that others do not reserve at least a certain portion of their park's capacity for their own customers. It appears that, on the whole, the majority of parks in which dealers have an ownership interest do not discriminate between tenants on the basis of where the unit was bought. However, it is possible that some dealers who have an interest in the ownership of a park (and thus control of park policy) may tend to restrict entrance into their parks to those tenants who purchase their units from them. This is known as a closed park. When zoning restricts mobile homes to parks and a dealer owns the only park in the vicinity, closed park policies give the dealer monopoly power that may have adverse social and economic effects not only on the consumer but also on the growth of the industry.

Delivery of Units

The dealer is usually responsible for the delivery of the mobile home to the buyer's park site or private lot. Trucks tow the unit on its own chassis to the site. Although most dealerships maintain at least one company truck for this purpose, some hire outside transport companies or use other means, such as truck rental. Of the dealers surveyed by PMHI, 74 percent relied on their own truck(s) to make all or part of their deliveries; outside help is often contracted when the larger numbers of mobile homes sold during peak seasons exceed the delivery capacity of a dealership's own fleet of trucks. Almost one-third of the respondents used outside towing services, but only 13 percent used them exclusively. It is highly probable that the return on investment for most of these dealerships does not justify the added costs of the purchase and maintenance of a company truck. However, small dealers who must rely on transport firms to deliver their units are at a disadvantage to the larger firms whose scale of operations enables them to purchase or lease their own trucking fleet. The higher costs of delivery by commercial carriers are most likely to be passed on to the consumer.

Although the considerations that enter into a dealership's calculations of average shipping costs per mile differ for each operation, it is interesting to note the variances in delivery costs between a company using its own truck(s), hiring local service companies, or employing other means of transportation to deliver a unit. Self-delivery, with an average cost of $0.62 per mile, is the least expensive method; it is only half as expensive as delivery by a hired trucking firm ($1.26 per mile average) and slightly less expensive than other means of delivery ($0.68 per mile average). (Further analysis of the movement of mobile homes can be found in chapter 14.)

Installation

The mobile home sales contract guarantees that the dealer will either set up the unit on the chosen site or hire mobile home movers or other professional installers to carry out the setup. The home is set upon concrete blocks or jacks on a site that has been checked to make certain that undue settling of the ground will not occur. Dealers who invest the time and money to ensure that the unit is properly blocked and leveled will have fewer service requests for corrections from buyers. Incorrect blocking and leveling can cause buckling and loosening of parts of the unit, as well as improper closing, binding, sagging of the windows, doors and cabinets, and malfunctions of plumbing and electrical systems. After it is properly blocked and leveled, the mobile home is connected to all utilities. The dealer or the installing technician is responsibile for testing the utility systems (water and drainage, gas or oil hookup, and electrical).

Most dealers can set up a mobile home in one day. The length of time varies with the type of unit to be installed, the number of installers assigned to the task, and the complexities encountered at each site. Half of the PMHI/DS respondents indicated that they required an average of only six man-hours to install a unit, 29.8 percent estimated fifteen hours, and 17.5 percent said twenty hours. State or local building codes usually require the inspection and approval of the setup and hookup of mobile homes. After the on-site installation of a home is approved by a local building inspector, a conscientious dealer makes certain that a customer understands the setup and obtains written approval from the buyer before turning over ownership of the home. Some dealers contact the owner within a specified period of time after initial occupancy in order to determine if the unit has remained level and if the utility systems function reliably.

Postsale inspections of the setup and hookup of units have become a topic of interest within the industry. Because a large number of warranty claims concern improper setup and leveling, the Federal Trade Commission intends to require inspection of the unit during and ninety days following installation. Because dealers have traditionally assumed this responsibility, such requirements would entail a restructuring of manufacturer and dealer activities and could prove costly to the manufacturers. If all dealers would guarantee full inspection of the home upon installation, the time- and cost-consuming FTC regulations would be unnecessary, as would many of the present warranty claims.

A mobile home dealer's obligation to a customer does not end when a unit has been delivered and set up on a buyer's site. Customers frequently encounter problems

Postsale Operations

when they assume occupancy of units, and they contact the dealer from whom the unit was purchased to perform necessary repairs and adjustments. Dealers have traditionally assumed the responsibility for making adjustments because they regard it as proper sales policy to retain the customers' goodwill or they are obligated under dealer warranties.

Maintenance and Servicing

The more carefully dealers inspect units before delivery and conduct on-site hookup and retesting, the fewer postsale maintenance difficulties are encountered. Many of the problems that do arise are the result of damages that occur during the transportation of the unit from the dealer's lot to the buyer's site; many warranty claims are attributed to insufficient preparation prior to delivery. Poor workmanship on the interior and exterior of the unit and defective parts installed at the manufacturer's plants cause problems that require servicing, as do defective appliances supplied by brand name manufacturers. Who must assume liability for these defects is addressed in our discussion below of warranty coverage.

Table 8.12 compares the problems reported by mobile home owners during surveys conducted by Owens-Corning in 1969 and 1974. For several problems, the percentage changes were large between 1969 and 1974. Plumbing problems were listed by 38 percent of the respondents in 1969 but by only 21 percent in 1974. Furnace/heating problems also decreased; these were mentioned by 25 percent of owners in 1969 and 11 percent in 1974. Fewer problems in these areas reflect the fact that the increasing sophistication of the mobile home industry has led to greater quality control on the part of the manufacturer, as well as the evolution of more mature dealers who can perform more competent on-site installations. On the other hand, some categories showed an increase in problems: The percentage of owners reporting faulty doors rose from 15 percent to 22 percent; window problems plagued 4 percent of 1969 respondents and 12 percent of those in 1974; more roofs leaked (10 percent in 1969, 14 percent in 1974); and there were more complaints about electrical systems and hot water tanks. This could be explained by the fact that the mobile home product's continuous evolution toward an ever more houselike appearance brings initial problems; the industry is simply not yet familiar enough with such elements as house-type doors and windows. However, the decrease in some problem categories shows that the difficulties can be solved, so we assume that as dealers become more familiar with the changes in the product, this new rash of problems can also be overcome.

The service problems most commonly handled by respondents to the PMHI/DS included faults in plumbing and electrical systems, roofs, floors, windows, doors, and

Table 8.12.
Problems Reported by Mobile Home Owners upon Moving into New Units

Problem	1969	1974
Plumbing	38%	21%
Furnace/heating	25%	11%
Doors did not close/stick	15%	22%
Electrical	11%	15%
Roof leaked	10%	14%
Oven	10%	10%
Hot water tank	8%	12%
Interior fixtures	6%	3%
Leveling	6%	8%
Carpet	5%	9%
Windows leaked	5%	9%
Window problems	4%	12%
Air conditioning	4%	5%
Doors leaked	4%	6%

Source: Owens-Corning Fiberglas, Inc., *The New Mobile Home Market* (1970, 1975).

furnishings. One-third of the respondents frequently serviced problems with the overall functioning of the electrical and heating/cooling systems, and another third often had to deal with leaks in various parts of the unit.

Many dealers employ such trained repair personnel as carpenters, plumbers, and electricians to perform postsales maintenance. Dealers may have up to eight of such service people but more commonly use between two and four. Dealers without their own servicing agents contract commercial repairpersons. Problems with appliances are often directed to the manufacturer's local service centers. Approximately half of all dealerships maintain one or more repair trucks. Several dealerships maintain service, supplies, and parts centers that are often also stocked with furniture, appliances, and accessories. Dealers offer buyers a discount on the cost of parts and supplies that may be needed once the warranty has expired.

Dealers occasionally send faulty parts to their manufacturers' factories for repair or replacement and service the units when the new or repaired parts are returned. Some manufacturers will dispatch repairpersons to perform service work on major repairs; others pay for the repairs that dealers have made. Dealers run into problems when the lot operation is far from manufacturers' plants. This may cause delays in servicing from manufacturers as well as additional costs. Similarly, problems often arise between mobile home dealers and brand name appliance manufacturers/suppliers because of lack of a direct buy-sell connection. Appliance suppliers usually have no means of identifying dealers who sell units equipped with their appliances. Dealers often experience difficulties in contacting the appliance suppliers if service outlets are not readily located in the area in which the dealership operates.

The majority of dealers regard maintenance and servicing as a necessary but not always profitable activity. Most dealers restrict their setup and servicing activities to mobile homes purchased from them. Few dealers service any home. In the late 1970s an increasing number of dealers continue to provide servicing after a warranty has expired. However unprofitable servicing may be to dealers, the fact that quite a few of all mobile home owners experience maintenance problems upon moving into their new homes indicates the important role that proper postsales servicing plays in the distribution function. An efficient dealer who provides continuous service will reap the "profits" of maintaining a reputable business in a reputable industry, which, in turn, will increase sales.

Communication between dealer and buyer is essential in effective postsales operations. (Some dealers request feedback from customers about the quality of their new homes.) Communication not only fosters a proper relationship with the consumer market, but it also gives dealers an indication of common defects occurring in production or transportation. Some of these defects may then be remedied by alerting the respective manufacturer or appliance supplier for correction in future production. The dealer may also be more alert to these specific problems that could be fixed before the sale of the units, thus avoiding the added costs of postsale servicing.

It is interesting to note the opinions on dealer responsibility for postsales maintenance of another major group of individuals who are instrumental in the mobile home industry: mobile home park owners, developers, and managers. Respondents to PMHI's Park Survey were asked to provide suggestions for changes in mobile home dealerships. Two-thirds of these respondents stated that dealers could or should provide better services during and after sales, and about one-fourth stressed the need for honesty and dependability in dealership operations. Respondents also indicated that dealers should insist on product perfection from their manufacturers and that manufacturers should also perform more service work on the mobile home units. Dealers not involved in park activities often request the opinions of park managers concerning the service work performed on the units placed in their parks. This sort of influence by park managers provides encouragement for more dealers to maintain improving levels of service and repair operations.

Warranty Coverage
Most of the mobile homes dealers sell carry warranties from the dealer as well as the manufacturer. Because of instances of inefficient warranty coverage and irresponsible postsales operations by both manufacturers and dealers, the mobile home industry and government agencies have devoted a great deal of attention to the improvement and clarification of warranty coverage performance. Those who guarantee products must assume costs of providing service for repairs and maintenance, yet these costs may be substantially reduced if product perfection is stressed in production and if dealers make careful examinations of the unit before sale. Warranties are essential to ensure good product performance, and the extent to which manufacturers and dealers provide service on warranties will influence the future image of the mobile home industry.

Manufacturer Liability
Manufacturer warranties on mobile homes certify that the product will be free from defects in workmanship and materials. Should any problems resulting from such defects occur under normal use of the mobile home, the manufacturer is obligated to repair the defective parts within a specified period after the delivery of the home to the original owner. According to the PMHI/DS, 98 percent of the manufacturers represented by the respondents offered warranties ranging from ninety days to over two years. The majority of manufacturers (59 percent) provided warranties of one year, 23 percent guaranteed service for a period of at least ninety days, and 12 percent provided coverage from ninety days to one year. Homes that are financed under VA or FHA programs require warranties of a full year, and a few offered warranty coverage extending beyond one year.

The extent of coverage authorized by manufacturers' warranties varies. Generally, manufacturers guarantee the durability of materials used in the structural body and frame construction of the mobile home such as sidewalls, ceiling, floor frames, roof coverings, and devices for anchoring the home to the ground. Manufacturers' warranties also usually cover interior-exterior parts (doors and windows) and interior features (flooring, ceiling, wood paneling, shelving, and cabinetry) as well as the function of the major systems (plumbing, ventilation, air conditioning, and electrical systems). Separate warranties for the various appliances are normally supplied by the respective appliance manufacturer/supplier.

Dealers depend on the quality of the manufacturers' products and rely on service offered by manufacturers' warranties. Forty three percent of the PMHI/DS respondents mentioned that their manufacturers' warranties extended into broad areas of and/or

causes for possible product defectiveness such as factory defects, faults in workmanship or poor quality construction, structural defects, and shipping damage. One dealer went so far as to say that the manufacturers' warranties covered almost everything. However, some manufacturers' warranties are vague. Sixteen percent of the PMHI/DS respondents' manufacturers guaranteed only "materials" or "construction" or both. Another 11 percent could not specify the particular items of manufacturer warranty coverage but answered that their manufacturers covered only what they build: the complete mobile home. Some dealers' manufacturers provided as little as possible in terms of guarantee of the mobile home. These warranties that do not assume liability for specified items often create difficulties for the consumer and dealer when determining the responsibility for repairs.

Dealer Liability
According to the PMHI/DS, 70 percent of the respondents offered warranties over and above those provided by the manufacturer. Dealers' warranties ranged from one month of free service to an indefinite amount of time. Almost 50 percent of the dealers who provided warranties offered free service for a period of one year; 15 percent service mobile homes for a period up to ninety days. Some dealers indicated that they offered free service for over one year or that the length of their warranty is variable or indefinite. Some dealers' warranties are designed to cover whatever pleased the customer. According to *Mobile Home and Recreational Vehicle Dealer Magazine*, 39 percent of the dealers surveyed between 1969 and 1972 offered one year's free service after delivery and another 39 percent offered ninety-day service. The results of interviews conducted in 1973 by the *Mobile-Modular Housing Dealer Magazine* revealed that almost 60 percent of the dealers offered one year's free service and 32 percent offered service for ninety days. It appears that more dealers are offering warranty coverage or that there has been a trend toward lengthening the term of warranty coverage demonstrated by mobile home dealers.

The extent of dealer warranty coverage varies. Two-fifths of the PMHI/DS respondents stated that their warranties covered almost anything that can happen to a mobile home: all items within the completed unit or any reasonable request for servicing. Several dealers mentioned that specific items covered included minor defects relating to the roof, plumbing, electrical and gas lines, materials, workmanship, scratches, loose paneling, or leaks. Some dealers' warranties covered service problems that were not provided in manufacturers' warranties or problems they considered to be the dealer's responsibility to service. These problems were often related to dealer workmanship or arose from setting up and hooking up the home. A few dealers did not provide written or oral warranty agreements, but, as a matter of protection and sales policy, provided customers with many of the above-mentioned services. Some dealers mentioned that they will go beyond what is considered normal service if necessary and if requested by a customer; however, this is rare.

Federal Regulation of Warranties and Servicing

The 1975 Owens-Corning Survey revealed that of the mobile home owners who received repair service for defects, 72 percent had the repair work performed by dealers and 21 percent were serviced by manufacturers. Thus it is evident that dealers are better equipped, or at least more accessible, to handle warranty-related problems. However, conflicts regarding responsibility for costly repairs do arise, and many times the defect or problem is never fixed or the owner must hire outside repair service. As a result, the consumer must often bear unnecessary costs and inconveniences. An additional victim of these disputes is the dealer, who is exposed to the multiplicity of warranties and the resulting confusion over their context and scope.

Federal and state regulatory agencies have recently recognized the necessity for warranty provisions to be clearly interpreted by manufacturers, dealers, and consumers alike and adhered to by the appropriate warrantor. Based on its belief that existing performance levels for warranty service are insufficient, the Federal Trade Commission initiated proceedings for a proposed Trade Regulation Rule (16 CFR 441, Mobile Home Sales and Service) in the mid-1970s. Public hearings were conducted in the late 1970s and it now appears possible that the rule may be imposed upon the industry by 1980. The proposed Trade Regulation Rule (TRR) would regulate warranty performance in three ways: It would specify time frames within which various classes of warranty service must be initiated or completed; it would require specific actions by warrantors that would formalize the inspection and defect reporting processes and provide records of services undertaken; it would regulate the relationships between warrantors and their designated service agents if such agents were utilized.

Mobile home manufacturers, suppliers, and dealers have generally recognized the legitimacy of a majority of the complaints associated with warranty performance. Industry representatives, however, maintain that the proposed TRR unduly restricts the ability of warrantors to define their warranty structure with respect to variable market conditions and that these restrictions may be to the ultimate detriment of consumers.

Of the three areas covered by the proposed TRR, only the first directly associates inferior performance with higher costs to the manufacturer. One basic concept of sound regulatory practice is to reward favorable actions and to penalize unfavorable actions. Those sections of the proposed TRR that deal with specific required actions by the warrantor and with the relationship between the warrantor and its designated representatives do not make such a distinction and therefore do not encourage favorable action. Thus warrantors who are presently in substantial compliance with the objectives of the TRR will be penalized along with warrantors who are less inclined toward adequate performance levels.

When hearings were begun in late 1977, no detailed studies of the probable implications of the proposed TRR had yet been made, so it is impossible to detail specific results of the regulation. It is possible, however, to suggest three possible changes that would result from the adoption of the TRR. First, there may be a tendency to decrease the number of low-priced units produced. This effect would be especially pronounced if warranty problems are inversely correlated with price. Second, because the TRR would impose significant costs even on firms with no warranty problems, it is reasonable to predict a decrease in the number of firms in the industry due to the exit of smaller firms and the presence of a disincentive to enter the industry. Finally, the nature of the manufacturer-dealer relationship would be changed by the TRR. The impact of the expected changes is presently a subject of debate, but it is clear that the impact upon the industry would be important.

Two problems that have long plagued the mobile home industry are the negative social image associated with mobile home living and the restrictive zoning practices that severely limit the placement of mobile homes in many localities. These two factors can especially affect the dealer, who often has difficulty selling the product under such circumstances. One way dealers and park operators could work together to overcome these problems in a particular area would be to underwrite "model parks" designed to correct the community's negative impressions of mobile home living. Although such an effort would certainly result in a short-term financial loss for the dealer and park operator involved, it could very well yield longer-term positive benefits. The successful establishment of an attractive park would not only help to upgrade the image of the mobile home but could also break down the zoning barriers in the locality, for the community would have visible proof that the mobile home park does not have to be an eyesore and does not have to attract "undesirable" low-income groups.

D. Policy Alternatives

A prerequisite to setting up a model park is, of course, obtaining permission from the local zoning board. The dealer and park operator might accomplish this by offering an attendant community service, such as subsidizing a certain number of units in the park for needy residents, perhaps the elderly. In order to help these tenants acquire and maintain their units, the dealer, working with a lender interested in generating future loans, could offer interest-subsidized loans and the park operator could absorb the park maintenance fees. The dealer and park operator might even be able to obtain funds from federal programs to help shoulder these costs.

As noted earlier, the mobile home industry's product mix has been shifting toward increasingly larger units, especially doublewides and "factory-built housing" or "sectionals." (Traditional doublewides are built in accordance with the federal mobile home construction and safety standards and usually have wheels; sectionals usually conform to statewide factory-built housing codes and are always placed on a foundation.) This emphasis on larger units is influencing the nature of the distribution activities conducted by individual dealerships. With more favorable zoning and the taxation of factory-built housing as real property, manufacturers are increasingly including in their product mix fixed-site housing and expanding their markets into medium- and high-density areas. This requires more sophisticated setup and servicing procedures and is usually directly tied to development activities. In many cases manufacturers already deal directly with developers for sectionals and with large park developers for mobile homes, thus bypassing the traditional intermediary, the dealer. These changes may ultimately create a situation in which many dealers will either face obsolescence or have to find ways to participate in the distribution of and developments for fixed-site factory-built housing as well as large-scale mobile home communities.

In order to remain in a competitive position, dealers could handle both mobile home distribution and the sale of fixed-site units, acting as brokers for the latter but not involved in actual land development. Individual dealerships that primarily sell singlewide models, and to a lesser extent doublewides, must be prepared to include larger models in their lot inventories. Larger dealership operations, having greater lot areas and access to more working capital, will be better equipped to accommodate the increasing number of model variations. Small dealers with less capital may forfeit participation in fixed-site unit sales totally and specialize in the "mobile" home. Another option for dealers would be to integrate into actual development activities in addition to selling usual mobile home models. Or they may slowly evolve into developers, as is the case with the "builder-dealer" relationship in the present manufactured building industry. As sectionals become increasingly popular, more dealers will have to mature at least into quasi developers. Once sectionals are marketed on a wider basis, those few dealers already involved in land development may have a distinct advantage because they have already acquired experience through these activities. The mobile home dealerships carrying sectional units will also have to become more skilled in other aspects of the distribution of these homes, including site installation and servicing of units placed on permanent foundations.

The transition of the "mobile home" industry into the "fixed-site manufactured housing" industry will have the greatest impact on those dealerships capable of extending operations to development. But the transition will certainly be felt by all dealers, especially through the slackened sale of smaller models. Those dealers who do not have the expertise or financial resources to enter development activities may continue previous operations, although it is evident that the mobile home market in the future will be largely dominated by fixed-site doublewides or sectional units. Large dealers, especially the ambitious, flexible entrepreneurs willing to develop expertise resembling that of the builder-dealer, will find themselves most suited to deal with the "unit and land" package characteristic of sectional distribution.

As the industry moves toward larger, fixed-site units, however, we would caution dealers against moving too far too fast. In order to be able to provide total service in distribution, development, setup, and maintenance of these new units, dealers must acquire more land development skills and real estate expertise. But we recommend attainment of these skills in a methodical, logical fashion, evolving within the industry rather than hastily jumping beyond it. Thus we suggest that dealers cut their teeth on the doublewides already in their product mix, paving the way for the sectionals that require similar services. If necessary, dealers should even create demand for doublewides in order to accomplish this. In this way the industry will also be preparing itself to market the product of tomorrow. Although the exact timing and form of the future product is still uncertain, we do know that it will be fixed-site; by acquiring the necessary skills now, the dealer, and the industry in general, will have established a solid experiential foundation that will make the transition into new products smooth and painless. However, the mobile home industry must not jeopardize the unique status that has allowed it to develop into such an effective entity. Only when the industry manages to alter strategically both its business and political environments in preparation for a move toward new products and hence markets can such a move succeed. We feel that the industry should concentrate on defending the mobile home status and then explore "fixed-site housing" by first working toward creating additional, effective demand and a supporting climate and then developing a new product for a new marketplace.

Yet another avenue for dealers to explore is the establishment of generally and strongly supported trade associations and the attendant development of greater political acumen. This, however, requires a widespread support and cooperation that has been noticeably lacking in previous attempts at such unification, especially on the regional and national levels. There is no viable, strong national organization representing dealers' interests. Dealer associations, whether on the state, regional, or national level, could function like any other professional group (such as the AMA or bar associations) to guarantee a certain degree of professionalism among their members. These groups could perform the necessary self-regulatory tasks of weeding out fly-by-night operations that give dealers a bad name and monitoring dealerships that give unprofessional or insufficient service. If the distribution system itself identifies and corrects its unprofessional elements, it will effectively avoid the kind of government intervention that occurred when the FTC believed it had to step in on the warranty issue.

A major problem faced by any industry trade group attempting to ensure the professional behavior of its members is the lack of power to enforce its regulations. One way a dealers' organization could overcome this hurdle would be to license all dealerships meeting certain basic requirements. These standards could include proven financial stability, posting of a bond attachable for failure to perform satisfactorily guaranteed warranty work, adequate warranty and service facilities and personnel, and proven knowledge of and compliance with statutory regulations affecting mobile homes and their dealers. Very much as the MHI in years past enforced compliance with the ANSI code, licensed dealers could be monitored by inspectors responsible only to the national association, which would eliminate any conflict of interest on the local level. Alternatively, the dealers' association could work with state or local government agencies to set up minimum performance standards for licensing. This would allow dealers to initiate and actively participate in shaping governmentally mandated regulations rather than merely to respond to those rules established after they have shown an inability to regulate themselves.

Such licensing would be beneficial to dealers in protecting their good reputations as well as helpful to the consumer in ascertaining the quality of a given dealer. It might also help dealers to establish their credibility as acknowledged experts in their work. For example, in 1976 and 1977 efforts were made by real estate interests in several states to require a real estate license of anyone selling a mobile home already in place; the reasoning went that because more states were considering mobile homes as real property for tax purposes, this classification should be extended to all other areas. Such a move, if successful, could seriously undermine dealers and threaten the growing trade-in market for mobile homes. (Approximately eight hundred thousand to nine hundred thousand used units now change ownership per year, about three times the total number of new units sold.) If the distribution system were to establish and enforce its own licensing requirements, other licensing measures for the sellers of mobile homes would not be necessary.

One important point that dealers must keep in mind is that they are part of a larger system: the entire mobile home industry and its total business environment. Because all parts of this system interact, what benefits one element will aid all the other components. It is to the dealers' advantage to consider the interests of the total industry and its supporting environments, even in situations in which there may be no immediate gains to the distribution component: Dealers should see themselves as part of the greater whole and work with the other components toward the greater long-term good of the industry. Thus the ideal would be for dealers to join with a larger industry group, such as the MHI, to enhance the political and economic strength of the whole industry. This might make sense especially because the regional nature of distribution activities may minimize the need for a separate national dealer organization.

In organizing itself the mobile home industry would do well to observe the smooth and effective operation of the National Association of Home Builders. That group's well-organized, three-tiered local-state-national structure gives it grass-roots supports as well as coordinated national strength. There is an apt analogy here: The home builder constructs an entire dwelling unit, and all the systems of the mobile home industry work together as a whole to accomplish the same purpose. Because dealers are now strong at the grass-roots level and manufacturers have national strength in the MHI, a synchronization of both types of groups in one larger trade association could lead to the same kind of integrated yet multi-tiered organizational structure that has proven so effective for the NAHB.

Chapter 9

Cost and Price Structures in the Distribution System

The mobile home distribution system constitutes a significant element of the total mobile home production and delivery system. The average value added for dealers represents 26 percent of the final purchase price of a typical mobile home. This relatively high value added is indicative of the important role dealers play in the production of a finished mobile home that is ready for occupancy. Two major steps in the delivery of the finished product, transportation from manufacturers to dealers and from dealers to lots and setup at the lot, account for 6.4 percent of the final purchase price and for 24 percent of total dealer value added. An accurate evaluation of the performance of the distribution system must therefore include an assessment of the transportation and on-site setup functions.

In order to assess the performance of the distribution system and to identify areas in which potential for cost reduction exists, we considered two basic areas of inquiry relative to the overall structure of dealer costs. First, because the system is composed of independent dealers who are generally free to explore varying combinations of services that are provided to the retail customer, the basic cost compositions for individual dealers are compared. A broad pattern of significant differences in the cost structures would indicate either that the distribution system has not achieved a consensus concerning the most efficient and most profitable method of delivering the final product or that demand differentiation in specific markets requires highly individualized approaches to the problem of dealer strategy. Cost structure stability among dealers would support the conclusion that one basic pattern of dealer behavior is only slightly modified to suit regional market differences. If the former condition is found, it could indicate a substantial potential for performance improvement through transfer of information and soft technologies among individual dealers. The latter condition would suggest that dealers have approached an optimal strategy within the context of existing industry structure; the most likely source for improved performance would therefore lie in modifications to the general structure of the industry.

Second, in order to isolate areas of potential improvement in dealers' cost performance, we must understand the principal determinants of variations in those costs. An analysis of such causal relationships serves a dual purpose. With respect to the existing dealer system it permits testing of hypothesized explanations of observed cost variations. Such an analysis is also the important first step toward the development of reliable predictions about changes in performance that would be associated with major structural modifications in the mobile home industry. These considerations are addressed in the first two sections of this chapter.

In section C comparisons of trends in retail prices of mobile homes with selling prices of conventional homes demonstrate a wide disparity between the two forms of housing. Whereas the cost of site-built homes has soared in the last ten years, mobile home prices have remained relatively stable. It is the uniquely effective synchronization of the many functions in the mobile home industry's production and distribution systems that has propelled the mobile home to the "number one" spot in low-cost housing.

Its new approach to shelter production enables the mobile home industry to deliver a finished home for a 1977 mean retail selling price of $13.23 per square foot. The distribution of reported selling prices is shown in table 9.1. Mean values for 1977 range from a low of $11.95 per square foot in the East and West South Central regions to a high value of $15.76 in the New England and Middle Atlantic regions. The four main regions' mean selling prices per square foot are expressed as a percentage of the national mean value:

Northeast	119.1 percent
North Central	93.1 percent
South	97.9 percent
West	98.2 percent

The retail price of a mobile home typically includes all furnishings: freestanding and built-in furniture, carpeting, curtains, and draperies. The kitchen is equipped with the same range and refrigerator that are standard in the traditional homes. The mobile home also has built-in cabinets and closets, automatic heating system, and water heater. On request, many dealers will sell mobile homes unfurnished at a discount. A variety of options is available to the purchaser, including central air conditioning, central vacuum

A. Retail Prices

Table 9.1.
Range of Values, Total Retail Selling Price per Square Foot, 1977

Total Retail Selling Price Per Square Foot	Number of Firms	% Respondents to Question
Under $9.00	1	1.6
$9.01–$10.00	4	6.5
$10.01–$11.00	6	9.7
$11.01–$12.00	18	29.0
$12.01–$13.00	16	25.8
$13.01–$14.00	12	19.4
$14.01–$15.00	3	4.8
$15.01 and over	2	3.2
Mean: $13.23		
Missing observations 9		

Source: PMHI/DS and 1977 follow-up survey.

cleaning system, washer and dryer, dish-washer, and garbage disposal. Retail prices include the cost of transporting the home from the dealer to the site and setting it up for the new owner.

During 1974–1975, recession-triggered high repossession rates gave new prominence to the previously owned mobile home market. Lingering high unemployment rates throughout the late 1970s and associated cautious consumer spending behavior contributed to the suddenly increasing importance of the "secondhand" mobile home. The preowned mobile home is by far America's best housing buy. The first owner has paid the penalty for the unrealistically high depreciation assumptions. The second owner reaps the windfall profit—"income redistribution" by default—of the common error in which the entire financial sector, government, and industry join: an assumption that the economic life of the mobile home may at best be fifteen to twenty years. To the contrary, we found that the economic life of a mobile home equals that of the site-built home if equally well maintained. As a result, the prices for preowned homes not only are very low (table 9.2) but carry over into low occupancy costs: The total cost is sufficiently low that the purchaser can make cash payment, thereby avoiding the high add-on interest burden of financing the unit. (Only "decent" to "excellent" shelter is considered in table 9.2; 10-wides are excluded because of their necessarily functional shortcomings in layout, even though 10-wides approach one-bedroom apartments in size and can be bought for as little as $4–$6 per square foot, or $2000–$3000 per home.)

difference between retail selling price and FOB factory price and represents those costs over which the dealer is assumed to have greatest control. Conceptually, value added represents the increase in the value of the final good attributable to dealer activities. As shown in table 9.3, reported values added range from a low of $1 per square foot to a high above $5 per square foot, with a majority of values between $2 to $4.

It is important to emphasize that mobile home dealers, like mobile home producers, are characterized by low fixed costs. The ranges of reported values for fixed and variable costs are shown in table 9.4. The average variable cost is $10.40 per square foot with 74.3 percent of the respondents in the $8.00 to $11.00 range; average fixed costs are $1.44 per square foot. Low fixed costs enable firms to maintain a high degree of flexibility in an industry characterized by significant seasonal and cyclical variation in demand.

The averages and ranges for the percentage breakdown of model selling price as reported by respondents to the PMHI/DS are shown in table 9.5. The costs include the variable costs associated with FOB factory price, salesman's commission, advertising, and floor planning and the fixed costs associated with transportation, setup expenses, general and administrative expenses, and overhead, as well as the residual profit and taxes.

These basic descriptive data provide an important insight into the structure of the distribution system. First, variable costs as defined constitute almost 79 percent of total retail selling price, indicating that dealers' cost structures are characterized by a high degree of flexibility. However, the largest single component of variable cost is FOB factory price. Once a unit arrives at the dealer's lot, this cost is no longer variable, and the remaining variable costs comprise only 27 percent of dealers' value added ex-

B. Comparative Dealer Cost Structures

Cost Structures

Although retail price is the ultimate test of the efficiency of the mobile home industry, the more relevant measure for understanding the composition of dealer costs is the value added by each dealer to the final value of the mobile home. Value added is defined as the

Table 9.2.
Average Price per Square Foot (in dollars) of Preowned Mobile Homes, 1977[a]

Region	"Excelllent" Condition (salable after general cleaning)	"Good" Condition (needed minor work—under $150—before resale)	"Fair" Condition (required repairs of $150 to $300 before resale)
North East	$11.04	$9.44	$8.85
North Central	10.02	8.57	8.33
South	8.86	8.20	6.75
West	NA	10.16	9.09

a. Six-month average, July–December 1977 (including only 12-wides, 14-wides, and doublewides; excluding 8-wides and 10-wides).

Source: Computed from raw data provided by *Mobile-Modular Housing Dealer Magazine*.

Table 9.3.
Range of Values, Value
Added per Square
Foot, 1977

Value Added per Square Foot	Number of Firms	% Respondents to Question
$0–$1.00	1	2.8
$1.01–$2.00	2	5.6
$2.01–$3.00	18	50.0
$3.01–$4.00	9	25.0
$4.01–$5.00	3	8.3
Above $5.01	2	5.6
Missing observations 36		

Source: PMHI/DS and 1977 follow-up survey.

Table 9.4.
Range of Values, Dealer
Average Variable and
Fixed Costs per Square
Foot, 1977

	Number of Firms	% Respondents to Question
Variable costs per square foot		
Below $ 7.00	1	2.6
$7.01–$ 8.00	3	7.7
$8.01–$ 9.00	8	20.5
$9.01–$10.00	14	35.9
$10.01–$11.00	7	17.9
$11.01–$12.00	3	7.7
$12.01–$13.00	2	5.1
$13.01 and over	1	2.6
Missing observations 32		
Mean: $10.40		
Fixed costs per square foot		
$.00–$.60	3	8.1
$.61–$.80	4	10.8
$.81–$1.00	6	16.2
$1.01–$1.20	7	18.9
$1.21–$1.40	8	21.6
$1.41–$1.60	5	13.5
$1.61–$1.80	1	2.7
$1.81–$2.00	1	2.7
$2.01–$2.20	1	2.7
$2.21 and above	1	2.7
Missing observations 34		
Mean: $1.44		

Source: PMHI/DS and 1977 follow-up survey.

Table 9.5.
Breakdown of Retail
Selling Price

FOB Factory Price
Average of all companies reporting: 73.92%
 2 show FOB cost 40% or less
 2 show FOB cost 41% to 60%
23 show FOB cost 61% to 80%
10 show FOB cost 81% to 100%

Salesman's Commission
Average of all companies reporting: 2.54%
14 show commission expense 1% or less
15 show commission expense 2% to 3%
 6 show commission expense 4% to 5%
 2 show commission expense 6% and over

Advertising Costs
Average of all companies reporting: .76%
29 show advertising expense 1% or less
 8 show advertising expense 2% to 3%

Floor Planning Costs
Average of all companies reporting: 1.56%
24 show floor planning expense 1% or less
 9 show floor planning expense 2% to 3%
 2 show floor planning expense 4% to 7%
 1 shows floor planning expense 8% to 10%

Transportation to Dealer
Average of all companies reporting: 2.27%
17 show transportation cost 1% or less
15 show transportation cost 2% to 4%
 4 show transportation cost 5% to 6%
 1 shows transportation cost 7% and over

Transportation to Lot
Average of all companies reporting: 1.81%
30 show transportation cost 1% or less
 5 show transportation cost 2% to 3%
 2 show transportation cost 4% and over

Set-up Costs
Average of all companies reporting: 2.30%
11 show set-up cost 1% or less
19 show set-up cost 2% to 3%
 5 show set-up cost 4% to 5%
 2 show set-up cost 6% to 7%

General and Administrative Expense
Average of all companies reporting: 1.69%
22 show general and administrative expense
 1% or less
11 show general and administrative expense
 2% to 3%
 2 show general and administrative expense
 4% to 8%
 1 shows general and administrative expense
 9% and over

Other Overhead Costs
Average of all companies reporting: 5.05%
 2 show overhead cost 1% or less
10 show overhead cost 2% to 3%
15 show overhead cost 4% to 7%
 9 show overhead cost 8% to 11%

Profit and Taxes
Average of all companies reporting: 8.10%
10 show profit 4% or less
14 show profit 5% to 8%
 5 show profit 9% to 12%
 6 show profit 13% to 16%
 4 show profit 17% to 20%

Source: PMHI/DS.

clusive of profit. Dealers' value added, therefore, is dominated by its fixed cost component and dealer flexibility is somewhat diminished. Dealers who maintain large inventories will face high fixed costs during periods of decreased demand until they are able to reduce inventory levels.

Factors Influencing
Variations in Costs

Although the previous simple descriptive statistics provide a valid overview of the structure of the dealer system, they do not permit analysis of variations in dealer costs. In order to test for patterns in cost variations, twelve elements of cost data were cross-tabulated with seven indexes related to individual dealer characteristics.

Dealer Characteristics	Dealer Cost Categories
Number of lots	FOB factory price
Total annual sales	Sales commissions
Total sales per lot	Advertising
Sales composition	Floor planning
Customer services	Total variable costs
Selling advantages	Transportation to dealer
Seasonality	Transportation to lot
	Setup
	General and administrative
	Overhead
	Total fixed costs
	Profit and taxes

The cross-tabulation analysis indicates no significant trends within the distribution system. Although the ranges of values for various costs were reasonably consistent, it is impossible to reject the hypothesis that variation within the ranges is totally random.

Drawing on the PMHI data bank, we used multivariate regression analysis to identify determinants of two cost categories, variable and fixed for the standardized model. A regression was run with each of the model cost categories as a dependent variable: FOB factory price, salesperson's commission, advertising, floor planning, transportation, set-up, general and administrative expense, and overhead. The regressions for salesperson's commission, advertising, floor planning, transportation, general and administrative expense and overhead were significant. The following factors were significant determinants in at least one equation:

Economies of scale: Economies of scale were approximated by TASLOT, total number of sales per lot; AIL, average inventory level; TAS, total annual sales; and LOTS, the number of sale lots.
Composition of sales: Composition of sales was measured by MANLOT, the number of manufacturers represented per lot; NBRN, the number of brands sold; and MANR, the number of manufacturers represented on all lots.
Seasonality: Seasonality was approximated through seasonal fluctuations using the

variable HMSLMS, the ratio of highest monthly sales volume to lowest monthly sales volume.
Brand loyalty: BRNP, the percentage of customers requesting a product by brand name, was used to measure brand loyalty.
Services: Availability of customer services was approached through the variables EWRT, the dealer's extra warranty; by SPS, the percentage of sales to customers with lots in the dealer's park; and ACT, the acceptance into the park of only those tenants buying from the dealer.
Regional variations: Regional variations were approximated by the dummy variable, WAGER, reflecting variations in natural resources, capital and labor markets.

A summary of the variables included in the regression analysis follows:

Variable	Explanation
TASLOT	Total number of sales per lot
AIL	Monthly inventory level
TAS	Total annual sales
LOTS	Number of sale lots
SUDZ	Percentage of sales other than singlewides
NBRN	Maximum number of brands sold
MANLOT	Manufacturers per lot
MANR	Number of manufacturers
HMSLMS	High monthly sales volume/ low monthly sales volume
BRNP	Percent of customers requesting product by brand name
SPS	Percent sales to cusomters with lots in dealers' parks
ACT	Are tenants only accepted in your park if they bought from your dealership?
EWRT	Are extra warranties offered?
WAGER	Regional wage rate
YRST	First year of business.

Average Variable Costs
Regressions for the variable cost categories are shown in table 9.6. Regressions were run, with FOB factory price of the standardized model, salesperson's commissions, advertising expenses, and floor planning costs as dependent variables. All regressions except for FOB factory price were significant.

The significant determinant of the salesperson's commission was:

Services: The variable SPS (t = 3.19) demonstrated that salespersons increased their commissions as they sold more units to be located in the dealer's park. This was probably due to dealers' incentives for renting park space.

The significant determinant of the advertising regression was:
Composition of sales: NBRN (t = 4.14)

showed that an increase in the number of brands a dealer carried increased advertising expenses.

The significant determinants of the floor planning regression were:

Brand loyalty: BRNP (t = 3.5) indicated that floor planning costs increased as the percentage of customers requesting products by brand names increased. One reason for this could be that well known brand names were priced higher resulting in a higher financing charge.

Services: The variable ACT (t = 2.12) indicated that floor planning costs will decrease if a dealer accepts as tenants in his park only those who buy units from him. It was not expected to find customer-oriented policies affecting floor planning costs, which should be determined by the financial market and the company's financial position. One explanation may have been that this policy allowed the dealer to buy the unit from the manufacturer either after the sale or with minimum financing time.

Average Fixed Costs

Regressions for the fixed cost categories are shown in table 9.7. Regressions were run, with transportation costs, setup expense, general and administrative expense and for overhead.

The significant determinants of general and administrative costs were:

Economies of scale: TASLOT (t = 2.86) showed that increasing sales per lot increased general and administrative costs. Increased sales, clerical and maintenance personnel, and paper work could have caused the result. The variable AIL (t = 3.75) indicated that a large inventory level decreased costs. If a large inventory meant a large dealer, then the reduced costs might have resulted from consolidation of activities and efficient management.

Services: EWRT (t = 2.67) demonstrated that an extra dealer's warranty increased costs substantially. This was expected since warranties increase paper work and labor requirements.

Regional variations: WAGER (t = 4.77) showed that the Northeast, East and West North Central regions experienced higher general and administrative costs than the South and West North Central. Higher personnel costs were probably the reason for this result.

The determinants of overhead costs were:

Economies of scale: The variable TASLOT (t = 4.34) showed that the higher the number of sales per lot, the higher overhead costs. This was expected since the bigger dealer must make a larger capital investment.

Regional variations: WAGER (t = 2.39) showed that the Northeast, East and West

Table 9.6.
Dealer's Variable Cost Regression Table

Variable	Price FOB	Salesperson's Commission	Advertising	Floor Planning
TASLOT		.00291 (.00222)		−.00189 (.00145)
AIL	−.01973 (.01594)			
TAS	.00082 (.00500)	−.00128 (.00157)	.00033 (.00024)	.00113 (.00108)
LOTS			−.05256 (.04345)	
SUDZ	−10.94550 (11.03657)			
NBRN	.37466 (1.63475)		.11959[a] (.02886)	
MANLOT				
MANR	.61044 (1.41879)			
HMSLMS	.09016 (.67882)	−.08358 (.20559)		
BRNP		−.02416 (.02239)		.05695[a] (.01624)
SPS		.06746[a] (.02117)		.00953 (.01734)
ACT				−3.03668[a] (1.43167)
EWRT				
WAGER	5.10148 (7.72431)	−1.69573 (1.84128)	.06725 (.37589)	−1.91309 1.18482
YRST				
R²	.23883	.47354	.54001	.49228
F	.58272	2.69849[b]	7.33734[b]	2.90878[b]
t−k	13	18	25	18

a. t significant at 0.05.
b. F significant at 0.05.

Source: PMHI/DS.

Table 9.7.
Dealer's Fixed Costs
Regression Table

Variable	Transportation Cost	Setup	General and Administrative	Overhead
TASLOT	.01279 (.01675)	−.00086 (.00168)	.00672[a] (.00235)	.00607[a] (.00140)
AIL	.01756 (.04503)		−.02218[a] (.00591)	−.00152 (.00351)
TAS	−.01045 (.01438)	.00057 (.00108)		
LOTS				
SUDZ	6.40775 (15.19170)	−.28636 (1.53678)	−2.84204 (2.94246)	−1.83772 (1.90598)
NBRN				
MANLOT	−1.29737 (1.42414)	.12895 (.15025)	.47768 (.26770)	−.20393 (.15169)
MANR				
HMSLMS	−.33975 (.75206)	−.03182 (.08487)	−.20497 (.14342)	−.22951[a] (.09163)
BRNP				
SPS				
ACT				
EWRT	4.86731 (9.90649)		5.09317[a] (1.90681)	
WAGER	−3.20875 (9.29543)	.22096 (1.11458)	8.47411[a] (1.77792)	2.89238[a] (1.21162)
YRST	.31700 (.42236)		.04115 (.07696)	−.07699 (.04881)
R²	.14363	.08820	.74528	.76576
F	.16772	.24184	3.65733[b]	5.13713[b]
t−k	9	15	10	11

a. t significant at 0.05.
b. F significant at 0.05.

Source: PMHI/DS.

North Central regions experienced higher overhead costs. This was more than likely associated with the higher cost of land and construction in these areas, since distribution is a land-intensive industry.

Seasonality: Seasonality fluctuation variable HMSLMS (t = 2.50) showed a reduction in overhead expenses. There were no *a priori* grounds for this result. It was thought that seasonality would cause inefficient operation and increased cost. Thus this result was questionable.

Implications

Cross-tabluation and regression analysis failed in general to provide significant explanation. Based upon the results of these two forms of statistical analysis, it is reasonable to state that the distribution system is still in the process of development, with random variations in cost structures that would be associated with a group of individual firms in the early stages of seeking an optimal operating structure.

The average retail price of a mobile home has remained remarkably stable over the years. Indeed, the mobile home was one of a few products whose price per square foot declined over the 1950s and 1960s. The same, however, cannot be said for the cost of traditional housing.

Clearly, the average selling price of a mobile home cannot, without adjustments, be compared directly with the corresponding price of a site-built home. The price of a mobile home typically includes all furnishings but excludes the cost of the site it will occupy. Conversely, the price of a site-built home excludes furnishings (except, occasionally, carpeting, drapes, and appliances) but includes the cost of the land. The U.S. Department of Commerce figures for conventional housing in figure 9.1 exclude the value of the improved site. The data in figure 9.1 also control for differences, however, in absolute size by reporting cost as price per square foot.

The gap between the two forms of housing is large and increasing steadily. The price of a site-built home is rising by leaps and

C. Retail Price Trends: Mobile Home versus Traditional Home

Figure 9.1.
Cost Comparison of
Mobile Homes and
Site-Built Homes.

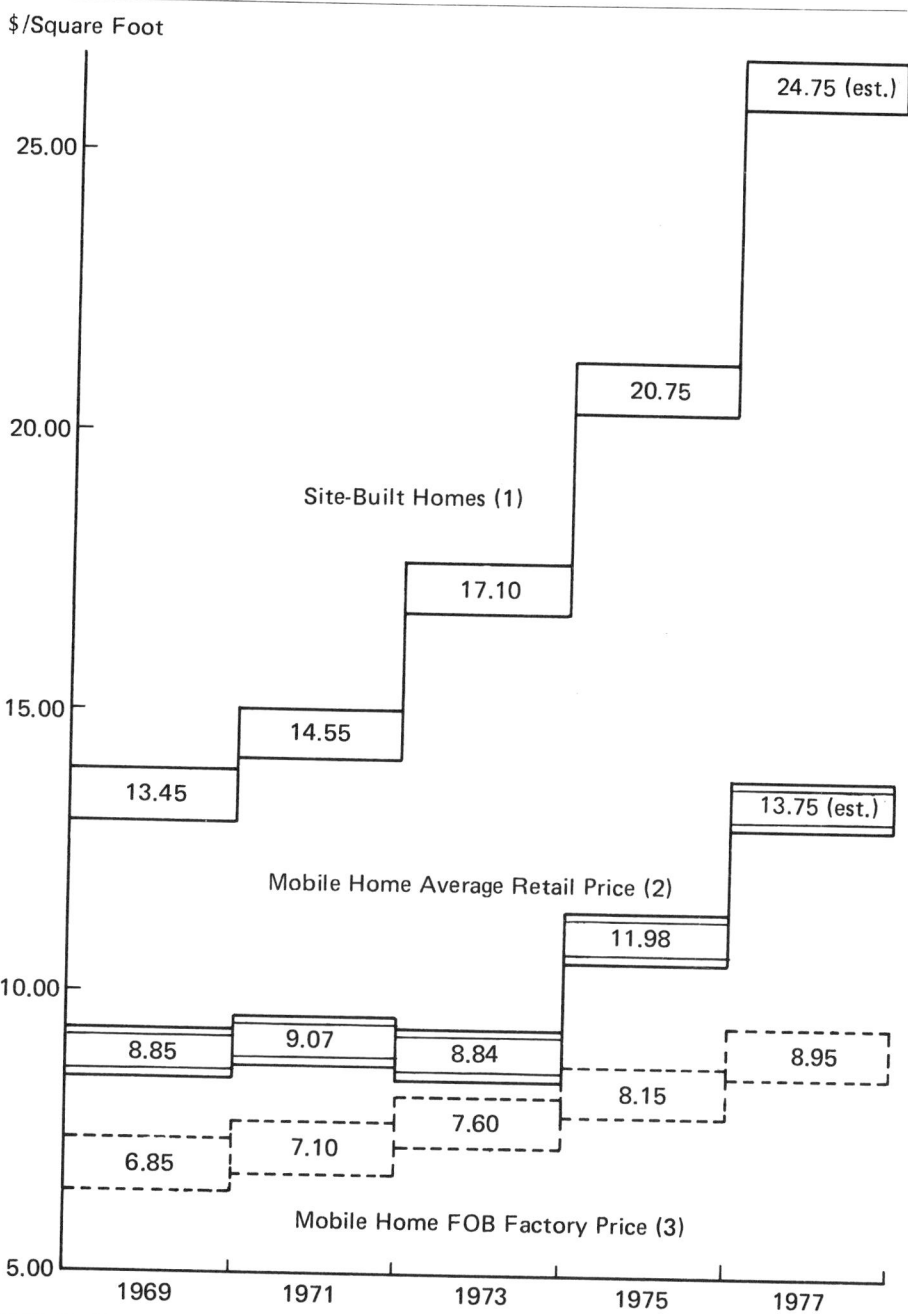

$/Square Foot

25.00

24.75 (est.)

20.75

Site-Built Homes (1)

20.00

17.10

15.00

14.55

13.45

13.75 (est.)

Mobile Home Average Retail Price (2)

11.98

10.00

8.85   9.07   8.84   8.95

8.15

7.60

7.10

6.85

Mobile Home FOB Factory Price (3)

5.00

1969   1971   1973   1975   1977

Sources: 1. Price per square foot, site-built homes; excluding land, furnishings, and appliances (U.S. Department of Commerce, Bureau of the Census, Construction Report Series C25).
2. Average retail price per square foot, mobile homes, excluding land, including furnishings and appliances (Elrick and Lavidge, Inc.).
3. FOB factory price per square foot, mobile homes (PMHI National Surveys 1969, 1971, 1973, 1975, and 1977).

bounds (by 23 percent in a single year, 1973–1974), but the price of mobile homes remains relatively constant. The apparent jump in price from 1973 to 1975 resulted in part from the lifting of federal price controls, signaling the end of artificially repressed inflationary trends. As evidenced by the comparatively low increase over the following two years, mobile home prices have again stabilized.

As figure 9.1 shows, however, there has been over the last eight years an alarming widening of the gap between FOB factory price and average retail price. In fact, this gap between wholesale and retail price is increasing at a faster rate than overall inflation. This trend reflects the increasing burdens imposed on dealers by government regulation, the effects of the last recession, particularly increasingly restrictive land use controls that place many dealers who control park spaces in a "quasi-monopolistic" situation.

Figure 9.2 illustrates the growth of the mobile home industry as a percentage of the new home market in two price ranges. The astronomical rise in conventional home prices has boosted the market for mobile homes to the point where the mobile home industry completely dominates the under-$20,000 new home market in 1977, and its share of the under-$30,000 market is rapidly approaching 85 percent.

D. Policy Implications

What characteristics of mobile home distributors (dealers) are responsible for their low value added per square foot? Three distinct observations can be made:

1. Because the production system is so highly specialized, the distribution system has developed as an independent sector. This allows dealers to develop the most efficient and economic means of distribution.
2. Even though variable costs are 79 percent of the retail selling price, the largest portion (74 percent) is the cost of the home (FOB factory price). Sales representative's commission and profit comprise only 10.7 percent of retail selling price.
3. Dealers have very low fixed costs, representing only 21 percent of retail selling price. This is the main factor in keeping overhead costs of distribution very low. Regression analysis has shown some minor determinants of fixed costs: Dealer size and increased customer services are both positively correlated with increased costs.

Regression analysis associated most of the determinants of variable costs to customer services or preferences. This suggests that the price of a mobile home is affected somewhat by the customer's tastes and desired services. All the determinants have only minor influences on all cost categories. It is

the interaction of all these factors in the marketplace that produces the variations observed in the value added statistic. Only if dealers consider all these factors is there any promise of reducing costs and increasing profits—the other alternative, increasing retail markup, would invite dangerous competition with the on-site builder.

As so often is the case, the most important policy implication was not detected by the computer but rather in numerous "human" conversations with dealers all over the country. We found no higher incidence of "fly-by-night" operations among dealers than we had found among manufacturers in this or any other subsector of the building industry, but we did observe that the occasional fast-buck, fast-sell dealer has a much more negative impact on overall industry image than the occasional fly-by-night manufacturer. Dealers are the ultimate link to the consumer and their performance directly shapes public perceptions. We observed in most states a generally low esteem for the dealer, even among manufacturers, who suspect that dealers' markups are unjustifiably high and blame dealers for thus discouraging consumers.

More than 99 percent of all dealers are respectable business people and many have to accept low profits and high risk. The issue is not that "only" less than 1 percent of mobile home dealers are disreputable. The issue is that this minority largely determines public perception and thus should be perceived by the distribution system as business problem "number one." The extent of government intervention in the 1970s can in part be attributed to the usually exaggerated accounts of isolated instances of excessive pricing that eventually reach Congress.

The most important policy implication is that dealers must never forget that the mobile home distribution system represents a major component of the total industry. They must never forget that a highly efficient distribution system is crucial to the continued growth of the industry. The mobile home industry's major market advantage is its low price relative to conventional housing.

Figure 9.2.
Percent mobile home
share of new home
market—under $20,000
and under $30,000.

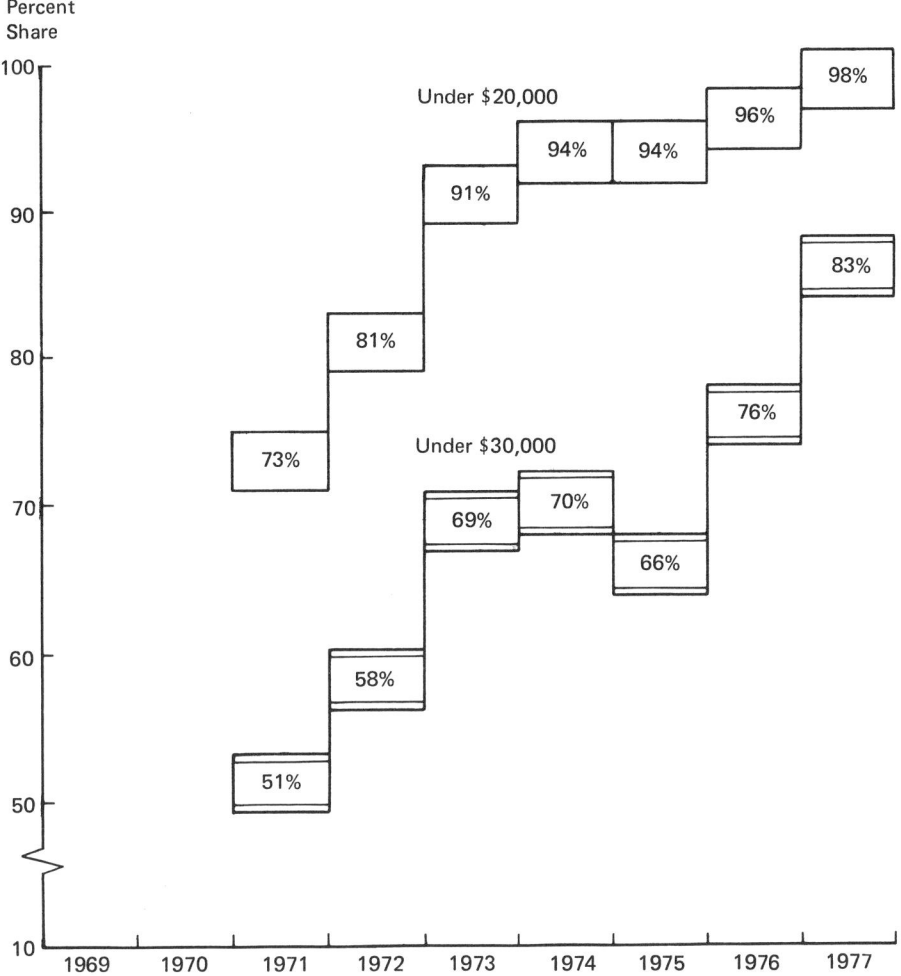

Percent
Share

Under $20,000

Under $30,000

Source: U.S. Department of Commerce, Bureau of Census data, Conventional Homes— Construction
Reports; Elrick and Lavidge, Inc. (Mobile Home Data).

Cost and Price Structures

Part III

The Mobile
Home
Park System

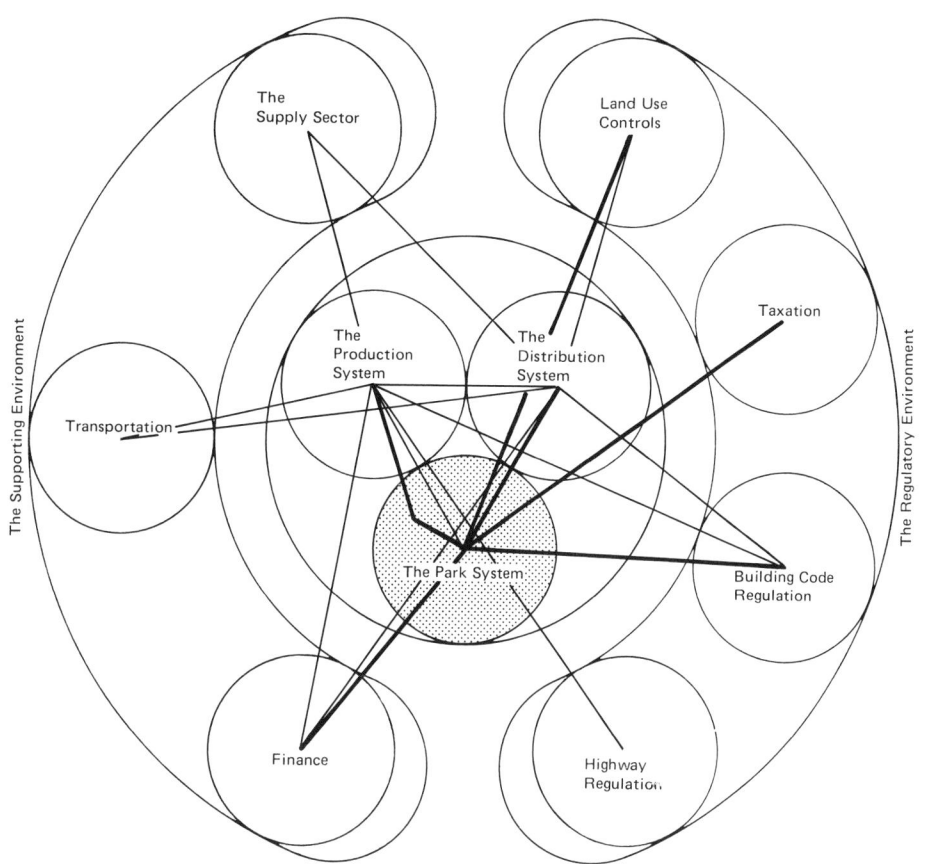

Chapter 10

Industrial Organization of the Park System

Relying on private initiative alone, the mobile home industry has developed from scratch an entirely new, separate industry: the mobile home park industry. This is a crucially important supporting industry because it is the very market without which the production system could not have survived and prospered.

The history of the mobile home park system dates back to the pre–World War II period. All over the country people had taken to the trailer coach for primary, year-round living even though the trailer coach had been intended as secondary housing. The industry suddenly found itself in the housing "business," and the demand for its product developed beyond expectations. Productive capacity was readily stepped up to keep pace with rising demand, but the industry quickly realized it could not satisfy this demand effectively. Now that its product was used as a home, the industry realized that it produced only one "part" of this home; it did not provide the other indispensable "parts"—the land upon which to place the home and the community into which to integrate its inhabitants.

Apart from largely substandard trailer camps and poorly maintained private lots, nobody had developed land for the industry's product. Even worse, whatever initiative in this direction did exist was discouraged if not terminated. Because of the prevailing highly negative "trailer" image, local government officials employed regulatory measures to prevent land from being made available for mobile homes. Examples of these tactics included exclusionary zoning practices or the imposition of local building codes that the mobile home by definition could not meet. The industry was left with the sobering realization that without an adequate supply of land it had no effective market and that public opinion and the regulatory climate seemed to make the creation of this market impossible.

The industry's reaction demonstrates an unusual degree of farsightedness. In the middle to late 1940s, the Trailer Coach Manufacturers Association (TCMA), the predecessor of the MHI, embarked on a major effort to build a new national industry that could provide a sufficient supply of needed land and new communities. The effort proceeded on many fronts. The TCMA developed engineering and planning standards for mobile home parks. It also launched an intensive campaign to overcome prejudice on the part of local governments and the financial sector because the TCMA realized it was crucial to develop more favorable land use control attitudes and greater willingness to finance the development of parks. Finally, the TCMA directed a general, sustained effort toward overcoming the negative attitudes of the population at large. The continuous upgrading of the quality of park developments was an equally important objective in this effort. Many regional and state associations worked in the same direction and deserve major credit for the emergence of today's high-quality mobile home park.

From the late 1940s to the 1970s, the development of the park system remained one of the highest priority areas of the MHI. By the early 1970s the MHI had become the world's largest residential land developer, with its in-house staff providing design, financing, and other assistance in the development of more than one hundred thousand park sites per year. The MHI then decided to discontinue the massive efforts of its land development division and to leave this function to the private sector. By the time this occurred, a rapidly-growing national industry, the mobile home park industry, had been created. The creation of this new, crucially important supporting industry is one of the most impressive achievements any trade association can claim. Without this sustained effort at building its own market, the mobile home industry probably would not exist today.

The implications of this achievement are far-reaching. Many advocates of "industrialization of building" have maintained for some time that public initiative in aggregating a high and stable demand volume for industrialized shelter is the imperative prerequisite for successful building industrialization. This notion, which originated in European countries with highly centralized government structures, has also been advocated for many years as the panacea to housing needs in the United States. Although reliance on the government as a nation's major "houser" should be questioned in almost any economy, it is certainly an unrealistic proposition in this country, which has such a long and strong history of private enterprise. The mobile home industry is by far the most successful paradigm of the "industrialization of building" in all countries with market economies. In fact, it probably can be considered the most successful example in the world. This industry and the park industry it built have been created by exclusive reliance on private initiative. This fact should stimulate the thinking of individuals in any country who are concerned with or involved in the development of the building industry.

A. Overview

It is important to define the term "mobile home park system" as we use it in this chapter. Mobile homes located on scattered sites are not included in the total mobile home park inventory. We define the mobile home park system to consist of the park inventory only. This definition was chosen for two reasons. First, park operations tend to view themselves as part of an "industry," while owners of non–park-located units do not. Second, the data available on units not located in parks are extremely limited.

Figure 10.1.
Evolution of the mobile home park system: a 1930 trailer camp. The first incidences of primary housing use.

Figure 10.2.
Evolution of the mobile home park system: a post-World War II trailer park at a defense project. The trailer camp becomes permanent housing.

Figure 10.3.
Evolution of the mobile home park system: a mobile home community today.

This chapter focuses on the park system as defined, but maintains a perspective on the total inventory of mobile homes. Section B deals first with the total inventory of park and non-park mobile homes. Then the remainder of the chapter deals exclusively with the park inventory—the mobile home park system.

B. Statistical Perspective

Mobile Home Inventory

Our calculations for 1974[1] show close to four million mobile units used as year-round housing in the United States. (At press time, no data beyond 1974 were available.) The following pages will cover the geographical distribution of these mobile homes and their contribution to the total housing inventory, as well as the historical development of present patterns. For two reasons, an unusually long period (1960–1974) has been chosen for tracing changes in numbers and distribution of mobile homes over time. First, before 1960 most of the mobile home inventory was still clustered close to production centers in the Great Lakes region, and the historically strongest markets—the retirement and tourist centers of Florida and California. In 1938, Florida alone claimed 25.4 percent of the park spaces in the United States; Florida, California, Michigan, and Ohio together contained 46.7 percent.[2] Since the 1930s a more homogeneous distribution has developed as the industry's product has evolved from a camping trailer into a viable housing alternative, as production has been decentralized and transportation has become less difficult, and as the industry has created a widespread market for itself by fostering the development of mobile home parks across the country. Second, the rapid economic growth of the South and West since 1960 has accelerated the growth of the mobile home industry and shifted its markets decisively.

Geographical Distribution of Mobile Homes

Mobile Home Distribution: 1974

Table 10.1 displays the distribution of the United States mobile home inventory across the four regions and nine subregions designated by the U.S. Bureau of the Census. The 1974 data for the four regions show a clear pattern: The South has nearly 50 percent of the nation's mobile home inventory (close to two million units); the North Central and Western regions each show less than half as many; and the Northeast has only about half of that. Data for the nine subregions show an even more striking pattern: Over one-quarter of the United States mobile home inventory is found in the South Atlantic subregion; only about 2 percent is in New England, and the seven other subregions cluster between 15 percent and 8 percent. State data (table 10.2) refine these regional pat-

terns. Florida and California, with their large retirement populations, have the largest shares of the national inventory: about 10 percent and 7 percent respectively. Over one-sixth of all mobile homes in the United States are located in one of these two states; over one-half are concentrated in ten states (in decreasing order of percentage share: Florida, California, Texas, North Carolina, Georgia, Pennsylvania, Michigan, Ohio, New York, Alabama). At the low end of the scale are sparsely populated Western states and the New England states.

Changing Distribution Patterns: 1960–1974

Two indicators of shifts in the distribution of mobile homes in the United States are regional differences in the growth rate of the mobile home inventory and changes in regions' percentage shares of the national mobile home stock (see tables 10.1 and 10.2). Between 1960 and 1974, the South experienced a 700 percent increase in number of mobile home units, more than twice that of any other region. Among the nine subregions, the three Southern subregions showed the highest rates of increase (East South Central, 950 percent; West South Central and South Atlantic, 650 percent). From 1960 to 1974, the South and all of the Southern subregions also increased their relative shares of the national mobile housing stock. All of the other regions and subregions experienced a decline in their percentages of the mobile housing stock.

The same indicators may be applied to state data. Fifteen states and the District of Columbia—listed below in decreasing order of rate of growth—showed increases in their mobile home inventories greater than 550 percent. However, Hawaii, the District of Columbia, New Hampshire, and Vermont have such low mobile home inventories that even very high inventory growth rates do not significantly increase their shares of the total United States inventory.

(Hawaii)	North Carolina
Georgia	West Virginia
Arkansas	Kentucky
Alabama	Oklahoma
Mississippi	(New Hampshire)
(District of Columbia)	Louisiana
Tennessee	Texas
South Carolina	(Vermont).

Thirteen states showed increases in their percentage shares of the United States mobile home inventory of more than one-half percentage point. These states are listed below in decreasing order of percentage growth. Of these states, all but Florida experienced very high inventory growth rates as well. Florida appears on this list only because its very large inventory—it is, after all, one of the oldest home states for mobile housing—made for a considerable increase

Table 10.1.
Regional Distribution
of Mobile Homes:
1960, 1974; Growth
Rate of Mobile Home
Inventories: 1960–
1974

Region	Year	Total Mobile Home Units[a]	% Change (1960–1974)	% of Mobile Housing Stock	National Rank[b]
Northeast	1960	98,042		12.8	IV
	1974	409,587	317.8	10.5	IV
New England	1960	26,146		3.4	9
	1974	94,165	260.1	2.4	9
Middle Atlantic	1960	71,896		9.4	5
	1974	315,422	338.7	8.1	8
North Central	1960	213,714		27.9	III
	1974	887,923	315.5	22.8	II
East North Central	1960	143,820		18.8	1
	1974	572,355	298.0	14.7	2
West North Central	1960	69,894		9.1	6
	1974	315,568	351.5	8.1	7
South	1960	239,066		31.2	I
	1974	1,818,209	660.5	46.7	I
South Atlantic	1960	143,650		18.7	2
	1974	1,026,135	614.3	26.4	1
East South Central	1960	36,127		4.7	8
	1974	365,964	913.0	9.4	5
West South Central	1960	59,289		7.7	7
	1974	426,110	618.7	10.9	4
West	1960	215,743		28.1	II
	1974	779,435	261.3	20.1	III
Mountain	1960	82,048		10.7	4
	1974	327,375	299.0	8.4	6
Pacific	1960	133,695		17.4	3
	1974	452,060	238.1	11.6	3

a. Must be a year-round dwelling to be included.
b. Includes the District of Columbia.

Source: U.S. Bureau of the Census, 1960 Census of Housing; PMHI, 1974 projections.

The Mobile Home Park System

Table 10.2.	State		Total Mobile Home Units[a]	% Change (1960–1974)	% of Mobile Housing Stock	National Rank[b]
Distribution of Mobile Homes by State: 1960, 1974; Growth Rate of Mobile Home Inventories: 1960–1974	Alabama	1960	9,932		1.3	25
		1974	112,723	1034.9	2.9	10
	Alaska	1960	3,039		0.4	46
		1974	13,218	334.9	0.3	47
	Arizona	1960	23,243		3.0	10
		1974	93,079	300.5	2.4	16
	Arkansas	1960	4,880		0.6	43
		1974	60,470	1139.1	1.6	26
	California	1960	101,601		13.3	1
		1974	294,031	189.4	7.6	2
	Colorado	1960	12,979		1.7	16
		1974	61,470	296.6	1.6	24
	Connecticut	1960	6,456		0.8	37
		1974	10,720	66.0	0.3	48
	Delaware	1960	3,569		0.5	45
		1974	16,429	360.3	0.4	44
	District of Columbia	1960	77		0.0	50
		1974	802	941.6	0.0	50
	Florida	1960	65,087		8.5	2
		1974	359,964	453.0	9.2	1
	Georgia	1960	12,689		1.7	18
		1974	172,316	1258.0	4.4	5
	Hawaii	1960	25		0.0	51
		1974	693	2672.0	0.0	51
	Idaho	1960	6,763		0.9	36
		1974	29,048	329.5	0.7	34
	Illinois	1960	32,470		4.2	5
		1974	111,564	243.6	2.9	11
	Indiana	1960	27,994		3.7	9
		1974	107,901	285.4	2.8	13
	Iowa	1960	11,735		1.5	20
		1974	41,141	250.6	1.1	31
	Kansas	1960	11,783		1.5	19
		1974	48,661	313.0	1.2	28
	Kentucky	1960	10,076		1.3	24
		1974	80,464	698.6	2.1	18
	Louisiana	1960	9,445		1.2	28
		1974	67,609	615.8	1.7	19
	Maine	1960	6,180		0.8	39
		1974	30,092	386.9	0.8	36
	Maryland	1960	9,521		1.2	27
		1974	27,534	189.2	0.7	35
	Massachusetts	1960	6,766		0.9	35
		1974	14,425	113.2	0.4	45
	Michigan	1960	29,400		3.8	8
		1974	148,540	405.2	3.8	7
	Minnesota	1960	10,702		1.4	23
		1974	61,516	474.8	1.6	25
	Mississipi	1960	6,327		0.8	38
		1974	71,603	1031.7	1.8	22
	Missouri	1960	16,613		2.2	13
		1974	93,712	464.1	2.4	15
	Montana	1960	7,077		0.9	33
		1974	33,171	368.7	0.9	32

Table 10.2. (Continued)

State		Total Mobile Home Unit[a]	% Change (1960–1974)	% of Mobile Housing Stock	National Rank[b]
Nebraska	1960	7,115		0.9	32
	1974	28,169	295.9	0.9	37
Nevada	1960	8,026		1.0	31
	1974	32,889	309.8	0.8	33
New Hampshire	1960	2,896		0.4	47
	1974	20,756	616.7	0.5	40
New Jersey	1960	9,156		1.2	29
	1974	22,044	140.8	0.6	39
New Mexico	1960	12,937		1.7	17
	1974	40,060	209.6	1.0	30
New York	1960	31,306		4.1	7
	1974	129,085	312.3	3.3	9
North Carolina	1960	19,133		2.5	11
	1974	199,988	945.2	5.1	4
North Dakota	1960	5,017		0.7	42
	1974	18,118	261.1	0.5	42
Ohio	1960	42,892		5.6	3
	1974	141,171	229.1	3.6	8
Oklahoma	1960	8,086		1.1	30
	1974	58,584	624.5	1.5	27
Oregon	1960	14,090		1.8	15
	1974	72,634	415.5	1.9	20
Pennsylvania	1960	31,434		4.1	6
	1974	164,293	422.7	4.2	6
Rhode Island	1960	1,513		0.2	49
	1974	3,437	127.2	0.1	49
South Carolina	1960	11,072		1.4	21
	1974	112,114	912.6	2.9	12
South Dakota	1960	6,929		0.9	34
	1974	24,031	246.8	0.6	38
Tennessee	1960	9,792		1.3	26
	1974	101,174	933.2	2.6	14
Texas	1960	36,878		4.8	4
	1974	239,447	549.3	6.1	3
Utah	1960	4,858		0.6	44
	1974	21,133	335.0	0.5	41
Vermont	1960	2,335		0.3	48
	1974	14,735	531.0	0.4	46
Virginia	1960	17,257		2.3	12
	1974	89,279	413.7	2.3	17
Washington	1960	14,940		1.9	14
	1974	71,484	378.5	1.8	21
West Virginia	1960	5,245		0.7	41
	1974	47,909	813.4	1.2	29
Wisconsin	1960	11,064		1.4	22
	1974	63,179	471.0	1.6	23
Wyoming	1960	6,165		0.8	40
	1974	16,525	168.0	0.4	43
U.S.A.	1960	766,565		100.0	
	1974	3,893,570	407.9	100.0	

a. Must be a year-round dwelling to be included.
b. Includes the District of Columbia.

Source: U.S. Bureau of the Census, 1960 Census of Housing; PMHI, 1974 projections.

in its share of the market even though its inventory increase rate was only moderate.

Georgia	Mississippi
North Carolina	Kentucky
Alabama	(Florida)
South Carolina	West Virginia
Tennessee	Louisiana
Texas	Oklahoma.
Arkansas	

Excluding Hawaii, the District of Columbia, New Hampshire, Vermont, and Florida, then, the convergence of these two measures is striking evidence of the growth of the mobile home industry in the South—the region that, once rural, has now become almost a synonym for economic boom.

The following states—again listed in decreasing order of growth rate—showed the lowest growth rates in their mobile home inventories between 1960 and 1974, less than 200 percent:

Connecticut	Wyoming
Massachusetts	Maryland
Rhode Island	California.
New Jersey	

Most of these states (with the dramatic exception of California, ranked first in 1960) had very low 1960 inventories (see table 10.2). However, a number of states with large 1960 inventories (California, Ohio, Illinois, Indiana, New York, and Arizona, all ranked among the top ten states in 1960) are among those whose percentage shares of the total United States mobile home inventory dropped most sharply (states are listed in decreasing order of percentage share drop):

California	Arizona
Ohio	New Jersey
Illinois	Connecticut
Indiana	Maryland
New York	Massachusetts.

In sum, the geographical distribution of mobile homes in 1974, though not yet homogeneous, is far more even than the tightly clumped inventories of the 1930s. Since 1960 two important trends are discernible in this leveling process: the decline, in inventory growth rates as well as national unit stock shares, of the dominant populous East North Central and Middle Atlantic states (Illinois, Indiana, Michigan, Ohio, Pennsylvania, New York), and the concerted rise of the South. Florida has, somewhat belatedly, caught up with the economic boom of the South, and in addition has become a major producer of mobile homes. As a result, it has displaced California, which is losing ground along with other high inventory states, as the first-ranked state.

The Contribution of Mobile Homes to the Total Housing Inventory

To what extent does the mobile home inventory contribute to the total inventory of year-round housing units? Figures for total year-round housing include mobile home units, but are made up primarily of conventional, nonmobile housing. We have coined the term "mobile housing percentage" as an easy reference term for the mobile home unit inventory expressed as a percentage of the total year-round housing stock. This index thus indicates the relation between the total number of year-round housing units and the number of mobile home units. Table 10.3 compares the distributions of all year-round housing units and mobile home units across the four Census regions. The national mobile housing percentage is 5 percent. Not surprisingly in view of the mobile home distribution figures presented earlier (table 10.1), the mobile housing percentage is highest in the South (7 percent) and lowest in the Northeast (less than 2.5 percent). The percentage for the West, at 6 percent, is close to the South's 7 percent although the West's mobile home inventory is only about half the South's, because the West's total year-round inventory is less. Similarly, the North Central region's mobile home inventory is not a great deal lower than the West's, but because its total year-round housing inventory is greater, its mobile housing percentage is only about 4 percent.

The national mobile housing percentage increased from 1.3 percent to 5 percent between 1960 and 1974, and all four regions also showed increases. Again, our previous inventory increase data (table 10.1) suggest that the South's mobile housing percentage would take the greatest leap (up nearly six percentage points). However, although table 10.1 indicates that the Northeast's mobile home inventory is actually increasing more rapidly than the West's, table 10.3 shows that the mobile home as a housing alternative is gaining in importance much more rapidly in the West than in the Northeast.

In table 10.4, the mobile housing percentage is used to compare the distributions of total year-round housing and mobile homes across areas of higher and lower population density. We use Standard Metropolitan Statistical Areas (SMSAs) and central city areas, as defined by the U.S. Bureau of the Census. Table 10.4 shows that nationally, the 1974 inventory of all year-round units is divided fairly evenly among central city areas, non–central city areas, and non-SMSAs, although concentrated slightly more in non–central city areas. By contrast, only 5 percent of mobile homes are found in the central city, and more than 60 percent are outside SMSAs altogether. Summing central city and non–central city figures, year-round units as a whole are seen to be concentrated inside SMSAs (about 70 percent), whereas, again summing central and non–central city inventories, only 40 percent of mobile homes are found inside SMSAs. These proportions reflect trends since 1960: an increase in the percentage of total year-round housing units located within SMSAs, and a steady decline in the percentage of the mobile home inventory found in these areas. Because of this discrepancy, the mobile housing percentage is very low in the central city, less than 1 percent, whereas in non–central city areas it is just under the national average of 5 percent, and outside SMSAs is nearly 10 per-

Table 10.3.
The Contribution of Mobile Homes to the Year-Round Housing Inventory, by Region: 1960, 1974

Region	Total Year-Round Housing Units	Mobile Home Units	Mobile Home Units as % of Year-Round Housing Units	Rank by Percentage
Northeast				
1960	14,507,801	98,042	0.7	4
1974	17,274,000	385,000	2.2	4
North Central				
1960	16,793,361	213,714	1.3	3
1974	20,211,000	792,000	3.9	3
South				
1960	17,171,181	239,066	1.4	2
1974	24,343,000	1,686,000	6.9	1
West				
1960	9,555,729	215,743	2.3	1
1974	14,059,000	853,000	6.1	2
U.S.A.				
1960	58,028,072	766,565	1.3	
1974	75,886,000	3,715,000	4.9	

Source: U.S. Bureau of the Census, 1960 Census of Housing, 1974 Annual Housing Survey.

Table 10.4.

National Distribution of
Mobile Homes and Total
Year-Round Housing
Units with Respect to
Standard Metropolitan
Statistical Areas: 1960,
1970, 1974

	Total		
	1960	1970	1974
Total year-round housing units	58,314,784	67,699,000	75,886,000
% year-round housing units	(100)	(100)	(100)
Mobile home units	766,565	2,073,000	3,715,000
% mobile home units	(100)	(100)	(100)
Mobile home units as % of year-round housing units	1.3	3.1	4.9

	Inside SMSAs								
	Total			Inside Central City			Outside Central City		
	1960	1970	1974	1960	1970	1974	1960	1970	1974
Total year-round housing units	36,374,700	46,083,000	51,645,000	19,615,456	22,584,000	24,009,000	16,759,244	23,498,000	27,636,000
% year-round housing units	62.4	68.1	68.1	33.6	33.4	31.6	28.7	34.7	36.4
Mobie home units	384,148	933,000	1,485,000	84,182	176,000	198,000	299,966	757,000	1,287,000
% mobile home units	50.1	45.0	40.0	11.0	8.5	5.3	39.1	36.5	34.6
Mobile home units as % of year-round housing units	1.1	2.0	2.9	0.4	0.8	0.8	1.8	3.2	4.7

	Outside SMSAs		
	1960	1970	1974
Total year-round housing units	21,940,084	21,616,000	24,241,000
% year-round housing units	37.6	31.9	31.9
Mobile home units	382,417	1,140,000	2,230,000
% mobile home units	49.9	55.0	60.0
Mobile home units as % of year-round housing units	1.7	5.3	9.2

Source: U.S. Bureau of the Census, 1960 Housing Census, 1974 Annual Housing Survey.

cent. These percentages increased in all three locations nationally from 1960 to 1974; slowly in the central city, moderately in non–central city areas, and very rapidly outside SMSAs.

Table 10.5 expands upon tables 10.3 and 10.4, contrasting the distributions of mobile homes and total year-round housing units by SMSAs for each region. First, comparing the distributions of year-round housing units in each region to the national data in table 10.4, we see that the North Central region shows a distribution similar to the national distribution. In the South, the proportion inside SMSAs is lower (both central city and non–central city), and the proportion outside SMSAs is higher, by more than 10 percent. The West and Northeast show just the reverse: the proportion inside SMSAs is higher (in and out of the central city), and the proportion outside SMSAs is lower, again by more than 10 percent.

We look next at the mobile housing percentage—the distribution of mobile homes with respect to the distribution of the total year-round housing inventory—as broken down in table 10.5. Looking back to table 10.3, which presented the mobile housing percentage for each region without considering SMSA categories, the regional rankings lead us to expect the highest mobile housing percentages in the South and West, a moderate percentage in the North Central region, and a very low percentage in the Northeast. Referring again to table 10.4, which presented national mobile housing percentages for the SMSA categories, we are led to expect mobile homes to make their greatest contribution to the total housing inventory outside SMSAs, and their lowest inside the central city. In general, the effect of this pattern is stronger than the effect of the regional pattern. As expected (table 10.5), southern and western non-SMSAs show the highest mobile housing percentages, 11 percent and 13 percent respectively; and the mobile housing contribution is lowest in Northeastern central city areas, at 0.1 percent. In only a few cases does the regional pattern have the stronger effect. In the West, for example, the ratio of non–central city mobile home units to total year-round housing units for the region is higher than the corresponding ratio for most non-SMSAs (that is, non-SMSA mobile home units/total year-round housing units for the region). In fact, the West is the only region that has more mobile homes in non–central city areas than outside SMSAs.

Important factors in accounting for variations in the mobile housing percentage are population density, restrictiveness of land use controls regarding mobile homes, and the method of taxing mobile homes. (A more thorough discussion of these factors will be found in chapter 16 on land use controls, and in chapter 17 on taxation.) In general,

higher mobile housing percentages are associated with lower population density, less restrictive zoning, and property taxation of mobile homes. Clearly the association with population density and land use controls agrees with our findings of the highest mobile housing percentages outside SMSAs and the lowest inside central cities. Lower mobile housing percentages in central city areas than in non–central city areas may be partially accounted for by certain inherent limitations of mobile housing as it is produced today; for example, the difficulty of transporting large mobile home units through central city streets and the low population density of mobile home developments compared to high-rise apartments. But the higher mobile housing percentages in non-SMSAs are probably a different effect of population density: in areas of lower density, outside SMSAs, the housing industry often is less developed (or, as in some parts of the West, nonexistent), and hence the consumer may be more dependent on the mobile home as a housing alternative. Also, less restrictive land use controls contribute to keeping the cost of land low (again, see chapters 16 and 17 on land use controls and taxation). Regional differences in zoning and taxation also reflect population density. In general, states in the New England, Middle Atlantic, and East North Central subregions are densely populated and have more restrictive land use controls than states in other regions. The West North Central states and all the Western states except California have lower population density and looser zoning restrictions. Like California, Florida is an exception within its region. All of the East South Central and West South Central states and most of the other South Atlantic states still have large rural populations and are experiencing rapid mobile home development.

Whether a mobile home is located in a park or on private property affects its legal status in the community. In most states, land use controls treat mobile homes in parks differently from those located on private property. Mobile homes on private property are more likely to be taxed as real property and may be required to conform to traditional building codes (see chapter 16 on land use controls, chapter 17 on taxation, and chapter 18 on building code regulation). The location of a mobile home also has implications for consumer financing. A unit located on isolated, private property is more likely to qualify for traditional, long-term mortgage financing, especially if it is permanently attached to the land and subject to real property taxation and traditional building codes, as are many doublewides (see chapter 15 on finance sector influence). Park or non-park location is directly relevant to market research, in particular to demand forecasts by the prospective park developer or the mobile home manufacturer.

Placement of Mobile Homes in Parks

Table 10.5.
Regional Distribution of
Mobile Homes and
Total Year-Round
Housing Units with
Respect to Standard
Metropolitan Statistical
Areas, by Region:
1970, 1974

| | Total | | Inside SMSAs | | | | | | Outside SMSAs | |
| | | | Total | | Inside Central City | | Outside Central City | | | |
	1970	1974	1970	1974	1970	1974	1970	1974	1970	1974
Northeast										
Total year-round housing units	16,198,000	17,274,000	12,943,000	13,556,000	6,201,000	6,204,000	6,742,000	7,352,000	3,255,000	3,718,000
% year-round housing units	(100)	(100)	79.9	78.5	38.3	35.9	41.6	42.6	20.1	21.5
Mobile home units	241,000	385,000	108,000	160,000	6,000	5,000	102,000	155,000	133,000	224,000
% mobile home units	(100)	(100)	44.8	41.6	2.5	1.3	42.3	40.3	55.2	58.2
Mobile home units as % of year-round housing units	1.5	2.2	.8	1.2	.1	.1	1.5	2.1	4.1	6.0
North Central										
Total year-round housing units	18,675,000	20,211,000	12,163,000	13,166,000	5,976,000	6,070,000	6,188,000	7,096,000	6,512,000	7,044,000
% year-round housing units	(100)	(100)	65.1	65.1	32.0	30.0	33.1	35.1	34.9	34.9
Mobile home units	499,000	792,000	216,000	292,000	39,000	52,000	177,000	240,000	283,000	500,000
% mobile home units	(100)	(100)	43.3	36.9	7.8	6.6	35.5	30.3	56.7	63.1
Mobile home units as % of year-round housing units	2.7	3.9	1.8	2.2	.7	.9	2.9	3.4	4.3	7.1
South										
Total year-round housing units	20,884,000	24,343,000	11,604,000	13,798,000	6,156,000	6,842,000	5,448,000	6,956,000	9,279,000	10,545,000
% year-round housing units	(100)	(100)	55.6	56.7	29.5	28.1	26.1	28.6	44.4	43.3
Mobile home units	868,000	1,686,000	329,000	550,000	72,000	74,000	257,000	476,000	539,000	1,136,000
% mobile home units	(100)	(100)	37.9	32.6	8.3	4.4	29.6	28.2	62.1	67.4
Mobile home units as % of year-round housing units	4.2	6.9	2.8	4.0	1.2	1.1	4.7	6.8	5.8	10.8
West										
Total year-round housing units	11,942,000	14,059,000	9,372,000	11,124,000	4,251,000	4,892,000	5,121,000	6,232,000	2,570,000	2,934,000
% year-round housing units	(100)	(100)	78.5	79.1	35.6	34.8	42.9	44.3	21.5	20.9
Mobile home units	465,000	853,000	280,000	483,000	59,000	68,000	221,000	415,000	185,000	370,000
% mobile home units	(100)	(100)	60.2	56.6	12.7	8.0	47.5	48.6	39.8	43.4
Mobile home units as % of year-round housing units	3.9	6.1	3.0	4.3	1.4	1.4	4.3	6.7	7.2	12.6

Source: U.S. Bureau of the Cenuss, 1974 Annual Housing Survey.

The Mobile Home Park System

In spite of the importance of the park or non-park location of mobile homes, no data have been available on this issue. Data on park versus non-park location of mobile home units had to be computed by PMHI, based on hand-tabulated raw data.[3] In the mid-seventies, HUD entered into a contract with the Bureau of the Census for an ongoing survey to identify the location of new mobile homes sold in the United States, but the survey does not distinguish park and non-park locations.[4] We urge that the contract scope be expanded to identify park versus non-park location, or alternatively, that HUD contract with a private organization to compile reliable data regularly on this issue.

The ratio of mobile homes not located in parks to mobile homes located in parks (see tables 10.6 and 10.7) for the United States as a whole is 1.4. The West is the only region with a non-park to park ratio of less than one; that is, with more mobile homes located in parks than on private property. The South has the highest ratio of any region, at 2.1. California and Florida are the only states with both a non-park to park ratio of less than one and very high mobile home inventories (table 10.2). But California's low ratio merely emphasizes the West's already low ratio; if California were excluded, the West would still have the lowest ratio of any region. Florida's low ratio is the exception in the South, however; if Florida were excluded, the South's ratio would jump from 2.1 to 3.2, double that of any other region, and the ratio for the South Atlantic subregion would jump to 3.4. The lowest ratios for subregions are 0.4 in the Pacific subregion, including California, and 1.1 in New England and the Mountain subregion. New England is an area of high income, restrictive zoning laws, and high property values; the Mountain subregion has had accelerated park development over the last decade, especially of retirement parks in the style of California and Florida.

Table 10.7 shows that only ten states have more mobile homes in parks than on private property. Most of these are sunbelt states (California, Florida, Arizona) favoring the development of mobile home parks built as retirement communities, or states where high property costs and/or stringent zoning laws discourage mobile home development on private lots (Connecticut, Massachusetts, New Jersey, Rhode Island, Iowa). In Alaska, much of the cost of a mobile home is shipping and installation costs; park developers, unlike private home developers, can take advantage of economies of scale. Most of the low growth states discussed earlier have low non-park to park ratios ranging from 0.1 to 1.1. The states which were historically dominant but are now losing ground (Illinois, Indiana, Michigan, Ohio, Pennsylvania, New York) have moderate ratios, from 1.1 to 1.9. The ten states with the highest non-park to park ratios, all greater than 3 (South Carolina,

Tennessee, West Virginia, Mississippi, North Carolina, Alaska, Georgia, Kentucky, Louisiana, Arkansas) are all among the high growth states discussed earlier. These states have largely rural populations, relatively low property costs, and fewer land use controls, all conducive to locating mobile homes on private property.

We can now turn toward the main objective of this chapter on industrial organization, namely, to describe the structure and operation of the mobile home park system and to gauge implications for the system's economic performance. The necessary perspective has been developed by surveying the entire mobile home unit inventory in the preceding pages of this chapter. The focus now will be exclusively on the park system—relying primarily on PMHI's national survey of park operators/owners (PMHI/PS) as the major data base.

Origins of the Park System
Our purposes in understanding and characterizing park owners' origins were to establish whether any current park owners have entered the mobile home park system from the traditional housing industry or fields related to it and to determine the relevance of park owners' past experience in providing guidance in their current responsibilities. Because the mobile home industry has evolved separately from the traditional housing industry, those entering the mobile home industry from the conventional housing industry may transfer knowledge important for the future growth of the park system—and more generally the mobile home industry—or may stimulate an ultimate integration of the mobile home industry and the larger housing industry.

The PMHI Park Survey indicates that a 64 percent majority of the current park owners did not have prior experience directly relating to the mobile home industry or the park system. Only one-sixth of all owners had related backgrounds involving dealerships (12 percent), recreational vehicle park development or operation (4 percent), and mobile home manufacturing (1 percent). A number of these owner-respondents reported two or more such experiences related to the mobile home industry. On the other hand, approximately one-fourth of the respondents were previously engaged in aspects of the traditional building industry. These occupations involved land development other than mobile home or trailer parks (12 percent), on-site residential construction (6 percent), and building manufacturing (6 percent).

Those owners surveyed who indicated they had also developed their parks revealed much the same background as the owners. Only a small percentage had had mobile home industry-related experiences: dealerships (15 percent) and recreation vehicle park

Table 10.6.
Distribution of Mobile
Homes in Park and
Non-Park Locations, by
Region: 1974

Region	Total Mobile Home Units	Mobile Home Units in Parks	% Mobile Home Units in Parks	Ratio of Non-Park Mobile Home Units to Park Mobile Home Units
Northeast	409,587	156,891	38.3	1.6
New England	94,165	44,081	46.8	1.1
Middle Atlantic	315,422	112,810	35.8	1.8
North Central	887,923	398,035	44.8	1.2
East North Central	572,355	263,865	46.1	1.2
West North Central	315,568	134,170	42.5	1.4
South	1,818,209	592,451	32.6	2.1
South Atlantic	1,026,135	397,871	38.8	1.6
East South Central	365,964	76,125	20.8	3.8
West South Central	426,110	118,455	27.8	2.6
West	779,435	467,068	59.9	0.7
Mountain	327,375	152,351	46.5	1.1
Pacific	452,060	314,717	69.6	0.4

Source: PMHI projections of park vs. non-park data.

development or operation (8 percent). None had prior experience as manufacturers of mobile homes. Those having backgrounds in the traditional building industry made up approximately one-fifth of the developer respondents, again an amount similar to the owner respondents. As an alternative to practical experience, 1 percent of the respondents had had prior school training in park management.

That many park owner-developers and owner-purchasers are able to enter and succeed in the park system without relevant experience is indeed remarkable; this is indicative of the mobile home industry's "youth" as well as its apparent lack of complex or established practices that would offer obstacles to development and operation. Many parks are still owned and operated by husband-wife teams who depend upon the parks for their livelihoods; these couples have neither large capital reserves nor prior managerial experience but must nonetheless risk the problems that befall their operations. Because of a number of factors, such as the increasing development and operation expenses, the expansion of the park system at the regional and national levels, the resultant increase in competition, and a stricter regulatory environment, it is clear that the one-park owner today faces a complex situation. The continuation of the recent growth of both the park system and the encompassing mobile home industry and the likely increase in complexities of start-up and operation seem to call for a corresponding injection of more sophisticated know-how. Thus it is likely that individuals who enter the park system

will increasingly require relevant prior experience or education.

One possibility for the prospective owner who wants to reduce the risks involved in the development or operation of a park is to employ a professional, specialized developer or manager. The owner who does so, of course, incurs greater expenses; but the likelihood of success, financially and in providing services, is greater as well. Ironically, the existing supply of professional developers or managers presently is not being used to its full potential. This implies that the park system and the mobile home industry as a whole could benefit from the education of park owners as to the advantages of better utilizing the pool of professionally trained talent.

Once better utilization of existing expertise is achieved, more effective training of future professionals must be the issue. We are aware of only two universities in the United States that currently offer special study programs in mobile home park management—one in Michigan and one in California. Educational programs, if offered by more universities, could be extremely valuable. Several private consulting firms also provide seminar-type instruction in mobile home park management (again, most of these firms have met with little success because of underutilization).

Little information is available to offer meaningful insights into park operations. Questions about monitoring cash flow, establishing rents, or choosing services are not discussed in any substantive fashion in the existing literature, nor have any commercial

Table 10.7.
Distribution of Mobile
Homes in Park and
Non-Park Locations, by
State: 1974

State	Total Mobile Home Units	Mobile Home Units in Parks	% Mobile Home Units in Parks	Ratio of Non-Park Mobile Home Units to Park Mobile Home Units
Alabama	112,723	25,155	22.3	3.5
Alaska	13,218	8,591	65.0	0.5
Arizona	93,079	56,119	60.3	0.7
Arkansas	60,470	14,384	23.8	3.2
California	294,031	240,551	81.8	0.2
Colorado	61,470	27,558	44.8	1.2
Connecticut	10,720	7,422	69.2	0.4
Delaware	16,429	7,085	43.1	1.3
Florida	359,964	247,061	68.6	0.5
Georgia	172,316	38,581	22.4	3.5
Idaho	29,048	12,231	42.1	1.4
Illinois	111,564	52,960	47.5	1.1
Indiana	107,901	46,243	42.9	1.3
Iowa	41,141	24,751	60.2	0.7
Kansas	48,661	18,336	37.7	1.7
Kentucky	80,464	18,591	23.1	3.3
Louisiana	67,609	15,872	23.5	3.3
Maine	30,092	9,047	30.1	2.5
Maryland	27,534	13,218	48.0	1.1
Massachusetts	14,425	10,459	72.5	0.4
Michigan	148,425	74,035	49.8	1.0
Minnesota	61,516	30,062	48.9	1.0
Mississipi	71,603	14,472	20.2	4.0
Missouri	93,712	33,895	36.2	1.8
Montana	33,171	10,431	31.4	2.2
Nebraska	28,169	13,200	46.9	1.1
Nevada	32,889	18,741	57.0	0.8
New Hampshire	20,756	9,989	48.1	1.1
New Jersey	22,044	19,667	89.2	0.1
New Mexico	40,060	13,162	32.9	2.0
New York	129,085	44,348	34.7	1.9
North Carolina	199,988	40,119	20.1	4.0
North Dakota	18,118	7,415	40.9	1.4
Ohio	141,171	66,171	46.9	1.1
Oklahoma	58,584	19,480	33.3	2.0
Oregon	72,634	32,122	44.2	1.3
Pennsylvania	164,293	48,795	29.7	2.4
Rhode Island	3,437	2,699	78.5	0.3
South Carolina	112,114	19,284	17.2	4.8
South Dakota	24,031	6,511	27.1	2.7
Tennessee	101,174	17,907	17.7	4.6
Texas	239,447	68,719	28.7	2.5
Utah	21,133	9,730	46.0	1.2
Vermont	14,735	4,465	30.3	2.3
Virginia	89,279	23,802	26.7	2.7
Washington	71,484	33,453	46.8	1.1
West Virginia	47,909	8,721	18.2	4.5
Wisconsin	63,179	24,456	38.7	1.6
Wyoming	16,525	4,379	26.5	2.8
U.S.A.	3,893,570	1,614,813	41.5	1.4

Source: PMHI projections of park versus non-park data.

services been formed specifically to treat such questions. As a supplement to direct classroom learning, some private organization(s) should take over the abandoned efforts of the MHI's Land Development Committee in developing and publishing continuously updated instructional material on mobile home park development and management. The formation of a private or public agency to provide advisory services is of primary importance to the continued growth of the park system. There are many companies all over the country with extensive experience in park operation gained from working within the park system for decades, and some of them should feel encouraged to become involved in this area.

The significant participation of people from the traditional building industry in the creation and development of the park system has forged a new, rapidly growing national industry. This trend of people entering the park system from the traditional building industry is ongoing and is likely to continue in the future. This has brought relevant know-how into the park system and may signal a slowly emerging trend toward integration of the mobile home and the housing industry. The existence of traditional building industry know-how in the park system suggests the potential capability of this system to move into markets not presently served by the mobile home industry, such as higher density suburban and urban housing.

Production of New Mobile Home Parks
Our estimations of annual production of new parks and spaces had to be based on fragmentary raw data obtained from several sources; no statistically reliable data base exists.

Between 1969 and 1973, annual production of new parks was hovering between nine hundred and close to two thousand parks. The number of new spaces produced annually in those years was between 110,000 and close to 200,000 (with the exception of 1971, when less than 100,000 spaces were produced). Except for 1971, the average number of spaces per new park increased from roughly 100 in 1970 to approximately 150 in 1973. After 1974, new park construction was negligible. Only now, in the late 1970s, is the production pace picking up slowly.

Annual regional production rates differ sharply. New England, for example, reached its peak with an estimated fifty new parks in 1973, while the West South Central region produced at peak more than 450 new parks in 1972. While annual production figures for new parks remained relatively constant or even declined in the New England, Mid-Atlantic, East South Central, and Pacific regions, production figures in other regions increased by as much as 100 percent. The peak years of park production do not coincide for all regions.

The average number of spaces per new park increased in most regions. The largest average number of spaces per park ever was recorded in the South Atlantic region (more than three hundred spaces/park in 1973), and the smallest average was shown in the West North Central region (27.1 spaces/park in 1971). The few parks constructed in the late 1970s continue to be large.

Three states—Florida, California and Texas —were consistent leaders in production of new spaces from 1969 to 1977. During this nine-year span, the average pre-1973/75 recession production per year both in Florida and California was more than twenty thousand spaces, in Texas almost ten thousand. There is a significant gap between the production of new spaces in these three states and the production in the seven other leading states, where the average yearly production was between three thousand and seven thousand. The areas with the greatest growth in production of spaces are the California-Arizona area and the Michigan-Ohio-Indiana area.

We compared the numbers of new mobile home units shipped by region and year with the total number of park spaces produced for each year, in order to test the degree of compatibility between unit volume shipped to the various regions and the number of new park spaces available for locating them.[5] The disparity between the units shipped and the spaces available is great, particularly in four regions: New England, Mid-Atlantic, South Atlantic, and East South Central. In the East South Central region, for instance, an annual average of more than five thousand park spaces was produced between 1969 and 1973, whereas the number of units shipped to this region averaged more than fifty thousand. Thus, the owners of only 10 percent of these new units would have had access to new park spaces. The rates of fit between the number of spaces built and the number of units shipped for the other three regions are also low, and indicate that most recently built mobile homes located in these fours regions are not placed in parks but are sited on private property. The best fit between the number of spaces produced and the number of units shipped is found in the Pacific region. Specifically, an average of about twenty-five thousand spaces/year were built during the 1969–1973 period and an average of close to fifty thousand units were shipped to this region, indicating that half of all new mobile home units in this region are likely to be located in parks.

From our analyses it became apparent that nationally there has been little reduction in the disparity between the number of mobile home units shipped and the number of park spaces developed. In 1969, the number of spaces constructed was 25.2 percent of the number of units shipped, and in 1977

this percentage peaked at 39.3 percent, but by 1973 declined again to 25.9 percent. The fact that the rate of fit exceeded 30 percent only once during the study period indicates a structural difference between these two production rates. Whether such low rates of fit are evidence of the real quantity of demand for park spaces is not clear. One reason for the disparity we noted is the fact that artificial limitations, such as restrictive land use control and local opposition, often impede mobile home park development. Beyond the necessity that the park system deal with this problem, it is not clear whether efforts should be made to encourage the park developers and the unit manufacturers to establish fit with each other. This may create artificial situations in which too many park spaces would become available or an insufficient number of units would be manufactured for sale to "other" purchasers (individual consumers, subdivision developers, government agencies, and so on) who will locate units in subdivisions or on private or government property, or who plan to export homes. An analysis of the character of the supply/demand relationship for park spaces, although beyond the scope of our supply-oriented study, is badly needed.

Quality and Size Characteristics of the System
While today no organization is maintaining anything even close to a reasonably reliable data bank on the park system, the Woodall Publishing Company had been rating mobile home parks from 1947 through the mid-1970s. Since new park construction practically came to a halt after the 1973/75 recession, the Woodall statistics still are useful for gauging some system characteristics. Parks were examined by Woodall to determine if they qualify to be listed on Woodall's one-to-five-star rating system. The staff considered and rated the condition of the units, the planning and upkeep of the park, its services and facilities, the competence of its management, and the characteristics of the occupants. Parks were reevaluated annually. Rated parks were listed in the annual *Mobile Home and Park Directory*. In general, Woodall-rated parks were newer, larger, and of better quality than non-rated parks. There are approximately 13,000 Woodall-rated parks. According to research conducted by Woodall and PMHI, there are an additional 11,000 parks that either were never inspected, or were inspected but not rated. Of the total of approximately 3,893,500 mobile homes in the country, about 42 percent (1,614,800) are located in nearly 24,500 parks. Of these mobile homes, 62 percent (994,240) are in the 13,000 parks that used to enjoy a Woodall rating.

Table 10.8 displays the regional distributions of total mobile home parks and park-sited unit inventories, and of parks and their unit

Table 10.8.
Distribution of Woodall-Rated Parks and Non-Woodall-Rated Parks and of Mobile Homes in Woodall-Rated and Non-Woodall-Rated Parks, by Region: 1974

Region	Total Parks	Woodall-Rated Parks	% Woodall-Rated Parks	Total Mobile Home Units in Parks	Mobile Home Units in Woodall-Rated Parks	% Mobile Home Units in Woodall-Rated Parks	Ratio of Mobile Home Units in Non-Rated Parks to Mobile Home Units in Rated Parks
Northeast	2,728	1,555	57.0	156,891	106,258	67.7	2.1
New England	763	459	60.2	44,081	30,077	68.2	2.2
Middle Atlantic	1,965	1,096	55.8	112,810	76,181	67.5	2.1
North Central	5,867	3,410	58.1	398,035	289,036	72.6	2.6
East North Central	3,511	2,127	60.6	263,865	198,167	75.1	3.0
West North Central	2,356	1,283	54.5	134,170	90,869	67.7	2.1
South	8,345	3,590	43.0	592,451	326,815	55.2	1.2
South Atlantic	4,463	2,089	46.8	397,871	230,545	57.9	1.4
East South Central	1,552	533	34.3	76,125	35,441	46.6	.9
West South Central	2,330	968	41.5	118,455	60,829	51.4	1.1
West	7,199	4,436	61.6	467,068	347,789	74.5	2.9
Mountain	2,614	1,328	50.8	152,351	101,669	66.7	2.0
Pacific	4,585	3,108	67.8	314,717	246,120	78.2	3.6

Source: PMHI projections based largely on 1974 raw data compiled by Woodall for PMHI (see note 6).

inventories that used to be Woodall-rated.[6] Four subregions are particularly noteworthy here. Considering the percentage of parks which were Woodall-rated developments, the Pacific and East North Central subregions show the highest percentages of Woodall-rated parks (67.8 percent and 60.6 percent respectively), and the South Atlantic shows one of the lowest percentages. This is precisely repeated in the data for percent of park-sited mobile home units located in Woodall-rated parks, reflecting the overall regional picture: all the Northeastern, North Central, and Western subregions fall above the national average (61.6 percent) of park-sited mobile homes located in Woodall-rated parks, whereas all the Southern subregions fall below it. For the South Atlantic subregion, however, this is misleading: because the South Atlantic has so many mobile home parks, it has over four times as many Woodall-rated parks as New England (2089: 459), even though its percentage of Woodall-rated parks is much lower. And even more telling, because of its large inventory of mobile homes, it has over seven times as many mobile homes in Woodall-rated parks as New England (230,545:30,077); in fact, the South Atlantic subregion is second only

to the Pacific subregion in number of mobile homes located in Woodall-rated parks.

These regional patterns correspond closely to state data. Many of the states with the greatest numbers of Woodall-rated parks are historically sites of large mobile home inventories: Michigan, Ohio, Illinois, Indiana (making up most of the East North Central subregion); New York and Pennsylvania; Florida in the South Atlantic; and, in the Pacific, California, Oregon, and Washington. The same states have the highest numbers of mobile homes located in Woodall-rated parks, except that Oregon and Washington are replaced by Arizona, indicating that parks are larger in the retirement states of California and Arizona than in Oregon and Washington. It is important to remember that Florida and California dominate their regions to a great extent. California claims over one-half of the park-sited mobile home units in the West, and over three-quarters of those in the Pacific subregion. Florida contains over 40 percent of the South's park-sited mobile homes, and over 60 percent of those in the South Atlantic subregion.

Bearing this in mind, we can compare the proportion of mobile homes located in parks to the proportion of park-sited mobile homes located in Woodall-rated parks, by region. The West has the highest percentage of mobile homes located in parks and the highest percentage of park-sited mobile homes located in Woodall-rated parks; the South has the lowest percentages of any region. As in the preceding discussion of park-sited and non-park mobile homes, California merely exaggerates the West's already high percentages, whereas Florida offsets the very low percentages in the rest of the South. Excluding Florida, the South's percentage of park-sited mobile homes located in Woodall-rated parks would drop even further, to 23.7 percent.

Between 1968 and 1974, the number of spaces in Woodall-rated parks increased by 443,289. Thus the national average number of spaces/park has increased markedly from 63.75 in 1968 to 95.91 in 1974, as newer, larger parks were added to the Woodall listing and older, smaller parks were dropped.

The regional distribution of the 13,059 Woodall-rated parks is as follows: The West has the greatest share, 34.5 percent; the Southern and North Central regions have 27.5 percent and 26.1 percent respectively, and the Northeast lags at 11.9 percent. The influence of park size, however, changes this picture (see table 10.9). The largest parks are found in the South Atlantic, averaging 125.35 spaces. Florida, which has the greatest number of spaces in this subregion, averages 169.23 spaces per park. Somewhat smaller parks are found in the Western region, averaging 89.94 spaces. As a result, the regional distribution of the 1,252,519 Woodall-rated spaces is rather different from the distribution of parks. The South and West have nearly equal percentages of park spaces (South, 33.0 percent; West, 32.2 percent); the North Central region claims 25.9 percent, and the Northeast, only 8.9 percent.

The East North Central subregion, near the mobile home production center in Indiana, has one of the highest average park sizes (103.60 spaces per park) and also has had a consistently large total inventory of park spaces, presently 220,370. This inventory is fairly evenly distributed among the subregion's states.

In both the South and West, however, high inventories are due to the dominance of one state; Florida has 50.1 percent (206,811) of park spaces in the South, and California has 56.3 percent (227,011) of the West's park spaces. The dominance of Florida and California is further reflected in the rankings of the South Atlantic and Pacific subregions, which together make up 45.6 percent of the nation's Woodall-rated park spaces.

The present equilibrium between South and West may well be a crossover point. From 1958 to 1968, the West's inventory of Woodall-rated spaces grew much more rapidly than the South's did (87 percent versus 57 percent increase), and as a result

the West overtook the South in total number of spaces by 1968. Between 1968 and 1974, however, the situation has been reversed. Florida's inventory of Woodall-rated spaces has increased at a higher rate (54.6 percent) than California's (42.7 percent). Moreover, the rest of the South's inventory is increasing even more rapidly than Florida's, at 64.1 percent; whereas the rest of the West is increasing its inventory more slowly than California, at 31.1 percent. In 1974 for the first time, the South again surpassed the West in total number of Woodall-rated park spaces.

Two other states besides Florida and California make heavy contributions to the total number of Woodall-rated park spaces in the South and West, both as a result of rapid recent growth. Both Texas and Arizona had experienced declines in park development between 1968 and 1972–1973 as did a number of states. Then Texas jumped from 217 rated parks with 18,775 spaces in 1972 to 513 parks with 47,963 spaces in 1974. The number of rated spaces in Arizona increased from 38,976 in 1973 to 47,602 in 1974.

All regions of the United States continue to experience increases in the number and size of mobile home parks. But the most rapid new park development is occurring in the sunbelt—for example, California, Florida, Arizona, and Texas—in response to continued demand for retirement communities, as well as to the strong economic growth in this area.

A majority of respondents to PMHI's national Park Survey (70.3 percent) work in (manage, develop, or own) parks whose owners possess only one mobile home park. The percentages of respondents working in parks whose owners have two or three parks are 12.4 percent and 8.6 percent, respectively. It is clear that some owners are engaged in at least a limited form of expansion, but the degree of expansion is low; this survey of the park system has revealed further evidence of the atomistic nature of this industry.

Although the frequency of owners possessing more than one park is higher in the Pacific and Western South Central regions, the incidence of multiple-park ownership still is a limited phenomenon. Most parks are currently built, filled, and then sold. This process occurs most frequently with the larger parks; many of these are purchased by husband-wife teams who run them for a livelihood and as an investment. Nevertheless, there are a number of organizations that are multiple-park owners. We have devoted a major effort to a comparison of the characteristics and motivations of the multiple-park owner and the one-park owner in order to estimate the degree of economic concentration within the park system and to predict future trends of park ownership and development.

Economic Concentration in the Park System

Table 10.9.
Total Woodall-Rated Park Spaces and Average Spaces per Park, by Region: 1958, 1968–1974(77)

Region		1958	1968	1969	1970	1971	1972	1973	1974	1975–1977[a]
Northeast	1)	56,069	75,796	78,929	83,627	95,471	99,721	107,807	112,374	
	2)	31.82	53.68	53.84	55.71	58.64	60.92	65.30	72.26	
New England	1)	15,390	21,668	23,698	25,388	28,198	29,584	30,470	31,103	
	2)	36.38	51.84	53.14	56.04	56.62	60.50	74.56	68.76	
Middle Atlantic	1)	40,679	54,128	55,231	58,239	67,273	70,137	77,337	80,812	
	2)	30.38	54.46	54.15	55.57	59.53	61.10	65.60	73.73	
North Central	1)	133,165	191,057	199,749	209,039	258,129	264,692	290,704	324,143	
	2)	40.91	60.83	67.48	75.49	82.39	83.68	87.46	95.28	
East North Central	1)	99,743	130,937	141,600	152,491	173,587	181,672	195,775	220,370	
	2)	47.70	71.28	76.67	80.60	87.36	90.79	95.08	103.60	
West North Central	1)	33,422	60,120	58,149	56,548	84,542	83,020	94,929	103,773	
	2)	28.71	46.10	52.25	64.48	73.77	71.45	75.04	81.39	
South	1)[b]	165,593	259,573	286,731	272,628	311,308	315,473	375,866	413,172	
	1)[c]	96,204	125,771	121,708	129,172	144,276	148,351	188,161	206,361	
	2)[b]	36.30	73.16	88.99	89.24	95.85	100.41	104.96	115.09	
	2)[c]	28.71	55.46	62.38	68.09	72.36	77.79	80.76	87.14	
South Atlantic	1)[b]	108,732	190,992	224,205	204,365	232,422	238,409	262,475	286,945	
	1)[c]	39,343	57,190	59,182	61,909	65,390	71,287	74,770	80,134	
	2)[b]	43.86	90.39	109.80	107.92	115.40	112.78	124.90	125.35	
	2)[c]							86.54	75.10	
East South Central	1)	14,127	23,227	24,410	21,026	28,111	31,541	37,376	43,331	
	2)	25.45	56.38	58.40	52.96	70.28	75.23	75.20	81.29	
West South Central	1)	42,734	45,354	38,116	46,237	50,775	45,523	76,015	82,896	
	2)	27.98	44.33	50.02	61.24	60.88	74.75	78.45	85.63	
West	1)[d]	156,762	293,526	295,402	305,472	336,796	350,155	376,774	403,289	
	1)[e]	69,061	134,489	135,295	132,272	144,059	153,192	160,803	176,278	
	2)[d]	33.95	63.91	65.56	70.16	75.19	78.88	83.83	89.54	
	2)[e]	28.62	29.28	55.27	58.04	61.75	64.53	67.23	73.63	
Mountain	1)	51,030	94,762	90,338	84,042	88,714	97,386	103,656	119,193	
	2)	28.74	64.55	61.74	66.75	71.72	76.08	78.17	89.75	
Pacific	1)[d]	105,732	198,764	205,014	221,430	248,082	252,769	273,118	284,096	
	1)[e]	18,031	39,727	44,907	48,230	55,345	55,806	57,147	57,085	
	2)[d]	37.20	63.60	67.39	71.54	76.52	80.02	86.18	89.45	
	2)[e]							53.61	53.55	

1) total park spaces
2) average spaces/park
a. Rating was discontinued, but new park construction also became negligible in the mid- to late 1970s.
b. Includes Florida.
c. Excludes Florida.
d. Includes California.
e. Excludes California.

Source: Compiled by PMHI from 1958–1974 statistics provided by Woodall.

Size and Age Characteristics of the Multiple-Park Ownership Organizations

Of course, many of the country's largest park chain organizations were not included in the PMHI/PS survey sample—the survey was designed to understand the park system at large, not the industry leaders only. Thus the mean size of the multiple-park ownership respondents to the PMHI/PS is small compared to the "giants" controlling well in excess of ten thousand spaces each. Of the multiple-park ownership organizations that responded to the PMHI/PS, 21 percent control one thousand or more spaces. The largest such organization responding to our PMHI Park Survey stated that it controls seven thousand six hundred spaces (based on an ownership of thirty-five parks).

The issue of park age in this study essentially implies a twofold question: How old are the multiple-park ownership organizations and how old are the parks that make up these organizations? We have undertaken a special survey of the largest chains only. This special survey shows that in general the multipark chain emerged as a child of the 1960s. For example, two organizations—a Colorado firm and a Los Angeles corporation—started in 1969 and 1971, respectively, and others were begun in the middle 1960s; this supports the supposition that these large multiple-park ownerships are a fairly recent phenomenon. However, a New England organization, claiming to be the oldest multiple-park ownership in the United States, dates from well before 1950.

We estimate the average age of the individual parks that make up the large ownerships at less than ten years. It is apparent from our special survey of a number of these organizations that many of the parks presently being added come about through those companies' own development efforts. It also appears that the large ownerships based in Florida and the western states are composed presumably of relatively new parks developed in the last ten years.

Concentration Ratios

From our special survey of the large multiple-park ownerships, it was clear that the national concentration level is quite low. At the highest level of apparent concentration is a Los Angeles-based group controlling approximately one hundred parks and over thirty thousand spaces; this organization represents only 2 percent of the national total of park spaces and only 0.4 percent of the total of national parks. Our estimates of the number of these multiple-park ownerships, drawn from this special survey, are correspondingly low: The number of organizations presently owning between two and five parks is set at about one hundred fifty ownerships, the number of companies owning between twenty and fifty parks is about five, and the number controlling more than fifty is projected as somewhere between one and

five. Our estimates reinforce the generally accepted image of the national park system as a highly atomistic and unconcentrated industry.

The several large multiple-park ownerships with whom we have communicated are all nationally based, own parks in two or three of the major geographical regions, and expect to continue their national character. However, significant local ownership concentrations do exist. Some of the large national or multi-regional companies have begun their growth through local expansion. The Colorado-based organization, for example, controls six different parks in Denver, Aurora, and Golden, Colorado, representing about 22 percent of the park spaces in the metropolitan Denver area. There are a limited number of other such instances of local concentration.

Policy Implications

Presumably, the reason for the low level of regional and national (as opposed to local) concentration is that the mobile home park system is primarily the product of many individual entrepreneurs who have entered the park system without the apparent interest in or capabilities for acquiring multiple-park ownerships. It appears that the motivations of the one-park owner and the multiple-park owner, whether an individual, a partnership, or a corporation, are expressly different. The one-park owner seeks to invest capital in a park that will provide a livelihood and will not necessarily foster significant growth; the multiple-park owner sets such growth as a primary goal from the start of the operation. Encouragement for the formation of large ownerships should be directed at new companies that start out with their goals set for growth rather than at current owners who are successfully operating a single park.

Large multiple-park ownerships come about either through initial development or the purchase of existing parks. It is not evident which route is the more efficient. Theoretically, the simultaneous development of a number of parks in one area would be optimal because of possible efficiencies in organizing labor and construction equipment and purchasing building materials. However, this sort of regional concentration is often impractical because of the difficulty in simultaneously acquiring a number of tracts, establishing suitable zoning, and securing sufficient capital. For example, two large park organizations indicated that they have grown primarily by buying existing parks. However, parks available for purchase, having been developed previously by others, often are not efficient in size, design, or operation. A senior official at one of the large organizations noted the difficulties faced by developers of the "Mom and Pop" tradition in dealing with zoning problems, tight money, and the problems of gaining managerial skills.

With the exception of the New England-

based corporation, these companies have begun the formations of such ownerships comparatively recently and with the explicit goal of acquiring a significant number of parks. The reasons for the recent formation of these large ownerships are not clear, although it is possible that a number of groups with sufficient capital realized that opportunities existed to make handsome profits in this industry. It is interesting to note that only a few established organizations with managerial experience in other related or nonrelated fields seeking opportunities for integration or diversification have entered this industrial area. Most of the organizations currently functioning as multiple-park ownerships began operation as new companies rather than as extensions of existing companies.

As to possible future trends in multiple-park ownerships, all surveyed organizations agree that the existence of large organizations will continue, although the number of such organizations will be relatively small for at least the next decade. For example, two corporations presently owning thirty and forty parks anticipate that they will each own approximately two hundred parks in the foreseeable future. Thus there might be ten such corporations owning one hundred or more parks by 1985. These large organizations will probably have a wide national base. A number of the surveyed corporations indicated that large regional organizations, each owning up to one hundred parks, will also come into existence in the next decade. These are thought especially likely to occur in such areas as Florida and California-Arizona.

It appears that a number of opportunities provided by the size of large ownerships (which are appreciably larger in terms of spaces per park than even large single-park ownerships) should encourage growth. It is unclear whether economies of scale exist for multipark ownerships. However, the likelihood of establishing highly developed managerial skills (at least at the corporate level) and the creation of workable practices for running parks based on a sharing of experience by the various managers could be real advantages. Large organizations should also have greater opportunities for securing funds for development and operation (presumably at lower rates than the one-park owners). Compared with the atomistic character and low rate of organization displayed by the park system, large ownerships should experience marked advantages over the one-park owners and be better able to provide a uniformly higher quality of site and service. It is probable that the formation of large ownerships will increase among investors from other industries who enter the mobile home park system for the first time upon discovering its potential for diversifying their holdings. The rates of return on investments in the park system have been good in the past and are likely to continue. However, the

The Mobile Home Park System

growth of large ownerships from within the park system would appear to be unlikely because existing levels of managerial and financial experience are generally inadequate for large-scale operations.

Integration

Two purposes sought in establishing vertical integration in the mobile home park system are an increase in stability and a limitation of competition. The first purpose, enhancement of stability, is widely employed by park owners who establish dealerships primarily to ensure that there will be tenants for their parks. Many park-owner-spawned dealers operate through contractual agreements with purchasers so that their homes will be located in that park the dealer is affiliated with. Limiting competition is of importance on a local level, depending on how closely competitive mobile home parks are clustered. If dealers are relatively distant in a region of many parks, the park owner who also operates the one dealership in the area may have some control over how easily rival park owners are able to find tenants.

Distinguishable Patterns of Vertical Integration in the Mobile Home Park System

There are two distinguishable paths of vertical integration that correspond to the two elements that combine to form the final mobile home park environment—the mobile home itself and the site upon which it is located. By integrating the earlier stages of the mobile home production process into a unified business concern, park owners may be able to increase their own stability and establish a position that will work to their advantage in competition with other park owners who are dependent on their manufacturing or dealership facilities. The same considerations must be made for vertical integration of park site development. Such integration would be exemplified by owners who had developed their own parks and who maintained the capabilities necessary for further land development.

The major emphasis of the PMHI Park Survey was to examine the vertical chain through which homes, as opposed to sites, are produced. However, the survey also shed light on integration of site development. In response to one question, nearly 42 percent of the park owners answered that they were also the developers of their parks. This shows a significant amount of vertical integration in the process by which mobile home sites are produced, extending from land development to the actual operation of the park, but it should be noted that the actual size of the park and of the developmental process in any given case will have much to do with the potential for limiting competition. The 42 percent includes many park owners who require a once-only operation to develop their parks instead of a continuing involvement in land development operations.

We have gathered data about the degree to which park owners are presently integrated with other parts of the mobile home production and delivery process, as well as their future plans. There is a significant degree of vertical integration in the mobile home park system insofar as the distribution system is concerned: 35.7 percent of the respondents had previously entered or were planning to enter the mobile home dealership business. Such integration results from a natural inclination to link the sale of product and the establishment of site and community more than from any tendency toward aggressive expansion. This explanation is reinforced by the extreme paucity of integration from the park system into the manufacturing system, which generally requires considerable capital outlay. Only 2.5 percent of the respondents to the survey stated that they were now or would become involved in mobile home manufacturing. This low percentage suggests that vertical integration of the entire mobile home production and delivery process is virtually nonexistent.

Cross-Sectional Analysis

To explore owner integration into the dealership system further, we examined a variety of geographic, demographic, and financial characteristics. The PMHI Park Survey indicates that a large proportion of park owners in the North Central and South Atlantic regions are also mobile home dealers. In the East North Central region, 47.1 percent of the owner/manager respondents also act as mobile home dealers. This region is followed closely by the West North Central with 45 percent and the South Atlantic sector with 40 percent. The percentages observed were generally much lower in the western part of the country. Only 16.7 percent of the Pacific park owners, 22.2 percent of the Mountain area owners, and 18.2 percent of owners in the West South Central subregion also engage in mobile home distribution. The number of survey observations for the New England, Mid-Atlantic, and East South Central regions are too small to permit any conclusions, even though high percentages in the first two regions (50 percent and 80 percent, respectively) seem in line with the intuitive experience of high degrees of upstream integration into dealerships in these regions. The regional analysis indicates little trend toward integration in the more developed areas of the system, such as the Pacific region. Rather, it suggests that some of the more generally dilapidated parks in the system—in the North Central and South Atlantic areas (with the exception of Florida)—have the highest proportions of park owners who are also dealers.

Our survey suggests no variance of integration by age. The percentage of park owners who are also dealers seems unrelated to park age. Of parks begun between 1950 and 1959, 38.2 percent of the owners stated they were also dealers. The proportion was scarcely different for the 1960s, 36.6 percent. The first five years of the 1970s produced a 36 percent rate. Thus no distinctions based on age are apparent from the data.

Similarly, there seems to be little variance of integration by park size. Of parks with fifty to one hundred spaces, 22.7 percent had adjoining dealership operations. The figure was somewhat higher for parks of one hundred to two hundred spaces, 31.4 percent. Together, these two categories included 59.4 percent of the parks involving dealership integration, but they contained 70.9 percent of the owners responding to the question. What is clear from the analysis is that most of the park system's integration with the dealership system is the work of those respondents owning parks with between fifty and two hundred spaces. There is little indication that size appreciably affects the likelihood of an owner's being a dealer-park operator.

Regarding the question of variance of integration by owner origin, the results of the PMHI Park Survey indicate that 46.3 percent of those engaged in park and dealership integration had originally gone into park operation. Alternatively, those who had evolved from being mobile home dealers to owning mobile home parks constituted 26.2 percent of the respondents to this survey question. We found some surprising results regarding the fields of land development and on-site residential contruction. Of the park owners who also own dealerships, 14.3 percent had original experiences in land development operations outside the mobile home industry and 9.5 percent had been involved in on-site construction. Such developmental operations have been noted previously in the discussion of the integration path by which the mobile home site is produced and owned by the respondents. As such, the data suggest a crossover from one vertical path to the other, intersecting at the mobile home park ownership level.

It is important to note that the survey question on "origin" was designed to elicit information on know-how transfer rather than on corporate expansion, integration, or diversification. Thus our cross-tabulations of park owners' vertical integration into dealerships with owners' origins provide more of an analysis of the work experience of these owners than the direction of corporate movement.

Finally, we did find a variance of integration by legal form of organization. The respondent's tendency to integrate park and dealer operation increased with the complexity of the legal form of organization. Of the park owners who stated that they were the individual proprietors of their

parks, 31.7 percent were also maintaining or planning to expand into dealerships. A larger percentage of those respondents (38.5 percent) involved in partnerships displayed integration. A still greater percentage of those respondents (45.8 percent) who said that their ownership was of a corporate nature exercised some control over dealerships. It seems, therefore, that as the system moves from more simple to more complex organization, the tendency toward integration increases.

Policy Implications

The considerable amount of integration between the mobile home park system and the distribution system found in the Eastern and North Central parts of the country suggests that the integration patterns observed are being caused largely by owners of the smaller and older parks typical for these parts of the country. As already stated, this integration pattern by small park owners will depend on the local availability of alternatives. Although the PMHI Park Survey suggests that 83.2 percent of the park owners have competition within ten miles, there are clearly areas where competition is inhibited because of local government's zoning policies.

The mobile home park system is tending toward complexity through increased size, expanded quality of services, and total costs. One would expect that integration, in this case the purchase of dealerships, would increase. Similar trends in the dealership system will result in increased park purchases. The entire mobile home system's growth as an industry would probably lend itself to increased integration. However, the considerable extent of present and future mobile home park system integration need not have major implications for the performance of the system, though implications are more likely when integration is occurring in highly restricted localities. In these localities, such practices as restrictive land use controls affect both parks and dealership activities. Because of such restrictions, it is not likely that the observed integration is responsible for major economic patterns in the system.

Diversification may increase a firm's market power by enabling it to compete in markets for goods that are reasonable substitutes for those it initially produced. Thus a park owner who begins to produce conventional housing is in the position of being able to fulfill a basic demand for housing in two different markets and is in a stronger market position in both. Diversification may also provide an alternative area for investment of funds when there are limited attractive investment opportunities within the firm's initial area of activity.

Diversification

Distinguishable Diversification Patterns in the Mobile Home Park System

The PMHI Park Survey polled park owners and operators on whether they had diversified or were planning to diversify. Our survey results indicate that the mobile home park system shows a sizable amount of overall diversification, though it is only slightly diversified into any one of the target industries. Of the survey respondents, 7.7 percent stated they were planning to enter the field of recreational vehicle park development and 6.4 percent were already in the field. This total of 14.1 percent was the largest single field of diversification noted. The second largest category on a national level, 9 percent of the respondents, was diversification into on-site residential construction. Other categories such as mobile home consumer financing, nonresidential construction, production and distribution of building supplies, or other businesses were far behind.

Because the categories of diversification with ease of entry and the greatest possibilities for concentrated market power were trailer and recreational vehicle park development and on-site residential construction, it is not surprising that they were also the major areas toward which firms diversified. (Consumer financing, although promising almost unprecedented market power, obviously has high entry barriers; only three respondents had diversified or planned to diversify into this field.) Because of the small percentages for many other categories of diversification presented in the PMHI survey, various cross-sectional analyses are impossible. Diversification into areas other than the two main target fields will therefore be discussed generally as one phenomenon rather than broken down into many categories of limited practical value when taken individually. The differential effects of the various larger categories of diversification may nevertheless serve as a measure of the industry's financial success.

Cross-Sectional Analysis

Distribution of mobile home parks with diversified business interests of any sort tends to be heaviest in the Pacific (24 percent), the West North Central (25 percent), and Mid-Atlantic (60 percent) regions of the country. The more successful regional parts of the park system show below-national averages for the two main target businesses: Diversification into recreational vehicle park development totaled 9.5 percent in the South Atlantic region and 7.7 percent in the Pacific region; in the case of entry into on-site residential construction, these figures are 4.8 percent and 7.7 percent, respectively. The reasons for this counterintuitive behavior are unclear.

There was a clear variance of diversification by park age; the tendency of mobile home park owners toward diversification decreased with park age. None of the respondents whose parks had been developed during the 1940s had diversified. Some form of diversification had been engaged in by 11.1 percent of those whose parks had been developed during the 1950s. This figure increased to 24.4 percent of park owners whose parks were developed in the 1960s. Finally, 44.4 percent of owners sampled from the 1970s stated that they either had already diversified or were planning to.

These trends changed somewhat in the particular cases of on-site residential construction and recreational vehicle park development. In the case of the former, a greater tendency to diversify was observed for the 1960s and 1970s than for any other period. The two periods were roughly comparable: 14.3 percent of those parks developed in the 1970s and 11.1 percent of those from the 1960s were owned by individuals or groups who either had diversified or were planning to diversify into on-site residential construction. None of the respondents whose parks had been built during the 1950s had diversified via on-site residential construction.

Quite different results were observed for those respondents diversifying into recreational vehicle park development. A great deal of diversification activity (28.6 percent of respondents) was initiated by parks developed during the present decade. For parks developed in the 1950s, 18.8 percent of the respondents indicated involvement in recreational vehicle park development. However, this is not, strictly speaking, diversification because the distinction between "mobile home" and "recreational vehicle" was not that sharply made during that decade.

Variance of diversification by park size is logical. It would be expected that the number of spaces in a park might be a crude indicator of the success of its owner(s) and, therefore, that diversification would tend to increase with size. This was the trend generally observed, with one unexplained drop in diversification activities occurring for the group between one hundred and one hundred fifty spaces. Of respondents owning a park of up to fifty spaces, 15.7 percent stated that they had either diversified or were planning to in the near future. That percentage increased to 25 percent for the park owner group between fifty-one and one hundred spaces. It fell to 13.6 percent for owners between one hundred one and one hundred fifty spaces, then returned to 25 percent for the next fifty, and was 100 percent for those owning parks with more than three hundred spaces. These last two categories were based on very few responses.

In the case of diversification into recreational vehicle park development, we find almost all of the activity in the low to moderate ranges (parks with under one hundred spaces). Of the parks diversifying, 72.7 percent fell into this range. The results were broadly distributed slightly more for owners who had specifically diversified into on-site residential construction. These observations seem convincing; entry into either field is relatively easy.

Variance of diversification by origin does exist. The examination of owner origins for parks engaging in diversification indicates that the major areas involved owners who had gone straight into park operation (40 percent) or had come from "traditional" land development (25 percent). These same patterns held for the two specific areas of diversification analyzed (recreational vehicle park development and on-site residential construction). It is clear that owners with "traditional" land development background are more likely to diversify than owners who originated in park operations, since fully 64 percent of all owners had gone straight into park operations as compared to only the 12 percent of owners who had originated in land development. (See the discussion of origins of the park system earlier in this chapter.) This is logical: People with a background in general land development not only have experience with diversification per se but also to some extent with the two target areas.

Finally, variance of diversification by legal form of organization follows expected patterns. There appears to be a markedly stronger tendency for partnerships and corporations owning mobile home parks to diversify than there is for individuals. Only 11.6 percent of those respondents who stated that their park was owned by one person were also engaged in some form of diversification. This provides a sharp contrast to the 38.5 percent of parks owned by partners and the 32 percent owned by corporations who had diversified.

The tendency toward diversification into recreational vehicle park development is consistent, but diversification in on-site residential construction seems to increase with the complexity of the legal form of organization. Of the individual proprietors surveyed, 2.9 percent answered in the affirmative to the question of diversification. That percentage increased to 10.5 percent in the case of partnerships and to 15.8 percent for corporations. As an indicator of the correlation of diversification to the degree of financial success and the scale of financial activity, it is interesting to note that 50 percent of all operations diversified into this field were owned by corporations.

Policy Implications
It may be concluded that the degree of diversification does serve as an indicator of the success enjoyed by the park owner. Our analyses of park age, the number of spaces in the park, owner origin, and the legal form of organization of the park all lead toward this conclusion. These patterns did not hold up as well for recreational vehicle park develop-

ment as they did for diversification into residential on-site construction.

The specific conclusion that success tends to stimulate diversification into on-site residential construction is important. In no small degree will the continued maturation of the park system depend upon the increasing presence of the on-site builders' or developers' know-how. We mentioned earlier how strongly builders and developers have been moving into the park system since the industry's beginning. The ongoing diversification by park owners into traditional building is a similarly effective transfer of on-site building experience into the park system and should be encouraged by public policy with maximum possible vigor. To the extent that new trends in the system are visible, they would seem to suggest a continuing general diversification. This diversification has neutral overall effects on economic efficiency, but it may be seen as an indicator of an industry undergoing new growth.

We have attempted to determine to what extent there are economies or diseconomies of scale in the mobile home park system, whether economies of scale act as barriers to entry, and whether an optimal park size exists above or below which efficiency is notably impaired.

Economies of Scale in Park Construction
Three main functions of park development offer potential economies of scale: planning, purchasing, and construction. Total costs per park space for design, planning, obtaining regulatory approvals, and securing financing decrease as the scale of operation increases. These economies are obviously greatest for companies specializing in park development and having in-house staff for these activities.

Large-scale park construction provides purchasing and technical economies. Material costs are likely to fall as park size and quantity of needed materials increase. Substantial cost savings per park space can be realized by large quantity purchase of asphalt, cement, piping, and so forth. Large firms, which are simultaneously or sequentially developing several parks in a given area, can achieve truly significant purchasing economies. Technical economies of scale are also realized in park construction because heavy equipment can be used more efficiently on large projects. The reduction of transportation of heavy equipment alone can achieve savings; no additional transportation costs are incurred in constructing an additional one hundred park spaces if the equipment has already been moved to the site to build the first two hundred. Larger-scale park projects will also probably have lower per-space labor costs and are more likely to capture the attention of large established construction firms with the highly specialized labor force, heavy equipment, and know-how to complete a quality job efficiently. More detailed information on economies of scale associated with park development is given in chapter 12 on cost and price structures.

Economies of Scale in Park Operation

The larger the park, the larger the resident population over which fixed and certain variable costs can be spread. This lowers the average operating costs per park space, achieves economies of scale, and makes possible many facilities and services less commonly found in small parks. It was evident from the PMHI Park Survey that larger parks were apt to provide more recreational, sporting, and religious facilities than smaller parks. Large parks are also able to take advantage of savings and benefits that accrue from the division of labor. Small Mom and Pop park operations often require the owners to assume many roles (manager, maintenance personnel, accountant, social director, and so forth), but large parks are able to hire specialized individuals. Our field experience as well as the data generated by PMHI's Park Survey suggest that these economies can be substantial. Economies of scale in park operation are important for both the park owner and the resident; economies influence owner profits and occupant costs.

Policy Implications

Economies of scale can be achieved in park development as well as in park operation. Average costs per park space fall as the size of the park increases. However, there is not yet a comprehensive enough base to quantify reliably the extent of existing economies of scale and to determine whether scale economies act as entry barriers or whether an optimal park size exists. A major study directed toward quantification of scale economies in park development and operation is needed. Hard quantitative evidence on this phenomenon would provide both the industry and the public sector with input necessary to determine and encourage an optimal industry structure.

Entry Barriers

We have examined two potential barriers to the entry of new competition into the mobile home park system: absolute cost barriers and product differentiation.

Absolute Cost Barriers

There are three major barriers: cost of land, cost of development, and cost of obtaining favorable zoning. Detailed information on factors contributing to these barriers can be found in other parts of this book, particularly in chapters 12 and 16 on cost/price analysis in this part and the chapter on land use controls in part V. The cost of land is substantial and varies dramatically by region and among rural, suburban, and urban areas. In certain regions and in many suburban and urban situations, this cost constitutes a significant entry barrier. Development costs, already high and steadily increasing, are as much of a hindrance to free entry as land costs. Development costs vary from area to area because parks in different areas are built to different quality standards and supply their customers with different services. For instance, retirement parks located in California or Florida will require greater construction funds than an average park in Vermont. The cost of obtaining zoning is the expense incurred in convincing the local government to alter restrictive zoning practices. In many cases these practices are immutable; no amount of money and effort will be enough to overcome discriminatory land use control attitudes. Such inhibitive zoning ordinances infinitely increase entry cost barriers. This fixes the available supply and allows those owners who were established before the adoption of an ordinance to collect rents in excess of the prices a competitive framework would permit.

It is difficult to assess the degree to which these absolute cost barriers inhibit competition. The vast majority (83.2 percent) of PMHI/PS respondents claimed that there were parks within ten miles offering similar services (a reasonable proximity). Although this would suggest a competitive environment, several other factors must be considered. First, there is the question of similarity of parks' orientation. For instance, a low-rent park would not normally be a serious competitor to a luxury park within ten miles. Second, truly similar parks located near one another may prefer to work together to realize the highest possible profits rather than compete. As mentioned earlier, overly restrictive zoning practices in Connecticut seem to have created monopoly pricing situations there.

Product Differentiation Barriers

A second barrier to entering the park system is the cost of overcoming product differentiation. Our analysis of product differentiation follows the most commonly used approach of studying advertising patterns and techniques. We found that advertising as practiced by park owners creates only minimal distortions in the consumer mentality and does little to contribute new entry barriers.

The major advertising techniques used by parks are newspaper advertisements (34.2 percent of the PMHI/PS respondents) and highway signs (22.8 percent). The other forms of advertising mentioned were less popular: radio messages (7 percent), television (3.5 percent), and signs in stores (1.8 percent). Word-of-mouth advertising played an important role for 78.9 percent of the respondents, and 36 percent used some additional unspecified means. From demographic cross-tabulations with a park owner's tendency to advertise, we found that the Pacific, South Atlantic, and Central regions tend to be the most active and that owners of parks developed during the 1970s consistently tend to advertise more than owners of older parks. High vacancy rates and the need to fill up new parks explain much of this tendency. Another consistent trend noted was that advertising methods of all kinds except word-of-mouth were more commonly used by those firms with greater numbers of spaces.

We also attempted to determine through a cross-tabulation process whether advertising was a proxy for product differentiation. It would be expected that low vacancy rates and a positive response to the question about waiting lists would accompany more sophisticated forms of advertising. However, exactly the opposite result was observed. The firms that tend to fund the most sophisticated and expensive forms of advertising are those experiencing greater difficulties in conducting their businesses. They tend to have more vacancies and fewer people on their waiting lists. When the influence of advertising on a firm's success is used as a measure of product differentiation, it suggests more that failure leads a firm to advertise rather than that advertising leads a firm to success.

It is understandable that the mobile home park system tends to advertise through non-mass media techniques. The system has many owners and very few have the resources to make use of radio or television advertisements. The owners do not feel the need to advertise and are not particularly concerned with the problems of product differentiation. Our demographic cross-tabulations reflect the trend toward more activity in larger parks in certain regions, such as the South Atlantic and the Pacific, at the present time.

Policy Implications

There are many entry barriers in the mobile home park system that are based on the costs of development, land, and obtaining favorable zoning. These costs are highly volatile from area to area and they may range from the moderate to the infinite. Because of exclusive control, a park owner may in many instances indiscriminately raise the price of the services supplied.

Barriers to entry caused by product differentiation are minimal. Except in a very few states such as California and Florida, where the industry is highly developed, most park owners do not perceive a need nor do they have the resources to carry on advertising through the major communications media—radio, television, or newspapers. In the 1970s this trend is slowly changing. Owners of parks constructed in the 1970s tend to engage in more mass media advertising than do their predecessors because more modern parks tend to be both large enough and financially sound enough to use mass media

techniques more effectively. We anticipate that this trend will continue; however, because of its slow rate of progress (indicated by the concentration rate of the park system) and the additional time that will be required for the eventual development of brand name identification through advertising, it will probably be a long time before significant product differentiation is seen within the system itself. Most park owner advertising still seems to be very much more a defensive than offensive weapon. Poor performance triggers advertising rather than advertising triggering high sales.

Absolute cost barriers to entry of the mobile home park system—the costs of development, land, and obtaining favorable zoning—are relatively high and increasing; it is important to note that the traditional home-building industry is also suffering from this situation. If these barriers continue to grow at the present rate, they may soon begin seriously to inhibit competition in the park system and in some areas lead to oligopolistic or even monopolistic situations. On the other hand, some entry barriers are desirable to avoid atomistic competition, which is still widespread in many parts of the country. Product differentiation in general (for example, the creation of more responsive service packages) could be one such desirable barrier and should be encouraged.

The mobile home park system in America is competitively structured. The distribution of members is extremely atomistic, with the largest firms in the industry controlling less than 1 percent of the national total of approximately twenty-five thousand parks. Integration is almost entirely restricted to the dealership system, though it is very significant on this level; for many purposes it is practical to consider the dealer-park combination as one operation. Diversification appears significant, but very little of it is directed into any one specific area. Diversification into areas providing for substitute goods seems rather limited. Two other significant structural conclusions were derived in the preceding discussion: Entry barriers due to product differentiation are slight, which encourages competition, and economies of scale do apply for different aspects of the park system, but their total impact is too weak to impair competition. These structural conditions suggest competition.

On the other hand, there are some significant entry barriers, particularly the costs of obtaining zoning and the costs of land and development, which would tend to inhibit competition. However, the PMHI Park Survey results indicate that parks offering similar services are, in the wide variety of cases, available within a reasonable distance. Our survey did not include a question concerning the number of such parks in proximity. The greater the number, the less likelihood of price collusion.

D. System Operation

Expectations Based on Structure

In conclusion, the mobile home park system should behave competitively with only limited and scattered local pockets of market control generated by high entry barriers. Rents will probably be determined by the costs facing park owners, as opposed to the amount they can extract from the market by contracting supply. Therefore, reasonable profits, based on the characteristics of economic rent, should be observed instead of profits at windfall levels. Prices should be relatively stable over time because bursts of predatory pricing to clear the market of occasional competitors should not be a characteristic of the system. Rents should be quite similar in an area facing similar costs over time, though they should not vary too closely in the short run, as might be expected from an oligopolistic system of tacit price coordination. Rents must also be examined in terms of price discrimination implications; there should be little discrimination based on the consumer's income, life-style, age, season of application, or other characteristics in a competitive system. Some of these expectations are examined in our discussion of price policy below.

Product policies and other dynamics, which can be expected to develop in a system with generally active internal competition, are examined in the balance of this analysis of system operations. Specialization of park services as a means of circumventing competition would be expected to develop, and those parks that do not go the specialization route would be forced to develop a very standard set of services in order to remain competitive. Finally, we expect this system to exhibit the innovative behavior that often characterizes truly competitive systems.

Price Policy

Analysis

As table 10.10 indicates, virtually all park revenue derives from park rentals. Of the respondents, 74.8 percent replied that between 81 percent and 100 percent of their revenue comes from this source. Furthermore, 54.4 percent of the sample stated that between 95 percent and 100 percent of their income comes from rent. For the entire survey population, a mean percentage of park revenue based on rent of 85.3 percent was recorded (table 10.10). Other sources of income are minor.

In certain census regions the pattern of the predominant contribution of rent to total revenue is altered, but on the whole the trend is stable. Some of the major exceptions to the pattern may be found in the Mid-Atlantic, South Atlantic, East South Central, and Pacific regions. On the mean, in the Mid-Atlantic, only 56.3 percent of revenues derives from rent; 49 percent of revenues comes from mobile home sales. In the South Atlantic lot sales are more than three times the national average, standing at 7.4 percent. East South Central respondents stated that

Table 10.10.
Sources of Park Owner Revenue

Revenue from Park Rentals

% of Total Revenue	% of Total Respondents
0–20	5.8
21–40	2.0
41–60	5.8
61–80	11.6
81–85	3.0
86–90	10.6
91–95	6.8
96–99	14.6
100	39.8

Park Site versus Other Sources of Revenue

Source	Mean % of Total Revenue	% of Respondents Deriving No Revenue from Source
(Park site rentals)	(85.3)	(1.9)
Mobile home sales	6.1	83.5
Mobile home unit rentals	2.7	81.7
Lot sales to mobile home owners	2.0	95.2
Overnight recreational vehicles, fees	1.7	85.4
Utilities	1.3[a]	88.5
Service fees	0.3	92.9
Concessions	0.2	88.8
Other	0.5	92.8

a. This percentage can easily exceed 10 percent if the parks in question include utilities in their rental fee. (See chapter 12 on cost and price analysis.)

Source: PMHI/PS.

10 percent of their revenue came from mobile home unit rentals, almost four times the national average, and that 10 percent (nearly seven times the national figure) came from overnight recreational vehicles.

The PMHI/PS also questioned park owners about charges in addition to continuing rent that they may assess to consumers on a one-time-only basis. These are few in number and are used in a minor way by park owners. Only 7 percent of the respondents charge an entrance fee to their customers; the mean entrance fee was $51.89. Of the owners, 27.5 percent have a requirement for a security deposit, averaging $47.81. A resale fee for home owners planning to leave the park is assessed by 11.2 percent of the respondents; no information on the average costs charged was available.

There was broad agreement with regard to the policies (entrance fees, security deposits, and resale fees) of owners in different regions. The only skewed results may be observed in isolated cases in the South

Atlantic, East North Central, West North Central, and West South Central regions. In the South Atlantic 13.8 percent of the parks have an entrance fee, which is approximately twice the national average. Security deposits are widely used in the West North Central area (42.9 percent of the owners require them) and in the West South Central (45.5 percent); they are also more commonly used in the East North Central region (41.2 percent). Of that region's park owners, 18.8 percent also have entrance fees.

There were a number of other charges for certain services that could be assessed to home owners and that could be included in rent or in the sale price of a lot. Although a detailed effort was made to categorize these services and to determine the contribution of their costs to rents placed upon consumers, relatively little about their actual contribution to rent prices could be determined because of the complexity of the data. The variety of services is displayed in table 10.11. There were strong differences in the behavior of owners selling lots from those renting them. In the former case the amenities most often included were the mobile home unit, supports and skirts for the home, an initial hookup of the home to the facilities, and other unspecified accessories and items. The most commonly included services in the rentals case seem to be water, sewers, park maintenance, the mobile home and its supports, and other accessories and items. Many other services to the home owner, such as gas, electricity, garbage disposal, and taxes, are included in about one-fifth of the rental cases. The percentages of these services included in lot sales is understandably much lower because of their continuing nature.

Almost all park spaces are rented and the predominant source of revenue is rent, so it seems reasonable to base a study of prices in the mobile home park system on an analysis of rents. Fortunately, extensive data on rent levels throughout the United States were available through annual rent statistics provided to PMHI by the Woodall Publishing Company. The analysis that follows is confined to Woodall-rated parks.

The Woodall's rent data (see table 10.12)[7] is divided into five categories: $29 or less, $30–$39, $40–$59, $60–$100, and more than $100 per month. On a national level, very few parks are located at either extreme. Of the parks, 5.8 percent fall in the lowest category and 1.6 percent fall in the highest. The data cluster in the $40–$59 range, with 46.4 percent of the sample in this category. Generally, the distribution is rather symmetrical, yet the data differ strongly from region to region. In New England 86.3 percent of the owners charge rents in the $30–$59 range. The South Atlantic region represents a less skewed, though still far from average aggregation, with 58.5 percent of the park owners receiving rents between $30 and

Table 10.11.
Services Included in
Sale or Rental

Item or Service	% Respondents Who Include in Sale	% Respondents Who Include in Rental
Initial hookup to utilities	17.1	23.9
Lot maintenance (private areas)	2.7	15.2
Mobile home unit	53.8	30.8
Mobile home supports	56.3	37.5
Mobile home skirts	81.8	9.1
Other accessories	50.0	50.0
Other items	22.2	60.0
Water	8.9	84.7
Gas (central system)	5.2	19.8
Sewer (central system)	8.3	76.7
Electricity	6.2	20.4
Garbage pickup	10.6	27.2
Taxes	6.4	22.7
Park maintenance (community facilities)	5.1	62.4

Source: PMHI/PS.

$39 a month. In several other regions the preponderance of rents tended to be in the second and third categories. The Pacific region is biased in just the opposite direction: 85.5 percent of this region's parks charge rents between $40 and $100, the third and fourth categories. Rents in excess of $100 were charged by 5.8 percent, a very large number relative to the national total. California alone contained 182 of the 197 parks in this category.

A crude attempt was made to use these data as an indicator of pricing of rents in the mobile home park system. Each of the five rent categories was assigned a consecutive number between one and five. These integers were multiplied by the percentage of parks in that category, summed for each region and then for the nation as a whole in order to produce a value analogous to a mean value. These regional values can then be compared with the national value as a measure of differences in prices and perhaps of competition.

For example, in table 10.12, .030 of the parks in New England had rents of $29 or less, which has been assigned the value 1. We multiplied .030 by 1 and then added it to .354 multiplied by 2 and to .509 multiplied by 3, and so forth. This eventually sums to 2.696. This same process used on the statistics available for the entire United States produces the value 2.870. On this basis we concluded that rent levels are lower in the New England area than for the country as a whole and that this may suggest a more competitive than average industry in that region. This technique crudely implies in general that the industry is more competitive in some places than in others.

We also tested qualitatively the degree of competition by comparing the rent level indexes with indexes of the extent of restrictive land use control practices. The latter were constructed by summing up the percentages of all municipalities in each state of a particular region that either completely exclude mobile homes or that restrict them to parks and by then computing the "average" from this total. (Data were taken from a PMHI fifty-state survey analyzed in chapter 16 on land use controls.) High index values suggest a regulatory climate not conducive to fostering competition; low values indicate that stimuli operate to increase competition. The indexes for each region are shown in the last column in table 10.12. For the Mid-Atlantic and the Pacific regions, high rent levels correlate with high restrictive land use control indexes, which corroborates the suspicion of low competition. On the other hand, the East, South, Central, and West North Central regions show very low rent level indexes and also very low indexes of restrictive land use controls, which suggests a very competitive climate.

A second test regarding the actual presence of competition was made by considering the return on equity (ROE) enjoyed by industry members in different areas. This may determine the extent to which different rent levels reflect greater than competitive profits and not merely higher costs and normal profits. Overall, the PMHI Park Survey indicates that the average ROE is 16.196 percent. Equity returns of less than 10 percent were

claimed by 51.1 percent of the respondents; 23.5 percent stated that their ROEs exceeded 20 percent.

Emerging Trends
Based on data from the PMHI/PS, most of the rent level and restrictive land use control indexes compare favorably with the ROE in most of the regions. The Mid-Atlantic, Mountain, and Pacific regions all had the most parks located in the higher ROE ranges. Smaller values than the national average were seen in the East South Central, New England, and West North Central regions. Only in the South Atlantic and West South Central regions do the rent and profit data diverge. On the basis of this second test, we may speculate more definitively about the extent of competition in different regions. The least competitive areas, based on price, extent of restrictive land use controls, and profits, appear to be the Mid-Atlantic, Pacific, and Mountain regions. The more competitive park owners may be found in the East South Central, the West North Central, and the South Atlantic regions.

Conclusions
Almost all revenue received by park owners derives from park rentals. There are many other amenities or services the owner may or may not provide within those rentals, but they seem to be of small significance in the development of pricing policy. A comparison of rental rates throughout the country, furthermore, suggests wide variation from a national average. This variance correlates well with variance of restrictive land use control attitudes and with variance of data on profit rates, leading to the following conclusions: The system is more competitive in certain areas than in others and public regulatory attitudes may in part tend to discourage competition.

Table 10.12.
Rent Levels in Woodall-rated Parks by Region

Region	1 $29 or less # Parks	%	2 $30–$39 # Parks	%	3 $40–$59 # Parks	%	4 $60–$100 # Parks	%	5 $100+ # Parks	%	Index for Mean Rent Level	Index for Restrictive Land Use Control Practices
New England	12	3.0	140	35.4	201	50.9	41	10.4	1	0.3	2.696	24.7
Mid-Atlantic	287	2.7	210	20.2	548	52.6	254	24.4	2	0.2	2.995	41.7
South Atlantic	149	5.3	1635	58.5	757	27.1	251	9.0	3	0.1	2.401	37.6
East South Central	119	23.4	226	44.4	156	30.6	8	1.6	0	0.0	2.104	13.6
West South Central	80	8.5	385	40.7	436	46.1	45	4.8	0	0.0	2.474	12.1
East North Central	63	3.2	521	26.1	1107	55.4	305	15.3	3	0.2	2.838	28.1
West North Central	190	1.5	463	36.8	527	41.9	76	6.0	1	0.1	2.253	23.0
Mountain	54	4.3	305	24.5	595	47.8	285	22.9	5	0.4	2.903	15.2
Pacific	22	0.7	250	8.0	1388	44.3	1291	41.2	182	5.8	3.434	30.5
United States	715	5.8	3119	25.4	5712	46.4	2558	20.8	197	1.6	2.870	

Source: Compiled from statistics provided by the Woodall Publishing Company and PMHI's 50-State Land Use Control Survey.

Thus far in the 1970s, profit rates are undergoing changes, a very radical movement toward a bipolar equity return distribution. Such a distribution would be consistent with the hypothesis of two different types of parks in the system. One type is the sophisticated, well-organized retirement community, which earns a high return on equity, and the other type is the Mom and Pop operation, which has a lower level of return.

We have attempted to approach the problem of price policy as an index of competition through regression analysis, introducing the factors mentioned above and a dummy variable representing local competition; however, the results were inconclusive, probably due to the difficulty of building an accurate enough data base. We have concluded that regression analysis does hold promise if more resources can be devoted to amassing an accurate enough data bank.

Product Policy

Analysis

The product the park owner offers the consumer is the mobile home space on which the home may be sited as well as a wide variety of supporting goods and services, some private and some communal. The types of services and facilities a park may provide for its occupants include the following:

A paved and curbed street system

An underground utility system

Automatic laundry or laundromat

Play areas for children and run areas for pets

Recreational facilities, including a swimming pool or a recreational program or both

Competent and helpful management available at all times

Mail delivery

Other facilities and services, such as everyday and casual shopping, religious services, and communitywide gatherings of a social or entertainment nature

The variation in goods and services park owners supply throughout the country was measured through two sources: data supplied by the Woodall Publishing Company and the PMHI Park Survey. The former source is the more comprehensive; the latter was used to examine particular aspects of product policy that could not be analyzed with the data made available by the Woodall organization.

The Woodall staff had been rating mobile home parks since 1947. Small teams, usually two persons, carefully inspected the various parks requesting to be listed. Before a park was listed, it was systematically examined on a number of points, such as condition of the mobile home units present, degree of park planning and upkeep, amount of services and facilities, management competence, and character of the occupant clientele. Parks examined were not listed if their quality levels fell below Woodall minimum standards. Not all parks were examined; in the mid 1970s the Woodall's directory listed only about thirteen thousand parks of the national total of about twenty-four thousand five hundred. By 1977 it was clear that Woodall would not continue its rating and directory publication activities—a fact, however, of little relevance for this analysis of product policy patterns.

Because of the competitive nature of the park system, the peer pressure to establish recognition and to prove that one's park is as good as the neighboring park, and the value in advertising the park's presence and quality, it is probable that most park owners felt they should be listed among the top parks and request that their parks be inspected. Therefore the Woodall listings were likely to provide an accurate picture of the better parks in the United States. It should be noted that the Woodall staff had continuously been reexamining previously rated parks and inspecting new ones, so incentives existed for the maintenance and establishment of a high-quality product.

The Woodall mobile home park rating system has undergone a constant process of revision and upgrading in the almost thirty years the directory has been published. As the mobile home has outgrown the image of the travel trailer and become more sophisticated and legitimate, so too did the scope and concerns of the Woodall rating system change. This was especially true since the advent of the larger, wider singlewide and doublewide units, which have significantly altered the spatial requirements for quality mobile home park developments.

A comparison of the star rating system in 1968 and 1972 reveals some interesting facts. The Woodall one-star rating—the lowest acceptable rating for parks that were at least "a decent place to live"—changed little over the five-year period. The only significant alteration was the elimination of the requirement of "adequate laundry facilities." The Woodall two-star rating, which required certain extra amenities (such as landscaping, storage areas, and so forth) in addition to those offered in a one-star park, also remained generally the same. One other alteration was the elimination of the requirement for the provision of play areas "if the children are accepted." Because families with children tend to be much more common in parks with lower star ratings, the elimination of this requirement was significant. Woodall three-star parks were of significantly higher quality than the one- and two-star parks. Many of the three-star parks may once have been rated higher, but original construction in these parks might prohibit utilization of the newer 14-wide or doublewide units or the 60-foot and overlength units. All modifications in the requirements for three-star parks were of a purely structural nature (changes in porches, cabanas, park signs, and so forth). However, it is important to note that in 1972 the following reference to children was eliminated from the introduction to the three-star section: "If children are allowed, there should be adequate play area. However, the disarray caused by children may at times be the determining factor that keeps a three-star park at that level when it otherwise could be rated higher." The Woodall four-star and five-star categories were the luxury park classifications. It is here that the rating system had undergone its most rigorous upgrading since 1968. Consequently, many parks formerly rated as four- or five-star have often "slipped" to a three-star rating. Luxury mobile home parks may have been defined primarily by the presence of certain extra features in the physical environment as well as by outstanding upkeep and management. In 1972 some of the ways in which the four-star parks were upgraded included the following: 75 percent to 98 percent of the homes must be covered with skirting of some kind; tanks and bottles must be concealed or eliminated; off-street parking must be provided. In addition, a new requirement concerning play areas for children was added.

The top Woodall rating was the five-star park. As the directory stated, "They should be nearly impossible to improve. Their quality must be diligently maintained." These parks must include outstanding recreational facilities (pool, recreation hall, and so forth), carefully planned layout (wide paved streets, sidewalks, setbacks, and so forth), only late model homes, and must be at least 75 percent occupied in order for Woodall "to judge the quality of the residents that indicates the park's ability to maintain five-star rating between inspections." Five-star mobile home parks had to meet the following upgraded requirements in 1972: 320 square feet of porch or patio space on all homes (except doublewides); paved two-car, off-street parking; all homes completely skirted with quality skirting; awnings or cabanas and carport on all homes; uniform shed at all homes; and superior on-duty management. In addition, an admonition that "most five-star parks were for adults only" was eliminated.

Given the last rating system, we attempted to determine differences in the quality of the product—the mobile home park—being made available by owners in different regions and, in some cases, different states. This effort was based on the same type of system used in the preceding discussion of price policy. A mean value star rating for each area was developed (table 10.13).[8] As the data indicate, the mean U.S. park star rating was 2.18. It is interesting to note that most regions fell below this mean, some very much so. The South Atlantic and the East South Central regions, for instance, stood at 1.59 and 1.78, respectively. The only regions

above the national average were New England, which is seldom viewed as a higher-than-average quality product area, and the Pacific region, which was rated 2.44, much higher than anywhere else in the system. A state-by-state analysis indicates that California's mean star rating was 2.69, Florida's was 2.50. Because this analysis corroborates what is generally known in the mobile home industry—that the mobile home park product is very different in quality in California and Florida from the rest of the country—the validity of our approach is supported. In the rest of the nation, regional analysis indicates broad similarities, with the exception of the South Atlantic, which except for Florida offers a lower quality product.

There was also close correlation between the ratings and the size of the parks (in terms of the number of units present). Progressing upward from the average one-star park to the average five-star park, the number of units present increased. This correlation is logical because the expenses for the installation of the various services required for a five-star rating inevitably necessitated a money pool that could be provided only by a larger park. Economies of scale play a significant role.

Certain aspects of product policy that were not included in the Woodall rating system were examined through the PMHI Park Survey. There was a variety of services involved based on the availability of community facilities. We found, for example, that only 2 percent of parks have shopping or religious facilities, but a sizable percentage maintain recreational, sports, or other communal facilities. In all cases, however, facilities outside the park are much more widely used than those within the park (table 10.14). Low percentages of parks making communal facilities available does not mean that park owners are unresponsive to their tenants' desires. It is clear from the data that the overwhelming majority of tenants perceive services located outside their park to be better than those inside the park, with the possible exception of athletic activities, and that the owners perceive that they cannot match the quality of outside facilities and design their product accordingly. These statistics suggest that the mobile home park system is a competitive one in which owners cannot afford to be unresponsive or to establish facilities that will generally not be favored by the tenant.

Other practices that should be considered as elements of product policy are leasing agreements, restrictive entry practices, and influence by the tenant in park decisions. A lease was required of 37 percent of the respondents. That figure reflects a preponderance of verbal agreements in the South Atlantic, meaning that the actual percentage of ironclad agreements arrived at is much higher. Of those parks in which a lease is required, 19 percent specify a one-month agreement, 51 percent between one month and one year,

Table 10.13.
Park Quality Levels

State/Region	1	2	3	4	5	Total
Conn.	23 (0.31)	28 (0.37)	12 (0.16)	9 (0.12)	3 (0.04)	75
Maine	22 (0.20)	57 (0.52)	28 (0.25)	3 (0.03)	0 (0.00)	110
Mass.	21 (0.21)	37 (0.37)	35 (0.35)	8 (0.08)	0 (0.00)	101
N.H.	17 (0.20)	36 (0.42)	24 (0.28)	7 (0.08)	1	85
R.I.	4	11	7	0	0	22
Vermont	3	17	12	0	0	32
New England (2.22)	90 (0.21)	186 (0.44)	118 (0.28)	27 (0.06)	4 (0.01)	425
N.J.	14	39	56	6	1	
N.Y.	195	188	66	10	0	
Pa.	78	226	140	17	2	
Mid-Atlantic (2.03)	287 (0.28)	453 (0.44)	262 (0.25)	33 (0.03)	3 (0.00)	1038
Delaware	13	17	11	1	0	
Florida	275 (0.25)	338 (0.30)	271 (0.24)	138 (0.12)	98 (0.09)	1900 (2.50)
Georgia	60	61	24	1	0	
Md.	17	40	18	3	0	
N.C.	121	90	26	1	1	
S.C.	44	38	10	1	0	
Va.	71	55	21	3	0	
W.Va.	18	25	7	1	0	
South Atlantic (1.59)	619 (0.32)	664 (0.35)	388 (0.20)	149 (0.08)	99 (0.05)	1919
Ala.	66	89	35	2	0	
Ky.	30	51	20	0	0	
Miss.	42	33	8	0	0	
Tenn.	40	47	21	3	0	
East South Central (1.78)	178 (0.38)	220 (0.47)	65 (0.14)	5 (0.01)	0 (0.00)	468
Ark.	60	31	25	3	0	
La.	36	56	19	1	0	
Okla.	52	49	37	4	0	
Tex.	109	149	126	31	2	
West South Central (2.03)	257 (0.33)	285 (0.36)	207 (0.26)	39 (0.05)	2 (0.00)	790
Ill.	126	137	88	16	1	
Ind.	70	143	132	19	0	
Mich.	82	177	144	49	0	
Ohio	116	197	169	29	0	
Wisc.	71	82	43	7	1	
East North Central (2.16)	465 (0.24)	736 (0.39)	576 (0.30)	120 (0.06)	2 (0.00)	1899

Table 10.13. (continued)

State/Region	1	2	3	4	5	Total
Iowa	60	115	66	14	0	
Kansas	42	52	38	1	0	
Minn.	76	90	47	12	0	
Mo.	100	138	78	15	0	
Nebr.	53	52	22	6	0	
N.D.	24	23	14	1	0	
S.D.	12	15	1	0	0	
West North Central (2.00)	367 (0.31)	485 (0.42)	266 (0.23)	49 (0.04)	0 (0.00)	1167
Ariz.	171	121	74	27	5	
Colo.	28	39	45	14	1	
Idaho	77	77	33	5	0	
Mont.	74	49	13	2	1	
Nev.	48	42	27	15	2	
New Mex.	31	23	12	2	1	
Utah	19	35	15	1	1	
Wyo.	13	13	1	0	0	
Mountain (1.93)	461 (0.40)	399 (0.34)	220 (0.19)	66 (0.06)	11 (0.01)	1157
Alaska	31	24	7	1	0	
Cal.	391 (0.21)	474 (0.25)	551 (0.29)	357 (0.19)	127 (0.07)	1900 (2.69)
Ore.	114	154	116	34	10	
Wash.	168	199	113	29	6	
Pacific (2.44)	704 (0.24)	851 (0.29)	787 (0.27)	421 (0.14)	143 (0.05)	2906
U.S. (2.18)	(0.29)	(0.36)	(0.25)	(0.08)	(0.02)	11788

Source: Computed from data provided by the Woodall Publishing Company.

Table 10.14.
Community Services Offered by the Park

Service	% Park Has	% Use Park's	% Use Community's
Shopping	2.1	0.0	82.1
Other Shopping	2.1	0.0	78.1
Religious	2.1	1.0	79.2
Recreational	36.1	22.7	48.5
Sports	28.4	20.0	64.2
Other	24.5	14.7	27.4

Source: PMHI/PS.

Table 10.15.
Park Tenant Mix

Group	% of Respondents
Racial/ethnic	
"Have you ever had these groups in your park?"	
White	99.1
Spanish-American	31.3
Indian	21.4
Black	17.9
Oriental	30.4
Other	8.0
Social/professional	
"Do you view these groups as potential occupants?"	
Elderly	94.0
Young couples	75.0
Widows/widowers	50.0
Couples with children	46.6
Single men	39.0
Single women	36.4
Divorced	31.4
Students	26.0
Persons with pets	24.6
Other	10.2

Source: PMHI/PS.

25.6 percent one year, and 20.5 percent have no set length. It is difficult to draw conclusions about owner responsiveness to consumer demand on the basis of this information. The requirement of a lease and its length will mean very different things to owner and tenant, depending on the type of park. In a young adult park it may be presumed that tenants would prefer a shorter lease, giving them more flexibility. In a retirement park, however, older tenants are likely to want the stability of a long-term lease. The only conclusion that can be drawn is that a movement of leasing arrangements from verbal to written form would be favorable as a matter of sound business practice.

PMHI/PS data indicate that mobile home parks tend to have a limited mix in terms of their ethnic, professional, or social populations. Although in many cases this may be the result of restrictive entry practices, no such conclusion can be drawn from the PMHI Park Survey (table 10.15). It should be noted in this context that 17.7 percent of park owners restrict entry to new units. This should be viewed as an attempt to maintain the quality of the park rather than a "restrictive" practice. Even if the tenant mix should be the result of restrictive practices, it is altogether likely that such practices are very responsive to tenants' wishes, that is, that there is a widespread desire to restrict certain population elements in the community. Such practices may well be due to the park owner's competitive needs to design the kind of community the tenant appears to want.

As a matter of policy, owners do not tend to buy homes back from their tenants when they leave. Of the respondents, 54.1 percent never buy homes back, 28.8 percent do so rarely, 15.3 percent do so occasionally, and only 1.8 percent do so most of the time. This information suggests that park owners are responsive to their tenants but that the actual power exerted by the tenants over the owner is very limited. This is confirmed by data on the influence that tenants enjoy over the decision-making process of the park. Of the respondents, 48.9 percent allow tenants to participate in deciding park activities, 26.6 percent allow tenant influence over new facilities, and 9.9 percent allow participation in expansion decisions. These figures indicate a level of responsiveness to tenants that a competitive framework would require, but they also show a clear delineation of management's right to make those decisions that determine the financial future of the park.

Of the respondents to the PMHI Park Survey, 95 percent stated that other parks are located within a ten-mile radius—most (but not all) with similar service orientation. Such a competitive framework suggests the development of product standardization within given states or regions, which would then serve to differentiate and specialize that region in terms of the entire nation. Regarding standardization, 83.2% of the park owners

stated that parks located nearby had similar orientations. This standardization of the parks throughout the system has been fostered by the presence of the Woodall rating method. Still today, the extent of standardization is strongly indicated by the number of parks that used to subscribe to the Woodall rating, and by the number of parks that existed at each rating level.

It should be remembered that the bases for rating the parks have been upgraded since the inception of the Woodall's directory. This improvement of standards over time has resulted jointly from the Woodall organization having raised its standards to match the improvement of various parks and the Woodall organization causing better development and operation of new parks and the upgrading of older parks. Because of its presence and recognition, the Woodall organization also used to wield the power to foster policy changes within the system. Although it did not directly initiate policy changes, the Woodall organization could strongly influence practices in the system by setting standards that many parks assiduously followed.[9]

The positive impact that the Woodall rating activities have had suggests that the mobile home industry at large (including manufacturers and dealers) should either encourage Woodall or another organization to resume or to start similar rating activities or should initiate some other method of self-policing in the park system. Although this would require some investment of managerial and financial resources by the industry, the alternatives threaten to be much more costly: A possible product quality deterioration in the park system and the implied possibility of government intervention would present a major business problem for the industry.

The need for a financial subsidy of self-policing is evident from another fact. In 1977 an Illinois-based firm, American Mobile Home Communities (AMHC), had planned publication of a national park directory, but in the interest of economic feasibility planned not to make any inspections. (Woodall, implicitly, did confirm the economic feasibility point by not resuming publication of its rating-based directory, thus potentially permitting AMHC to invade its long-monopolized territory.) But, as AMHC told us, they had to abandon their plan; national tests indicated that the park system seemed unwilling or unable to underwrite the costs of listing, even without inspection.

Emerging Trends
As can be seen from a comparison of tables 10.16 and 10.13, the quality of mobile home parks has increased over a five-year period since 1969. During this period the mean star rating for the total United States increased from 2.07 to 2.18, some 5.3 percent. However, regional variations were much stronger. The largest increases were in the central part

The Mobile Home Park System

Table 10.16.
1969 Park Quality
Levels (for Comparison
with Table 10.13).

State/Region	1	2	3	4	5	Total	State/Region	1	2	3	4	5	Total
Conn.	18	22	23	15	1		Ill.	175	115	53	12	3	
Maine	74	17	8	0	0		Ind.	119	117	82	7	0	
Mass.	23	39	35	7	1		Mich.	102	121	97	26	1	
N.H.	16	27	23	5	2		Ohio	151	165	114	34	1	
R.I.	8	11	5	3	0		Wisc.	94	71	24	4	1	
Vt.	9	18	8	2	0		East North Central	641	589	370	83	6	1689
New England	148	134	102	32	4	420	(1.94)	(0.38)	(0.35)	(0.22)	(0.05)	(0.00)	
(2.08)	(0.35)	(0.32)	(0.24)	(0.08)	(0.01)								
							Iowa	136	64	37	8	1	
N.J.	13	23	57	32	1		Kansas	79	33	13	1	0	
N.Y.	141	201	72	15	1		Minn.	97	61	48	12	0	
Pa.	152	160	78	18	1		Mo.	77	70	37	8	0	
Mid-Atlautic	302	384	207	65	3	961	Nebr.	62	41	23	5	0	
(2.05)	(0.31)	(0.40)	(0.22)	(0.07)	(0.00)		N.D.	27	11	5	1	0	
							S.D.	34	32	4	4	0	
Dela.	4	11	16	5	1		West North Central	512	312	167	39	1	1031
Fla.	363	400	223	123	49	1158	(1.74)	(0.50)	(0.30)	(0.16)	(0.04)	(0.00)	
	(0.31)	(0.35)	(0.19)	(0.11)	(0.04)	(2.22)							
Ga.	88	31	9	1	0		Ariz.	146	131	75	60	9	
Md.	14	17	27	15	1		Colo.	105	53	22	31	3	
N.C.	109	60	19	0	1		Idaho	99	48	16	1	1	
S.C.	59	17	4	1	0		Mont.	108	25	4	3	1	
Va.	85	40	11	0	0		Nev.	62	38	20	7	1	
W.Va.	16	3	1	0	0		N.M.	50	28	20	11	2	
South Atlantic	738	579	307	145	52	1821	Utah	37	20	12	14	0	
(2.00)	(0.41)	(0.32)	(0.17)	(0.08)	(0.03)		Wyo.	22	17	10	0	0	
							Mountain	629	360	179	127	17	1312
Ala.	82	48	16	1	0		(1.899)	(0.48)	(0.27)	(0.14)	(0.10)	(0.01)	
Ky.	25	22	4	0	0								
Miss.	64	39	10	0	0		Alaska	82	48	16	1	0	
Tenn.	22	24	6	0	0		Cal.	404	522	474	322	153	1875
East South Central	193	133	36	1	0	363		(0.22)	(0.28)	(0.25)	(0.17)	(0.08)	(2.61)
(1.57)	(0.53)	(0.37)	(0.10)	(0.00)	(0.00)		Ore.	169	105	45	23	9	
							Wash.	193	122	71	7	12	
Ark.	59	33	22	4	0		Pacific	848	687	606	353	174	2668
La.	57	25	22	7	0		(2.40)	(0.32)	(0.26)	(0.23)	(0.13)	(0.07)	
Okla.	64	32	16	0	0								
Tex.	140	100	56	14	1		U.S.	4309	3451	2089	872	258	10979
West South Central	320	190	116	25	1	652	(2.07)	(0.39)	(0.31)	(0.19)	(0.08)	(0.02)	
(1.77)	(0.49)	(0.29)	(0.18)	(0.04)	(0.00)								

Source: Computed from data provided by the Woodall Publishing Company.

of the country: the East South Central (+13.4 percent), the West South Central (+14.7 percent), the East North Central (+11.3 percent), and the West North Central (+14.9 percent). The next highest increase was New England's 6.7 percent, followed by slight changes in the Mountain and Pacific regions, which increased 2.1 percent and 1.7 percent, respectively. There were declines along the East Coast, with the Mid-Atlantic quality rating going down 2.4 percent and the South Atlantic, 20.5 percent. Considering the states individually, California increased in quality rating by only 3.1 percent; Florida went up by a hefty 12.6 percent. Given Florida's growth, the decline in the rest of the South Atlantic by comparison was very severe.

The overall trend, then, would seem to be one of rapid growth in the center of the country and Florida, a tremendous decline in the other South Atlantic states, and a relatively static situation everywhere else. This trend must be judged in the light of the changes in the Woodall ratings that have occurred during the period in question—given the decreased quality implied by the lower star ratings and the increased quality of the higher star ratings, the changes observed in each direction are probably even more substantial.

Conclusions

The product policies of the mobile home park system are those of a highly competitive system. This had been reinforced by the Woodall's directory, which has caused a much greater product information flow throughout the system. There has been considerable differentiation of the product from region to region as each area has undergone its own standardization process.

Park owners seem generally responsive to the wishes of their tenants with regard to maintaining certain types of communities. They have allowed a reasonable level of input from tenants in the decision-making process while retaining their control over financial affairs. Furthermore, they have generally upgraded the quality of their product throughout the 1970s. It is worth re-emphasizing that these trends are in no way uniform on the national level but vary markedly from region to region. Our information indicates that the highest-quality product can be found in California and Florida but that the central region of the country is making rapid gains.

E. Policy Alternatives

There are a number of potentials for performance improvement in the park system, and these are eminently achievable. As noted previously, the park system is a young industry with only a short history; few growth constraints have developed within the system itself. Instead, most inhibitions to further development result from external factors, notably from land use controls. The system must increase its efforts at overcoming these external forces.

One opportunity for the system to continue to grow and mature is especially evident: extending the system's presence and allowing it to acquire a greater share of the housing market by increasing its responsiveness to the consumer's needs. In the early years of development (the 1930s and 1940s), many of the parks resembled ghettos and were treated as such by the occupants and the surrounding communities. The parks of that period were developed with little planning and operators paid little attention to tenant needs beyond simply providing unit sites. Now the system is developing environments that begin to feature many of the same attributes of the standard suburban community. The park system, however, can move beyond that. It can offer the housing industry a unique opportunity to explore innovations in community development and housing services that would normally be inhibited by long-established and constraining practices within the conventional home-building industry. The park system has the potential to pursue such innovations because it is not bound by the many regulations directing the conventional housing industry.

Perhaps the most important advantage is that the park system and the mobile home industry already treat housing as a total service. The prospective unit owner is able to purchase a dwelling unit from a dealer who is often a park operator. The occupant may then secure a place in the dealer/park-owner park, which may have all the supplementary services of shopping, recreational facilities, religious facilities, and established social programs. It is entirely possible that occupants will find a relatively homogeneous community into which they may be immediately accepted. Nowhere else in the housing sector is such an opportunity for further experimentation with the "housing-as-a-comprehensive-service" concept even approximated.

The park system has reached a stage in its growth at which a shortage of professional talent is beginning to develop. Three opportunities should be explored or created: Improve and make more widely accessible methods for training and educating prospective developers, owners, and managers to allow them better to start up and operate the park; increase consulting services for developers or owners who wish to obtain assistance during start-up and initial operation (a case in point are several organizations, which have recently begun to establish such services) and make developers and owners more aware of their need for such services; and encourage knowledgeable groups or individuals to enter the park system as both developers and owners. A key question is what kind of encouragement is appropriate and are there specific incentives for attracting qualified

Figure 10.4.
Mobile home communities today.

Figure 10.5.
Mobile home communities today.

Figure 10.6.
Mobile home communities today.

Industrial Organization

individuals or groups? Part of the solution may be to make the potential investor more aware of opportunities in the park system. Chapter 15 on finance sector influence deals specifically with key opportunities.

The continued growth and further creation of large multiple-park ownerships offer the development of greater expertise within the park system. The organizations quickly generate understanding of the development and operating procedures and create high-quality parks that are stable elements within the system. They also offer the possibility of generating some degree of concentration for securing more favorable treatment in the marketplace. (For example, they may be able to locate and obtain more money for purchasing or developing parks or for developing know-how for arranging land acquisition and code variances.) Multiple-park ownership by firms with relatively sophisticated financial techniques should be encouraged.

If economic concentration can be increased and if it increases equally throughout the system, integration and diversification will naturally increase. A greater integration of activities provides two primary opportunities for evolving a more efficient park system. First, more vertical integration can be created by manufacturers or manufacturer-dealers who enter the system as developers or owners; presumably such people will have a higher level of insight and background relevant to the mobile home industry. Such integration would also appear to offer opportunities for establishing better ties between the various members of industry and for providing a streamlined process of the supply of unit, site, and services. Second, vertical integration, like diversification, may provide a means of protecting the participant against financial difficulties. Greater diversification into the various subsectors of the "traditional" building sector will secure on-site, building-specific know-how for the park system.

By employing more sophisticated and pervasive advertising methods, the park system should be better able to display its product and foster growth. Advertising the nature of the park system's product is as important as stressing the range and quality of services the system offers. In order to overcome the image fostered primarily by the old trailer camps of the 1930s and 1940s, the park system must inform the public of its new character. To promote more widespread acceptance, the park system should communicate its ability to provide a total housing service, including dwelling unit, land, maintenance, community, and community services. Such advertising should be based on existing demographic data (for example, census information or specifically commissioned studies) to ascertain who would be most receptive to the park system's product and what advertising methods would be most

rewarding. It should be noted that well-employed advertising will help fill existing park spaces and create a demand for new parks and spaces.

Strong incentives should be created to encourage park owners and managers of substandard parks to upgrade their parks. For example, an organization could be commissioned to develop incentives designed to encourage more park operators to request inspection. An inspecting organization would require financial assistance of some private or public agency such as the MHI or the Small Business Administration. Such assistance would make the organization amenable to reflecting input from the mobile home industry at large, from the public sector, or from both in its rating criteria. The purpose of inspecting presently substandard parks would be to provide the park owners and managers with insights into their parks' deficiencies and methods of improvement. Possible incentives might include the ease of acquiring capital for such improvements, the establishment of higher rents (without eliminating existing tenants) resulting in potentially greater profits, peer pressure from nearby parks, and increased rental of existing or newly developed spaces.

In its further development, the park system should continue to rely on its own initiative. It should not forget its proud historical record, the successful building of a new industry, the park system, by private enterprise. Government action should focus on making growth and maturation easier for the industry while allowing the industry to grow independently.

Notes to Chapter 10

1. PMHI's projections have drawn upon many data bases, including Subject Report HC(7)–6, Mobile Homes, a publication of the 1970 Census of Housing, U.S. Bureau of the Census, and the "Monthly Market Letter on Mobile Home Shipments" published by Mobile-Modular Housing Dealer. The figures for the total number of mobile homes per state were derived by allowing for deterioration of older mobile homes, for the percentage of all mobile homes shipped that are used for temporary office functions or for other non-residential purposes. The error factor is in the range of 5–12 percent.

2. Donald O. Cowgill, Mobile Homes, A Study of Trailer Life (Unpublished Ph.D. dissertation, University of Pennsylvania, 1941).

3. PMHI's projections of the state-by-state non-park versus park data were primarily based on two sources. The first source was annual Woodall compilations of the rated park inventory by state. Second, at the request of PMHI, Woodall Publishing Company extracted from its files and hand-tabulated a state-by-state, yearly compilation of the number of deleted parks, the number of deleted spaces, and the number of parks never listed. The error factor in our projections is in the range of 5 percent to 10 percent.

4. HUD News, No. 74–256, U.S. Department of Housing and Urban Development, Washington, D.C., August 2, 1974.

5. Because the time lag between production decision and "marketing" is much longer for park development than for unit production (it may take years just to obtain the many public regulatory approvals), a same-year comparison would be meaningless. At best a comparison of several-year averages is justified. Thus, this approach was used.

6. The projection for the distribution by state of the number of all parks vs. the number of parks that used to be Woodall-rated, was based primarily on the sources given in footnote 3.

7. Woodall's 1974 Mobile Home and Park Directory Plus Vacancies and Monthly Rentals (Highland Park, Ill.: Woodall Publishing Co., 1974). The 1974 data reflect pre-1974/1975 recession conditions. Most important are the ratios of indexes rather than absolute rent levels, which are distorted in recession periods.

8. Ibid.

9. Correspondence with park operators, 1975–1977.

Chapter 11

Park Development and Operation

A. Occupant Profiles

Income

An accurate occupant profile is a prerequisite for evaluation of user needs and park design. Income, ownership, occupation, age, and family size are the most important factors affecting park design and performance. Mobile home occupants differ significantly from the rest of the population in each of these aspects. Our profiles, constructed with data drawn largely from surveys published in 1977, indicate that the primary demand for mobile homes comes from moderate-income groups: blue-collar working families and retirees. The average income of mobile home families is much lower than that of families in conventional housing who are, however, less likely to own their homes. There are more young families, which results in smaller families with more children under six and fewer under eighteen. The number of families with children is surprisingly high.

Income is the most important difference between families in mobile homes and those in conventional housing. The income gap affects expectations and determines the quality of life mobile home occupants can afford. The industry's greatest success is that it can provide home ownership for lower-income families without subsidy.

Recent trends to increase the size and upgrade the quality of mobile homes and parks will not only gradually attract consumers who presently do not consider mobile home living an acceptable housing alternative but also continue to meet the needs of the group the industry now serves, thereby decreasing the gap between mobile home families and conventional housing families.

The income of mobile home families is much lower than the income of conventionally housed families, particularly those in suburban areas. In rural areas this difference is the least pronounced. The latest census data available in 1977 for family income are summarized in tables 11.1a and 11.1b. The median incomes of both mobile home-owning families, $9500, and mobile home-renting families, $6500, are significantly lower than the median of $13,500 for all home-owning families.[1]

There is evidence that the gap between income levels of mobile home families and conventional housing families remains constant in the middle-income levels and is widening in the upper-income levels. For example, in 1969 the proportion of mobile home families in the income group $5–9999 was 40 percent compared to 34 percent of all families in this group—a 6 percent difference. The latest census data show this difference to be 8 percent (see table 11.1a). At the upper-income levels ($15,000 and over), the income gap between mobile home families and all families in 1969 was about 15 percent; the most recent census data show that this gap has now widened to about 25 percent. It is clear that the mobile home

industry has not been attracting families in high-income groups.[2]

These income characteristics have significant implications regarding demand and design standards for mobile homes and parks. On the positive side, the generally higher incomes of mobile home owners compared to conventional housing renters indicate that mobile home ownership is a matter of choice and that these families simply prefer it to renting conventional housing of generally higher density. Table 11.2 shows a Veterans' Administration survey of seven hundred mobile home residents indicating that over 40 percent prefer mobile home ownership over other housing, cost and other factors considered.[3]

However, the relatively lower incomes of mobile home families compared to the population as a whole suggest that cost plays a dominant role in housing selection. The

Table 11.1a.
Distribution of Family Income

Income Ranges	Mobile Home Families	All Families
Under $5,000	25.2%	11.5%
$5–6,999	12.8%	8.0%
$7–9,999	18.5%	15.2%
$10–14,999	23.5%	20.9%
$15–24,999	16.1%	28.5%
$25,000 and over	3.9%	15.9%

Table 11.1b.
Median Family Income

| Area | Median Income | |
	Mobile Home Owners	All Owners
Central City	$9300	$13,500
Suburban	$9400	$16,400
Rural	$9600	$11,000

	Mobile Home Renters	All Renters
Central City	N.A.	$7200
Suburban	$6800	$9800
Rural	$6400	$6800

Source: U.S. Bureau of the Census.

Table 11.2.
Attitude Toward Mobile Home Living

Attitude	%
Prefer over all housing	21
Prefer over any other affordable housing	22
Like as well as any housing	20
Like as well as any other affordable housing	22
Dissatisfied	15

Source: U.S. Veterans' Administration.

relatively lower expectations of lower- and moderate-income groups explain to some degree the relatively lower design standards found in mobile home parks compared to conventional single-family subdivisions. However, the mobile home industry has the potential to meet user needs as well as expectations without incurring significant cost increases by improvements in mobile home community design.

Ownership

The desire for privacy and ownership inherent in the "American dream" is the most important user preference affecting mobile home demand. Mobile home families are more likely to own their own homes (85 percent) than families in conventional housing (65 percent).[4] This characteristic provides a measure of stability for mobile home parks that is not found in rental housing. It refutes the obsolete, stereotypic characterization of the mobile home occupant as a transient whose contribution to the community is temporary in nature. Over 75 percent of mobile home families are planning to live in their homes for at least five years, as table 11.3 indicates. In addition, approximately 60 percent of all mobile home families plan to live in mobile homes at their present site.[5] We estimate that mobile home families move less often than families in rental housing. Community opposition to mobile home parks based on transience would be understandable only if conventional rental units in the community were restricted for the same reason.

Occupation

The proportion of blue-collar workers is higher and white-collar workers lower in mobile home communities than in conventional housing. An estimated 15 percent of mobile home families are professional or technical workers as compared to 25 percent of the total population. Crafts persons and other blue-collar workers comprise over 25 percent of the mobile home population, while only about 15 percent of all workers in the United States are blue-collar workers. In both mobile home families and the population in general, approximately the same proportion of workers comprise the service, farm, and clerical forces.[6]

Surveys based on selected samples, such as service-intensive adult parks in resort areas, or parks near military installations, yield different occupant profiles. Surveys of high-quality parks indicate a greater proportion of retirees than are found in most parks.[7] This reflects the fact that parks are often oriented toward particular occupant groups.

Age

There are more young families in mobile homes but proportionally fewer senior citizens than in conventional housing. Table 11.4 shows that there are also fewer mobile home families than conventionally housed families in the thirty to sixty-four age group.[8] The relatively large number of young families

(twice as many as in conventional housing) differs from the results that some industry sources have obtained by other surveys. For example, 70 percent of a sample of parks surveyed by the Urban Land Institute were restricted to adults only, yielding a higher percentage of middle-aged and elderly occupants in contrast to the national sample.[9] Such parks are usually oriented more toward retirees than young marrieds, accounting for the survey differences.

Family Size

Mobile home families are somewhat smaller, with a median of 2.3 persons per household, than conventionally housed families, which have a median of 2.7 persons per household, as table 11.5 illustrates.[10] Mobile home families tend to have more children under six and fewer under eighteen.[11]

Table 11.3.
Number of Years Planned on Living in Mobile Home

Years	%
1	4.5
2	4.5
3	5.0
4	3.7
5–10	34.6
Permanently	43.7
Do not know	4.0

Source: Owens-Corning Fiberglas Corporation.

Table 11.4.
Age of Household Head

Age	% Mobile Homes	% All Households.
Under 25	19.7 ⎫ 38.3	8.2 ⎫ 18.7
25–29	18.6 ⎭	10.5 ⎭
30–34	12.5 ⎫	10.4 ⎫
35–44	13.6 ⎬ 49.4	16.7 ⎬ 61.2
45–64	23.3 ⎭	34.1 ⎭
65 and over	12.3	20.1

Source: U.S. Bureau of the Census.

Table 11.5.
Household Size

Number of Persons	% Mobile Homes	% All Households
(Median)	(2.3)	(2.7)
1	20.4	19.6
2	38.5	30.6
3	18.4	17.4
4	14.0	15.6
5	5.6	9.0
6	1.6	3.4
7 or more	1.5	3.7

Source: U.S. Bureau of the Census.

The number of children, although varying with the type of park, is an extremely important factor that should be considered in designing mobile home parks and in determining the impact of proposed parks on the community. Various surveys (Urban Land Institute and PMHI) indicate that in parks oriented toward adults the number of children per unit (0.2) is significantly lower than the number of children per conventional single family home (1.5). At the other extreme, parks oriented almost exclusively toward families, such as parks on military installations, may have almost as many children as conventional housing projects.[12]

More important in determining a mobile home park's impact upon schools is the number of children in various age groups. About 40 percent of all mobile home families have children under eighteen, compared to 42 percent of all families. A greater proportion of mobile home families have only young children (under six), with 16 percent as compared to 10 percent of all families.[13]

The number of bedrooms per unit is a significant factor in determining the attraction of the various types of housing to large families and to families with older children. For example, only about 25 percent of all existing mobile homes have three or more bedrooms compared to approximately 50 percent of conventional year-round housing; accordingly, 8 percent of mobile home families have three or more children, but about 12 percent of conventionally housed families have three or more children.[14]

Adult, Family, and Student Parks

Mobile home parks can be grouped into three broad categories based on their primary source of occupants: adult parks, family parks, and student parks. Adult parks are oriented toward senior citizens and tend to be located in warm weather areas. Children may be excluded entirely or families with children may live in a separate section of the park. Community facilities play a dominant role in encouraging group activities. Parks oriented toward families with children place greater emphasis on economy and tend to have fewer community facilities than adult parks. Park locations near employment centers are needed for this group. Parks for students serve a pressing need for low-cost housing near education centers, especially for young married students who are not in the labor force. The remainder of mobile home parks include parks for temporary use for such groups as construction and seasonal workers, but these parks are relatively small in number. Each of these occupant groups has different priorities, and parks vary in design and scope to accommodate these differences.[15]

B. Park Design and Construction

Analysis of mobile home park design and construction focused on seven areas of concern: user preferences, factors affecting park location, park size and density, community

facilities, street and lot patterns, utilities and services, and construction. In each of these areas we compared existing mobile home parks and conventional housing projects and identified trends in park design and construction. (Although much of this analysis draws on firsthand experience in the field, primary sources used include designs made available to PMHI by park developers, managers, and professional design firms and information provided by many industry-affiliated organizations.)

User preferences affect mobile home demand, mobile home design, park location, and park design. In examining those factors that affect mobile home park design, we identified five broad areas into which these preferences can be grouped: privacy, landscaping and open space, community activity, variety and individuality, and economy.

Respondents to many surveys stressed privacy; this is usually more important for families on private lots than for families in parks. Dominant among the responses to our national park survey was a desire for lower densities and larger lots, which clearly relate to privacy. More extensive user surveys regarding privacy features have been accomplished for housing forms other than mobile homes and their findings have relevancy: Mobile home parks are simply another residential land use and families within them have the same or similar user needs as families in conventional housing. A recent study of seventeen hundred town house residents stressed landscaping, open space, space around buildings, and other features that affect privacy.[16] Sixty-three percent preferred an enclosed patio with fencing on all three sides as an effective means of achieving privacy.

Landscaping and open space were the two user needs stressed most in the responses of town house residents. Forty-two percent wanted more trees, woods, and landscaping; 27 percent wanted more open space. The density range of the town house projects, six to ten units per acre, was higher than most mobile home parks, but it is unlikely that the items mentioned in a similar survey of mobile home families would be significantly different. These are just the features most often lacking in typical mobile home parks.

Community activities are important to town house and mobile home park residents alike. In the town house survey play or recreation space ranked third on the list of priorities, followed closely by convenience to shops. The isolated location of many mobile home parks causes even greater emphasis to to placed on community facilities, particularly in adult parks.

Variety and individuality are important to most home owners, particularly single-family and town house residents. The wide variety of unit accessories and landscaping

User Preferences

Figure 11.1.
A planned mobile home
community today.

Figure 11.2.
A planned mobile home
community today.

Figure 11.3.
A planned mobile home
community today.

features with which owners "decorate" their homes is sufficient evidence of the strong desire for individuality. Despite the overall sameness of most mobile home designs, families are remarkably successful in achieving this objective. The preference for parking cars off-street, on a lot beside each home (75 percent), is due in part to convenience but also to the desire to have a clearly defined space under the control of the owner.[17]

Economy remains a major user need and limits the number of improvements mobile home occupants are willing to pay for. Features residents of conventional housing might find mandatory may greatly exceed the expectations and income of mobile home residents or may not be desired at all. The design and performance of mobile home parks must be evaluated with this in mind.

Factors Affecting Park Location

There are several complex factors affecting mobile home park location. Chance, user needs, community opposition, and site characteristics play major roles in site selection. These related factors are affected by the trend toward suburbanization of America, particularly employment centers, and by the recent countertrend toward urbanization instigated by the energy crisis.

Chance

Chance was the dominant factor affecting the location of early trailer camps and it has only recently decreased in importance. Tailers were found on empty lots, behind gas stations, on the edge of town, and in farmers' fields: "Having discovered the cheapest living in the U.S., many of these gasoline Bedouins settled down at congenial oases; they unhitched the tow car, hiked up the trailer on blocks and called it home." ("200,000 Trailers," *Fortune*, March 1937.) In short, the first trailer camps were not planned—they just happened. Traces of these parks linger on today, particularly in rural areas. In 1972 even the Urban Land Institute's survey of only high-quality mobile home communities stressed the elements of "chance and the presence or absence of public regulation rather than of choice."[18] Similarly, during interviews we conducted with park owners as recently as 1976 and 1977, many stated that they had not consulted anyone regarding the location of their parks. However, because proximity to the main highway, shopping, residential areas, and flourishing communities were cited as major factors affecting location, the sites were not selected entirely by chance.

The haphazard siting of mobile homes and parks resulting from this lack of planning has contributed substantially to the industry's unfavorable image in many areas. Surprisingly, the situation has not much improved during the last two decades. Two park surveys conducted in the early sixties in Arizona and Oklahoma, for example, found 82 percent of the parks in Oklahoma and 47 percent of those in Arizona in commercial surroundings,

21 percent of those in Oklahoma adjacent to flood plains, and 19 percent of the Arizona parks in industrial surroundings.[19] Although the two hundred twenty quality parks in the 1972 survey were more likely to be in residential areas than the Oklahoma and Arizona parks surveyed ten years earlier, a relatively high proportion still remained in commercial, industrial, and institutional areas. Chapter 16 shows that discriminatory zoning frequently relegates parks to nonresidential areas; thus these survey results cannot be blamed on lack of planning alone. Rather, a vicious circle does operate: Haphazard placement leads to parks in poor surroundings, which reinforces anti–mobile home zoning attitudes, which in turn force new parks to be located in undesirable areas—and the circle begins anew.

User Needs

Since the late 1940s, the Manufactured Housing Institute has recognized that improving the location and design of mobile home parks in response to user needs is necessary. Planning officials are now beginning to recognize mobile home parks as simply another residential land use option chosen by families with the same user needs as families in conventional housing. The most important user needs affecting park location are economy, privacy, and proximity to work.

Land cost has a significant influence on total initial costs, even though most parks are located in suburban areas or on the rural fringe of cities. The low cost of mobile homes combined with relatively low density limits the price most users will pay for a developed site. The cost of land plus site development, in some cases, approaches the cost of the mobile home itself, and this is rarely true in conventional housing. This supply/demand relationship has forced park developers to seek lower-cost land in areas farther from the center city or in less desirable locations than conventional housing projects.

The desire for privacy inherent in the preference for single-family living also affects park location. Typical new parks have densities of five to seven units per acre; older parks maintain up to ten units per acre. Although these are higher than conventional single-family densities and are in the same range as town houses, they are not high enough for mobile home parks to compete successfully for high-priced land in desirable suburban locations.

Proximity to work is a major user need affecting park location for working families. Economy and privacy versus convenience to work are trade-off values that are typically in opposition. Mobile home parks have proportionately more blue-collar workers and fewer white-collar workers than the population as a whole, not least because the location of most parks in suburban/rural areas does not create major commuting problems for blue-collar workers, who are more likely than white-collar workers to be employed in the suburbs. As recent trends toward the suburbanization of retail trade and other white-collar employment centers progress, this could change. However, suburbanization may not continue indefinitely. Trends halting the outward growth of cities are beginning to emerge as a result of the energy crisis and increased availability of mass transit. These trends could accelerate demand for higher-density, low-cost housing, which is currently not being produced by mobile home manufacturers.

Proximity to work is clearly not important for retirees. Rather, the desire for economy and a pleasant environment in which to live are decisive. Shopping and other community facilities that all families need limit to some degree how far from the central city a retirement-oriented park can be. Resort parks in isolated locations tend to have more community facilities and self-contained activities than suburban family parks.

The overriding importance of the above user needs factors and their effect on park location was addressed in a survey of park occupants conducted in the 1960s.[20] (No more recent survey on this subject exists.) The survey distinguished responses of owners and renters and distinguished families in parks from those on private lots (table 11.6). The survey clearly indicates that economy is more important for owners than renters, particularly for families on rural private lots. Proximity to work and shopping are most important for renters. Privacy is stressed by occupants of private lots, as might be expected. Availability of services ranks behind these factors and is closely related to convenience to work and shopping. Although mentioned, ties with family and friends are clearly considered less important than other factors.

Community Opposition
Community opposition to mobile homes because of their appearance and the lower-income characteristics of their occupants is also an important location factor. This opposition most often takes the form of zoning regulations that exclude mobile homes entirely or restrict them to parks, often in the least desirable areas. (See chapter 16.) The availability of land that can be zoned for mobile home parks is one of the developer's primary concerns. Many sites in residential areas that would otherwise be very desirable are ruled out because of zoning restraints. Community opposition, however, often leads to unusually high standards in park design. When prospective developers realize they can only obtain zoning by proposing a mobile home community that would clearly be a great asset to the community, they often devote unusual resources in terms of money and time to design and planning. In the final analysis, of course, the community "wins" anyway:

The "approved" mobile home community, so carefully planned and developed, ultimately often becomes so expensive that it effectively excludes lower-income groups.

Site Characteristics
Site characteristics, such as surroundings, vegetation, community facilities, topography, availability of utilities, views, and numerous other features, also affect park location. Such characteristics are compared by developers to site characteristics of other mobile home parks in the area in order to determine the probability of success.

Chance, User Needs, Community Opposition, and Site Characteristics
The PMHI Park Survey confirms that location by "chance" becomes the exception and that concern for user needs, community opposition, and site characteristics are primary location factors (table 11.7).

From the point of view of both the user and the developer, user needs, community opposition, and favorable site characteristics are primary factors affecting park location. The developer is primarily concerned with profit, but a site that does not respond to user needs will not be as profitable as one

Table 11.6.
Factors Affecting Park Location for Owners and Renters

Factor	Owners		Renters	
	In Park	Private Lot	In Park	Private Lot
Economy	30%	47%	18%	19%
Privacy	38%	66%	19%	58%
Proximity to work/shopping	36%	33%	72%	42%
Services	26%	11%	22%	9%
Family ties	13%	24%	9%	23%
Close to friends	6%	15%	10%	10%

Source: Mobile Home Journal.

Table 11.7.
Factors Affecting Park Location

Factor	% Respondents Mentioning Each Factor
High demand for park spaces in area	53
Favorable location (to shopping/employment/transportation)	53
Attractive natural features	37
Favorable zoning	35
Attractive surroundings	28
Low land costs for the area	20
Low construction/utility costs	20
Other	15

Source: PMHI/PS.

Table 11.8.
Average Rentals
Compared to Park Size

| | Rent | | | |
Size	$20–29	$30–39	$40–59	$60–100
Number of parks	4	26	38	23
Percentage of total parks	4	29	42	25
Average number of spaces	26	53	93	215
Smallest park (spaces)	16	6	13	44
Largest park (spaces)	50	180	274	940

Source: PMHI/PS.

that does. Increased interest in the elements that distinguish one site from another provides evidence that the location of mobile home parks is less a matter of chance than it once was. This relatively new land use form will become an integral element of the entire residential community in the future. As mobile home design comes closer to conventional housing design, community opposition will diminish, increasing the availability of land.

Table 11.9.
Range of Unit Sizes,
1977 Shipments

%	Unit Size	Trend
1	8′, 10′, 16′ singlewides	
15	12′ singlewides	decreasing
53	14′ singlewides	increasing
31	Expandables/doublewides	increasing

Source: MHI.

Park Size and Density

The size of mobile home parks, their density, and land use patterns are important design parameters that affect the quality of life parks provide. Park sizes have increased rapidly in recent years, and there has been a gradual decline in density to accommodate increasing numbers of large singlewide and doublewide mobile homes. Land uses in most parks are primarily residential, but some large high-quality parks provide a wide variety of community facilities as well. Park size is a major factor in determining the feasibility of development, the amount of funds available for community facilities, and the sense of "neighborhood" or "place."

We estimate that new parks planned or under construction in 1977 had an average size of one hundred seventy-five spaces each, up from an average size of all existing quality mobile home parks of ninety-six in 1974, of seventy-five in 1970, and of only thirty-six in 1958. We estimate that in the almost twenty years between 1958 and 1977 average size of all quality parks has risen by 230 percent, that is, at an average rate of 12 percent per year. From the state-by-state analysis of park size over time in chapter 10 it is clear that the growth rates among the states have differed significantly—in some states average park size has increased by more than 400 percent during the last twenty years.

Larger parks tend to command higher rentals because they are generally newer and provide more community facilities. PMHI's Park Survey corroborated that rent levels tended to be higher for larger parks (table 11.8).

Park density is a second major design parameter that affects park quality. As density increases, the amount of usable open space is diminished and must be compensated for by additional privacy features. Density trends in mobile home parks are significant. Current densities are typically around five to seven units per acre, compared to about ten units per acre for older parks. Responses to PMHI's Park Survey indicate a desire for larger lots and lower densities—similar to those user preferences commonly expressed by the conventional low- and medium-density housing population. The demand for larger lots to accommodate doublewides and larger singles has made many older parks prematurely obsolete. The trend in industry sales is clearly toward larger units (table 11.9).

If this trend continues as projected, developers and park owners would benefit by reducing density even further to accommodate large units on most, if not all, future sites. This trend may be halted by increases in land cost, in which case modifying unit design to permit more successful medium-density siting in high-cost areas will be required.

Density can be related to lot size in more specific terms. The general range of lot sizes found in single-family housing is shown in table 11.10. Efficient designs that provide little public open space will use about 10 percent of total land area for streets, walks, and community space. Inefficient designs, or designs that provide a large amount of open space and community facilities, use about 30 percent of land area for public use and yield smaller lots at the same density. Some designs fall outside this range at either end. The "typical" low-density project, single-family or mobile home park, will probably have 20 percent of its land area devoted to streets and public land. In such a typical project, a density of six units per acre will yield lots averaging just under 6000 square feet. Subtracting the area occupied by the unit itself yields the usable yard area indicated in table 11.11. From this table it is apparent that doublewide units must be sited at about one unit per acre lower density than singlewide units to yield the same yard area.

Considering lot size in relation to unit size is important, but the quality of the space provided is a more effective measure of performance. In a typical park, windows of adjacent units face the only "yard"—the space between units—and privacy would be achievable only by providing either more space or better landscaping than most mobile home owners can afford. Additional space can provide privacy at relatively low cost in rural areas. In suburban areas even a slight increase in density can free sufficient capital to permit intensive, privacy-ensuring landscaping of the space between units.

Expressing density in terms of people rather than houses is a more effective measure for evaluating the impact of proposed designs. After all, most density-related problems are caused by and affect people. The range for most low- and medium-density developments is shown in table 11.12. One relatively simple way to measure people density is to determine the number of bed-rooms in a project because family size and bedroom count are closely related. As table 11.13 illustrates, the mobile home park has a people density range close to that of conventional single-family projects even though "house density" is twice as great.

Similarly, "people density" in terms of children per acre differs little between mobile and conventional homes even though conventional singles have twice as many children per unit (table 11.14). This indicates that designing mobile home parks with children in mind is more important than most designers realize, particularly for parks outside the retirement center states of California, Florida, and Arizona. From the point of view of environmental impact, particularly on schools, the children density indicates that some family parks (as opposed to adult parks) may affect a community in much the same way as a conventional single-family project—this does not hold true for town houses and apartments, which have roughly twice as many children per acre.

Community facilities play an mportant role in most mobile home parks, particularly those located in isolated areas. As social centers, they provide a focal point for group activities, even if the facilities are limited to a laundry

Community Facilities

Table 11.10.
Density and Lot Size

| Density (Units per Acre) | Public Land (Streets, Sidewalks, Open Space) | | |
	10% Land Area (Sq. Ft./Lot)	20% Land Area (Sq. Ft./Lot)	30% Land Area (Sq. Ft./Lot)
3	13,070	11,615	10,165
4	9,800	8,710	7,620
5	7,840	6,970	6,100
6	5,535	5,810	5,080
7	5,600	4,980	4,355
8	4,900	4,355	3,810
9	4,355	3,872	3,390
Total private land area	39,205 sq.ft./acre	34,850 sq.ft./acre	30,490 sq.ft./acre

Source: Range of land area devoted to public land based on PMHI inspection of varied low-density site plans, conventional housing.

Table 11.11.
Density and Lot
Dimensions, Yard Area,
20 Percent Public Land

Density (Units per Acre)	Lot Size (Ft.) Singlewide	Lot Size (Ft.) Doublewide	Yard Area (Sq. Ft.) Singlewide	Yard Area (Sq. Ft.) Doublewide
3	116 × 100	155 × 75	10,610	10,140
4	87 × 100	116 × 75	7,710	7,240
5	70 × 100	93 × 75	6,010	5,540
6	58 × 100	78 × 75	4,810	4,340
7	50 × 100	66 × 75	4,010	3,540
8	44 × 100	58 × 75	3,410	2,940
9	39 × 100	52 × 75	2,910	2,440

Note: Assumptions: lot depths and yard areas based on 14 × 75' (71') singlewide units and 24' × 65' (61') doublewide units.

Table 11.12.
"House Density," Units
per Acre

House Type	Density		
	Low	Typical	High
Single family	1	3	7
Mobile home	3	6	9
Town house	5	8	15
Walk-up apartment	15	20	30

Source: Direct development experience.

Table 11.13.
"People Density,"
Bedrooms per Acre

House Type	Typical Density (DU/AC)	Bed-rooms per Unit	Bed-rooms per Acre
Single	3	3	9
Singlewide mobile	6	2	12
Doublewide mobile	5	3	15
Town house	8	3	24
Walk-up apartment	20	2	40

Source: Direct development experience.

and a small pool. The lack of outdoor privacy found in many parks makes informal encounters more likely, and this contributes to the small-town atmosphere many families consider an advantage of mobile home living. The emphasis placed on community facilities varies. Retirement-oriented adult parks generally offer more facilities and higher-quality features than family or student parks. Higher occupant incomes in some of the retirement parks make a large complement of facilities more feasible, but the main factor is probably greater need for group activity and the higher proportion of time senior citizens spend at home. In many of the adult parks, more features are provided than in conventional moderate-income projects of the same size.

Many surveys of mobile home families indicate that an approximate 60 percent prefer a basic park to one with a pool, clubhouse, and recreation facilities, considering costs. Only one-quarter of families surveyed seem willing to pay $10 to $15 per month

more to have such features. This reflects the emphasis placed on economy by many young families, and it does not mean that such families do not seek group activity. Better returns on investment can often be achieved by omitting such facilities—this, at least, was increasingly becoming common thinking among park developers in the late 1970s. And this investment strategy, of course, tends to result in a lower rent burden, which is not only important to many young families but to many senior citizens as well.

Features oriented toward children, such as landscaped play or recreation space, would appeal more to families with children and generally cost less. Very few quality parks advertise such features in directories or regional trade journals.

The cost of providing community facilities is discussed in detail in chapter 12. Increasing the number and scope of community facilities becomes more feasible as park size increases because costs per space will be lower. However, for many features, such as landscaping and privacy fencing, the cost does not significantly decrease as the park grows in size.

The sample of quality mobile home parks surveyed by the Urban Land Institute provides a quantitative accurate picture of community facilities. In addition to the almost universal laundry and community hall, 61 percent of these parks had pools, 22 percent had playgrounds, 16 percent had a lake or a waterfront, 11 percent had a sauna, and 8 percent had a golf course. An average of 20 percent of total land area was devoted to community facilities.[21] The parks were primarily oriented toward retirees (70 percent were for adults only). Family parks would yield lower figures.

It is important for developers to identify occupant groups and park quality/rent objectives early in the design process, as prerequisites for an accurate evaluation of the need for and scope of community facilities. In family parks in particular, the optimum community facilities blend may differ considerably from the norm for other parks in the area.

Street and lot patterns in most mobile home parks are similar to those in conventional linear single-family subdivisions, except that densities are higher, lots are smaller, and

Street and Lot Patterns

Table 11.14.
"People Density,"
Children per Acre

House Type	Typical Density (DU/AC)	Children per Unit	Children per Acre
Single family	3	1.5	4.5
Mobile home	6	0.75	4.8 (family parks)
Town house	8	1.0	8
Walk-up apartment	20	0.5	10

Source: PMHI estimates.

the units differ considerably from conventional housing in appearance and in their relationship to the site. The function of outdoor space is compromised by the uncoordinated design of mobile homes and mobile home sites, as well as by the economic restraints imposed by shipping dimensions. Cluster site plans, "zero-lot-line" designs with windows of only one unit facing the side yard, and other innovations are beginning to emerge in industry attempts to improve site plans.

A typical design based predominately on cul-de-sacs is shown in figure 11.4. The design illustrates the relatively narrow but deep lots found in most mobile home parks. The long and narrow shape of singlewide mobile homes has had significant impact on park designs. Entrances to such units usually face the sideyard rather than the street, although entrances for doublewides vary more. Turning homes parallel to the street more clearly defines the entrance, but it also increases street frontage and cost. The pattern of relatively deep, narrow lots perpendicular or angled to the street remains most common (figures 11.5 and 11.6) even though site plans increasingly resemble those of traditional single-family housing subdivisions.

The narrow lot reduces the space between units. The average yard width reported in the Urban Land Institute's survey of two hundred twenty quality parks was 17 feet between units; the range averaged from 12 to 30 feet.[22] Without landscaping, sideyards this small are hardly usable and achieving privacy outdoors is virtually impossible. The sideyard serves as the only outdoor space available to mobile home families; front and back yards typically do not exist.

Landscaping is not the only element available to create privacy between units in narrow lots. "Zero-lot-line" approaches to unit design create privacy with a blank sidewall on one side of the unit, or at least a wall with high windows. In such designs the space between units "belongs" entirely to one unit and is much more usable. This design approach is now quite common in California single-family and town house units but has not yet been realized in mobile home designs.

Many parks provide marginal car parking space. Off-street parking, at least for occupants, is preferred by most mobile home families. Responses to PMHI's Park Survey indicated that 86 percent of occupant cars and 59 percent of visitors' cars were parked off-street. Most parks provided two car spaces per lot. Clustered parking, although sometimes more economical, is provided less often for occupant spaces in new parks.

Within the restraints currently imposed on park designers, the overall quality of the best new parks is surprisingly high. The uncoordinated design of unit and site remains the major restraint to improved performance. As the popularity of mobile home subdivisions increases and more manufacturers produce units that reflect potential site conditions, this constraint will gradually disappear.

Utilities and services generally follow a linear pattern comparable to the linear pattern of streets and lots in most parks. Mains may parallel streets, as in a conventional subdivision, with service laterals running to mobile home pads on both sides of the street. However, the lack of permanent foundations and the light weight of mobile homes makes it possible to eliminate service laterals entirely or reduce their length, running smaller "mains" directly under the units. Electrical distribution systems, particularly underground systems and their service connections, are typically toward the rear of most mobile home stands. The economics of alternate utility layout patterns should be carefully considered once the basic unit layout is determined.

Utilities represent the major cost (about 40 percent) of mobile home park construction. Design efficiency has direct bearing on cost. Designs that vary considerably from the average unit component costs shown in the cost analysis in chapter 12 demand a close look. From an efficiency point of view, the primary design objective is to minimize the length of runs and provide optimum sizing of utility lines for each layout. The efficiency of proposed layouts can be tested by comparing solutions in these terms.

Typical parks provide a basic water, sewer, and electrical system. Gas or oil systems are not provided in all parks, although when these fuels are available, they are usually more economical than all-electric systems. Underground storm drainage systems are rare—surface drainage systems and roll-edge curbs and gutters are more common. Street lights provide additional safety and encourage outdoor activities in quality parks.

Design criteria for mobile homes, sponsored by the MHI and the American National Standards Institute, standardize to some degree the location of service point connections and have suggested compatible locations for service risers. Design solutions vary considerably in practice, however. In one park near Washington, units were custom-made with connections to the rear, where they are somewhat less conspicuous. The assortment of exposed utility risers under and near mobile homes contributes visually to the sense of disorder in many parks. Even when connections and transformers are placed to the rear of each lot, they will still be noticeable if landscaping is minimal. The most attractive solutions involve a combination of carefully selected location and screening or landscaping. Combining utility risers and meters with a storage shed is another solution. Poorly located risers are not only unattractive but also can compromise the function and privacy of outdoor spaces.

Figure 11.4.
Site plan. Source:
Douglas M. Ruth / H. W.
Behrend.

Park Development and Operation

Figure 11.5.
Site plan. Source: H. W.
Behrend Associates.

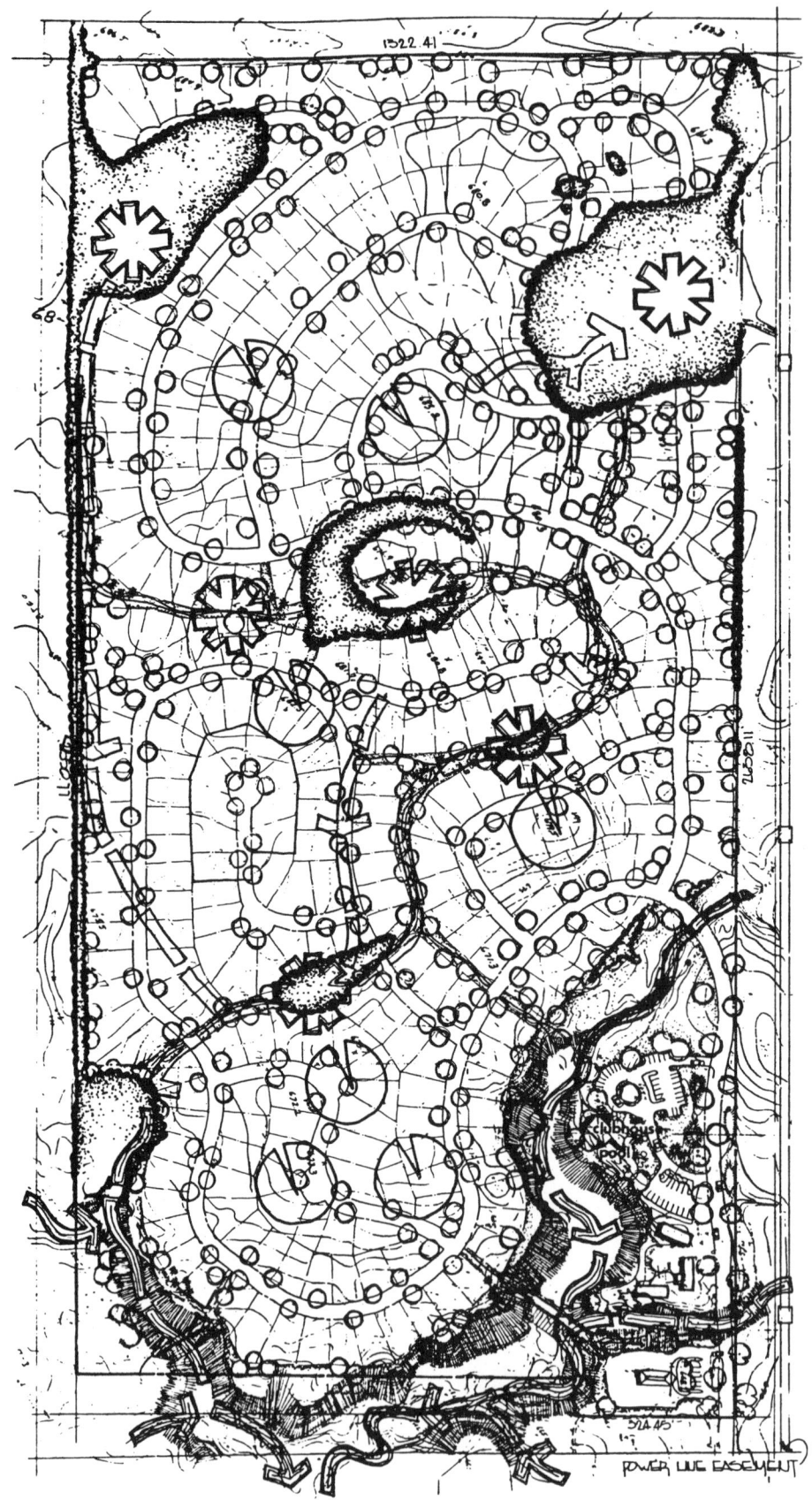

Figure 11.6.
Site plan. Source:
Herbert Behrend.

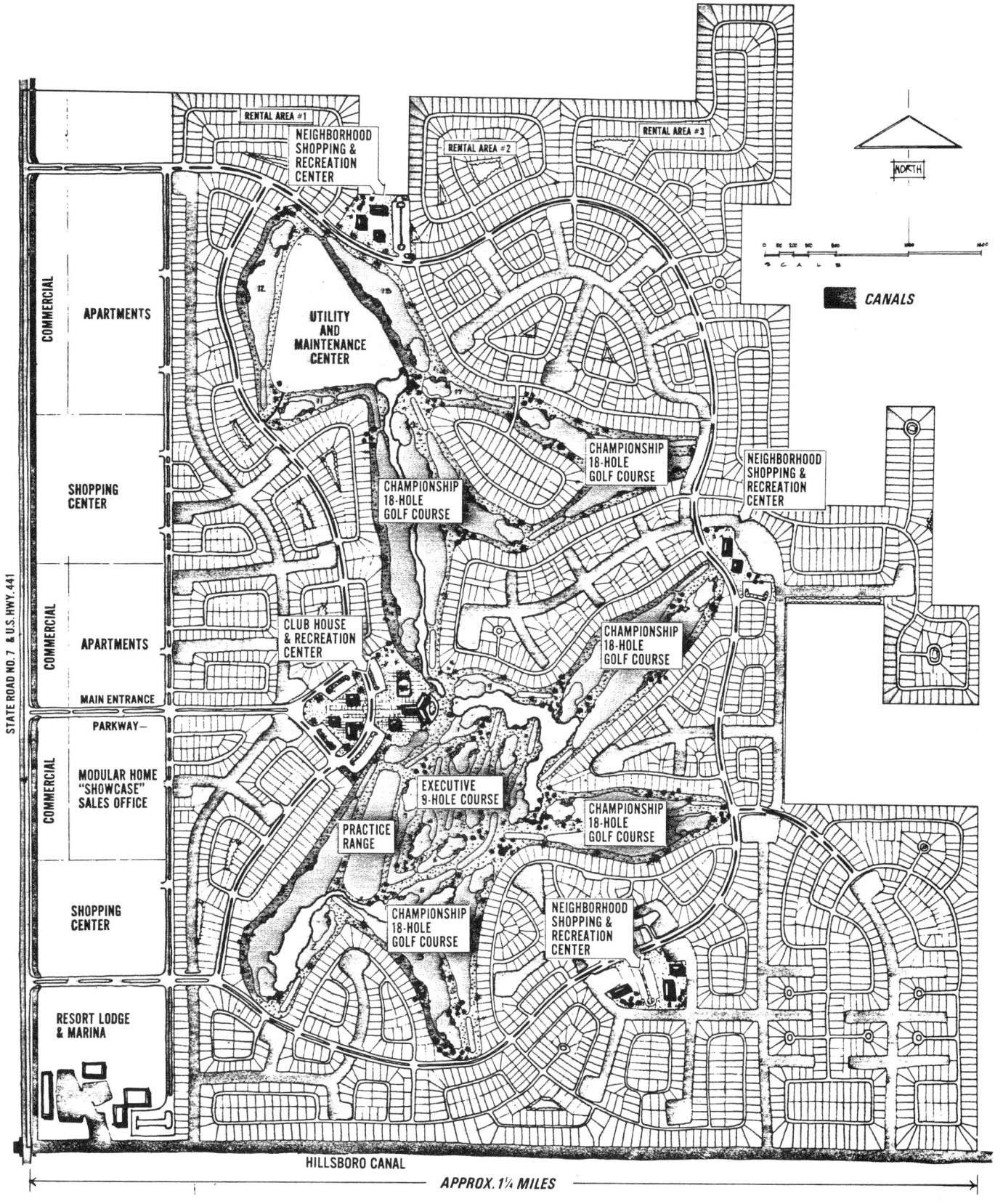

Park Development and Operation

Figure 11.7.
Utility connections.
Source: H. W. Behrend
Associates / ANSI
A119.3–1977.

Optimum Location
of Utility Connections

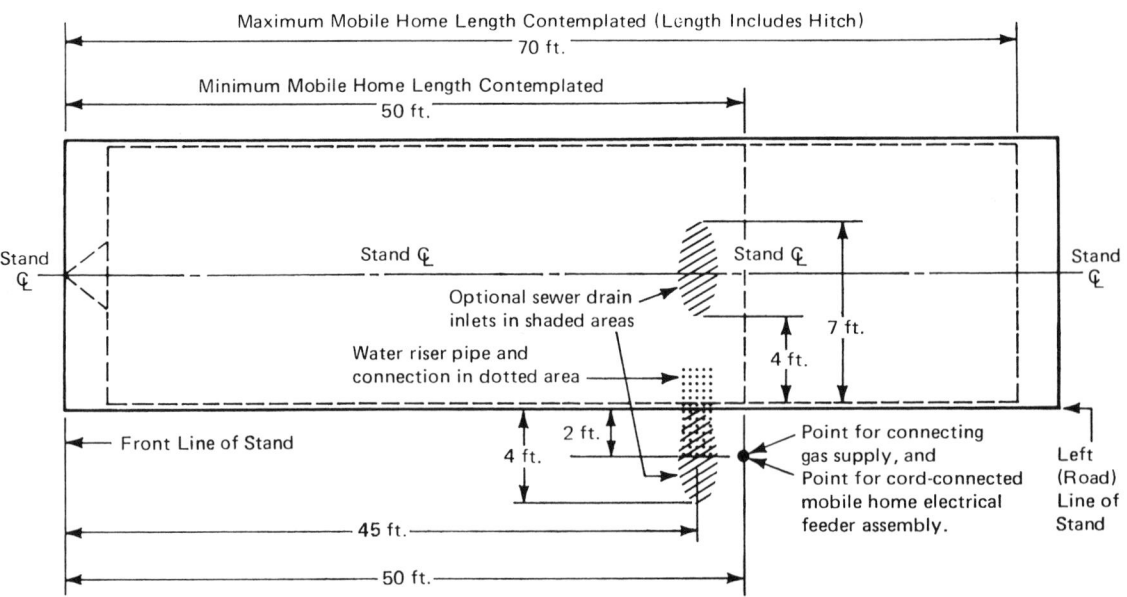

Note: Dimensions vary with mobile home size.

Typical Pipe
Connections to
Mobile Homes

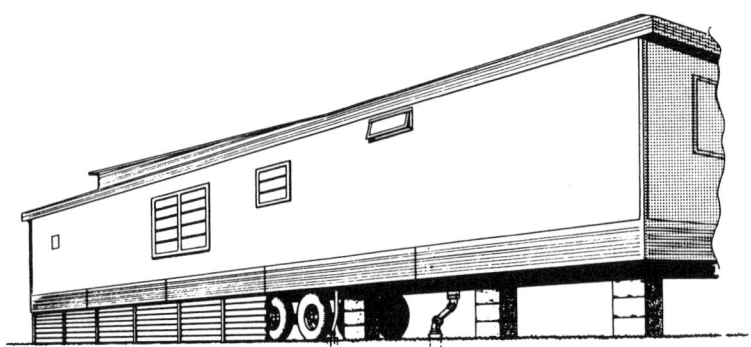

A. Non-freezing wall hydrant
B. Main shut-off valve
C. Water connection (3/4″ copper tubing)
D. Water riser pipe
E. Mobile home drain outlet
F. Sewer connections
G. Sewer riser pipe

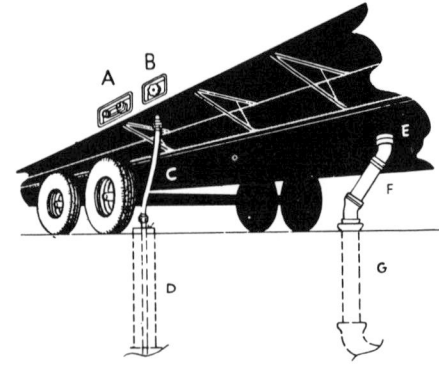

Trash service is often overlooked in design solutions. Individual trash pickup is more convenient but is usually more expensive in use. A carefully located, screened pedestal can add a permanent element to each lot. Bulk storage containers are more common but usually less attractive.

Despite the importance of efficient engineering, the optimum utility/service solution is one that considers not only the cost but also the quality and visual impact of each design element.

Construction

Construction schedules vary according to park size, location, and firm capability. Construction innovations and designs are subject to code and zoning requirements and review by building officials in the same manner as conventional housing projects. Although the mobile homes for a project can typically be produced in a month or less, a construction period of a year or more may be required for site work.

The typical minimum development schedule for a one hundred-unit mobile home park allows for one year; about half the time is slated for preliminary planning and design, half for actual construction. The schedule does not allow any prediction for certain planning elements such as zoning approvals, as the reader will appreciate after having read chapter 16 on land use controls. Zoning approvals can easily take a year or longer in some communities, effectively doubling the actual development time required. Construction periods can range from three months to more than a year (see figure 11.8). Although an extremely short time schedule can adversely affect bids, interest costs and other carrying charges can be significantly reduced.

The dollar volume represented by most projects attracts smaller construction firms than do typical conventional housing developments, which affects schedules. Most of the parks providing cost data in the PMHI Park Survey were actually built in two or more different increments over a period of several years. Only 30 percent were built at one time.

Time-phased overlapping of design and construction can reduce time and costs, particularly in large projects. A two-month period for actual design is reasonable and the advantage of a single advertise/bid package may offset the advantages offered by time-phasing.

Construction innovations in park development are just as rare as in site work for conventional housing. Although part of this is due to restraints imposed by local codes and building officials, the volume economies inherent in assembly line production have limited application at the site. The scale economies that do occur result primarily from purchasing materials in large volumes and reduced mobilization time.

The mobile home industry would benefit from review of code and zoning restraints, firm capabilities, and design standards to identify areas in which the entire planning/design/construction process could be expedited. Development of standard design details and specifications is underway in other industry segments and could be applied to park construction. The length of time needed to develop a mobile home park, particularly to obtain zoning approvals, remains one of the primary restraints to improved cost performance.

Figure 11.8.
Mobile home community development: Flow chart and time schedule.

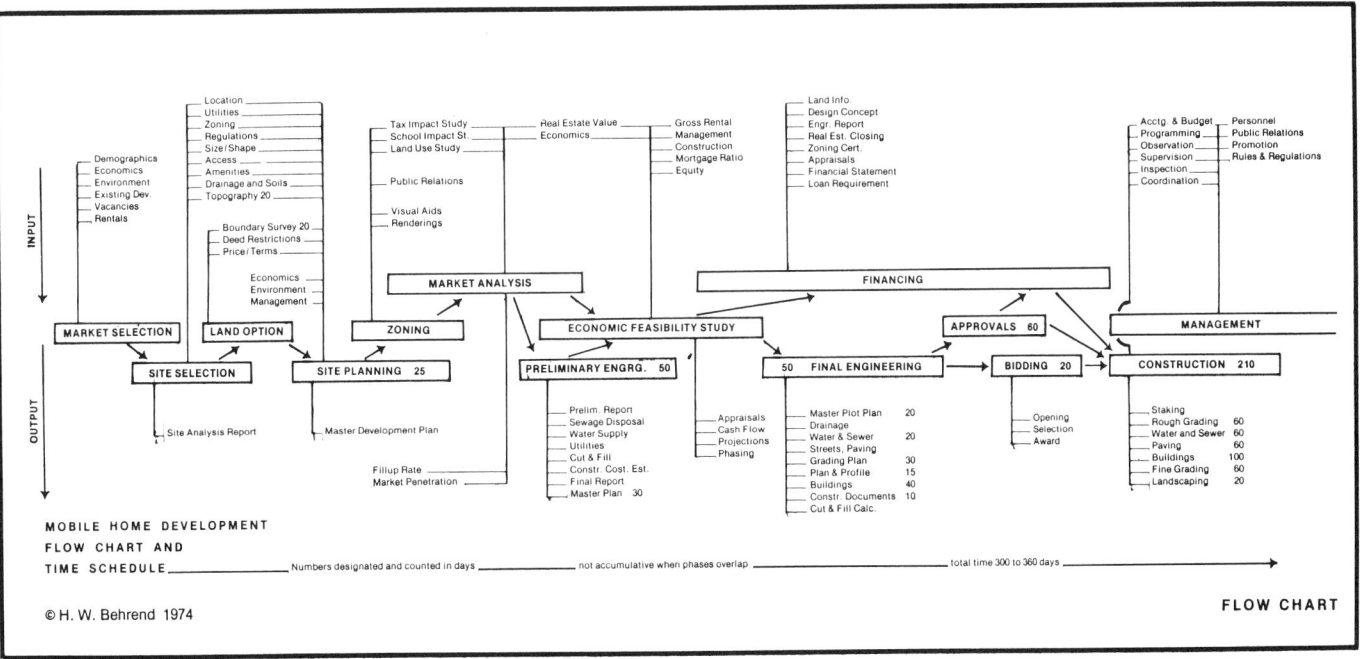

© H. W. Behrend 1974

FLOW CHART

Figure 11.9.
A mobile home community today: Street design. Source: H. W. Behrend.

Figure 11.10.
A mobile home community today: Court design.

Figure 11.11.
A mobile home community today: Landscaping.

C. Park Operation and Management

Park Managers: Characteristics

In evaluating the park operation and management process, we found that park management characteristics correlate with certain specific policy and management decisions. By examining type, background, experience, and other variables, it seems possible to predict with some degree of accuracy a manager's policies and park facilities.

There are a number of management variables to consider when approaching the question of determining park policy as an approximate function of manager characteristics. One of the more important of these characteristics is "manager type." The PMHI/PS found that 58 percent of the questionnaire respondents answering the type question identified themselves as park managers. However, 43 percent identified themselves as owners and managers and 30 percent said they were owner and developer as well as manager. This leads us to consider the difference in management response (that is, park policy) among these three groups: manager, manager/owner, and manager/owner/developer.

Full-time professional park managers (as opposed to manager/owners, and so forth) tended to operate larger parks. They made fewer suggestions for improvements in their parks, indicating satisfaction with services offered, which were more numerous than those of other manager types. These managers also operated with smaller personnel/space ratios, although they were generally more experienced than other groups. Manager/owners and manager/owner/developers seemed more willing to offer improvement suggestions. They seemed to run smaller parks, with less variety of tenants. Most managers favored "management changes" as the most important improvement to the park system; only manager/owner/developers and manager/owners offered "better mobile home design" as a frequent suggestion.

Comparison of the three management categories leads to some interesting conclusions. We found that respondents who identified themselves as manager or manager/owner/developer primarily had construction backgrounds, while manager/owners had more diverse backgrounds. Managers tended to have more managerial experience than manager/owner/developers; manager/owners had the least experience. Manager/owner/developers showed the highest degree of expansion. This is probably the result of their construction backgrounds and development experience. Though both managers and manager/owner/developers recommended "management changes" as the most frequent suggestion for improvement, manager/owners chose "physical park change" with the same frequency. There was little variation among the categories regarding personnel/space ratios, although manager/owners seemed to operate with higher ratios than the other groups. Parks operated by full-time managers offered the most services, although not a significantly greater number.

The managers' prior experience might be a prime factor in their response to a given management difficulty. Table 11.15 lists expected and observed percentages of specific Standard Industrial Classification (SIC) occupational groups. The "expected" percentages consist of the percentage, determined from census data, of each group that one might expect to find in a random sample of the population.[23] The PMHI/PS found that a statistically significant proportion of mobile home park managers had SIC construction backgrounds. The manufacturing and public administration SIC groups were represented by a significantly small number of managers and more than expected came from finance and construction. It is easy to understand why a significantly large number of managers are coming from finance and especially from construction. Fully 54 percent of PMHI/PS respondents were either manager/developer or owner/developer of their parks. Because developing a park requires a construction background and some knowledge of the financing involved, the significance is not surprising.

In order to form a clearer picture of the influence of background on park management, we ran a cross-tabulation of background versus manager response to problems. Of all "on-site residential construction" respondents 55.6 percent checked

Table 11.15.
Observed versus Expected Park Manager Occupational Categorization, Using Standard Industrial Classification Major Divisions

SIC Major Divisions	Observed % of Managers	Expected % in Random Sample
A. Agriculture	5.5	4.2
B. Construction	21.1	4.4
D. Manufacturing	6.4	25.1
E. Transportation	2.8	5.8
F. G. Wholesale and retail trade	19.3	20.6
H. Finance	11.9	5.1
I. Services	22.0	16.3
J. Public administration	1.8	17.6
B. K. Other	9.2	0.9

Note: An overall Chi Square of the data showed overwhelming significance (p < .01). Tests of independent proportions showed that three categories were significant to the .01 level. Finance required a one-tail test to achieve significance to the .05 level.

Source: PMHI/PS, U.S. Bureau of the Census.

"physical park change" as one of their suggestions for improvement. When one compares this to the small 15.4 percent of the "dealer" respondents in this category, manager background is clearly a determining factor. Background also seems to have some effect on the degree of expansion. Based on the percentage of owners not expanded versus percentage expanded, those responding "dealer" to the background question had higher levels of expansion than any other group, which is understandable in the light of dealer integration into park management. Second was the "construction" group, whose members are able to branch out because of their experience in the type of work required for starting new parks.

A cross-tabulation of background versus number of mobile home park spaces showed little significant deviation from the previous breakdown of "background." In the 51 to 100-space and 151 to 200-space parks, "dealer" was a more frequent response than "on-site residential construction"; however, this demonstrates that the parks of respondents with a dealer background do not tend to be small family operations. We assume that many of the respondents with dealer backgrounds are still dealers, and it is in their interest to seek more park spaces in which to place their homes.

It is clear from analysis of the PMHI/PS data how background affects other variables of the PMHI/PS. With additional substantiation one can begin to build a profile of mobile home park management simply by looking at operator variables. For example, managers operating a park with an expanded owner may differ significantly from other managers in their response to management problems. Operators with dealer backgrounds tend to manage parks for owners who are expanded into other areas, to own larger parks, and to offer fewer suggestions for improvement. On-site residential construction respondents, however, lean toward recommending physical park changes when asked about park improvement.

One of the most obvious manager characteristics that must be explored is an operator's degree of training or experience. The spread of the PMHI/PS variable on training/experience was interesting: Only 2.4 percent of the respondents had had any formal training; 31 percent had over sixteen years of experience; 19.5 percent had eleven to fifteen years of experience; and the remainder fell fairly evenly into the zero-to-five-year and six-to-ten-year brackets. Less-experienced managers operated parks with more service facilities and offered more suggestions for improvement than did the more experienced operators. A cross-tabulation of experience versus services offered shows that 70 percent of the newest managers (zero to five years' experience) offered two or more services: 55 percent of the six-to-ten-year group and 53.9 percent of the sixteen plus-year group offered two or more services.

The cross-tabulation on suggestions offers few surprises; as might be expected, managers with over ten years of experience offered the fewest suggestions, with the under-ten-year group offering from 30 percent to 40 percent more. This might occur simply because of the time factors involved— an "old hand" at park management who stayed at the same park would tend gradually to incorporate most, if not all, of the features thought desirable. The one trend that emerges is that 50 percent of the managers with zero to five years of experience checked "physical park changes." Though most other respondents suggested "management changes," 57.1 percent of all respondents checking both "management" and "physical" were in the zero-to-five-year experience bracket.

We ran a cross-tabulation in an attempt to determine whether degree of experience would lessen the personnel/space ratio. One could reason that a more experienced manager would require less help and that the personnel/space ratio would thus decrease as experience increased. However, 24.4 percent of the respondents had ratios greater than .05; of these, 40 percent had from zero to five years of experience, 10 percent had six to ten years, and 40 percent had more than ten years. This is probably due to the large number of so-called Mom and Pop park operations; these have comparatively few spaces but two or more park personnel, which raises the ratio. Although the data are too sketchy to indicate any major trend, it would seem that the newer managers are working with slightly higher personnel/space ratios.

One important issue is the effect of expansion on park management. To test our theory that owner business expansion would tend to make park management less responsive to problems and varying situations, we ran cross-tabulations of degree of owner expansion versus personnel/space ratios, services offered, and variety of tenants. As owner expansion increased, several trends became evident. The most definite trend was a reduction in the personnel/space ratio, which may merely reflect increasing park size. As expansion increases, a small decrease can be noted in the number of services offered. Park owner expansion does not affect park operation to the degree that might be expected. Evidently, owners with other interests do not let their parks decay but still take considerable care to ensure proper service to their tenants.

Examining the correlation of management characteristics with specific policies and discussions, should suggest not only the managers' policies for that specific park but also the policy trends of the system in general. In summary, less experienced (newer) managers work with higher personnel/space ratios, have parks with considerably more services, and offer the most suggestions for improvement. More experienced managers tend to offer fewer services and suggestions, a majority indicating "management change" rather than "physical change" as the crucial improvement factor. The increasing emphasis on physical improvement and better performance indicates that new operators are spearheading an upgrading process in the park system, which should have positive ramifications for the entire industry.

Principal Types of Park Managers
The evolution of mobile home parks from transient trailer camps to stable. planned communities has effected a dramatic change in the role of the park manager. Although the levels of expertise still vary widely, a new profession has evolved: the professional park manager. This new professional, usually employed to run one of the many new, large parks, has frequently had prior relevant experience and is able to impart expertise into the operation of these parks. In contrast to the professional manager is the continued presence of the husband and wife ownership teams with little relevant experience who develop or purchase their parks and then operate them without the assistance of hired professional managers. Though many of the newer, larger parks are managed by professionals with delegated authority from absentee owners, many of these parks and other smaller ones, both new and old, are run by owner/managers. Thus the park owner who also functions as caretaker, troubleshooter, and accountant continues to be a major participant in the park system. Park managers are most frequently employed in one of three roles, depending on the park's size and type:

1. The owner/manager, who directs a small or large park with varying services in order to establish a livelihood
2. The professional manager, hired by an owner who may be absent, whose responsibility is to run the park according to regulations set by the manager or the owner and to achieve a reasonable profit
3. The professional manager employed by a cooperative or condominium mobile home community, who most often is responsible to a community association that establishes the regulations for the park

The owner/manager and the professional manager hired by an absentee owner are frequent forms of management. In the PMHI Park Survey, 43 percent of the respondents identified themselves as owner/managers and another 15 percent as professional managers. The fact that 40 percent of all the respondents identified themselves solely as owners suggests that most, if not all, of these owners employ managers. Thus the

PMHI survey shows that the occurrence of the hired professional manager and the owner/manager are close to equal. Only a small number of professional managers in the park system work in cooperative or condominium-based communities, primarily because of the rare occurrence of mobile home parks under such ownership.

Professional managers can be split into two groups according to their origin: those who are relatively experienced in the operation of parks and for whom such work is their life occupation and those who are residents of the park they manage and have taken on the managerial role as a part-time or full-time occupation. It is probable that in most instances this latter type of professional manager has no prior experience in park management and operation. This differentiation between these two types of professional manager suggests a difference in the degree of commitment each exhibits: The first type is presumably committed to the park system in general, whereas the latter is more likely to be interested only in the park in which he or she lives and works. A difference in remuneration also exists: The first receives s salary and living accommodations, and the second usually receives a rent-free site on which to place his/her mobile home.

The type of professional manager needed depends on the size of the park and the amount of work required. In a larger park, many of which have been developed during the last decade, a professional manager is expected to have prior experience in park operation or at least some other relevant work experience. This manager directs the park on a full-time basis and may have a staff of one or more full- or part-time people as assistants. The complex operation of a large park and the responsibilities that the position entails will be more rigorous than for the live-in occasional manager. The professional manager may be responsible for virtually complete direction of the large park, including such tasks as financial management, regulation setting, and tenant selection. The amount of direction required and maintained depends on whether the owner is present and takes an active role in park operation. Alternately, the occasional manager is likely to be employed in smaller and older parks. This manager will also probably be responsible for a park with less extensive services, which demands less time. It is likely that the managers of these smaller parks, who are often employed on a less formal basis than the managers of the larger parks, do not have the same level of authority and the responsibilities for setting regulations and financial policy.

A primary difference between the owner/ manager and the professional manager is that the latter must necessarily institute policy that will be acceptable to the owner, whereas the owner/manager has no such intermediary. The owner/manager will often exercise more exhaustive enforcement of the rules and regulations under which the park is operated. Such owner/managers are most frequently found in parks of fewer than one hundred spaces, which indicates that both prospective and present tenants may be subject to more rigorous screening and closer scrutiny than would be the case in a larger park, particularly one operated by a professional manager.

Flexibility is another advantage of owners who manage their own parks. Unlike traditional apartments or housing developments, mobile home parks can adjust to changes in tastes, layout, and demand for unit size. Shifts in product styles and resident incomes can be accommodated by unit turnover. As manager, the owner/manager is aware of trends in tastes; as owner, he or she can direct necessary adjustments to trends. The park owner/manager has the flexibility to adapt to dealers' and home owners' demands while maintaining a profitable operation.[24]

The professional manager who works for an absentee owner is necessarily responsible to the park owner for operating the park and ensuring optimum returns on the owner's investment. The owner must clearly delineate the responsibilities the manager must perform. The absentee owner will frequently provide the resident manager with a reasonable amount of autonomy, allowing him or her to set the regulations and admit tenants of his or her own choosing. Park operation in terms of its financial status will be worked out by the owner with the assistance and consultation of the professional manager. Most owners seek to employ professional managers who will ensure a smooth-running, profit-making, virtually trouble-free operation. The owner naturally wishes to be kept well informed of what issues have arisen and how they are handled.[25]

The park manager in condominium and cooperative mobile home communities has essentially the same role as the manager working for the absentee owner. Here, though, the park manager has the additional task of implementing policies for a governing board that represents the residents. It is interesting to note that some mobile home owners are wary of condominium and co-operative situations, fearing lack of control by the management over resales, maintenance, and use of communal facilities. Some elderly park residents worry that upkeep of land and property taxes would be prohibitive in anything other than a rental arrangement.[26]

Managerial Responsibilities

Management activities within a mobile home park would typically include the following:

Screening of applicants and eviction of disruptive tenants

Ensuring that tenants comply with regulations and, in the case of manager/owners, the formulation of those rules

Informing residents of ordinances and of their own responsibilities

Ensuring that the park is kept in good repair and is clean; yard and common area maintenance

Establishing rents and fees

Functioning as an intermediary between owner and residents (in the case of absentee ownership)

Supervising recreational and social activities

Purchasing products necessary for construction in and upkeep of the park, as well as products to be sold to tenants and the public

Interacting with dealers concerning the sale of mobile homes for placement within the park

Acting as a mediator between the mobile home community and the outside community, responding to possible community opposition

In addition to the tasks listed above, the park manager may also be responsible for directing and approving the resale of mobile homes within the community. Removal policies vary with the size of the park, but managers generally have concrete strategies for the updating and upgrading of mobile home units. With the departure of the unit owner, the manager will often buy the home and then sell it on the used market or scrap it and replace it with a new unit for sale to the next tenant on the space. The commission on the new unit may be calculated to cover any loss that might be sustained to the old unit.[27] Such phase-out activities are considered an important management task and essential in maintaining the park's appearance. An Urban Land Institute survey found that 83 percent of their manager respondents controlled the type, appearance, and essential physical features of their mobile home parks; only 2 percent placed no restrictions at all.[28]

Normally, the park manager is also responsible for purchasing in large quantities products for park maintenance and improvement as well as products necessary for enlargement of individual sites. Many operators also conduct extra businesses such as small stores, restaurants, motels, gas stations, and repair shops for mobile homes to serve tenants and the public. Though the availability of such goods or services is usually a matter of convenience for park residents, there are alleged instances where management exerted some pressure on residents to purchase these goods or services.[29] However, we have found no evidence to support these claims.

The manager may require an assistant in conducting the community's recreational program. For instance, a social director elected by the residents is often employed to aid in the collection of money for trips, entertainment, and other outside activities and to assist in organizing park programs. Family parks, which are by nature more home-oriented than community-oriented, usually need less supervised recreational provisions than retirement parks. In the former case, play facilities for the children are considered an important recreational asset.

Additional assistance to the manager includes resident associations (especially popular in service-oriented parks), which are formed to organize daily events and large-scale recreational activities. Moreover, information dissemination within the park is usually accomplished via a bulletin board and a newspaper. The latter covers upcoming recreational events, specific park business, general mobile home news, and personal items such as birthdays, anniversaries, visits, and trips.

Relationship of Managers to Residents

The manager's role as either a professional hired from outside or as an occasional manager hired from within the park will most likely have an effect on the relationship between the manager and the residents of the park. A study of smaller adult parks in California found that in many cases park managers had lived in mobile home parks for some time before deciding to look for a manager's job.[30] Some of these people had slowly worked into a manager's or assistant manager's position within their own communities. As a result, such managers generally had cordial and harmonious relationships with the other tenants. The relationship between park occupants and the professional manager hired from outside is likely to be more formal and distant at the outset, although this does not preclude the development of a comfortable manager-occupant relationship.

Historically, the number of mobile homes has far exceeded available park sites, and spaces for newly purchased units have been at a premium. As a result, park managers exercise considerable control over resident mobile home owners. The PMHI Park Survey found that 47 percent of the respondents had no vacant spaces and 41 percent had a waiting list of prospective tenants. Parks oriented toward retired groups are more likely to have waiting lists (table 11.16). Thus managers usually have little difficulty in finding replacements for tenants whom they consider unsuitable. The politics of scarcity can give park managers substantial discretion over prospective tenants. Determining what characterizes a "suitable" tenant is often a matter of preference. Park managers, then, can afford to select their prospective residents carefully. If someone applying for admittance does not appear suitable, there is little difficulty in finding other residents. The practice of establishing entrance fees arose when new tenants

Table 11.16.
Waiting List Frequency
by Park Type

Park Type	% Parks With Waiting List	% Parks Without Waiting List
Retirement-oriented	60.6	17.4
Non-retirement-oriented	39.4	82.6
Total	100.0	100.0

Source: PMHI/PS.

paid the manager a sum of money to encourage approval of their application. Many park managers can currently demand high fees because of the scarcity of park space in many areas of the nation.

The problems confronting park managers vary with the type of park they operate (closed, adult, family, resort), the kind of home owners with whom they must deal, and the state and county in which the park is located (zoning and taxation laws are not nationally consistent). Most operators and owners have responded to this set of issues by structuring a detailed list of rules designed to regulate park operation, to please investors, and to ensure a minimum of friction with the surrounding community. The professional manager must balance several vested and sometimes conflicting interests.

The rules and regulations of mobile home parks are usually determined by two factors: the desires of the actual or potential park occupants as perceived by the manager and the desires of the community at large as it expresses them or as perceived by the park owner or manager. Those regulations established in response to the wishes of the park residents themselves are legitimate ones; it is reasonable to expect that because these rules most likely reflect the wishes of the majority, few individuals would feel constrained by them. For example, the occupants of a park composed primarily of elderly residents might prefer not to have children in the park.

The validity of those restrictions imposed by the wishes of the community at large, however, may be called into question; such rules are instituted not in response to the residents' desires but solely as a result of prevailing pressure from the surrounding community. A prime example of this type of regulation would be prohibitions against children and low-income groups, which are a direct result of local zoning procedures. In many parts of the country, it is difficult for developers to obtain favorable zoning without an implicit or explicit guarantee that the park will prohibit children (to save the locality additional educational costs) or low-income groups (to preserve the "good appearance" of the community). A similar situation also exists in traditional housing in terms of half- or full-acre lot zoning, which assures that low-income groups are excluded by high

prices. If such zoning practices reflect the fiscal consensus of the community, the responsibility for these regulations lies with the local government that institutes such practices, not the park owners and managers who must implement them. If this vicious circle is to be broken, fiscal zoning policies must be reexamined and the problems of mobile home taxation dealt with (see chapter 17).

In a sense, explicit rules can be traced to the transition period of park development. As trailer camps evolved into mobile home parks, the need arose for a new image of parks as stable, ordered communities of responsible citizens. Owners and operators extended their authority to include not only the physical setting and maintenance of the site but also the behavioral and social interactions of the residents. Once admitted to a park, mobile home owners may find that they are "tenants at will." Often lacking a legal agreement such as a lease that would give leverage in negotiating with the management, the mobile home owner may be threatened with eviction by the park operator for noncompliance with park rules.

In most situations residents who move from a park cannot transfer the right to their park space. They either sell their unit to the park management or, if a private sale is made, the new buyer may have to tow the unit out of the park and try to find a new location. In extreme cases when the new owner is allowed to occupy the same site, management may charge a fee for connecting the utilities even though they have not been disconnected.[31]

It is not unusual for park operators to require prior approval of the sale to a new owner and to ask for character references and credit checks. Owner/operators may charge a resale fee. Generally taken as a commission for the sale of the unit, the resale fee is payed by the new owner in exchange for the guarantee of space availability. This commission can be levied whether or not the professional brokerage function is performed by the manager.[32] In Massachusetts, the Salem Superior Court has struck down this type of fee as a violation of the Consumer Protection Act, stating that resale fees constituted "unfair and deceptive trade practices."[33]

Relationship of Park Management to Mobile Home Dealers

Professional park managers must sustain business relationships not only with their employer and park residents but also with their colleagues in other parks and in other sectors of the mobile home industry. Of this latter set of relationships, interaction with mobile home dealers is perhaps the most important. Mobile home dealers usually make the initial contact with prospective park occupants. The impression an individual dealer makes on the buying public has a direct effect on the success of neighboring park operations.[34]

The mobile home dealer's influence on the relationship between managers and residents can extend beyond the choice of a unit and the first entrance of new home owners into the park. Park selection and initial unit maintenance are two categories of responsibilities for which dealers as well as park managers and home owners are liable. A dealer may often lease sites in a mobile home park so that a sale may be facilitated by the existence of a readily available site on which to locate the new unit. Where park spaces are at a premium and dealers selling homes are plentiful, such dealers will often pay a park manager a fee in order to secure a site. In some cases it is impossible for a dealer to make a sale without this kind of arrangement. Aware that park space is limited, most new mobile home owners are willing to comply with the dealer's settlement. Dealers thus may have a great influence over their customers' choice of parks.[35]

If maintenance problems occur shortly after a new unit is in place, they are often handled by the dealer, though it is the park manager who must act as an intermediary in facilitating dealer service. Plumbing and heating malfunctions are among the most frequently cited difficulties. The level of customer satisfaction with the dealer and the unit is largely dependent on how competently these problems are handled. The park manager's relationship with the dealer can also be affected by the consistency with which such problems occur and are resolved.[36]

It is interesting to note that a substantial number of park operator-respondents to the PMHI Park Survey cited increased dealer cooperation as one of the most positive changes that could be made in the industry. Though in some instances dealers are accused of getting an unfair percentage of profits, many suggestions have been made for creative dealer cooperation. Some managers wanted to foster interaction between dealers and state officials so that more enlightened mobile home legislation could be passed. Many felt that park rules and regulations should be structured only after dealers are consulted. Still others felt that local boards of mobile home dealers should be set up to act in an advisory capacity to "amateur" park developers.

Relationship of Park Management to the Community at Large

The completion of a mobile home park is not necessarily the end of opposition from the surrounding residential communities. Motivated by fears of rising school costs, possibly decreasing real property values, lost property tax revenue, and municipal service overload, citizens in the community surrounding a park want many questions answered. Much of the public relations responsibility is delegated to the park manager, who may find that alliances with local businesses and the local Chamber of Commerce are his most successful source of support.[37]

Inviting local residents to participate in open house tours and other events scheduled in the mobile home park can be a means of allaying doubts about the physical image of the park. Encouragement of interaction between park and community people becomes important in establishing positive public relations between mobile home dwellers and their conventionally housed neighbors.[38]

In the course of park operation there are, then, a number of potential conflicts that may prevent a trouble-free relationship between the park manager and the people who must be dealt with—owners, dealers, residents, and people in the community at large. This, however, is not a situation that occurs only in mobile housing; it happens in other forms of housing as well.

One of the primary recommendations of our study is that mobile homes be treated like conventional housing with regard to consumer financing, taxation, and land use controls. Mobile homes have become another legitimate form of permanent housing and should not be excluded from residential neighborhoods and restricted to mobile home parks.

If, however, the widely practiced restriction of mobile homes to parks cannot be swiftly abolished, the mobile home industry could and should turn this restriction to its own advantage. The prevalent confinement of the industry's product, and hence its consumers, to the mobile home park need not be a liability in industry development. If it is used creatively, the park concept can be an asset in the development of mobile housing communities. In many respects, the mobile home park is still a "legal vacuum," not subject to many regulations governing traditional residential developments. Because the park can thus escape the restrictive nature or redundancy of many of the conservative controls operating within the traditional housing industry, innovations in housing design, construction, and operation can be achieved more easily and with better cost performance than is possible in conventional housing development. An apt analogy is the "Made in Germany" labeling requirement the Allies imposed upon German industry after

D. Policy Alternatives

World War I in order to inflict the stigma of inferior products; the Germans, however, succeeded in achieving the opposite by building the "Made in Germany" label into a recognized trademark of excellence. Similarly, the mobile home park concept can tactically be used as a protective legal umbrella for innovation; the industry can exploit the "legal vacuum" in which it now operates to turn the negative image of the mobile home park into an image of excellence in serving housing needs.

Daring innovation must be accompanied by formulation of rigorous development and construction standards in order to ensure excellent design, sound construction, and efficient land use. The absence of standards has contributed to the poor public image of parks, the bias against them, and their consequent relegation to nonresidential land, side by side with factories and junkyards. A set of park development standards (ANSI A119.3) has been formulated, but neither the scope nor the extent of official adoption of ANSI A119.3 is wide enough to accommodate innovation of the order suggested above. The further development and adoption of such standards and the introduction of conventional mortgage financing and real property taxation will upgrade park development and increase community acceptance of parks—an essential step toward the "trademark of excellence" concept.

If both innovation and development of standards are pursued, there is no reason why the mobile home park industry could not become a market leader, in the vanguard of the development of creative, user-responsive housing. The advantages to the industry of a radical change in direction are great: Public opinion of mobile homes would improve and the market would expand enormously.

An analysis of emerging trends in park development reveals that the present trend is toward larger parks, developed with larger amounts of capital than older ones and operated by professional managers. New parks attract larger families because they are built at a lower density and accommodate larger units such as doublewides. Because of rising land costs, developers have to look for more remote park locations in order to maintain these low densities at affordable rentals. Large professionally run parks will have a wide range of community services that fulfill luxury wants that often far exceed essential community needs. These new high-quality parks are attracting higher income groups to mobile home living. Another attraction of new parks is site design improvement to ensure greater privacy.

Trends toward development of parks with low densities, rural locations, and luxury services may be presently productive, but they do not indicate where the greatest potential for growth lies. The future demand will be for low-cost high-density housing in

close-in locations because of rising land and transportation cost. Trends toward large, heavily capitalized parks with design innovations for high-density siting, efficient planning, and a complete range of community services will best respond to this demand. The policy alternatives discussed here are suggestions for future park development—ideas based on the general notion of turning into advantage the legal vacuum in which the mobile home industry still operates.

If the industry is to expand its market significantly to include more of the general population, it must offer a wider range of living environments than it does today. A variety of environments means variety in park locations, housing density, housing types, and community types.

In addition to low-density suburban-rural parks, there should be high-density urban parks. Mobile home parks with higher densities will be able to compete with conventional housing such as town houses and walk-up apartments for higher-priced desirable residential land. But if parks are to become an important element in urban housing, heir present sprawling suburban character must be radically altered. The potentials for clustering and stacking demand that the mobile home no longer be considered as a separate single-family house only but as a building component capable of achieving many different architectural configurations. Consequently, unit design must better respond to site design constraints to ensure privacy as the individual lot shrinks in size and importance and the park assumes a tight urban form. Steps have been made toward this type of coordination with zero-lot line and cluster site plans. Mixes of single-family, clustered, and stacked housing in various densities would encourage the development of a balanced community of young and old, with small and large families. Such mixes are usually difficult, if not impossible, to achieve under conventional zoning but could be possible by tactically using the park concept as a legal vehicle, that is, by exploiting the legal vacuum.

Thus mobile homes can perform not only many of the functions of conventional housing but also different creative functions within the park concept. A fully developed model of a future park might be comparable to a small town in density, size, and self-sufficiency, with the advantages of rapid prefabrication and low cost. In rapidly growing cities where mobile homes play an important role in expansion, parks should not merely be a housing adjunct to that expansion but the actual organizational basis for new communities.

A greater emphasis is being placed on efficient planning of utility and road systems, but as yet there are no innovations that

A Range of Living Environments

Utilities and Services

Figure 11.12.
Mobile home
communities today.

Figure 11.13.
Mobile home
communities today.

Figure 11.14.
Mobile home
communities today.

would reduce the excessively long site development and construction phase and erase the dichotomy between traditional on-site park construction and off-site unit prefabrication. What is needed, at least as an option, is a system for site preparation that is the logical counterpart to mobile home production. The mobile home is advanced, low in cost, and flexible; but the infrastructure on which it rests is conventional, expensive, permanent, and inflexible.

Site drainage and road systems as presently installed require a permanent alteration of the landscape by conventional methods. Innovation is conceivable, however, in the utilities system. The various services (water, sewer, electrical, telephone, gas, steam heat, and so forth) could be combined in large prefabricated, insulated pipes laid out above ground, topped by pedestrian walkways. Trenching and refilling for each individual service would be eliminated, thereby reducing on-site costs and disturbance to the landscape. Once initial grading and roadwork are completed, the prefabricated components for a complete utility grid would be transported to the site and set in place, followed by the placement of the mobile homes. If rising land values and exorbitant taxes were to dictate the removal of the mobile home park, the utility grid's components could be disassembled and transported along with the mobile homes to a new location. The land could then revert to other uses.

Energy

The self-contained nature of the mobile home park would make appropriate the development of a total energy system as part of the prefabricated utility system. Such systems are now used by institutions with large physical plants and by some small communities in order to increase efficiency through the recycling of waste heat. The park would also be an ideal testing ground for alternative energy sources that are especially suitable for powering a small community.

The Total-Service Community

The mobile home park has the potential to be largely self-sufficient in social services. The mobile home industry has already developed a tradition of housing as a total service, especially in serving retirees' special needs. When one buys a mobile home, one is often buying a package for living, including space in a park complete with basic utilities, amenities, and a life-style. The concept of total service is presently expanding only in the luxury market, where the mobile home park approximates a country club. The real potential, however, lies in providing the general population with essential services. In addition to presently provided services such as trash collection, a laundry, and a community center, a mobile home park might include a day-care center, stores, a health clinic, and recreation facilities.

A complete range of services implies large-scale development and professional management, accompanied by higher costs to park residents. In order to determine if the concept of total service is viable, the industry should conduct research into the needs of the present and potential mobile home populations and analyze those services for which people are really prepared to pay. Although a total-service community might duplicate services in an already developed urban area, it would be vital in an isolated area where the community infrastructure is weak.

Notes to Chapter 11
1. U.S. Department of Commerce, Bureau of the Census, *Current Housing Reports*, Series H–150–75, *Selected Housing Characteristics for Mobile Homes and Trailers: 1975*, p.14, and *Financial Characteristics of the Housing Inventory: 1975 and 1970*, p. 10., Washington, D.C: U.S. Department of Commerce, 1977.

2. U.S. Department of Commerce, Bureau of the Census, *Current Housing Reports*, Series H–150–75, *Financial Characteristics of the Housing Inventory: 1975 and 1970*, p.10, and *Current Population Reports* Series P–60, No. 75, *Income in 1969 of Families and Persons in the United States.*

3. "Veterans Administration Survey," *Mobile-Modular Housing Dealer*, November 1976, p.65.

4. *Financial Characteristics of the Housing Inventory: 1975 and 1970*, p.10, and *Selected Housing Characteristics for Mobile Homes and Trailers: 1975*, p.14.

5. "Mobile Home Consumer Survey," Owens-Corning Fiberglas Corporation, *Mobile-Modular Housing Dealer*, June 1976, p.72.

6. PMHI estimate based on 1970 and 1975 occupational statistics. "Mobile Life Consumer Survey, Mobile Homes," *Mobile Life Magazine*, 1965, and *1976 Statistical Abstract of U.S.*, Bureau of the Census, *Employed Persons—Percent Distribution, by Occupation and Race, 1960–1975*, p.373.

7. Max S. Wehrly, *Mobile Home Parks, Part 2: An Analysis of Communities* (Washington, D.C.: Urban Land Institute, 1972).

8. *Selected Housing Characteristics for Mobile Homes and Trailers: 1975*, p.17, and *Characteristics of the Housing Inventory: 1975 and 1970*, p.4.

9. Wehrly, *Mobile Home Parks*.

10. *Selected Housing Characteristics for Mobile Homes and Trailers: 1975*, p.17; *Characteristics of the Housing Inventory: 1975 and 1970*, p.3.

11. *Selected Housing Characteristics for Mobile Homes and Trailers: 1975*, p.18; *Characteristics of the Housing Inventory: 1975 and 1970*, p.5.

12. Wehrly, *Mobile Home Parks*.

13. *Selected Housing Characteristics for Mobile Homes and Trailers: 1975*, p.18; *Characteristics of the Housing Inventory: 1975 and 1970*, p.5.

14. Ibid.

15. Dr. James Gillies, *Another Look at Mobile Home Parks* (Los Angeles, Cal.: Trailer Coach Association, 1968).

16. Carl Norcross, *Townhouses and Condominiums* (Washington, D.C.: Urban Land Institute, 1973).

17. "Mobile Life Consumer Survey, Mobile Homes," 1965.

18. Wehrly, *Mobile Home Parks.*

19. Unpublished Oklahoma Mobile Home Park Survey, done by the state of Oklahoma in 1961; Max E. Fieser, "Arizona Mobile Home Park Survey," Arizona State University, October 1962.

20. "Consumer Survey," *Mobile Home Journal,* September, 1963.

21. Wehrly, *Mobile Home Parks.*

22. Ibid.

23. Before actual statistical "background" tests could be made, a classification system had to be used to establish accurate statistical weights for given industrial occupations; and the system had to be applied to standardize the listed previous occupations. For this particular application, SIC guidelines were used because they represent an official classifying system and a well-documented list of occupation categories. A study of table 11.15 reveals major discrepancies between expected and observed percentages in construction and manufacturing, and to a lesser extent in finance and public administration. As might be expected, a Chi Square of the data shows overwhelming significance ($p < .01$). Individual tests of significance (independent proportions) of these four occupational groups also show significance to the 1 percent level, except the finance group, which required a one-tail test to achieve significance of ($p < .05$).

24. Wehrly, *Mobile Home Parks,* p.31.

25. D. and R. Nulsen, *Mobile Home and Recreational Vehicle Park Management* (Beverly Hills, Cal. Trail-R-Clubs of America, 1971), p.376.

26. "Amenities Build Sense of Community," *Project Builder,* August 1971, pp.52–61.

27. George Gade, "Economics of Operating a Mobile Home Park," *The Appraisal Journal,* July 1965, pp. 351–356.

28. Wehrly, *Mobile Home Parks,* p.32.

29. Office of Legislative Research, Joint Committee on Legislative Management, The General Assembly of the State of Connecticut, *Report on the Use of Mobile Homes in Connecticut* (Hartford, Conn.: State Printing Office, 1972).

30. S.K. Johnson, *Idle-Haven: Community Building Among the Working Class Retired* (Berkeley, Calif.: University of California Press, 1971), p.139.

31. C.B. Gibson, *Policy Alternatives for Mobile Homes* (New Brunswick, N.J.: Center for Urban Policy Research, Rutgers University, 1972), pp. 29–30.

32. Ibid.

33. *Boston Sunday Globe,* December 10, 1972, p.2.

34. *Focus on the Mobile Home Market,* Survey by Market Facts, Inc. for Owens-Corning Fiberglas, Pub. No. 5–BL–4954, May 1975.

35. Nulsen, *Mobile Home and Recreational Vehicle,* p.384.

36. *Focus on the Mobile Home Market.*

37. Nulsen, *Mobile Home and Recreational Vehicle.*

38. Correspondence with park operators, 1975–1977.

Chapter 12

Cost and Price Structures in the Park System

In order to determine whether the mobile home park system is best serving consumers, it is necessary to understand the nature of park costs. We believe that the consumer's interests are served if park costs are as low as possible, as long as cost reductions allow adequate incentives for developers and are consistent with quality standards. Therefore our goal in this discussion is to determine where cost reductions can be most effectively made. The discussion is divided into development and operating costs, followed by a brief section on policy alternatives. Predominant sources of information for this analysis are PMHI's national surveys of park developers, owners, and managers. Other sources include direct development experience of PMHI staff, extensive field interviews, and correspondence with professional park development firms, as well as industry and government publications.

A. Development Costs

Land Costs

Land costs vary tremendously for mobile home park developments, from about $600 to $35,000 per acre. Land for a typical park cost about $6000 per acre in 1977 or $1,200 per space at a density of five units per acre. PMHI's attempt to determine land prices empirically met with limited success because few land developers responded to our surveys. However, land costs are a major influence on the location and density of mobile home parks.

In rural locations land costs remain relatively low and lower-density parks are typical. Even at $1000 per acre, a density of two units per acre yields a very reasonable land cost of $500 per space. Land in prime suburban locations near major metropolitan areas typically costs $20,000 per acre, depending on parcel size, amenities, and surroundings. Even though most park developers seek lower-cost land on the suburban fringe, land prices are the prime reason mobile homes in suburbia are rarely sited at typical single-family densities of three or four units per acre. At $20,000 per acre and $10,000 per space for site development, a density of three units per acre will yield $16,700 per space for a developed site, about the price of a mobile home.

To justify high land costs, a park in a prime location often will be oriented toward doublewide and expandable units. Continually increasing land costs will encourage mobile home developers to develop high-density parks. However, high-density conventional parks are likely to be unattractive to many mobile home owners. Developers may increase park densities by utilizing higher-density forms of housing. For instance, current forms of cluster designs can make single-family housing feasible at densities of up to ten units per acre.

It is still possible to buy low-cost land in far-out locations. However, increasing highway congestion, energy costs, and commuting expenses are creating demand for park spaces on high-priced land near employment and recreation centers. This provides incentives to develop higher-density mobile home parks. If the industry does not anticipate the impact of land price escalation, this trend will severely restrain growth.

Zoning Costs and Fees

Zoning costs and fees must be estimated for specific locations. Costs range from almost nothing in rural areas to perhaps $2500 per space if rezoning is difficult and utility tap fees high. Parks built in many rural areas are not subject to zoning; building permits are of nominal cost; and there are no connection fees. However, these potential savings may be offset by higher site development costs.

Zoning changes may take years and require costly public displays and public hearings. Litigation is necessary in some cases. The emerging no-growth stance of many communities faced with school or environmental problems may delay any new project, especially a mobile home park. In most instances an extensive environmental impact report will be required to outline the project's advantages and disadvantages to the community. A strong no-growth attitude can result in exorbitant charges for utility connections or government services even after zoning is approved.

The difficulties of coping with zoning and environmental problems are substantial. It has been estimated that a zoning court case at the county or circuit court level averages $5000 to $15,000, plus the indirect cost of a three-month to one-year delay while waiting for the case to be heard. An appeal may add six months to a year and bring the total court cost to $30,000 or more. Although this would only be $200 per space for a typical one-hundred-fifty-space park; the figure includes only direct costs and represents money that must be invested before financing can be obtained.

Professional presentation drawings, impact studies, and other exhibits prepared for public zoning hearings can cost another $40,000. These costs, if required, are supplemental to the costs of design documents prepared for construction purposes. Another significant indirect cost of zoning and court battles is the impact of delay on financing and construction costs. Front money for land and design documents yields no return until the park is built. A one-year delay will add at least 5 percent to construction costs.

Initial contacts with zoning officials are important first steps for the developer, both in evaluating the chances of obtaining a zoning change and in estimating its cost. Government officials will also provide information about documents required for review and typical connection charges.

Design Costs

Professional design services for a one-hundred-fifty-space park will average $250 per space. Per-space costs for smaller parks will be higher because a significant portion of the design work involves preparation of details and specifications for which the amount of effort is the same regardless of park size. This size factor can be minimized if the same details and specifications are used for more than one project.

Design contract variations are numerous, and the type of contract can significantly affect costs. Design fees often are expressed as a percentage of the total project cost; as inflation increases construction costs, design fees rise. It may be to the developer's advantage to negotiate a contract on some basis other than percentage of construction cost.

Actual design fees reported to PMHI ranged from $75 to $425 per space. The smallest parks had the highest per-space design costs for a given level of design work. To reduce costs, many small parks are not designed professionally; the basic layout may be designed by the owner or developer and built with a minimum of detailed drawings and specifications. Although this technique may be feasible in rural locations, it is no longer common for parks in suburban areas.

The community's attitude toward the park will affect design costs. If a tough zoning battle is anticipated, nothing less than a first-class professional design effort with attractive presentation drawings will be required to convince the community that the park will be an asset. Environmental impact statements normally are prepared by professional firms and will increase the design fee.

Construction Costs

The number of features included in a project affects costs more than any other factor. The time span of each construction phase and park location are significant. Construction costs also are affected by site conditions, design efficiency, and the quality of materials. Within the density range of most new parks, density has only a slight impact on total park construction costs. In this range density primarily affects per-space land costs. It should be noted that all cost data presented here exclude the cost of land, design, and zoning variances.

Construction costs reported to PMHI in 1977 ranged from $700 to $68,000 per space, the latter number from a unique luxury park. A typical one-hundred-fifty-space park in Washington, D.C., cost $4500 per space and a quality park, $7000 per space, excluding community facilities. Costs for outdoor accessories, normally paid for by the mobile home owner rather than the park developer, add about $2000 for a singlewide mobile home. Total construction costs for parks vary with size and quality. In 1977 a

fifty-space park with minimum features cost $160,000, and a high-quality five-hundred-space park, $3,850,000.

The impact of community facilities is shown in table 12.1, which illustrates typical 1977 costs for each major construction feature in a one-hundred-fifty-space park near Washington, D.C. The total cost, $7000 per space without community facilities, includes features comparable to those in moderate-quality subdivisions. Approximately $2500 of the total is for such optional features as curbs and gutters, walks, a gas or oil system, street lights, storm drains, trees and shrubs, patios with privacy fencing, and pads for storage sheds. It would be possible to build a $4500 park without changing the design or compromising the park's basic features. However, it is apparent that the overall quality of the park would suffer from deleting these optional features.

Assuming that scope and quality are comparable, there is no question that park size has an impact on per-space costs. Table 12.2, compiled from actual bids for mobile home parks that were designed to approximately the same quality standard, indicates that a fifteen-space park will cost twice as much per space as a two-hundred-space park of comparable quality.

The impact of park density is less significant. Typical lots having densities of four, six, and eight units per acre, with 20 percent of total land area allowed for streets and common community/recreation areas, are compared in figure 12.1. Decreasing density while maintaining the same lot depth increases the space between units, as shown in figure 12.1. However, costs are higher because utility lines, curbs, gutters, and street paving are more expensive for the lower-density configuration.

Costs attributable to low densities can be minimized by efficient design. Techniques such as limiting grass area and increasing lot depth or common open space, rather than increasing lot width, reduce costs by minimizing utility and street runs. Lot width is a more important cost variable than lot size or density. In many cluster designs lots are not as clearly defined and may be neither parallel nor perpendicular to the street. In such designs the critical cost factor is not the density but the length of streets, utilities, and walks required to serve each cluster of units.

Design efficiency is a more important cost factor than density. Park density can be relatively low but costs will remain moderate if streets and utilities are designed to minimize the length of runs. This does not necessarily mean that narrow lots on both sides of the street will yield the most efficient design; many cluster designs compare favorably with conventional linear designs in terms of street and utility length. The conventional linear designs can be used as a yardstick to measure the performance of other alternatives. For example, single-loaded streets, with units on only one side, or collector streets, with no units facing them, almost always add costs. Utility lines that serve isolated units tend to be more expensive than lines that serve compact clusters of units. Wide lots, particularly those for units having the long entry side facing the street, add considerably to utility and street lengths. Individual off-street parking with two cars per unit will be more expensive than off-street parking for one car and common parking areas for guests and second cars. Surprisingly, on-street parking for all cars is usually more expensive than narrower streets with all parking off-street. All of these examples illustrate design decisions that have a cost impact.

Site conditions affect costs in a variety of ways. On a regional scale the project location determines the availability and costs of materials and labor. The impact of these variables on park design can be estimated for specific locations by referring to commonly used residential cost indexes. These indexes permit direct comparison of current costs in major American cities with a common bid date and location. On a local scale the proximity of the site to access roads and utilities is significant. Within the site natural features such as topography, vegetation, water table, and soil conditions affect costs. From a regulatory point of view, the site may be subject to zoning and building code requirements that increase costs.

The quality of materials is another significant cost factor. Although the material variables in site work are more limited than those in dwelling unit design, the cost of obtaining a given level of performance varies from site to site. For example, roll-edge asphalt curbs and gutters may provide water control in Arizona, whereas Seattle may require a conventional 6-inch concrete curb. The extent and type of landscaping, quality of patio and fencing materials, tie-down anchors, and gravel pads or concrete runners are further examples of material variables that affect costs. In many cases the most cost-effective option is not evident. Initial and long-term costs must be considered as well as the interrelationship of materials. For example, concrete runners are normally more expensive than gravel pads, but it may be easier to provide an anchor for tie-down straps in concrete than to bury screw-type anchors in the soil. Each material choice must be considered as part of a system of choices that relate to one another.

The scope and quality of community facilities feasible in a park are directly related to park size. Increased demand for such facilities has been a primary factor in the trend toward larger parks. Table 12.3 illustrates the total funds available for community

Table 12.1.

Cost Estimate (Excluding Land Cost), Mobile Home Park Components, One Hundred Fifty Spaces, Five Units per Acre, Washington, D.C., 1977

Item	Cost per Space($)		%
Community facilities	700		9.1
Unusual costs	200		2.6
Utilities		100	
Roads		100	
Site preparation	500		6.5
Paving	1600		20.8
Curbs/gutters		330	
Parking/driveways		300	
Streets		670	
Walks		300	
Utilities	3000		39.0
Water		670	
Sewer		700	
Gas		400	
Electrical		750	
Street lights		150	
Storm drainage		330	
Landscaping	650		8.4
Grass		325	
Trees/shrubs		325	
Fencing	250		3.2
Unit accessories	800		10.4
Pad/tie-down anchors		450	
Storage shed pads		75	
Patios		275	
Total: With community facilities	7700		100.0
Without community facilities	7000		

Source: Estimate based on responses to PMHI letter to park designers/developers and correspondence with H. Behrend, 1977.

Table 12.2.

Park Size/Cost Trends (Excluding Land Costs)

Number of Spaces	Park Cost($) per Space
200	6,500
150	7,100
100	7,700
50	9,000
25	11,000
15	13,000

Source: Responses to PMHI letter to park designers/developers and correspondence with H. Behrend, 1977.

Figure 12.1.
Typical lots. Source: PMHI.

Typical Lots
20% land area: streets/community
$30–$50/lin. ft. streets/utilities
$.10/sq. ft. grading/grass
14 × 70 singlewide with patio cover
and expandable room or deck

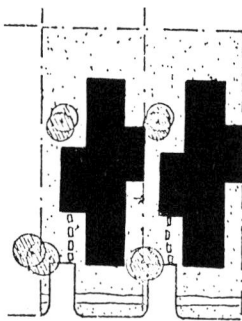

Density: 8 units/acre
4400 sq. ft. lot

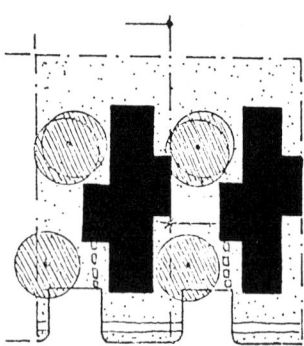

Density: 6 units/acre
5800 sq. ft. lot
$350–$480 *more* than
8 units/acre

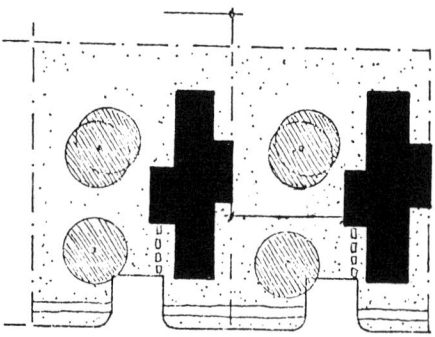

Density: 4 units/acre
8700 sq. ft. lot
$675–$950 *more* than
6 units/acre

facilities in parks of various size, depending on the amount spent per space. The typical new park of one hundred fifty spaces will have $75,000 available for community facilities at $500 per space. This amount is just enough for a small laundry, community center, and pool, which are almost mandatory for a high-quality mobile home community today. For additional amenities to be feasible, either the park size or the cost per space must increase.

The costs of outdoor accessories normally are paid by the mobile home owner and are not part of the park's cost. However, they must be included in total occupancy costs. As shown in table 12.4, these accessories add about $1950 to the cost of a singlewide mobile home. Tie-down requirements vary according to wind conditions and unit size. Skirts for a doublewide mobile home are about 20 percent more expensive than for a singlewide unit. The height of the unit above the ground also affects costs. Custom-size patio covers cost more per square foot than the standard size. Deck costs vary considerably according to size and material; many decks are low enough to omit railings. Custom-built steps, storage sheds, and carports would cost more than prefabricated metal designs.

A number of items on this list would not be required at all if unit design in relationship to the site were changed. For example, if the unit is placed 8 inches above the ground, no entry steps, skirts, and decks are required. Savings resulting from the deletion of these items exceed the added costs of site work to reduce the height of the unit above the ground. Design changes will occur as manufacturers realize that the unit and its site must be designed as an entity and that the least expensive unit design may not be the least expensive unit/site design.

Total Development Costs

The total development cost of a mobile home park is the sum of its four major components: land, zoning and fees, design, and construction. From the preceding analysis it is apparent that these costs vary considerably. In a rural area where land and zoning costs are low, the owner provides design services, and the park has few features, total initial costs can be as low as $3850 per space. A quality park in a prime suburban or resort location could cost six times as much. The typical suburban park with land at $7000 per acre, average zoning and connection fees, a professional design, and limited amenities will cost about $6500 per space to develop. Table 12.5 indicates the range of development costs. Costs of interim construction financing are reflected in the construction figures shown. These initial development costs can be used as a basis for projecting lot sale prices or rental charges, the user cost of a mobile home park.

Table 12.3.
Funds Available for
Community Facilities
(Excluding Land Costs)

	Number of Spaces per Park				
$/Space	50	100	150	200	500
100	$ 5,000	$10,000	$15,000	$ 20,000	$ 50,000
200	$10,000	$20,000	$30,000	$ 40,000	$100,000
300	$15,000	$30.000	$45,000	$ 60,000	$150,000
400	$20,000	$40,000	$60,000	$ 80,000	$200,000
500	$25,000	$50,000	$75,000	$100,000	$250,000

Table 12.4.
Mobile Home
Accessories

Item	1977 Cost per Unit ($)
Tie-down straps (8 frame, 2 roof straps)	100
Skirts (170 linear feet, 24 inches high)	325
Patio cover (10 × 20 foot, standard prefab metal)	250
Deck/stair (8 × 8 foot metal frame, wood floor, rails)	400
Steps (prefab metal with railings)	200
Storage shed (prefab metal 50 square feet)	225
Carport (prefab metal, one car)	450
Total	1950

Source: PMHI/PS and 1977 follow-up survey.

B. Operating Costs

Table 12.6 shows a breakdown of operating revenues and expenses as a percentage of total revenues per park. The figures are based on an analysis of several conventionally financed mobile home parks. For the most part the income and expense categories are self-explanatory. For example, "Rentals" includes income based on monthly space rentals, fees for use of recreation facilities, and additional charges for guests, pets, or a third adult. "Advertising and Promotion" expenses vary according to the mobile home park's age as well as the vacancy rate. A new park will incur heavier advertising costs than a well-established park with a low vacancy factor. "Land and Building Taxes" vary widely according to local and state tax rates.

Table 12.5.
Total Development
Costs, 1977

	Cost ($) per Space		
Item	Low	Typical	High
Land @ 6 units/acre	75	1,000	6,000
Zoning and fees	0	700	2,500
Design	75	250	500
Construction	3,700	4,550	6,000
Total cost	3,850	6,500	15,000

Source: PMHI/PS.

Table 12.6, derived from PMHI surveys, compares favorably with information found in FHA and other literature in that gross expenses including utilities but not depreciation or interest are about 40 percent of total revenue.

The key to park profitability is the rent level because this is the major revenue source. Only by charging the appropriate rent can a park compete with those nearby and still turn a profit. It is in determining the initial rent level that the expense rule of thumb shown in table 12.6 becomes useful to the developer.

In order to maintain full occupancy, the rent must be compatible with that for nearby parks offering the same amenities. On the other hand, rent must be adequate to cover direct expenses, interest, and taxes while providing a reasonable return to the developer. Finally, rental receipts must be sufficient to cover cash demands of running the park and paying back principal. It is the careful balance of these factors that determines park profitability, and most lenders will require developers to demonstrate their understanding of this principle by asking them to provide a *pro forma* balance sheet, income statement, and cash flow statement before considering the project to be a feasible investment opportunity.

Table 12.6.
Operating Revenues
and Expenses

	Range (%)[a]		
	Low	Average	High
Income			
Rentals and utilities	90.0	95.0	100.0
Washing and vending machines, etc.	3.0	5.0	7.0
Total income		100.0	
Expenses[b]			
Advertising and promotion	0.5	1.0	1.5
Dues and permits	0.2	0.5	0.8
Insurance	0.5	1.0	1.5
Legal and accounting	0.3	0.5	0.7
Office expenses	0.3	0.5	0.7
Salaries and wages	5.5	9.0	12.2
Repairs and maintenance	3.5	6.0	7.5
Services purchased	0.3	1.0	1.3
Supplies	0.4	1.0	1.5
Telephone	0.4	0.5	0.6
Taxes—land and building	6.0	8.0	12.0
Utilities—gas, water, electric	8.0	10.0	16.1
Miscellaneous	0.2	0.5	1.5
Total expense		39.5	
Depreciation	10.0	14.6	20.0
Interest on loan payments	10.0	15.0	20.0

a. Based on several current projects.
b. Items of expense are expressed as a percentage of total income.

Source: PMHI/PS.

C. Policy Alternatives

Potential for Reducing Development Costs

If government agencies were to reduce code restrictions and speed the approval process for mobile home parks, development costs would decrease substantially. Without this government support the developer must look to potential savings in land costs and park size to effect economies. Land costs could be reduced if parks were built in rural areas, but energy considerations do not favor such a trend and the marketability of remote sites may be a problem. If park densities are increased, land costs per space can be significantly reduced, even where land costs are high. The shortage of desirable land will encourage manufacturers to develop totally different unit designs suitable for higher-density park developments.

Per-space construction costs are affected by park size, even if quality and scope are held constant. This partly explains why park sizes have increased steadily in recent years. Land costs tend to be lower if large parcels are purchased; and front-end costs, such as design and zoning fees, are less per space as park size increases. Per-space construction costs are lower for larger parks because costs of common facilities, such as community centers and recreation space, are shared by more users. Also, bid costs for large parks tend to be lower for any given quality level because of construction economies.

Apart from density and park size, however, possibilities for reducing development costs are limited. Standardizing design details and simplifying bid packages yield some savings, as does careful design control to ensure maximum efficiency. Simultaneously constructing several parks to the same standard and advertising them at the same time offers some volume economies. However, this option is only available to large developers.

As land prices continue to escalate, mobile home manufacturers and park developers will be encouraged to produce higher-density housing. With cluster design even single-family homes are feasible at densities up to ten units per acre without creating insurmountable environmental problems. Planned unit developments with conventional housing have demonstrated successful cluster densities of six to eight units per acre, and mobile homes are usually smaller than conventional homes. However, cluster designs cannot be accomplished successfully simply by placing existing mobiles closer together. Complete redesign of units to be compatible with higher-density site conditions would be required, as would a thorough rethinking of site planning principles.

Potential for Reducing Operating Costs

Inflation results in large cost increases for park construction and all aspects of park management. If rents for mobile home spaces are to remain low, park management must seek ways to reduce these costs. On balance, there are few ways to limit operating costs once the park is constructed. One way is to build parks with more rental spaces. Not only are construction costs reduced on a per-space basis, but some fixed operating costs are substantially lower for larger parks. Wages for park personnel, costs of operating community buildings, advertising, insurance, legal and accounting costs, and office expenses will decrease per space as the number of spaces increases. There is a point where more personnel and facilities must be added to provide services for a larger number of tenants, but an economic analysis before the park is constructed should indicate an optimum operating size.

Another way to reduce costs is to use more sophisticated park financing methods in order to improve financing terms. If the interest rate can be reduced, yearly interest expense will be lower on a per-space basis. If the loan term can be extended, both interest and principal payments will be reduced on a per-space basis.

Perhaps the most effective way to reduce park operating costs is by considering alternatives to rental parks. Mobile home subdivisions and condominiums provide consumers with lower living costs because they are eligible for low-cost mortgage financing and profits from an equity buildup on land. Mobile home cooperatives provide consumers with a potentially appreciating asset, shares in the cooperative. All of these park arrangements can lead to lower monthly costs than do rental parks, thereby ensuring a growing demand for mobile homes and park spaces at the expense of conventional housing.

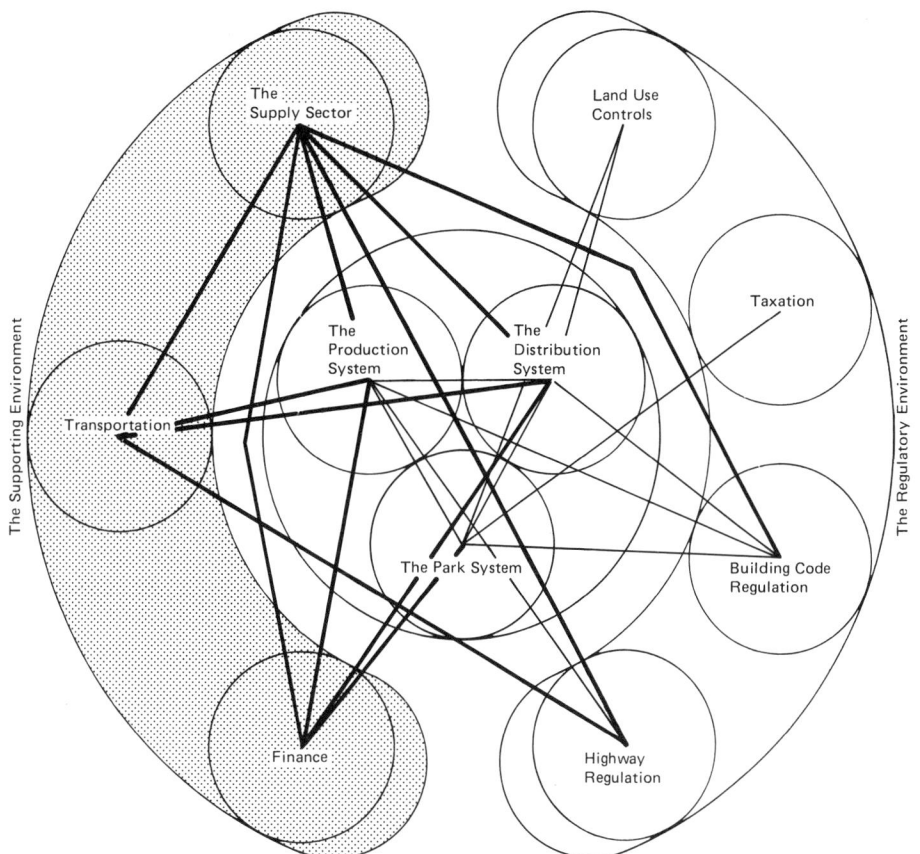

Chapter 13

Supply Sector
Influence

A. Model of the
Supply Sector

Statistical Overview
of the Supplying
Industries

There is little reason to expect suppliers to the mobile home industry to have anything more in common than the fact that they all provide this service function for the industry. Indeed, the differences between suppliers are great; the different companies offer a tremendous range of large and small products, and the proportion of business devoted to the mobile home industry varies greatly. On the other hand, it is interesting to note the extent to which these suppliers' behavior is similar. The following discussion stresses the extent to which the firms differ; we later consider the extent to which they behave similarly.

Figure 13.1 is a flow chart that traces the important movement of materials from the most basic industries to the final consumers of structures. Although this chart does not begin to capture the full flavor of the complexity of the supply sector, it does amply demonstrate the breadth of the supplying industries.

PMHI's Supplier Survey (PMHI/SS) polled all companies that are known or that we could identify as suppliers to the mobile home industry. To facilitate analysis of the nationwide survey, we classified products into eight relatively distinct categories. Table 13.1 presents the definitional platform for this classification, which we used because it seems that on a priori grounds supplier behavior will be more uniform within a category than between categories. (Any further reference to "product category" refers to this classification.)

The products of all known suppliers and the products reported by survey respondents were categorized in order to compare the sample with its universe. A total of 259 firm-category combinations were reported in the sample. The survey is representative in the middle six categories. The extremes are underrepresented both in percentage and absolute terms, which suggests that no conclusions based on statistical inference will be reached regarding these categories.

The PMHI/SS gives information on entrance into a supplying field but does not consider exit. Annual industry directories are useful in this respect because they present the total number of suppliers at any one time. Examination of these numbers suggests that change is one constant suppliers share. In a sample of 100 products manufactured in 1971 and 1972, the number of suppliers declined for almost three out of four products. Equally interesting is the amount by which the number of suppliers changed in one year's time: In 23 percent of the sample cases, the number of suppliers in 1972 was less than half the number in 1971. A similar comparison of a larger period, 1969 to 1974, displayed the same phenomenon. Declines outnumbered advances in almost the same ratio.

The responses of surveyed firms that reported their sales for 1967, 1972, and 1977 indicate that, as a rule, suppliers have not shared in the expansion of the mobile home industry. We computed the percentage change in sales over the pre–1974 recession period, 1967–1972, using 1967 sales as a base. Some suppliers contracted; in fact, 7.2 percent showed less than zero growth. More than 50 percent showed 1 percent or less growth. One firm grew 91 percent over this period, but the vast majority lost ground to inflation. The growth record is broken down by the category of the principal product in table 13.2. The standard deviations are so large that none of these means is significantly different from zero statistically, and they are clearly not significantly different from each other.

Although the manufacture of mobile homes today requires less intrafirm self-reliance, this has not prevented some mobile home producers from increasing their self-sufficiency. Over 10 percent of the PMHI/SS respondents stated that upstream integration of manufacturers had eroded their sales. Mobile home manufacturers are apparently unlikely to integrate into raw materials or accessory add-ons. The latter is particularly surprising because manufacturers would seem to have a comparative advantage in this area. There are some mobile home manufacturers involved in the production of raw materials, a few quite deeply. In general, this category should be fundamentally immune from erosion until mobile home manufacturers become considerably more advanced. The erosion is spread evenly across categories 3 through 7. Manufacturers that we interviewed are predicting an uneven pace of integration through the early 1980s, with some activities being increasingly turned over to suppliers and some being taken away. One manufacturer estimated a substantial reduction in the number of plants producing framing members and roofing trusses in-plant and a substantial increase in the number involved in chassis, heating ducts, and doors. This manufacturer also felt that by 1985 all firms would leave the production of furniture to suppliers.

Although erosion of sales through manufacturer integration may be one factor behind the general decline in the many product fields before 1974, integration could hardly be held responsible for the incredible turnover. It should be remembered that exiting from the role of supplier to the mobile home industry does not mean exiting from business: Supplying the mobile home industry often requires a more committed approach than supplying other sectors of the housing industry.

Because the mobile home industry utilizes conventional building materials as well as materials and equipment not traditionally

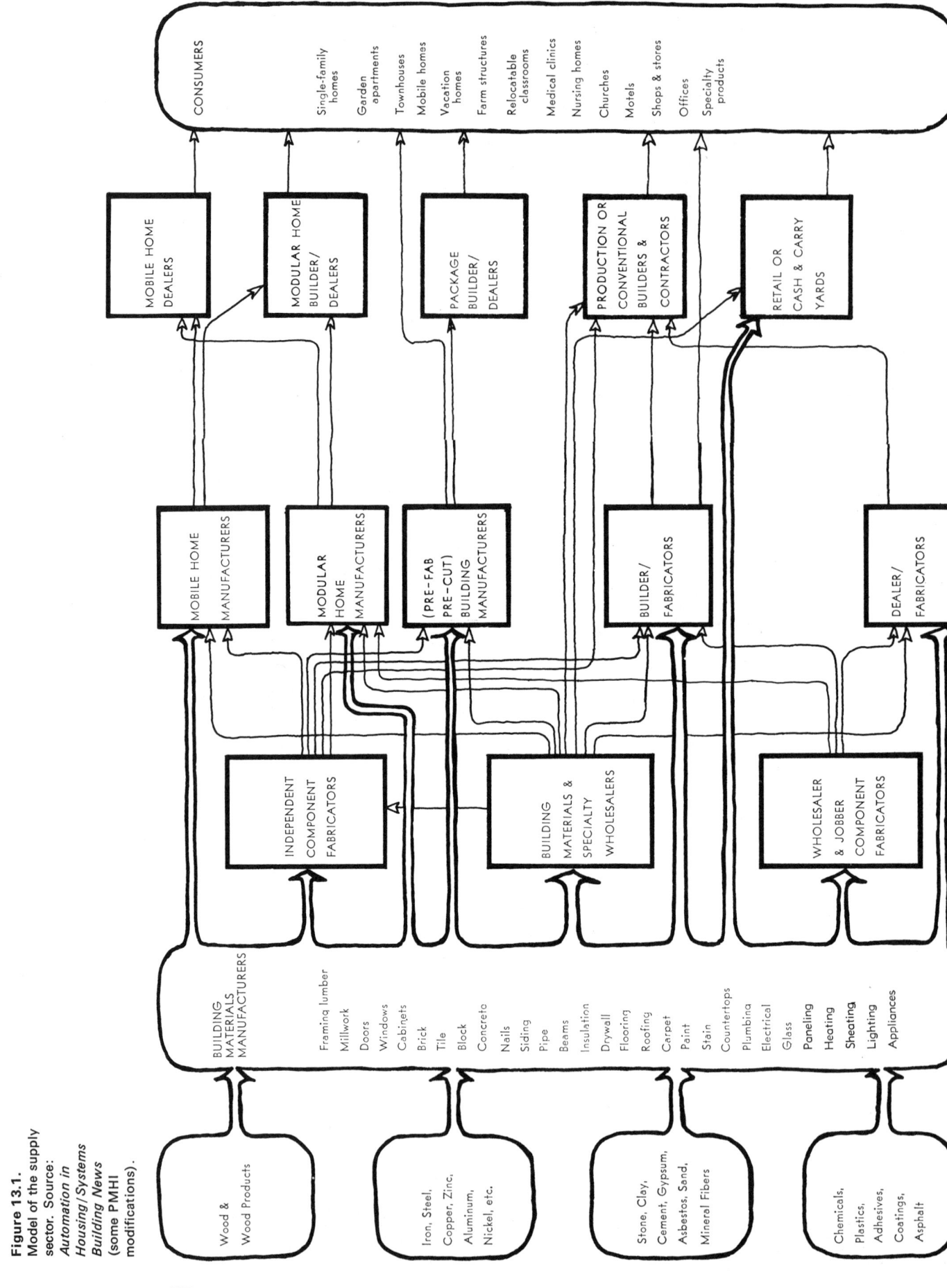

Figure 13.1.
Model of the supply
sector. Source:
*Automation in
Housing/Systems
Building News*
(some PMHI
modifications).

CONSUMERS

Single-family homes
Garden apartments
Townhouses
Mobile homes
Vacation homes
Farm structures
Relocatable classrooms
Medical clinics
Nursing homes
Churches
Motels
Shops & stores
Offices
Specialty products

MOBILE HOME DEALERS

MODULAR HOME BUILDER/ DEALERS

PACKAGE BUILDER/ DEALERS

PRODUCTION OR CONVENTIONAL BUILDERS & CONTRACTORS

RETAIL OR CASH & CARRY YARDS

MOBILE HOME MANUFACTURERS

MODULAR HOME MANUFACTURERS

(PRE-FAB PRE-CUT) BUILDING MANUFACTURERS

BUILDER/ FABRICATORS

DEALER/ FABRICATORS

INDEPENDENT COMPONENT FABRICATORS

BUILDING MATERIALS & SPECIALTY WHOLESALERS

WHOLESALER & JOBBER COMPONENT FABRICATORS

BUILDING MATERIALS MANUFACTURERS

Framing lumber
Millwork
Doors
Windows
Cabinets
Brick
Tile
Block
Concrete
Nails
Siding
Pipe
Beams
Insulation
Drywall
Flooring
Roofing
Carpet
Paint
Stain
Countertops
Plumbing
Electrical
Glass
Paneling
Heating
Sheating
Lighting
Appliances

Wood & Wood Products

Iron, Steel, Copper, Zinc, Aluminum, Nickel, etc.

Stone, Clay, Cement, Gypsum, Asbestos, Sand, Mineral Fibers

Chemicals, Plastics, Adhesives, Coatings, Asphalt

Table 13.1.
Product Category
Schema

Product Category	Production Requirement				
	Manufacturing, Fabricating (Subtracting, Forming)	Assembly, Normally Off-line	On-line Installation	Little or No Assembly (Hook-up, Plugging in, Loading)	Prototypical Product
1. Tools, machines, supplies used in production					Stapler, staples
2. Raw materials	×				Lumber, particle board
3. Prepared materials (precut, prefinished, preformed)	×				Paneling
4. Parts (one-piece, one material)		×			Casters, wheels
5. Components (several pieces, several materials)		×			Prehung doors
6. Subassemblies (major, 3-D)			×		Chassis, wet cores
7. Finished elements				×	Refrigerator
8. Add-ons				×	Awnings, skirts

Source: Developed by PMHI.

Table 13.2.
Growth by Category
of Principal Product

Category	Mean	Standard Deviation	N
1. Tools	1.393	1.926	5
2. Raw materials	1.605	1.260	20
3. Prepared materials	1.375	2.094	15
4. Parts	7.971 (3.084)	21.017	18
5. Components	1.185	1.150	15
6. Subassemblies	1.377	1.855	23
7. Finished elements	1.515	1.081	15
8. Add-ons	.482	.328	2
All firms	2.445 (1.638)	74.8483	113

Source: PMHI/SS.

used in on-site building, the variety of corporate backgrounds is understandable. Mobile homes are generally supplied furnished and with a complete set of appliances, so it is far from surprising that fourteen PMHI/SS respondents reported a background in furniture and sixteen in electrical machinery. A great deal of metal is incorporated into mobile home design, and sixteen firms were in metal and metal fabrication. A background in lumber, which includes traditional building supplies as well as firms created to supply the mobile home industry, was reported by thirty-four firms. Wholesaling, an important function of suppliers because many of them rely on independent wholesalers, was the background of twenty-three firms.

When asked to define their corporate activities, as production, marketing, warehousing, or other, most PMHI/SS respondents (79.3 percent) listed production, 38.3 percent reported warehousing, 44.7 percent were involved in marketing, and 13.9 percent noted other activities, which ranged from consultant to importer. The most common mix of activities is production, warehousing, and marketing, which is a reasonable combination for a supplier. The pairing of production and marketing is a viable strategy given the concentrations of mobile home manufacturers and the presence of independent distributors in these markets. Many firms report that their activities include production but not marketing, which is understandable because many products do not require marketing in the sense that consumer goods do. Independent distributors abound, as do manufacturer's representatives who specialize in mobile home accounts.

There are several measures of size that could be used to classify suppliers. One measure is simply the number of products sold to the mobile home industry. A substantial number of firms sell a single product for use in mobile homes, and eleven of the PMHI/SS respondents sell as many as six or more. A product is not clearly defined: A firm that said it produced ornamental iron work could only be counted as selling one product when in fact it may be producing a variety of railings, light posts, and mailbox supports. This measure of size is rather simplistic and merely indicates that the modal firm produces one product. It does, however, lead to questions regarding the nature of multiproduct firms. The internal diversity of suppliers is a matter of some interest because it may provide further clues to their nature. A diverse firm will be defined as one whose second most important product is in a different category than its first. Any firm that produces more than one product has shown some diversity when categories are so broadly drawn. Statistical analysis indicated that the category of the first product is an excellent predictor of the second's category. Such a finding should not be allowed to cloud the fact that 68 percent of multiproduct firms are

defined as diverse. One explanation for this diversity is the adaptability and dynamism of these firms: Opportunity is exploited. This may be one factor accounting for the apparent rapid entrance and exit of suppliers; similarly, merger activity may result in declining numbers and diversity.

In classifying suppliers by size, firm size has traditionally been measured either by assets or by sales. Two measures of sales are available from the PMHI/SS: sales of the individual products and total company sales. Some firms in the sample had fifth product sales of over $8 million per year, and one firm's sales were this large for its sixth product. It is almost as likely for a multiproduct firm's second product to have sales of perhaps more than $1 million as a randomly chosen firm's first product. The small size of some of these suppliers is best shown by examining total company sales as well as sales by product. Almost one-third (31.9 percent) of the PMHI/SS respondents had sales of less than $2 million. A little more than one-half (55.8 percent) had sales between $2 million and $50 million. The remainder had greater sales, with 8 percent recording more than $100 million. In terms of numerical importance, relatively small firms predominate; but this picture changes dramatically when these numbers or percentages are weighted by sales. If small firms average $1 million and if those in the next category average $25 million, their combined sales would be equal to the combined sales of the top 8 percent of firms if these companies averaged $175 million. Some firms in the sample had sales of over $1 billion. This suggests that two equally important tiers of suppliers exist. One tier contains a small number of large and very large firms, and the other consists of a large number of small and smaller firms. What is true of one tier may have little bearing on the other.

One thing that distinguishes suppliers is the importance of the mobile home industry to them. A measure of this is the percentage of their total sales derived from the industry. For example, the mobile home industry is important to Georgia-Pacific, which in 1977 derived 4 percent ($163 million) of its sales of over $3.5 billion from the industry. Although it is debatable whether a firm that does 100 percent of its business of $163 million feels that the mobile home industry is more important to it than Georgia-Pacific does, it is clear that both value this business highly. We would expect, however, that a comparison of two firms with identical total sales would indicate that the percentage to the mobile home industry would be reflected in the firm's behavior. Of the PMHI/SS respondents, 37.6 percent did no more than 10 percent of their business with the mobile home industry and 75.1 percent did no more than 75 percent. There is a tendency for firms to be either heavily dependent on the mobile home industry or relatively independent of it.

The first element of a model of interaction between suppliers and manufacturers is the nature of a "product." In selecting a supplier of a particular product, the manufacturer will not decide solely on the basis of price and quality but will also consider service. We thus extend the concept of product to include the elements of service: The manufacturer must choose a package that includes quality and may also include frequency and reliability of delivery, credit policy, availability of support, and other aspects.

The mobile home manufacturer is a potential competitor of any supplier, although this potential varies with the particular product. Suppliers must therefore provide manufacturers with a package that is superior to one they could provide for themselves. This is particularly true for the service elements of the package. A manufacturer could buy a discount product, denuded of service elements, and supply the services itself if the discount adequately compensated for the increased costs. The maximum discount a supplier would offer is the saving from services unperformed. Suppliers will provide those service elements they can perform less expensively than the manufacturer. Indirect costs are also important. If the user has limited financial capital and a range of open opportunities, the rational user will utilize the capital in those opportunities that offer the highest rates of return. A mobile home manufacturer with limited capital may purchase a product it could manufacture at lower cost if producing it means diverting capital from activities with higher rates of return.

Users ability to produce for themselves establishes an upper limit on the price a supplier can charge. The presence of substitutes may establish a lower limit price: The maximum price a supplier can charge without losing a customer is governed by the price of substitutes. A supplier of lumber for studs is limited by the availability, actual and potential, of aluminum or steel framing. In the limit substitutes become perfect; the availability of substitutes for lumber becomes the availability of lumber from other suppliers. Competition may not only establish a limit price but will also usually establish it within a range in which the market price will fall. The threat of competition will often moderate the market price. If there are two suppliers in a market, each may be able to do quite well—well enough to encourage a third to enter. To forestall such entry, existing firms may attempt to create entry barriers. One barrier is to keep the price within reason so that entry is not as profitable. Users of a product can either increase this power or threaten to. Merger or growth may enable users to supply themselves at a cost not much higher than that of the most efficient supplier.

The supplier must determine the elements of his or her product package. By expanding the service component, the supplier has a superior product that will command a higher price. The supplier has an incentive to provide every increment to his or her service and product quality for which the user is willing to pay. No service will be offered that users value for less than the supplier's expense to provide it. If all suppliers provided such a service, an adroit supplier would offer a reduced price and less service and increase its profits. It is important to recognize that suppliers do not provide such an extensive range of services because they are the docile servants of the mobile home industry but rather that they serve their own self-interest, which coincides with that of the users. A very large and secure supplier wishing to guarantee a return on its "investment" might take steps to nourish a growing industry in order to expand its market in the future. However, it is unlikely that the services mobile home suppliers offer are designed to encourage industry growth. The service behavior of suppliers is too uniform for this to be the case because many suppliers are not large and secure. In addition, we found that suppliers as a rule have not shared in the industry's growth.

Mobile homes have had a relatively short history as a major force in the building industry. Originally, products used in mobile home manufacture were frequently adapted from those intended for use in conventional housing construction. The development of supplies specific in their application to mobile home production has been an important element in the reduction of costs and the development of product quality in the mobile home industry. Respondents to the PMHI/SS identified their principal product as being specific to the mobile home industry 53.6 percent of the time, and 47.7 percent of all products were so listed. As the mobile home industry continues to develop, the need for additional specific products will presumably grow. Approximately two-thirds of the responding suppliers intended to expand their product lines in the near future, with the proposed expansion being nearly equal in all product lines.

Responses to the PMHI/SS revealed that many of the two-thirds of suppliers planning to expand their product lines were actively engaged in ongoing research and development (R&D) efforts. Many of these suppliers indicated that their R&D efforts were specifically aimed at the mobile home industry; 38 percent were oriented exclusively in this direction. This is an extremely high figure, especially when combined with the 31.5 percent of this set oriented toward the mobile home industry, the manufactured building industry, and the on-site building industry and the 16.5 percent oriented toward both the mobile home industry and the manufactured building industry. The R&D orientations of all sampled firms and those that supply at least one mobile home-specific

B. Product Development

Supplier Research and Development

product are compared in table 13.3. In categories 2 through 6, suppliers with a mobile home-specific product are a higher percentage of firms doing R&D with a mobile home orientation than they are of all suppliers. Although the expected pattern develops, it is not as marked as one might expect. It indicates that suppliers without a mobile home-specific product are as often at work developing one as firms that already have one. Mobile home specificity was interpreted as an expression of supplier concern for and understanding of the constraints of the mobile home industry, and the amount of this concern and understanding was found to be considerable. This concern is obviously not compassionate; rather, it represents the dispassionate belief of suppliers that such efforts are rewarding to them.

R&D with specific reference to the mobile home industry is surprisingly prevalent. Table 13.4 shows that this macro picture is true for all sizes of firms in all categories. Although the smallest firms report a surprising amount of R&D, their activity should be weighted by the resources they have to devote to this effort. Among small firms, only parts suppliers seem to have become complacent. Larger suppliers in this category seem to take up the slack. We investigated the growth record of all suppliers now doing R&D and found that these firms have shared in the growth of the mobile home industry to a greater extent than have firms that are not now performing R&D. Their current R&D posture may result in part from their higher rate of growth or their current R&D posture may reflect past successes that resulted in growth.

Devoting resources to R&D without understanding what the market wants is often not a fruitful use of resources. The supplier may have the clearest conception of what is possible and the best way to attack a problem, but the mobile home manufacturer is most likely to have a better idea of what is needed. There is in fact much communication between suppliers and mobile home manufacturers and necessary information is often exchanged through this channel. Of the PMHI/SS respondents, 76.1 percent rely on this method, 65 percent rely on indirect communication via salesperson feedback, and 36.3 percent utilize both. Some mobile home manufacturers have reported making frequent visits to suppliers' facilities.

Other means of obtaining information are also employed. Some firms, typically large ones, have in-house market research facilities and staffs. Private market research consultants may also be hired. The mobile home industry, in its collective interest and through its national association, created the Design Council of Industrialized Housing (now defunct) to help spur new product development through direct work with suppliers and potential suppliers. One firm in the PMHI/SS commented that its products are designed

within well-defined constraints; there is no need for any explicit communication in this situation. This attitude is undoubtedly more general than the sole response indicates. Influences like an energy crisis or new regulations have an impact on the likely direction of future R&D, and little communication is required for suppliers to comprehend this. One firm said that it relied on spies. In breaking down the methods used for generating information by firm size we found that all sizes of firms work closely with mobile home manufacturers. If there is any tendency, it is for larger firms to make greater use of the "other" means of generating information.

Collectively, mobile home manufacturers are cognizant of the importance to them of R&D oriented to mobile home supplies. However, mobile home manufacturers, with notable exceptions, are unlikely to devote their own resources to R&D, which is an expensive and risky enterprise. An industry with R&D-conscious suppliers need not undertake any risk or expense but simply has to pay the price to be provided with a stream of new and improved products.

Role of the Manufacturer

Firms likely to do their own R&D are large companies active in both the supply and manufacturing functions that possess both the resources and expertise to make this feasible. These companies have a large enough market to benefit from any progress and have the facilities to capitalize easily on any results.

The MHI created the Design Council for Industrialized Housing in large part to encourage the improvement of suppliers' products. The Design Council took the concrete step of becoming directly involved in supply development by establishing as a nonprofit corporation a Research Center designed to serve the best interests of industrialized housing as a whole. However, by the mid-1970s both the Design Council and the Research Center were inactive, and by 1977 they had been phased out.[1] Although the Center was intended to finance itself by performing client research for a fee, research results were available to all at no charge in order to serve wider interests. Some clients did come forward with research fees, but the Center's structure was not conducive to widespread utilization of its resources. The Center fell short of its potential to influence the direction of supply R&D to accomplish the wider and best interests of the mobile home industry and other segments of industrialized housing.

Although joint supplier-manufacturer R&D work is not reported by any of the respondents to the PMHI/SS, these two groups have often worked closely to guarantee that products developed by the supplier will be applicable to the specific uses of the manufacturer. For example, a supplier of plumbing

Joint Product Development

Table 13.3.
Comparison by Category of R&D Orientation and Mobile Home Specificity of Principal Product

Category of Firm's Principal Product	A Number of Firms with MH R&D Orientation	B Number of Firms with MH-Specific Product & MH R&D Orientation	C B/A × 100	D Specific Products as % of all Products	E Sign of C − D
1. Tools	6	1	16.7	80.0	−
2. Raw materials	13	9	69.2	57.7	+
3. Prepared materials	6	3	50.0	36.4	+
4. Parts	13	7	53.8	50.0	+
5. Components	14	4	28.6	28.6	0
6. Subassemblies	12	6	50.0	40.0	+
7. Finished elements	7	4	57.1	61.9	−
8. Add-ons	1	1	100	75.0	+

Source: PMHI/SS.

Table 13.4.
Size-Category Breakdown for All Firms with Mobile Home R&D Orientation and for Firms with Mobile Home-Specific Products with a Mobile Home R&D Orientation

Sales		Tools	Raw Materials	Prepared Materials	Parts	Components	Sub-assemblies	Finished Elements	Add-ons	Row Totals
$0–$2M	(a)	3[a]	4	1	2	3	7	2	—	22
	(b)	4[b]	5	3	14	5	14	4	3	52
	(c)	75.0[c]	80.0	33.3	14.3	60.0	50.0	50.0	0.0	42.3
$2–$50M	(a)	—[a]	8	4	9	6	8	5	1	41
	(b)	1[b]	16	10	14	12	19	12	1	85
	(c)	0.0[c]	50.0	40.0	64.3	50.0	42.1	41.7	100.0	48.2
$50–$100M	(a)	—[a]	—	—	—	1	—	—	—	1
	(b)	—[b]	1	1	—	1	—	3	—	6
	(c)	—[c]	0.0	0.0	—	100.0	—	0.0	—	16.7
$100M+	(a)	—[a]	1	1	1	2	1	—	—	6
	(b)	—[b]	2	4	2	2	2	1	—	13
	(c)	—[c]	50.0	25.0	50.0	100.0	50.0	0.0	—	46.1
Column Totals of a)		3	13	6	12	12	16	7	1	70

a. Firms with mobile home R&D orientation and mobile home-specific product.
b. Firms with mobile home R&D orientation.
c. a/b × 100.

Source: PMHI/SS.

fittings may work closely with a particular manufacturer to ensure that its product will match the dimensions selected by the manufacturer. The PMHI/SS reveals that twenty-one firms have worked with manufacturers to achieve dimensional coordination, twenty-five have worked jointly to achieve standardization, and seventy-five have worked for both.

The achievement of both dimensional coordination and standardization has immediate positive impacts. Dimensional coordination means that mobile home manufacturers have less trimming and fitting to do, and standardization increases their flexibility vis-à-vis suppliers by increasing the number of suppliers who produce a suitable product. Suppliers may be better able to take advantage of economies of scale, and these benefits may be passed in full or in part to the mobile home manufacturer. On the other hand, the mobile home industry has been criticized for sterility of design, which in turn has been blamed on the development of standardized supplies.

The mobile home specificity of a supplier's product is not a good predictor of whether joint work will occur. Presumably, firms without a mobile home-specific product have no less of an interest in dimensional coordination or standardization. Both raw and prepared materials suppliers exhibit a little higher than average joint work, and component and subassembly suppliers show even greater amounts. These results confirm a priori expectation because individual suppliers have the most to gain in these areas. A subassembly manufacturer who can offer a near perfect fit is better off than a competitor who cannot; thus the competitor will also strive for the same. Finished elements show considerably less than average joint work; again, this is in accord with a priori expectation. This does not imply that standardization and dimensional coordination have not been important or that they have not occurred, quite the contrary. For example, many range manufacturers make a 30-inch model, and refrigerators have standard sizes. For the most part, suppliers have instituted these standards without reference to the mobile home industry; rather, the mobile home industry works to the suppliers' standards. The exceptions are important and tend to occur in such products as furnaces and air conditioners; the mobile home market is more distinct than conventional markets in these areas than it is for furniture and appliances.

C. Sale and Distribution

Marketing

Mobile home supplies display a wide range of consumer anonymity. A product is anonymous if the tastes of the final consumer in no way impinge on the mobile home manufacturer's selection. Dimensional lumber rates very high in anonymity, and refrigerators, very low. For this reason, successful marketing of refrigerators requires a substantially different strategy than marketing of 2 × 3s. An anonymous product is in effect sold to the mobile

home manufacturer, not to the consumer. A consumer is interested in sound construction; but if the construction is guaranteed, a consumer would not generally care how, with what materials, or by whom the shell was built. Thus the supplier of an anonymous product directs its marketing efforts toward the mobile home manufacturer.

Nonanonymous products are in effect sold through the mobile home manufacturer to the final consumer. All other things being equal, consumers who prefer brand X refrigerators will most likely prefer mobile homes that contain these refrigerators. Manufacturers will want to supply those nonanonymous products that consumers prefer, other things being equal. This last qualification is especially important. The mobile home producer's involvement is more than simply as agent of the final consumers; the manufacturer has a real interest in the product as well. Products designed for conventional housing and with wide consumer acceptance may require modification or redesign to accommodate a mobile home environment. The supplier of nonanonymous products plays a major marketing role. The supplier must not only attempt to gain and maintain consumer loyalty but must also convince mobile home manufacturers and dealers that consumers prefer these products.

The importance of the consumer's tastes and the selection of nonanonymous products to the success of any mobile home manufacturer and the industry in general cannot be overstressed. When *Mobile/Manufactured Housing Merchandiser* surveyed dealers for their opinions on consumer preferences,[2] price was rated as the principal selling point, with second place shared by interior design and quality of construction. (We would note, however, that because only first choices were included in the survey, it does not present a complete picture of dealers' opinions.) Dealers rate the kitchen as the room consumers show the most interest in most often; the living room ranks second. These two rooms, which dominate the ratings, rely heavily on supplied products for their qualities. Kitchens in particular require design effort in the location of facilities because they cannot be inexpensively rearranged. The kitchen components themselves also play a major role. Appliances rate the highest for consumer brand name preference. Because air conditioning and furnaces are rated separately, most appliances are in the kitchen. Brand names are also important in the second most important room, the living room, and were considered somewhat or very important in carpeting, paneling, and furniture. It should be clear that mobile home manufacturers are extremely dependent on suppliers to provide what consumers desire and that it is the supplier's responsibility for marketing aimed at the consumer. The supplier's marketing effort aimed at manufacturers consists of pointing out the strength of consumers' preferences for the product.

There is one classic example of how a supplier, by understanding the mobile home industry and its unique constraints, was able to dominate the market for its product. The case involves furnaces, which are not a completely anonymous product. The consumer wants a furnace with a guarantee and the mobile home manufacturer wishes to provide it; but some furnace manufacturers will not supply furnaces for mobile homes because they have no control over where these units are going to end up and thus will not guarantee the service factor on them. The dominant heating plant manufacturer in the mobile home industry captured the lion's share of the market because it not only designed a product specifically for mobile homes but also created a service organization to deal with the unique problem of a heating plant that is installed one place and operates somewhere else. Intertherm, Inc. is this leading furnace supplier to the mobile home industry; it offers a one-year warranty, maintains sixteen hundred service personnel across North America, provides prompt delivery from seventeen warehouses, and offers an extensive line of furnaces tailored to the needs of the mobile home industry. Ninety-five percent of Intertherm's business is mobile home-related and it is prepared to keep this business.

The marketing of anonymous products differs substantially from that of nonanonymous products. If the mobile home manufacturer is regarded as the final consumer of anonymous products, what does it take to market these products successfully? The key points of interest to the manufacturer are price, quality, and service, in no specific order. A manufacturer is prepared to trade off service for price or quality and by assumption knows the nature and results of such trade-offs. A low-quality item can be sold only at correspondingly low price. The producer's calculus and the consumer's calculus may differ; if an improvement in quality is worth less to the consumer than it costs the supplier to provide, such an improvement would not be offered. There is a very powerful incentive for suppliers to provide every increment of quality or service or both that is worth the effort. The level of expertise on both sides makes this imperative. Mobile home manufacturers are receptive to innovations, which is evidenced by the fact that the industry itself is an innovation utilizing innovative materials and applying original techniques (for the housing industry) to them. Price is a self-explanatory variable in the user's calculus; quality and service are not. Fundamental mobile home production materials change as prices change. Where once aluminum was used to support walls, wooden studs are now the industry standard. If relative prices change, mobile home manufacturers adjust.

Quality is a catchall concept and includes such things as style, performance, useful life, ease of handling and installation, and coordination with other inputs. Any product that is easier to work with or results in a more valuable final product is a higher-quality product. Any firm that offers such a product can expect, other things being equal, to sell more of its product or collect a higher price or both. The furnace example is a case in point and there are others. For instance, particle board is made by compressing wood fibers in a matrix of adhesive. It is a very strong material and is less expensive to produce than plywood. It makes an excellent material for subfloors provided that it is kept dry; it loses its strength when wet. Because particle board can be kept dry during construction in a mobile home assembly plant, it is not surprising that it is used almost universally for mobile home subflooring. Another case in point is insulation. Fiberglass mat insulation is supplied in widths to fit stud pockets in conventional housing. Mobile home construction is different; Owens-Corning, for instance, supplies rolls of insulation in widths that exactly fit mobile homes.

The components of service include credit, warehousing and delivery, and technical advice and support. A supplier that increases its service stands to gain business from alert mobile home manufacturers. It might be thought that an R&D effort on the part of suppliers should be characterized as a service, but this is not really the case. Although such an effort may result in a service to the industry, it provides no immediate incentive to the individual mobile home manufacturer to do business with this supplier.

How do suppliers market their products to the mobile home industry? Major firms in the building materials industries have established specially trained sales forces to handle these accounts. National Gypsum teaches its salespeople servicing the mobile home industry to be attuned to it, both technically and psychologically. Not only are they set up to call on members of the industry and provide them with goods and services, but they are also trained to inform the company of new ideas the manufacturer might have or immediate or future products and service needs. Suppliers also provide technical support in the proper use of new products.

A successful marketing strategy for suppliers is long on service and quality. One reason for this is that mobile home manufacturers are appreciative and discriminating buyers. Suppliers could use such a marketing strategy to maintain their market power. By possessing good foresight and meeting the needs of mobile home manufacturers, suppliers may carve a niche for themselves in a specialized corner of the housing market, a market that is theirs to exploit.

Distribution is an important component of a comprehensive marketing strategy. The better the distribution, the easier the product is to sell. Furthermore, because distribution is one vehicle for entering new markets, effective distribution can be essential for firm growth. Suppliers are keenly aware of the importance of effective distribution. Ineffective distribution, in the words of one executive, is "tantamount to withdrawing from some markets."[3]

For the smallest firms, the decisions on distribution and plant location are coincident; the firm will serve the market in which it is located. Somewhat larger suppliers may require more than a single market area to justify this scale. If economies of scale in production are unimportant, the product is expensive to transport, or both, a reasonable means of entering a new market is to open a production facility in that market. If either of these conditions is not met, other options become viable. The firm may open a distribution center, warehouse, sales office, or all three or it may contract with an independent distributor to distribute its products. The extent of the new market plays an important role. A small market may justify independent, but not in-house, distribution or it may justify in-house distribution but not a production facility. Independents have an advantage in that they can distribute many firms' products; thus each supplier can have its products distributed in markets in which no individual firm could afford to distribute.

In-house distribution is expensive. An executive of Waste-King Corp. noted that he is "painfully aware that it takes dollars to do this [in-house distribution], dollars that we would normally use in the development of new products or the expansion of our product line. And it takes manpower and management talent." Boise Cascade distributes its own products in a number of states. According to one executive, "We do that to know what is going on in the field, but we demand a return on investment from that [each] distribution point." This firm relies heavily on independent distribution. In fact, when difficulties develop, "Our first desire is to find another one [independent distributor] and help build him up." Of those firms that rely on independents, this seems to be the strategy for improving the effectiveness of distribution. Fortunately for those firms that rely on independents, "It is a strange market that doesn't have one good distributor or one which could be built into a good distributor." But there are also costs associated with reliance on independents since "nobody is as interested in selling a product as the manufacturer."[4]

In many respects, mobile home manufactures are more demanding of distribution than is the conventional building industry. To do business with a single mobile home manufacturer a firm may have to be prepared to supply a number of geographically separate plants because mobile home manufacturers prefer to purchase principal materials centrally and to produce regionally. Mobile home manufacturers are also demanding in that they hold little inventory and thus require frequent delivery and more backup warehousing.

There are three identifiable stages of the distribution system. The first stage is the location of each industry's production facilities. As an example, in plotting the locations of the known suppliers of frames and frame components, we found that all of the top ten producing states (Alabama, California, Florida, Georgia, Idaho, Indiana, North Carolina, Oregon, Pennsylvania, Texas) are served by at least one supplier. The nature of this product suggests that proximity to mobile home manufacturers is a powerful locational influence; this is evidenced by the sometimes close proximity of one firm's facilities to each other.

We also plotted the state locations of all the coded production and warehouse facilities of the firms in the PMHI/SS. Many of the suppliers' products are used by other industries; every state has a housing industry, and 50 percent of the products are not mobile home-specific. But it is clear that states that produce a great many mobile homes do receive special attention. Suppliers cannot rely solely on their own warehouses for distribution. When we plotted the location of every known independent distributor, we found that there are so many that their locations define almost every center of mobile home production in the country. Greater Boise's production ranks Idaho high in mobile home production. Three production and nine warehouse facilities from the sample are in Idaho, and one frame facility and ten distributors are located in Boise. This latter concentration of distributors makes Boise one of the largest centers of independent distributors. Michigan, on the other hand, has access to one frame facility located conveniently in Elkhart, Indiana, as well as fifteen production and nine warehouse facilities, but only three distributors. One explanation for these phenomena is that so-called Michigan firms are extremely integrated and self-reliant; obviously, a firm that manufactures a product for its own consumption need not rely on an independent distributor. Another factor is history; suppliers may be slower than distributors to respond to the switch in mobile home emphasis from Michigan to Idaho.

Suppliers have two options for entering a market: They can sell directly to the mobile home manufacturer or indirectly through an independent distributor. We have generated a number of hypotheses as to what kind of firm will choose which option. Table 13.5 divides the PMHI/SS firms into thirty-two size and category cells and reports the number of firms in each cell that utilize local dealers to some degree, the number that do not, and the percentage of the total that do. In six categories there is less reliance on local dealers as sales pass the $2 million mark.

Table 13.5.
Size-Category Classification of Firms That Do and Do Not Utilize Local Dealers

Sales		Tools	Raw Materials	Prepared Materials	Parts	Components	Sub-assemblies	Finished Elements	Add-ons
				Category of Firm's principal Product					
$0–2M	a)	4[a]	3	3	11	3	6	2	3
	b)	(–)[b]	(2)	(–)	(3)	(2)	(8)	(2)	(–)
	c)	100[c]	60	100	78.5	60	42.8	50	100
$2–50M	a)	—[a]	7	4	10	4	11	2	1
	b)	(1)[b]	(9)	(6)	(4)	(8)	(8)	(10)	(–)
	c)	—[c]	43.7	40	71.4	33.3	57.9	16.7	100
$50–100M	a)	—[a]	1	1	—	1	—	1	—
	b)	(–)[b]	(–)	(–)	(–)	(–)	(–)	(2)	(–)
	c)	—[c]	100	100	—	100	—	33.3	—
$100M +	a)	—[a]	2	3	1	1	2	—	—
	b)	(–)[b]	(–)	(1)	(1)	(1)	(–)	(1)	(–)
	c)	—[c]	100	75	50	50	100	—	—

a. Number of firms in cell that market through a local dealer.
b. Number of firms in cell that do not market through a local dealer.
c. a/(a+b) × 100.

Source: PMHI/SS.

This suggests that small firms require more assistance to distribute their products to the mobile home industry than slightly larger firms, which can afford to take over some or all of the distribution responsibilities. Large firms with sales over $100 million seem to rely on local dealers to a major degree. These firms require more distribution services and rely on local dealers to provide some portion of these services. The largest firms thus reverse the tendency observed among smaller ones. These suppliers are distributing their products to corners of the mobile home market that in-house distribution cannot profitably reach, and thus there is need for independent distribution. In addition, large firms are more likely to be supplying other, more geographically dispersed segments of the housing industry, which may account for some portion of their increased reliance on independent distribution.

Inventory and Delivery

Service is an integral component of suppliers' marketing strategies. Mobile home manufacturers maintain extemely low supply inventories. Convenient, frequent, and reliable delivery is necessary to make such a policy viable; and this requires good distribution and warehousing. Inventory is a continuity guarantee and as such is of the utmost importance to an assembly line. Mobile home manufacturers place a very high value on quality inventory services, but inventory services are expensive. This is especially true at low volumes, for inventory is characterized by economies of scale. Because of these economies of scale, mobile home manufacturers will trust such an important function as inventory to outside agents. There are at least two economies of scale associated with inventory. The first is straightforward: It simply takes less than twice the resources to manage an inventory twice as large, and this is especially true with electronic data processing. The second economy is more subtle and treats inventory as a continuity guarantee. The larger the inventory, the better the guarantee. A family maintains a medicine chest for similar reasons. Doubling the size of the family does not necessitate doubling the size of the medicine chest to provide each member with the same level of guarantee that they had previously. Such an economy will exist unless sickness and accidents strike every member at the same time. If two mobile home manufacturers inventory, a third party could provide both with the same guarantee while holding less than their combined inventory.

When suppliers are hard pressed to supply inventory, they can and do rely on independent local dealers who can exploit the same economies of scale. The allied services that combine to provide inventory services display a maximum price mobile home manufacturers will pay that is greater than the minimum price that suppliers and their agents require to provide it. The existence of the independent dealer rests on this differential.

Rapid and frequent delivery is the cornerstone of the inventory-by-supplier policy. Most suppliers deliver directly to some of their clients; many of these firms also deliver to local dealers for future delivery. Even firms with no warehousing report direct delivery. This is sensible when a product is relatively inexpensive to transport because production at one point will be competitive with production at many other points. It also makes sense when transportation is expensive because in such a case production for local consumption is to be expected. When asked whether they delivered daily, weekly, monthly, or other, a surprising number of PMHI/SS respondents offered daily delivery; thirty-two firms delivered daily to small firms and forty-five offered such service to large firms. With both sizes the modal response was weekly delivery. Weekly delivery to small firms is offered by 51.7 percent of suppliers and to large firms by 57.6 percent.

Trade Credit

Most suppliers offer some form of credit to users and other purchasers of their products; thirty days credit is the standard policy. Of 184 PMHI/SS respondents who reported their accounts receivable policy, 152 offered a thirty-day term, 6 offered a sixty-day term, and 3, a ninety-day term; 48 said they offered some other policy.

Much has been made of independent distributors' ability to provide services to the mobile home manufacturer that the supplier can or will not provide. One of these services is credit, which is expensive. A small firm may be competitive with a large firm only if its products can be sold on credit; the existence of distributors makes this competition feasible. Comparison of suppliers' delivery and credit policies provides some insight: Firms that deliver to mobile home manufacturers are more likely to offer credit than firms that do not.

Many mobile home manufacturers rely on suppliers to finance the construction of mobile homes at least to some extent. A strategy that might be followed is to order supplies on credit, build presold mobile homes, collect for these upon delivery, pay off suppliers within the credit period, and order anew. Because materials make up the large part of the costs of a mobile home, a substantial reduction in the amount of "front" money is achieved by such a policy. A given amount of front money also builds more mobile homes. For the most part, mobile home manufacturers have a thirty-day period to build and collect before interest is charged, and this is generally enough time to avoid paying the interest. This is especially true when small inventories are held, which is often done by mobile home manufacturers.

Many suppliers provided details of their credit posture, though this was not requested by the PMHI/SS. It is difficult to judge the generality of these postures on the basis of such responses. Many firms reported that interest is charged on the balance only after the balance has been due for thirty days. An interesting feature, however, is that cash discounts are offered. A representative example is 2 percent for payment within ten days. It is a mistake to think of this as thirty-day

credit; it is ten-day credit. There is a rather large penalty involved for payment within ten to thirty days. For example, if one ordered supplies nominally worth $100, they would cost $98 if paid for within ten days and $100 if paid for within ten to thirty days. Delaying payment past the tenth day costs $2 (2.04 percent of $98); this is equivalent to borrowing $98 for ten days at 6.12 percent per month or $98 for thirty days at 2.04 percent per month. These are rather large annual rates. Purchasing supplies nominally worth $100 and delaying payment for thirty days is equivalent to borrowing $98 at an annual rate of 24.48 percent. Generally, 1.5 percent per month is charged on balances due for more than a month. In the above example, delaying payment sixty days is equivalent to borrowing $98 at an annual rate of 21.6 percent compounded monthly.

The PMHI/SS does not reveal how common cash discounts are. If it is a general policy and if mobile home manufacturers rely heavily on suppliers for financing, mobile home manufacturers pay very dearly for balances due past ten days. These are big ifs. If both conditions exist, they raise the question of why mobile home manufacturers rely on such an expensive form of credit. Because the answer to this question has important implications but relies on the above-mentioned conditions for validity, a more complete investigation of supplier credit is necessary.

Warehousing plays a central role in the service component of suppliers because it partially determines the quality of their inventory performance. We have seen that pockets of mobile home manufacture are accompanied by production and warehouse facilities. We found that as the percentage of sales to the mobile home industry rises, firms more often report that proximity is important in their decision to locate warehousing and production facilities. This is a very statistically significant relationship. Proximity seems to be relatively important for all categories, though there is a slight tendency for the importance of proximity to increase as the product category increases.

Production and warehousing facilities combine to provide a supplier's distribution system. The location of final demand is an important, but far from the only, determinant of the location of production facilities. Only 44.2 percent of the PMHI/SS suppliers felt that proximity was important for their production facilities. Parts and finished element manufacturers in particular do not as a rule consider proximity important. The location of final demand is also an important determinant of warehouse facilities; the difference, of course, is that there are few other determinants. Parts and finished elements have shown a remarkable turnaround. The percentage considering proximity important has

Warehousing

increased in every category save the extremes, where the number of observations is very small. The gross percentage favoring proximity has risen to 63.1 percent.

It is to be expected that the larger the firm, the more warehouses it can and will afford. A smaller firm is apt to make relatively more use of independent warehousing and distribution. These hypotheses were borne out at exceptional levels of significance. Of the PMHI/SS firms with sales under $2 million, 21.3 percent maintain two or more warehouses; 35.8 percent of the firms with sales between $2 and $50 million and 46.7 percent of the firms with sales over $100 million maintain three or more. (It is interesting that 40 percent of the firms with sales over $100 million maintain one or fewer warehouses; but this last finding is based on a small sample, so no attempt was made to analyze further the characteristics of these firms.)

There can be little doubt that suppliers as a group recognize the importance of providing high-quality delivery service; locating warehouses at critical points is one way of providing this. This is clear not only from suppliers' statements but also by their collective behavior, which has resulted in extensive distribution networks supplemented by local distributors.

Technical Support Services

Suppliers offer mobile home manufacturers a variety of special services, including maintenance of specialized sales forces and expert support. The specialized sales force often works with other experts to provide technical assistance. This is an extremely valuable service and is a partial guarantee that mobile home manufacturers are using the most effective methods of dealing with these supplies. Such staffs also benefit suppliers because their knowledge is of particular interest in the development and creation of supplies. The presence of these experts is a major input in the problem-solving function. A mobile home manufacturer in isolation may recognize that he or she has a problem but may not try to solve it because problem solving is expensive. A supplier's expert can afford to solve problems that a manufacturer cannot. The expert can use the results to solve other mobile home manufacturers' problems as well. An expert invests energy in learning all there is to know about product installation. Because this learning is a valuable resource to mobile home manufacturers, suppliers have an incentive to offer such services. It is clear that such a staff of experts and their commitment makes it almost mandatory for a competitor to offer equivalent service or to sell at a considerably lower price.

D. Policy Alternatives

The single most encouraging fact regarding the potentials for the improvement of the performance of the supply sector is that many of them will be realized as the natural outcomes of suppliers' business routines. However, there are others that either will not be

realized without concerted effort to bring them about or that need assistance to be realized. The suggestions we tender are not the only or the best solutions; only time and continued research can provide clearer perspectives on both potentials and viable strategies to fulfill them. The ideas we offer range from potentials for improving suppliers' products and services to potentials for reduced dependency upon suppliers. Supplier behavior is such that changes in one aspect are likely to be felt in others as well.

There will always be the potential for new and improved products and services, and suppliers are actively engaged in the process of tapping this potential. It is in the supplier's interest to be responsive to the expressed needs of the mobile home manufacturer and consumer. The potential for improvement lies in the development of mechanisms that will guarantee the full articulation of user needs. In the case of anonymous products, consumer desires pass through a number of levels before reaching the supplier. This presents no problem for a truly anonymous product for which consumers' preferences are irrelevant. However, interest in the characteristics of nearly anonymous products is growing, which makes communication between final consumer and supplier increasingly more important. The rapid growth of consumer advocacy and governmental watchdog agencies attests to this importance. Suppliers would be well advised to open direct channels with consumers rather than rely on secondhand inputs. The MHI can become more effective as a vehicle for the articulation of values that individual firms cannot express. Historically, the MHI's accomplishments have included comprehensive building standards and the Research Center, which expressed collective values to suppliers. The MHI must be encouraged to initiate more effective communication mechanisms, for it is the most likely vehicle for expressing the industry's collective desires to its suppliers.

Despite the various problems that led to the demise of the MHI's Research Center, we consider the concept of the Center a good one. We therefore suggest the establishment of a similar organization that would benefit from the lessons learned from the Research Center's failure. The Center resources would have been more effectively utilized under alternative financing schemes. As it was, the firm that financed research had no more right to the results than any other member of the industry. A supplier is not likely to pay for research that benefits others when it has its own research facilities. Suppliers might make greater use of a new organization's resources if the results were restricted, perhaps if the organization were structured along "club" grounds. Results would be restricted to the set of dues-paying members; suppliers would have an incentive to join, provided the results are valuable, and the new organization would have the financing to generate valuable results.

A less preferred alternative would be to encourage the formation of supplier consortiums for the purpose of financing the new organization's projects. Some supplying industries maintain associations, which are natural vehicles for instituting this alternative. The possibility is less preferable, however, because such consortiums may be used to establish and enforce monopoly practices. An interesting option is to encourage the MHI to finance projects in the interest of its manufacturing members. One way in which its members' dependence on suppliers is manifested is in the limited commitment to R&D. The new organization would be one vehicle that could be used to provide the industry with more control over its own destiny. The implementation of such a policy is complicated by the fact that not every manufacturer will view this policy in the same light. To some it will appear a waste of money; to others it will pose a threat to their own R&D programs.

Forward integration by suppliers, backward integration by manufacturers, and mergers offer a potential for improved supplies and services because there can be no communication problem when the same decision makers are involved in both the supply and manufacturing sectors. Manufacturers have shown more proclivity for the production of mobile home supplies than suppliers have for the production of mobile homes. (Boise Cascade was an important exception to this.) Mobile home manufacturers have been involved in the production of supplies from the beginning of the industry; therefore, it is not really new ground for them. Backward integration can improve communication and it can increase the effective competition between suppliers. Forward integration offers suppliers of anonymous products the ability to gain direct experience with both manufacturers' and final consumers' concerns. Assuming that nonsupply considerations would not contradict the desirability of increased integration, it is not immediately obvious in what ways integration or mergers can be stimulated. It is clear, however, that information and experience play a crucial role. Because there is already considerable variation among manufacturers in the extent of integration, the lack of experience will not necessarily retard the development of integrated firms.

There could be more standardization, dimensional coordination, and mobile home specificity of products supplied by the supply sector. At the same time, a potential for greater architectural variety exists. Suppliers are working in these directions and have achieved an impressive amount of specificity as well as standardization and dimensional coordination. In general, these are areas in which mobile home manufacturers can articulate the value they place on suppliers' accomplishments. Standardized supplies need not imply standardized homes. There can be greater standardization of architecturally neutral supplies without jeopardizing variety. Supplies that do not predetermine architectural expression possess a potential for greater variety.

There is the potential for increased interchangeability of parts and components between the different forms of housing offered today. This contradicts the potential for increased specialization of supplies. Increasing interchangeability to improve performance will require that the products be designed to the parameters and constraints of all segments of the housing industry. The mobile home consumer may find that purchasing replacement and accessory parts is more convenient as a result. Moreover, the development of such "multimarket" supplies would generate cost benefits through economies of scale, ease of distribution, and minimization of seasonality and would greatly increase the market of a specialized supplier. Interchangeability will allow mobile home-specific suppliers to expand into other segments of the building industry without jeopardizing their mobile home position. Expansion would lessen the suppliers' reliance on the seasonal mobile home market and reduce the costs of materials and services that seasonality influences. It might then be possible to reduce the price manufacturers pay for supplies and thus the price consumers pay for mobile homes.

There is some possibility of reducing the lead time for product development. Suppliers have been late in providing supplies in the appropriate dimensions required by new developments in the mobile home industry; this has been especially evident whenever permissible highway transportation width increased. The reason for this lengthy lead time may be the expense of new plant and equipment, which firms are hesitant to incur when demand is untested. If it is felt that the gains from shortening the lead time are positive and extend beyond the confines of the industry, it may pay to consider favorable tax treatment or other subsidization of these investments. Another reason for this lag may be the inadequacy of communication. Suppliers may hesitate when demand is untested and manufacturers may be slow to test demand without appropriate supplies. Improved communication could presumably eliminate such traps. More suppliers could be encouraged to join the MHI, and MHI activities could revolve with even greater emphasis around this nexus.

The seasonality of the mobile home industry forces its suppliers to accept higher costs than they would have in the absence of seasonality. Reducing this seasonality could decrease the price manufacturers pay for supplies and services and thus the price consumers pay for mobile homes.

Nowhere in the housing industry is there greater potential for reducing the dependence upon suppliers than there is in the mobile home industry. The industry has the potential to apply countervailing power to the many giant firms that inhabit the supply sector. The dependence on suppliers has hampered the maturation of many mobile home manufacturers. Manufacturers' interests and perspectives are often overly narrow, to the harm of the industry. By retarding the maturity of manufacturers, the dependence has limited the countervailing power. The industry has not had a very long history, and increased maturity may come with age; but there is no guarantee of this. Suppliers keep the industry flexible and the entrance requirements low. Neither of these is bad in and of itself, but they do not contribute to the development of mature firms whose perspectives encompass the industry and beyond.

One possibility that may speed the maturation of the industry is forced weaning. Eliminating the manifold services of suppliers would force the industry's members to fend for themselves. It should be clear that this would be a very expensive means of attaining decreased dependency upon suppliers. A more fruitful approach may be for the MHI and the trade journals to encourage and publicize the developing tier of more mature manufacturers. The behavior of these firms could serve as models for others. A somewhat subtle distinction is being made here between utilizing suppliers and depending upon suppliers. The benefits from utilizing suppliers are clear. Depending on suppliers for the performance of critical functions provides them with the ability to exploit the relationship. Manufacturers can utilize suppliers without being dependent upon them.

Notes to Chapter 13

1. Correspondence with the MHI's Suppliers Division, November 1977.

2. "The Dealer, The Manufacturer, The Customer," *Mobile & Recreational Housing Merchandiser*, August 1973, pp. 30–39.

3. "How to Speed New Products From the Men Who Make Them to the Men Who Use Them," *House and Home*, June 1966, p. 114.

4. All quotes in this paragraph are from ibid.

Chapter 14

Transportation System Influence

The mobile home transportation system serves as the vital link between the manufacturer, the dealer, and the consumer of the mobile home. In order to facilitate safe, rapid, and efficient delivery of units, the mobile home industry has stimulated the development of a separate national industry, specializing solely in such transportation, which has become an integral component of the larger production and delivery system. Although movement of mobile homes by rail, water, or air is possible under certain circumstances, the hauling of units on highways is the most common and currently feasible transportation method, and therefore will be the focal point of our discussion.

A. Origins

The commercial transportation of mobile homes over highways began with the establishment of the first businesses concerned with moving trailers for hire in 1936. These early transporters used their own passenger cars, pickup trucks, or jeeps to tow trailers from manufacturers to dealers and were paid on a mileage basis. In the late 1930s trailers were sometimes moved by railroad flatcars or automobile boxcars. With the growth of the mobile home industry as well as the size of the unit itself, the transportation of mobile homes over highways developed into a more specialized industry and became the primary method of movement. Railroads were used less frequently because the larger size of the mobile home made loading and unloading difficult and increased the risk of damage to the unit. Rail transport was also inconvenient in that it added yet another step in moving the home from the railroad siding to the dealer's lot. In response to the need for vehicles specially designed to accommodate mobile homes, the shortened wheelbase truck, the telescoping frame truck, and the variable length toter were developed.[1]

The expansion of the mobile home industry to include the movement of units across state lines necessitated approval by the Interstate Commerce Commission (ICC); the first such authorities were granted in 1941. Enterprising drivers acquired ICC authorities to operate in particular areas, arranged contracts with manufacturers and dealers to deliver their units, and then hired other truckers to service these routes. As the original drivers acquired more authorities and hired additional truckers, the modern mobile home transport companies evolved. Today the mobile home transportation industry has grown to include approximately twenty large firms offering nationwide service as well as numerous small local companies operating intrastate. Thus the mobile home industry has created a specialized supporting industry: its transportation system.

B. Industrial Organization

Industry Structure

The mobile home transportation industry is composed of nationwide firms that have ICC authorities for interstate routes, local firms that operate intrastate, and independent truckers who primarily handle intrastate business. Mobile home transporting firms utilize an owner-operator system: Each driver owns his or her own truck, is under exclusive contract to a particular company, and is paid on a per-trip, per-mile basis. The driver absorbs the costs of gas, truck maintenance, permits, and tolls over an allotted amount; the insurance on the mobile home is usually split evenly between the driver and the transport company. This system is particularly beneficial for the transport company, which does not have to purchase and maintain trucks or train drivers.

There are two forms of mobile home movement: primary and secondary. Primary movement involves hauling the unit from the manufacturer to the dealer and accounts for approximately 70 percent of all hauling. Secondary movement (about 30 percent of all movement) has two aspects: transporting the unit from the dealer to the home site and from site to site. A lesser function of secondary movement is the transportation of mobile homes to and between military bases and to natural disaster areas.

Services/Costs

Operations

The basic service mobile home transport firms offer is the movement of a unit from the point of origin to its destination. The company may also provide such extra services as unblocking the home and reblocking it at the new site or preparing the home and the items it contains for the trip (securing furniture, packing loose items, and so forth). Transport firms carry insurance at least meeting minimum requirements set by the ICC and the states in which they operate. This insurance can cover the unit and its manufacturer-installed equipment against damage caused by collision, theft, or other causes due to carrier negligence.

Transportation charges are usually based on the length and width of the mobile home and the points of origin and destination. In addition to the basic rate, indirect costs related to conditions and regulations in individual states may be included in the total charge. The rates can absorb such costs as permits or road and bridge tolls but may not include such indirect costs as the escort vehicles required to travel with the home or the special equipment needed in some states. (The cost for each escort, for example, can vary from $0.30 to $0.50 to more than $1.00 per mile.) Extra services (unblocking, packing, and so forth) are not included in the base rate and are usually charged at an hourly rate. Rate levels are set by the ICC interstate and by state authorities intrastate.

Highway Regulations

When mobile homes are transported on public highways (figure 14.1), their movement is subject to state highway regulations, which usually include dimensional limitations, the need for permits, equipment requirements,

Figure 14.1.
Rigs hauling mobile
homes.

and traffic regulations. (Chapter 19 discusses this area in further detail.) In almost all states mobile homes exceed the length and width requirements of a "normal-sized" vehicle and thus are classified as "oversized" and must obtain a special permit to travel on the highways. All states allow the transport of 12-wides and almost all allow movement of wides, but very few allow movement of 14-16-wides. The transporter must obtain at least one permit (and sometimes more) from each state through which the mobile home travels. These permits often specify route restrictions' equipment requirements, and a bond or proof of insurance or financial responsibility. Most states usually require a separate permit for each trip or unit transported, although the practice of issuing an extended time permit to cover periods of up to one year is becoming more common.

The mobile home transporter is also subject to the special traffic regulations imposed on oversized vehicles. These can include a need for escort vehicles to travel with the unit, restriction of travel times (usually during the daylight hours of weekdays), route restrictions, and requirements for special equipment such as warning lights or signs. Although these highway regulations are necessary to ensure the safety and convenience of the state's residents, they pose major difficulties for transporters. The primary problem is the variance of rules from state to state. Not only must a transporter always be aware of the current regulations in each state and locality in which it operates, but a hauler must also have a separate permit and in some cases different equipment for each state. This is a costly and time-consuming process that can cut down on the speed and efficiency of mobile home delivery and may result in increased costs being passed through to the consumer.

The mobile home transportation industry presents an interesting paradox. On the one hand, several firms dominate the industry and there are effective entry barriers. On the other hand, there is substantial intraindustry competition in the form of providing rapid, complete, and efficient service. A few of the approximately fifteen to twenty nationwide firms have the lion's share of the market. (It is estimated that three companies account for about 85 percent of the revenues received in transporting mobile homes.[2]) There are several plausible reasons for this concentration.

In order to transport mobile homes across state lines, transporters must obtain approval to travel certain routes from the ICC. (Firms operating within one state receive route permission from local authorities.) The ICC approval ("authority") can be obtained in one of two ways: direct application to the ICC, which requires proof of the need for transporters in that particular area and the ability of the applicant to meet that need, or purchase of an authority already held by a firm or individual. The ICC sets price levels for interstate hauling and grants more than one authority in the same area if there is a proven need for several haulers.

Because several of the top nationwide transporters have been in business for at least twenty-five years, these companies have had the opportunity to acquire numerous and well-placed authorities that enable them to make the most direct deliveries. A direct route should entail less time in transit, mileage, gas, and vehicle use than an indirect one and thus allow the transporter to realize substantial cost savings. The larger and older transporter's operation is also more efficient than that of a new firm in that the company has made its initial capital outlays for start-up expenses and has a full complement of drivers under contract. In addition, these firms have established terminals across the country; drivers reaching their destination can pick up another unit to deliver, effectively solving the problem of costly empty back hauls.

Thus lack of authorities and the cost efficiency of established operations provide effective entry barriers for a firm attempting to begin an interstate business. Buying an authority can entail a major capital outlay. Because the long-established companies have authorities for many of the choice direct routes, the fledgling firm can either acquire an alternate route (which is usually less direct and thus less economical and less desirable) or it can attempt to prove the need for another hauler on an established route. In the latter case the new firm might face opposition from the companies holding the authorities to transport in that area, which could lead to lengthy delays.

An important psychological barrier to entry is posed by the established firms' experience and reputation. Because there is no real product differentiation in the mobile home transportation industry, firms must rely on reputation and advertising to attract customers. It is difficult for a new company to compete with an older firm that has experienced drivers and an established name. Another barrier to entry is posed by the new firm's lack of knowledge of the different highway regulations in each state.

The dominance of the mobile home transport system by a few large firms was recognized in 1974, when three of the top companies pleaded no contest to criminal antitrust charges filed by the U.S. Department of Justice. In 1976 a similar civil antitrust suit, charging the same companies with price fixing and conspiring to maintain a monopoly, was settled as the companies consented to a court order prohibiting them from trying to monopolize the mobile home transportation market.[3]

There has been renewed interest in deregulation of the trucking industry in order to spur competition and lower rates. Should either the ICC or Congress mandate deregulation, the dominance of the mobile home transport system by a few companies would be further weakened.

Despite the entry barriers that effectively leave the bulk of the nationwide mobile home transportation business in the hands of relatively few firms, the industry does exhibit competitive characteristics. If there is a proven need for more than one hauler in a particular area, the ICC can grant additional authorities; thus there is potential for competition on a given route. Transporters also vie with each other to develop better routes. Because prices are relatively fixed, transporters strive to attract customers by providing the most rapid, efficient, and expert service. Thus they must be attuned to and meet the challenge of innovations and efficiences introduced by their competitors.

Competitive characteristics would seem to be most pronounced intrastate because there is relative ease of entry and operation on the local level. The process of obtaining route permission for intrastate transport is not as difficult or complicated as that for getting ICC authorities. In addition, local granting agencies are more inclined to give routes to local haulers than to nationwide firms. There is less concentration on the local level; shorter distances are involved in intrastate transport than interstate so there is no need for the network of terminals that give established nationwide firms the edge in interstate hauling. It would also seem likely that local haulers would have a knowledge of the area in which they operate and might have developed more personal relationships with local manufacturers, dealers, and park operators in order to get more business from them.

Although transportation of mobile homes by truck on overland routes has become the dominant form of movement, other methods have been and are used with varying degrees of success and applicability. These forms of transit include movement by rail, water, and air.

Rail

In the late 1930s mobile homes were often moved by rail, but as mobile homes became larger and heavier, this method became outmoded because of the difficulty of loading and the increased risk of damage to the unit. Rail transport briefly came into vogue in the mid-1950s when 10-foot-wide units were introduced because the new units exceeded the legal width restrictions for highway movement in most states.[4] Railroads again fell from favor when highway regulation caught up to the progress being made in the industry; almost all states now allow transport of 14-wides, whereas the width restriction by rail is 11 feet 8 inches. However, railroads are occasionally used for special train movements of mobile homes that allow transport of wider loads, such as 12-foot and 14-foot units. These special train movements are routed in such a way that there is no train traffic coming in the opposite direction to interfere with the oversized load.

There is increasing potential for the use of railroads in the transportation of mobile homes. As railroads become viable again after the major reorganizations that have taken place in the last few years, they are seeking more business and may be willing to accommodate wide loads and provide the more careful handling needed in transporting mobile homes. Train transport can be very economical for long-distance hauling.

Train transport still involves the extra step of transporting the mobile home unit to and from the railroad siding. However, many manufacturers already have rail sidings at their factory sites in order to facilitate deliveries from suppliers. These manufacturers might also be able to arrange for pickup of finished units from these sidings, and it might be economically feasible for other manufacturers to construct factory-site rail sidings for the same purpose.

Water
Transportation of mobile homes by water also has few practical applications at the present time. Mobile homes can be carried by barge or baby flat-top carrier; but, like railroad transport, this form of movement requires the additional step of getting the home from the port to the final destination. Transportation by water could be useful in mass shipment of mobile homes, particularly to developing countries with critical housing shortages that lack local production facilities. An interesting twist on this application is presently being used in Saudi Arabia, where an American company is supplying mobile homes built in the United States to the employees of American firms there. The company ships the fully furnished units to Saudi Arabia on specially outfitted freighters; the units are then trucked to the home site from the port of entry.[5]

The further development of transportation of mobile home units by water would be advantageous in that this mode does not put any limitations on the size of the unit, as highway transport does; thus the unit could be designed for functional adequacy and efficiency rather than to meet the dimensional standards imposed by highway regulation.

Air
Because of the size and weight of the present mobile home unit, air transport is currently unfeasible on a large scale in terms of both logistics and economics. However, it is possible that crane helicopters could be adapted to transport mobile homes under certain circumstances. Crane helicopters are now used for offloading ships (for example, from crowded harbors), for heavy construction (for example, lifting equipment to the upper stories of high-rise structures), and in specialty construction for which no other mode of transportation is possible (for example, placing ski lodges on mountains). A major U.S. aircraft company has developed a crane helicopter strong enough to lift the equivalent of a doublewide mobile home unit (see figure 14.2). With certain modifications in both design and usage, it is possible that crane helicopters could be used effectively in the mobile home industry, especially in the transport of building components (three-dimensional units like mobile homes, conceived to become part of a larger structure) to high-density areas.

Crane helicopters face none of the logistical problems involved in truck transport of building components to urban areas. Truck transport entails compliance with highway regulations that limit load width and thus stifle functional design and engineering of building components; because crane helicopters could conceivably carry units as large as 16 feet or 18 feet wide, manufacturers can produce to the width consumers need, not to the width highway regulations necessitate. Truck transporters must deal not only with traffic congestion, which lengthens the time of delivery, but also with the logistics of moving very large loads on narrow urban streets; this could well be physically impossible, or the truckers might be denied permission from local authorities. Air transport obviates all of these problems.

Use of crane helicopters to transport mobile homes would necessitate a modification in the labor environment. Crane helicopter operators would have to be specially trained to position the homes on site, which could lead to problems with existing construction unions fearing that already-scarce work would be taken away from their members. However, because this application would be fostering work that would not even exist otherwise, it should be perceived as a positive development. Training of crane helicopter operators can also be done within the unions. An Operating Engineers local in New Jersey is actively training its men in the use of helicopters for construction at its own expense, thus anticipating the probability that this will become a reality.

The major drawback to use of crane helicopters is their prohibitive costs. Not only does such a craft cost millions of dollars to develop, but it is also expensive to operate; thus, it must be used constantly to be at all cost effective. In addition, its use would make sense only if it obviated the need for any other crane (the use of which is also very expensive per hour). However, if a more simple and less expensive crane helicopter were developed or if existing models (such as the large surplus of crane helicopters left over from the Vietnam War) were modified, this mode used in concert with mass transportation by rail or water could be especially effective for purposes ranging from urban renewal to new high-rise developments. For example, building components could be shipped en masse by barge or train from a manufacturer in the South to a high-rise developer in the Northeast. The components could be offloaded by crane helicopter and flown to the site, where they would be stacked or positioned. However, this combination of modes can be economically feasible only with use of advanced construction management techniques that would keep costs down by ensuring close synchronization of operations.

Summary
Thus, although transportation by rail, water, and air can be used in isolated cases to deal with special circumstances, it must be

Figure 14.2.
Skycrane lifting
sectional home.

repeated that these methods are currently economically unfeasible for widespread industry use. This situation could change as the mobile home industry and its supporting and regulatory environments evolve to make greater use of these alternatives, but highway transportation remains the most rapid, effective, and cost efficient method of transporting mobile homes in most cases.

Manufacturers

Most mobile home manufacturers own and operate their own fleets for delivery of units over short distances. For long hauls it is economically advantageous for manufacturers to retain the services of a transporter for two primary reasons: the cost inefficiencies of long-distance hauling and the intricacies of highway regulation.

Although maintenance of a fleet for short-distance hauling can reduce a manufacturer's costs, the expenses increase with the distance traveled. Manufacturers also shy away from using their own fleets for long-distance hauling because of the cost involved in maintaining a full complement of equipment and operators in a seasonal industry. Because most hauling is done during the peak spring and summer seasons, manufacturers would have the majority of their fleets lying idle during the slack periods. In addition, manufacturers would have to absorb the costs of empty back hauls, a primary cost problem. (Transporters avoid this cost by using a nationwide network of terminals.)

Manufacturers also use transporters for long-distance hauling to avoid the complexities of the various highway regulations involved in interstate transport. Transportation

companies are familiar with the highway regulations in the states in which they operate, know which permits are required to travel through the state and how to get them, and have the ICC authorities to travel certain routes. Thus, it is to the distinct advantage of manufacturers to avoid spending time and money duplicating services already available.

The existence of a well-developed transportation system facilitates entry into the mobile home production system because there is already a viable method for the crucial function of getting the final product to its destination. A new manufacturing firm can thus concentrate its efforts on developing its own expertise. Commercial carriers have also become increasingly important to those manufacturers who either had to cut back or eliminate their own fleets during and after the 1973–1975 recession.

Dealers

Mobile home dealers tend to use transportation firms less frequently than do manufacturers. Not only does secondary movement from dealer to home site make up at most 30 percent of all movement, but these hauls tend to be over shorter distances than primary moves from manufacturers to dealers. Most dealerships maintain at least one company delivery truck; 74 percent of all dealers surveyed by PMHI relied on their own trucks for all or part of their deliveries.

Dealers may make use of local transporting firms during peak seasons when the number of homes sold exceeds the delivery capacity of the dealer's own fleet. The PMHI Dealer Survey found that although 54 percent of dealers could make all deliveries with their own trucks, approximately 20 percent relied at least in part on additional means of delivery. Only 13 percent of the dealers surveyed used transporting companies exclusively, while almost one-third used them at some time. It is highly likely that for a small dealership the return on investment does not justify the capital outlay of owning its own trucks.

The PMHI Dealer Survey found that delivery by dealer-owned truck was about half as expensive as delivery by a commercial transporter. Because most dealer deliveries are made within a relatively small radius of the dealership, it is cost effective for the dealership to maintain its own truck for short hauls. However, given the cost of empty back hauls involved in long-distance trucking, it would be more economical for dealers to use transporters for distance hauling.

D. Performance of the Transportation Industry

The transportation system serves as the bridge of the mobile home industry, connecting the manufacturer and the dealer as well as the dealer and the consumer. One of the main attractions of the mobile home over conventional housing is that the consumer can occupy it more quickly (about ten days from manufacturer to consumer as opposed to a few months for construction of an on-site home); the mobile home is also appealing because of its potential mobility. The existence of a well-developed transportation sector facilitates rapid and safe delivery of the mobile home from manufacturer to dealer to consumer as well as from home site to home site.

Because of the transportation system, manufacturers can ship to dealers located far from their factories; thus dealers have a greater choice of manufacturers from which to buy units, which affords the consumer greater variety in design and price of mobile homes. A ready-made and widely available transportation system also allows greater entry into the manufacturing system. The cost efficiencies developed by the transporters may help to stabilize the price of units by reducing manufacturers' hauling expenses. The reliability and expertise of the mobile home transporters reflect well on the industry and help to mitigate the negative image of the mobile home still held by many consumers.

The smooth functioning of the transportation system makes the difference between accessibility and inaccessibility of the product (the mobile home); having access to all parts of the country enlarges the market for the product and fosters the growth of the mobile home industry. The strengths of the mobile home transportation system (primarily its economic efficiencies and its expertise) have been discussed in length throughout this chapter. Although we have also touched on the problems facing the transport industry, a further explication of these difficulties is

in order because of their importance for the performance of the system. The primary problems of this sector can be categorized as seasonality, sensitivity to economic variables, lack of standardization in manufacturing, bootlegging, lack of qualified drivers, and difficulties with transporting increasingly larger mobile homes.

The seasonality that is characteristic of the mobile home industry also extends into its transportation system. Hauling peaks during the spring and summer seasons, when there is sometimes even a shortage of experienced drivers to handle the volume of units being shipped. In the slack fall and winter seasons, however, the transportation companies face gross underutilization of their resources. The rigs used to move mobile homes are specially designed and cannot be used to haul anything else, so there is no opportunity for transportation companies to diversify into other types of hauling. (Some of the major mobile home transport companies are themselves diversification efforts of larger corporations.)

During slow seasons drivers are underemployed and must often look outside the industry for work. (Because drivers are under exclusive contract to one transportation company, they cannot haul for another, even if another company has work when theirs does not; however, drivers are free to do other kinds of off-season work.) Seasonality fosters a high driver turnover rate because many truckers want more secure year-round employment. This in turn can lead to a lack of qualified drivers, especially during peak seasons, which has two ramifications: It hurts the transportation industry because less experienced drivers may not be as quick or efficient as seasoned ones, which could lead to dissatisfied customers and thus tarnish the reputation of the company and the industry; it also reverberates in other sectors of the mobile home industry in that both the production and distribution systems are affected if shipments are delayed. Several transport companies have attempted to deal with the seasonality factor by setting up programs to train drivers to use leased equipment, but none of these efforts has proven successful.

As a link in the mobile home production and delivery process, the transportation sector is also plagued by the mobile home industry's sensitivity to economic variables. The reduction in mobile home sales caused by the 1974 recession affected the transportation sector as much as it affected the rest of the industry. Transportation industry sources estimate that total mileage reduction during the recession could have ranged from 30 percent to 50 percent; levels vary among different regions depending on the relative concentration of manufacturing facilities. Although the transportation sector has made a slow comeback, business has yet to reach prerecession levels.

A problem often cited by transporters is poor manufacturing and lack of standardization of mobile homes. If a unit is either poorly constructed or has unusual physical characteristics, damage such as broken axles, frames, and flat tires can occur when the home is in transit. The transporter then suffers the wrath of the consumer and the manufacturer for delay and rough handling and loses time that could be used in making another delivery in returning a unit to the factory. The transporters' charges of poor manufacturing are countered by the producers' contention that mobile homes are damaged in transit by careless handling. Although there could be some validity in both sides of the issue, the problem should be somewhat alleviated by two factors: the uniform federal construction and safety standards for mobile homes that became effective in 1976 and the 1974 recession, which caused a shakeout in the industry that eliminated some of the less professional producers.

Transportation firms must also deal with bootleggers, unauthorized haulers without insurance who transport homes at cut-rate prices. Bootlegging is primarily an intrastate problem because these haulers are usually employed by dealers and by home owners moving to another site. Not only do bootleggers take business away from authorized haulers, but they also hurt the image of the transportation industry by careless handling and inadequate insurance that leaves the home owner to bear the costs of any damage done to the unit in transit.

E. Emerging Trends Recent developments both within and without the transportation system are bringing changes to this sector of the mobile home industry. The increasing size of the mobile home unit is having a major effect on several aspects of the transportation system. By the mid-1980s, 12-wides will be obsolete, 14-wides will be the norm, and 16-wides will be gaining popularity. As mobile home manufacturers move toward production of larger units, there should be increasing perception and treatment of mobile homes as permanent. Although this does not discount the attractive element of mobility, transportation industry sources see a market shift into more primary movement (manufacturer to dealer). Two factors are contributing to the decline in the number of secondary moves from site to site: most mobile home dwellers consider their units permanent, and those mobile home owners moving to a new location are more apt to sell the unit and buy another at the new location rather than move the old one.[6] The increasing size of units is also fostering greater demand for qualified drivers. Larger units pose problems for highway transportation in terms of possible inadequacy of present roads and highway regulations that do not yet allow the transport of wider and longer units. Thus mass transport of mobile

homes by rail or water and offloading and positioning by crane helicopter could well become more important methods of transport if they can be developed to the point of economic feasibility.

The recent establishment of the federal code for uniform construction and safety standards for mobile homes should prove a major boon to transporters; standardizing the construction and ensuring the quality of units will make delivery safer and more rapid because it will cut down the potential for damage and thus delays caused by return of the unit to the manufacturer.

The 1974 recession and the attendant debacle in the housing industry have caused major changes in the mobile home industry that have directly affected its transportation system. The shakeout that occurred at this time rid the industry of some of its less sterling elements, and the companies that survived are those that tend to offer products of higher quality and sounder construction that thus hold up better in transit. Even more important to the transportation system is the fact that the production decline caused many manufacturers to cut back or completely eliminate their own fleets. Although most manufacturers will continue to maintain a fleet of some size to deal with short-distance hauling, it is unlikely that they will ever rebuild their fleets to prerecession levels because of the increased costs of fuel, maintenance, administration, and drivers. This benefits transporters in that it increases the manufacturers' dependence on them; this is especially important given the fact that primary movement (manufacturer to dealer) now accounts for 70 percent of all transport business and should increase in the future.

F. Policy Alternatives As the mobile home industry assumes a greater role in alleviating the need for high-quality, low-cost housing, its transportation system will also become proportionately more important. Thus it is necessary for the transportation system to work on several fronts to improve its cost performance as well as to increase its effectiveness in the safe and rapid delivery of mobile home units.

Through strategic collaboration, mobile home manufacturers and transporters can reduce seasonality in both the production and transportation systems by negotiating off-season delivery contracts with developers of large-scale projects in return for unit and transportation price cuts. Under these circumstances, manufacturers are prepared to reduce unit prices; many have expressed to us their willingness to cut profits or even take losses on off-peak orders if these are scheduled so that the added volume would enable them to produce at full capacity during the slack seasons. Similarly, transporters might reduce prices in order to generate business during the off-season; even if the off-season compensation for drivers were lower, some revenue would be better than none for otherwise under- or unemployed owner-operators. This seems to represent an "all-win" system. Mobile home producers and transporters increase business volume (albeit at lower profit) while at the same time reducing seasonality; developers (and, potentially, consumers) benefit from lower prices.

The transportation system can also develop methods to increase the effectiveness of highway movement, especially in terms of transporting larger units. Revision of state highway regulations to allow shipment of larger units would have a positive impact in two ways. Mobile home units could be built not to meet artificial dimensional requirements or physical limitations but rather to satisfy design criteria that would result in the functionally most responsive product for the consumer.

Standardization of the highway regulations that now differ from state to state would allow transporters to save a great deal of unnecessary time and expense. This standardization could include use of extended time permits and uniform equipment regulations. Standardization would pose no safety hazards yet would allow transporters to realize substantial cost savings that conceivably could be passed on to the consumer. (These cost savings are detailed in chapter 19.)

Notes to Chapter 14

1. Carlton M. Edwards, *Homes for Travel and Living: The History and Development of the Recreation Vehicle and Mobile Home Industries* (East Lansing, Mich. Carl Edwards & Associates, 1977), p.206.

2. *The Wall Street Journal,* January 22, 1976, p.16.

3. *The Wall Street Journal,* December 6, 1974, p.12, and January 22, 1976, p.16; *The Manufactured Housing Newsletter,* VII, 6, February 6, 1976.

4. Edwards, *Homes for Travel and Living,* p.207.

5. *The New York Times,* September 15, 1977, p.25.

6. Based on a 1977 survey conducted by National Trailer Convoy, Inc.

Chapter 15

Finance Sector Influence

As a result of its low-cost product and unique financing structure, the mobile home industry offers three major benefits to the prospective home owner. First, it is the primary supplier of low-cost housing in America. Second, the mobile home industry provides the home buyer with an alternative to conventional construction that has lower down payment and initital cost requirements. Third, the industry provides an alternative that has lower monthly cost requirements.

An overview of the financing structure is shown in figure 15.1. Although extremely complex, the industry has four principal actors: manufacturers, dealers, consumers, and park developers. They receive support from suppliers, lenders, stockholders, service companies, insurance companies, and others. Judging from this wide range of participants, one might expect to see a clear division of responsibilities. However, our study of the industry found that a significant overlap exists.

Mobile home manufacturers are capable of producing the lowest-cost shelter units in America, and with few exceptions they concentrate solely on the production aspect of the mobile home delivery system. Most attempts by manufacturers to develop parks, enter into special relationships with dealers, and engage in wholesale and retail financing have been unsuccessful. The primary challenge facing manufacturers in the 1980s is to find capital sources for operations and expansion in light of a slackening interest on the part of stock market investors.

Dealers represent the broadest overlap of responsibilities in the industry. Although their primary function is to sell mobile homes, many dealers derive a greater part of their income from lender and insurance company commissions. Dealers also are active in park development, and some tie park entrance to the purchase of a mobile home from the dealership. Perhaps the most serious problem results from the relationship between wholesale dealer financing and retail consumer financing prevalent in the industry. All these factors work to increase monthly costs to the consumer. We believe that the challenge for dealers will be to redefine their responsibilities in such a way as to maintain profitability while reducing the consumer's financing costs.

Consumers are the recipients of the industry's end product. Their power is that of the marketplace, casting a vote each time a purchase is made. As consumers are priced out of the market for conventional housing, they are confronted with the retail financing system prevalent in the mobile home industry. Although the mobile home itself is far less costly than a comparable conventional home, the existing financing structure results in monthly payments that are surprisingly high. We believe that the entire finance mechanism must be restructured to distinguish between retail and wholesale financing and encourage mortgage loans for mobile home purchasers.

Mobile home parks have unique advantages over conventional real estate developments. Parks have lower capital requirements than do comparably sized conventional projects. A larger percentage of a mobile home park investment is dedicated to the purchase of land, which tends to increase in value as time passes. A mobile home park can be removed if the land becomes valuable enough to support another type of development. Despite these advantages, mobile home park developers often have difficulty obtaining financing. Among the primary reasons are the lingering trailer park image of the developments and the belief that park occupants do not carry a fair share of the local tax burden. These perceptions lead to community and lender resistance. We believe that park operators, indeed the entire industry, must dispel these false notions. In addition, creative financing techniques must be utilized to develop parks.

This chapter deals in detail with the financing issues raised above. How will manufacturers raise necessary capital? How will dealers maintain profitability while reducing consumer financing costs? How will the consumer's disproportionately high monthly payments be reduced? How will park operators obtain capital to develop in unreceptive areas? We conclude that the industry's finance structure must be altered from its present form, a historical accident, to one that maximizes the consumer's interest. Only then will manufactured housing reach its full potential as an alternative to conventionally constructed housing.

A. Manufacturer Finance

Arthur G. Sherman, the original travel trailer mass producer, floated a convertible preferred stock issue of thirty thousand shares at $25 per share in 1937. However, it was not until the 1950s that investment bankers would give serious consideration to floating an issue of mobile home stock. For financing, mobile home producers depended on their own savings, stock sale to relatives and friends, and cash flow generated by sales.

Two industry characteristics reduced the need for capital investment. First, because space requirements were flexible, leasing was feasible, resulting in monthly payments in lieu of initial investment. Second, because suppliers delivered components as needed and the production system operated on an order-only basis, a low inventory of raw materials and finished goods was maintained. Plant expansion customarily was financed with internally generated funds. Other sources included leasing agreements, the sale of additional common stock to friends, mortgages and equipment loans, and assistance from communities seeking new industry.

Figure 15.1.
PMHI model of the financial structure of the mobile home industry.

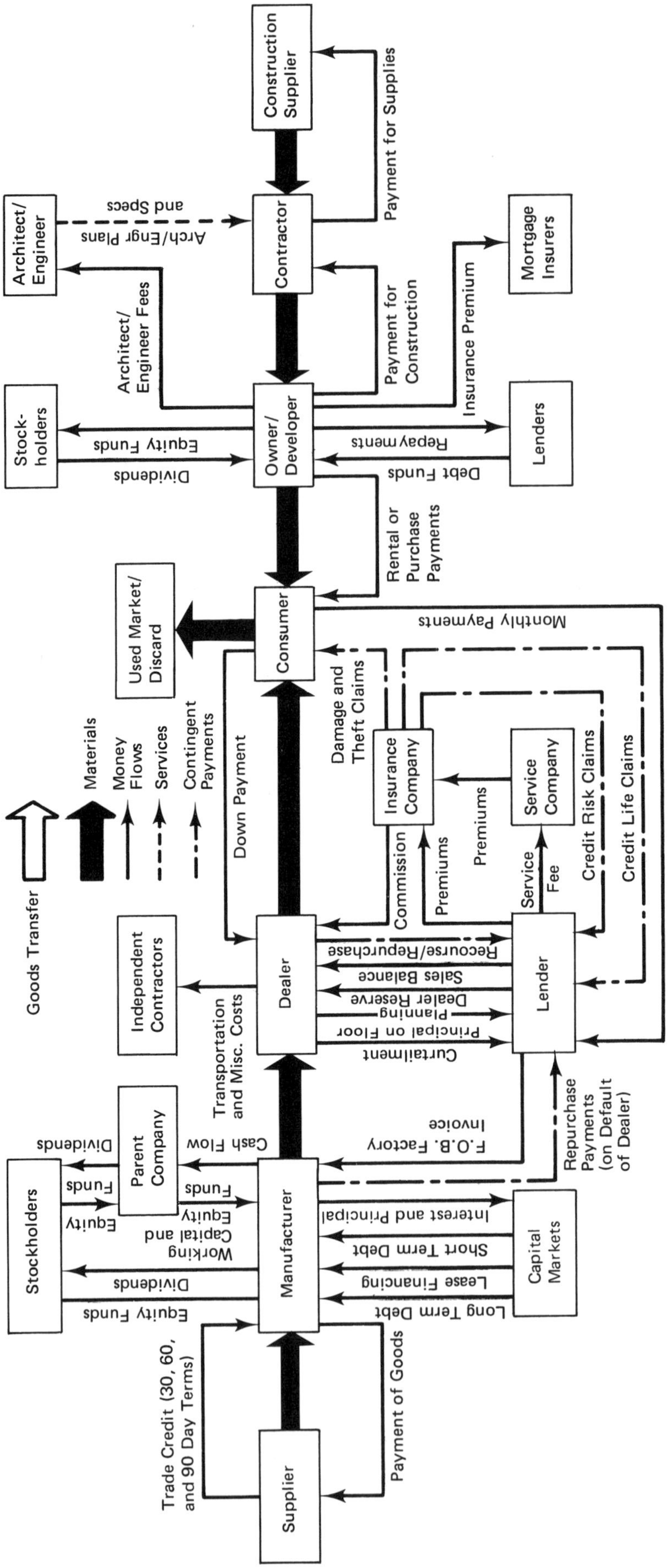

Goods Transfer

Materials

Money Flows

Services

Contingent Payments

In this highly competitive industry, with its uncertain market, manufacturers adopted a number of conservative practices to maintain minimum investment and maximum liquidity. These included extensive leasing of plant and equipment, extended credit from suppliers, high inventory turnover, emphasis on variable rather than fixed costs, and cash on delivery. Long-term commitments, especially debt, were avoided.

This situation changed in the late 1950s when some of the stronger companies began to expand and build regional plants in order to reduce transportation costs and respond more effectively to regional demand patterns. During the 1960s, integration and diversification became a factor. Rapidly developing conglomerates, attracted by forecasts of 15 percent to 20 percent annual sales growth and promises of higher earnings, began to show interest in acquiring mobile home manufacturers. These pressures to expand forced mobile home manufacturers to seek external financing. Price/earnings ratios for mobile home stocks were at record highs in the mid- and late 1960s, so common stock was a popular source of funds.

It was the infusion of capital through stock offerings and by conglomerates, coupled with increased use of commercial bank credit, industrial revenue bonds, and lease financing, that allowed mobile home manufacturers to expand capacity for a record production of 601,250 units in 1972. However, inflation, recession, and tight money plagued the economy in the mid-1970s. Stock prices fell sharply and the market for equity financing disappeared. Further expansion was therefore financed primarily out of retained earnings and leasing. As a result of this economic downturn, the concept of expansion itself was reevaluated. Competition in the industry became intense as profit margins began to erode. Many small and medium-sized firms found themselves in precarious positions, unable to compete with industry giants. By 1975 even large firms were feeling competitive pressure. The key industry strategy became consolidation rather than expansion.

During the early 1970s, many manufacturers had intensified their quest for integration and diversification. However, by the mid-1970s some firms saw that they lacked the expertise and capital to carry out their plans successfully. As a result companies such as Redman Industries eliminated mobile home park operations and Fleetwood closed nine of its thirty-eight plants. By 1977 mobile homes represented 98 percent of all new homes priced under $20,000 and 83 percent of those priced under $30,000. The surging market of purchasers in this price category, combined with the general economic recovery, encouraged many manufacturers to reopen facilities in 1977 that had been closed a few years before and open new facilities to increase production capacity from low 1975 levels. In the late 1970s, more than two hundred mobile home manufacturers are gearing to satisfy an increased demand for their products. How will this production be financed? In this section the financing options are discussed, and those that will play a dominant role in the early 1980s are identified.

In simple terms, a firm's directors have four sources from which to obtain capital for daily operations and expansion. They may utilize the firm's cash flow, rely upon creditors for financing, seek debt funds from lending institutions or bond offerings, and seek equity funds from stock offerings. The source they select is dependent upon their finance goals for the firm and the relative cost of each alternative. A financing model of a typical mobile home manufacturer is presented in figure 15.2.

Cash Flow and Trade Credit
Funds obtained from cash flow often are thought of as free money in that there is no interest or penalty associated with their use. Of course, this is not true because an opportunity cost accompanies the expenditure of internally generated funds. This cost results from the opportunity of obtaining a return from this cash if it is invested elsewhere. In general, however, internally generated funds are less expensive than investment funds from outside sources.

Trade credit from suppliers through inventory warehousing and liberal payment terms can be another form of low-cost financing, as long as suppliers do not penalize the manufacturer by raising prices for goods and services provided. The financing and control of inventory has been an important short-term financing strategy for mobile home manufacturers. An attempt is made to maximize the inventory turnover ratio in order to reduce cash requirements, improve the profit/investment ratio, and obtain a higher rate of return on capital.

From a practical standpoint, internally generated funds and trade credit often cost less than funds associated with equity or debt financing. However, sound business practice requires a cash cushion for contingencies and good relations with creditors. At some point the directors probably must choose between the other alternatives, debt or equity financing. The cost of debt financing is easy to determine because the interest rate and term are specified when funds are borrowed. The cost of equity financing is somewhat more difficult to ascertain, but an attempt to do so must be made or management will be unable to make a rational financing decision.

Debt Financing
Debt financing increases a firm's risk because the debt is a fixed obligation that must be paid. If the firm is doing poorly,

Financing Options

Figure 15.2.
PMHI model of a
typical mobile home
manufacturer.

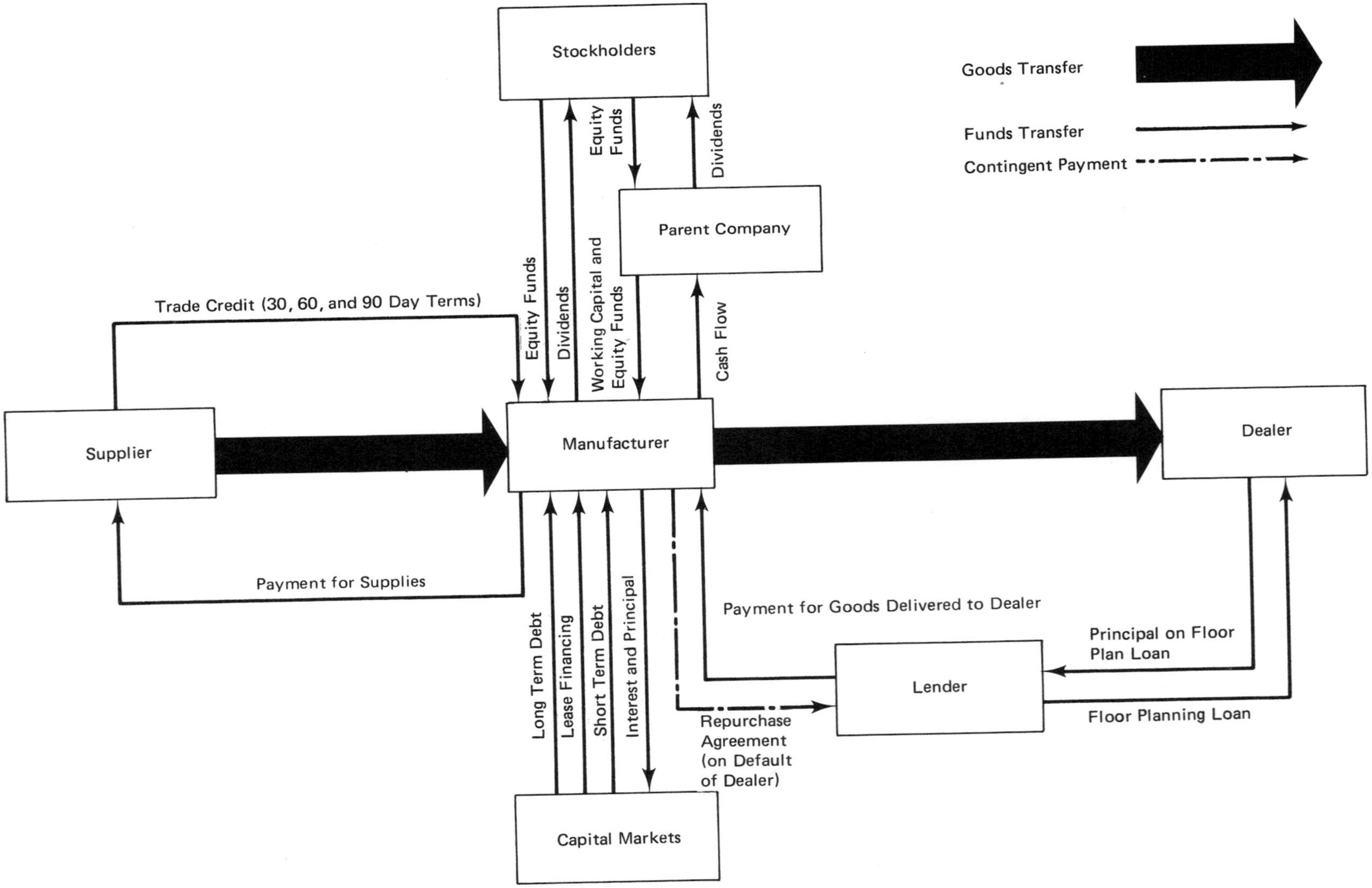

Goods Transfer

Funds Transfer

Contingent Payment

Dealer

Principal on Floor
Plan Loan

Floor Planning Loan

Payment for Goods Delivered to Dealer

Lender

Repurchase
Agreement
(on Default
of Dealer)

Parent Company

Dividends

Cash Flow

Stockholders

Equity
Funds

Working Capital and
Equity Funds

Dividends

Equity Funds

Manufacturer

Interest and Principal

Short Term Debt

Lease Financing

Long Term Debt

Capital Markets

Trade Credit (30, 60, and 90 Day Terms)

Payment for Supplies

Supplier

this fixed obligation can force bankruptcy. Although debt initially may be a relatively inexpensive financing option, its costs are directly related to risk. Therefore, as the firm's indebtedness increases, so do its risks and the costs of obtaining a loan.

Mobile home manufacturers traditionally have refrained from entering the capital markets for debt financing. The risky, high-growth characteristics of the industry, which had been so attractive at the stock market where investors buy future potential, were disadvantageous for borrowing. Creditors are more interested in the firm's soundness and its ability to repay than they are in future growth because they receive no added compensation for growth. In fact, creditors penalize risk with a higher interest rate.

By the late 1960s many of the larger manufacturers were of sufficient size and financial strength to obtain long-term debt financing. Nevertheless, relatively few of them engaged in this form of financing to any extent. Those who did maintained low debt/equity ratios. A number of reasons can be advanced to explain this situation. First, internal cash flows were sufficient to finance expansion for many manufacturers. Second, mobile home stocks were selling at high multiples and therefore equity capital was less expensive than debt. Third, manufacturers felt that debt would result in high fixed-interest expense, a higher breakeven point, less financial flexibility, and more volatile profit rates.

It is interesting to note the trends in debt financing for some of the largest mobile home manufacturers between 1967 and 1977 (table 15.1). Most firms on the list show a stable debt ratio over this period, and three have no long-term debt at all. Of the firms included in the sample, Commodore shows the greatest fluctuation in leverage factor. However, Commodore was discharged from Chapter XI bankruptcy proceedings in 1976, and its behavior is not typical of an ongoing concern during this period. Town and Country, Champion, Vintage, and Redman lost money between 1973 and 1977. Of these four firms, the latter two have increased long-term debt substantially since 1967.

Although some successful mobile home manufacturers have been criticized for using equity rather than debt financing, it must be remembered that the firm's long-run stability is more important than the short-term price of the firm's common stock. It is true that a number of these firms might have shown higher earnings per share in the early 1970s if they had relied more heavily on debt financing. However, some firms with high debt/equity ratios were not able to weather the mid-1970s recession.

There are other forms of debt financing, such as leasing, that have seen widespread use in the mobile home industry. Lease financing is relatively easy to obtain because

Table 15.1.
Leverage Factors for Selected Mobile Home Manufacturers

Company[a]	Leverage Factor[b]		
	1967	1973	1977
Skyline	100.0	100.0	100.0
Fleetwood	100.0	100.0	100.0
Town and Country	100.0	100.0	100.0
Commodore[c]	100.0	46.2	NA
Vintage	93.0	75.9	83.8
Redman	69.5	54.0	59.4
Champion	72.0	79.0	81.1
Conchemco	78.0	73.1	81.6

a. From 1967 list of twenty-five largest firms.
b. The leverage factor is the common equity as a percentage of invested capital (which includes common equity, preferred stock, and long-term debt). Long-term lease arrangements were not included.
c. Incorporated in 1968; first set of figures for fiscal 1969. Not applicable in 1977 because of common equity deficit.
Source: Annual reports and Standard & Poor's Standard N.Y.S.E. Stock Reports.

it is not strongly dependent on market conditions or the risk structure of the firm. This factor is especially important for new firms. Lease financing by mobile home manufacturers typically involves the sale and leaseback of a plant facility. Under a sale and leaseback agreement a firm sells an asset it owns to another party and this party leases the asset back to the firm. The prime advantage is that it is off-balance-sheet financing. Therefore the mobile home manufacturer is able to maintain the flexibility of a no-debt balance sheet. In such a transaction the annual lease payments appear as a deduction on the company's income statement and are treated as such for tax purposes. Of course, the manufacturer loses interest and depreciation deductions that would apply if it owned the asset.

Industrial revenue bonds are another form of debt financing that mobile home manufacturers have used to a limited extent. Because these securities are tax exempt, the cost of funds is lower than with conventional debt financing. The bonds are issued by a municipality to fund facilities constructed by a manufacturer in expectation that this will provide employment and improve economic well-being in the community. Local commercial banks often will purchase the bonds in order to stimulate economic growth in the area. This enables mobile home manufacturers to meet their capital requirements by tapping a new source of funds.

Term loans provide funds so that manufacturers can carry out expansion or other business operations. In addition term loans normally are renewable if the business has been operating successfully. A term loan has

a maturity of more than one year but not more than ten years, and a majority of term loans arranged by mobile home manufacturers mature in five years. Interest rates on these loans range from 1/4 percent above the agent bank's prime rate for the industry's best credit risks to 4 percent above prime for higher risks.

An important aspect of term loans is that they usually are amortized over the life of the loan. Therefore the borrower must repay the loan gradually instead of paying interest periodically and the large principal payment at the end of the term. This protects both manufacturer and lender from the possibility that the manufacturer may not be able to meet the lump sum payment. Lending institutions normally require collateral for term loans. This often is provided in the form of plant, equipment, land, common stock, and airplanes.

Equity Financing
The final financing alternative is equity, selling part ownership of the firm to stockholders. For their investment stockholders expect a return in the form of a future increase in the firm's market worth (market stock price times the number of outstanding shares) and, perhaps, periodic dividends. Because stockholders are part owners of the firm, their position is subordinate to creditors that have loaned funds to or performed services for the company. To compensate for this risk, stockholders generally will expect a higher return on funds than do lenders.

It is possible, especially for a firm in a relatively immature industry, that future growth expectations will be unusually high. Because of these expectations, stockholders bid up the price of the firm's stock. By carefully timing stock offerings, a firm can take advantage of these inflated market prices and obtain equity funds that are less expensive than debt funds. This was true of many mobile home stocks during the 1960s. However, as the industry matures and the firm's future growth expectations decrease relative to those of other stock market offerings, the cost of equity financing increases.

In December 1968 fewer than twenty mobile home manufacturers actively traded common stock on the security markets. In 1969, however, a boom began in public offerings of mobile home stocks, and by December of that year there were fifty actively traded public firms that manufactured mobile homes. There are six reasons for this increase.

First, during the late 1960s manufacturers found their markets expanding and needed new funds to finance plant expansion, equipment, and working capital. Because mobile home stocks were commanding high multiples, many manufacturers went public while they could still realize high prices relative to earnings. From 1967 to 1969 the price/earnings ratios of five leading mobile home stocks increased from 10 to 30. Since then the multiples have reached as high as 60.

Second, by selling common stock, the mobile home industry engaged in a form of public relations. As more and more people became stockholders in mobile home manufacturing firms, they could not help but change their image of the mobile home.

Third, by having a public market for their stock, manufacturers were able to see a tangible value for their firm. This was especially important to entrepreneurs who sold their companies to conglomerates. Without the value of the outstanding shares of stock, it is unlikely that sellers would have been able to command attractive sales prices.

Fourth, going public facilitated acquisitions of firms. By offering stock rather than cash to the other company's stockholders, a mobile home manufacturer avoided taxation on the transaction. Thus the manufacturer could make acquisitions and expand operations for a lower price.

Fifth, going public helped mobile home manufacturers attract and retain more qualified personnel by enabling the firms to offer stock options, which can be exercised and sold for capital gains.

Finally, by going public and then continuing to present profitable opportunities to investors, mobile home manufacturers found it easier to raise additional equity capital. Furthermore, the manufacturers improved their equity base, so credit agreements with financing institutions became easier to arrange.

Financing Sources for the Future

Equity financing has traditionally been the major source of capital for mobile home manufacturers. Because mobile home stocks were commanding high price/earnings (P/E) ratios during the late 1960s, equity financing was the natural choice. However, the lackluster stock market typical of the mid-1970s caused the P/E to drop and made public sale of stock unattractive. Although the stock market is stronger now than it was in the mid-1970s, many mobile home manufacturers will continue to turn elsewhere for expansion capital. Typical of most maturing industries, mobile home stocks have lost some appeal for investors. The investing community is discounting future potentials and evaluating risk more carefully.

One measure of risk to investors is the turnover rate of firms in the industry; the more firms that fail, the higher the risk. Short of failure, a firm can be risky to investors if the return is lower than anticipated. There is a positive correlation between risk and return; an investor will put capital into riskier than normal ventures only if the expected return is correspondingly higher.

Return-on-investment (ROI) figures for mobile home manufacturers, although considerably higher than those found in most industries, currently are lower than they were during the late 1960s. A survey of manufacturers conducted by PMHI indicates that average before-tax ROI dropped from 25.6 percent in 1968 to 18.6 percent by 1972 and is lower today. This is typical of a market that has begun to mature. As profit margins continue to decline because of increased competition, saturation of new markets, consumerism, and other characteristics of a maturing industry, ROI can be expected to decrease further. As ROI declines, so will investor interest.

This anticipated decrease in industry ROI probably will increase the cost of equity capital and may result in greater reliance on debt financing instruments. As a result we would expect to see higher debt/equity ratios among manufacturers during the rest of this decade. Of course, much expansion will continue to be financed by internal cash flow. In addition, trade credit will play a major part in providing cash for investment. However, we expect a major shift from equity to debt instruments for funding that cannot be supplied by these less expensive sources.

Although mobile home issues may lose glamor status among equity investors, there will continue to be a steady market for the stock of successful mobile home manufacturers. As a result of the clear competitive edge mobile homes have over conventional housing and the large market of potential mobile home buyers, major firms in the industry will continue to attract equity investors with promises of exceptional earnings potential. In fact these prospects, combined with the rapid cash turnover typical of many mobile home manufacturers, make some firms in the industry ideal targets for takeover bids by other corporations. For these firms, efforts to avoid being swallowed by a conglomerate may be the prevailing consideration in selecting appropriate financing instruments for the early 1980s.

B. Dealer Finance

A mobile home has high unit value, and one would not expect a dealer to finance inventory from cash flow. Instead a dealer typically seeks intermediate financing that allows possession of inventory until the units can be sold. This practice, called "floor planning" or "flooring," enables the dealer to maintain an adequate supply of mobile homes and accessories for display and sales purposes.

In the mobile home industry floor planning and retail financing are closely related. Floor planning is an accommodation granted by a financial institution to a mobile home dealer for two basic reasons: to secure from the dealer the majority of lucrative retail paper resulting from the sales of mobile homes and to gain other dealer business such as facilities improvement loans, expansion loans, and general banking accounts. Were it not for these two considerations a lender would have little interest in extending floor plan financing because interest rates for floor planning are low and the loans are difficult to administer. Consequently, floor planning should not be considered in isolation but rather as an integral part of a financing package that includes retail financing.

Wholesale Financing

A dealer typically turns to a commercial bank, finance company, or savings and loan association to finance inventory. The lender usually advances 100 percent of the dealer's inventory costs, including freight, taxes, and extras, and pays the manufacturer directly for units shipped to the dealer. The dealer, in turn, repays debts to the lending institution as sales are effected and inventory is depleted.

The lien instrument used for flooring inventory is the "trust receipt," which represents a three-way transaction involving the manufacturer, dealer, and lender. The lender holds title to the mobile home inventory that it floor plans. Because title to the merchandise passes directly from the manufacturer to the lender, the possibility of an intervening lien is eliminated.

A trust receipt also is a written contract between the lender and the dealer whereby the lender agrees to release to the dealer certain specified property, mobile homes and accessories itemized by serial number. In turn the dealer agrees to hold the property "in trust" for the lender and to use such property in a specified manner. The dealer is granted the right to sell inventory, usually for not less than a specified "release price," and is obligated to remit proceeds to the lender promptly. Because this arrangement allows the dealer to maintain possession of mobile homes owned by the lender, the lending institution must be prepared to do the following to protect itself against losses:

Demand that certificates of origin and invoices for the units be mailed directly to the lender when the manufacturer ships units to the dealer.

Make periodic checks at the dealership in order to ascertain that all sales have been reported and every mobile home unit is accounted for. This check normally includes reconciling units sold and inventory on hand with the lender's own statements. Discrepancies may indicate that some sales are not reported to the floor planner. These commonly are known as "sales out of trust."

Determine that adequate insurance protection is provided and that the lending institution retains the policy with a loss-payable clause in its favor.

Investigate a dealer whose billings for interest, curtailment, and other charges are not paid within ten days of the due date.

Notify an endorser or guarantor on a floor plan note of any irregularities, even those that may appear to be minor.

For its services the lender usually charges a small percentage above the prime lending rate, although the specific rate varies among dealers and states. In addition to the interest charge, some floor planners may levy a small service fee. As previously mentioned, these financial charges are rather low because the lending institution provides a dealer's floor planning to secure most of the profitable retail financing business generated by dealer sales.

In order to protect itself against losses due to dealer failure, the lending institution commonly requires some form of dealer endorsement on both wholesale and retail paper. The two basic types of endorsement employed in the industry are repurchase agreements and full recourse endorsements. In addition to the dealer's endorsement, principals of the dealership are sometimes required to execute personal and continuing guarantees on both wholesale and retail paper. The personal guarantee eliminates protection afforded the principals by the corporate structure. The continuing guarantee ensures that the principals remain liable until such time as all endorsed paper has been liquidated.

As a further security measure most lenders require that manufacturers enter into a repurchase agreement to cover all units of their manufacture under a whoesale line of credit. In the event of dealer failure, the manufacturer is required to buy back those floor planned units on the dealer's lot that have not been sold. Consequently, it is not uncommon for lenders to inspect a manufacturer's operation and periodic financial statements. It should be noted, however, that because many manufacturers are small and undercapitalized, lenders cannot realistically expect manufacturers to honor repurchase agreements on a large scale. Thus lenders must rely primarily upon the dealer's credit for repayment.

As a reciprocal arrangement under the repurchase agreement, the lender generally is required to protect the manufacturer by collecting from the dealer reductions of the outstanding balance on wholesale units, a process known as "curtailment." A common curtailment provision requires the dealer to reduce the outstanding wholesale balance on each unit by 10 percent after ninety days, with an additional 10 percent reduction every thirty days until the unit is either sold or paid for completely. A curtailment provision may be part of any wholesale financing package between a dealer and a lender, whether or not the lender requires a repurchase agreement from the manufacturer. Thus curtailment serves to protect the interests of the lender and the manufacturer in the event of dealer failure. In addition curtailment decreases the lender's investment in floored inventory, thereby enhancing the lender's collateral position; encourages the dealer to exert greater sales efforts; and alerts the lender to a dealer's financial condition if the dealership is unable to meet curtailment payments.

It has been widely acknowledged in the industry that retail financing is the most profitable segment of mobile home financing. This is supported by data obtained in the PMHI survey. Although cash sales are not uncommon, 75 percent to 80 percent of mobile home sales are financed. The standard financing instrument is a conditional sales installment credit contract, with interest usually computed on an add-on basis.

Until 1972 mobile home paper was regarded by lending institutions as relatively safe. In 1967 the American Bankers Association Credit Survey reported that mobile home paper had the lowest average dollar amount of losses, computed on the basis of liquidations, of all forms of installment credit loans. The alarming upsurge in delinquencies and repossessions of the mid-1970s raised serious questions in lenders' minds. It also caused an influx into the industry of dealers specializing in repossessed units. Presently, however, the upward trend in delinquency and repossession rates is reversing.

Perhaps the delinquency situation of the mid-1970s was the result of imprudent lending and rapid expansion during the peak sales years of 1970–1973. During this period lending institutions may have been lulled into a false sense of security as a result of the low delinquency rates at the time. Perhaps they underestimated the severity of the general economic recession. Whatever the reason, the industry must restore lenders' confidence if consumers are to receive low-cost financing.

Indirect Financing
There usually is an unwritten agreement that dealers provide their floor planner with retail paper, and roughly 90 percent of the retail financing business that goes to lending institutions is channeled through dealers. Dealers may or may not guarantee payments on the retail paper they generate. Financing of dealer-endorsed paper is known as "indirect financing" because the customer does not go directly to the bank for a loan, but goes through the dealer. With dealer endorsement comes dealer income and responsibilities. The interrelationship between dealer-lender responsibilities and expectations provides the basis for indirect financing arrangements. Arrangements between the dealer and lender for the sale of mobile homes often take the form of repurchase agreements, full recourse endorsements, or nonrecourse financing.

Repurchase Agreements
As indicated in the wholesale financing discussion, a lender sometimes requires a repurchase agreement from the manufacturer in order to reduce the risk of possible dealer failure. In retail financing, repurchase agreements take a somewhat different form. Whereas wholesale financing repurchase agreements are negotiated between the lender and the manufacturer, retail financing

repurchase agreements represent an endorsement of the ultimate purchaser by the dealer to the lender. Throughout the remainder of this section, the term "repurchase agreement" will be understood to apply only to the retail financing situation.

Basically, a repurchase agreement requires that the lender locate the mobile home and obtain any necessary releases in case of consumer default. After ascertaining that the mobile home has been vacated, the lender advises the dealer to move the unit back to the lot at the dealer's expense. Under this type of arrangement, the dealer attempts to resell the unit based upon the "Blue Book" value and the condition of the unit. If the sales price is greater than or equal to the outstanding balance of the defaulted contract, the lender is repaid in full and the dealer keeps whatever is left over. If the sales price is less than the unpaid balance outstanding, the lender absorbs the loss. Given this situation, the dealership also loses to the extent that it is unable to recoup transportation, setup, and overhead costs incurred in reclaiming and reselling the unit. In the event that the lender cannot repossess the unit, the dealer is not responsible for the loss.

Full Recourse Endorsements
Full recourse endorsement places the entire burden of collection activity upon the dealer; thus the dealer is required to locate the unit, obtain necessary releases, and transport the unit back to the lot if the consumer defaults. Under full recourse endorsement the lender may require the dealer to repay the outstanding balance of the defaulted conditional sales contract at any time, whether or not the unit has been repossessed or even located. In exercising this provision, the lender passes to the dealer all title rights to the mobile home representing security for the defaulted contract. Of course, the dealer may exercise the right to renegotiate with the original purchaser or may try to resell the unit. In any case the dealer acquires title to the unit, even if it cannot be located, and the lender calls for repayment.

It should be noted that, although in theory the lender is fully protected against any loss, indiscriminate exercise of the recourse provision could force a dealer into bankruptcy. Should that situation occur, the lender would be left with virtually no protection for the unpaid balance of any other paper originated by that particular dealer. Thus the lender must carefully choose when and how to exercise provisions of a full recourse endorsement agreement.

Nonrecourse Financing
A recent development, nonrecourse financing releases the dealer from any legal obligation for repayment of delinquent accounts. Of course, there is nothing to prevent the lending institution from seeking such guarantees from other sources, such as service com-

panies. Although nonrecourse financing imposes no legal obligation upon the dealer if customers default, the dealer must still be concerned about delinquencies and repossessions. Continued dealer referral of poor credit risks results in losses for the lender. When that happens, wholesale financing of dealer inventory is jeopardized. The danger of losing floor planning, coupled with the fact that few dealers have the financial liquidity to honor full recourse endorsements on a large scale, implies that nonrecourse financing is not as risky for the lender as it might, at first glance, appear to be.

Service Companies

Service companies have emerged in the retail segment of the mobile home industry as a response to the intricacies involved in acquiring a portfolio of mobile home paper. These firms, which specialize in the solicitation and origination of mobile home paper, experienced rapid growth during the early 1970s but were severely affected by the recession of the mid-1970s. Their early growth can be attributed to two factors. First, banks doing business with high-volume dealers found that they had five-figure net worths and six-figure contingent liabilities. Because these dealers would find it difficult to redeem many repossessions, recourse agreements provided limited protection to the lender. Hence, service companies, which guarantee loans, represented a real service to lenders. Second, service companies are uniquely equipped to handle all phases of mobile home financing that require highly specialized and experienced personal supervision. It could be costly for bankers to maintain a knowledgeable and sophisticated mobile home department. Service company personnel handled most problems that arose and provided equivalent services to lenders at lower cost than if lenders provided these services internally. In effect the service company acted as a mobile home department for the lender, thereby enabling both large and small lending institutions to participate in the market for mobile home paper.

Service companies currently play a minor role in the mobile home industry. However, some provide a wide range of services to lenders and dealers, including the following:

Advising dealers on legal requirements for perfecting a security interest in collateral and on procedures for compliance with the Truth in Lending Act, the Federal Consumer Protection Act, and similar legislation

Insuring the lender against credit losses on chattel paper purchased by the lender through the service company and insuring direct loan chattel paper that the lender wishes to bring into the service company's plan

Procuring physical damage insurance, including fire, theft, embezzlement, and conversion, with the lending institution (the lender is listed as the loss payee)

Checking the inventory and floor plan on new and used mobile home sales volume and making retail commodity checks with customers at the lender's request

Providing personal appraisal services to lenders on used mobile homes

Soliciting, investigating, and screening the credit position of potential participating mobile home dealers

Physically repossessing mobile homes when necessary because of defaulted contracts

Providing for the disposal of repossessed homes and full recovery of funds

Investigating customer complaints on services performed under warranty

In order to examine whether the existing dealer financing system serves the best interests of dealers and consumers, it is necessary to consider a dealer's cash flow attending the sale of a mobile home, the income that is generated and the expenses that result. PMHI has found that dealers profit as much from insurance commissions and other indirect income sources as they do from the markup on new mobile homes. To the extent that such indirect sources lead to inflated dealer profits, the system works to increase the cost of mobile home living and ultimately may not be in the dealer's best interests.

Sources of Funds

In the PMHI study of mobile home dealers, we addressed the question of dealer markup by analyzing the selling price of a typical mobile home with furnishings, as shown in table 15.2. Percentages in the table represent averages of the responses given by dealers surveyed by PMHI. From the table it can be seen that the FOB factory invoice price accounts for approximately 74 percent of the total sales price of the typical mobile home, with various other cost items totaling about

Table 15.2.
Percentage Breakdown of Mobile Home Retail Selling Price

Item	% of Selling Price
FOB factory price	73.9
Transportation Manufacturer to dealer	2.3
Dealer to lot	1.8
Setup costs	2.3
Sales person's commission	2.5
Advertising costs	.8
General and administrative expenses	1.7
Other overhead expenses	5.0
Floor planning cost	1.6
Profit (pretax)	8.1
Total	100.0

Source: PMHI/DS

18 percent. This leaves an average 8 percent pretax profit for the dealer from new mobile home sales. The rest of the dealer's profit primarily comes from such sources as dealer spread, insurance commissions, sale of used mobile homes, sale of accessories, and income from park participation.

Dealer Spread

The lender providing inventory financing usually receives most of the retail financing generated by the dealer's sales. In arranging financing for customers, the dealer quotes an interest rate that is higher than that at which the lending institution would normally discount the paper. This difference between the interest rate charged consumers and the discount rate offered the dealer is known as dealer spread.

The income from dealer spread becomes the basis of the dealer reserve account. The reserve account, deposited with the lender, sometimes is divided into a special reserve and regular reserve. Usually the lender stipulates that the special reserve must contain from 4 percent to 6 percent of the aggregate amount of retail paper outstanding before the dealer can withdraw any money. However, some banks give a dealer with a good credit rating up to half the total dealer reserve when the dealer enters into contract with the lender to obtain retail financing for a customer. The remainder of the total reserve is transferred to the dealer when half the consumer loan is paid. These lenders are willing to pay the dealer reserve quickly in order to obtain a large volume of retail paper from dealers with good credit ratings.

Insurance Commission

Another source of dealers' income results from their activities as agents to an insurance company. This practice is consistent with the dealers' involvement in retail financing of their products because a purchaser financing a mobile home is required by the lender to carry credit life insurance and, in some cases, credit risk insurance for the duration of the contract. Dealers often are required to endorse financial contracts through such mechanisms as full recourse endorsements and repurchase agreements, and they have a vested interest in obtaining proper insurance protection for their customers. Accordingly, most dealers are agents for all types of mobile home insurance. As agent to an insurance company, the dealer receives a commission, which may run as high as 35 percent to 50 percent of annual premiums. In some cases this amounts to 1 percent of gross annual sales.

Used Mobile Home Sales

Used mobile homes are becoming an increasingly significant portion of the mobile home market. The 8-wides and 10-wides have proved to be exceptionally versatile, adapting to such uses as construction trailers, vacation cabins, and low-cost shelter for those who cannot afford or do not desire a new mobile home.

Dealers normally base their trade-in allowance for used units on their appraisal and the value quoted in the Official Mobile Home Market Report (the "Blue Book"). Industry publications estimate a 20 percent to 25 percent dealer markup on used mobile homes. This is confirmed by the PMHI Dealer Survey, which found that a typical trade-in value allowed by dealers is about $2800 and a typical sale price of used units is about $3500. Because the dealer's average cost to refurnish a used unit is $420, the dealer is left with a gross profit of about $280 or 10 percent.

Sale of Accessories

Dealers generally sell new mobile homes at about a 20 percent to 30 percent markup, but the markup on accessories is normally 30 percent to 50 percent. Although the markup is rather substantial, revenue generated from selling accessories is only a very small portion of the total revenue received by mobile home dealers. The PMHI study indicates that 29 percent of the respondents sold accessories valued from $50 to $150 per unit. This figure appears to be low, probably because some dealers consider accessories to be part of the retail price. However, even with $200 worth of accessories sold per unit, there is a gross profit of only $60 to $100 per mobile home. Thus it appears that dealers do not rely on the sale of accessories as a major source of income.

Participation in Park Operation

Many dealers obtain additional income from ownership interests in mobile home parks. The PMHI study revealed that a little over half of the dealers surveyed had some ownership interest in at least one park, with a mean total park capacity of 316 units. Of this group, half had connections with only one park. Some dealers who have park interests link the availability of rental space in their parks to sales from their dealership. Roughly 12 percent of the dealers surveyed in our study reported that about 90 percent of total units sold were located on park sites in which they had a financial interest.

Uses of Funds

At one time a couple with $5000 in the bank and a bit of land could seriously consider going into the mobile home dealership business. Today things are quite different because of two major factors. First, mobile home display has become an expensive and important outlay for the dealer. The sales lot must be attractively landscaped and roads within the lot should be paved. Mobile homes displayed for sale must approximate the actual use situation as closely as possible. Utilities must be connected, appliances must be in working order, and accessories must be neatly placed to give the customer a view of how the mobile home will look in actual use. In addition there must be personnel on hand to take care of the display units, and the sales lot must have an attractive office in which to finalize a sale. Second, there is a growing trend toward multilot operations. The PMHI survey shows that about 40 percent of the dealers operate from more than one sales lot, with one-fourth of this group employing four or more lots. Some dealers rotate mobile homes, especially slow-moving units, around various lots. These and other current business practices have substantially increased the minimum starting investment in a dealership.

Display and Setup Costs

Certain finishing touches to a mobile home can only be accomplished at the dealer's lot. Units are shipped to the dealer with furnishings partially assembled, crated, and strapped down, and these furnishings must be assembled and installed so that models intended for display on the dealer's lot appear ready for occupancy. These setup costs become increasingly important in the case of doublewides, which are shipped as individual components and then assembled at the dealer's lot, only to be dismantled after sale for transportation to the purchaser's site.

Although the actual amount of setup costs incurred by the dealer depends on both the type of unit and the manner of transportation, the PMHI survey indicates that it costs about $200 per unit for a dealer to set up units for display. In addition to the more direct expenditures for labor and transportation mentioned above, setup costs can include such indirect items as the installation of utility hookups so that display homes may be heated during the winter months. As a convenience and selling point during home inspections, customers often like to turn on the lights, stove, fans, water faucets, and appliances. Therefore this mechanical equipment must be kept in good working order.

Advertising and Sales Promotion

Unlike their counterparts in the automobile industry, who rely upon the automobile manufacturers for media exposure of their products, dealerships undertake most of the advertising in the mobile home industry. Advertising expense typically ranges from 1/2 percent to 2 percent of total sales. According to the PMHI Dealer Survey, dealers spend their advertising dollar according to the following general breakdown by medium: newspapers, 65 percent; radio, 15 percent; television, 10 percent; and other outlets, 10 percent. Advertising media in the "other" category include displays at mobile home fairs, billboard advertising, and direct mailings.

Sales promotion in the form of trade shows sponsored by the industry or local dealer associations is becoming an increasingly important expense for mobile home dealers. Dealers can spend over $1000 per unit per show, with added costs when doublewides are displayed. Usually transportation to and from the shows, setup, and take-down costs account for most of these expenses. In addition the dealer is required to pay an entry fee and rent the spaces on which mobile homes are displayed.

Many manufacturers give their dealers an advertising allowance, which takes the form of a deduction from factory invoice when tear sheets or other proof of insertion are submitted. Those manufacturers large enough to employ advertising managers supply dealers with materials that range from newspaper ad copy to sales brochures, signs, and banners. Some companies furnish scripts and tapes for radio advertising as well as slides, scripts, and films for those dealers who can afford television advertising.

After-Sale Expenses
Once a sale has been consummated, the dealer must unhook the unit from the sales lot, perform whatever repacking of appliances and equipment is necessary, and provide for transportation to the purchaser's site. Normally all transportation costs within twenty-five to fifty miles are absorbed by the dealer as part of the sales package. When the unit arrives on site, it must then be reinstalled.

In addition dealer-to-dealer competition has encouraged the group as a whole to assume responsibility for the manufacturer's warranty. In fact, the PMHI survey indicates that over 70 percent of the responding dealers offer warranties beyond those manufacturers provide. Generally, such additional dealer warranties range up to a year in duration. Under the manufacturer's warranty any necessary repairs must be promptly made by the dealer and settled with the manufacturer at a future date. In some cases, however, manufacturers subsidize warranty assumption by the dealer through a system of rebates or discounts from factory invoice.

Conclusions from the Funds Flow Analysis

Although mobile home dealers derive a substantial profit from indirect sources, there is a close relationship between much of this income and costs. For example, to sell accessories and used mobile homes, the dealer incurs advertising and after-sale costs. However, two sources of income, dealer spread and insurance commissions, cannot be justified by corresponding costs. Although there is some administrative work involved, the resulting expenses to the dealer for ongoing retail financing and insurance programs are small.

This does not imply that the elimination of dealer spread and insurance commissions

would result in lower costs for the consumer. Dealer profits, including income from these sources, are not excessive; the PMHI survey found that dealerships typically generate pretax profits of 15 percent or less. If insurance commissions and dealer spread were eliminated, dealers would try to make up for the income loss by charging more for mobile homes. Therefore arbitrary changes that reduce dealer income may not have the desired impact on costs to the consumer. If consumer costs are to be lowered, a comprehensive strategy is required that reflects a thorough understanding of the mobile home industry.

At present, wholesale and retail financing at the dealership level are very much entangled in the mobile home industry. This entanglement results from lenders' expectations that by providing low-cost wholesale financing they will obtain the lucrative retail financing generated by dealer sales. However, this expensive retail financing paper has a considerable impact on the cost of mobile home ownership. If retail financing costs are to be reduced, a method must be devised to lower lender participation without affecting dealer profits and costs of floor planning.

Consider, for example, a scenario in which a dealer receives inventory on consignment from manufacturers. Now the lender does not have to provide low-cost funds for floor planning and does not require as high a retail finance charge to profit from the dealer's account. Such an arrangement could result in lower total costs to the consumer, assuming that the manufacturer is financially able to support sales by providing a sufficient number of units on consignment. Another approach would be for manufacturers to provide low-cost floor plan financing to dealers as an incentive for them to concentrate on that particular manufacturer's product. The financing costs to the manufacturer in this arrangement might be compensated for by a higher sales volume.

There are other ways to reduce the cost of mobile home ownership, and most of them involve a change in the relationship between wholesale and retail financing at the dealer level. Substituting mobile home manufacturers for traditional lenders to finance inventory would enable manufacturers to forge stronger ties with selected dealers. At the same time sales would increase because the ultimate costs of the manufacturer's products to the consumer would be reduced. Such an arrangement might be to the manufacturer's and dealer's mutual advantage, although it would provide a competitive hurdle for small manufacturers.

Among the major concerns of new home buyers are the initial cost and monthly payments associated with the purchase. Although a mobile home is the least expensive form of housing and requires a lower down

Policy Alternatives

C. Consumer Finance

payment than conventional homes, monthly costs often are surprisingly high. This is a result of the complex consumer financing mechanism that prevails in the mobile home industry. This finance structure is shown in figure 15.3.

Some mobile home buyers pay cash, but most finance their purchases through lending institutions. Unlike the conventional home buyer who obtains a simple interest mortgage for twenty-five years or more at a relatively low interest rate, the mobile home buyer pays a relatively high add-on interest rate for a term of twenty years or less. In addition the dealer receives a portion of the interest consumers pay in the form of dealer spread, which drives the rates higher than they need be. The net result of these factors is that although the mobile home buyer generally pays lower monthly costs than do conventional home owners, the costs are disproportionately high considering the mobile home's significantly lower price. This financing disparity tends to reduce the desirability of mobile home living. In this discussion of consumer finance we explore the ramifications of the financing structure depicted in figure 15.3 and show how major changes in the finance structure might benefit the consumer and dealer.

Considerations in Retail Financing

The financial intermediary involved in supplying money to a mobile home purchaser faces certain risks in making a loan and must carefully consider the factors that determine the magnitude of contingent losses. Lenders tend to stress the risks of retail mobile home financing when justifying their high interest rates. In general they consider the risks of such loans to parallel those implicit in other forms of consumer credit installment loans such as automobile purchase financing. However, some believe that the risks faced by the investing institution more closely resemble those of a conventional site-built home mortgage loan.

Whether one agrees that mobile home loans should be placed in the same risk category as conventional mortgages, the appropriateness of the installment loan classification must be seriously questioned. For a number of reasons there was a considerable improvement in risk conditions on mobile home paper during the late 1960s. First, lenders' fears that a mobile home owner could hitch the home to a car and disappear became unwarranted; new, larger mobile homes required a crew of professional movers. Second, most mobile homes were purchased to be the borrower's principal residence and default would mean loss of shelter. Finally, measures were taken directly by the lenders to reduce risks; use of vendors-single-interest (VSI) insurance coverage to protect the lender against embezzlement, credit risk insurance, dealer recourse and repurchase agreements, and dealer reserves became widespread.

Although mobile home loans may be less risky than other installment loans, they do have some disadvantages. The longer term of mobile home loans implies lower reinvestment costs but also means less flexibility to reinvest when desired. Also, the large average investment per borrower compared with other types of installment loans implies a less diversified investment portfolio and hence a greater overall lender risk. Finally, although mobile homes are inconvenient to move, they are still more mobile than a site-built home.

Depreciation

On balance, the factors above tend to push the mobile home out of the consumer loan risk category into the conventional home mortgage risk category. However, depreciation dictates against this reclassification. Depreciation is a measure of the yearly decrease in the resale price or market value of a capital good. The depreciation rate for mobile homes is much higher than that for conventional housing.

The most controversial and important factor influencing the depreciation rate is the life of the mobile home. The economic life of the mobile home, rarely taken to exceed twenty years, depends upon many factors. Among these are size, make and model, date of manufacture, quality of maintenance, regional climatic differences, and site. Extensive nationwide PMHI interviews of traditional builders and developers as well as mobile home manufacturers and park operators suggest that the economic life of the mobile home is considerably longer than is commonly assumed and may be close to the life of a conventional home.

Depreciation is influenced by other factors. Furniture and appliances supplied with a new mobile home, which represent 10 percent of the purchase price and may have to be replaced several times during the home's life, increase depreciation. Depreciation rates tend to vary by mobile home model and year of production. This characteristic causes the resale value for mobile homes to resemble that for automobiles in that prices are determined by age and Blue Book estimates rather than by an appraisal of the true value. Consumer tastes also influence the depreciation rate; many mobile home shoppers prefer a new home of the latest style, thereby depressing the value of used homes.

Lenders view the depreciation rate as a significant risk. In the event of repossession, the lender must recoup some of the lost investment by selling the used unit. Because the mobile home may lose a significant portion of its value in the first few years, the lender stands to lose this amount in the event of default. Today, some mobile homes actually are appreciating in value. However, because of previously mentioned market factors, they are not increasing in value as rapidly as conventional houses. Until mobile home apprecia-

Figure 15.3.
PMHI model of the
dealer/consumer
relationship.

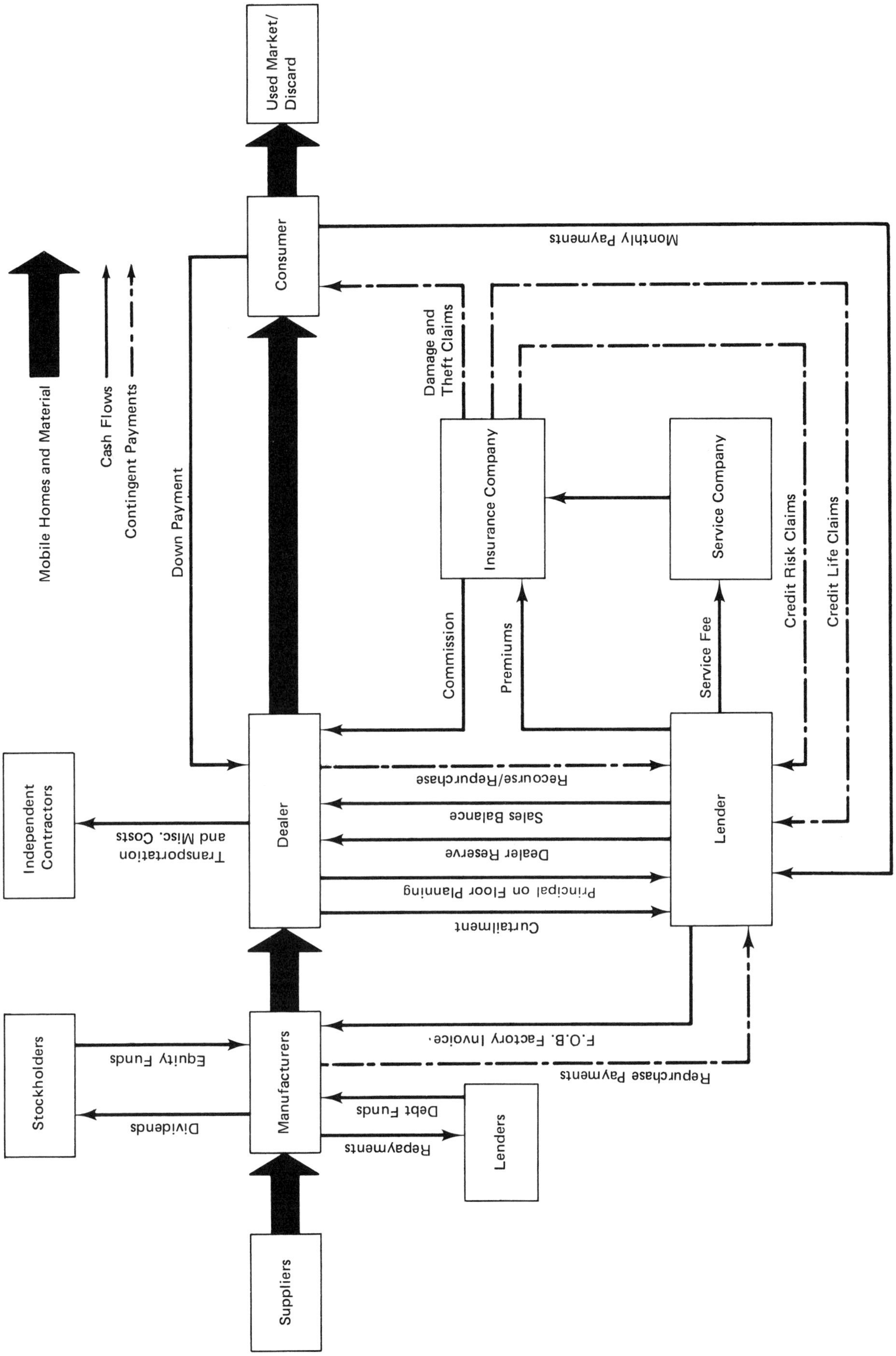

tion is comparable to that for conventional homes, lenders will not put mobile homes in the same risk category.

Credit Risk

The effect of general economic conditions on mobile home buyers has become obvious to financial institutions holding mobile home paper. When the economy is doing well, a large group of potential mobile home purchasers exists. During a recession, some of this group lose their source of income because of layoffs. Others may be unable to meet payments, resulting in an increase in defaults. Without sound credit practices, lending institutions are vulnerable to the changing risk patterns caused by variations in either the national or regional economies.

Lenders can control expected losses through their credit allocation practices. Although lenders cannot control exogenous factors such as the mobile home depreciation rate and statutory maximum interest rate, they can adjust credit practices to reduce the magnitude of contingent losses. Several important factors influence lenders' credit policy in the field of retail and wholesale mobile home financing. Among these are the dealer's operations, the terms of the retail and wholesale contracts, and the customer's credit standing. Cautious lenders maintain strict screening policies in order to lower risk.

Some lending institutions handle credit screening and enforcement practices through service companies. Others protect themselves against credit losses by requiring risk insurance. Though included in the package plan offered by service companies, credit risk insurance can be purchased without their intermediation. This type of insurance is designed to protect the lender against contract default and the resulting losses from delinquency or repossession. Lenders pay credit risk insurance premiums in a lump sum at the inception of the loan contract. Premium size is based upon the loan amount and the lender's customer screening history.

The development and widespread use of credit risk insurance has had two effects on the financing sector of the mobile home industry. First, costs to the lender have stabilized. By utilizing credit risk insurance, mobile home loans can be classified as low-risk investments. Because the premium costs of credit risk insurance are known, the lender can project future yields with certainty. Second, the use of credit risk insurance has caused greater division of labor in the financing sector. Dealers no longer need to be tied to recourse agreements and lenders no longer need to venture into the used mobile home business to sell repossessed mobile homes. Both may concentrate resources on primary business objectives.

Government Loan Insurance Programs

In order to make the mobile home industry a more readily available source of low-cost

housing, the federal government initiated loan guarantee programs through the Federal Housing Administration (FHA) and the Veteran's Administration (VA). The objective of these programs was to reduce the financing costs for mobile home purchasers, primarily by lowering interest rates, lengthening contract terms, and alleviating costly credit insurance policies. In the VA and FHA programs the lender is induced to make mobile home loans at the lower specified interest rates because government agencies underwrite the risk.

These programs appeal to different audiences and therefore are structured somewhat differently. They are constantly being revised by Congress, and their specific conditions are subject to change. As of this writing in 1978, the FHA program insures loans for singlewide mobile homes to $16,000 at terms up to twelve years and simple interest rates ranging to 12 percent. The FHA program has a down payment requirement of 5 percent for the first $3,000 borrowed and 10 percent for the balance. For doublewides, the FHA insures loans up to $24,000 for fifteen years. The VA program requires no down payment and has a maximum guarantee on loans up to $17,500 or 50 percent of the loan, whichever is less. The permissible loan terms are fifteen years for singlewides and twenty years for doublewides. Both FHA and VA programs allow for larger loan limits if the mobile home is attached to improved land. There are also provisions in each program for insuring loans taken to purchase mobile home lots and used mobile homes.

To date these programs have not been successful. FHA and VA credit insurance have typically been employed in fewer than 4 percent of all mobile home transactions. In 1977 approximately three thousand lenders maintained portfolios containing mobile home loans. Of these only six hundred made the government programs available to borrowers and fewer than seventy actively promoted the programs. Lenders are reluctant to provide loans at the specified maximum interest rates when they can loan funds elsewhere at higher rates. Dealers also find the programs unattractive; they are unwilling to forego income generated from dealer spread, which is not permitted with FHA- and VA-insured loans.

The federal government has been attempting to improve the FHA and VA programs. However, simple modifications to existing programs will result in only marginally greater use. More extensive steps may be required if the FHA and VA programs are to become major factors in mobile home retail financing.

Advantages and Disadvantages of Mobile Home Paper

Financial institutions interested in mobile home paper must consider both the pros and

cons of holding such paper before plunging into the mobile home arena. Once the lender has made an affirmative decision concerning mobile home investment, time and money will have to be spent to develop a successful mobile home loan department.

The disadvantages of mobile home paper can be understood only relative to other forms of financing. Relative to conventional site-built mortgage financing, mobile home financing involves the added risk of a higher depreciation rate. Compared to consumer installment loans, mobile home paper generally has a longer term and is less flexible for reinvestment. Furthermore, mobile home paper involves a larger investment than that required for other installment loans, which results in a greater quantity of invested funds per borrower and reduces the diversification of risk. Additional disadvantages of mobile home paper arise from the indirect nature of mobile home retail financing. In order to obtain retail financing business through mobile home dealers, the lender typically must provide wholesale financing for the dealer's inventory. This floor plan financing often involves a substantial amount of funds loaned at a low interest rate, offering only a marginal yield.

Many financial institutions believe that the advantages of retail mobile home paper outweigh the disadvantages. Relative to conventional mortgage investments in site-built homes, investments in mobile home paper return a higher interest rate, provide for a more rapid turnover rate, require less effort per transaction, and involve a level of risk comparable to that of financing site-built homes. Relative to other credit installment loans, mobile home paper provides a similar interest rate level, a low degree of risk, and lower transaction costs. The last factor is due to the greater average amount and term of mobile home contracts compared to other installment loan contracts. An additional advantage to those financial institutions that purchase mobile home paper is the likelihood that borrowers will consider the specific lending institution when searching for other financial services.

Stability of Credit: Tight Money Considerations

What have been the effects of tight money on the mobile home industry? Mobile homes and conventional housing respond similarly to changes in the interest rate; when the economy is strong and interest rates increase, both mobile and conventional housing sales drop. However, because mobile homes are financed with relatively high interest loans compared to conventional housing, loan funds are not exhausted as rapidly for mobile homes when capital is short. The higher interest rate and shorter term of mobile home loans give lenders an incentive to seek out mobile home loans when conventional home mortgages are unattractive.

There is evidence that the mobile home industry does not recover quickly from a deep recession, such as that of the mid-1970s. Although the housing industry recorded major gains in 1977 over 1976, the mobile home industry saw only modest improvement. The position of mobile homes as a percentage of total new housing production has been steadily eroding from a peak of 22 percent in 1973 to 12 percent in 1977. Part of this drop is explained by the mobile home financing mechanism, which results in high interest rates and disproportionately high monthly payments considering the low cost of the home. This high interest characteristic proves to be an advantage in channeling funds to the industry at the onset of recession but a disadvantage as the recession ends and funds are available for lower-interest loans. However, the drop also reflects consumers' apparent preference for site-built homes and their willingness to pay the higher price when the economic outlook is favorable.

Conventional Mortgage Financing

In the early 1960s, when sectionals and doublewides began rolling off the assembly line in increasing numbers, lenders began to consider conventional mortgage financing for these larger and more costly mobile homes. There were necessary prerequisites, however, to the use of mortgage financing for mobile homes. First, the land upon which the mobile home was placed had to be included in the purchased package. The appreciation rate of the land value helped to offset the normal high depreciation rate of the mobile home and thus reduced the magnitude of the contingent losses to the lender from potential repossession. Second, lending institutions insisted that the mobile home be secured to the land, arising perhaps from the lenders' fear that their collateral might vanish in the night. As a final precaution lenders generally insisted that undercarriage and wheels be removed from the mobile home.

There are many incentives for lenders to extend credit terms through mortgage financing. If land is included, the appreciation of a mobile home package is comparable to that for a conventional home. The improved quality of mobile homes has increased their expected lives to the point where lenders can safely extend the contract terms. Also, the higher prices of better-quality and larger mobile homes have necessitated the use of longer-term contracts, without which the monthly payments could be prohibitive.

Offsetting these incentives are some disadvantages associated with conventional mortgage financing of mobile homes. First, lenders usually are required to provide unprofitable floor plan financing for dealers. To compensate for this loss, the lucrative installment-type retail paper is preferred by the lender over the less profitable mortgage paper. Second, dealers are not motivated to promote conventional financing because their dealer reserve would be eliminated. Third, land usually is not included in the purchase of a mobile home. Finally, some customers prefer to have their mobile homes treated as personal property rather than real property because personal property is often taxed at a lower rate.

Price and Terms of Purchase

The average price for a new mobile home has increased significantly over the years. Three factors combined to produce an overall rise in the price level. First, mobile home quality has improved. Second, new mobile homes are increasing in size; as more middle- and upper-income families choose the mobile home living alternative, a greater demand is created for increased interior space provided by expandables and doublewides. Third, inflation is driving up manufacturing costs. As prices continue to increase, financing terms will play an even greater role in defining the market of mobile home buyers.

Since mobile home financing was first instituted in the 1930s, the average length of the contract and the down payment requirement have shown definite trends. The term has lengthened from two to twenty-five years, and the down payment required has dropped from 35 percent to the point where it is waived in some transactions. More liberal terms have evolved for several reasons. The perceived risk of a mobile home loan has declined over the years as the character of the mobile home changed with improved construction quality and park conditions. Retail paper has exhibited good performance in terms of delinquencies and repossessions. The average life of a mobile home is greater than it once was. Public pressure for low-cost housing has resulted in government insurance programs that specify longer terms and lower down payments. Also, increased competition among lenders for the profitable retail paper has resulted in more lenient terms.

Government policies have been implemented to reduce interest rates for mobile home loans. These include the authorization of savings and loan associations to buy retail paper, which increases lender competition. The policies also include the FHA and VA programs to reduce risks to the lender. These policies have served to lower maximum rates on mobile home paper as well as to narrow the gap between the typical mobile home retail interest rate and the conventional home mortgage rate. However, given the current financing structure, mobile home rates will never be competitive with conventional home mortgage rates. As long as the dealer reserve results from the high interest charge and lenders require lucrative retail interest rates to offset unprofitable wholesale mobile home financing, high rates will be maintained.

Risks to the Lender

The perceived depreciation rate in the value of mobile homes has shown a decline over the years. Reasons for this decline include the higher quality and longer expected lives of newer mobile homes. A lower depreciation rate, in turn, implies a lower level of risk to the lender in terms of expected losses due to repossession. A trend to unbundled finance packages, in which the home and furniture are separately financed, should further decrease the impact of depreciation.

The use of credit risk insurance, including that provided by the FHA and VA programs, appears to be increasing. Lenders have come to recognize credit risk insurance as a mechanism through which uncertain margins can be converted to predictable profits.

The delinquency and repossession ratios on outstanding mobile home paper decreased impressively during the 1960s and bottomed out in 1970 and 1971 before rising during the recession of the mid-1970s. A direct determinant of the level of these ratios is the degree of conscientious credit screening and dealer supervision effort by the lender. Another major determinant is the level of economic activity. Inadequate screening and a low level of economic activity combined to produce the increase in delinquencies and repossessions that occurred during the mid-1970s. Improvement in both factors will be necessary for delinquency and repossession ratios to return to 1970 and 1971 levels.

Conventional Mortgage Financing

The use of conventional mortgages for mobile home financing has been gradually increasing since becoming available in 1963. Among the reasons are higher prices, longer terms, lower perceived depreciation rates, and lower delinquency ratios of mobile homes, all of which have improved the compatibility of mobile home parameters with mortgage contract terms. Nonetheless, mortgage financing still plays a minor role.

The growth rate of mobile home mortgage financing has not been outstanding. Neither has it reflected the view that mortgage financing is the inevitable goal toward which retail mobile home financing is headed. The ultimate direction that mobile home financing will take may not be fully described by installment credit financing or conventional mortgage financing, but by a hybrid of the two. Prerequisite to this however, is a new basis for a mobile home purchase in which the home is attached to land and appliances are separately financed.

Performance of the Consumer Finance Sector

In order to analyze the performance of the consumer finance sector, it is necessary to consider the impact of the system on all participants: lender, consumer, and dealer.

Lender

From the lender's viewpoint mobile home paper has been a high-yield, low-risk investment. Retail mobile home paper offers a yield at least equal to that from other installment loans. In addition, the cost of acquiring and servicing mobile home loans is less than that for other installment paper because the loan amount tends to be larger and the term longer. On balance, the risk associated with mobile home paper has proved to be relatively low. Lenders who maintain carefully supervised mobile home loan portfolios therefore have good reason to be satisfied with the present structure of the consumer finance sector.

Consumer

The consumer's welfare should play a substantial role in an analysis of the performance of the consumer financing sector. The consumer is the pivot upon whom the success of the mobile home industry depends; he or she represents the ultimate target toward which mobile home units flow and the source from which all funds originate. How well are the consumer's desires being met within the present structure of the financing sector?

Unfortunately, this question cannot be as decisively answered as that concerning the lender. The reason for ambiguity is that consumers have dissimilar financial and social conditions and, hence, differing priorities. The mobile home consumer market can be divided into four distinct interest groups: elderly individuals and couples whose mobile homes function primarily as retirement or vacation homes; middle-income people who voluntarily have chosen mobile home living as an alternative to a conventional home; the youthful segment such as newly-weds, who often have limited credit; and low-income families, who are constrained by their lack of money and credit. Different consumer segments assign varying degrees of importance to different aspects of the consumer financing sector. One group of consumers may be satisfied with the current performance of consumer financing; another may not benefit from its structure. Factors most important to consumers are discussed below.

Monthly Payments

The monthly cost of owning a mobile home is one of the most influential factors affecting a consumer's decision to buy. To the low-income segment, however, it is all-important. The lower the consumer's income, the larger the percentage that must be devoted to monthly payments. In some sense the consumer financing sector has performed well regarding the monthly payments factor. Monthly payments have remained below, or at least comparable to, the monthly payments on a conventional mortgage for a site-built home. Longer terms have accompanied rising prices to keep monthly payments at a reasonable level. However, some

Figure 15.4.
Flow diagram showing
relationship of retail
markup to interest rate.

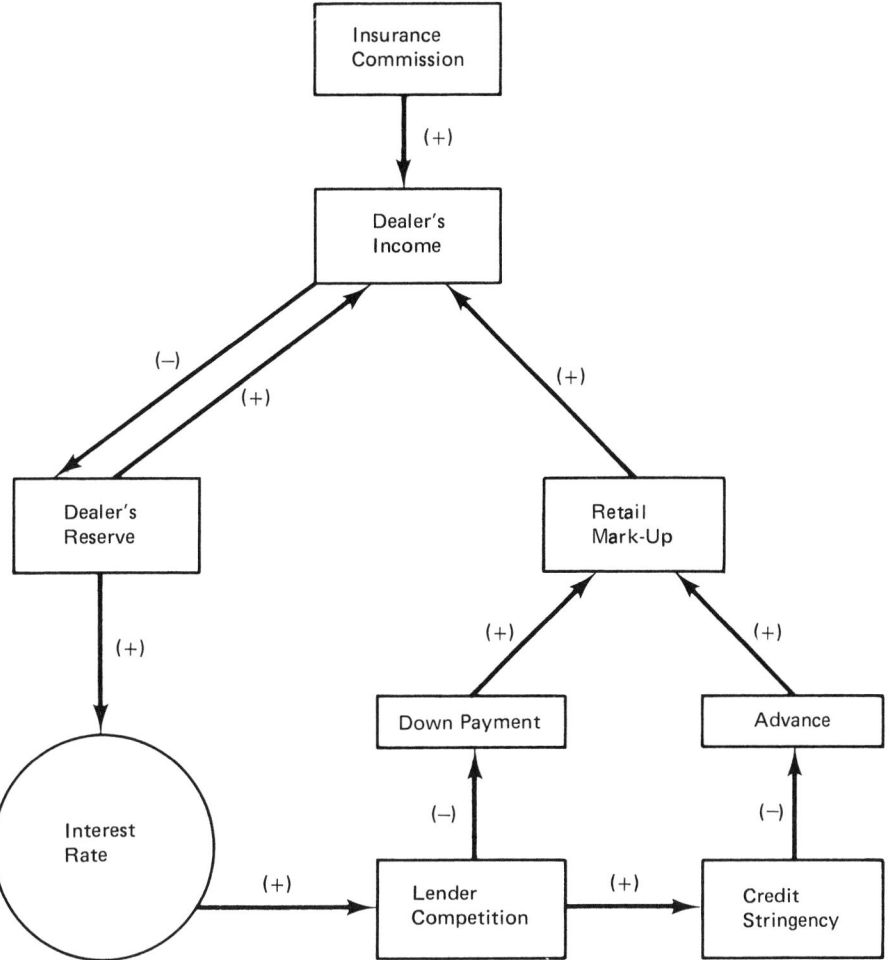

groups, such as low-income consumers and
federal government agencies, have felt that
monthly payments are too large considering
the lower price of mobile homes compared to
the price of site-built homes.

Availability of Credit
The availability of credit to mobile home
purchasers is of primary concern to youthful
and low-income buyers because the need for
credit is most strongly felt by these groups.
Fortunately for these consumers, the retail
financing sector generally has been successful in maintaining a liberal supply of credit.
Historically, financing has been available in
periods of tight money, when mortgage lending on conventional homes was severely
curtailed. The primary reason for this is the
high interest rate of mobile home paper and
the resulting high yield to the lender.

Down Payment Requirement
The low down payment the lender requires
has been advantageous to the consumer.
Lender competition has driven the down payment requirement of mobile home buyers to
10 percent of the unit's retail price or less.
Because the retail price is lower than the
price of a site-built home, the required down

payment for a mobile home is substantially
lower than for a conventional home. This
advantage is weighed most heavily by those
consumers having a poor liquid asset position, primarily young and low-income consumers.

Interest Rate
The high interest rate charged on a mobile
home loan is one of the most negative indicators of consumer financing performance. The
degree of its importance depends upon the
consumer segment analyzed. Many consumers
seem indifferent to interest rates and prefer to
finance through the dealer rather than shop
for a lower rate. Others are so concerned
about obtaining manageable monthly payments that they pay little attention to total
interest costs. However, under the current
retail financing system and dealer structure
there is little the consumer can do about high
interest rates.

Dealer
The existing dealer structure contributes to
high interest rates for the consumer. Because
the markup on retail mobile home sales often
is inadequate, dealers must supplement
profits with income from other sources such
as dealer spread. Figure 15.4 is a causal flow

diagram presented to clarify this point. A plus sign between two variables in the diagram indicates that they work together; as insurance commissions increase, so does dealer's income. A minus sign indicates that the variables work in opposite directions; as lender competition increases, down payment requirements decrease.

Figure 15.4 indicates that the dealer's income is affected by the retail markup, dealer reserve, and insurance commission. The dealer reserve and insurance commission depend upon a sale being made and are incentive payments to the dealer by lenders and insurance agencies for business referrals. The markup is determined by two factors: the down payment requirement and the percentage of invoice price the lender is willing to advance the dealer. For example, consider a mobile home that costs the dealer $8000. If the lender is willing to advance 115 percent of manufacturer's invoice and the down payment is 10 percent, the markup computation is

$ 8,000	Invoice
$ 9,200	Advance (115% of invoice)
$ 1,022	Down payment (10% of retail)
$10,222	Maximum retail price

The resulting gross profit to the dealer is

$10,222 − $8,000 = $2,222   Markup

$$\frac{\$\,2,222}{\$10,222} = 21.8\%$$ Actual gross profit.

This percentage may be inadequate to sustain the dealer's operations.

The gap between actual margin and necessary margin results from the low down payment requirement, dictated by a competitive market, and from the lender's unwillingness to advance an adequate percentage of invoice cost. The ultimate effect of these constraints is that many dealerships are marginal operations. The greater the dealer's reliance on supplementary financial returns such as dealer reserve, the greater the pressure for higher interest rates.

Policy Alternatives

One of the most promising methods to reduce inefficiencies in the consumer finance sector is to encourage specialization among the participants. One step toward a clear division of labor might be the elimination of dealer reserve. For many dealers income is inadequate if dealer reserve is eliminated and it must be supplemented in another manner. Consider an arrangement whereby lenders are willing to advance 125 percent of manufacturer's invoice rather than 115 percent. The dealer's markup computation would be

$ 8,000	Invoice
$10,000	Advance (@ 125% of invoice)
$ 1,111	Down payment (@ 10% of retail)
$11,111	Retail price.

The gross profit would then be

$11,111 − $8,000 = $3,111   Markup

or as a percentage,

$$\frac{\$\,3,111}{\$11,111} = 28\%$$ Actual gross profit.

In general this would be adequate to cover the dealer's expenses and provide a fair return.

The result of such a change might be to eliminate the dealer's need for a financing participation fee and an insurance commission. Dealers would be forced to compete among themselves on the basis of service and price. Financing considerations would not complicate the consumer's decision of where to buy the mobile home. A specific financial institution probably would still be floor planning for a given dealer, so it is inevitable that dealers would direct consumers to their preferred lender. However, interest rates would be lower on retail paper because the dealer reserve is not extracted from the consumer's financing charge.

How would this change affect aspects of mobile home financing important to the consumer? Assuming that the lender advances the dealer 125 percent of manufacturer's invoice rather than 115 percent, the retail price would increase as follows:

Before (115%)	After (125%)	
$ 8,000	$ 8,000	Invoice
$ 9,200	$10,000	Advance (115% and 125%)
$ 1,022	$ 1,111	Down payment (10% of retail)
$10,222	$11,111	Retail price.

The increase in retail price is $889, less than 9 percent of the original retail price, and the increase in down payment is $89, again less than 9 percent above the original down payment figure. This change affects the interest rate, monthly payments, term, credit availability, and consumer's equity. The interest rate will decline because dealer's reserves will be eliminated. However, many mobile home buyers are more interested in monthly payments than in the interest rate level. The important question is whether interest rates will decline sufficiently to maintain the previous level of monthly payments.

Continuing with the example, assume that the original interest rate is 7 percent add-on and the term is ten years. The monthly payments are

$10,222	Retail price
1,022	Down payment
$ 9,200	Advance
$ 6,440	Interest charge (7% × 10 year × $9,200)
$15,640	Total payment
$130.33	Monthly payment (120 payments)

What interest rate will produce the same monthly payments at the higher retail price, assuming the term remains constant at ten years?

$11,111 Retail price
 1,111 Down payment
$10,000 Advance

$15,640 = $10,000 + ($10,000 × X% × 10 years)

X% = 5.64% Add-on interest rate.

Assuming that 7 percent add-on is the normal retail financing rate with dealer spread, 5.64 percent is not an unreasonable interest rate to the lender when dealer spread is eliminated. Therefore from a consumer's viewpoint the net results of a higher advance are a lower interest rate and a higher down payment. Availability of credit and monthly payments are approximately the same following the change. Finally, the consumer's equity probably will be higher because the same mobile home will now sell at a higher price.

Financial institutions are motivated by programs that result in maximum profits. Therefore policies tending to lower interest rates to lenders without providing offsetting compensation will not work. If the advance increases, interest rates would decrease but dealer reserves would be eliminated. Therefore yield probably would remain at a satisfactory level. A higher advance results in larger loans and a greater volume of business from the same number of outstanding mobile home loans. On the other hand, the lender's risk will increase. Lenders who rely on dealer recourse agreements would hold no dealer reserve to back up these agreements. Also, lenders would stand to lose a significantly greater percentage from contract defaults and repossessions because they would have advanced more money per mobile home. Therefore the policy of increased advances would have to be accompanied by a policy of more stringent underwriting requirements.

Other policies might be implemented, some that affect the relationship between lenders and service companies. Large lenders generally do not require service companies to generate and service their mobile home portfolios because they have their own experienced mobile home loan departments. Only the small and often inexperienced lenders must resort to service companies if they want to become involved in mobile home financing. Do service companies cause inefficiency by introducing unnecessary steps in the financing process or do they promote efficiency by providing services that strictly belong to neither the dealer nor the lender?

During the recession of the mid-1970s many lenders terminated relationships with service companies. In part this resulted from reduced activity in the mobile home financing market. However, some lenders felt that service companies were a luxury they could not

afford when the market softened. This loss of new business, combined with financial pressures created by an increase in consumer defaults, caused many service companies to fail.

We believe that as mobile home markets become strong again service companies will see a growth resurgence. Their function of providing expertise and support to small lenders is important if small lenders are to participate in the mobile home retail finance market. It is up to the service companies, however, to improve credit screening procedures if they are to be insulated from economic recessions.

Another area of policy change focuses on mobile home manufacturers. Manufacturers are able to influence financing sector performance through their ability to control the quality and retail price of mobile homes. As the quality of the unit is improved, its value and expected life increase. A consumer can realize two direct advantages from this improvement. The first is a potentially lower level of monthly payments, because a longer contract term may result from the longer expected life. The second advantage is that of higher consumer equity. A better-quality mobile home will appeal more strongly to those investment-minded shoppers who place significant emphasis on their future equity. These consumers include middle- and upper-income purchasers, and they represent a growing portion of the mobile home market.

Summary

The installment method of consumer financing in the mobile home industry is a product of tradition. It continues to be the most widely used method of financing, primarily because of its relationship to other components of the industry's financial structure. Although the use of installment financing has made mobile home living available to many, it has limited the possible future evolution of the industry.

Using installment financing, lenders have been able to obtain rates of return on mobile home loans that are higher than those available on mortgages. Increasing loan terms have offset the higher interest cost of these loans, with the result that monthly payment levels have remained within the means of most consumers. However, the interest rate differential between mortgages and mobile home installment loans has resulted in considerable extra cost to mobile home consumers. This higher cost often has been explained by alluding to greater risks associated with mobile home loans, primarily because of mobile home depreciation and the financial status of many mobile home owners.

Until recently, the risk of default associated with mobile home loans was low relative to most other consumer loans. During the past few years a lack of adequate credit screening by lenders, the energy crisis, and the recession have caused an upsurge in the number of repossessions. This has led to considerable stress in financial institutions serving the industry. In view of this negative experience, lenders are sure to strengthen screening procedures on future mobile home loans, at least temporarily. This new policy and the abatement of the recession should reduce risk.

The financial and physical similarities between mobile homes fixed to a site and conventional homes suggest a change in financing from the traditional installment methods to mortgage financing. This would be a desirable change for mobile home consumers because home ownership costs would be reduced. It also is attractive to the industry because such a cost reduction would cause an expansion of consumer mobile home demand. However, poor quality of mobile home furnishings, changing demand for used mobile homes, and exclusion of land from most mobile home sales packages have prevented lenders from viewing the two types of housing as equivalents.

The accepted method of installment financing is only one element in the complex financing pattern prevalent in the mobile home industry. Changes should be made to lower consumer financing costs. These must be accompanied by changes in other financial relationships if the manufacturer, lender, and dealer are to maintain profitability. Thus an improvement in consumer financing should be one part of a comprehensive effort, which perhaps would include extension of greater trade credit by manufacturers, the elimination of floor planning and the dealer reserve, and complete lender control over the loan process.

D. Park Finance

To a developer, real estate investments generally have one or more of the following financial goals: capital gain, rapid recovery of equity, cash flow, leverage, and tax shelter. Mobile home parks can offer the investor all of these financial incentives. In fact, the structure of mobile home park financing, shown in figure 15.5, is similar to that for other real estate investments.

Despite financial incentives to develop mobile home parks, however, there is a shortage of park space in many parts of the country. In order to understand the reasons for such shortages, one must be aware of the local politics involved, lending agency attitudes, state and federal government policies, and developer characteristics. This section on park financing will explore these aspects of the financing problem, emphasizing factors that have impeded the growth of the mobile home park industry.

Over the years the nature of mobile home park developers has changed. Small developers initially found a 14 percent to 30 percent pretax return on equity an adequate incentive to build parks with fewer than 100 spaces. Beginning about 1965 large land developers entered the park development business and built mobile home developments with 500, 1000, 2000, or more spaces. By 1977 over 24,500 mobile home parks existed containing 16 million spaces. Although most new parks have 150 to 175 spaces, some are quite large.

Large developers have brought more sophistication to the industry. The time horizon of their potential investments has taken on greater importance. Many wealthy individual investors and corporations owning large tracts of unused land have been looking at mobile home parks as ten- to fifteen-year investments; it is possible that, as a result of suburban sprawl, this land could be used more profitably in another type of development at the end of this time period. On the other hand, many owners have been developing subdivision or condominium parks in which the cash flow primarily occurs during the first two years, when homes are sold to to consumers.

Rental Parks

It is commonly held that a majority of the nation's population prefers to own a home. However, mobile home parks have been predominantly rental parks, where the consumer owns a mobile home and rents the site. By looking into the financial implications of rental, subdivision, cooperative, and condominium parks, we may be able to explain this apparent contradiction.

The developer of a rental park traditionally has been able to secure large profits by offering a unique style of living at a monthly occupancy cost lower than anything available in the conventional housing market. However, a comparison of rental parks with other types of mobile home developments, noting that the only advantage of rental parks is ease of consumer mobility, leads one to wonder why more than 90 percent of all mobile home parks are rental developments.

Some incentives for a rental park developer are the benefits of income tax deduction, depreciation charges, and potential capital gains from land appreciation. Also, lenders support rental parks because they realize a high 12 percent to 14 percent return from the add-on consumer loans to purchasers of mobile homes.

Subdivision

In a subdivision the home owner normally purchases a packaged lot and mobile home from the developer. The mobile home subdivision, however, should not be confused with cooperative or condominium parks, which usually have common recreational facilities. The absence of such facilities has been one limitation on subdivision development.

From the consumer's standpoint a subdivision represents the lowest available cost of home ownership. Because the mobile home is attached to land, a borrower is able to obtain a mortgage having a relatively low

Figure 15.5.
PMHI model of mobile
home park financing.

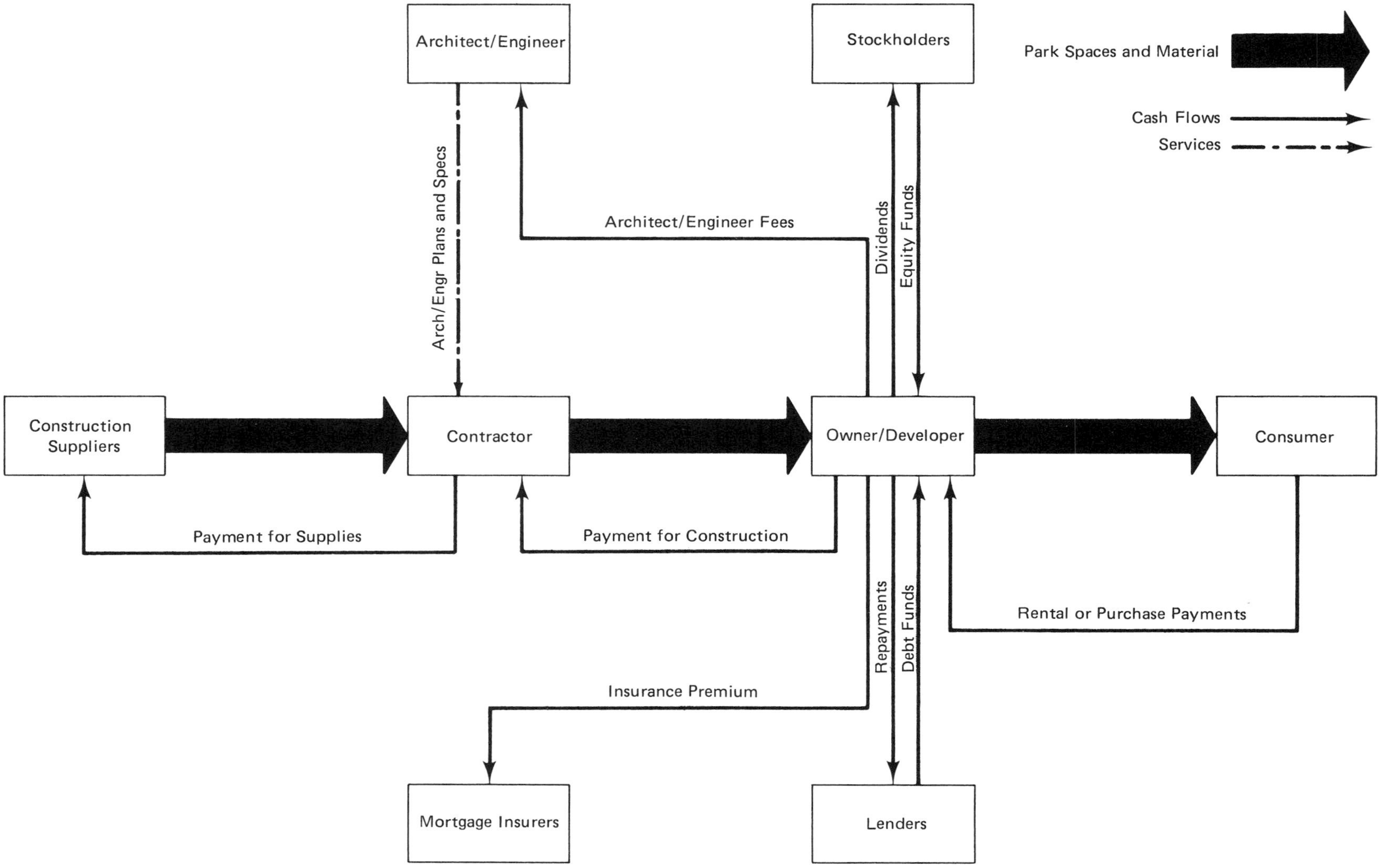

Park Spaces and Material

Cash Flows

Services

Consumer

Stockholders

Owner/Developer

Lenders

Equity Funds

Debt Funds

Dividends

Repayments

Rental or Purchase Payments

Architect/Engineer Fees

Payment for Construction

Insurance Premium

Architect/Engineer

Contractor

Mortgage Insurers

Arch/Engr Plans and Specs

Payment for Supplies

Construction
Suppliers

interest rate and long term. As a result, monthly mortgage amortization and interest payments are much lower than for add-on financing, the method traditionally used in mobile home transactions. Furthermore, because consumers have decided to forego recreational facilities, they need not pay any park rental or management fees. For higher-income subdivision residents there is an added benefit because they are able to deduct real property taxes and the interest paid on the mortgage from personal income tax.

As a result of its low cost we might expect mobile home park subdivisions to have the lowest associated risk to the lender. This does not appear to be the case in practice. Both developers and lenders, fearing low consumer acceptance and resulting high vacancy levels, have been reluctant to participate in this type of venture. Lenders also fear that subdivisions, lacking the strict regulations and sound management of conventional parks, may deteriorate into trailer slums.

Cooperative
In a mobile home cooperative each household owns corporate shares proportional to the value of its land. Householders receive a proprietary lease, which sets rules and regulations pertaining to commonly used facilities and may set limitations on the model, quality, and age of mobile homes in the park. Under the lease agreement a home owner must make monthly payments to the cooperative to cover the cost of community facilities, maintenance, and the cooperative's debt obligation. These payments can become a burden if vacancies should arise because shares revert to the cooperative when people leave the park. Under these circumstances existing stockholders own a greater percentage of the project and pay a greater percentage of the park's obligations.

By joining a cooperative, a household indicates its intention of maintaining the mobile home as a long-term residence. The household, however, is unable to translate the permanence of home ownership into more equitable mortgage terms because the cooperative holds title to the land and the individual shareholder cannot use this title as collateral for a loan or mortgage. Also, shares of the cooperative and the proprietary lease generally are not considered real property; most lenders will not accept them as collateral for a mobile home loan. Finally, the household may have difficulty selling its share of the cooperative because it must find a purchaser able to pay both the equity in the cooperative and down payment on the mobile home. Thus the adverse consequences of a cooperative arrangement are additional liability, possible restricted resale market, traditional high-interest-rate mobile home financing, and two substantial down payments—one for equity in the cooperative and the other for the mobile home.

On the other hand, there are financial benefits to cooperative ownership. Owners can deduct their share of the cooperative's interest payments and taxes from personal income tax. Because interest payments on mobile home loans can also be used as federal income tax deductions, some of the households in rental and cooperative parks may find that itemized deductions exceed the standard deduction. The cooperative arrangement also eliminates the possibility of arbitrary rent increases. As a result, monthly payments are utilized for the benefit of the residents rather than a park owner. In addition there is the potential of capital gains from land appreciation upon the sale of a household's cooperative shares.

Condominium
In some respects condominiums are similar to cooperatives. Tax benefits, potential land appreciation, protection against arbitrary rent increases, and elimination of a park owner's profit are common to both arrangements. The fundamental difference between the two is that a condominium household takes title to the land and is able to use this title as collateral for a conventional mortgage covering the cost of both the mobile home and the land. It is relatively easy to resell a condominium because the new purchaser will be able to obtain a mortgage without making a large down payment. Also, the condominium owner's liability is not as extensive as that of the cooperative shareholder. If park vacancies should rise and existing owners fail to meet their monthly condominium payments, the condominium owner would lose only the rights to those facilities that are shared in common with other residents.

Because condominium park developers sell the land and pay off a large part of the loan over a short period of time, they should find it easier to secure financing than developers of a rental or cooperative park. This, however, has not been the case in practice. Experienced lenders who finance parks also try to finance the mobile homes; they are reluctant to relinquish the high interest rates typical of traditional mobile home financing. Lenders cannot justify these rates in a condominium park and must provide a conventional mortgage loan. To avoid this the lender will encourage the developer to build a rental park. In the future, as more lenders engage in mobile home financing and traditional rates decline, the incentive to encourage rental parks will diminish.

As a result of advantageous financing terms to both purchasers and developers, monthly occupancy costs to the consumer in a condominium park are lower than in a rental or cooperative park. Only a subdivision has lower cost for the consumer than a condominium, but the owner in a subdivision does not receive the same social amenities and recreational facilities.

Parks are being developed and financed through conventional financial institutions, many without FHA or other government insurance. The loans are based entirely on the security of the mobile home park itself but may have additional guarantees such as the personal endorsement of developers, guarantees by corporations, or a pledge of marketable securities. Parks that are financed with only the park itself as security depend on the value of the improvements, land, and income to establish valuation upon which to place loan limits.

Mortgage officials generally view mobile home parks as single-purpose properties that require careful consideration. Certain fundamental practices are followed, and they relate to all project loans whether they are mobile home parks or other types of specialty loans. In presenting lenders with applications for park loans, the developer should study factors that lenders consider when making a financial decision. Among these are park location, competition, consumer acceptance in the area, project quality and cost, and cash flow projections.

Market research is an essential element of any real estate venture. Before starting a project, both the developer and lender should be convinced that an adequate market exists for the proposed development. As a specialized segment of the residential housing sector, mobile home parks require, in addition to standard market research techniques, attention to details that are unique to the mobile home housing market. For example, the concept of "highest and best use" must be considered. Associated with mobile home parks is an unusual amount of flexibility in land use. The investment time horizon for a mobile home park development can be significantly shorter than for most other developed land uses. Tracts of land on urban fringes can be developed as parks and converted after ten or fifteen years to another use as land value appreciates.

Community receptivity is another factor. In many areas of the United States, people have negative attitudes about mobile home parks. These community attitudes can be changed by a demonstration of improved industry standards, tasteful advertising, and tactful presentation of potential benefits associated with well-managed mobile home parks.

Other problems may threaten the success of a mobile home park. There continues to be a significant amount of building trade union resistance to the increased use of manufactured homes. These unions often have an impact on zoning or planning board decisions. Unions also influence building codes that may effectively exclude mobile housing from certain areas.

Although this list is not exhaustive, it presents a picture of the unique real estate market factors facing mobile home park developers. Careful consideration of factors such as these allows the developer to design a park that will satisfy consumer demand, thereby improving the prospect of a successful venture.

Commercial Banks

Commercial banks with experience in mobile home financing have found park financing to be especially profitable when they are able to tie high-yield consumer loans to the park mortgage. Of course, this can be done only when the developer is also a dealer, and PMHI/PS indicates that only one-third of developers sampled are mobile home dealers. In such tie-in arrangements the dealer normally has an option of taking consumer contracts elsewhere if the bank is not providing competitive rates and terms. Upon exercise of this option the owner/dealer relinquishes the park loan with its ten- to twenty-year maturity and enters into a new agreement with another lender.

The attractiveness of tie-in arrangements is one reason commercial banks have been reluctant to finance FHA-insured parks. FHA guidelines prohibit park owners from selling mobile homes on the park premises.

Savings and Loan Associations

Federally chartered savings and loan associations (S&Ls) are very active in providing construction and working capital financing to park developers. Many savings and loan officials view park development as a natural extension of their prime function, supplying mortgage credit. Since passage of the 1968 Housing Act, which allowed federally chartered savings and loan associations to engage in wholesale and retail financing of mobile homes, S&Ls have increased their level of park financing. Like other lending institutions, S&Ls usually require park owners to steer high-yield consumer credit their way. Regulations set forth by the Federal Home Loan Bank Board allow S&Ls to lend up to 80 percent of the park's appraised value for a term of eighteen months, and thereafter the ratio drops to 70 percent for a term not exceeding twenty years.

Park developments are classified as improved real estate and are considered part of the S&Ls commercial loan portfolio. Although they are allowed to invest as much as 20 percent of their assets in commercial loans, most S&Ls lack the expertise necessary to evaluate such loans and therefore limit them to less than 10 percent of their portfolio. In addition, the FHA mortgage insurance program permits any approved savings and loan association to originate FHA-insured loans and purchase existing FHA-insured mortgages from other lending institutions.

Joint Ventures

In recent years joint ventures have been used to develop real estate projects that otherwise might not have been possible. Although most joint ventures are formed to develop conventional real estate projects, a limited number of mobile home parks have been financed in this way.

Participants in these ventures are typically a local investor or small developer who also manages the park and a large developer, mobile home manufacturer, or corporation. The local partner provides an understanding of the local market, which facilitates the initiation of project proposals and feasibility studies. Local partners also often provide the land and develop the park. Because local partners generally have equity in the operation, there is a strong incentive for them to work for the project's success. The other partner usually provides financial resources, additional feasibility study expertise, accounting and financial control systems, and a wide range of services that may include planning and design, financing, and marketing expertise. As of 1977 the amount of capital entering mobile home park projects by way of joint venture has been limited. However, this marriage of skills and resources may provide a significant source of funds for future mobile home park development.

Parks Developed by Manufacturers

For many years mobile home manufacturers have felt that manufacturing offered a higher return per dollar invested than park development. Behind this reasoning is the fact that, assuming an 80 percent mortgage, 20 percent equity invested in a park will yield at most around 20 to 25 percent before taxes. Further, debt from the park mortgage will show on the balance sheet and depreciation will decrease earnings. These factors may adversely affect the price of the firm's common stock. As a result mobile home manufacturers have refrained from development.

When manufacturers have developed parks, they usually limited home sales in the park to their brand. Local dealers who lost business to the manufacturer then notified their fellow dealers in other parts of the country. Fearful that the manufacturer would do the same in their area, the dealers would begin to favor other manufacturers' units.

In many cases manufacturers found that mobile home park development required expertise they did not have. The resulting unprofitable parks were a financial and managerial drain on the firm. These problems caused most manufacturers to withdraw from the park development business.

Other Sources of Park Financing

In addition to the primary sources of funds listed above, there are other sources that provide financing for park development. These include real estate investment trusts, insurance companies, and pension funds. Financing can also be obtained by utilizing government insurance programs, such as the Title I program administered by the Federal Housing Administration.

Performance of mobile home park financing can be assessed using many measures. For example, one might consider the availability and cost of capital for mobile home projects, the return on equity realized by park owners, or the amount of tax shelter provided investors. In the final analysis, however, the appropriate measure of overall industry performance is whether the mobile home market has reached economic equilibrium, a condition existing when the supply of park spaces equals the demand for them.

Finance is a major variable in the equilibrium formula, and good financial performance incorporates the appropriate incentives and rewards that lead to good overall performance. In many parts of the country demand for mobile home park space far outweighs supply. The survey of mobile home dealers conducted by PMHI indicates that some dealers could have sold over 30 percent more homes if enough park space were available. One manifestation of an excessive demand situation is the "closed park." Data from PMHI/PS show that almost 9 percent of all parks are closed. Many of these parks reap monopoly profits by charging entrance fees and requiring that park dwellers purchase homes from the park owner's dealership at premium prices. Poor financial performance is one major cause of excess demand.

Economic disequilibrium prevalent in the mobile home industry can be resolved by the development of more mobile home park space. However, this will occur only if incentives are sufficient to developers and lenders so that they are willing to invest more capital in the industry. In order to promote a successful mobile home project, developers must overcome many obstacles; zoning barriers and lack of capital are two. Zoning restrictions increase preconstruction costs for public relations and governmental lobbying. Lack of capital can result in greater equity requirements and interest charges than would be the case in other real estate developments. The net effect is a lower return on equity for the developer and less incentive to build a quality mobile home park.

Zoning

Zoning restrictions directly affect the feasibility of a mobile home park development. However they also can affect financing arrangements in a more subtle fashion. One of the greatest constraints working against mobile home park financing is the psychological effect of stringent zoning restrictions on lenders' willingness to make mobile home park loans. Where mobile home parks are considered a blight by the community, lenders are unwilling to upset the local populace by providing funds.

Although restrictive zoning is a handicap at first, it can turn into a great advantage for the park owner. If one is the only developer in the area, it is possible to maintain high occupancy levels at high rentals. Thus strict zoning results not only in fewer park spaces but also in higher costs to the consumer.

Lack of Available Capital

Historically there has been a lack of capital to finance mobile home parks, which results in fewer park spaces built and fewer homes sold. Lenders who have never made mobile home park loans are reluctant to enter a field they do not understand. Furthermore, they are still influenced by the image of the old trailer court. In areas such as Florida, California, and Arizona, reputable developers with well-planned and carefully analyzed projects can obtain funds at interest rates and terms that compare favorably with other housing developments. Unfortunately, this financial climate does not exist in most parts of the country.

The shortage of low-cost capital in many areas results in lower-quality parks that add to the bad image of mobile homes. This in turn leads to stricter zoning laws and a decrease in the amount lenders are willing to invest in mobile home park loans. Lack of park space also results in a large number of mobile homes located along the roadside, further contributing to the bad image and resulting lack of capital. These relationships are shown in figure 15.6.

Incentives for Mobile Home Park Development

Considering all the problems, one might ask why developers would consider a mobile home park rather than a conventional real estate investment. There are several incentives associated with mobile home parks. For example, mobile home parks can be less risky than many other types of real estate investment. Because mobile homes are the least expensive form of new housing and conventional housing costs are increasing rapidly, more people are turning to the mobile

home living alternative. This increasing market improves a park developer's chances for success.

In addition to lower risks, mobile home parks require a substantially smaller investment than comparable conventional housing projects. Park investment costs are closely associated with land values, whereas conventional construction is associated with labor and material costs. Although land, labor, and materials are becoming more expensive, the park developer can reduce a major portion of costs by selecting a site that has a relatively low price. Also, a developer probably will realize land value appreciation. The conventional real estate developer, having a greater part of the investment tied up in construction costs than does the mobile home park developer, may not realize the same relative gain as land value increases.

Another advantage of mobile home park development is added flexibility. Conventional construction is more permanent than mobile home park construction. The mobile home park developer can turn the land to a more profitable use in ten or fifteen years as increasing land values justify other types of projects, but the conventional developer is constrained to a greater degree by the physical presence of the buildings.

In general, mobile home park development suffers from a lack of low-cost capital, which results in higher costs to the consumer and lower returns to the developer than would otherwise be the case. The net effect has been a demand for mobile home park spaces that exceeds the supply in many sections of the country. There are several ways to reduce the imbalance. For example, it is possible to remedy this condition by raising rental prices so that demand decreases. However, this solution would alter the low-cost nature of the mobile home living alternative. From the

Policy Alternatives

Figure 15.6.
One result of lack of capital.

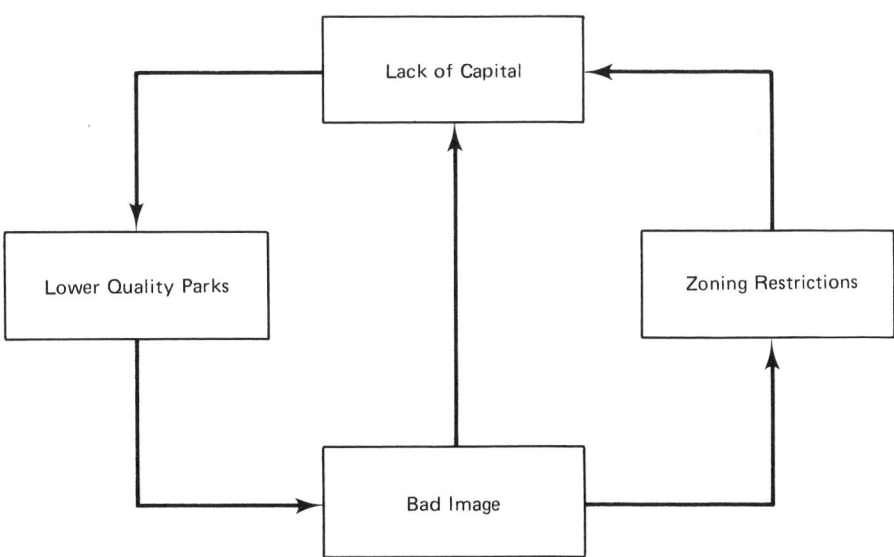

consumer's perspective, a more desirable solution probably would consist of three broad elements:

Government incentives that would encourage developers and lenders to become involved in mobile home park projects

The use of creative financing by developers, mortgage brokers, and lending institutions

Willingness of lending institutions to view park developments as they do other real estate developments, requiring a similar percentage down payment and offering similar interest rates and terms.

Policy Alternatives for Government

Closed Parks
In order to reduce closed park owners' excess profits, which tarnish the industry's image and increase costs to consumers, it is necessary to prohibit practices that require consumers to purchase a mobile home from a particular dealer and pay an entry fee. Such legislation would reduce consumer costs and therefore improve industry performance. It should be noted, however, that the park owner still will be able to charge excessive monthly rents unless more spaces are built.

Zoning
Local zoning has had an impact on mobile home sales. Many communities have exclusionary zoning policies that preclude any form of factory-built housing within their boundaries. Although these policies are a response to the trailer court image that many have of mobile home parks, they also often are an effort to exclude from a community those who do not have the resources to buy a conventional home.

Government must oversee zoning restrictions if *de facto* ghettos resulting from zoning policies are to be eliminated. If local government is unable to act, state agencies may be able to rise above local considerations and recognize those areas where well-designed mobile home parks should be encouraged.

Taxation
There is a wide variation in state tax policies applying to mobile homes. For tax purposes some states treat mobile homes as personal property, other states, as vehicles, and others, as real estate. A uniform approach to taxation must be developed. Mobile homes are real property and serve as personal residences. Taxation parity between mobile home owners and conventional housing owners will play an important role in settling disputes such as those concerning zoning and community acceptance.

Government Insurance Programs
Government loan insurance programs such as those offered by the Federal Housing Administration can promote park development only if they are attractive to both developers and lenders. Developers must be allowed a reasonable return on their investment. Lenders must have the ability to charge realistic interest rates, geared to the prime rate, or they will invest funds in more lucrative areas. If government programs are to have a major impact on park development, they must be restructured to accommodate developers' and lenders' requirements.

Financial Alternatives for Developers
Like other real estate investors, mobile home park developers are faced with rapidly increasing land, construction, and management costs. Their response to these cost increases will determine whether park development continues to be attractive to the large market of low-income families. If developers are to minimize their capital costs and the impact of rising prices on mobile home park dwellers, they will have to adopt more sophisticated financing approaches. The following are examples of techniques that might be used to maintain mobile home living as a low-cost alternative for the consumer.

Leasing
In most forms of commercial real estate development the practice of leasing land for a project has become widespread. Mobile home parks are no exception. In many circumstances developers have found that their profits from a proposed park are maximized by a land-lease agreement. The necessary conditions usually are high land costs, future alternative uses for the land, and reluctant sellers.

In areas of high land costs, some parks become feasible through leasing because the initial investment is reduced, rents can be deducted as expenses, and more funds are available for financing improvements. If a more profitable use for the land is anticipated as its value increases over the years, the landowner may be unwilling to sell and leasing is the only alternative. In either case a leasing arrangement makes the development possible.

With land becoming more expensive and representing a larger percentage of the total project cost, mobile home park developers should begin to examine the subordinated sale-leaseback as a source of capital. In this arrangement a developer builds a park, sells to investors for an immediate return of capital, and leases back the park to operate it.

Standby Commitment
Park developers have used the standby commitment in recent years to obtain a construction loan. Usually the commitment is written for an interest rate well above market levels with the intent that it never will

be funded. The high interest rate provides the developer with a strong incentive to obtain permanent long-term financing.

By obtaining the commitment, the developer can build a mobile home park without being locked into a permanent loan that has no prepayment privileges. If the park rents as well as expected, the developer will be able to refinance and obtain a permanent loan with a longer amortization period and lower rates than provided for in the commitment. At the same time, the developer is establishing a track record that may lead to better terms on future construction loans and permanent loans.

The fee for a standby commitment is one-half to one point for every six months that the commitment is outstanding, but longer-term commitments generally have lower rates. Although this may seem a heavy charge, for many developers it has been a vehicle for obtaining funds that otherwise would not be available. Furthermore, it has acquainted many lenders with mobile home park financing and established a foundation upon which park developers can build a business relationship with lenders.

Mobile Home Rental
One park arrangement that has not been used extensively provides for renting both the park space and mobile home to residents. This mobile home apartment scheme allows a park owner to maintain the value of the homes on the balance sheet. Tax shelter resulting from the depreciation of this asset would play a part in the feasibility analysis of the project. This scheme opens a new market of potential residents: those who do not have sufficient funds to purchase a mobile home. Although this could decrease the vacancy rate, a developer must take care that park quality does not deteriorate.

Lease-Option-to-Buy for Consumers
Many developers who want to build condominium parks are concerned that consumers may not be able to obtain adequate financing to purchase both the land and the home. One possible solution is to establish a condominium park and sell lots to those who can obtain the necessary funds. Those who do not have funds to purchase the lot can rent a space with an option to buy it within a fixed period, such as seven years. This will give a consumer enough time to accumulate funds needed to meet down payment requirements on the land. In such cases individuals should obtain a liberal prepayment provision on the mobile home loan so that when they do purchase the land they can refinance the home and land with a conventional mortgage. In fact, if purchasers have a lease-option-to-buy, perhaps the FHA could insure a conventional mortgage from the time they purchase the home.

These are only a few examples of sophisticated financing techniques that have been employed by conventional real estate developers for years. Park developers of the late 1970s and early 1980s will respond to rising commuting costs and the increasing potential market of young, working families by seeking park land closer to their jobs. As a result park developers will be competing with conventional real estate developers for desirable land. If the park developer is to prevail, he or she must adopt the methods that have been so successful for conventional developers.

Interactions between Developers and Lenders
Perhaps nothing has restrained park development, indeed development of the entire mobile home industry, as much as the lack of low-cost capital. Reacting to images of trailer parks and responding to community pressures, many lenders have been reluctant to support the industry.

It is the developer's responsibility to rectify this problem. Lenders will recognize good business opportunities, and mobile home parks must be well-conceived from a financial standpoint. To ease public pressure on lenders, planned parks must be attractive. Resources should be dedicated to generating public support. Among other things, local citizens must be convinced that the park will not detract from their property values and that park residents will contribute their fair share of taxes.

In states such as Arizona, California, and Florida, developers and lenders have joined forces to create many successful mobile home parks. As a result these developers are able to obtain low-cost capital. We suggest that developers in other states make an effort to establish an equally good rapport with lenders. In the final analysis these efforts not only will benefit consumers by providing a lower-cost housing alternative but will benefit the entire industry by increasing consumer demand.

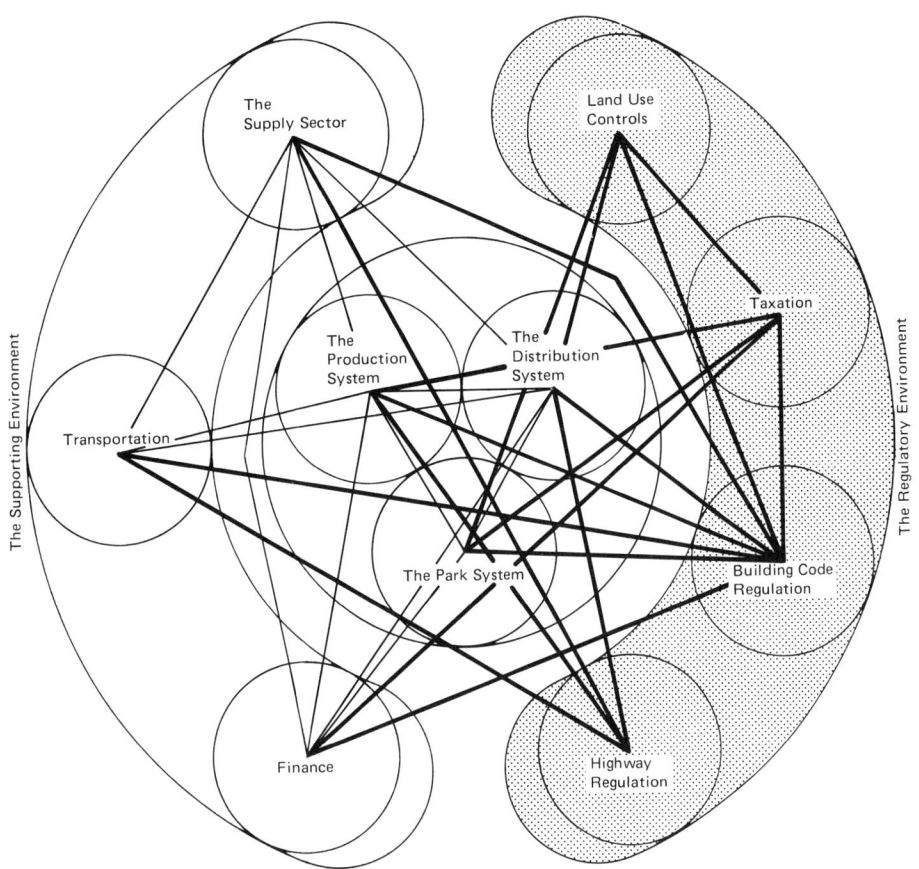

Chapter 16

Land Use Controls

A. Historical Perspective

Governments have been controlling land use since as early as 1285 and in the Americas from as early as 1573.[1] Although the European tradition of public land acquisition affected early American cities, widespread ownership of land by ordinary freemen after the American Revolution led Americans to regard land as a kind of property like any other, to be owned outright. The rights accorded property owners became so important that by 1780 the Commonwealth of Massachusetts had included acquiring, possessing, and protecting property in its definition of basic human rights. Many other state constitutions followed Massachusetts' lead.

As America bought or conquered new territories, land became a major resource for the federal government, which regarded land as the most readily available source of revenue.[2] Because land was often a man's only possession and his major source of livelihood, the new definition of "property rights" was important to Americans. As one commentator notes, "Americans have interpreted the right of 'protection' of property to mean protection not only (or even primarily) from impingement by government, but also from impingement by competing private interests."[3] Although the right to freedom from government encroachment has been a major factor in preventing the widespread use of many land use controls, the right to freedom from competing private interests has fostered the widespread use of one important land use control—zoning.

Land use was first controlled through zoning in San Francisco in the late 1800s; at that time control was not motivated by the desire to protect property rights but rather by the desire to exclude ethnic minorities.[4] Zones were used in New York, Massachusetts, and Washington, D.C., in the late nineteenth century to regulate the height and bulk of buildings. In 1909 the Supreme Court upheld the Massachusetts legislation, but it was in New York City in 1913–1916 that property rights began to be the primary motivation for zoning.[5] The city was growing rapidly, not only in size but, more important, in density; new downtown skyscrapers, themselves highly valuable properties, deflated the property values of surrounding buildings.[6] Property owners in fashionable downtown shopping districts felt that their businesses were jeopardized by the influx of low-paid laborers who worked in the skyscrapers.[7] The combined efforts of merchant associations concerned with declining property values and social reformers appalled by the environmental problems created by skyscrapers led to the establishment of the Advisory Commission on the Height of Buildings in 1913. Three years later New York City was divided into three types of districts: residential, business, and unrestricted; separate height and bulk districts were also established. Amended more than two thousand times, this comprehensive ordinance was in force until 1961 and served as the model for subsequent zoning ordinances across the country.

In the 1920s protection of property value began to supersede protection of freedom of use. John Delafons observes that the interest protected "may be that of private property owners against both speculative developers and unwanted newcomers . . ." and that "it is a very significant fact that the American system of regulating private development— 'zoning'—is a legacy of the 1920s, the heyday of private enterprise."[8] By 1925, 368 municipalities had passed zoning ordinances; and by 1931, more than 1000 had done so.[9] State legislation giving municipalities the authority to zone became common in the 1920s. In 1924 an advisory committee on zoning in the Department of Commerce issued the State Zoning Enabling Act, which, if adopted by state legislatures, granted their towns and cities the police power to zone.

The constitutionality of the concept of zoning was settled in 1926 when the Supreme Court decided the case of *Village of Euclid* v. *Ambler Realty*.[10] The Court sustained the validity of zoning despite Ambler's claim that the town's zoning ordinance violated his Fourteenth Amendment rights by depriving him of property without due process. The Court regarded the intrusion of industry and apartments into single-family zones as analogous to a public nuisance: "A nuisance may merely be the right thing in the wrong place, like a pig in the parlor instead of the barnyard." In effect, the Court sanctioned the creation and maintenance of residential neighborhoods and the insulation of the single-family district. The Court also approved comprehensive zoning, declaring it immune to constitutional attack unless a given ordinance was found to be "clearly arbitrary and unreasonable, having no substantial relation to the public health, safety, morals, or general welfare." The constitutionality of zoning was thus firmly established, and apart from *Nectow* v. *City of Cambridge* in 1928 (the Court, without invalidating the ordinance, refused to support the zoning of a particular lot on due process grounds), the Supreme Court has refused to hear zoning cases, leaving it to the various states to apply the constitutional principle of reasonableness to individual cases as they arise.[11]

Zoning laws vary greatly among local governments but usually include the following aspects: a designation of permitted uses, usually divided into three basic categories (residential, commercial, and industrial); a limitation on population density, usually accomplished through minimum lot size requirements; and a regulation of building bulk, accomplished by limiting building height and lot coverage. Traditional zoning (or Euclidean zoning, from the historic court case of *Euclid* v. *Ambler*) established a hierarchy of land use categories with the single-family residential district at the top.

Uses considered mutually incompatible are thus separated and "less desirable" uses excluded from land use districts considered "harm sensitive." Within each zone or district a uniform set of regulations dealing with such aspects as uses and bulk apply.

The second major method of land use control, subdivision regulation, has its origins in the land claim recording system enacted after the American Revolution. At first dealing only with the mechanical and legal aspects of registering deeds and surveys, this method was gradually expanded to regulate street widths and other details when the rush of homesteaders caused problems for growing towns in the West. In 1882 the village of Oak Park, Illinois, required that parcels of land be filed in advance of their sale and that they conform to certain standards.[12] However, these early regulations were not intended to protect property values or limit development but rather to ensure orderly street layout and legal documentation.

Although zoning controls as a means of controlling the type of development in a given area were coming into widespread use at this time, no control was placed on the size of proposed developments. As a result many subdivisions were begun and never completed, causing a drain on municipal services. As Delafons says, "the vast land speculations of the 1920s showed the folly and ruinous expense to local governments of unrestricted subdivision."[13] When subdivision developments again became economically possible after World War II, many communities adopted subdivision regulations to prevent a repetition of the mishaps of the 1920s. More recently, subdivision regulations have gone beyond simply limiting the size of developments; they now typically govern site design and relationships (to assure that subdivisions are related to their surroundings and their own sites) and allocation of facilities (subdividers are often required to dedicate internal streets and pave them to specification as well as to provide drainage, water, sewage systems, street lights, and so forth). The legal rationale behind subdivision regulation is different from that of zoning, and this may explain why there have been many fewer court challenges. The registration of a subdivision is considered a privilege granted by a municipality—a favor from which the developer will make a profit. In return the developer is expected to meet the standards of the community. The standards can go further than zoning because, unlike zoning, these regulations confer an advantage.

The administrative structure of the land use control "system" permits adjustments to and departures from the basic scheme. Though there are many variations, some administrative procedures are basic. Upon a denial of a permit from a building official, a party may appeal on the grounds that the ordinance has been misinterpreted or has been applied arbitrarily. Appeals are usually taken to a local board of zoning appeals. A variance is designed to rectify problems that arise from the strict application of the ordinance. The granting of a variance is intended to mitigate potential hardship to the property owner. The variance poser most often belongs to the board of appeals. The special exception, a discretionary procedure (also known as conditional use and special use), involves an identification of particular uses within a zone that may be permitted by a review body on application of a developer or landowner. Amendments, commonly known as "rezoning," involve a basic alteration of the original ordinance. To assure that regulatory actions conform to the federal and state constitutions and statutes and to local ordinances, zoning statutes further provide for review by the courts.

The inevitable result of the way in which planning powers have been allocated is our present "system" of local land use ordinances that vary greatly from community to community. According to the Douglas Commission Report, some ten thousand governments in the United States now exercise regulatory powers. Within Standard Metropolitan Statistical Areas (SMSAs), fifty-two hundred jurisdictions have zoning ordinances. The extent to which localities have made use of their authority is summarized below.

	Governments					
	Number Surveyed	With Planning Boards	With Zoning Ordinances	With Subdivision Regulations	With Building Codes	With Housing Codes
Within SMSA	7,609	4,963	5,199	4,509	4,527	2,780
%		65.2	68.3	59.3	59.5	36.5
Outside SMSA	10,384	5,754	4,396	3,577	3,817	2,124
%		55.4	42.3	34.4	36.8	20.5
Total[a]	17,993	10,717	9,595	8,086	8,344	4,904
%		59.6	53.3	44.9	46.4	27.3

a. Total omits all municipalities and townships outside SMSAs with populations under 1000 and township governments in states where these governments lack municipal-type powers.

Source: Douglas Commission. *Building the American City.* U.S. National Commission on Urban Problems: Report to Congress and the President of the U.S. (Washington, D.C.: U.S. Government Printing Office, 1969).

The fragmentation of land use control responsibility is especially important within metropolitan areas, where many land use concerns are properly regional in scope. The degree of decentralization within metropolitan areas becomes apparent when specific areas are examined. For example, in the New York area, as defined by the Regional Plan Association, more than 500 jurisdictions have zoning ordinances; in Chicago's Cook County, the figure is 112, and in the San Francisco area, 100.[14]

B. The Current Situation

Frequency of Use of the Most Common Controls on Mobile Homes

Early mobile homes were principally used as vacation trailers, but the housing crisis of the Great Depression forced many impoverished families to use them as permanent residences. As a result, congested, poorly planned trailer camps grew up almost overnight. Hostility toward mobile homes was understandably prevalent. The trailers were viewed by many as a shoddy and unattractive departure from conventional housing. The mobile home dweller was usually considered an undesirable transient. Property owners feared that location of mobile homes near their property would result in depreciation of land values. Regulatory bodies initially reacted in a negative fashion: They prohibited the trailers or forced them into areas where no one else wished to live. The relegation of mobile homes to industrial or commercial areas where amenities were lacking in turn helped to foster the negative image of mobile homes. This cycle perpetuated the animosity to mobile homes that was incorporated into many zoning ordinances in the post–World War II era.

Despite radical changes in the appearance of mobile homes and parks over the years, the stance of communities and regulatory bodies has remained fundamentally the same. To some extent the current hostility is still attributable to memories of the shantytowns of the past, but there are other reasons. Property owners feel that mobile homes present many of the same problems as low-income, high-density housing, that property values will be depressed by neighboring mobile home parks, and that the aesthetics of the community will be detrimentally affected. Those concerned with keeping the tax rate down argue that mobile home units will not return in taxes what they add to the municipal budget in terms of education costs and other governmental services. Whatever its causes, the general hostility has given rise to discriminatory land use regulation.

Because the power to control land use has been delegated to local governments, information regarding the nearly ten thousand zoning ordinances in the nation is incomplete and unwieldy. Only a small number of studies is available on state and regional ordinances, and we found them insufficient for this project's purposes. To secure the information we needed, we undertook a major study. Through correspondence or personal interview we contacted the governor of each state and the president of each state and regional trade association, requesting all the information available on the status of land use controls relevant to mobile homes. The information we received ranges, depending on state, from reliable censuses to estimates by knowledgeable individuals. Using this data on the situation in all fifty states, we were able to uncover some of the trends in land use regulation and some of the reasons behind these trends.

Complete Exclusion

Complete exclusion is usually accomplished by an outright ban or by a failure to make provision for mobile homes in the local ordinance. Courts have disagreed on the validity of local regulations that effectively exclude mobile homes or mobile home parks from a locality, but in a majority of the states in which this approach has been challenged the courts have ruled that the total exclusion of mobile homes from a political unit is unconstitutional.[15] One rationale adopted by the courts is that mobile homes do not constitute a nuisance and that therefore their complete exclusion is an abuse of the police power. And courts have invalidated ordinances that completely exclude mobile homes for the reason that every state legislature has provided for the regulation of mobile homes in the state enabling act. According to the courts, the concept of regulation implies the promulgation of reasonable rules—not outright prohibition. Courts in a few states have sustained regulations prohibiting mobile homes. As recently as 1962 the New Jersey Supreme Court sanctioned the complete exclusion of mobile homes.[16] However, the promulgation of regulations for mobile homes rather than their outright prohibition has been the overriding trend in judicial opinion. In some states none of the municipalities completely exclude mobile homes, but in other states, such as New Jersey, as many as 95 percent of the municipalities completely ban mobile homes. The frequency of use of complete exclusion is presented in table 16.1 and figure 16.1. Note that the data given reflect only the percentage of municipalities with an excluding ordinance, not the percentage of a state's developable land or population affected by it. For instance, only 1 percent of Colorado's municipalities exclude mobile homes, but this 1 percent is Denver, which accounts for 30 percent of Colorado's population.

Restriction of Mobile Homes to Parks

Either by choice or by necessity, nearly half of all mobile home dwellers reside in mobile home parks.[17] It is often more economical to locate in a park than to buy land, but consumer choice is limited, for mobile homes are commonly prohibited from locating in any area except a mobile home

Table 16.1.
Percentage of All
Municipalities That
Exclude Mobile Homes
or Restrict Them to
Parks

Region	Exclusion	Restriction to Parks
New England		
Maine	18	4
New Hampshire	2	3
Vermont	2	12
Massachusetts	65	28
Rhode Island	51	13
Connecticut	87	12
Middle Atlantic		
New York	50	11
New Jersey	95	4
Pennsylvania	60	30
East North Central		
Ohio	50	40
Indiana	10	25
Illinois	3	38
Michigan	15	40
Wisconsin	10	50
West North Central		
Minnesota	15	85
Iowa	2	80
Missouri	1	10
North Dakota	1	50
South Dakota	1	33
Nebraska	1	15
Kansas	5	—
South Atlantic		
Delaware	29	35
Maryland	20	80
Virginia	11	55
West Virginia	40	60
South Carolina	1	60
North Carolina	25	75
Georgia	1	30
Florida	5	75
East South Central		
Kentucky	10	30
Tennessee	1	35
Alabama	5	10
Mississippi	5	13
West South Central		
Arkansas	0	5
Louisiana	0	25
Oklahoma	1	50
Texas	1	10
Mountain		
Montana	5	5
Idaho	1	10
Wyoming	1	10
Colorado	1	40
New Mexico	4	10
Arizona	1	65
Utah	1	63
Nevada	1	25
Pacific		
Washington	10	75
Oregon	25	50
California	40	52
Alaska	1	2
Hawaii	25	25

Source: 50-State PMHI Survey.

Figure 16.1.
Percentage of all municipalities that exclude mobile homes or restrict them to parks. Source: 50-State PMHI Survey.

Exclusion

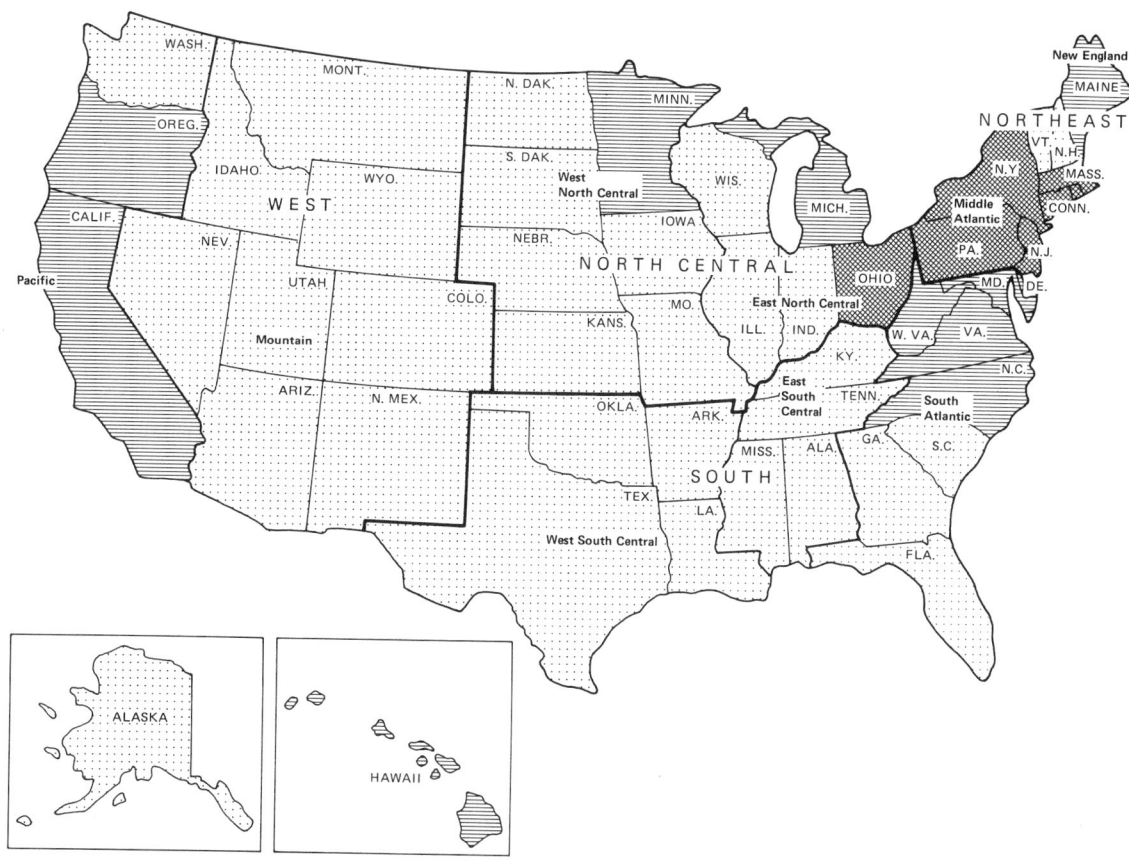

Restriction to Parks

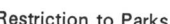

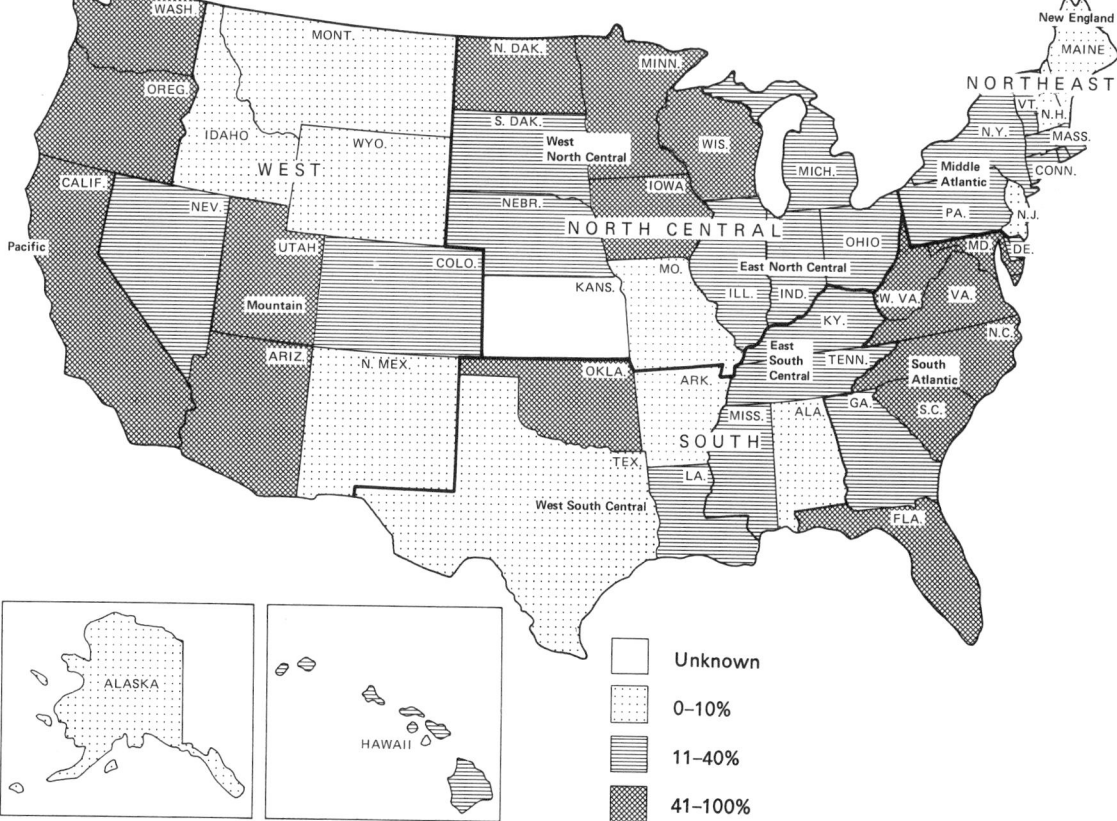

Unknown

0–10%

11–40%

41–100%

Land Use Controls

park. Such confinement is usually "justified" on the grounds that there are sanitation problems inherent in mobile home living that require periodic inspection and that government control can be maintained more efficiently if such dwellings are confined to designated areas. Although confinement on these grounds may have been reasonable in the early days of trailers, it is not now, for mobile homes are built and maintained as good-quality, low-cost housing. It has also been argued that the grouping of mobile homes in parks reduces the architectural disharmony that results when mobile homes are scattered throughout residential districts. This argument—another leftover from the the days of the tin can trailer—has become absurd. Today roughly half the mobile homes sold in many states are doublewide units indistinguishable from conventional housing, and the dominance of these and of "sectional" homes in the industry's product mix is accelerating.

Provisions restricting mobile homes to established mobile home parks are generally upheld in court. This has been the result even when a statute restricted mobile homes to parks and there were none.[18] In *People v. Clute,*[19] in a jurisdiction that does not permit outright exclusion, the court upheld the park-only designation on the grounds that sewage, water supply, and other problems it felt were connected with mobile home maintenance require that all units be located in parks where services can be strictly supervised. In following this precedent, the court, in *Mobile Home Owners Protective Association v. Town of Chatham,* upheld the park-only restriction, although it felt compelled to state that "it would appear somewhat anomalous to consider a residence some twelve feet wide by sixty feet in length set upon a permanent foundation to be anything other than an ordinary house. . . ."[20] There does seem to be general agreement that zoning ordinances restricting mobile homes to parks are legally justifiable, and to a large extent the restriction is consistent with the needs of those mobile home dwellers who cannot afford to buy land or who desire to be mobile.

Subdivision controls also usually restrict mobile homes to parks. The details vary from municipality to municipality, but many use the FHA's "Minimum Property Standards for Mobile Home Courts."[21] Often, the subdivision regulations are more enlightened than most zoning ordinances: Parks are located in residential districts only; a minimum area and number of spaces are required to create the economic base necessary for provision of required common facilities, open space, and services; travel trailers are prohibited; and good park design is rewarded with density bonuses. These controls have been subject to far less litigation than zoning. They have never been ruled upon by the Supreme Court and have usually been upheld in the lower

courts. Unlike zoning, they have usually been administered by an appointed planning department rather than by an elected city council.[22] The close relationship between planners and developers may be one reason subdivision controls are so infrequently litigated—even though they are much more specific than zoning in their application.

The frequency of the restriction to mobile home parks is summarized in table 16.1 and figure 16.1. The absolute frequency of this restriction is misleading when compared between states without considering the number of municipalities that do not exclude mobile homes. For example, 3 to 4 percent of both New Hampshire's and New Jersey's municipalities require mobile homes to be in parks, yet this represents 80 percent of all New Jersey municipalities allowing mobile homes and only 3 percent of New Hampshire municipalities allowing mobile homes. To compensate, the percentage of all municipalities in a state allowing mobile homes that require location in a mobile home park is shown in table 16.2 and figure 16.2. The use of this device displays less of a pattern than does the use of complete exclusion; however, we can see that the densely populated, urbanized states generally show higher percentages than other areas. Note that in table 16.2 the Middle Atlantic, South, East, North Central, and Pacific regions have mean percentages of greater than 40.

Exclusion from Residential Districts and Restriction to Commercial/Industrial Districts

The majority of municipal ordinances, though not explicitly prohibiting mobile homes and mobile home parks, do restrict their location. Mobile homes are typically excluded from residential districts, the desirable locations for homes of any sort, in three ways: An ordinance may expressly exclude mobile homes from residential districts; an ordinance may permit mobile homes only in nonresidential areas; or an ordinance providing for only dwellings or residences can be interpreted as barring mobile homes.

Most litigation concerns the third category. Although the wording of the ordinances varies, the question before the court is always the same: Does a mobile home deposited on a permanent foundation fit with the provisions of the local ordinance limiting an area to single-family dwellings? In the past this problem was treated as one of semantics—is a mobile home a vehicle or a residence? An extreme position excuding mobile homes from single-family districts was taken by the Massachusetts courts, which assumed that "once a trailer always a trailer," even if a structure is permanently attached to a foundation, landscaped, and in compliance with local housing codes. The Massachusetts courts have insisted that a mobile home does

Table 16.2.
Percentage of Municipalities Allowing Mobile Homes That Restrict Them to Parks or Exclude Them from Residential Areas

Region	Restriction to Parks	Exclusion from Residential Areas
New England		
Maine	4.9	3
New Hampshire	3.1	11
Vermont	12.2	0
Massachusetts	80.0	70
Rhode Island	26.5	3
Connecticut	92.3	0
Middle Atlantic		
New York	22.0	90
New Jersey	80.0	98
Pennsylvania	80.0	80
East North Central		
Ohio	80.0	95
Indiana	27.8	20
Illinois	39.2	80
Michigan	47.0	20
Wisconsin	55.6	0
West North Central		
Minnesota	100.0	5
Iowa	81.6	20
Missouri	10.1	0
North Dakota	50.5	0
South Dakota	33.3	8
Nebraska	15.2	0
Kansas	—	10
South Atlantic		
Delaware	49.3	2
Maryland	100.0	60
Virginia	61.8	23
West Virginia	100.0	20
South Carolina	60.6	15
North Carolina	100.0	20
Georgia	30.3	20
Florida	79.3	0
East South Central		
Kentucky	33.3	5
Tennessee	35.4	5
Alabama	10.5	25
Mississippi	13.6	5
West South Central		
Arkansas	5.0	0
Louisiana	25.0	20
Oklahoma	50.5	25
Texas	10.1	25
Mountain		
Montana	5.3	5
Idaho	10.1	0
Wyoming	10.1	0
Colorado	40.4	5
New Mexico	10.4	8
Arizona	65.6	0
Utah	63.6	0
Nevada	26.3	0
Pacific		
Washington	83.3	0
Oregon	66.6	10
California	86.7	40
Alaska	2.0	0
Hawaii	33.3	33

Source: 50-State PMHI Survey.

Figure 16.2.
Percentage of munici-
palities allowing mobile
homes that restrict them
to parks or exclude them
from residential
districts. Source: 50–
State PMHI Survey.

Restriction to Parks

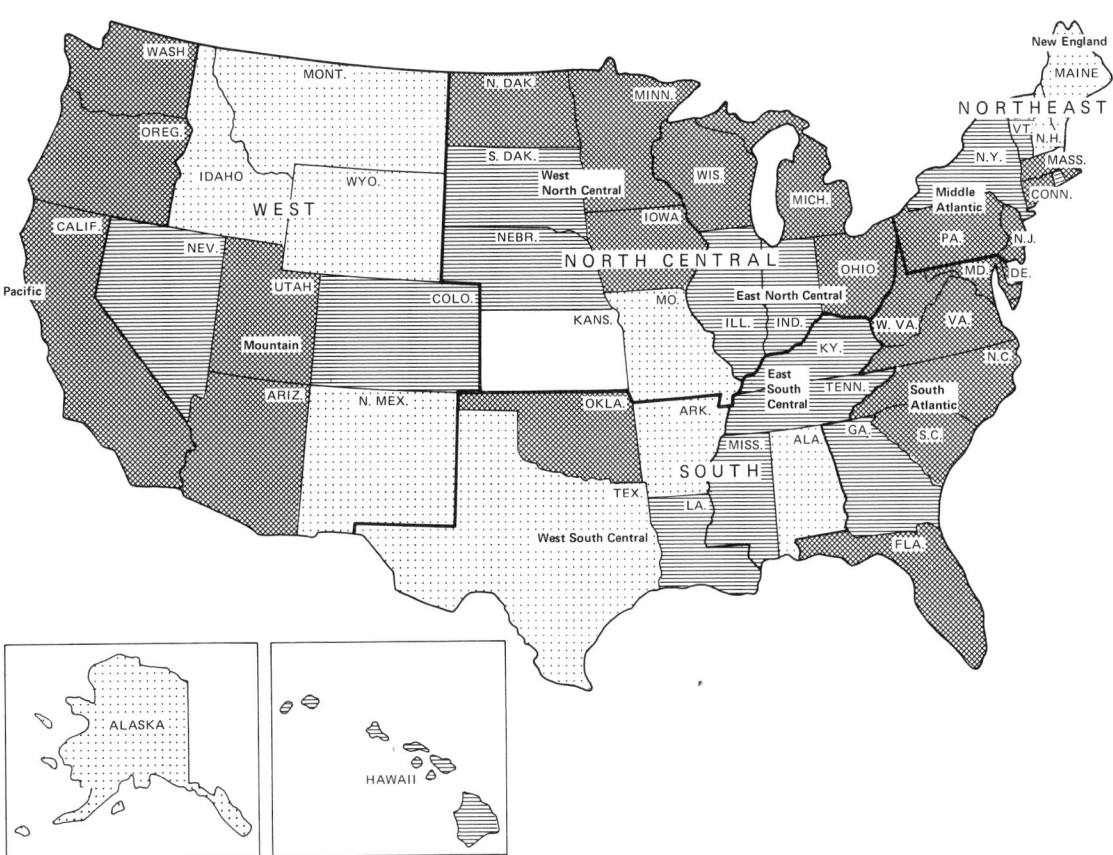

Exclusion from
Residential Districts

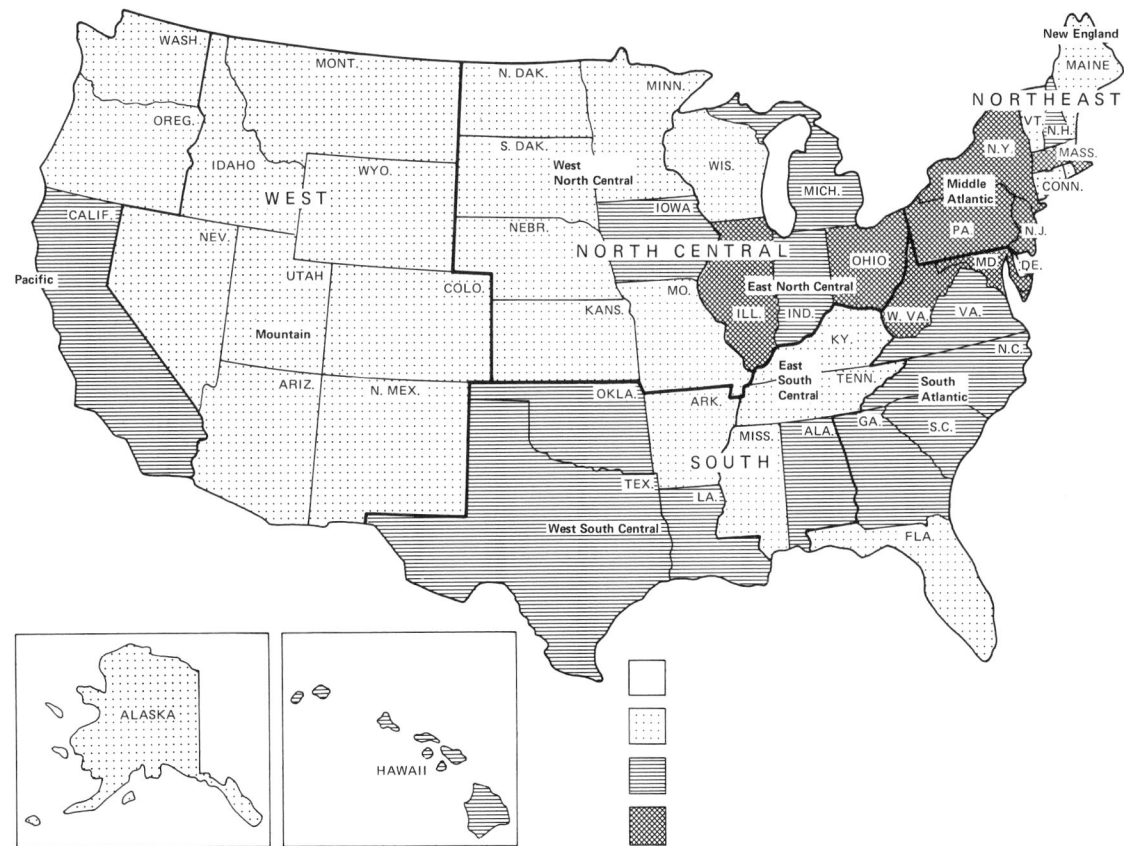

Land Use Controls

not constitute a one-family residence within the meaning and intent of the various ordinances and thus is properly excluded. Courts in other states have also held, with varying degrees of emphasis and in different situations, that mobile homes, even if immobilized, remain trailers and thus are within the prohibition of such an ordinance.[23]

However, a Vermont court, in the case *In re Wiley*, considered the owner's intent, found that he clearly intended to make his mobile home a permanent residence, and noted that structures, including prefabricated houses, brought to a site do not become vehicles.[24] In *State of Washington* v. *Work* a court went further and held that the mobile home was never a vehicle but always a home and that as long as a structure meets the applicable code regulations, it should not be prohibited.[25] These cases indicate a growing awareness that the essential difference between mobile homes and other housing units is the manner in which they are produced and distributed and not necessarily the manner in which they are used. With greater emphasis on "home" rather than "mobile," the courts will increasingly look to the actual use of the mobile home before deciding whether or not it violates the homogeneity of the residential district.

Most zoning ordinances dealing with mobile home parks treat them as commercial ventures and thus draw the dubious conclusion that they belong in nonresidential areas. As a result, mobile homes and parks have been relegated to commercial areas at best, industrial areas at worst. Although mobile homes are undeniably a different form of residential use, they nevertheless are residential facilities, not unlike apartments. The forced location of mobile homes in commercial or industrial zones is similar to the forced location of an apartment house in commercial or industrial zones—the ownership and operation of an apartment house is a business in the same sense that a mobile home park is. Municipalities that relegate mobile homes to commercial and industrial areas mistakenly use the incidental profitability of the park to its owner rather than the primary purpose of its use by the consumer as a basis for its designation. The two court cases most often cited for the proposition that a commercial classification is legitimate are *City of New Orleans* v. *Louviere* and *City of New Orleans* v. *Lafon*.[26] On the other hand, a trial court in South Dakota pointed out that the constitutional rights of mobile home occupants to due process and equal protection would be infringed upon if they were forced to live in areas unsuited for residential living.[27]

Our data on the incidence of exclusion from residential areas or restriction to industrial-commercial areas is summarized in table 16.2 and figure 16.2. Except in agricultural regions, these two devices have a similar impact and, for the most part, are indistinguishable.

Limits on the Number of Mobile Homes or Parks in a Municipality

Mobile homes will usually not only be restricted to parks but also the number of parks, acreage per park, and number of homes per park will be explicitly limited. Park size can also be implicitly limited by zoning a limited amount of suitable land or setting a minimum lot size for each unit within the park. Many of these restrictions are reasonable land use measures designed to protect residents' health and to control area density, but the controls can be unreasonable and overly restrictive. The various limitations on parks may have the effect of creating monopolies, which in turn reduces the incentive to establish efficient, high-quality developments. In *Town of Yorkville* v. *Fonk* an ordinance limiting the number of park spaces to twenty-five was upheld on the basis that it bore a direct and substantial relation to the general welfare.[28] The court reasoned that the impact of allowing more units would be to overburden the already crowded schools and deferred to the community's judgment of devising this solution. This type of restriction may be reasonable but it may prevent a developer from achieving the necessary size to provide services at a price a mobile home consumer can afford, and thus the restraint can effectively prohibit parks.

Time Limits

Even today there are ordinances limiting the period during which mobile homes may remain within a municipality, and these take a number of forms: prohibition of habitation in excess of a stated time; requirement of a nonrenewable permit to occupy; or imposition of stringent building code provisions upon mobile homes remaining longer than a certain time. This form of regulation clearly dates back to the days when the units were truly mobile and were similar to the vehicles we now call vacation trailers. Nevertheless, as late as the 1960s courts have upheld this method of regulation as applied both to individual mobile homes and to mobile home parks. No distinction has been made between temporary vacation homes and permanent mobile home residences; the regulation has been upheld across the board. Although the common use of mobile homes as permanent residences has now rendered this method of regulation anachronistic, some courts still rest their decision on health and safety grounds or on the "legitimate" need to promote transiency. An Ohio court saw permanent mobile home residences as a cause of slums and felt that any method designed to enforce the transiency of mobile home dwellers was in the public interest.[29]

A time limitation on mobile homes located outside parks or in tourist camps may be reasonably related to health and safety considerations if, after the time has expired, there is a provision allowing the unit to remain if it complies with health and safety regulations;

but even this reasoning cannot logically be applied to mobile homes within parks. Neither occupants nor community is healthier or safer if a dwelling designed for permanent residence is allowed only a temporary stay. Once a park complies with local code and licensing regulations, individual homes within the park can create no additional burdens on the community.

The imposition of time restrictions on mobile homes located in parks designed for permanent living is inconsistent with the nature and purpose of the product. Modern mobile homes are not mobile. Once sited, they are moved as infrequently as most conventional housing. Time restrictions, even if not uniformly enforced, will discourage potential mobile home occupants who desire permanency. Moreover, because of the inconvenience and cost of moving a modern mobile home, these provisions in most cases constitute a form of indirect exclusion. The courts' reluctance to examine the assumptions underlying the imposition of a nomadic existence on mobile home dwellers is indicative of their failure to recognize the improvements in modern mobile home living. Communities, however, may have recognized that time limits have become anachronistic and unreasonable: According to the results of our survey, limitation of stay apparently occurs or is enforced very infrequently.

Frontage Consents
Certain ordinances regulating mobile home parks contain provisions making the right to locate a park contingent upon the consent of nearby property owners or residents. This type of regulation, commonly referred to as a "frontage consent" provision, was upheld in two decisions, *Huff* v. *City of Des Moines* and *Cady* v. *City of Detroit*, handed down over twenty years ago.[30] A contrary result was reached in a recent case, *Williams* v. *Whilten*, where the ordinance required consent of all landowners within 200 feet of the proposed park.[31] The court found this requirement invalid as an unlawful delegation of legislative power by the state to adjacent property owners. Perhaps, then, frontage consent ordinances are rarely employed to restrict or exclude mobile homes because their constitutionality is suspect. Nevertheless, in those areas where they are still applied to mobile homes, private citizens may withhold consent at their whim. This is yet another situation in which the single-family mobile home dwelling is often accorded different treatment than the single-family conventional dwelling.

Constructive Exclusions
Aside from all these methods of control, political units have power to exclude mobile homes indirectly. These "constructive" exclusions take on many forms. Some municipalities exclude mobile homes by classifying them as residential dwellings but requiring them to conform to ordinances applicable only to conventional dwellings. For example, a provision requiring a minimum amount of floor space, minimum lot size, side yard footage, and so forth may have the practical effect of excluding mobile homes. In *Ostek* v. *Barone* the court upheld an ordinance requiring a minimum floor area of at least 900 square feet.[32] In its opinion the ordinance did not constitute a practical exclusion of mobile homes or mobile home parks, although testimony indicated that only about 6 percent of the mobile homes in 1967 had 900 or more square feet of floor space. (Today most singlewide mobile homes have 950 square feet and doublewides have around 1800 square feet.) Testimony also maintained that the lot size requirement, 10,000 square feet, was inconsistent with mobile home park design needs. However, the court rejected the contention that the ordinance operated as an arbitrary or discriminatory exclusion of mobile homes because it had equal application to mobile homes and conventional homes, reasoning that legitimate planning regulations should not be invalidated merely because they indirectly exclude mobile homes.

As already noted, communities may also exclude mobile homes by providing for their location in specified districts but failing to zone any available land for such use or by providing land for parks in areas where it would be economically unfeasible to run a park. In *Rottman* v. *Waterford Township*, for example, the ordinance provided a small amount of land for mobile homes and had a provision for further allotment later; but when the designated land was entirely consumed, no more was allotted.[33] Courts usually uphold the validity of such an ordinance on the ground that it is not a complete ban, focusing on the formal qualities of the ordinance and ignoring its practical effect.

Communities can even exclude mobile homes by allowing them as special exceptions but in practice denying the mobile home owner's application for a permit.[34] This is undoubtedly a common occurrence, but it is infrequently litigated because there are few standards by which to judge the review body's decision. The zoning body that considers special permit applications may have general guidelines to abide by, but by and large the process is a discretionary one.

Information on the frequency of the use of legal devices such as these is difficult to obtain, for the very reason that they are often implicit attempts at exclusion where explicit bans are impossible. However, some idea of the frequency of their use can be gained by comparing two views of exclusion compiled by this study. In the course of gathering our data, we contacted both a state planning official and the president of each state and regional trade association. The planning official quoted the percentage of municipalities in his or her state that explicitly exclude mobile homes and sometimes added that through other techniques, such as minimum floor area requirements, quotas, or building code regulations, an additional percentage effectively excluded mobile homes. This additional percentage was usually close to the percentage quoted by the trade association spokesperson. The difference between the percentage given by the president of the trade association and the one given by the state planning official can be interpreted as a measure of the frequency at which constructive exclusions, restrictions on the number of mobile homes and parks in a municipality, and frontage consents occur. The reliability of the figure is, of course, not clear and it is presented only as an indication of the present situation and not as hard data.

The difference between the pair of the percentages was tested statistically with a one-tailed t-test. The mean difference was computed to be 3.31 percent. This proved to be insignificant (table 16.3). The probability of .317 is not nearly low enough to reject a hypothesis that there is no significant difference between the two groups. Nevertheless, the differences between them are presented in the table.

Analysis of Local Zoning Preferences

Several studies have attempted to explain why municipalities adopt particular zoning ordinances to regulate mobile homes. Their explanations are usually theoretical and often only suppositions. The arguments generally assume that each municipality makes a rational decision reflecting the costs and benefits of mobile homes at the local level, without much consideration for the larger impacts of their actions. But most analyses make no distinction between complete exclusion of mobile homes and other restrictive measures. With all forms of exclusion and restriction lumped together, none of the arguments can distinguish between what may be different motivations behind the various exclusions and restrictions. Therefore we formulated a series of hypotheses designed to find the different reasons behind the various restrictions and then tested them out on a sample of ninety-six localities with populations above twenty-five-thousand. Though heavily biased toward the more restrictive East, this sample, derived from our national survey, consists of all cities and towns whose zoning practices were known and for which observations on the other variables were available.

Hypothetical Factors Cross-Tabulated with Exclusion
If a consideration behind zoning is indeed the fiscal impact of various land uses, then the exclusion of mobile homes in municipalities where mobile homes are not subject to real estate and property taxes would be an understandable action. Where such taxes are imposed, the municipality receives direct revenue from its mobile home citizens and can use this revenue to offset the costs of municipal services. Where mobile home dwellers are not subject to such taxation and are only charged nominal vehicular licensing fees, they may be seen as less desirable. Hence, our first hypothesis:

A municipality will have a greater propensity to exclude mobile homes if it is in a state where mobile homes are not subject to the property tax.

Table 16.4 lends little support here. Indeed, there is a slight pattern showing the opposite of what we expected. However, dividing the system of taxation into the two categories of property tax and license systems does not directly take into account the varying assessment procedures and tax rates in each category and may not adequately reflect the per-dwelling tax on mobile homes in each municipality.

It has been suggested that mobile home dwellers are perceived as paying less than their fair share of taxes, considering the municipal services they "consume," and are therefore excluded to protect the municipal budget and out of fears of rising property taxes. If this is accurate, then it will be true to the extent of a municipality's dependence on the property tax for revenue. In localities where sales, income, and other taxes are a significant portion of its revenue, the motivation to engage in such fiscal zoning should be correspondingly reduced. The hypothesis:

A municipality will have a greater propensity to exclude mobile homes if most of its revenues are dependent on the property tax.

The cost of most municipal services is difficult to assign to specific users, but the cost of education can be broken down easily. Because this is a large portion of a community's expenditures, sometimes over half, it is often applied as an easily understood yardstick when a municipality considers the impacts of alternative land uses. Multifamily dwellings are often excluded or restricted to one-bedroom units for this reason. Because mobile homes are also seen as dense land users, the percentage of a municipality's expenditures spent on schools would be positively correlated with its propensity to ban mobile homes for fiscal concerns. This would be true for two reasons. First, a few municipalities that are predominantly retirement communities (such as those in Florida) would have smaller school budgets and less need to engage in fiscal zoning. Second, municipalities that are not directly responsible for raising money for schools would not be immediately concerned with the school budget. In cases where schools are the responsibility of an autonomous school district with its own posers to raise money, the local governments, although ultimately affected, are not as strongly motivated to concern themselves with the impact of their actions on the school population. Thus we arrive at hypothesis number three:

A municipality will have a greater propensity

Table 16.3.
Percentage of
Municipalities in Each
State Using
Constructive Exclusion,
Frontage Consents,
and/or Restriction of
Number of Mobile
Homes and Parks

State	%
Alabama	11
Alaska	2[a]
Connecticut	2
Hawaii	75[a]
Indiana	10[a]
Kansas	5[a]
Kentucky	5
Massachusetts	3
Minnesota	—[b]
New Hampshire	19
New Jersey	—[b]
Ohio	—[b]
Rhode Island	5[a]
South Carolina	49
Vermont	40[a]
Virginia	0[a]
West Virginia	—[b]
Average of 17 states	13.3

T-Test Between Pair of Variables

Variable	Mean	Standard Deviation	Standard Error
% of municipalities			
banning MH per state	33.3077	33.611	9.322
banning MH per assn.	36.6154	24.975	6.927

Number of Cases	Corr.	Sig.	Difference Mean	Standard Deviation	Standard Error	T Value
13	0.691	0.933	3.3077	24.363	6.757	0.49

Degrees of Freedom	1 Tail Prob.
12	0.317

a. States where explicit information on the frequency of the use of the three devices in known. The average use of the devices is shown.
b. Those states where the state claimed a higher exclusion level than the trade association.
Source: 50-State PMHI Survey.

Table 16.4.
Cross-Tabulation of
Hypothetical Factors
with Exclusion of
Mobile Homes

	% of Municipalities That	
Factor	Do Not Exclude	Exclude

Taxation (method by which mobile homes in a municipality
are taxed)

Property tax	41.9	58.1
License system	54.7	45.3

Corrected Chi Square = 1.09791
with 1 degree of freedom
Phi = 0.16694
Contingency Coefficient = 0.10634

Revenue (percentage of municipal revenues derived from
property tax)

Below 95%	81.5	18.5
Above 95%	36.2	63.8

Corrected Chi Square = 14.14160
with 1 degree of freedom
Phi = 0.38381
Contingency Coefficient = 0.35832

Schoolex (percentage of municipal budget spent on schools)

Below 40%	68.8	31.3
Above 40%	29.2	70.9

Corrected Chi Square = 13.50586
with 1 degree of freedom
Phi = 0.37503
Contingency Coefficient = 0.35119

Wealth (median value of single-family homes in a municipality)

Below $18,500	68.6	31.4
Above $18,500	26.7	73.3

Corrected Chi Square = 15.20675
with 1 degree of freedom
Phi = 0.39800
Contingency Coefficient = 0.36979

Growth (percentage of growth in municipal population,
1960 to 1970)

Below 8%	39.2	60.8
Above 8%	60.0	40.0

Corrected Chi Square = 3.34279
with 1 degree of freedom
Phi = 0.18460
Contingency Coefficient = 0.18344

Density (municipal population per square mile)

Below 4,700	62.9	37.1
Above 4,700	23.5	76.5

Corrected Chi Square = 12.09261
with 1 degree of freedom
Phi = 0.35491
Contingency Coefficient = 0.33447

Source: PMHI study of ninety-six municipalities with populations over twenty-five thousand; various
series, U.S. Bureau of the Census.

to exclude mobile homes if a significant amount of its expenditures goes for schools.

The extent of municipal dependence on the property tax and level of expenditures on education are both significant determinants of exclusion (table 16.4), suggesting that although there may not be a direct causal relationship between these variables and exclusion or nonexclusion, fiscal consideration in general may be a cause of municipal preferences regarding the exclusion of mobile homes. In both tables the null hypothesis can be rejected at beyond the 99 percent level; and although phi does not come close to approaching unity, it is at a level that is not unreasonable for a cross-sectional sample like the present one.

Mobile homes are probably excluded for other reasons besides fiscal ones. Communities fear depressed property values and individuals desire to live in a community of a single socioeconomic status. Because occupants of mobile homes are for the most part in low-income brackets, wealthy communities may be more likely than the less wealthy ones to exclude mobile homes. Of course, the exclusion of low-income housing may have ensured a community's wealth in the first place, but it does provide a test for socioeconomic exclusion of lower-income groups. When wealth is measured by the median value of single-family dwellings in the community, it provides a possible test for the property value argument:

A municipality will have a greater propensity to exclude mobile homes if it has a high per-capita wealth.

Measuring wealth by the median value of single-family dwellings in a municipality, the data in table 16.4 lend strong support to this hypothesis.

Legal arguments justifying restrictions often note that "because (mobile homes) can be sited rapidly and in a relatively small area, they are capable of imposing a sudden and severe load on all municipal facilities."[35] This is difficult to test in the scope of our analysis. Municipalities experiencing rapid growth might be more apt to exclude mobile homes when each of the previously mentioned reasons would be more immediate and the threat of mobile homes establishing themselves more prominent. This will be true if one assumes that mobile homes are not an important component of growth when an ordinance was passed or amended, as is the case in most municipalities.

A municipality will have a greater propensity to exclude mobile homes if it is experiencing rapid growth.

In this case the percentage of population growth from 1960 to 1970 tabulated with exclusion shows an unexpected pattern. Table 16.4 indicates that if a community is experiencing rapid growth, it is more likely not to exclude mobile homes than to exclude

them. It may be that mobile homes are a more significant component of growth than was assumed when the hypothesis was developed. Intuitively, the pattern is convincing—rapid growth and a likely accompanying acute housing shortage make exclusion of the most quickly available remedy (the mobile home) unlikely. Further, it is possible that rapid-growth areas are generally lax in development standards, and this could account for the figures.

There is another possible reason for excluding mobile homes: They may be excluded where they would be unable to compete economically with other land uses, such as dense cities where land values dictate more dwelling units per acre than the traditional mobile home can provide. Though there may be no need to exclude mobile homes (in most cases they will not be able to locate there anyway), they may still be excluded on paper because one view of the purpose of zoning is to correct market imperfections. An area can be zoned for commercial or multifamily uses, excluding mobile homes, to ensure the highest and best use of the land and at the same time increase its value.

A municipality will have a greater propensity to exclude mobile homes if it has a high population density.

The cross-tabulation of density per square mile in table 16.4 does not contradict this hypothesis.

Cross-Tabulation with Restriction and Exclusion

The restriction of mobile homes to non-residentially zoned areas is almost as predictable a response to the fiscal considerations inherent in the first three hypotheses as is the complete ban. By restricting mobile homes to industrial or commercial zones, a municipality can produce tax revenues from otherwise vacant land while holding it open for future more intensive and higher revenue producing industrial and commercial uses that can command higher land prices. A mobile home is one of the most temporary and easily displaced of all land uses. There is still a question of the costs to a municipality in services provided mobile homes, but if a locality cannot or will not completely exclude, a temporary cost (real or imaginary) is preferable to the more permanent one that would occur if mobile homes were permitted in residential areas.

The desire to prevent a feared decline in residential property values, however, seems a more plausible reason. The exclusion of mobile homes from residential areas is as "adequate" a solution as the complete exclusion of mobile homes, protecting both adjacent home owners' investment in their property and the municipality's tax base. The restriction of mobile homes to mobile home parks can be explained by the same reasoning. Likewise, the exclusion of mobile

homes from residential areas and the restriction to mobile home parks adequately satisfies the desire to live among individuals of similiar socioeconomic status. It is unlikely that there are any direct fiscal motivations in the restriction of mobile homes to mobile home parks. However, the restriction ensures that the land remains in one unbroken tract, increasing the feasibility of later conversion to industrial and commercial uses. When this restriction is combined with the restriction to industrial and commercial zones, the fiscal reasons for restriction to industrial or commercial zones are enhanced.

It was observed that municipalities experiencing rapid growth do not exclude mobile homes (perhaps because of sheer need for any type of housing or out of general laxness in development controls), so it is expected by the same reasoning that exclusion from residential areas will not occur in these communities either. It is unclear, however, whether the restriction of mobile homes to parks will occur more frequently in fast-growing communities; although it can be interpreted as a restriction in development, it may also facilitate development by encouraging the development of mobile home parks. Needless to say, any results of cross-tabulation with growth will have little meaning for the hypothesis growth was introduced to test.

One would still expect that more heavily populated communities would restrict mobile homes to parks, if not excluding them altogether. This segregation of mobile homes would help ensure the best use of other areas while keeping the land used for mobile home development in large tracts, facilitating future reuse in the more intensive development that would be likely in dense cities. This also applies to the restriction of mobile homes to industrial and commercial areas when it is used in conjunction with the restriction of mobile homes to mobile home parks.

The same six variables used in table 16.4 are computer tabulated with both restriction to parks and exclusion from residential areas in table 16.5. The zoning restrictions are divided into five categories: no restriction, the use of the restriction of mobile homes to parks, the use of an exclusion from residential areas, the concurrent use of the restriction to parks and exclusion from residential areas, and the use of a complete exclusion. In this case, the 95 percent confidence level for chi square is 9.488.

A glance at the figures on taxation shows that municipalities operating under a property tax system restrict or exclude mobile homes less often than those operating under a license system. And, as in table 16.4, municipalities in a property tax system exclude mobile homes slightly more often than those in a license system. The interesting observation in this table is the frequency with which municipalities employing one or both restrictions are found to be in a license system. The

Table 16.5.
Cross-Tabulations of
Hypothetical Factors
with Various Forms of
Restriction and
Exclusion

Factor	% of Municipalities Using Restrictions				
	None	Parks Only	Nonresidential Areas Only	Parks and Nonresidential Areas	Exclusion
Taxation (method by which mobile homes in a municipality are taxed)					
Property tax	32.6	2.3	2.3	4.7	58.1
License system	5.7	77.6	7.5	18.9	45.3

Chi Square = 22.78459 with 4 degrees of freedom
Cramer's U = 0.48717
Contingency Coefficient = 0.43797

	None	Parks Only	Nonresidential Areas Only	Parks and Nonresidential Areas	Exclusion
Revenue (percentage of municipal revenues derived from property tax)					
Below 95%	11.1	48.1	7.4	14.8	18.5
Above 95%	20.3	0.0	4.3	11.6	63.8

Chi Square = 42.44003 with 4 degrees of freedom
Cramer's U = 0.66499
Contingency Coefficient = 0.55868

	None	Parks Only	Nonresidential Areas Only	Parks and Nonresidential Areas	Exclusion
Schoolex (percentage of municipal budget spent on schools)					
Below 40%	14.6	27.1	10.4	16.7	31.3
Above 40%	20.8	0.0	0.0	8.3	70.8

Chi Square = 27.23007 with 4 degrees of freedom
Cramer's U = 0.53258
Contingency Coefficient = 0.47007

	None	Parks Only	Nonresidential Areas Only	Parks and Nonresidential Areas	Exclusion
Wealth (median value of single-family homes in a municipality)					
Below $18,500	23.5	19.6	7.8	17.6	31.3
Above $18,500	11.1	6.7	2.2	6.7	73.3

Chi Square = 17.04109 with 4 degrees of freedom
Cramer's U = 0.42132
Contingency Coefficient = 0.38827

	None	Parks Only	Nonresidential Areas Only	Parks and Nonresidential Areas	Exclusion
Growth (percentage of growth in municipal population, 1960 to 1970)					
Below 8%	13.7	5.9	5.9	13.7	60.8
Above 8%	22.2	22.2	4.4	11.1	40.0

Chi Square = 7.93695 with 4 degrees of freedom
Cramer's U = 0.28754
Contingency Coefficient = 0.27634

	None	Parks Only	Nonresidential Areas Only	Parks and Nonresidential Areas	Exclusion
Density (municipal population per square mile)					
Below 4,700	24.2	21.0	4.8	12.9	37.1
Above 4,700	5.9	0.0	5.9	11.8	76.5

Chi Square = 18.02487
Crame'rs U = 0.43331
Contingency Coefficient = 0.39759

Source: PMHI study of ninety-six municipalities with populations over twenty-five thousand; various series, U.S. Bureau of the Census.

type of taxation used seems to matter greatly in the decision to restrict mobile homes. In a property tax system, if a municipality does not exclude mobile homes, it is not likely to use either of the two restrictions, restriction to parks or restriction to nonresidential areas. On the other hand, a municipality in a license system, if it does not exclude mobile homes, will be likely to use one of the restrictions.

The percentage of municipalities restricting mobile homes to nonresidential areas and those employing both restrictions, when separated by their dependence on the property tax, differ little from the sample. This does not contradict the argument that there are few fiscal motivations for restricting mobile homes to mobile home parks. The fiscal reasons for restricting mobile homes to industrial and commercial areas may not be as great as was thought.

The distribution for school expenditures by zoning is similar to that for dependence on property tax and supports the same conclusions. The principal difference between the tables is the percentage of municipalities with school expenditures less than 40 percent of their budget that restrict mobile homes to nonresidential areas.

The tabulations of wealth by zoning restrictions indicate that wealthier communities more frequently restrict or exclude mobile homes than the less wealthy, though a significant percentage of the less wealthy employ some restrictions on them. One may conclude that although most municipalities exclude or restrict mobile homes, those with the strongest reasons exclude mobile homes while others generally restrict or control them in some fashion.

When growth rates are tabulated by zoning restrictions, municipalities with high growth rates restrict mobile homes to parks more often than the sample of those with low growth rates. This supports the contention that a restriction to parks is less of a development control than was thought while the other restrictions are effective.

The relationship between density and the use of the restriction to parks turns out to be the opposite of what was expected. Instead of the denser municipalities using the restriction to parks more often, communities below forty-seven hundred population per square mile are the exclusive users of this restriction. This is almost entirely due to the frequent use of the complete exclusion of mobile homes by cities with denser populations.

In summary, most municipalities either exclude or place a restriction on mobile homes. Not surprisingly, communities with more incentive, fiscal or otherwise, do so more often. These communities, however, are much more likely to exclude mobile homes completely, and others, with less incentive, restrict them to mobile home parks and nonresidential areas. However, the pattern in this second set of tables does not conclusively show that the restrictions are

not a result of the same motivations that cause a municipality to exclude mobile homes. The method of taxation is associated with the decision to restrict but not significantly with the decision to exclude. Dependence on the property tax, school expenditures, and wealth are associated with the decision to exclude. A municipality with over a 95 percent dependence on the property tax or with school expenditures over 40 percent, if it does not exclude mobile homes, is more likely to place no restriction on mobile homes than to restrict them.

Linear Probability Model
The cross-tabulation on the preceding pages considers the simple relationship between two variables and ignores the possible influence of other variables on this relationship. It is possible to construct tables that hold the other variables constant, but this is a tedious process. Rather than do this, we decided to set up a regression where the left-hand dependent variable could be considered the conditional probability of an event occurring, given the right-hand dependent variables.

Essentially, this is simply performing ordinary least squares where the left-hand variable takes on only two values, so that one may use unity to indicate the occurrence of an event and zero to indicate its nonoccurrence. By running a multiple regression on such a dependent variable Y on several explanatory variables X, one can then interpret the calculated value of Y, for any given X, as an estimate of the conditional probability of Y, given X.[36] The linear probability model allows only two values for the left-hand variable. This permits only one restriction or exclusion to be tested at a time. Complete exclusion of mobile homes is considered below. We decided that to do the same for the other two restrictions would be misleading because they often occur simultaneously and a municipality does not make a simple decision to restrict mobile homes; it is part of a larger decision about both controls.

A linear probability model was formulated using the same variables that were examined in the preceding section. BAN is a dummy variable; it has the value 1 when a municipality excludes mobile homes and 0 when it does not. Taxation is included as a dummy variable. This yields

$$BAN = C + a_1 \text{ WEALTH} + a_2 \text{ SCHOOLEX} + a_3 \text{ REVENUE} + a_4 \text{ DENSITY} + a_5 \text{ GROWTH} + a_6 \text{ TAXATION}.$$

Using ordinary least squares with t-statistics in parentheses:

$$BAN = -0.61 + 0.000017 \text{ WEALTH}$$
$$(-2.47) \quad (1.73)$$
$$+ 0.0064 \text{ SCHOOLEX}$$
$$(2.31)$$
$$+ 0.0043 \text{ REVENUE}$$
$$(1.58)$$

$$+ 0.000049 \text{ DENSITY}$$
$$(4.26)$$
$$+ 0.000054 \text{ GROWTH}$$
$$(1.27)$$
$$+ 0.025 \text{ TAXATION},$$
$$(0.29)$$
SSR = 14.259, Std. Error = 0.398.

Dropping TAXATION because it is insignificant here and also in the cross-tabulation and dropping GROWTH because it also is insignificant and has a small contribution to the fitted value of BAN (note that GROWTH is positive, opposite of what would be expected from the cross-tabulation results):

$$BAN = -0.54 + 0.000017 \text{ WEALTH}$$
$$(-2.30) \quad (1.77)$$
$$+ 0.0070 \text{ SCHOOLEX}$$
$$(2.70)$$
$$+ 0.0034 \text{ REVENUE}$$
$$(1.29)$$
$$+ 0.000048 \text{ DENSITY},$$
$$(4.28)$$
SSR = 14.512, Std. Error = 0.399.

Each coefficient has the expected sign, but one cannot reject a null hypothesis that the coefficient of PCTTAX is zero or of the opposite sign at the 95 percent level. The others are significant at a 95 percent one-tailed level. The importance of each variable is demonstrated by its effect in BAN over its range in the sample. WEALTH ranges from 33,000 to 11,000, which can produce a difference of as much as .37 in BAN. Similarly, SCHOOLEX varies from 99 to 21 or a difference of .34; DENSITY from 16,000 to 782 or a difference of .77 in BAN. This gives some feeling for the importance of density, but to be rigorous, the standard error of each coefficient must be considered. For example, 90 percent confidence interval for REVENUE includes zero, at which point a municipality's dependence on the property tax does not affect complete exclusion at all.

A plot of the actual and fitted values (which can be interpreted as conditional probabilities) proved the model to be rather reliable. One additional way of evaluating this model is to tabulate the number of times it fails to discriminate between the occurrence of BAN and the nonoccurrence of BAN. Because the sample is more or less evenly divided between occurrence and nonoccurrence, a probability of .5 is an adequate dividing point. The failures are tabulated below.

		Actual	
		BAN	no BAN
Predicted	BAN	47	14
	no BAN	5	30

19 failures, 77 successes, out of 96 cases

Summary
We can summarize our test results as follows:

A wealthier municipality, all else being equal, has a greater propensity to exclude mobile homes than does one with less wealth.

Fiscal considerations are important. The more a municipality must directly spend on schools, all else being equal, the greater its propensity to exclude mobile homes. In a simple two-way relationship the same holds true for a municipality's dependence on the property tax for revenue; though when considering the other variables, the effect of a community's dependence on the property tax is not significant in predicting whether it will exclude mobile homes.

It could not be established whether the way mobile homes are taxed in a state bears a relationship to the propensity of a municipality in that state to exclude mobile homes; the taxation method is, however, a significant determinant of restrictions to parks and non-residential areas.

Denser municipalities, everything else being equal, have a greater propensity to exclude mobile homes.

The effect of the rate of population growth is not conclusive. Communities with high population growth exclude mobile homes less than slower-growing communities; however, all else being equal, the effect is positive though small and only 90 percent significant.

Impact of Land Use Controls on Industry Performance

The impact of land use controls is generally negative. In only three instances do zoning regulations have positive impact on any industry actors: Subdivision controls, sometimes linked with a restriction to parks, can ensure an attractive environment for the consumer (though this will add cost); requirements that mobile homes be in parks support the mobile home park system; and constructive exclusions can give monopoly status to any existing park owner—a positive impact, of course, only from the owner's perspective and likely to affect the consumer negatively. Otherwise the results of land use controls, as described below, have negative effects on all actors of the mobile home industry.

Land Supply

The most obvious effect of land use control has been the limitation of the supply of land available for location of a mobile home. The most severe limitation occurs in areas of complete exclusion, but many other land use controls, although appearing less severe, can have the same effect on land supply: Municipalities may zone only minuscule portions of land for mobile homes or mobile home parks; the land that is legally available may be unsuitable for development because of topography or surrounding environment; competition from other permitted uses may make a park infeasible; or limitations on length of stay, inconsistent with modern mobile home living, may prevent development.

The limitation on land supply is manifested most clearly in the continuing shortage of park spaces available for mobile homes. From the late 1960s through the late 1970s the annual volume of new mobile home unit production has consistently outpaced annual new park space production volume by a ratio of approximately four to one. If this discrepancy continues on the present scale, site shortage is bound to become an increasingly serious impediment to the growth of mobile home sales. Waiting lists of three years or longer for park spaces are common in parts of the country with highly restrictive zoning practices. The shortage of land presently zoned to permit mobile home parks, without constructive exclusions, priced at and developable at a feasible cost, and in a marketable location, is one major reason for the lack of park space.

This shortage affects park developers most directly, for their primary interest is in developing land for mobile homes, but all actors are affected. Consumers cannot or will not buy a mobile home if they have no space for it at an acceptable cost in an acceptable location. Dealers therefore cannot sell mobile homes for which there are no spaces. And the original actor in the industry—the manufacturer—receives only a limited number of orders from dealers and thus production is limited as well.

In a 1971 survey of dealers, 59 percent identified lack of park space and 55 percent identified local zoning as "the major problems facing your business." These figures rose, respectively, to 79 percent and 70 percent among dealers in the generally more restrictive North. The same survey reported that 24 percent of all dealers (42 percent of the dealers in the North and 5 percent in the South) had from 81 percent to 100 percent of their retail sales "dependent on your ability to provide an adequate park site."[37] Our own national survey of dealers further investigated sales lost because of lack of land (that is, park space). One respondent claimed he could have sold 700 percent more mobile homes had space been available, but the average claim among respondents was 49 percent. Responses from dealers in both Florida and California (states with the largest number of respondents) had an average of 42 percent.[38] A 1977 dealer survey that we conducted on this very issue only yielded an average "lost sale" claim of 63 percent, suggesting that the regulatory climate, at least through the early 1980s, is unlikely to improve. In the same 1977 survey 9 percent of all interviewees claiming lost sales larger than 75 percent were from the South; 68 percent were from the Northeast.

Not only the amount of land available for mobile homes and parks but also its quality is adversely affected by land use controls. Where mobile home parks are restricted to industrial, commercial, or equally unattractive (for permanent residence) environments, developers are understandably pessimistic of the rents that can be demanded from such sites. The present land use control system and the economics of competing uses relegate mobile home parks to the most marginal quality land. The prevalence of restrictions to mobile home parks excludes from the market those consumers who are uninterested in living in a park. The potential market for mobile homes is therefore limited to those customers willing to live in the limited range of environments actually available.

Product Cost

Land use controls affect the final consumer occupancy cost of a mobile home in several ways. Simple economics argues that when the supply of suitable land is limited, competing demand will drive the price up. An increased cost of raw land for the park developer is subsequently translated into an increased final occupancy cost. Land use controls have a similar effect on any land thus limited, of course. The legal constraints on a piece of land are as much a factor in its value or cost as any physical assets: What a developer can do with a piece of land determines what he or she will pay for it. The impact of public regulation on the price of "mobile home land" is great, however, because mobile homes and parks are more severely restricted than other uses.

Further, when a site only marginally attractive for residences (and thus presumably priced low) is the only site in the area where mobile homes are legally permitted, the local government confers, in effect, a monopoly status upon the buyer. This adds to the present value of the land and increases the cost to the potential consumer. Furthermore, land zoned for industrial, commercial, or high-density use is generally more expensive on a per-square-foot basis than residential and because of its higher income-producing potential or opportunity value. Mobile home parks that are restricted to such zones must compete with businesses for the higher-cost land.

Land costs are a significant portion of total costs. The value of an improved urban lot typically makes up to 20 percent of the total value of a conventional single-family dwelling on that lot.[39] We found that the typical mobile home owner's park space rental constitutes a significantly higher percentage of the total housing bill. Land costs, therefore, have a disproportionately greater impact on the mobile home owner than on the conventional home owner. The direct relationship between high raw land costs and final occupancy costs is somewhat obscured because the space is rented, but clearly the developer must charge rents that will repay the investment in the land, pay for improvements, and still yield a profit. The current low-density nature of mobile home parks (often as low as four to five homes per acre) emphasizes the land cost component. In apartment development, for example, the cost of expensive land (appropriately zoned) can be divided among a flexible number of units; the more apartments there are, the smaller will be the fixed land cost per unit. In mobile home parks the per-acre carrying costs of land can only be divided among an upward limit of about five to eight spaces. The developer cannot afford to buy and improve land whose carrying charges per space will require unmarketably high rents. However, with no cheaper alternatives available, the consumer continuously drives up the price ceiling or "marketable space rental."

Two other elements of the present land use control system affect mobile home occupancy costs: Costs are associated with litigation and costs are associated with subdivision controls. Special zoning costs can occur in any district that does not permit mobile homes "by right." They may include filing fees, special permit fees, and legal counsel fees. Appeals to local boards of appeal involve similar zoning costs. In any situation where developers feel they must seek judicial review of the local decisions or statutes, they must bear the costs of litigation. Our national survey on park owners found that the average amount spent "obtaining the desired zoning" was $785 and the maximum spent was $8000.[40]

Table 16.6 summarizes the information

Table 16.6.
Park Owners' Attempts to Obtain Desired Zoning

Process used	Frequency (%)
Variance	7
Special permit	19
Zoning amendment	17
Other appeal process	7
No appeal necessary	39
Don't know	11
Authority appealed to	
Building inspector	5
Board of appeals	45
Municipal court	2
Superior court	2
Appellate court	2
Other appeal involvement	17
Don't know	24

Length of time required to obtain approval from authority	Months	Number of respondents
Financing sources	4.7	20
Building inspector	4.7	12
Zoning officials	4.7	29
Planning officials	4.5	8
Municipal court	36.0	1
Superior court	1.0	1
Appellate court	20.0	2
Other	7.4	8
Total length of time		
Mean	6.3	58
Standard deviation	12.5	
Minimum	0.0	
Maximum	84.0	

Source: PMHI National Park Survey.

collected pertaining to zoning: the type of appeal process, to whom the appeal was directed, and the mean amount of time spent acquiring approval. Whatever extra time is added to the development period by any of these processes adds to the developer's ultimate cost. Developers in turn pass the additional cost on to the consumer in the form of higher park space rentals; nevertheless, these added costs act as deterrents to potential park developers.

Subdivision controls, although in many respects representing a more enlightened land use control attitude toward mobile homes than zoning, frequently do restrict mobile homes to parks and allow park construction in certain districts only if the developer agrees to provide excessive improvements as specified by the municipality (we have seen street width requirements that would permit an emergency landing of a Boeing 747). Subdivision controls typically regulate park density and design and ensure the provision of certain amenities and the existence of a good residential environment. These controls may be, in effect, constructive exclusions of mobile homes and, whatever the effect, they do cost money. In a 1972 study of zoning and housing costs in New Jersey, George Sternlieb found subdivision requirements in general a highly significant determinant of final selling price but one that could not be adequately measured "given the present uniformity of a high level of standards." The costs necessitated by subdivision controls are passed on to the consumer. According to Sternlieb, "public policy decisions pertaining to minimum zoning requirements are significant factors explaining selling price variation."[41] Where restrictions are most severe, as with mobile homes in many municipalities, the impact on costs will be similarly severe, given a constant demand.

Park Location and Design
The impact of the present land use control system on the location and design of mobile home parks is, with the exception of subdivision controls, essentially negative. As the United States Court of Appeals found in a 1972 decision, some towns are determined "that there be metaphorical tracks for a mobile home park to be on the other side of."[42] Originally the common restriction of mobile home parks to industrial or commercial districts seemed justified because trailer parks were considered businesses; but our surveys found that though mobile homes are now stationary primary housing, 20 percent of all municipalities still force them into nonresidential areas that the community, presumably for good reasons, judged best suited for industry or commerce and inappropriate for residential use. Location in these areas adds to the impermanence of a mobile home park, partly because of the undesirable environment and partly because chances of redevelopment in such zones grow as more intensive and

more economical users of the land bid to replace the low-density mobile home park. Although this impermanence could be an advantage if properly planned for, it now functions as a restriction.

In some cases the land use control system is not the primary cause of poor location. A great deal of land in high-density urban areas is priced so high that a low-density mobile home park cannot support the cost.[43] Removal of the legal restrictions would have no impact on location in such cases; legally permitting mobile homes on Park Avenue is a meaningless gesture. However, technological changes that make higher-density mobile home development possible could change the economic factor.

Park location may suffer through overly severe local zoning restrictions, but park design may suffer through lack of proper regulation. Conventional single-family detached dwellings have typically been subject to various density, set-back, and other requirements that reflect a concern for quality of housing; mobile home parks have not. Developers may often create crowded densities (particularly if they must pay off high-priced land) and ignore design amenities —layout, landscaping, roadways, and services—if they are not required. What may be short-term savings to the developer (and initially, perhaps, to the consumer) are long-term losses to the consumer and the community.

Where sites are restricted in size, or parks in number of spaces, the developer may not be able to achieve the scale necessary to support or justify many amenities. Recreation centers and pools, for example, are typical only in the larger mobile home parks. Provision of more basic amenities such as landscaping and community facilities are discouraged by two other factors: impermanence and the original undesirable location. Owners will be unwilling to invest in greenbelts or quality roadways, for example, when they are under economic pressure to relocate or when the park is located in a thoroughly undesirable environment. Expert landscaping cannot overcome the odor of a factory next door, and recreational areas will not cover the noise of a nearby freeway. Parks classified as "nonconforming uses" may have design problems caused by legal restrictions. Improvements and alterations to such parks have sometimes been banned and expansion, sometimes necessary for improvements, prohibited.

Thus we have a vicious circle. Ordinances that relegate mobile home parks to the least desirable locations and fail to assure design standards contribute to the general low quality of parks. Inferior parks are unattractive to live in and to look at and understandably feed a community's desire to discourage them and to keep them on the "other side of the tracks."

The Consumer
An important measure of any industry's performance is the extent to which it satisfies user needs. Present land use control practices have produced frequent lapses of responsiveness and flexibility in the park system, which ultimately affect the production system's image.

The consumer has very little choice in location or style of his or her home where land use controls are most strict. Local land use controls, first of all, may have effectively excluded lower-cost conventional housing units (possibly in the form of multiple-family dwellings) in the community and pushed a segment of the population or potential population into the mobile home market. Local controls may further limit the consumer by allowing mobile homes only in a park. The more strict the local regulations and the less land zoned for parks, the less choice the consumer has in deciding in which park to locate a mobile home. The consumer may have to accept an undesirable living environment. Space shortages and waiting lists are evidence of this situation.[44]

Local restrictions may be so severe that a parks monopoly is created. Existing parks that are deemed "nonconforming uses" are almost invariably secured from new competition. The United States Court of Appeals was so convinced of a municipality's complicity in creating a monopoly situation that it overturned an eviction case (*Lavoie* v. *Bigwood*) within a park on the grounds that "state action," and not a purely private action, was adequately demonstrated.[45] Of course, in some municipalities the limitation of choice problem is avoided because the municipality excludes mobile homes or mobile home parks altogether.

The monopoly or near-monopoly situation has worse consequences than lengthy waiting lists. Monopoly status alters the fundamental landlord-tenant relationship by conferring considerable dominance on the park owner. This puts consumers in a very weak bargaining position; they may be subject to many park owner excesses: entrance fees, exit fees, sales fees, service fees, association fees, guest fees, lack of a lease, eviction without cause, and park rules and regulations (no children, no pets, no noise, no "improper conduct," who can sell milk, who can make deliveries, and so on) that may be unreasonable. Such intimidation can be fought—in the case of *Lavoie* v. *Bigwood* a park owner tried to evict a tenant, allegedly because he complained about the park and was active in a tenants' association. The United States Court of Appeals held that "an ejectment action instituted to punish the exercise of a tenant's constitutional rights of speech and association, by a mobile home park owner whose monopoly has been created by zoning" was invalid.[46]

The statistical frequency of such intimidation is very low, but such abuses do represent serious problems for many individual mobile home owners. Basically, a landlord is restrained in dealings with tenants by the law, what the market will bear, and his or her own ethics and conscience. State law dealing with tenant-landlord relations generally ignores mobile home parks. Currently only a very few states—Delaware, California, Florida, and Michigan, among others—have laws that to some degree protect the mobile home park tenant. With annual average occupancy rates in mobile home parks often exceeding the 95 percent level, many park owners do not need to be overly concerned about filling the space of an evicted tenant. That leaves the mobile home consumer with only the park owner's ethics and conscience. Of course, in most cases these suffice, but they are hardly a businesslike substitute for institutionalized protection of park tenants.[47] Aggravation of any single consumer indirectly builds up a major business problem for the entire industry because the news media give many single incidents wide negative coverage, hurting the industry image.

A less identifiable but perhaps more severe negative impact of the present land use control system on the consumer segment of the mobile home industry is sociological. Where mobile homes are forced into parks and parks are forced into isolated or unattractive sites, it may be assumed that they are inferior housing and that differential treatment and segregation are justified and should continue. A psychological ghetto may be formed: Park tenants feel isolated from the outside community and keep to themselves.[48] The surrounding community, already prejudiced, becomes more and more suspicious of the segregated enclave and another circle is created.

Other Impacts
The influence of land use controls is powerful in a least three other ways. It is largely responsible for the fractionalized nature of the industry; it fosters uncertainty and thus may inhibit investment in the industry; and it prevents full realization of the industry's potential.

The fractionalized nature of the present land use control system, where some ten thousand local governments have the power to regulate land use, heightens the fractionalization of the mobile home industry. In order to deal with the particular problems of each locality's zoning, the park industry must operate on a small geographic scale. Mobile home manufacturers, on the other hand, cannot justify the initial costs of manufacturing facilities unless they work in a very large geographic market—they cannot deal with the hundreds of separate zoning jurisdictions that impinge on park development. These two subsectors of the industry—the production system and the park system—must deal with very different market sizes because of the fractionalization of the land

use control system. A third subsector, the distribution system, must bridge the gap between the production and parks systems. These differing concerns have inhibited consolidation within the industry.

Although consolidation is not necessarily the ultimate goal of a "rationalized" industry, a lack of consolidation can foster uncertainty within the industry. Any industry is limited by the most severely restricted facet of its production and delivery process. The mobile home industry is limited by land supply in its production of a total housing environment. The manufacturer and dealer must be able to place their product onto a park space if they are to market their goods (thus the great overlap between dealer and park owner). The localized land use control system makes the manufacturer and dealer uncertain of their future market. The local park developer/owner is not certain of success in changing restrictive regulations and overcoming other constraints to provide new park spaces. Uncertainty is thus apparent throughout the industry. Uncertainty, almost by definition, means higher risk. Higher risk dampens investment; investors are less likely to invest in a manufacturer's expansion of capacity if the uncertain land factor must shape the market's growth. The relative impermanence of a mobile home park may also discourage any considerable investment. New York City proposed a mobile home ordinance that, for example, anticipated the redevelopment of mobile home parks and offered special permits with a period of only ten years.[49] Whether impermanence stems from legal or economic pressure, no industry can expand to its fullest without a relatively stable and coherent environment.

The land use control system inhibits the full realization of the industry's potential. Typical local restrictions still reflect prejudices formed in the days of the nomadic trailer and are highly resistant to change. Land use controls have not been upgraded to reflect the improvements that have made mobile homes so like conventional homes, and this basic inflexibility hinders the entire industry.

Subdivision controls and planned unit development (PUD) codes, which allow densities to be moved around large sites, and special districts, which offer bonuses in return for specified developer performance, are part of a new genre of land use controls involving negotiations and bonuses to achieve highest-quality development. These more flexible regulatory devices typically require some form of decision or approval from a local administrative body; so subdivision control legislation must be carefully detailed to ensure against capricious or arbitrary decisions and to ensure that once a certain specified performance level is achieved, the zoning benefits do become, in effect, "as of right." Another danger to guard against is the possibility that subdivision controls could be

C. Emerging Trends and Their Effects on the Industry

Subdivision Controls

written so strictly as to be, in reality, constructive exclusions.

It is difficult to measure the degree to which communities are turning to these new regulatory devices, but the trend is clearly growing and its impact is generally favorable. The single possible negative effect is economic: Park spaces developed under subdivision controls will cost more and those costs will be passed on to the consumer. Whether this affects sales is yet to be seen—it depends on the consumer's willingness and ability to pay for a better designed and located mobile home environment. Total demand might actually expand if people who would not consider living in the old parks see substantially different living conditions in parks developed under subdivision controls.

The clearly positive aspect of this trend is more widespread community acceptance of mobile homes. Mobile home park development has been seriously hampered by restrictive zoning practices. Subdivision controls, however, by addressing the root causes of hostility to mobile homes and by requiring the developer to create a park aesthetically and economically acceptable to the community, could positively affect the industry.

Zoning Restrictions

During our survey on zoning practices we obtained from fourteen states information on the past use and estimated future use of complete exclusion, restriction to mobile home parks, and exclusion from residential districts (see table 16.7). The use of each of these three devices has steadily increased over the past thirteen years. However, only restriction to parks is projected to increase over the next five to ten years; use of the other devices is expected to remain constant or drop slightly. The increases in the use of complete exclusion as well as the frequency of use of exclusion from residential zones have both followed a slow growth trend, and overwhelming expectation for the future is for no significant change. The restriction to mobile home parks, which has experienced a much greater growth rate in the past than application of the other two devices, is presently at a higher absolute level, with further increase expected.

Although restriction to parks has frequently been used in the past when localities were unable or unwilling to exclude mobile homes completely, it has recently been used

as an instrument to improve the quality of life in mobile homes. Concern for the quality of life in mobile homes is not new, but the use of this restriction to improve it is. Yet the desire to restrict and control mobile homes remains, and restriction to parks will continue to increase as a factor in mobile home life as it becomes more difficult to exclude mobile homes completely from the community.

A one-state survey of officials and lawyers involved in zoning was conducted by the Illinois Zoning Law Study Commission in 1971. The commission's conclusions deal with the difference between urban and rural areas with respect to permission of mobile homes in residential and multifamily residential zones. First, comparing on the basis of total cases (612), rural respondents were twice as likely to report mobile homes in residential areas (4.2 percent urban, 10.9 percent rural). The same held true for multifamily dwellings (4.7 percent urban, 10 percent rural). Urban area respondents indicated mobile homes were most prevalent in light industrial (20.4 percent), commercial (17.3 percent), and industrial (16.8 percent) districts. Rural area respondents indicated that, overall, mobile homes were more evenly spread among residential (17.4 percent), agricultural (17.1 percent), multifamily residential (15.8 percent), and commercial (15.8 percent) districts.

The American Society of Planning Officials' Planning Advisory Service Report no. 265 presents the results of a survey of 287 jurisdictions that shows the pattern of exclusion of mobile homes very clearly. Mobile homes on individual lots, in mobile home parks, and in mobile homes subdivisions (where one owns a lot instead of renting) are distinguished. The distinction between urban and rural is disaggregated to central city, urban county, suburban city, rural county, suburban county, and independent city. It is interesting to note that mobile home subdivisions are excluded almost as often as mobile homes on individual lots. The county is less restrictive than the adjacent city in urban, suburban, and rural situations for all three forms of mobile home siting configurations. Also, the suburban city and county are much more exclusionary than their urban and rural counterparts. The independent city is more restrictive than the central city; the

Table 16.7.
Future Zoning Trends

Device	Number of States Expecting:			
	Increase	Decrease	No Change	Unknown
Complete exclusion	1	1	9	3
Restriction to mobile home parks	9	0	2	3
Restriction from residential zones	0	1	10	3

Source: 50-state PMHI Survey.

rural county about equals the urban county. However, rural counties often restrict parks but urban counties do not, and urban counties are more likely than rural counties to restrict mobile homes on individual lots.

Of course, restrictive or exclusionary zoning regulations have been used by communities not only to exclude mobile homes but also to impede or absolutely prevent the construction of any other form of low-cost housing. For reasons similar to those that motivate restrictions on mobile homes, suburban communities have enacted zoning regulations that have the effect of barring prospective lower-income residents, many of whom are members of minority groups. These exclusionary or "snob" ordinances take a number of forms, most of which constitute constructive exclusions of mobile homes. And these ordinances have been successfully challenged in court.[50] Nevertheless, there is a growing body of judicial opinion that reflects a different view on exclusionary zoning regulations. Some courts are looking beyond the zoning municipality to determine the areawide impact of local land use restrictions, and they are requiring that zoning power be exercised in terms of the general welfare of the broader community. Although these cases do not specifically consider mobile homes, their reasoning is applicable to the problem of mobile home exclusion or restriction.

Two different lines of antiexclusionary argument are emerging. The first, referred to as the "Pennsylvania rationale," uses the Fourteenth Amendment due process clause as the basis for eliminating exclusionary zoning schemes.[51] The Pennsylvania Supreme Court in *National Land & Investment Co.* v. *Easttown Township Board of Adjustment* struck down a four-acre minimum lot requirement as an unreasonable use of the police power.[52] Examining the implications of the ordinance in terms of the regional needs of Philadelphia, the court stressed "the town's responsibility to those who do not yet live in the township but who are part, or may become part of the population expansion of the suburbs" and concluded that a zoning ordinance is not in the general welfare if its "primary purpose is to prevent the entrance of newcomers in order to avoid future burdens, economic or otherwise, upon the administration of public services and facilities. . . ."[53]

The Pennsylvania court followed this decision in two recent cases. In *Appeal of Girsh* the court invalidated a local ordinance excluding all apartment houses from the town.[54] In *Appeal of Kit-Mar Builders* the same court invalidated a two-acre minimum lot size requirement, declaring that "an exclusionary purpose or result is not acceptable in Pennsylvania."[55] In both cases the court stressed the town's responsibility to bear the burden of development and population growth. Preservation of aesthetic character, lack of public services, and fiscal prudence

were rejected as justifications for exclusionary practices. Nevertheless, it should be noted the court also emphasized property owners' right to use their property as they see fit, mistakenly assuming an identity of interest between developers and those who are excluded from access to housing.[56] The weight accorded by the court to the property owner's interests makes the precedent value of these decisions questionable.

A second and perhaps more significant development may be the court cases that are being initiated on the basis of the social implications of exclusion rather than the restriction on a builder's right to develop land more intensively. These cases usually involve a third party representing the low-income or minority persons who claim to be excluded from the area rather than a developer. In these cases it is argued that zoning practices that have a discriminatory effect on low-income and minority groups violate the equal protection clause of the Fourteenth Amendment. This argument has been most successful to date when racial discrimination is evident. For example, in *Dailey* v. *City of Lawton* the court invalidated the city council's denial of a rezoning request for a federally subsidized low-income housing project in a predominantly white area.[57] The suit was brought by a group of blacks. The court found the council's action to be racially motivated and thereby a violation of the Fourteenth Amendment and the Civil Rights Act of 1866.

Judicial opinion has begun to recognize that under the equal protection clause a local government is obliged to plan for all groups in the population, and specifically for low- and moderate-cost housing. Two federal court decisions—the lower court in *Kennedy Park Homes Association* v. *City of Lackawanna* (invalidating a refusal to give subdivision approval) and *Sasso* v. *City of Union City* (invalidating the annulment by referendum of a rezoning permit for a low-income project) —have made fairly explicit statements on this point.[58] Nevertheless, the equal protection argument may have limitations in the courts; exclusionary zoning does not merely exclude racial minorities, it also excludes low- and middle-income whites. Although courts will not theoretically tolerate racial discrimination, economic or wealth discrimination has yet to be declared a suspect classification; and housing has not yet been held to be a fundamental right by the Supreme Court. In fact, in *James* v. *Valtierra* the Supreme Court held that Article XXXIV of the California State Constitution, which required a referendum before public housing could be built in a community, did not violate the equal protection clause because it applied to "any low-rent public housing project, not only (to) projects which will be occupied by a racial minority."[59] Although this case has been interpreted by some as an indication that the Court will not expand the equal protection doctrine to reach exclusionary zoning, there is ample support for the contention that *James* should be narrowly construed and that there are still satisfactory constitutional rationales for overturning exclusionary zoning ordinances left unaffected by the decision.[60]

These cases, despite the setback in *James*, indicate a general rethinking of the proper function of zoning and a new realization that zoning should not be used as a means of shifting economic burdens from the suburb to the city. There is no reason why the same kind of approach should not be applied to mobile homes. As yet no challenge to a zoning ordinance as applied to mobile homes has been brought by a third party—the racially and economically disadvantaged—but it is clear that the time is not too distant when a court will be asked to invalidate a restrictive ordinance on the ground that it constitutes a denial of equal protection. It will be argued that the low-income and racial miniorities are effectively precluded from seeking improved or different housing opportunities and having access to educational and job opportunities by the unavailability of mobile home sites. The likelihood of this argument succeeding grows as mobile homes play an increasingly important role in alleviating the housing crisis in this country. It is apparent that the importance and use of mobile homes as a source of low-cost quality housing will continue to accelerate, thus increasing the pressure on the courts to re-evaluate their thinking.[61] The probable future success of zoning challenges should help to reduce the negative impact of land use controls on the mobile home industry.

State and Federal Assumption of Land Use Policy

By now it is obvious that the case-by-case approach to challenging local control devices is at best fragmented. The court cases indicate little possibility for a broad-based attack on exclusionary zoning, for the precedent set by each case is limited to a specific factual situation. As court challenges prove successful, some barriers are lowered, but the housing problem remains. As a result, a more direct approach has been adopted by some states and considered by the federal government.

Several states have enacted legislation that enables the state to assert strong planning authority to control land development directly. Vermont's 1970 Land Use and Development Act designates specific spheres of state jurisdiction (commercial, industrial, and residential development larger than ten acres in size or subdivision developments of ten or more lots), calls for the development of a statewide land use plan, and establishes an environmental board and nine district environmental commissions. The act establishes specific environmental, social, and economic criteria a development must meet before receiving the required permit from a district commission. The Florida Environment Land and Water Management Act of 1972 empowers the state to designate "critical areas," to establish principles to guide the development of those areas, and to adopt guidelines and standards to be used in determining "developments of regional impact."

In other states legislation has been enacted to preempt local zoning power in designated areas. For instance, California and Wisconsin have legislation that gives the state power over coastal development.[62] In 1970 Maine passed an act that gives a state agency some control over the location of industrial and commercial development that may substantially affect the environment.[63] In 1968 New York created the Urban Development Corporation, which is essentially a state housing authority with the power to raise funds to build low- and moderate-income housing throughout New York. Originally the UDC was the only authority in the country with a total range of powers, including the authority to plan, regulate, and develop as well as override local zoning ordinances. Despite the serious legislative and financial difficulties that began to plague UDC in the mid-1970s, the model from which UDC was created remains viable and important.[64] Another important example is Massachusetts, which created a housing appeals committee with the power to override local zoning decisions in those cases where local zoning boards have denied permits for subsidized low- and moderate-income housing in towns that have not met the established quota for subsidized housing. This,"anti–snob zoning act" only requires that a small percentage of vacant residential land in each community be available to nonprofit or limited-profit housing sponsors for development and has had little impact to date.[65] Nevertheless, the legislation is expected to discourage communities from being overly protective by allowing the state to supervise the activities of local zoning boards and to facilitate low-income housing construction starts.

In some states the power to review, overrule, or regulate the development decisions of local governments has been given to the counties or regional planning development agencies. For example, in 1968 the New Jersey legislature created the Hackensack Meadowlands Development Commission to exercise zoning and taxing powers and to control the use and development of land in an area of meadows (twenty-one thousand acres) located within the boundaries of fourteen separate local governments. The commission has the power to undertake development projects and to regulate all subdivisions in the district. The property taxes from any new development, regardless of the city in which it is located, go into an intermunicipal fund. This tax-sharing device is designed to remove a major obstacle to rational planning for metropolitan areas—competition among local governments for new developments. Other examples include the San Francisco Bay Conservation and Development Commission, which was created in 1965 and designed to control and monitor the development of the bay.[66] The commission is authorized to deny or approve all building permits that request permission to fill or extract from the bay. The Minnesota legislature created the Twin Cities Metropolitan Council with extensive review authority over the plans of local governments within the metropolitan area. Ohio designated fifteen official planning regions that cover the whole state and are charged with developing "coordinated solutions to problems that overlap local jurisdictions."[67]

These various state legislative enactments reflect the current widespread thinking that state and regional agencies must assume a greater responsibility in land use planning and policy formulation. The basis for preemption is that state or regional land use and control will optimize the utilization and preservation of land resources or ensure equal protection and due process in the placement of low-income housing in all communities or both.

Much of this activity for state land use policy and control has been boosted directly or indirectly by increasing federal involvement in land use. Legislation in this area may be coming in the form of the Land-Use Policy and Planning Assistance Act, introduced by Senator Henry Jackson as far back as January 1970. The bill seeks to establish a national land use policy that favors social and environmental goals. It would provide $1 billion over eight years to states to aid them in the development of state land use policies and controls. One of the most controversial amendments to the bill would withhold certain federal aid from states that failed to perform statewide land use planning. Jackson's bill has consistently passed in the Senate, but support in the House has wavered at just below the level required to pass. This bill is only the latest effort in a trend toward federal action in land use. More important have been other environmental bills—the National Environmental Policy Act of 1969, the Environmental Quality Improvement Act of 1970, the Clean Air Act of 1970, and so forth—all of which have the effect of controlling how local land users can depreciate environmental resources.

Whether the motivation has been environmental or social justice, the new state and federal activity in this area is based on the realization that "local control has failed to deal with land use problems of more than local significance."[68] As *Business Week* puts it, "through all these examples of new land-use activism runs a common effort: to wrest some control over the land from local governments."[69] These movements have definite implications for the mobile home industry.

Local government decisions on land use are generally made by lay people who do not have the time or resources to acquire sophistication in housing policy or to examine what mobile homes are and what they could be-

come. As the sanctity of local zoning is eroded, it will become more and more difficult for a municipality to shift what it sees as a problem to other municipalities. Of course, there is no reason to believe that the mobile home industry will be the favored stepchild of future state or federal land use regulation, but we can expect that it will be dealt with in more sophisticated and less fractionalized ways.[70]

Exclusionary zoning practices help prevent the mobile home industry's production of a greater amount of higher-quality housing at a lower cost. The location and quality of the mobile home site or the mobile home park is closely tied to the industry's final product capabilities. Rigid land use control reduces the industry's responsiveness to user needs and limits the consumer's choices. The mobile home industry could potentially provide good low-cost shelter for a large portion of the population if the land use control system—as well as other regulatory systems—were geared for it. This industry can provide low-cost housing for a variety of densities without the amount of subsidization allocated to site-built housing, and it should be encouraged to do so.

Nowhere is our limitation in choice of living environments more severe than in this nation's suburban areas. Large segments of our population are barred by economic constraints from living in conventional suburban housing, and exclusionary zoning of mobile homes is also greatest in suburban areas. Thus even if one purchased a mobile home, one would be unable, because of exclusionary zoning, to locate it in suburbia. Recently, however, judicial and legislative action on this matter has been increasing. For example, the Massachusetts Zoning Appeals Law requires that every city and town permit construction of its "fair" share of low-income housing. The problem of ensuring equal opportunity in housing is by no means confined to the mobile home industry, but the potential of this industry to provide low-cost housing more efficiently than the conventional housing industry is not being developed.

Of course, our need for low-cost housing is not confined exclusively to the suburbs; and although reduction of exclusionary zoning practices would unquestionably improve the industry's overall performance, urban areas would reap only marginal benefits from the change. Where mobile homes are not now economically feasible because of the low-density nature of their present application, reduction of exclusionary zoning, although necessary, would not be enough. However, the mobile home industry has the technological capability to efficiently utilize the building materials necessary in higher-density construction. It proved this in the past when it relied extensively on aluminum-

D. Policy Recommendations

Reduction of Exclusionary Zoning Restrictions

and steel-frame construction. Technological capabilities for efficient utilization of concrete and stacking of three-dimensional shelter units based on materials other than wood are economically feasible means of providing low-income housing in urban areas. Constructive, supportive changes in land use controls are one of the most important prerequisites for realizing this potential.

Increased Integration with Conventional Housing

Differences in financing, taxation, purchase and sales agreements, and so forth, contribute in various ways to the difference between mobile homes and conventional homes. The major impact of the land use control system is its spatial segregation of the mobile home component from the conventional housing stock. The segregation of individuals living in mobile homes to parks may reinforce an economic difference already present and give it social dimensions as well. In municipalities where mobile homes are forced into parks and parks are forced into isolated or unattractive areas, mobile homes may be seen as inferior housing that must be treated differently and isolated from the rest of the community. To some extent, the stigma of the location must rub off on the tenants, regardless of the quality of the park. An important potential step toward correcting the separation of the two estates would be a reversal of the present trend to restrict mobile homes to mobile home parks.

The land use control system contributes to the stigma surrounding mobile home parks by neglecting their quality, after requiring their existence. The design of mobile home parks is seldom regulated to the same extent as that of conventional single-family housing. The lack of concern for the quality of mobile home parks and their frequent exclusion from residential areas contributes to the existence of shoddy parks in poor locations. The industry has improved its product and made it more like conventional housing, but the land use control system has not kept pace and now only reinforces the problems it was to solve. By isolating mobile home parks from conventional housing, the restriction to parks fragments the housing market and prevents direct competition between the mobile home and the conventional housing industries. The industry is confined to the production of a product with only one major application, limiting its further development to minor refinements. Public regulation determines and is largely responsible for the nature and character of the present product. Upon elimination of the restriction to parks, the expanded market would enable the industry to produce a physical environment more responsive to user needs. The industry would no longer be required to produce a product for the traditional mobile home park but could develop a product different from today's mobile home and better able to fulfill the new demands placed on it.

Though the restriction to parks at present fosters inertia in product development, the existence of segregation could be used to the industry's advantage. Compared to conventional housing developments, the regulatory environment of the mobile home park can be described as a legal vacuum: Codes governing land development are simpler and less stringent; siting requirements are not restrictive, if they exist at all. Innovation that would be difficult under conventional public regulation can be accomplished more easily in the mobile home park. The concept of the mobile home park as a planned development of exclusively (or primarily) mobile home components can encompass mobile home products vastly different from those employed today.

Innovative site design could utilize a mixture of single-family, town house, and multi-family housing. These would be impossible in conventional housing developments except under the most flexible planned unit development ordinance. A new town could be constructed using production efficiencies that the overregulated conventional housing industry cannot match. The mobile home industry has long been a testing ground for new and better products not yet accepted by the conventional housing industry. This laboratory concept can be extended to the mobile home park. New technical systems for things such as vacuum sewage disposal and solar energy systems could be perfected. Innovative social service delivery systems could be set up. By expanding beyond its present application, the mobile home park concept could become an area of progress in the development of new urban technologies and services.

Development of the Mobile Home Park Concept

Notes to Chapter 16
1. J.H. Beuscher, *Cases and Materials on Land Use Controls* (St. Paul, Minn.: West Publishing Co., 1969[1964]), p.1.

2. John Delafons, *Land Use Controls in the United States* (Cambridge, Mass.: Joint Center for Urban Studies of MIT and Harvard University, 1962), p.17.

3. Ibid., p.18.

4. Barbier v. Connolly, 113 U.S. 27 (1885); *Soon Hing* v. *Crowley*, 113 U.S. 703 (1885).

5. *Welch* v. *Swasey*, 214 U.S. 91 (1909).

6. Seymour I. Toll, *Zoned American* (New York: Grossman Publishers, 1969), p.71.

7. Delafons, *Land Use Controls*, p.20.

8. Ibid., p.18.

9. Douglas Commission Report, *Building the American City*, U.S. National Commission on Urban Problems: Report to Congress and the President of the U.S. (Washington, D.C.: U.S. Government Printing Office, 1969), p.200.

10. *Village of Euclid* v. *Ambler Realty*, 276 U.S. 365 (1926).

11. *Nectow* v. *City of Cambridge*, 277 U.S. 183 (1928).

12. Delafons, *Land Use Controls*, p.25.

13. Ibid., p.26.

14. Douglas Commission Report, *Building the American City*.

15. See B. Hodes and G. Roberson, *The Law of Mobile Homes*, 2d ed. (Chicago: Commerce Clearing House, 1965); Annot., 42 A.L.R. 3d 601 (1972); and Annot., 96 A.L.R. 2d 232 (1964).

16. *Vickers v. Township Committee of Gloucester Township*, 37 N.J. 232, 181 A. 2d 129 (1962); *Oakwood at Madison, Inc. v. Township of Madison*, 117 N.J. Super 11, 283 A. 2d 353 (1971).

17. PMHI estimates that approximately 42 percent of the mobile homes in the country are located in mobile home parks.

18. *Napierkowski v. Township of Gloucester*, 29 N.J., 481, 150A. 2d 481 (1950).

19. *People v. Clute*, 278 N.Y.S. 2d 231,18 N.Y. 2d 999 (1966).

20. *Mobile Home Owners Protective Association v. Town of Chatham*, 305 N.Y.S. 2d 334 (1969).

21. Frederick Bair, "Mobile Homes—A New Challenge," *Law and Contemporary Problems*, Spring 1967, p.112.

22. Delafons, *Land Use Controls*, p.63.

23. *Town of Brewster v. Sherman*, 343 Mass. 598, 180 N.E. 2d 338 (1962); *Town of Manchester v. Phillips*, 343 Mass. 591, 180 N.E. 2d 333 (1962); *Town of Marblehead v. Gilbert*, 334 Mass. 602, 137 N.E. 2d 921 (1956); *City of New Orleans v. Louviere*, 52 So. 2d 751 (1a. 1951); *People v. Clute*, 278 N.Y.S. 2d 231, 18 N.Y. 2d 999 (1966); *Bixler v. Pierson*, 188 So. 2d 681 (Fla. App. 1966).

24. *In re Wiley*, 120 Vt. 359, 140A. 2d 11 (1958). See also, R.W. Bartle and H.R. Gage, "Mobile Homes: Zoning and Taxation," 55 *Cornell L. Rev.* 491 (1970).

25. *State of Washington v. Work*, 75 Wash. 2d 212, 449 P. 2d 806 (1969).

26. *City of New Orleans v. Louviere*, 52 So. 2d 751 (La. App. 1951); *City of New Orleans v. Lafon*, 61 So. 2d 270 (La. App. 1953); see also *Appeal of Groff*, 1 Pa. Cmwlth 439, 274 A. 2d 574 (1971).

27. *Sioux Falls v. Cleveland*, 75 S.D. 548, 70 N.W. 2d 62 (1955). See also *City of Aurora v. Burns*, 319 III. 84, 149 N.E. 784 (1925).

28. *Town of Yorkville v. Fonk*, 3 Wis. 2d 371, 88 N.W. 2d 319, appeal dism'd. 358 U.S. 58(1958). See also *Town of Plainfield v. Hood*, 108 N.H. 502, 240 A. 2d 60 (1968); *Lavoie v. Bigwood*, 457 F. 2d 7 (1st Cir. 1972).

29. *Town of Southport v. Ross*, 132 N.Y.S. 2d 340, 284 A.D. 598 (1954); *Karen v. Town of East Haddam*, 146 Conn. 720, 155 A. 2d 921 (1959); *Rezler v. Village of Riverside*, 28 III. 2d 142, 190 N.E. 2d 706 (1963); *Cady v. Detroit*, 289 Mich. 499, 286 N.W. 805 (1939), appeal dism'd., 309 U.S. 620 (1940); *Renker v. Village of Brooklyn*, 139 Ohio St. 484, 40 N.E. 2d 925 (1942); *Town of Hartland v. Hensen's, Inc.*, 146 Conn. 697, 155 A. 2d 754 (1960); *Gilliam v. Board of Health of Sangers*, 327 Mass. 621, 100 N.E. 2d 687 (1951); *Stary v. City of Brooklyn*, 162 Ohio St. 120, 121 N.E. 2d 11 (1954), appeal dism'd., 348 U.S. 923.

30. *Huff v. City of Des Moines*, 244 Iowa 89, 56 N.W. 2d 54 (1952); *Cady v. City of Detroit*, 289 Mich. 499, 286 N.W. 805, appeal dism'd., 309 U.S. 620 (1939).

31. *Williams v. Whitten*, 451 S.W. 2d 535 (Texas Cir. App. 1970).

32. *Ostek v. Barone*, 60 Misc. 980, 304 N.Y.S. 2d 350 (Sup. Ct. 1968); see also *Town of Huntington v. Transon*, 43 Misc. 2d 912, 252 N.Y.S. 2d 576 (Sup. Ct. 1964); *Kimsey v. City of Rome*, 84 Ga. App. 671, 67 S.E. 2d 206 (1951); *Corning v. Town of Ontario*, 204 Misc. 38, 121 N.Y.S. 2d 288 (Sup. Ct. 1953); *County of Will v. Stanfill*, 7 III. App. 2d 52, 129 N.E. 2d 46 (1955).

33. *Rottman v. Waterford Township*, 13 Mich. App. 271, 164 N.W. 2d 409 (1968). Accord, Appeal of Groff, 1 Pa. Cmwlth 439, 274 A. 2d 574 (1971).

34. *Wright v. Michaud*, 160 Me. 164, 200 A. 2d 543 (1964); *Township of Honey Brook v. Alenovitz*, 430 Pa. 614, 243A. 2d 330 (1963). Contra, *Zoning Board of Adjustment v. Dragon Run Terrace*, 222 A. 2d 315 (Del. 1966).

35. Robert M. Anderson, *Zoning Law and Practice in New York* (Rochester, N.Y.: The Lawyer's Co-operative Publishing Company, 1963).

36. J. Johnston, *Econometric Methods* (New York: McGraw-Hill, 1972), p.183.

37. Survey for Owens-Corning Fiberglas by Market Facts, Inc., *Focus on the Mobile Home Market* (Washington, D.C., 1971).

38. PMHI Dealer Survey.

39. Mason Goffney and Richard F. Muth, "Land as an Element of Housing Costs," *Institute for Defense Analysis*, October 1968.

40. PMHI Park Survey.

41. Lynne Sagalyn and George Sternlieb, *Zoning and Housing Costs* (New Brunswick, N.J.: Center for Urban Policy Research, Rutgers University, January 1973), pp.15, 52.

42. *Lavoie v. Bigwood*, 456 F. 2d 7 (1st Cir. 1972).

43. Unpublished NYC Planning Commission Study, 1970.

44. L. Mayer, "Mobile Homes Move into the Breach," *Fortune*, March 1970, p.126; Lyle F. Nyberg, "The Community and the Park Owner Versus the mobile Home Park Resident: Reforming the Landlord-Tenant Relationship," 54 *B.U. L. Rev.* at 812 n. 27 (1973).

45. *Lavoie v. Bigwood*, 457 F. 2d 7 (1st Cir. 1972).

46. Ibid.

47. "Tyranny in Mobile-Home Land," 38 *Consumer Reports* 442 (July 1973); "The Community and the Park Owner," 54 *B.U.L. Rev.* 810 (1973).

48. Douglas E. Kneeland, "From 'Tin Can on Wheels' to the 'Mobile Home'," *New York Times Magazine*, May 9, 1971.

49. Con Howe, "Mobile Homes in NYC: A Case Study" (Unpublished working paper, January 1972), and Calendar of the NYC Planning Commission, March 17, 1971.

50. Note, "Large Lot Zoning," 78 *Yale L.J.* 1418 (1969). See also Douglas Commission Report, *Building the American City*, pp.214, 215.

51. Note, Robert M. Anderson, Norman Williams and Thomas Norman, "Exclusionary Land Use Control: The Case of North-eastern New Jersey" 22 *Syracuse L. Rev.* 465 (1971).

52. *National Land & Investment Co. v. Easttown Township Board of Adjustment*, 419 Pa. 504, 215 A. 2d 597 (1965).

53. Ibid.

54. *Appeal of Girsh*, 437 Pa. 237, 263 A. 2d 395 (1970).

55. *Appeal of Kit-Mar Builders*, 439 Pa. 466, 268A. 2d 765 (1970).

56. "Exclusionary Land Use Controls: The Case of North-eastern New Jersey," 22 *Syracuse L. Rev.*, at 499 (1971).

57. *Dailey v. City of Lawton*, 425 F. 2d 1037 (10th Cir. 1970).

58. *Kennedy Park Homes Association v. City of Lackawanna*, 318 F. Supp. 669 (W.D.N.Y. 1970), *Sasso v. City of Union City*, 424 F. 2d 291 (9th Cir. 1970). See also *Oakwood at Madison, Inc. v. Township of Madison*, 117 N.J. Super. 11, 283A. 2d 353 (1971).

59. *James v. Valtierra*, 402 U.S. at 141 (1971).

60. Note, "Exclusionary Land-Use Techniques: Judicial Response and Legislative Initiative," 22 *De Paul L. Rev.* 388 (1972); "The Equal Protection Clause and Exclusionary Zoning after Valtierre and Dandridge," 81 *Yale L.J.* 61 (1971); Note, "Zoning: Closing the Economic Gap," 43 *Temple L.Q.* 247 (1970); Richard Reeves, "Counterattack by Cities," *The New York Times*, March 8, 1971, p.30.

61. Comment, "Mobile Homes in Kansas: A Need for Proper Zoning," 30 *Univ. of Kansas L. Rev.* 87 (1971).

62. Water Resources Act, Wisconsin Laws of 1965, c. 614; 1972 Coastal Zone Conservation Act—California.

63. An Act to Regulate Site Location of Development Substantially Affecting Environment, Maine Public Laws of 1970, c. 571.

64. E.F. Roberts, "The Demise of Property Law," 57 *Cornell L. Rev.* 1 (1971).

65. "The Massachusetts Zoning Appeals Law: Lessons of the First Three Years," Unpublished working paper, Community Affairs Department, Commonwealth of Massachusetts, August 1972.

66. McAteer-Petris Act, California Government Code, Title 7.2, enacted 1965, amended 1968 and 1969.

67. *ASPO Journal*, June 26, 1973, p.25.

68. "Exclusionary Land-Use Techniques," 22 *De Paul L. Rev.* 388 (1972).

69. "The Land Use Battle That Business Faces," *Business Week*, August 26, 1972.

70. Richard P. Fishman, ed., *Housing for All under Law: New Directions in Housing, Land Use, and Planning* (Cambridge, Mass.: Ballinger Publishing Company, 1977).

A. The Present Situation and Emerging Trends

Organizational Basis for Taxation of Mobile Homes

The federal government derives the power to collect income and other taxes from the federal constitution. Although federal income taxation significantly affects housing consumption, investment in rental housing, and home ownership patterns, the central government has not levied a direct tax upon conventional housing or mobile homes. It is state and local governments that have subjected mobile homes to an array of tax measures, including motor vehicle taxes, real and personal property taxes, and in lieu fees.

The state governments derive the power to tax mobile homes from state constitutional provisions. Revenues so raised may be used to defray the costs of governmental services provided to mobile homes. However, the power of state legislatures to raise funds by statute is subject to the due process limitations of the federal constitution. State constitutions further limit this power by requiring that taxes be proportional and reasonable. This has been interpreted to mean that general taxes must be in proportion to the value of the property and that special taxes must be in proportion to benefits received.[1] Local governments are entities of the state and as such possess only those powers to tax mobile and other homes that have been delegated to them by the state. Granting of such power to municipalities may be contained in general "home rule enabling statutes" and in state statutes concerning health and welfare of the local units. Local tax ordinances are subject to the same federal and state constitutional limitations but enjoy a presumption of validity. When litigated, they have been attacked as violative of the due process clause of the Fourteenth Amendment.[2]

In addition to constitutional constraints, municipal governments must act within the bounds of the power delegated to them. Therefore local governments may be unable to tax individual mobile homes on private lots, to enact tax ordinances that operate as revenue measures, or to levy charges not specifically provided for by the state enabling statute.

A further problem arises when a local government enacts a revenue measure under a general grant of power from the state when the state has its own taxation legislation applicable to mobile homes. In such cases it must be decided whether the state legislature intended to preempt local measures and the local tax measure is void as conflicting with state statutory provisions or whether the state legislature intended to allow the municipalities concurrent power to tax with ordinances not inconsistent with state statutes and not repugnant to state public policy.

Statutory Definitions

Although the mobile home evolved from the travel trailer, it has become a generically different unit. Yet this split has not been noted by many public bodies and there have been difficulties in classifying mobile homes for various purposes. In terms of the arson statutes and a health ordinance, it has been held that a mobile home is a "dwelling-house," it is a building within the double indemnity clause of a life insurance statute, and it is a vehicle subject to forfeiture by statute if used to transport contraband.[3] On the other hand, a mobile home has been held not to be a home within a testamentary directive nor a "homestead" entitled to exemption from execution.[4] This confusion is particularly evidenced in the realm of taxation, where mobile homes have been characterized as motor vehicles subject to license and registration fees, personal property subject to personal property tax, and real property subject to real property tax.

But the confusion concerning taxation goes beyond that. The states differ widely in the details included in their definitional schemes. Three states do not define mobile home at all; others use a generic definition of "house trailer"; still others have one definition for tax purposes, another for other statutory chapters; some states have no definition for tax purposes but a detailed definition for other purposes. Our 1977 state-by-state survey of the taxation of mobile homes included the definition of "mobile home" used by each state for tax purposes; the responses revealed regulatory chaos.

Although the definitions vary greatly in detail, in substance they generally reflect in whole or in part the MHI's official definition: "A mobile home is a structure, transportable in one or more sections, which is 8 body feet or more in width or 32 body feet or more in length, built on a permanent chassis and designed to be used as a dwelling with or without a permanent foundation when connected to the required utilities, and includes the plumbing, heating, air conditioning, and electrical systems contained therein" (1977 version). But little comfort can be derived from this observation because the single greatest variance from the norm is a serious one. Only eighteen states make a distinction between structures that exceed certain dimensions (usually 32 feet long, 8 feet wide) and those that do not. Since as a rule structures exceeding the stated dimensions represent "mobile homes" and those that do not are designated "travel trailers," most states make no distinction between primary and secondary housing.

This chaotic situation points to two problems. First, definitional vagueness and interstate differences invite regulatory error and added administrative expense. Second, the prevalent failure to distinguish primary housing from secondary, temporary housing injures the mobile home population by reactivating "transiency" suspicions on the part of the population at large.

State Taxation of Mobile Homes
We are not concerned with the sales tax or other indirect forms of taxation but rather

Taxation Methods

with the various types of direct fees and taxes imposed on the mobile home owner by the different states. These can be grouped into four basic categories: motor vehicle taxation, personal property taxation, real property taxation, and tax measures falling under the heading of "fees in lieu" of property taxation.

Since the full-scale introduction of mobile homes in the 1930s, the method by which the units have been taxed has not remained static, in part reflecting the historical societal attitude toward this hybrid product. The mobile home was initially considered a "travel trailer" and was subject to a moderate annual state motor vehicle fee. In 1936 only twenty states imposed additional personal property taxes on travel trailers.[5] The use of travel trailers as permanent housing increased during the 1940s, which usually meant that the travel trailer population was enjoying municipal services without contributing to the local coffers. To alleviate this situation, many states adopted additional taxes. By 1956 the most common method, employed by thirty states, was taxation of mobile homes as personal property.[6] However, this was still an ineffective means of ensuring that mobile home owners paid their share of municipal revenues: Of these thirty states, sixteen provided that the owner would be exempt from personal property taxation if the mobile home were registered as a motor vehicle. The concept of taxing mobile homes as realty had been introduced by this time but had not been widely accepted; only Michigan, New York, Wisconsin, and Pennsylvania allowed the taxation of mobile homes as real property.

During the last twenty years more and more states have adopted either or both forms of property taxation of mobile homes; by 1977 all fifty states provided for such taxation if certain conditions were met. These conditions vary widely from state to state; forty-four states provide that in given circumstances the mobile home is to be taxed as realty, but the states differ greatly in the conditions imposed to warrant such taxation. The most common criteria for real property taxation of mobile homes seem to be that the unit be permanently affixed to the land, have its wheels removed, and be on owner-occupied land. The remaining six states either treat the mobile home uniformly as personalty or apply this tax if certain conditions are met.

Table 17.1 presents an analysis of the taxation situation today in all fifty states, showing in simplified and condensed form information from our 1977 state-by-state national survey of taxation departments. Generalizations about the taxation of mobile homes in the United States are difficult to make: Few states employ one taxation method exclusively; most use a combination of two or three methods. The predominant taxation method in each state is shown in figure 17.1.

The most common form of taxation is dual:

Real property tax imposed in certain circumstances, personal property tax imposed in all the rest. We gave states of this type a property tax label. In those states that employ a realty tax in some circumstances and impose a fee in others, the state was categorized according to how it taxes mobile homes located in parks. There are three salient factors pertinent to our fee classification. First, the fact that the mobile home owner must pay nominal registration or licensing fees or both in addition to property taxes does not change the categorization of such states as a "property" state. Second, the fact that all mobile homes are charged highway registration fees for the privilege of moving on the highways was disregarded for categorization purposes. Third, if the state differentiates between larger and smaller mobile homes, imposing a tax on the former but a fee on the latter, the method employed for the larger mobile home determined the categorization of the state. The "mixed" classification categorizes a relatively rare taxation method: either the state imposes one form of tax but gives the local taxing unit the choice of whether to use the state system or employ its own, or the state has no statutory authority to tax mobile homes and delegates that power to the local taxing authorities.

In calculating how many states allow a particular method of taxation, we have been more concerned with actual practice than with strict statutory definition. Thus, because the statutes of Alaska and New Jersey do not permit these states themselves to tax mobile homes, but rather empower their localities to do so, we have considered the methods allowed by the localities. We likewise list California as allowing real property taxation, although the state technically considers a mobile home to no longer be a mobile home once it has met the requirements making it eligible for real property taxation.

Emerging Trends

We conducted nationwide taxation surveys in 1969, 1973, 1974, and 1977 and had access to regional surveys done by various states in 1956. Examination of this information clearly reveals that the taxation of mobile homes has been and still is in a state of flux, with several states currently considering changes. The many changes that have occurred since the 1950s have not been entirely random; they show three discernible trends. The least dramatic of these is the decrease in the number of states that tax certain mobile homes (generally those in mobile home parks) as personal property; in 1956 forty states imposed such a tax; in 1968, thirty-five; and by 1977, 31.[7] A second trend is the decrease in the number of states that impose fees on mobile homes in certain circumstances. There were twenty-four such states in 1956, twenty-two in 1968, and twenty in

Table 17.1.
State-by-State Taxation
Methods, 1977

State	Type of Taxation Method Employed	Description of the Taxation Method Employed
Alabama	Property	If the unit is located on owner-occupied land, it is taxed as realty. In this case, the homestead exemption would apply. Otherwise it is taxed as personalty, and a registration tag must be obtained. Those units classified as personalty pay higher taxes than those classified as realty.
Alaska	Mixed	Mobile homes are not taxed by the state, as statutes permit taxation of real and personal property by local municipalities only.
Arizona	Property	Ad valorem tax is imposed on personalty and realty. There are 6 statutory classes of property. The rate of valuation for tax purposes depends upon the statutory class. Generally, personal property used for residential purposes is placed in the same class as improved real estate. If the mobile home is under the dimensional limits of the definition, it is classed as a travel trailer and an "in lieu" fee is imposed. The homestead exemption applies to mobile homes used as the personal residence of the owner.
Arkansas	Property	Taxed as personal property unless it can be determined that the owner intends his mobile home to be a permanent dwelling, in which case it is taxed as realty. Factors relevant to the determination of this intent are whether the mobile home is on a permanent foundation; whether the wheels are removed; whether permanent-type additional rooms have been installed; whether public utilities have been attached.
California	Fee	In addition to a registration fee, a license fee based on 2 percent of the market value must be paid. (This is in lieu of other property taxes.) If the mobile home has been attached to a permanent foundation and has been modified so as to satisfy all applicable building code and land use requirements as a residential building, then it has ceased to be a mobile home (and a vehicle), and can be lawfully occupied as a building, and the local tax assessor is empowered to assess the former mobile home in the same manner as other residential buildings are assessed.
Colorado	Property	Mobile homes are assessed on the same basis as that for real property (conventional housing), but at no more than 75% of the retail delivered price when they were new less the cost of built-in furnishings. No home-rule city, county, or other local government can impose a license or other special fees on the ownership or occupancy of mobile homes that is not similarly imposed on conventional homes.
Connecticut	Mixed	Classified and taxed as personalty at local mill rates. Any municipality by ordinance can adopt a monthly fee in lieu of this property tax.
Delaware	Property	Ad valorem property tay which is calculated at the same rate as the real property tax of the county and school district in which the mobile home is located.
Florida	Fee	A license fee is imposed unless the mobile home is classified as realty. The license fee is determined by the length of the unit and varies from $20 to $80. A mobile home is classified as realty if it is permanently attached to owner-occupied land.
Georgia	Property	If the unit is on owner-occupied land and is used as a residence, it is taxed as realty and is eligible for a homestead exemption. If the unit is on leased land, it is subject to an ad valorem personalty tax with no homestead exemption allowed.
Hawaii	Fee	If the unit is permanently attached to utilities, it is taxed as real property; otherwise it must pay a nominal registration fee plus a certain amount per pound which varies from county to county.

Source: PMHI national survey, 1977.

Table 17.1. (Continued)

State	Type of Taxation Method Employed	Description of the Taxation Method Employed
Idaho	Property	Mobile homes shall be assessed in the same manner as other "residential" housing. The state tax commission shall issue a regulation setting forth the method by which all "residential" housing will be appraised for ad valorem taxation purposes. The method shall provide uniformity in the assessment of all "residential" housing. County assessors shall assess the values to compute property taxes as prescribed in this regulation.
Illinois	Fee	If the unit is on permanent foundations, it is taxed as real property at local mill rates; if not, the owner must pay a special privilege tax in lieu of the ad valorem tax. This fee is based on 15¢ per square foot.
Indiana	Property	Generally taxed as personalty; a county assessor may classify as realty if he finds that the owner intends to make the unit his permanent home. In such cases the unit becomes eligible for the homestead exemption. Otherwise it is taxed at the rate uniformly imposed whether realty or personalty is involved.
Iowa	Fee	A semiannual tax is levied on mobile homes in lieu of a property tax. The amount of this tax is dependent upon the square footage of the unit and declines with age. A mobile home can be taxed as realty if on a permanent foundation and impossible to reconvert to mobility. If there is a security interest, permission to do so must be obtained from secured party. Elderly and disabled persons with annual incomes of less than $9,000 are eligible for reduced tax rates.
Kansas	Property	A mobile home, for purposes of taxation, shall be considered to be personal property, unless title to said mobile home is vested in the same person who holds title to the real property upon which such mobile home is located and such mobile home has a permanent foundation, such foundation being of a type not removable intact from the real property. Whether real or personal, mobile homes are appraised at market value and assessed at 30% thereof; the assessed value is then included in the valuation base for determining the levy to be applied for taxation.
Kentucky	Property	There is an annual registration fee of $19.50. Mobile homes are generally classified and taxed as personal property. If the wheels are removed and the unit is on permanent foundations, the mobile home is taxed as real estate. Both personal and real property are assessed at 100% of fair market value. The rate for personal property is approximately $1.15 per $100; the rate for real property is approximately $1.00 per $100. Realty is eligible for the homestead exemption of $8,900.
Louisiana	Mixed	A $35 per year registration fee is charged to mobile home owners. Parishes are allowed to tax mobile homes as realty; they further can allow a homestead exemption to be taken.
Maine	Property	The real estate tax is assessed on all mobile homes. The fact that an excise tax has been paid does not render the mobile home exempt from real estate taxation; but the law provides that where an excise tax has been paid and the mobile home is later in the year taxed as real estate, the excise tax paid shall be allowed as a credit on the real estate tax.
Maryland	Fee	If the unit is on leased land, it is subject to a locally imposed excise tax; if the unit is used or can be used for residential purposes and is either permanently attached to the land or connected to water, gas, electric, or sewage facilities, it is taxed as real estate.
Massachusetts	Fee	The owner of each licensed registered mobile home park must collect and turn over to the collector of taxes of the municipality in which the park is located a monthly fee of $6.00 collected from each mobile home occupying space in said park and in the event that a city or town votes, the amount of such license fee may be increased to an amount not exceeding $12.00 a month. If the unit is placed on privately owned land, it is taxed as realty.

Table 17.1. (Continued)

State	Type of Taxation Method Employed	Description of the Taxation Method Employed
Michigan	Fee	When located in a mobile home park, a fee of $3.00 is charged in lieu of real or personal property taxes. When located on private property, the mobile home is generally taxed as real property unless the mobile home is licensed for use on the public highways. Legislation is pending to change the method of taxation.
Minnesota	Property	If on permanent foundations on owner-occupied land and permanently attached to utilities, the mobile home is classified as real property, and eligible for the homestead exemption. All other mobile homes constitute class 2a and are valued and assessed at 40% of the market value thereof. Taxes assessed on class 2a property are considered personal property taxes but are eligible for homestead classification and tax credit the same as real property.
Mississippi	Property	If the mobile home is on owner-occupied land with the wheels removed, it can be taxed as real property at the option of the owner. Otherwise an ad valorem personalty tax is imposed.
Missouri	Property	The owner of a mobile home may convert his mobile home to real estate by attaching his mobile home to a permanent foundation; and by the destruction or modification of the vehicular frame rendering it impractical to reconvert the real property thus created to a mobile home. After complying with these provisions, the owner shall notify the assessor of the county in which the mobile home has been converted to real estate who may inspect the new premises for compliance. When the mobile home is properly converted, the assessor shall then collect the mobile home vehicle title, registration, and license plates from the owner and enter the property upon the tax rolls. The assessment of a mobile home as real estate by these methods prohibits any political subdivision of this state from declaring or treating that mobile home as other than real property for tax purposes.
Montana	Property	Ad valorem personalty tax which decreases automatically with age is imposed. The county assessor has the power to tax the house trailer as realty if he determines that it has lost its character as a house trailer. This determination is based on the permanency of the foundation upon which the unit rests and upon whether the unit is still fit for use as a conveyance.
Nebraska	Property	If the mobile home is located on property held by the owner of the mobile home and is permanently attached to the realty, then it is taxed as realty; otherwise it is taxed as personalty. The three tests to determine permanent attachments are: actual annexation to the real estate (most important aspect of test), conformity to the use to which the land is intended, and intent of owner. Mobile homeowners must obtain an annual permit. Failure to timely comply with permit provisions subjects mobile homeowner to penalty.
Nevada	Property	If the mobile home is on owner-occupied land it is taxed as realty; otherwise it is taxed as personal property.
New Hampshire	Property	If the mobile home is permanently affixed to owner-occupied land, it is taxed as realty; otherwise an ad valorem personalty tax is imposed. The mill rate varies with locality.
New Jersey	Mixed	In view of the lack of any legislation specifically dealing with "mobile homes" and their general treatment as applied to real estate, each case must be determined on an individual basis by the local tax assessor. Recent court decisions have held that in considering the taxability of "trailers" and similar structures as realty or personalty, the distinction is to be determined mainly by the physical aspects of the improvements in each case and the intention of the parties, the relation and situation of the party making the annexation, and the purpose or use for which the annexation was made.

Table 17.1. (Continued)

State	Type of Taxation Method Employed	Description of the Taxation Method Employed
New Mexico	Property	The owner of a mobile home, subject to valuation for personal property taxation purposes shall report the mobile home annually for valuation to the county assessor. The valuation method used for determining the value of mobile homes for property taxation purposes shall be a cost method applying generally accepted appraisal techniques and shall generally provide for the determination of initial cost of a mobile home based upon classifications of mobile homes and sales prices for the various classifications; deductions from initial cost for allowable depreciation, which allowances for depreciation shall be developed by the department; and deductions from initial cost of other justifiable factors, including but not limited to, functional and economic obsolescence.
New York	Property	Unless the unit is within the boundaries of the assessing unit less than 60 days or is for sale and unoccupied, it is taxed as real property.
North Carolina	Property	As a general rule, mobile homes are considered to be personal property. They are considered to be real property when the mobile home is situated on land owned by the owner of the mobile home, and the owner int ends forit to become more or less permanently affixed to the land, and the owner takes action to carry out the intention, such as attaching the mobile home to a permanent foundation and making additions to it—i.e., additional rooms, porches or carports. The determination of whether a mobile home is real or personal property is made by the local assessor, but the above guidelines have statewide application. Mobile homes treated as real property are appraised every eight years as is all other real property. Those classified as personal property are reappraised each year, the effect of which is to allow annual depreciation. Mobile homes are treated as the principal residence for purposes of the property tax exemption for low income elderly and disabled persons.
North Dakota	Fee	A "Mobile Home Decal Tax" is levied on mobile home owners. This tax is determined by taking into account the unit's age, square footage, and the local mill rate where it is located. If permanently attached to owner-occupied land and assessed as real property, it is exempt from this tax.
Ohio	Property	Annual license fee required if used on highways; annual tax in nature of property tax applicable if capable of use or occupancy for human habitation. House trailer subject to ad valorem tax calculated upon cost or value, similar to personal property tax, regardless of owner of land where it is located. If house trailer has been so acted upon as to become a permanent part of land it is assessed as real estate.
Oklahoma	Fee	The mobile home is subject to motor vehicle licensing fees in lieu of ad valorem taxation. If the unit is permanently attached to owner-occupied land, it is classified as personal property and subject to ad valorem taxation. In this latter case, it is exempt from the motor vehicle licensing fee and is eligible for the homestead exemption.
Oregon	Property	If the mobile home is located on owner-occupied land it is taxed as real property; otherwise it is classified and taxed as personalty. If the unit is not more than 8 feet wide, it is classified as a motor vehicle and regulated and taxed as such.
Pennsylvania	Property	Mobile homes permanently attached to the land or connected to utilities are considered real estate and taxed as such.
Rhode Island	Property	Mobile homes are uniformly classified as personal property and subject to taxation imposed by the municipality.
South Carolina	Property	All mobile homes are considered real property and are classified and assessed for ad valorem taxation.

Table 17.1. (Continued)

State	Type of Taxation Method Employed	Description of the Taxation Method Employed
South Dakota	Property	When the unit is on permanent foundations on owner-occupied land, it is classified and taxed as real property; otherwise mobile homes are taxed as personalty. Each unit is subject to a 3% tax on the book value for the first registration in the state.
Tennessee	Property	If the mobile home is used as a permanent residence it is taxed as real property; if the mobile home is not owned by the owner of the land on which it rests, the tax actually can be collected by either the mobile home owner or the owner of the property. In most counties within the state, mobile homes in trailer parks are likewise assessed against the mobile home owner and the owner of the park is held responsible for collection. Usually his rental fees include the pro-rata share of the real estate taxes.
Texas	Mixed	If the mobile home is located on owner-occupied land, it is classified as realty. Otherwise it is generally considered personalty. Some cities have opted to employ a permit system, in lieu of property taxation, for mobile homes located in mobile home parks.
Utah	Property	When the unit is attached to owner-occupied land, it is classified as real property. Otherwise it is taxed as personalty.
Vermont	Property	If the mobile home is attached to land, it is taxed as real property. Otherwise it is considered as personalty and taxed as such.
Virginia	Property	Mobile home purchaser must pay a 3% sales and use tax and a nominal registration fee. Although classified as tangible personal property, the tax on mobile homes is imposed by the locality at the same ratio of assessment and rate of tax as real property. Some localities impose a license fee in addition to the property tax, but the law authorizing the license fee is repealed as of 12/31/79.
Washington	Property	An ad valorem property tax is imposed. If the wheels are removed and the unit is placed on permanent foundations on owner-occupied land, the mobile home is classified and taxed as realty. Otherwise it is taxed as personalty. The valuation and tax rate are the same on real and personal property.
West Virginia	Property	If the mobile home is located on owner-occupied land, it is treated as Class II real property; if it is located on leased land, it is generally classified as Class II personal property.
Wisconsin	Mixed	If the value of annexes, foundations and other additions exceeds 50% of the total assessed value of the mobile home, the unit is classified and taxed as real property. Otherwise it is subject to an in lieu fee which is imposed in the following manner: if the home is in a city or village, it is exempt from the personal property tax but may be subject to an ordinance-imposed monthly fee; if the mobile home is in a town, it is subject to the personal property tax unless the town has passed an ordinance imposing the monthly fee system.
Wyoming	Property	If the unit is over 8 feet wide, it is subject to property taxation. If not, the owner must pay an in lieu registration fee. Mobile homes in the former category which are placed on permanent foundations on owner-occupied land are taxed as real property; otherwise they are placed on the personal property tax rolls.

Source: PMHI national survey, 1977.

Figure 17.1.
State taxation of mobile
homes: 1977. Source:
PMHI national surveys.

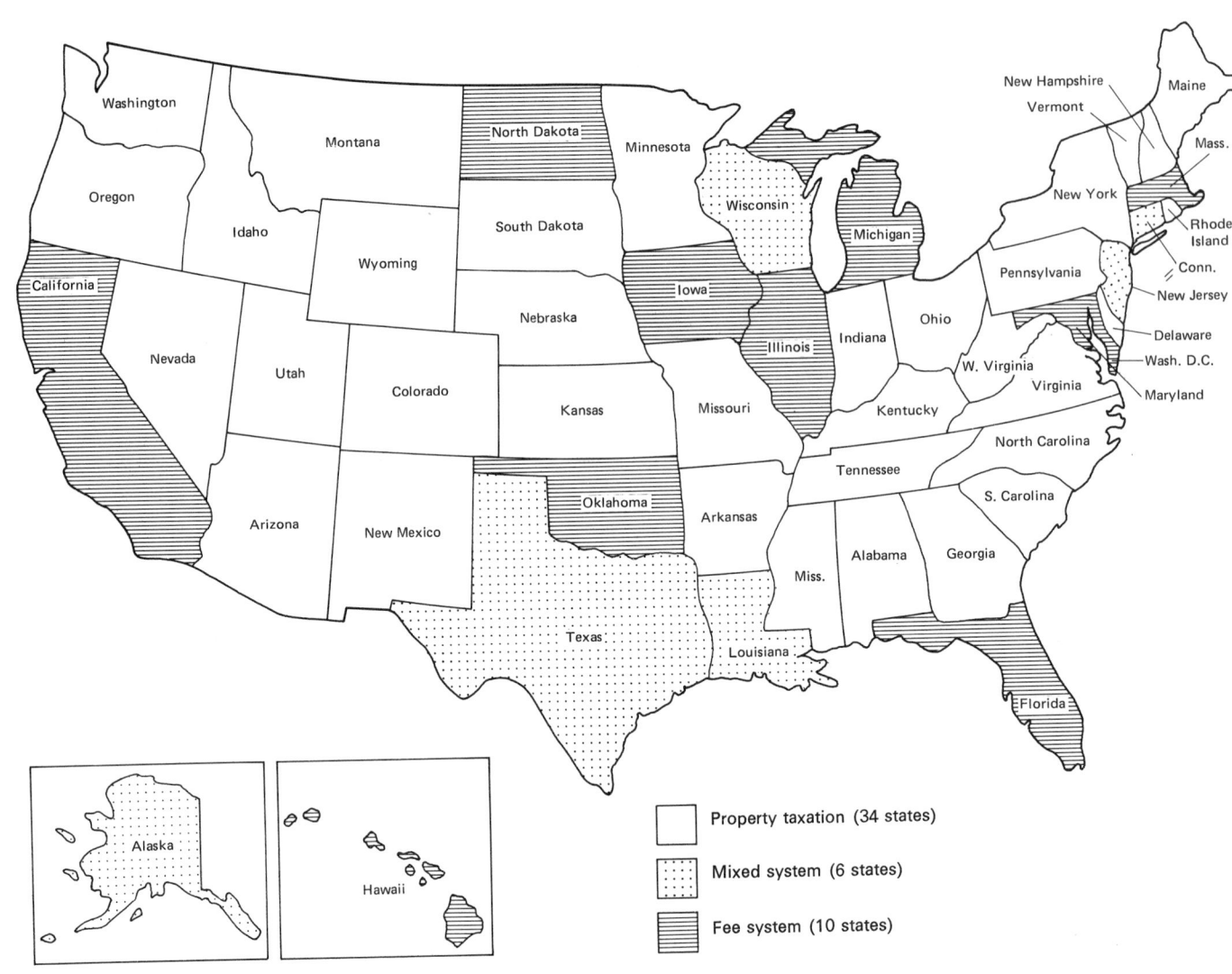

Property taxation (34 states)

Mixed system (6 states)

Fee system (10 states)

1977. The most significant trend has been the dramatic increase in the number of states that tax certain mobile homes as real property. In 1956 only four states provided for such taxation; by 1968 this number had increased to twenty, and by 1977 it had jumped to forty-four. Furthermore, the states considering change are contemplating either the introduction of real property taxation of mobile homes or the expansion of the present systems to include more mobile homes as realty. We believe that in the future an increasing number of mobile homes will be subject to real property taxation (figure 17.2).

Advantages/Disadvantages of Each Type of Taxation
Today most states use complex, individualized methods of taxing mobile homes. The system employed depends on many factors, including the state constitution, judicial history, and the strength of the industry lobby. Thus it would be misleading to declare categorically that one taxation method is better than others. However, the particular advantages and disadvantages inherent in each taxation method can be isolated.

Motor Vehicle Taxation
When mobile homes were merely travel trailers, there was no practical or theoretical reason against taxing them as motor vehicles. This method is by far the least expensive to administer: The state simply treats the mobile home, whether on the highway or attached to the ground, as if it were a motor vehicle. No additional administrative machinery is necessary, so the state motor vehicle department licenses the vehicle and collects the fees. Theoretically, this system is effective in keeping track of mobile homes: A license is required when the owner moves the mobile home from the dealer's place of business and must remain on the vehicle when it is permanently located.

Despite the simplicity of this system, it has such serious drawbacks that no state now uses it as the sole means of taxing mobile homes. In theory the state can impose motor vehicle licensing fees as a function of its police powers. Because of this connection to the police powers, the amount of such fees must be related to the cost of regulating mobile homes. When the fee is more than this cost, it runs the risk of being struck down as a revenue measure.[8] Because such regulatory costs do not include the expense of many municipal services (such as hospitals and schools), the license fee cannot reflect the burden conventional home owners bear.[9] The feeling that mobile home owners are not bearing their fair share of the taxation burden engenders much hostility, which often leads to exclusionary or lesser forms of discriminatory zoning, which may outweigh the initial monetary advantages of lower taxes. In this

regard, the fact that the mobile home owner originally paid nothing for municipal services magnified the hostility of the rest of the community: License fees went directly into the coffers of the state government. Although this drawback has largely been rectified by the state's redistribution of a large percentage of such fees to municipalities where the mobile home is located, the redistribution process is not as visible as direct contribution to the local coffers.

Even if the regulation/revenue hurdle is overcome, the motor vehicle fee cannot accurately reflect the taxes that conventional property owners pay because mill rates are determined locally but motor vehicle fees are uniform statewide. Furthermore, because the amount of the license fee is dependent on some sort of Blue Book value, individual characteristics that might affect the actual resale value of the mobile home are not considered. A mobile home located in a poorly designed, badly kept park in a deteriorating neighborhood will be worth much less than the same unit found elsewhere. Similarly, if the park is becoming more attractive and the neighborhood improving, the value of the home may actually appreciate. In both cases the Blue Book value will differ from the true resale value. License fees also fail to reflect improvements such as skirting, porches, and other additions the owner may have installed. In many states the depreciation allowance for mobile homes presupposes the same useful life as automobiles. This is totally unrealistic, as was shown in chapter 15.

The realty tax assessment of conventional homes does not include the value of furnishings. This would appear to give conventional home owners an advantage over the mobile home occupant because the assessment of the mobile home is generally based on the factory price of the fully-equipped unit. Because of the much higher cost of the conventional home, this advantage is illusory: Conventional home owners pay higher taxes for a standard of living often equaled by the mobile home. In addition, the rate structure used for motor vehicle taxation remains fixed for various periods of time and cannot easily be altered to reflect changing conditions within the state, let alone within particular counties. Conventional homes, on the other hand, are subjected to local mill rates that can be and often are changed yearly.

To retain the motor vehicle classification of mobile homes, certain states have begun to define "mobile" home in order to differentiate it clearly from other forms of housing. This trend is especially unfortunate; it tends to restrict the evolution of the mobile home industry and to slow down the realization of its potentials for developing products designed for higher-density situations.

Thus, in spite of the low cost of implementation and the ease of administration,

motor vehicle taxation remains too inflexible to act as the sole means for taxing mobile homes equitably.

Privilege or Excise Tax
In its simplest form a privilege or excise tax is one imposed on mobile homes for the privilege of being allowed to place the unit within the municipality. This fee is in lieu of all other taxes and is calculated in various ways. Illinois, for example, charges mobile home owners a certain amount per square foot of floor space; other states, such as Massachusetts and Wisconsin, impose a flat monthly fee, regardless of the value or size of the mobile home.

There are certain advantages in this type of taxation. Like motor vehicle licensing fees, it is relatively easy and inexpensive to administer; unlike state licensing fees, the in lieu privilege tax is paid directly to the local assessing unit, which is therefore less likely to view the mobile home as a parasite. Fees are often graduated according to the number of spaces in a mobile home park and collected directly from the park operator. This avoids the necessity for local authorities to find the park-located mobile home and tax it. Furthermore, when the fee is graduated according to the number of park spaces, a predictable, collectible minimum contribution from each mobile home owner is ensured.

In a number of states in which the mobile home is classified as personal property, there is no taxation levied on personal property. In these cases the in lieu fee is the only mechanism to ensure some contribution from each mobile home owner. Because the privilege tax is a tax and not a fee, it does not face the monetary limitations placed on regulatory devices.

Unfortunately, the privilege fee system is beset with a number of disadvantages. Uniform fees poorly reflect differences in mobile home values, particularly where the owner has added improvements. Thus the owner of a mobile home in an inferior park pays the same privilege tax as an owner whose unit is located in a higher-quality park. When imposed statewide, flat fees do not reflect local revenue requirements. Privilege taxes are often determined on a pro rata, benefits received theory. Why tax mobile home owners on a benefits received basis when conventional home owners are taxed on a straight ad valorem basis? If a special tax is justified on the theory that the mobile home is mobile, should not the owners be exempt from collections for permanent community improvements?[10] Basing mobile home taxation upon a benefits received theory raises the difficult question of valuation of park-provided services that lighten the financial load of the local municipality. The crux of this problem is the difficulty in rationalizing different tax treatment of residents according to whether the home is mobile. As the incidence of per-

Figure 17.2.
States that could/can tax mobile homes as real property: 1956, 1968, 1977. Source: PMHI National Surveys, 1969–1977.

1956

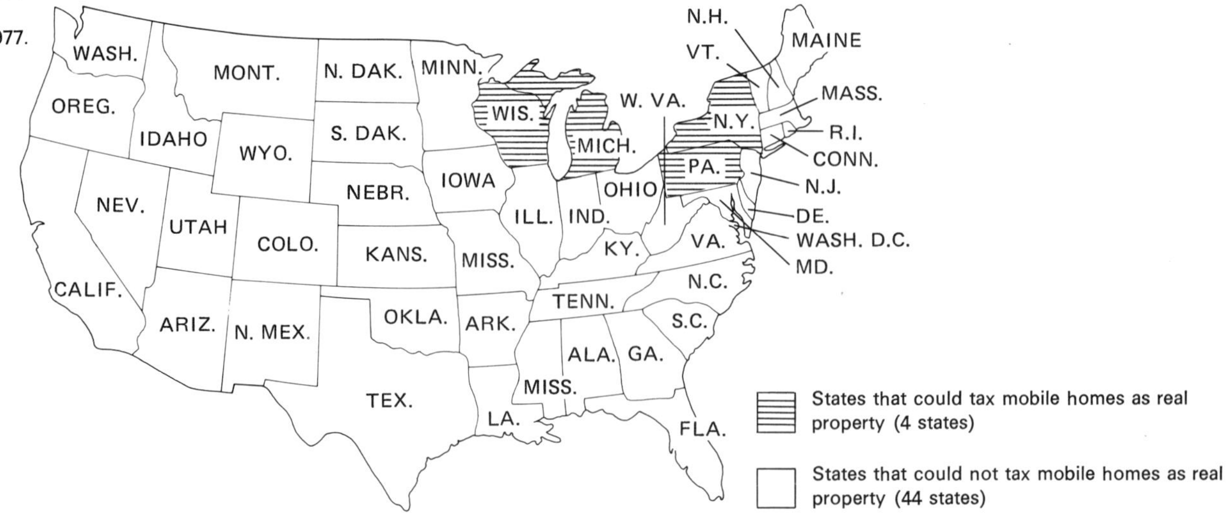

States that could tax mobile homes as real property (4 states)

States that could not tax mobile homes as real property (44 states)

1968

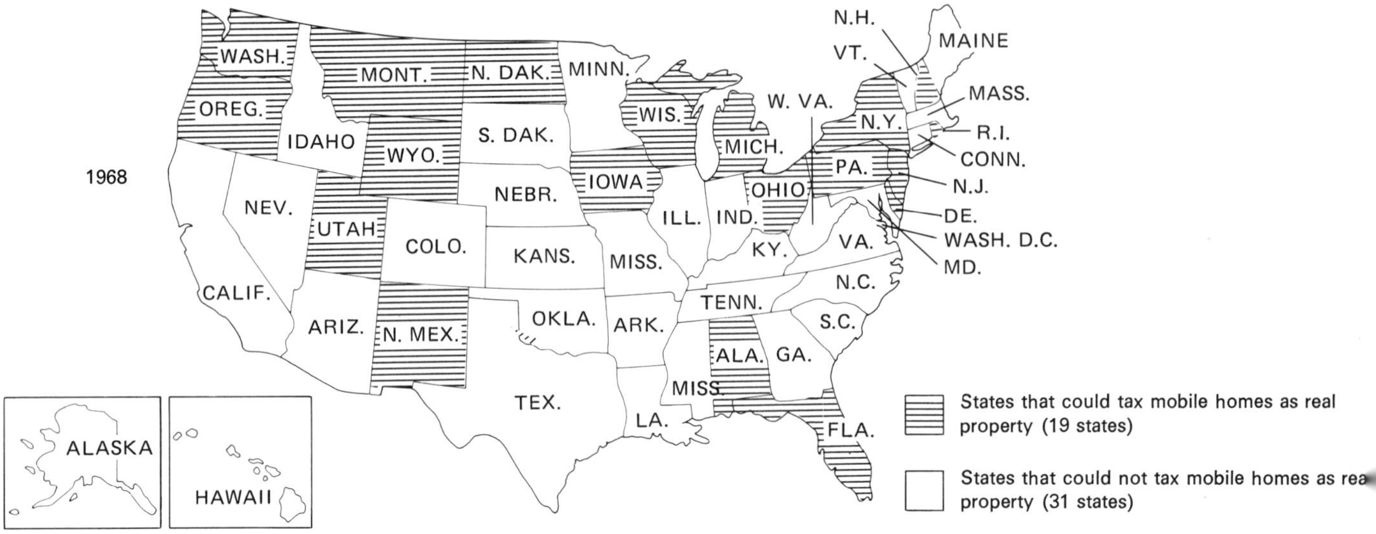

States that could tax mobile homes as real property (19 states)

States that could not tax mobile homes as real property (31 states)

1977

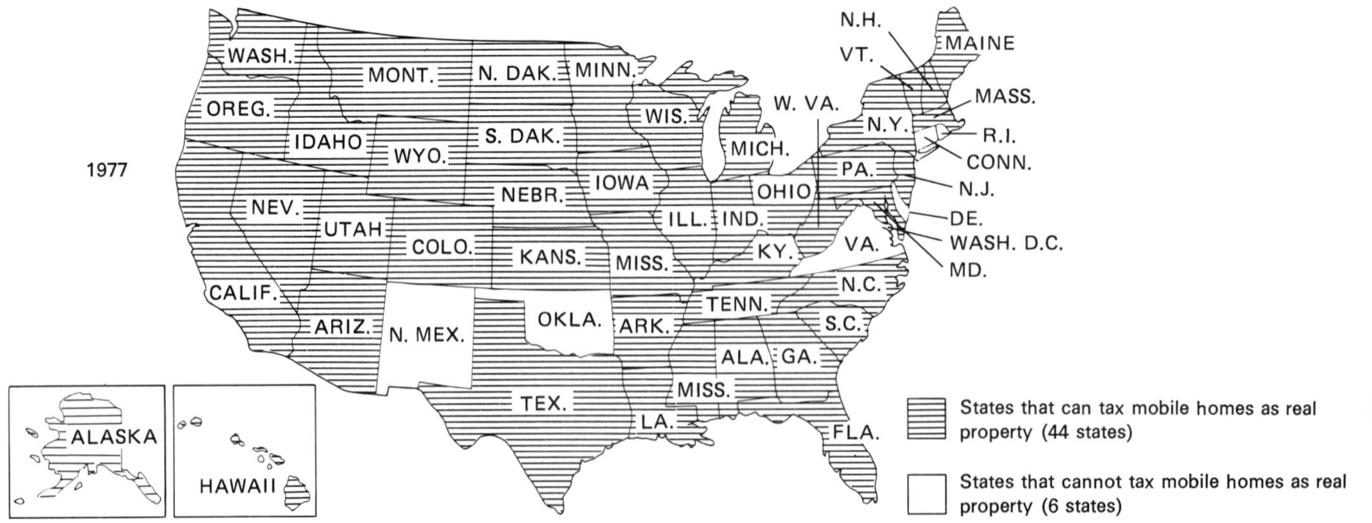

States that can tax mobile homes as real property (44 states)

States that cannot tax mobile homes as real property (6 states)

anent attachment increases and the standard of living provided by the mobile home approaches that of the conventional home, it seems likely that these differences in tax treatment will be challenged as violative of equal protection under the law.

Personal Property Taxation
In general, "personal" property is property that is not "real." The term embraces all objects and rights capable of ownership except freehold estates in land.[11] By definition mobile homes are personal property unless otherwise deemed by statutory law. Thus there is no theoretical objection that can be made against taxing mobile homes as personalty. Because the taxation rate depends upon the county, taxation as personalty is a much more flexible means of fulfilling county needs. Finally, property taxes (both real and personal) can be deducted from gross income in determining federal taxable income; this is not true for motor vehicle fees and in lieu fees.

There are, however, serious disadvantages to taxing mobile homes as personalty. Almost no successful methods for accurately assessing mobile homes have been devised. Several of the most commonly used assessment methods are seriously flawed. For instance, the *Judy-Berner Blue Book* and the *Unicomp* publication do not include values for all models, types, and years of mobile homes, and the valuations given are being widely questioned. Even if the industry depreciation schedule against sale price were accurate, assessors would still have difficulty in ascertaining the original sales price of older homes. The American Appraisal Company formula is unacceptable because the assessors must distinguish between standard, deluxe, and custom-made models, a task for which they are untrained. The need for assessor categorization pressures the assessor to assess all mobile homes at rates applicable to standard models. When the mobile home is moved to a new assessing jurisdiction, consistency in categorization is difficult to achieve.

A separate, though related, problem is encountered when depreciation of the mobile home is calculated according to a statewide formula. The causes for depreciation include physical deterioration as well as economic obsolescence—the changes in value due to changes in the neighborhood. How much depreciation has been caused by these two factors can be found only on a case-by-case determination. For instance, because of the upgrading of the neighborhood and improvements made by the owner, the mobile home may actually have appreciated in value. All of this points to the need for mobile home assessment on an individualized method similar to real estate assessment procedures.

Classification of mobile homes as personalty rather than realty has a number of consequences, most of them negative for the mobile home owner. Because mobile homes are not real property, the owner is unable to get mortgage financing but is eligible for consumer installment loans. The latter provide a greater rate of return for the lender, so in times of tight money financing of mobile homes has been available where mortgages on conventional homes were not. When borrowing money on such a basis, the mobile home owner not only faces higher costs but also does not have the legal protection of the mortgagor: In an installment sales agreement the vendor/lender retains the title until successful completion of all vendee obligations. Upon default the lender can repossess, a much simpler legal procedure than foreclosure.

Other advantages and disadvantages result from this classification, even though the taxation rate in the state may be the same for all property. Mobile homes are popular in areas surrounding military bases. By federal law, personal property of servicemen cannot be taxed by the state in which they are stationed. Thus military personnel living in mobile homes escape taxation in those states classifying mobile homes as personalty. On the other hand, veterans and widows living in conventional homes often enjoy statutory exemptions not applicable to those living in mobile homes classified as personal property. California's reluctance to give "homestead" exemptions to mobile home owners was one of the reasons it hesitated to amend its real property tax laws to include mobile homes.[12]

Because classification as personal property can entail both advantages and disadvantages, many factors must be considered before one taxation method is adopted; any change in the method of taxation will have far-reaching and perhaps unexpected results. For example, a 1974 study found that for Idaho, which at that time usually taxed mobile homes as personalty, the across-the-board reclassification of mobile homes as real property would not only necessitate a substantial change in the assessment methods (which would have to be brought in line with those methods used for conventional housing) but would also substantially increase the maximum limit for school bonds because such limits are keyed to the amount of real property on the tax rolls.[13] (Idaho has since adopted real property taxation of mobile homes to provide uniformity in the assessment of all "residential" housing.)

In the final analysis, the imposition of personal property taxes upon mobile home owners can be criticized as being discriminatory. There is little justification for imposing different rules, procedures, and taxes on residents simply because they live in mobile homes rather than in conventional housing. In Georiga, for example, a mobile home owner who has paid his/her taxes receives an emblem that must be displayed on the front door of the home; this is not demanded of conventional home owners. In many states summary proceedings are available to creditors against the mobile home; distraint and attachment are seldom if ever applied to conventional homes.

Real Property Taxation
In most states (see table 17.1), the mobile home located on owner-occupied land and permanently attached to the ground or utilities is classified and taxed as real property. Based on our determination of the percentage of the total national mobile home unit inventory located outside of parks, we estimate that approximately 60 percent of all mobile homes are already subject to real property taxation. In this case the mobile home has become nearly indistinguishable from conventional housing, so there is little disagreement among commentators and industry spokespersons that this is the proper treatment. Commentators, however, strongly disagree about real property as the proper classification of units found in mobile home parks.

There are several disadvantages to taxing units located in mobile home parks as real property. Real property has been defined as property that is fixed, permanent, and immovable, such as land and dwellings.[14] Simply because of their potential mobility, mobile homes do not theoretically fit within the confines of this traditional definition. To classify a mobile home as real property, although it is located on rented land with its wheels intact, is offensive to theorists who feel that legal fictions should be used seldom if at all. This is perhaps the greatest disadvantage of real property taxation of mobile homes: In the majority of cases it does not coincide with the rigidly interpreted definitions.

A related problem arises from the practicalities of administering the real property tax. For administrative convenience, the mobile home being taxed as real property is assessed as part of the rented land upon which it is located. What is to prevent the mobile home owner from simply towing the unit elsewhere, leaving the park operator with a lien on the land? Real property taxation of mobile homes has been attacked as violative of the Fourteenth Amendment due process guarantees because it entails taxing one individual for property owned by another.[15] Such attacks have been unsuccessful.

One argument often made in support of real property taxation is that mobile homes are functional equivalents of conventional homes and should be taxed similarly. It has been countered, however, that this is fallacious: Mobile homes are functionally equivalent to conventional homes simply because they provide shelter for human inhabitants. This equivalence is also found in apartment buildings, yet apartment dwellers are not assessed for real property taxes.

An interesting argument against imposing a new method that would result in higher taxation of mobile homes holds that new taxes on mobile homes, by increasing their costs relative to conventional housing, will make mobile homes less affordable and attractive for the population and will result in a shift of this population to conventional homes.[16] The long-range effect would be a disruption of the housing market equilibrium that could exacerbate rather than ameliorate the present housing shortage. Implicit in this argument is the assumption that mobile home prices will remain constant. However, it has also been theorized that increased use of the realty tax might indirectly lower the cost of mobile homes, perhaps offsetting the increased taxes (see chapter 16).

The extension of real property classification burdens would also entail the extension of the benefits. Thus, if the state grants homestead exemptions to certain segments of the population who live in conventional homes, equal protection demands that the state afford the same benefits to a now similarly situated (that is, paying real property taxes) mobile home inhabitant. The cost to the state could be significant. If mobile homes were classified as real property, assessment would be on an individual basis rather than according to industry Blue Book figures and statewide depreciation allowances. There is no doubt that such a system would be more expensive and complex to administer.

Experience in the courts has indicated that state assessors' efforts to tax mobile homes as real property without specific authorization from the state legislature will fail.[17] Thus, in order to ensure the legality of real property taxation of mobile homes, enabling legislation will have to be passed. In some states the state constitution would have to be amended before mobile homes could be taxed as real property. Finally, classification of mobile homes as real property would probably lead to much litigation. Unless the state classifies all mobile homes as real property, the owner's intent to attach the unit permanently will be the *sine qua non* of real property taxation. Such a determination would be fact finding and open to dispute in the courts.

On the other hand, there are also numerous advantages to taxing mobile homes as real property. Previous efforts by assessors to tax mobile homes as real property have failed for lack of statutory authorization. Would such authorization be constitutional? A New York case held that it would.[18] The court's rationale has been strongly attacked,[19] but it appears fairly certain that as long as the legislation classifying mobile homes as real property conditions such classification upon attachment of some sort, it will be upheld.[20]

Real property taxation provides a more efficient solution for a basic problem of taxing mobile homes. Classifying mobile homes located in parks as real property and leaving it to the park owner to collect pro rata shares by rent increases largely solves the problem of getting the unit on the tax rolls and keeping it there. In states classifying mobile homes as personal property, the county assessor has the task of keeping track of mobile homes moving in and out of the area. In some states persons who allow a mobile home unit to be located on their land must report such fact to the county assessor. However, this law is not effectively enforced and the county assessor remains heavily burdened. When park owners are required to pay the tax, they have a vested interest in seeing that all mobile home owners pay their share in the form of increased rents. Thus real property taxation benefits the taxing unit in that tax payment is ensured and its assessors no longer have to account for mobile homes existing on park land.

It has been argued that to change the tax structure and tax mobile homes as real property would add to the financial problems of low-income mobile home residents by increasing the unit's occupancy cost. There are three arguments against this view. First, although the median income of mobile home families is lower than that of the population at large, mobile home owners are not, by and large, poor. Second, it is debatable whether tax incentives (in the form of lower taxes) are the most economical means of effectuating social ends (here, better housing for all segments of the community). Third, it is arguable that there is a fallacy in helping low-income families by exempting them from real property taxation: To do so may be to shift the burden to the poor living in conventional housing.

Taxation of mobile homes as real property would subject units to the type of appraisal used for conventional homes. This would result in a much more accurate evaluation of the mobile home's worth because it is obvious that not all units depreciate at the same rate. In most cases the imposition of real property taxes would increase the total amount of revenues collected in spite of the additional costs of administration and the exemptions (such as homestead rights) that would have to be granted. In addition, as was indicated in the discussion of personal property taxation, such imposition would have other beneficial effects, such as increasing the maximum amount of possible school bonding.

The strongest argument that can be propounded in support of real property taxation of mobile homes is that it would lead to a greater acceptance of the mobile home population by the rest of the community. According to one commentator, it is universally accepted that horizontal equity should exist in municipal taxation, that is, similarly situated should be similarly taxed.[21] As long as a special scheme is employed to tax mobile homes, there is no assurance that such horizontal equity will result. If such equity does not exist, hostility is sure to appear: The conventional home owners will view mobile home owners as parasites who do not pay their share of municipal costs. It is not really relevant that mobile home owners may pay as much (but to the state) or that they do not use municipal services (if they live in a park). What is important is that they are part of a community and bound to suffer from its hostility. Thus the "lighter taxation" of mobile homes has been frequently used as an excuse to exclude them entirely from a municipality.[22] If mobile homes were taxed on the same basis as conventional homes, the general population might look upon the mobile home with less hostility and would begin to conceive of it as a type of conventional housing. This could lead in turn to a relaxation of the zoning laws in favor of mobile homes. The ultimate result could be that mobile homes resembling site-built homes in appearance would be allowed wherever single-family detached homes are found. As the physical separation of the mobile population from the rest of the community is decreased, the psychological distance would diminish. Feeling more a part of the community, the mobile home population would be much more likely to become involved in the community's affairs.

The imposition of real property taxes on mobile homes will generally increase the amount of taxes the mobile home owner must pay. Primarily for this reason, the mobile home industry has vigorously opposed real property taxation. Until the industry and the mobile home population realize the indirect benefits accruing from the realty classification, this vigorous opposition will continue. Although there would be clear disadvantages to taxation of mobile homes as real property, we feel that in the long run the overall impact would be beneficial.

Comparison of Land Use Control Attitudes and Taxation Methods in Each State

Although we found no absolute correlation between any tax method and high/low exclusionary land use policies in the various states,[23] some qualitative conclusions can be drawn. Table 17.2 summarizes our analysis. This table lists the states, arranged in increasing order of population density.[24] Population density is an important control factor in testing for such correlation—in states with low population density the traditional home-building industry is less developed and the cost of land is lower; because of this, mobile homes are more necessary as a housing alternative, exclusionary land use control attitudes are less likely, and mobile homes are more likely to represent a higher percentage of the housing stock. The third column shows the predominant method of taxation of mobile homes employed by the state. The fourth column indicates the "exclusion percentage,"

which roughly represents the state's attitude toward mobile homes: The higher the percentage, the less tolerant. Column five shows the percentage of state housing consisting of mobile homes.[25]

The qualitative assessment that can be made is that property taxation of mobile homes, as well as the lowest exclusion percentages, are found most frequently in the least densely populated states. Of the first seventeen states ranked by density, fourteen tax mobile homes as property; the average exclusion percentage for these seventeen states is 3.8 percent. In the second seventeen states, thirteen states classify mobile homes as property and the average exclusion percentage is 8.1 percent. In the final sixteen states, only seven states categorize mobile homes as property and the average exclusion percentage is 38.6 percent. Table 17.2 also shows that mobile homes as percentage of total housing stock decrease as the property taxation incidence decreases and as population density and the "exclusion percentage" increase.

These figures, of course, cannot reveal clear cause-and-effect relationships. But when the obvious impact of population density is discounted, the figures do lend qualitative support to our belief that taxing mobile homes by methods other than property taxation invites a more exclusionary zoning attitude.

Local officials and conventional home owners often attempt to justify their hostility to mobile homes—hostility which often manifests itself in restrictive and unfavorable zoning regulations for the mobile home—by alleging that mobile home owners do not pay their fair share of the tax burden. This attitude dates from the early days of mobile home use when, in fact, the mobile home population paid few if any taxes to the municipal coffers. Although this situation has greatly changed, the hostility lingers. Is there any validity to these allegations?

This question can be approached from two angles: the "horizontal equity" approach or the "benefits received" analysis. Horizontal equity is achieved when the mobile home owner pays the same tax per dollar of shelter as the conventional home owner. Tax theorists posit this approach as the ideal of municipal taxation. Unfortunately, few states have achieved it in mobile home taxation. As stated earlier, fee or mixed systems (presently used by sixteen states) often lead to inequalities in the tax treatment of mobile home owners vis-à-vis their conventional home neighbor: Fees are set statewide without reference to local mill rates and without regard to the unit's actual value as determined by neighborhood quality. Personal property taxes, when keyed to local mill rates, more closely approach the ideal of "horizontal equity." In most cases, however, the assessors valuate the unit without reference to its

B. The Fair Share Controversy

The Issue

Table 17.2.
State-by-State Comparison of Taxation Methods, Land Use Control Attitudes, and Contribution of Mobile Homes to Total Housing Inventory, 1977

Rank	State	Method of Taxation		Exclusion %		Total MH Inventory as % of Housing Units	
1	Alaska	Mixed		1		11.4	
2	Wyoming	Property		1		9.0	
3	Nevada	Property		NA		12.0	
4	Montana	Property		5		7.0	
5	New Mexico	Property		4		5.9	
6	Idaho	Property		NA		6.7	
7	South Dakota	Property		1		5.3	
8	North Dakota	Fee		1		4.8	
9	Utah	Property	14 Property	1	3.8	2.9	6.0
10	Arizona	Property		9		9.0	
11	Nebraska	Property		1		2.9	
12	Colorado	Property		1		4.2	
13	Oregon	Property		NA		5.0	
14	Kansas	Property		5		3.4	
15	Maine	Property		18		4.8	
16	Arkansas	Property		NA		4.4	
17	Oklahoma	Fee		1		2.9	
18	Texas	Mixed		1		2.5	
19	Mississippi	Property		5		4.4	
20	Vermont	Property		2		6.3	
21	Minnesota	Property		15		2.4	
22	Iowa	Fee		2		2.5	
23	Washington	Property		10		3.6	
24	Missouri	Property		1		3.1	
25	Alabama	Property		5		4.6	
26	West Virginia	Property	13 Property	40	8.1	4.6	4.1
27	Georgia	Property		1		5.2	
28	Louisiana	Mixed		NA		3.3	
29	Wisconsin	Mixed		NA		2.0	
30	Kentucky	Property		10		4.1	
31	New Hampshire	Property		2		5.1	
32	South Carolina	Property		1		6.2	
33	Tennessee	Property		1		3.7	
34	North Carolina	Property		25		6.1	
35	Virginia	Property		11		3.4	
36	Hawaii	Fee		25		0.1	
37	Florida	Fee		5		6.9	
38	California	Fee		40		2.8	
39	Indiana	Property		10		4.0	
40	Michigan	Fee		NA		2.6	
41	Illinois	Fee		3		2.0	
42	Ohio	Property	7 Property	50	38.6	2.5	2.4
43	Pennsylvania	Property		NA		2.3	
44	Delaware	Property		29		5.1	
45	New York	Property		50		1.3	
46	Maryland	Fee		20		1.6	
47	Connecticut	Mixed		87		1.0	
48	Massachusetts	Fee		65		0.6	
49	Rhode Island	Property		51		0.8	
50	New Jersey	Mixed		95		0.7	

Note: NA = not applicable.

Source: PMHI national survey, 1977.

location, actual physical deterioration, or improvements and additions. In short, the most practical method of achieving horizontal equity is by classifying and assessing all mobile homes as real property.

The other approach depends upon a "benefits received" analysis. Oversimplified, the goal of this approach is to tax property owners to the extent they benefit from living in the municipality. There are theoretical objections to this approach and it has not been widely accepted by tax theorists. Such an approach places the greatest burden on those least able to pay, and it is in practice very difficult to apply. The benefit received from society varies greatly from person to person and cannot be accurately valuated.

This approach, however, is emotionally attractive and cannot be deflated by mere theoretical arguments. Researchers have tried to evaluate the allegation that mobile home owners do not pay their fair share according to the "benefits received" approach. Unfortunately, most of the work that has been done clearly reflects the bias of the individual researcher. For example, if the bias is pro mobile home, the likely measure of amount of taxes paid is per acre; this results in higher tax figures for mobile homes because the average acreage of each unit is much less than that of the conventional home. If the bias is anti–mobile home, the unit of measurement is likely to be per unit; with this method, mobile home owners pay substantially less because of the lower assessed value of mobile homes.

This discernible bias raises questions about the validity of these studies' findings. The data we have collected on this issue have proven inconclusive, so we can present no definitive answer to the question of whether mobile home owners pay their fair share for benefits received. Instead, we will concentrate on elements that are relevant to a successful resolution of this question.

Demographic Characteristics of the Mobile Home Population

Most mobile home residents generally place the same demands on the municpalities as do conventional home dwellers. Our demographic studies have suggested, however, that the extent of the demand may be less than that of the population at large.[26] The median size of the mobile home family is smaller than that of the total population: 2.3 persons per family versus 2.7 persons. Mobile home owners have fewer school-age children than conventional home occupants. Of the married couples living in mobile homes, 40 percent have children under 18, which almost equals the 42 percent for the population at large. However, 46 percent of the mobile home families with school-age children have only one child in school, while 63 percent of the conventionally housed families with school-age children have two or more children in school. Of all the services provided,

education places the greatest burden on the municipality, so such statistics are revealing.

Roughly 30 percent of all U.S. household heads are under thirty-five, but we estimate that approximately 51 percent of all heads of mobile home households are under this age. This suggests that the mobile home population may be more apt to purchase durable goods (not having purchased them already) and thus stimulate the local economy. Furthermore, the median income of the mobile home population is lower than that of the population at large. This could mean that the mobile home occupant will be more likely to purchase locally produced or locally sold basic necessities rather than journey to suburban shopping centers or urban areas, as more affluent people might. This not only stimulates the local economy but also increases the amount of direct taxes paid (such as sales tax), taxes that will be returned in part to the local coffers.

A significant factor to consider when examining the public services consumed by the mobile home population is the amount of services provided by the mobile home parks themselves. We estimate that 42 percent of all mobile homes are located in mobile home parks, which furnish a wide range of facilities and services that would otherwise have to be provided by and at the expense of the local government. Park operators are required to supply water, utilities, sewage treatment, lighting, internal walkways, and street systems and to maintain and upgrade these systems. Other "public" services may include garbage collection, first aid, and small-scale police and fire protection. Many parks also provide social and recreational facilities such as swimming pools, bowling lanes, and playgrounds. In areas where there is competition among parks, these facilities vie to provide the best and most complete services to residents.

Services Provided by Mobile Home Parks to Residents

Having mobile home parks provide needed public services to their residents realizes an actual savings for the local government and should be considered a positive contribution to the local budget. For example, if a mobile home park provides $100 worth of services that the local government would normally have to supply, the local government saves $100 and can put the money to other uses. When the large amount of "public" services actually provided by the parks is considered, the savings to the local government are substantial.

The provision of services by the mobile home park operator to the residents effects a savings for the municipality, which is relieved of the burden of providing such services itself. Because the park passes the cost of these services on to the mobile home owner in the form of increased rents, the amount of money saved by the municipality should be considered a

Fees and Taxes Paid by Mobile Home Park Operators

contribution of the mobile home population. Similarly, the fees and taxes paid by the park to the municipality should be considered in calculating the amount of money paid by the mobile home dweller located on park land.

Mobile home parks are taxed as improved realty. Because the improvements are often extensive, the assessed value of the land is greatly enhanced and the tax levied is often considerable. Many states impose additional fees or excise taxes for the privilege of operating a park. Although these fees/taxes are in theory limited by the costs of regulation, they will not be struck down as excessive except in the most egregious examples. These property and excise fees are passed on (like the costs of services) to the mobile home owners in the form of increased rents and are, in fact, a form of hidden tax. However, this "tax" is rarely recognized by local officials or the population at large and is almost never considered in valuating the contribution of the mobile home owner to the municipal coffers.

Comparison of Indirect Taxes Paid by the Mobile Home and Conventional Housing Populations

The mobile home population and the conventional housing population consume the same types of public services, but not necessarily in the same amount. The demographic characteristics of the mobile home population, especially the smaller percentage of school-age children and the services provided by the mobile home parks, suggest that the mobile home population, in absolute terms, places a lighter demand on local public services than do their conventional housing counterparts.

Both groups are subject to indirect taxes (sales taxes, fees, and so forth) that are included in the cost of goods and services they buy. These taxes are regressive in nature and weigh more heavily on the lower-income groups than on upper-income groups. The regressiveness of these taxes, the income levels of the mobile home population, and the local orientation of the mobile home population again suggest that mobile home owners actually pay more in the form of indirect taxes than do their conventional housing counterparts. This may be offset, however, by the fact that many of the basic items for which the majority of the mobile home owner's budget goes are exempt from indirect taxes in some states (especially the sales tax, which often exempts food and clothing).

The mobile home owner who rents a park space is assessed part of the cost of services provided by the park operator and part of the cost of the taxes assessed against the park operator. This is an invisible tax that is often overlooked by public officials. Because conventional home owners pay taxes directly, their contribution to the local government is more visible. Thus the mobile home population probably consumes fewer public services yet contributes more, in indirect taxation, than

those persons living in other forms of housing. This difference is significant enough to merit consideration in any serious cost-revenue study of mobile homes.

We acquired information from the taxation departments of the fifty states concerning the relationship between mobile homes and other forms of housing as to the amount of taxes and fees each pays to the various levels of government and the cost of public services consumed by each form of housing. Although cooperative, many departments were unable to supply concise enough information because most states and many municipalities do not compile the needed statistics.

However, information we did receive indicates that the fair share conflict is a false one.[27] Rarely does any form of housing—single-family, multifamily, or mobile home unit—pay its true share of the community costs. All municipalities run deficits and are subsidized by taxes paid by industry and contributions from the state and federal governments.

We did receive detailed studies from a number of states. Each study had certain faults, failing to consider one or more of the elements mentioned earlier as crucial for dealing with this issue. Thus many studies failed to take into account differences in demography or the services provided by the parks at no cost to the local government or the fees and taxes paid by park operators. Other studies failed to take into account the amount of indirect taxes paid by mobile home owners. Nevertheless, most of these studies reached similar conclusions: Mobile homes do not pay a sufficient amount of taxes to cover the cost to local governments for services provided to them; all other forms of housing similarly do not pay a sufficient amount in taxes to cover local governmental services provided; mobile homes are undertaxed because of the method of taxation employed; and the method of taxation should be reformed.

The situation found in these studies is probably indicative of what would be found if a nationwide study were undertaken. It seems that the key factor for the local community is not the total amount collected versus the total amount expended but rather the marginal rate of cost expended for each new unit of housing versus the marginal rate of revenue received from each new unit of housing. By this measure mobile homes are acceptable because they have fewer school-age children, smaller families, and so forth. They add less per-unit cost than one new unit of conventional housing. This is often overlooked by local officials, who are concerned with aggregate amounts. The real problem lies not in some inherent shortcoming in mobile homes, but in the method by which they are taxed. The methods used are simply incapable of collecting sufficient amounts from mobile homes.

C. The Impact of State Taxation on the Mobile Home Industry

Social and Psychological Impact on the Consumer

We consider two impact indexes:

1. Social effect: What effect does the taxation method have on the integration of the mobile home population into the community?
2. Psychological effect: How does the taxation method affect the mobile home population's perception of itself?

Integration of the mobile home population into the community at large is discouraged by the widespread practice of restricting mobile homes to parks, and there is some evidence that nonproperty taxation encourages the practice. Table 17.3 shows that those states with a large percentage of municipalities that either ban mobile homes entirely or restrict units to mobile home parks often employ nonproperty taxation (see, for example, New Jersey, Massachusetts, Connecticut, Iowa, and Maryland). In many instances there seems to be a relationship between three factors: nonproperty taxation, a high percentage of exclusion of mobile homes or restriction to mobile home parks, and a comparatively low incidence of placement on private property. (Those few cases in which there is a high percentage of placement on private property despite a relatively high exclusion or restriction percentage most likely result from the fact that much of the mobile home inventory had been placed on private property prior to the passage of exclusionary or restrictive legislation concerning mobile homes.)

As table 17.3 indicates, we estimate that 58 percent of the mobile homes in the United States are found on private property. In the thirty-four states that tax mobile homes as real or personal property, 69 percent of the units were located on private property versus 48 percent for those sixteen states using fees or a "mixed" system of taxation. It would be simplistic to contend that property taxation leads to a greater tendency to place the mobile home on private property (and, hence, encourages integration); our data do suggest, however, that the method of taxation plays a role in this decision. It is logical to presume, for example, that if a low fee is levied against a mobile home located in a park, whereas a higher realty tax is imposed on the unit placed on owner-occupied land, there would be an added reason for remaining in the park. Similarly, if all mobile homes were taxed as real property, mobile home owners would probably more seriously consider buying their own plot of land upon which to place their unit.

But restriction to parks further militates against integration in more indirect ways. The mere fact that mobile homes located in parks tend to be taxed differently from conventional housing does not encourage integration. Because of this difference, the rest of the community often feels that mobile home owners are not paying their fair share of the community tax burden. This feeling often turns to hostility (in itself injurious to

mobile home dwellers), which manifests itself in exclusionary or at least unfavorable zoning regulations. Thus, as is detailed in chapter 16, mobile homes are often banned from residential zones. This ban forces mobile home parks to locate in commercial or industrial zones, where the surroundings are often unpleasant and mobile home residents feel inferior to and isolated from their conventional home counterparts. The mobile home park becomes a community in and of itself, which may have been one of the early factors in the development of park recreational and service facilities. This in turn further decreases the interaction of the mobile home population with the rest of the community and does nothing to soften the community's negative attitude about parks and mobile homes.

The negative social impacts, in turn, have negative psychological effects. Different tax treatment enhances the feeling of inferiority shared by many mobile home dwellers. Smaller subgroups usually assimilate the attitudes of the dominant subgroup. The classification and taxation of mobile homes as motor vehicles is a statement by the community that it considers mobile homes poor substitutes for conventional housing. This attitude is adopted by the mobile home community, whose perception of its status is generally already less than favorable. Taxing mobile homes as realty, like other forms of housing, may not eliminate the negative attitude toward mobile homes but would lessen the reasons for it.

Economic Impacts on Consumer and Producer

The two types of cost we examine are:

1. Production cost (the cost to produce the mobile home from the raw material to the finished product ready for shipment)
2. Occupancy cost (the cost to the owner of the mobile home to use the structure).

The type of taxation imposed has an indirect effect on the production cost and a direct effect on the occupancy cost.

The characterization and taxation of mobile homes as something other than realty has no direct effect on the cost of producing the unit but has a substantial indirect effect. The mobile home industry enjoys a major advantage over the conventional housing industry in that its product is not considered a "real" building; therefore it is not subject to myriad and often anachronistic local building codes and does not have to build a specialized product for each locality. This has allowed the industry to realize the substantial cost savings that accompany mass production. Thus the failure to classify mobile homes as realty has been a major benefit to the mobile home industry in terms of production costs. However, the danger that the mobile home industry could become subject to local building codes no longer exists; the new federal construction and safety standards for

Table 17.3.
Taxation and the
Location of Mobile
Homes

State	Type of Taxation	% of Municipalities That Ban MH Entirely	% of Municipalities That Restrict MH to Parks	% of MH Unit Inventory Located on Private Property[a]
Northeast				62
Connecticut	Mixed	87	12	31
Maine	Property	18	4	70
Massachusetts	Fee	65	28	28
New Hampshire	Property	2	3	52
New Jersey	Mixed	95	4	11
New York	Property	50	11	66
Pennsylvania	Property	NA	NA	70
Rhode Island	Property	51	13	22
Vermont	Property	2	12	70
East North Central				54
Illinois	Fee	3	38	52
Indiana	Property	10	25	57
Michigan	Fee	NA	NA	50
Ohio	Property	50	40	53
Wisconsin	Mixed	NA	NA	61
West North Central				57
Iowa	Fee	2	80	40
Kansas	Property	5	NA	62
Minnesota	Property	15	85	51
Missouri	Property	1	10	64
Nebraska	Property	1	15	53
North Dakota	Fee	1	50	59
South Dakota	Property	1	33	73
South Atlantic				61
Delaware	Property	29	35	57
Florida	Fee	5	75	31
Georgia	Property	1	30	78
Maryland	Fee	20	80	52
North Carolina	Property	25	75	80
South Carolina	Property	1	60	83
Virginia	Property	11	55	73
West Virginia	Property	40	60	82
South Central				75
Alabama	Property	5	10	78
Arkansas	Property	NA	NA	76
Kentucky	Property	10	30	77
Louisiana	Mixed	NA	NA	76
Mississippi	Property	5	13	80
Oklahoma	Fee	1	50	67
Tennessee	Property	1	35	82
Texas	Mixed	1	10	71
Mountain				53
Arizona	Property	9	65	40
Colorado	Property	1	40	55
Idaho	Property	NA	NA	58
Montana	Property	5	5	69
Nevada	Property	NA	NA	43
New Mexico	Property	4	10	67
Utah	Property	1	63	54
Wyoming	Property	1	10	74
Pacific				30
Alaska	Mixed	1	2	35
California	Fee	40	52	18
Hawaii	Fee	25	25	Unknown
Oregon	Property	NA	NA	56
Washington	Property	10	75	53
United States (Excluding District of Columbia)				58

a. For explanation of computation of data, see discussion of "Park Versus Non-Park Location" in chapter 10, Section B.

Note: NA = not applicable.

Source: PMHI national survey, 1977.

mobile homes, which became effective in 1976, ensure nationally uniform code regulation, independent of the mobile home's taxation status.

Municipalities depend in large part on realty taxes for their revenues. Growing demand for services plus inflation have caused frequent increases in the effective mill rates in most communities. When mobile homes are classified as something other than realty, they escape this frequently increasing mill rate and often pay lower taxes. Thus occupancy costs are generally lower in those states that impose fees or a personalty tax on mobile homes. Lower occupancy costs in turn stimulate sales: Everything else held constant, sales increase with the fee system and, at the other extreme, decrease with real property taxation.

Potential purchasers of mobile homes are generally unable to get mortgage financing, in part because of the lender's perception of the mobile home as something other than conventional housing. The state can help to change this perception by classifying the mobile home as realty. Financing mobile homes through long-term mortgages would substantially lower the monthly installments due the lender. Thus realty classification coupled with mortgage financing could indirectly decrease the cost of occupancy significantly.

Impact on Industry Development

The type of taxation of mobile homes has an impact on two aspects of industry development: the growth of the industry's potential market and the evolution of the industry's product mix. The effect of the differential tax treatment has translated into discriminatory zoning ordinances. Discriminatory zoning retards industry growth in that it limits the available land supply for the placement of mobile homes. These exclusionary policies have had predictable effects on industry development. For example, in the more industrialized urban areas of the Northeast, complete exclusion runs from 51 percent of the communities in Rhode Island to 95 percent of the communities in New Jersey; this partially explains why only 11 percent of the mobile homes in the United States are located in the Northeast. From the viewpoint of the industry (and the consumer), this is particularly unfortunate: Given the high cost of conventional housing in the Northeast, there would seem to be a large potential market for mobile homes were it not for the exclusionary policies of the region. On the other hand, the different tax treatment accorded mobile homes helped the industry during its early years. The classification of mobile homes as something other than realty has permitted the industry to use the cost savings associated with mass production to capture the low-cost housing market.

In terms of product mix, the tax treatment accorded mobile homes has had a detrimental effect. To secure the tangible advantages of the personalty classification (for example, exemptions from local building codes and lower taxes), the industry has had to restrict changes in the basic outward appearance of the mobile home. Classification of mobile homes as realty would free the industry from the need to maintain the motor vehicle or personalty classification of the mobile home; the wheels, which serve no useful purpose, could be removed, and the industry could change its designs to approximate more closely those of conventional housing. It could also experiment with new structural applications of mobile home building components such as stack-up configurations for higher-density situations. (Chapter 20, "The Product Tomorrow," explores such possible designs.) This development would attract wider markets and would make the product more acceptable to a wider segment of the population.

Summary of Impact

The effect of each tax on industry performance is summarized in table 17.4. The realty tax and classification have a positive influence on intangible performance measures (effect on consumers and effect on industry development). In the long run the realty tax and classification will prove the most beneficial, but in the short run they have a negative effect on cost and possibly on growth. All other forms of taxation—motor vehicle, fee, personalty—have positive effects on cost and negative effects on the intangible measures, except possibly growth, where they as well as the realty tax have both positive and negative effects.

D. Policy Alternatives

Potential Definition

The interstate differences in definition and the related differences in tax treatment of mobile homes underscore the need for a clear and uniform definition of terms. With the traditional units now available and with the development of "stabile" building components on the horizon, much confusion would be eliminated by the adoption of a statute distinguishing between full-scale residence and temporary portable housing. Such definitions could carry through taxation and other modes of public regulation and should be broad enough to cover both present and emerging mobile home forms. (The official 1977 MHI deunition, which governs many statutory definitions, is identical to the one contained in the federal building code for mobile homes, the National Mobile Home Construction and Safety Standards, which took effect in June 1976.)

But the MHI definition still alludes to mobility ("built on a permanent chassis and designed to be used . . . with or without a permanent foundation . . .") and is too narrow to fit the industry's future product: "im-mobile" shelter (see chapter 20, "The Product Tomorrow"). A promising legal definition that would cover both today's mobile

Table 17.4.
Summary of Impact on
Performance

| | Type of Tax | | | |
	Realty	Motor Vehicle	Fee System	Personal Property
Performance Measure				
Impact on consumer:				
Social	+	−	−	−
Psychological	+	−	−	−
Impact on cost:				
Production cost	+ −	+	+	+
Occupancy cost	+ −	+	+	+
Impact on industry development:				
Industry growth	+ −	+ −	+ −	+ −
Product mix	+	−	−	−

homes and the future building components provided by the mobile home industry could be developed by defining the mobile home as a dwelling unit with all of the following characteristics:[28]

1. Designed for primary residential use, functionally equivalent to traditional housing, meeting the essence of basic housing codes
2. Designed for use as a detached single-family home or for assembly into a two-family or multifamily structure
3. Designed to be essentially completely factory produced and factory finished, including all major standard fixtures and appliances and, as an option, all furniture; leaving the factory ready for occupancy except for on-site utility hookup and setup
4. Designed to withstand the stresses incurred in transportation from the factory to the dealer or site; designed to be transported via highways on its own wheels, on detachable wheels, on flatbed, lowboy, or other trailers, or by other modes of transportation including rail or waterways
5. Designed to be ready for occupancy upon arrival at the site except for minor and incidental unpacking, correcting, or assembling operations; location on foundation supports or integration into site-built supporting structure; and hookup to on-site utility systems
6. Designed to meet or exceed the Federal Mobile Home Construction and Safety Standards, Title VI of the Housing and Community Development Act of 1974, which became effective on June 15, 1976
7. If the industry's production of shelter for nonresidential uses is to be covered, the definition of course would have to be broadened.

A companion statutory provision should clearly distinguish between a "mobile home" and a "recreational unit," for example, by defining the latter as "a motorhome, travel trailer, pick-up camper, converted bus, tent-trailer, tent, or similar device used for temporary portable housing." Such a definition would be beneficial in that it would clearly recognize the distinction between today's

mobile home and its ancestor, the travel trailer. It would recognize mobile homes as a form of permanent shelter equivalent to traditional forms of housing.

Throughout this discussion of taxation, we have held two hypotheses: The mobile home industry has the potential to become a major source of high-quality, low-cost housing, especially for higher-density urban areas; and differential tax treatment is detrimental in the long run to such development of the mobile home industry. The real property tax meets the need for a system of taxation that will aid industry growth while ending differential tax treatment. Today the real property tax is the most widely used general method of taxation and most important source of revenue at the local level. Local governments are more likely to extend this tested method than experiment with new and untried ones, especially because an estimated 58 percent of the mobile home unit inventory in the United States is located on private property and is already taxed as real property. This is not meant to be an endorsement of the real property tax per se as a revenue-gathering method. If more equitable nonregressive methods are developed to replace the property tax, they should be applied uniformly to both traditional and mobile housing.

All traditional forms of housing are taxed as real property. Most of the attempts that have been made to include mobile homes under this realty tax have been resisted by mobile home park operators and dwellers. In the long run their opposition to the real property tax is not in the industry's best interest. The atmosphere of tension and distrust between mobile home park operators and residents and the local taxing authorities was created in the early 1930s and today is perpetuated in some measure by the local tax structure. Antiquated tax laws have allowed mobile home park operators and mobile home owners legally to secure tax benefits; local officials have retaliated with restrictive zoning and discriminatory ordinances. Some of the emotionalism that clouds this issue can be

Toward a Realty Tax

blunted if for tax purposes mobile homes are treated like other forms of housing. The mobile home population will usually be a minority in any community, so it must propose and support legislative measures that will lessen the tension between itself and the majority. This in turn will lead to a decrease in restrictive zoning, a wider availability of land, a larger market, and a product more widely accepted as a legitimate form of housing.

The fifty state taxation departments we canvassed generally felt that if any change in the manner of taxing mobile homes is imminent, it would be toward the realty tax. Past experience in New York and Pennsylvania indicates that the legal problems of mobile homes permanently attached to the ground can easily be overcome legislatively. Today's mobile homes and tomorrow's three-dimensional housing units for multistory structures will, as a practical matter, be permanently affixed whether judged by physical integration with the land or by the owner's intent. Moreover, we suspect that as the product becomes visually indistinguishable from housing constructed on-site, the states will meet little judicial resistance to the imposition of real property taxes on mobile homes.

There are still three major concerns about the extension of the realty tax: the discovery of the new homes, the valuation of the homes, and against whom to assess the tax. The first phase of the taxing process, finding the object, still presents certain unique problems in relation to the present mobile home. Unlike on-site constructed homes that take weeks to assemble, mobile homes can be placed on a lot within a day. This creates problems of timely discovery and entails added administrative costs if more inspectors must be hired to check for mobile homes entering a new area. A number of possible solutions are available. The community could require a permit, similar to a building permit, before a mobile home could locate in the community. Any home located without a permit would be subject to fine. Local landlords could be required to report all mobile homes located on their property. Alternatively, the state could require the registration of all mobile homes with the department of motor vehicles before movement on the highway. The state motor vehicle department would determine the destination of the home and whether any taxes were due before it issued a permit to move. This information could be forwarded to the local community. If the mobile home is to move interstate, the information could be forwarded to the state of destination and some type of reciprocal agreement could be developed. A nominal fee could be charged to cover the administrative cost of this program.

The second major concern is with the valuation of mobile homes. Most local assessors may not be sufficiently familiar with mobile homes to compute accurately the assessable value of the home. This problem could be overcome by state-issued valuation schedules. These schedules could be based on factory price lists, square feet, or some other acceptable measure of value. If a factory price list is used, the cost of furnishings should be subtracted; furnishings should be treated in the same manner as those in traditional housing. The valuation schedule should be developed at the state level to ensure fairness and uniformity. Additions to the home as well as other tangible and intangible factors increasing or decreasing the unit's value could be determined at the local level.

A related issue is depreciation. The traditional home often appreciates over time; mobile homes often depreciate at a technically totally unrealistic rate. Two factors seem to be at work here. The first aspect includes alleged lighter construction material and obsolescence of built-in, nonreplaceable parts, subjective taste factors, and forced location in undesirable areas. Second, unlike buildings whose values increase with the rise in land values, mobile homes remain separate for valuation purposes and do not benefit from an appreciation of the land value. The first factor can be overcome by improvement in quality control and code enforcement, better marketing techniques, the realization that mobile homes are legitimate alternatives to conventional housing, and the end of discrimination in zoning. Occupant ownership of both the unit and its site can overcome the second factor.

A third major concern is whom to assess, the owner of the home or the owner of the land upon which the home is located. Obviously, when they are one and the same person there is no conflict. But when the homes are placed in mobile home parks or on rented spaces outside of parks, a conflict does exist. Assessing the land owner (park operator) for this tax has administrative advantages. The park operator becomes the tax collector and acts for the city. The land serves as security for unpaid taxes if the home owner should depart. There is no need to take into account the various types of people in the park because the only person eligible to claim exemptions or deductions would be the land owner. This would eliminate a quantity of paperwork and also increase the amount of revenue collected.

There are two disadvantages to this method of collection. The park operator passes on the tax by increasing the rents pro rata, without considering the varying values of the different units within the park. Thus the owner of an inexpensive model pays the same share of the tax as the occupant of the deluxe model home. In addition, the tax is often calculated according to the number of spaces in the park. The fact that the park has fallen into disrepair or that vacancies have occurred is not taken into account. This leads to an increased rent burden on those occupants remaining, which in turn may cause

additional departures. The park operator could guard against this by requiring larger security deposits and higher income standards for acceptance into a park. This, however, would result in the exclusion of those people most likely to want and need mobile homes and a lessening of the demand for the p oduct.

An alternative would be to levy one tax on the land and improvements thereto (roads, lighting, utilities, and so forth) and another on each mobile home located in the park. Each owner could then take advantage of any special exemptions or deductions available. Furthermore, each individual would be able to deduct these property taxes from his or her gross income for federal tax purposes; when only one tax is imposed, the operator is allowed a deduction for a tax that he or she in fact did not pay but rather passed on to the tenants. Although this method would be more burdensome and expensive to administer, it would be more equitable for the mobile home owner. This collection method has been criticized because the municipality is not protected against any mobile home owner who may move out of the jurisdiction rather than pay the tax. However, this is unlikely to happen because the cost of moving would usually exceed the taxes due.

The pressure on the local taxing authorities to find more revenue has led many to tax the mobile home as real property. This raises the possibility of double taxation: property taxation at the local level, fees at the state level. Furthermore, there is no assurance that the state judiciary would uphold an extension of the realty tax to mobile homes without legislative authorization. Hence, to avoid lack of uniformity and ensure success, a realty tax should be imposed by the state legislature.

We believe that the adoption of the realty tax would be beneficial not only to the mobile home owner but also to the industry. The industry must realize that widescale acceptance of the mobile home will come about only when the community begins to perceive the mobile home as an alternative form of housing. Financial demands on municipalities are greatly increasing, and tax officials are searching for new sources of revenue. By 1977 an estimated 1.7 million mobile homes were located in mobile home parks, providing an attractive target. Many communities feel that mobile home owners are not paying their fair share of the fiscal burden. Whether they are or not is rather immaterial; what is important is the community's attitude. When the mobile home is viewed as a parasite living on the host of the community, it is likely to be excluded from the attractive residential areas by zoning. Unpleasant surroundings in nonresidential areas enhance the negative impression of mobile homes and increase the isolation of the mobile home population. A first step in breaking this vicious cycle would be to tax all mobile homes as realty.

The mobile home is fast becoming nearly indistinguishable from conventional housing. As this process continues, the courts will become increasingly sympathetic to the local assessors' efforts to tax them as real property.[29] The major resistance to realty tax imposition comes from mobile home owners and park operators. The basis for their opposition is economic: The real property tax is believed to represent a greater tax burden. Although in the short run this is undoubtedly true, the indirect benefits of the real property tax outweigh the fiscal disadvantages. The continued opposition must be seriously reconsidered.

Notes to Chapter 17

1. *In re Opinion of the Justices*, 220 Mass. 613, 108 N.E. 570 (1915).

2. In *Hoffman* v. *Borough of Neptune City*, 137 N.J. 485, 60 A.2d 798 (1948), the plaintiff had been forced to pay 43 percent of his gross revenues to the city coffers and operate his mobile home park at a deficit. Even though he could have passed these costs on to the owners renting spaces in his park, the court upheld his claim that the tax was oppressive, confiscatory, and unreasonable. This type of attack will be successful only in extreme cases such as *Hoffman*. In *Konya* v. *Readington*, 54 N.J. Super 363, 148 A.2d 868 (1959), the court upheld the constitutionality of a local revenue measure even though the amount collected exceeded administrative and regulatory costs. The court concluded that the reasonableness of the amount collected could be determined only through comparison with other similar fees.

3. *Gendreau* v. *State Farm Insurance Co.*, 206 Minn., 237, 288 NW 225 (1939); *Aetna Life Insurance* v. *Aird*, 108 F2d 136 (5CCA 1939); *Blasoti* v. *Clark*, 51 F. Supp. 608 (R.I.D. Ct. 1943).

4. *In re Foley*, 97 F. Supp. 843 (Neb. D. Ct. 1951); *Clark* v. *Vitz*, 190 SW 2d 736 (1945); compare to *Gann* v. *Montgomery*, 210 SW 2d 255 (1948).

5. T. Meloan, *Mobile Homes, Study #37* (Homewood, Ill.: Richard D. Irwin, Inc., 1954), pp. 101–104.

6. Ohio Department of Taxation, *Taxation of House Trailers in Ohio and Other States* (July 3, 1958), pp.14–15.

7. Information for 1956 was drawn largely from the report compiled by the Ohio Department of Taxation, *Taxation of House Trailers*; 1968 and 1977 information was drawn from surveys made by PMHI and from PMHI files.

8. See *County Bd. of Supervisors* v. *American Trailer Co.*, 193 Va. 72, 68 SE 2d 115 (1951).

9. See "The Search for an Equitable Approach to Mobile Home Taxation," 21 *De Paul L. Rev.* 1008 (1972).

10. "Toward an Equitable and Workable Program of Mobile Home Taxation," 71 *Yale L.J.* 702, 710 (1962).

11. 63 Am. Jur. 2d, PROPERTY, Section 22.

12. August 8, 1973, letter from the California State Board of Equalization to PMHI Director Arthur Bernhardt. In spite of this disadvantage, the letter predicted that it was only a matter of time until mobile homes were treated as real property, which indeed has occurred

13. *Mobile Homes in Idaho* (Boise, Ida.: Center for Business and Economic Research, School of Business, Boise State University, 1974), p.87.

14. 42 Am. Jur. PROPERTY, Section 13 (1942).

15. R.W. Bartle and H.R. Gage, "Mobile Homes: Zoning and Taxation," 55 *Cornell L. Rev.* 524 (1970).

16. Robert F. Rooney, "Micro Analysis of Mobile Home Characteristics with Implications for Tax Policy: A Reply," 44 *Land Economics* 414 (August 1968).

17. *Stewart* v. *Carrington*, 203 Misc. 543, 119 N.Y.S. 2d 778 (1952).

18. In 1952 an assessor in New York taxed mobile homes in parks as real property. In the case of *Stewart* v. *Carrington*, 203 Misc. 543, 119 N.Y.S. 2d 778 (1952), the court held that this was beyond the powers of the assessor. In 1954 the state legislature responded by classifying all mobile homes used as homes or offices as real property. This legislation was attacked as being unconstitutional. In the case of *N.Y. Trailer Coach Association* v. *Steckel*, 9 N.Y. 2d 533, 175 N.E. 2d 151, 215 N.Y.S. 2d 487. App. dismissed 369 U.S. 105 (1962), the New York Court of Appeals held that classification of property as real was a legislative function and was not dependent upon common law definitions. As long as there was a rational basis for the classification (the mobile home is attached to the ground), the classification would not be judicially invalidated.

19. "The Search for an Equitable Approach to Mobile Home Taxation," 21 *De Paul L. Rev.* 1008, 1020 (1972).

20. *Streyle* v. *Bd. of Property Assessment*, 173 Pa. Super 324 (1953); *Coyle Assessment*, 17 Pa. D&C 2d 149 (1958).

21. R. Berney and A. Larson, "Micro Analysis of Mobile Home Characteristics with Implications for Tax Policy," 42 *Land Economics* 451 (November, 1966), p.458.

22. "Mobile Homes: Zoning and Taxation." 55 *Cornell L. Rev.* 491, 492 (1970).

23. Land use information was drawn from chapter 16 of this book.

24. U.S. Bureau of the Census, *Statistical Abstract of the U.S.*, 98 edition (Washington, D.C.: The Department of Commerce, 1977).

25. U.S. Bureau of the Census, *Census of Housing: 1970, Volume I: Housing Characteristics for States, Cities, and Counties*, Parts 1–52 (Washington, D.C.: U.S. Government Printing Office, 1972).

26. Demographic characteristics have largely been drawn from the 1970 Census of Housing and the U.S. Bureau of the Census *Annual Housing Survey: 1975*, Series H–150–75 (Washington, D.C.: U.S. Government Printing Office, 1977).

27. Fair share information received by PMHI in partial response to PMHI's 1973 national taxation survey: Donald R. Crow, California Department of Housing and Community Development, *Fair Share Study of California*; Graduate City Planning Program, Georgia Institute of Technology, *Fair Share Study of Georgia*; Southeast Regional Planning Agency of Connecticut, *Fair Share Study of Connecticut*; Margaret Drury, *Mobile Homes—The Unrecognized Revolution in American Housing* (Ithaca, N.Y.: Cornell University Press, 1967), p.163.

28. Based on definitions suggested by Drury, *Mobile Homes*.

29. For example, *Ellis* v. *Bd. of Assessors of Acushnet*, 265 N.E. 2d 491 (1970). Also feedback from interviews with state officials during PMHI 50–State Taxation Survey, 1977.

Chapter 18

Building Code Regulation

A. Evolution of Mobile Home and Manufactured Building Codes

Public safety regulations for mobile homes did not exist in the early years of the industry. Manufacturers generally were not required to conform to conventional building code standards because mobile homes were commonly treated as personal property rather than as real estate. They were thus able to move ahead in the market by using technologically advanced materials and construction methods that substantially reduced production costs. These advances enhanced the market for mobile homes as a form of low-cost housing. At the same time, however, some mobile home manufacturers were marketing poor-quality and, in some cases, dangerous products. Because the public strongly identifies any mobile home it sees with all mobile homes, responsible industry leaders saw the need for high standards of quality for the entire industry. Quality control became increasingly important as municipalities began to impose local construction standards on mobile homes, often in an effort to exclude them.

To remedy the situation, the Manufactured Housing Institute (MHI) undertook the task of developing and promoting its own standards.[1] The MHI sought to avoid industry subjugation to the kind of complex and contradictory standards that still prevail throughout the on-site residential building industry. MHI members were aware that compliance with the existing maze of local codes would result in custom building units for each code jurisdiction, thereby losing much of the price advantage they held in the market.

In the 1950s the MHI began to institute a long-term program of self-regulation to build a national performance-type building code over the next twenty years. Using as its basic tactic the enlistment of respected, impartial, national institutions, the MHI and the Trailer Coach Association approached the National Fire Protection Association (NFPA) and the American National Standards Institute (ANSI) to seek their cooperation in developing mobile home standards geared to the special conditions of mobile home production. The resulting code, known as NFPA 501B, was the first set of comprehensive standards published solely for the benefit of the mobile home industry. In 1963 ANSI endorsed NFPA 501B's heating and electrical code and added its own plumbing code to produce American Standard A119.1-1963, for Installation in Mobile Homes of Electrical, Heating, and Plumbing Systems. Compliance with this code became a prerequisite to continued membership in the MHI. Meanwhile, by 1967, the MHI had developed the structural code Minimum Body and Frame Design and Construction Standards.

Under ANSI auspices groups from MHI and NFPA met to work out a compromise code. The mutually accepted code was incorporated into ANSI A119.1 in 1969. Thereafter NFPA 501B and ANSI A119.1 were jointly developed as one code. The joint ANSI/NFPA code has been called the most complete single-package building standard of any available in the United States. The joint code is generally known in the industry as ANSI A119.1 or the ANSI code, as it will be referred to here.[2]

Revised editions of the code were published regularly, and revisions were researched and drafted by specialists coordinated by NFPA. The code used performance requirements rather than specifications whenever possible. The distinction is important. A specification code describes current or historical building methods and materials and requires that these methods and materials be used on every new structure. A performance code isolates critical factors in the construction of a unit and prescribes performance criteria for evaluating building methods and materials. Although specification codes are generally easier to draft and administer, they unfortunately tend to freeze technology; performance codes tend to be more difficult to develop but allow maximum flexibility for innovation.

In the early 1960s, as a result of continued MHI pressure, states began to recognize ANSI A119.1 as a comprehensive code. By June 1974 forty-five states had adopted the ANSI code, or a derivative of it, largely because of MHI lobbying and state recognition of the need for public safety and quality standards. The basic problem, however, remained: State acceptance of the ANSI A119.1 was completely voluntary. Although the codes were based on ANSI A119.1, they were not all the same. Some states adopted the ANSI code in whole, others, in part, and still others, with modifications and amendments.

These state-by-state variations prevented full interstate reciprocity and uniformity. Project Mobile Home Industry called attention to the resultant negative impact on industry performance. PMHI showed that multiple inspections of the same unit in-state, out-of-state, and on-site raised costs and damaged interstate marketing. Variations in inspection were inevitable when identical units were inspected in different places or at different times. Individual inspectors interpreted and enforced the same code with different levels of strictness. Furthermore, only a minority of states with mobile home programs actively administered reciprocity in certification of manufacturers. Technological currency and interstate conformity were limited because most states lacked an automatic procedure for adopting amendments to ANSI A119.1. Differing state requirements forced manufacturers to produce the same model under various structural and mechanical standards or else overdesign to the toughest specifications. Either alternative increased the cost of mobile homes. State-by-state approval of new materials and processes also raised costs and discouraged innovation.

In addition, separate state administrative agencies for mobile home and factory-built housing subjected manufacturers that produced both types of housing to a wasteful duplication of time and effort.

While PMHI first identified and articulated many of these problems, groups affiliated with the mobile home industry also began to recognize these issues. At the same time, PMHI drew attention to the business potential of resolving industry problems through a unified national code. PMHI showed that uniform and efficient intrastate inspections could be achieved through a model training program for building officials, a viable funding and fee structure, and the development of cost-effective inspection methods and frequencies. Greater interstate uniformity of inspection could be achieved through a reciprocity system or a single third-party inspection system. Streamlining of the certification process for manufacturers' plans would eliminate the high cost of recertification by each state. In addition, cost-saving methods could be applied as quickly as possible through automatic nationwide acceptance of innovations in materials or methods that had been cleared by a single, sanctioned evaluation agency.

In addition to the PMHI initiative, the National Conference of States on Building Codes and Standards (NCSBCS) began encouraging states to adopt a single nationwide mobile home standard by consensus. NCSBCS had been formed in 1967 as an official interstate organization with delegates appointed by state governors. Created in response to the legitimate concerns of code enforcement officials, NCSBCS was committed to achieving building code uniformity by avoiding unnecessary differences in all areas of regulation and enforcement. In 1971, as part of this effort, NCSBCS asked the National Bureau of Standards (NBS) to evaluate various state mobile home and manufactured building standards. Following its analysis, NBS recommended the adoption of uniform interstate regulations for mobile homes and began developing a model enforcement program. Unfortunately, consensus agreement proved unworkable in the mobile home industry. In those cases when a consensus was reached, individual NCSBCS delegates would sometimes change a few provisions upon returning to their home state, thus rendering the agreement meaningless on a national level. Despite the efforts of NCSBCS, regulatory inconsistency continued to be costly, particularly for mobile home manufacturers with markets in more than one state.

Consequently, when Congress first began to discuss the idea of a federal mobile home code, it was greeted with support from the mobile home industry as well as consumer groups. In 1972 Representative Louis Frey, Jr. (R.-Fla.) introduced a bill to standardize mobile home building code regulation on a national scale. This action was partly prompted by insurance companies who realized that higher mobile home standards would mean lower insurance costs. Shortly thereafter Senator William E. Brock III (R.-Tenn.) introduced similar legislation in the Senate, but with a major difference. Representative Frey's bill allowed state and local codes to be equal to or more stringent than federal standards, but Senator Brock's bill required state and local codes to be equal to the federal standards. The mobile home industry supported the concept of total interstate reciprocity and endorsed Senator Brock's bill. Industry spokespeople also stressed the need for state participation in enforcement, recognizing that existing state enforcement agencies would need to adjust as rapidly as possible to the federal code.

The issue of mobile home standards was a popular subject in Congress from 1972 on. Shortly after the introduction of Representative Frey's bill, thirty cosponsors were gathered. At one point five bills dealing with mobile home safety legislation under separate sponsors were pending before Congress. Some of the proposed measures, like the one introduced by Senator Frank E. Moss (D.-Utah), would have imposed drastic changes. His bill would have grouped mobile homes with waffle irons and pep pills as "dangerous products" in the Product Safety Bill then before Congress. Senator Moss's bill failed to gain passage.

In 1973 Senator William Proxmire (D.-Wisc.) introduced a bill with stricter measures than Senator Brock's bill. The Proxmire bill was developed by the Center for Auto Safety, a Ralph Nader study group. Senator Proxmire's bill would have allowed states to set higher standards than those set in the federal code. The final Senate format, however, was a compromise between the Brock and Proxmire proposals. The bill enjoined HUD to develop the highest federal standards feasible but prohibited state and local standards that were not identical to the federal code.

Congressional legislation was finally passed as a compromise between the Brock-Proxmire bill in the Senate and a nearly identical but less stringent bill introduced by Representative Robert G. Stephens (D.-Ga.) in the House. The final compromise considerably softened the Proxmire version. For example, provisions were dropped for a federally required warranty and for two special HUD secretaries to deal with mobile homes; instead of requiring manufacturers to submit all plans to HUD for approval, the compromise only required manufacturers to certify their unit's compliance with the federal standards. Although the industry at first had somewhat hesitated to accept total federal regulation, both the industry and MHI cooperated fully in the drafting of the bill to assure themselves of a favorable standardization program.

The legislation became officially known as the National Mobile Home Construction and Safety Standards Act of 1974, Title VI of the Housing and Community Development Act of 1974. HUD was directed to establish a federal enforcement program and to formulate national construction and safety standards in consultation with the National Mobile Home Advisory Council, a group of representatives from the mobile home industry and from federal, state, and local governmental bodies concerned with mobile homes.

HUD published notice of its proposed rule making in the June 25, 1975, *Federal Register* and solicited public comment on the proposed standards, allowing thirty days for submission. Out of the more than 1000 comments received from mobile home manufacturers, suppliers, national code organizations, state and federal government agencies, consumer organizations, and individual consumers, 825 urged that ANSI A119.1 be adopted by reference as the federal mobile home standard. This overwhelming support of ANSI A119.1 affirmed its technical soundness.

HUD reacted responsively to these recommendations and based the federal technical standards on the ANSI code. Although it was clear that the adoption of a different set of federal standards would have perpetuated an even more difficult period of adjustment, HUD did not simply adopt the complete ANSI code by reference. One reason was HUD's concern that outright adoption of the ANSI mobile home standard would commit HUD to a de facto delegation of its authority to develop national standards. It must also be remembered that the ANSI code was the basis for the federal technical standards only because ANSI A119.1 does not include any enforcement procedures. HUD developed enforcement regulations based on an examination and consolidation of existing state procedures.

The new federal standards took effect on June 15, 1976. HUD made a conscious effort to keep the federal regulations reasonably compatible with the existing ANSI code. The federal code developed by HUD continues to be a performance code, permitting flexibility and innovation within the performance standards. In addition, HUD is aware of the need for more data in several areas of building code regulation, so provisions for systematic updating in tune with developing technology have been built into the code. Federal standards are expected to evolve in an orderly manner under the direction of the newly created HUD Office of Mobile Home Standards. Furthermore, HUD has acknowledged the expertise represented by the ANSI/NFPA Sectional Committee on Mobile Homes. HUD intends to use the committee's data and recommendations to formulate revisions in the code. This process allows HUD to continue to rely on the industry's aid in shaping the technical content of the mobile home code.

HUD has appointed NCSBCS as the contract agent to monitor the administration of federal standards at the state level, although HUD remains the final administrative authority. Local governments no longer play a direct role in mobile home regulation. The federal standard preempts all state and local regulations affecting mobile homes. States and localities may conduct their own construction and safety standards programs for building code areas not specifically covered by the federal standards, but only with the approval of HUD. In no case may states and localities amend the federal standards themselves.

States are encouraged to develop their own enforcement plan with the assistance of HUD. States having HUD-approved enforcement programs must grant reciprocity in their inspections: A mobile home inspected and certified as meeting the federal standards in any one state must be accepted for sale in all other states having HUD-approved programs. Reciprocity will help realize the full production and marketing potential of the mobile home industry; and the establishment of federal standards, along with authorized research and development, will further improve the safety, quality, and durability of the mobile home industry's product.

The federal code, however, does not promise to be an immediate panacea. Administrative inconsistencies may continue during the transition period because HUD has largely delegated code enforcement to the individual states. Ultimately, when the federal standards program is fully implemented, a manufacturer will no longer have to face costly duplicate approvals and inspections. This could mean a tremendous cost savings for manufacturers and consumers.

The development of a national performance building code was an important step for the mobile home industry, but its significance reaches beyond that industry. In the future all building construction may well be overseen by the federal government. Through the mobile home standards of Title VI, the federal government initiated its participation in building regulation outside of federally financed housing. It appears likely that the federal initiative on mobile homes will set a precedent for future building code regulation, especially when one examines the problems caused by diverse state and local regulations in the manufactured building industry. Just as the pendulum of regulatory power for mobile homes moved from the local to the state level and from the state to the federal level, the same movement could occur in the similar manufactured building industry.

Mobile homes and manufactured houses can be distinguished in terms of the industries involved. Confusing definitions have been a source of considerable trouble throughout the history of both industries because similar terms have been used to describe the two products. The generic term "manufactured building" refers to the componentized or panelized package (which is generally two-dimensional and is erected on-site) and the sectional building (which is three-dimensional and is often called modular building). The product of the manufactured building industry in the past was often known as prefabricated shelter but today is usually referred to as factory-built shelter. We use the terms manufactured building and factory-built housing interchangeably.

The mobile home industry, in contrast, primarily produces mobile homes. Terms continue to be somewhat misleading because some members of the industry have recently begun to rename mobile homes manufactured housing for the same public relations reasons that lay behind exchanging the term trailer coach for the term mobile home. Regardless of vocabulary, the manufactured building industry has shared many frustrations with the mobile home industry. Furthermore, mobile home manufacturers are increasingly including sectional units in their product lines. Many other mobile home manufacturers are connected to manufactured building firms under a shared corporate roof. Because similar distribution channels are used by both industries, regulation proceeding from the same governmental level could produce favorable results.

Until the recent past, when mobile home regulation advanced to the federal level, manufactured building regulation closely paralleled the evolution of mobile home codes. Factory-built shelter, however, remains regulated at the state level, subjected to much of the same kind of legislative chaos and multiplicity that has troubled traditional on-site building. Since colonial times, local governments have been the architects of building codes. All forms of building construction have historically been regulated at the local level based on the belief that municipalities should control their own environments. Most codes were drafted to cover all types of buildings, starting with conventional on-site structures. As a result, most lacked specific provisions for manufactured shelter. The control of manufactured shelter was arbitrarily left to traditional building codes, housing occupancy codes, or even zoning ordinances.

The situation has resulted in a hostile regulatory environment for the manufactured building industry. Local acceptance of technologically advanced shelter has been dependent on the maze of conventional building codes as well as the discretion of local building inspectors who interpret and, in some cases, amend codes. As a result, factory-built shelter has often been at the mercy of building inspectors, whose interests may be linked with those of local builders and material suppliers and who may be prejudiced against alien housing producers and production methods.

Municipal code writers and inspectors have also often been closely allied in outlook with local contractors and material producers. These groups often view building codes as a local concern intended to reflect and favor local needs and interests. Consequently, the local power structure has been a strong force in maintaining home rule and blocking attempts by state and local officials to preempt local jurisdiction with uniform statewide codes. The United States is unique among industrialized nations in its massive proliferation of local codes. It has been estimated that there are between 5500 and 8830 local codes in existence in the United States.[3] Code proliferation has resulted in a complicated tangle of obsolete, costly, and time-consuming regulations. Dissimilarity among codes of adjacent communities, differing interpretations of code provisions, political pressure causing administratively unsound decisions, and zoning exclusion by local interest groups are all factors creating a costly and confusing regulatory environment. If manufacturers build in accordance with the most stringent specifications, costs are inevitably increased for everyone.

Several national code associations now exist for the purpose of unifying building code regulation. Each advances a model building code that may be adopted on a mandatory or voluntary basis by states or localities according to their enabling legislation. The codes seek to incorporate current technology and protect the public safety. Each association includes representatives from its member states, usually appointed by the state government.

The oldest model code is the National Building Code, sponsored by the American Insurance Association. The Building Officials Conference of America (BOCA) sponsors the Basic Building Code, which is most influential in the eastern and north central states. The International Conference of Building Officials (ICBO) sponsors the Uniform Building Code, which is most influential in the western states. The Southern Building Code Congress (SBCC) sponsors the Southern Standard Building Code, which is most influential in the southern states. In addition to the fairly complete codes of these four associations, the National Fire Protection Agency (NFPA) publishes the National Electrical Code, the only nationally recognized electrical code.

Although few dispute the technical soundness of the national codes, the presence of four major codes inherently creates a significant problem. Even though the four code associations are widely respected within their member states, approval by one association does not necessarily guarantee approval by a local building inspector in one of the member states. Individual municipalities sometimes fail to update model codes and individual local inspectors sometimes amend codes. Until recently, the four code associations rarely approved complete systems because of the prohibitive testing expenses required of manufacturers. Only separate modules or components of a complete assembly were tested and approved. Accordingly, many local building inspectors were hesitant to approve an entire system. Furthermore, the codes contained enough differences that new methods and materials frequently were acceptable under one code but not under another.

Reacting to this inefficiency and expense, as well as to the growing nationwide housing shortage, factory-built housing advocates urged states to pass legislation aimed at greater uniformity in building code regulation. In 1967, the year it was formed, NCSBCS began to lobby for legislation to establish unified statewide building regulation for factory-built housing.

In 1972, in response to the aggressive actions of NCSBCS, three national model code publishers consolidated many parts of their codes. ICBO, BOCA, and SBCC established the Council of American Building Officials (CABO) to eliminate unnecessary code differences. CABO seeks to create a uniform code while maintaining regional autonomy. Considerable progress has already been made through CABO. For example, any new material or method found acceptable to one of the three code associations is then approved by the other two. CABO's actions, however, have not been successful enough to override the ongoing move toward state enactment of factory-built housing codes.

In 1969, in response to a congressional mandate to improve the national housing situation, HUD established Operation Breakthrough to encourage greater efficiency and use of new technology in industry. In particular HUD encouraged use of innovative procedures in the building industry. As one aspect of the program, HUD tried to furnish a supportive regulatory environment. By encouraging statewide factory-built housing codes, HUD sought to improve the efficiency of the total housing production and delivery process.

HUD's emphasis on statewide factory-built housing codes proved to be one of the most tangible benefits of Operation Breakthrough. Before Operation Breakthrough, no state had a uniform preemptive code; but in 1971 came the landmark California Factory-Built Housing Law, which established the first complete system of state approval and inspection of factory-built housing. The law enabled California manufacturers to circumvent the hundreds of different local codes. By the summer of 1972, twenty-seven states had enacted mandatory statewide regulations governing the use of factory-built housing.

In 1974, as part of HUD's efforts to bring about the passage of statewide laws and at the request of NCSBCS, the National Bureau of Standards developed and published a complete set of model documents for the evaluation and testing of factory-built housing. These documents provided states with a complete and authoritative model on which to base their factory-built housing codes. States can adopt such codes in one of two forms. The first type, formerly common among mobile home codes, is a mandatory preemptive state code in which any building meeting the minimum requirements of the state code must be accepted on the local level. The second type of model code is voluntary and relies on local jurisdictions to accept the model code. In either case there may or may not be a provision in the law regarding the rights of the local jurisdiction to amend the code without state approval.

As of September 1974, thirty-one states had either enabling legislation or pending legislation for statewide manufactured building codes. Finally, by the late 1970s the figure encompassed most states. Despite the encouraging prospects, the industry must ensure that individual state codes become fully uniform so that true reciprocity among states can be achieved. Fifty different state codes would, of course, be better than a multitude of local codes but would only achieve part of the potential benefit of a fully reciprocal code system for the entire United States. The federal government has not yet intervened directly to establish a factory-built housing code, but the passage of the federal mobile home safety and construction standards set a precedent that points significantly in that direction and this threat may energize state governments to achieve uniformity and full reciprocity on their own.

Title VI of the Housing and Community Development Act of 1974 directed HUD to create national mobile home construction and safety standards.[4] The standards are primarily based on ANSI A119.1 with further emphasis on energy conservation and fire safety features. The standards cover six basic areas: structural, plumbing, heating, electrical, fire safety, and energy conservation. HUD also makes provision for standardizing testing procedures. Each section provides a definition of terms and attempts to cover all significant design and construction issues. Performance standards are stressed rather than specification standards, that is, the code emphasizes quality standards stating how a system must perform but leaves the manufacturer free to fulfill them in a variety of ways rather than dictating itemized specifications on material types and quantities and assembly methods to be used.

Each section sets forth minimum performance standards for materials, fixtures, installation, and required capacity of each area.

B. Technical Regulations of the Mobile Home Building Code

Sometimes the code discusses other considerations such as accessibility of appliances and posting of operating instructions.

The structural standards contain an outline of fundamental provisions for architectural planning: floor area, lighting, ventilation, ceiling height, exits, windows, doors, and interior space. Body and frame construction standards are also evaluated from the standpoint of materials, equipment, and workmanship. The structural standards are based on strength and rigidity; protection against destructive forces such as corrosion, decay, and insects; protection against windstorms and resistance to other elements; and durability and economy of maintenance. The standards require the mobile home to be designed to withstand transportation shock and vibration. The code gives performance standards for assembly of springs, axles, brakes, and other parts subject to the adverse effects of transportation.

Plumbing standards concern the water supply, drain, waste, and vent systems. The code provides individual standards for joints, traps, fixtures, supports, water distribution, drainage, and venting.

The heating, cooling, and fuel burning standards pertain to all systems installed inside or outside the mobile home. The code discusses fuel supply, gas piping, installation of heat-producing appliances, cooling appliances, venting and combustion air systems, and circulating air systems.

The electrical standards largely refer back to the NFPA's National Electric Code (which was incorporated into the ANSI code, as previously explained). Issues involving power supply, circuiting, protective equipment, receptacle outlets, wiring methods, and calculations for computing supply cord and distribution-panelboard loads are covered in the code.

The fire safety segment deals with measures intended to protect occupants through reduced fire hazards and increased detection methods. Flame spread limitations, combustibility of materials, and location of fire detection equipment are the chief considerations.

The thermal protection section examines energy conservation standards for the mobile home. It sets out requirements for condensation control, air infiltration, thermal insulation and heat loss, as well as regulations for making heat gain and cooling calculations.

The testing section stipulates standards for testing structure load, roof trusses, glass surface areas, exit windows, and doorways.

The code is generally performance oriented, although there are occasionally explicit specifications. Usually one finds guidelines such as those given in the description of drawbar design for protection against transportation hazards, which represents a typical performance approach: "The drawbar shall be constructed of sufficient strength, ridigity and

durability to safely withstand those dynamic forces experienced during highway transportation. It shall be securely fastened to the mobile home frame by either a continuous weld or by bolting." Elsewhere the code refers to accepted engineering practices or already established codes. For example, the section on testing covers workmanship of swinging exterior passage doors: "All construction methods, materials and workmanship shall be in conformance with accepted engineering practices to insure durable, livable and safe housing."

At times, however, the federal code does run counter to the performance orientation of ANSI by adding precise specifications regarding materials or assembly. For example, the plumbing systems section gives specifications for antisiphon trap vent materials: "Cap and housing shall be listed acrylonitrile-butadiene styrene, DWV grade; stem shall be DWV grade nylon or acetal; spring shall be stainless steel wire, type 302; sealing disc shall be neoprene, conforming to ASTM C 564-70, or, silicone rubber, low and high temperature and tear resistant, conforming to F.S. ZZ-R-765B and MIL-L-10547."

It is informative to compare HUD's economic impact statement summary for the federal mobile home construction and safety standards with impact estimates made by the mobile home industry. Following congressional mandate, HUD examined cost, productivity, competition, employment, and energy consumption under the new code. The study concludes that the new regulations will add approximately $380 to the retail price of a typical mobile home, or a total gross increase of approximately $1 billion over five years. It is estimated that fuel savings from additional insulation will total $300 million; at the cost of $200 million for insulation materials, the standards are expected to result in net savings of approximately $100 million to the public. HUD points out that future savings from reduced insurance and maintenance charges and increased life expectancy of mobile homes through improved durability will also offset the cost increase. HUD notes that manufacturing to meet the standards will not cause a significant increase in energy consumption. Negligible effect is expected on materials and supplies. Furthermore, HUD concludes competition will be enhanced by eliminating restrictions on interstate commerce arising from conflicting state regulations and inspection procedures. Lastly, the study estimates 2.3 percent increase in workers (approximately 1370 workers) for the same level of production (five hundred thousand units per year). HUD claims the standards will mean decreased depreciation and higher resale value on mobile homes, decreased insurance costs, decreased warranty costs, decreased human and material losses not covered by insurance or warranty, decreased maintenance and repair costs, decreased energy consumption, and increased acceptance of mobile homes within communities because of their higher quality. HUD admits higher installation costs may result from compliance with the new federal standard but notes that HUD's authority applies only to mobile homes and does not extend to installation procedures such as anchoring.

Industry estimates on the economic impact of the new regulations differ sharply from HUD's calculated estimates. The MHI maintained that the $380 retail price increase was an underestimate. A mid-1976 survey of mobile home retailers tried to determine the cost impact of HUD regulations on homes sold.[5] The responses from sixty dealers showed no real agreement. Dealers reported cost increases ranging from $80 to $1500. Five dealers reported $400 increases, five reported $300 increases, five reported $200 to $400 increases, and four reported $1000 increases. Forty of the responding dealers attributed the increased costs not last to increased administrative burden. At the same time, however, more than two-thirds of the respondents felt the new HUD regulations would improve the industry's image. More important, and the increased cost arguments notwithstanding, by the late 1970s the mobile home industry began to realize that it had gained the all-important national uniformity in code content.

C. Procedural and Enforcement Regulations of the Mobile Home Building Code

Title VI of the Housing and Community Development Act of 1974 authorized HUD to establish federal mobile home construction and safety standards and to promulgate procedural and enforcement regulations.[6] The standards and regulations, known as the National Mobile Home Construction and Safety Standards Act, apply to all mobile homes manufactured for sale in the United States on or after June 15, 1976.[7] The act preempts all existing statewide mobile home codes and obviates passage of any future state or local codes.

Organizational Structure

HUD has delegated all authority except the power to sue and be sued to its Assistant Secretary for Consumer Affairs and Regulatory Functions (CARF). HUD established the Office of Mobile Home Standards as a central source for code development, enforcement, and information. The CARF assistant secretary names the director of the office.

The standards begin with a careful definition of terms, particularly those pertaining to faulty manufacture. Safety hazards and defects are carefully differentiated by level of severity. Noncompliance is defined as a failure to comply with the code that does not constitute a defect, serious defect, or imminent safety hazard. A defect is a failure to comply with the code that does not pose an unreasonable risk of injury or death to occupants. A serious defect is a failure to comply with the code that does pose an unreasonable risk of injury or death to occupants. An imminent safety hazard is a hazard that may or may not be related to failure to comply with the code but that poses an unreasonable risk of injury or death.

The code does not govern imported mobile homes, mobile homes intended for export, or recreational vehicles.[8] Add-on units such as car ports, cabanas or extra rooms attached to the mobile home after it has left the factory (for example, by the dealer or the user) are not covered by the code, but the regulations note that HUD in the future may choose to govern add-on units.

It may be of general interest to note that the enforcement regulations provide for a blanket authority to impose civil penalties, criminal penalties, and injunctive actions for failure to comply with the rules and regulations.

The act prohibits states from having laws on mobile home construction and safety standards unless they are identical with federal standards. This provision guarantees full reciprocity among states by forbidding preemption of federal authority through stricter or more lenient state standards. States are encouraged to participate in the program as State Administrative Agencies (SAAs) or Primary Inspection Agencies (PIAs), but states may not establish independent inspection procedures outside federal regulations. States may, however, have consumer protection regulations such as warranty requirements, which are not considered a part of the federal enforcement system.

Disclosure of Information

The act seeks to protect manufacturers' right to privacy; the disclosure of trade secrets or confidential commercial and financial information could put a manufacturer at a competitive disadvantage. The Secretary of HUD is responsible for determining what information on safety issues and faulty manufacture shall be available to the public and is also responsible for judging requests for nondisclosure of information.

Rule-making Procedure

Any interested person is welcome to participate in the rule amendment or repeal process by submitting comments in writing. Within 180 days of receipt of a proposal, the Secretary must initiate rule making or deny the proposal and notify the petitioner, unless further deliberation is necessary. When appropriate, "advance notice" and "notice" bulletins are posted for all rule making and proposed rule making. HUD also issues bulletins to interpret ambiguous standards when necessary. After any final ruling is made, a petition for "reconsideration of final rule" may be submitted within 60 days of publication of the rule in the *Federal Register*. The Secretary of HUD may grant or deny the petition with or without opportunity for further submission of comments.

The HUD regulations are constructed to provide ample opportunity to bring issues forward and to maximize public participation. Several levels exist through which interested persons may make their views known. There are two basic procedures, the informal and nonadversary "presentation of views" and the formal and adversary "hearings." The presentation of views may be written or may include oral presentation of evidence; it is intended to gather information to "allow fully informed decision making," but it is not carried out under oath or subject to cross-examination. The presiding officer has ten days to give the Secretary of HUD documentary materials, transcript, and a recommendation; the Secretary then has thirty days to make a final determination with a statement of findings and appropriate order.

At a hearing witnesses testify under oath and may be cross-examined at the presiding officer's discretion. The presiding officer files an initial written decision with statement of findings and appropriate order. This constitutes the final determination, unless the Secretary of HUD modifies or reverses the order.

All hearings and presentation of views are open to the public unless the secretary of HUD deems otherwise. "Notice" of hearings and presentation of views gives the name of the presiding officer and indicates what format will be used to allow interested persons to participate. In all cases any interested person may participate in writing and may participate in the oral presentation unless the presiding officer decides it would delay proceedings or "prejudice the rights of the parties directly involved."

Beyond the presentation of views or the hearing is the investigation. A formal investigation and inquiry involving an alleged, suspected, or threatened violation is a totally formal procedure. Any person may petition the Secretary of HUD to open an investigation or may file a statement with the Secretary once an investigation has begun. The Secretary may issue subpoenas requiring testimony or attendance of a witness and may issue subpoenas requiring access to documents. The transcripts are open to the public unless the Secretary deems otherwise.

Manufacturers participate in a system of design approvals and inspections intended to assure that mobile homes conform to the federal standards. There are two types of Primary Inspection Agencies (PIAs) that oversee manufacturers. The Design Inspection Primary Inspection Agencies (DAPIAs) evaluate and approve or disapprove mobile home designs, quality control procedures, and quality control manuals. The Production Inspection Primary Inspection Agencies (IPIAs) evaluate and provide surveillance over manufacturers' ability to produce mobile homes according to approved designs and follow approved quality control procedures. An individual organization may perform both DAPIA and IPIA functions. Either states or third-party agents may be PIAs. A manufacturer enters contracts with as many DAPIAs as it wishes and with enough IPIAs to provide services for each manufacturing plant, but with only one IPIA to a plant. Fees are established between the manufacturer and PIA or by the state if the state is acting as exclusive IPIA.

The DAPIA performs the design and manual approval. The manufacturer submits a copy of each mobile home design and each quality assurance manual for evaluation by the DAPIA of its choice. For the design the manufacturer submits all the information the DAPIA requires, including construction drawings or specifications or both; materials specifications; structural analysis and calculations; test data or other methods used to validate the design; heat loss calculations; floor plans showing fire safety features; diagrams of fuel, water, waste, and vent systems, showing materials and safety equipment; wiring diagrams; air flow diagrams; chassis design; performance ratings of appliances; hookup and installation; and report of tests conducted to show the mobile home conforms to federal performance standards. The DAPIA also inspects the quality assurance manual, which includes descriptions of the manufacturer's quality assurance program, tests, accountability, and manufacturing process. If the design information or quality assurance manual is incomplete, the manufacturer must submit supplemental information. If a manufacturer wants to change a design or quality assurance manual, the DAPIA must approve the design or manual before production for sale begins. All information submitted to the DAPIA may be prepared either by the manufacturer's staff or by outside consultants. The consultants may include DAPIAs, but not the DAPIA that will be performing approvals for the product.

The IPIA performs the factory inspection. The manufacturer provides the IPIA for each plant with copies of the DAPIA-approved quality assurance manual and the DAPIA-approved drawings and specifications. The factory inspection is then conducted based on the DAPIA-approved articles. A design or manual approved by any one DAPIA must be accepted nationwide by all IPIAs. The product must conform with the DAPIA-approved articles, and the manufacturer must make adjustments to conform if the IPIA issues a deviance report. The IPIA must make a complete inspection of the manufacture of at least one mobile home through all operations of the factory. Furthermore, IPIAs are responsible for ongoing surveillance, with visits scheduled so every mobile home is inspected at some stage of the production process. Inspections are made by one or more engineers who have reviewed the design and an inspector who has been briefed on the design. The IPIA issues a certification report once any necessary corrections are made to IPIA satisfaction, and certification labels are then affixed by the manufacturer or IPIA to completed mobile homes. The manufacturer must furnish the dealer or distributor with certification that the mobile home conforms to federal standards. Any IPIA-certified home must be accepted by any unit of government nationwide.

A manufacturer may request a presentation of views or a hearing when it disagrees with DAPIA or IPIA evaluations but may not continue to produce mobile homes under the unapproved plans. The manufacturer is required to cooperate with DAPIA, IPIA, or state and federal administrative officials in the course of investigation or remedial action. A manufacturer may be requested to notify mobile home owners and dealers of any nonconformity, defect, serious defect, or imminent safety hazard and furthermore may be required to correct the deviant elements.

Dealer and Distributor Responsibilities

Dealers or distributors (that is, any intermediaries between manufacturer and user) may not sell, lease, or offer to sell or lease any mobile homes they know do not conform with the federal standards. The ruling does not, however, apply to used mobile homes. If a dealer already possesses a faulty mobile home or is notified of faults in a mobile home, the manufacturer is responsible for correcting the items in question. Dealers who receive a customer complaint or who otherwise believe they have a faulty product must refer the matter to the manufacturer. The dealer or distributor may not alter the mobile home to create a deviance from federal standards, and no mobile home may be put on the market until all deviances are corrected.

State Administrative Agencies

The HUD code is designed to ensure that any state wishing to participate directly in the overall administration of the approval and inspection program may do so by making application to become a State Administrative Agency (SAA). An SAA is a state agency that has been approved to carry out an individual state plan for enforcement of federal regulations. The application procedure requires a description of the state agency that will be responsible for enforcement and an outline of procedures for notification, fees, complaint oversight, and remedial actions. These must be in accordance with federal guidelines. SAAs are required to perform monthly reports on their monitoring, notification, and correction activities; their hearings and presentations; and their handling of consumer complaints. In addition, a state has the option of performing a number of other possible functions, although the federal program does no more than suggest that these other functions be included in the state plan to provide consumer protection and safety assurances. It strongly urges SAAs to develop provisions for monitoring dealers' lots for transit damage, seal tampering, and dealer performance; approving alterations to make sure they comply with standards; monitoring final on-site installation (setup as well as hookup) of mobile homes to make sure it is being done properly; inspecting used mobile homes; and regulating certain aspects of mobile home transportation over the road.

Once a state plan is approved, HUD monitors state performance and has the right to withdraw approval of a state plan that has become inadequate. If a state decides to stop participating after being accepted into the program, the state must give HUD ninety-day notice. By the late 1970s most states participated as SAAs, indicating that HUD's respect for home rule had been a wise move.

The HUD code delineates specific application procedures for states or private organizations wishing to qualify as PIAs. HUD approves and monitors the proposed organizations after receiving applications describing the fee schedules, tests, reports, and evaluations they would make. Any state with an SAA may monopolize IPIA activities: A state accepted as an IPIA may act as the exclusive IPIA in the state. Without an SAA the state may still perform these functions but may not exclude competition from private agencies. Any state with an SAA may also act as a DAPIA but may not monopolize DAPIA activities. Separate fee schedules are established for the two functions.

An organization applying for approval as a DAPIA must submit a mobile home design and quality assurance manual it has approved or evaluated. An organization applying for approval as an IPIA must submit a certification or evaluation report on a mobile home plant. An organization that has not inspected mobile homes previously may be accepted "on the basis of the qualifications of its personnel and its commitment to perform the required functions." A private organization must submit a statement of its background experience, personnel, and engineers. HUD requires the organization to testify that there are no conflicts of interest that might hinder impartial judgment.

DAPIA approval is given by stamp or authorized signature on the manufacturer's documents. IPIA approval is given by a certification report, after which the IPIA continuously provides the manufacturer with a two- to four-week supply of labels. The sequentially numbered 2-inch by 4-inch aluminum plate certifying inspection is attached to the mobile home so it cannot be removed and reused. IPIAs must account for all labels and be able to identify the serial number of each mobile home to which an identification plate has been attached. The IPIA must also make sure each mobile home

Primary Inspection Agency Procedures

has a data plate furnished by the manufacturer that identifies the manufacturing plant, serial number of the unit, date of manufacture, and various other statistics.

Federal monitoring is intended to check the continued acceptability of PIAs. When a PIA is disqualified because of inadequate work, HUD tries to assure that the manufacturing process is not disrupted.

Consumer Complaints and Remedial Actions

Consumer complaints about faulty mobile homes are sent directly to the manufacturer so the manufacturer can begin to take remedial actions as soon as possible. The manufacturer is responsible for assessing and classifying the severity of a complaint within ten days. The manufacturer must determine whether there is an imminent safety hazard, serious defect, defect, or noncompliance and then notify the inquiring parties. If there is a faulty situation, the manufacturer must determine whether the problem is unique to the one mobile home in question or other mobile homes are affected.

A problem unique to one mobile home must be corrected within thirty days. If it is not unique, the problem must be reported within five days, including a statement from the IPIA to the SAA where homes are located. If homes are located in more than one state, the report is sent to the SAA where they were manufactured. If manufactured in more than one state or if there is no SAA, then the report must be sent to HUD.

The Secretary of HUD makes the final determination classifying imminent safety hazards or serious defects; the SAA or Secretary of HUD decides on defects and noncompliance. If a consumer complaint is referred to the SAA or Secretary of HUD, these agencies then contact the manufacturer. The manufacturer must explain whether it knew of the complaint and what action was taken; if it did not know of the complaint, it is requested to classify the complaint. Manufacturers must correct at their own expense any imminent safety hazard or serious defect related to design or assembly or reimburse owners who have already made the correction on their own. Manufacturers must notify purchasers through a statement that classifies and locates the problem and mentions precautions, repair facts and instructions, potential hazards, and risk evaluations. For all affected mobile homes, a manufacturer has thirty days to repair an imminent safety hazard or serious defect and sixty days to repair a defect or noncompliance, dating from the discovery or final determination. If repair cannot take place in that time, the manufacturer must either replace the mobile home with its equivalent in size and condition or take possession of the mobile home and refund the purchase price, minus depreciation for homes used over one year. The manufacturer is also responsible for remedial actions on mobile homes that have been released to dealers but not yet sold to purchasers.

HUD monitors PIAs through joint monitoring teams comprising personnel supplied by SAAs and HUD. Seventeen three-member teams monitor all PIAs. The teams include one representative from each of three participating states who visit each plant to monitor the PIAs. The members of each team must combine among them expertise in the mechanical, electrical, structural, and plumbing fields. These teams operate on a regional basis. As with SAAs, states are encouraged but not required to participate. States may monitor IPIAs if the state is not acting as an IPIA. The monitoring parties randomly review at least 10 percent of the design and quality assurance manual approvals made by DAPIAs. They also assure that IPIAs are carrying out effective inspections as far as frequency and maintaining complete label control. The teams also review remedial action records of manufacturers and PIAs.

Each PIA must be monitored four times per year unless HUD asserts that a PIA's performance is superior, in which case the monitoring may be decreased to a minimum of once per year. Reports are submitted regularly by manufacturers, IPIAs, and SAAs. The manufacturer submits a monthly report to the IPIA giving serial numbers and locations of all mobile homes manufactured the previous month. Each month the IPIA must send a report to the SAA, or to HUD if there is no SAA, giving the numbers provided by each manufacturer and the number of inspection visits made and faulty mobile homes discovered the previous month. The SAA also files a monthly report to HUD giving status of hearings, of presentation of views, and of legal actions, as well as describing oversight activities, consumer complaints, and corrective actions. HUD's oversight over SAAs and PIAs is maintained by reviewing SAA reports and monitoring reports on PIAs. The act instructs the Secretary of HUD to make random visits to oversee the activities of SAAs and the Secretary's agent.

Departmental Oversight and Monitoring of PIAs

Coordination of the federal enforcement standards has been delegated to NCSBCS, which began operating under an initial five-year contract of approximately $7 million. State or private agencies received about $6.5 million of the total sum through NCSBCS for their participation. After the phase-in period, NCSBCS's funds are being raised by charging a $19 labeling fee for every mobile home manufactured and a $2000 membership fee from each member state. NCSBCS funds state participation mainly through a $32,000-per-year contract between NCSBCS and the state and secondarily through NCSBCS reimbursement for per diem and travel expenses.

HUD has emphasized its commitment, as set forth by Congress in Title VI, to develop a program to maximize state participation. It

Funding

stated this clearly in the *Federal Register* before the standards took effect in 1976, despite a number of objections from manufacturers and other parties who felt that the system would be simplified by eliminating SAAs. The objecting parties feared that the existence of SAAs in some states but not mandatory throughout would pose confusion in reporting procedures.

State participation in enforcement is wholly optional, albeit the only fiscally rational alternative. If a state elects not to participate, it loses any rights to inspection or design approval. All revenue generated from regulatory activities then reverts to a third-party regulator. A state participating in the program as a PIA controls intrastate mobile home enforcement and keeps 90 percent of the funds generated by the $19 label fee. Given these incentives, extensive state participation seems likely. This would guarantee reciprocity throughout the United States and remove all restrictions on interstate mobile home commerce.

Although the HUD procedural and enforcement rules will ultimately give a simplified regulatory structure to the mobile home production system, many of the problems characteristic of pre-HUD days will persist regardless of federal coordination because enforcement procedures remain based on the state mobile home programs of the immediate past. Differently trained inspectors, corrupt third-party agents, and differing interpretations of the law will continue to crop up and pose enforcement problems.

If the federal standards program works to its full potential, a manufacturer will no longer have to face costly duplication of approval and inspection. Instead there will be one plan approval, one label, one data plate, and one review. If the mobile home industry can submit plans to and be inspected by one agency and thereby be automatically approved by all other states with no further submissions, the potential savings could amount to tens of millions of dollars.

D. Policy Alternatives

As the federal mobile home standard becomes an accepted way of life for industry and government alike, the predictable consequences are coming to pass: Firms and associations in the other subsystems of the building sector, on-site and factory-built housing producers, are also beginning to press for nationwide codes.[9] This impulse is logical but unfortunate. Although on-site and other off-site builders have dreamed of uniform, nationwide codes ever since the early decades of this century, accelerating the push now is, in our judgment, a premature if not a dangerous action.

Before there is further pressure for nationwide codes, the existing model codes in the other building sector subsystems must be refined and must undergo more field testing.

In hindsight the federal standards now seem to have turned out a blessing to the mobile home industry, but it must be remembered that this blessing was the product of historical accident. Luckily, when Congress empowered HUD to develop a mobile home code, HUD had the wisdom to base the technical code on the excellent code already developed within the industry itself. Given blanket authority by Congress, HUD could have decided on a specification-oriented code such as the ones that now exist in many local sectors of the building industry. Taking a pessimistic view, HUD could have wasted consumers' money and manufacturers' time by choosing to rewrite laws from scratch, overlooking the existence of the thorough industry code. At worst, HUD might have created a new code that could have seriously handicapped the mobile home industry.

The other subsystems of the building sector must learn from the example of the mobile home industry and perfect their existing model codes. The factory-built shelter codes developed by NBS and NCSBCS look promising at this point, and the on-site codes developed by the major code-writing associations also seem viable. All of these model codes would benefit from further observation of the refinements suggested by the successes and failures of the federal mobile home standards trial enforcement machinery. The federal mobile home standards encountered relatively few problems because a good, debugged code was present and ready for adoption. If on-site and factory-built housing producers demand a national code before they have perfected their model codes, they risk undesirable intervention. An incomplete, inefficient, untested, or otherwise imperfect code invites the danger of having a modified code imposed on the industry, a code created by an outside, possibly unsympathetic, state or federal government agency.

Who should take the initiative of working for building code uniformity? We do not recommend that the industries wait for the federal government. Intervention and enforcement at the federal level should only be regarded as the regulator of last resort. We generally favor state government as the upper limit of authority rather than federal government preemption of state authority, and we deplore the fact that the federal government did step into code regulation of the mobile home industry. Nevertheless, the federal government felt compelled to intervene because of the chaotic condition of state regulation of mobile home construction. Aside from general respect for home rule, there is the more pragmatic realization that federal supervision of the mobile home industry at the present level of involvement usefully coordinates state participation in the general program without encroaching on state autonomy. HUD involvement in the other building sector subsystems would at best be useful as a temporary catalytic force, if the federal government steps back once uniformity is taken for granted and enforcement authority is returned to the state governments.

HUD's intervention in the mobile home industry should be regarded as a warning. Such intervention is likely elsewhere only if state governments and the building industry subsystems fail to create effective code regulatory systems. By the same token, if a workable system can be devised jointly by industry and a national body such as NCSBCS, then the likelihood of federal intervention is forestalled. The rest of the building industry must not look toward Uncle Sam as a panacea because the outcome might not be as lucky as in the mobile home industry's case.

The move toward national code uniformity must follow a cautious and logical sequence. First, the mobile home regulatory system must be given several years to mature. At present some 60 percent of all mobile home plants also produce modular units or sectionals subject to BOCA or similar codes. For this reason the first move should be toward a code regulatory system for modulars and sectionals, a code system compatible with the mobile home production standards. We can expect that the mobile home standards will have been fine-tuned and functioning smoothly by the mid-1980s. Then, at least at the individual plant level, other building codes will be able to operate compatibly. Only after some years pass to permit maturation of this expanded system should nationally uniform performance-type codes be introduced by and for the remainder of the manufactured building industry and the on-site building industry. If this scenario seems slow, it must be remembered that it took more than forty years for the mobile home code to come of age. It was in 1937 that the NFPA formed the original committee on trailers and trailer camps that in time evolved into the first mobile home standards.

There are basically only two policy alternatives as we approach the 1980s: pushing too hard for an immediate nationwide code governing all building construction and probably resulting in an injurious situation or moving continuously and slowly toward a national code, building on previous experience, and finally achieving the dream of efficient code regulation.

Notes to Chapter 18

1. The MHI was known until 1975 as the Mobile Home Manufacturers Association (MHMA).

2. Formally published as ANSI A119.1/NFPA 501B *Standard for Mobile Homes.*

3. "Building Codes are Like Rabbits," *Automation in Housing,* October 1976, p.41.

4. Organization of the material on construction and safety standards is largely taken from the structure of the HUD code as it appears in U.S. National Archives, *Federal Register,* Vol. 40, No.

244, December 18, 1975, pp.58751–58792. The important revisions appear in the following *Federal Registers:* Vol. 41, No. 236, December 7, 1976; Vol. 41, No. 249, December 27, 1976; Vol. 41, No. 252, December 30, 1976. HUD intends to publish the regulations as a single volume.

5. "Dealers Appraise HUD Regulations," *Mobile-Modular Housing Dealer,* August 1976, pp.52–54.

6. Organization of the material on procedural and enforcement regulation is largely taken from the structure of the HUD code as it appears in U.S. National Archives, *Federal Register,* Vol. 41, No. 94, May 13, 1976, pp. 19845–19877.

7. A mobile home is defined in the May 13, 1976 *Federal Register* as "a structure, transportable in one or more sections, which when erected on site measure eight feet or more in width and designed to be used as a dwelling, with or without a permanent foundation, when connected to the required utilities and includes the plumbing, heating, air-conditioning, and electrical systems contained therein." Mobile homes subject to the effective date of the standards are defined as those that entered the first state of production on or after June 15, 1976.

8. A recreational vehicle is defined in the May 13, 1976 *Federal Register* as "a vehicle regardless of size, which is not designed to be used as a permanent dwelling, and in which the plumbing, heating, air-conditioning, and electrical system contained therein may be operated without connection to outside utilities and which are self propelled or towed by a light duty vehicle".

9. "National Code," *Manufactured Housing Newsletter,* October 21, 1977, pp.1–2.

The mobile home, like any other home, is a permanent dwelling. Unlike other homes, however, the mobile home is moved at least once—from the factory to its permanent site. Consequently, the mobile home industry is greatly affected by transportation regulations. Although the initial move may be over land, sea, or even through the air, the use of railroads, ships, and crane helicopters is very much limited at this time. Highway transportation is still the chief transportation method. For this reason we shall focus on the impact of highway regulation on the mobile home industry.

The two facets of the mobile home industry most affected by highway regulation are the industry's economic performance and the industry's responsiveness to users' needs. If governmental units legislate unnecessarily restrictive regulations, the industry must make extra expenditures in order to comply; if governmental units do not allow the wider homes on the highways, the industry cannot give consumers the functionally better layouts associated with wider mobile homes.

Highway regulation is the concern of various governmental units, the most prominent of which is the state. Each state imposes certain restrictions, regulations, and controls on the use of its highways in order to ensure the safety and convenience of its residents. Although these controls may in some cases burden interstate commerce, the Constitution assures an individual state's right to regulate its highways. In some cases Congress may determine that the burdens imposed on interstate commerce by state highway regulations are too great and then may curtail the state's regulatory power. In this curtailment Congress must weigh the state's authority to regulate its own highways against the congressional authority to improve interstate commerce.

All states exert some level of control over the movement of mobile homes on their highways. State highway regulations usually state maximum dimensions, permits, or special considerations for oversized vehicles (those exceeding the maximum dimensions).

Dimension Limitations

Every state sets dimension limitations for vehicles using its highways. Commonly regulated dimensions are the load length, the combination length (hauling vehicle length plus load length), the width, and the height. The maximum dimensions for vehicles without permits vary from state to state. They range as shown in table 19.1. Mobile homes that do not exceed the maximum size limitations are subject only to the normal controls imposed on all vehicles using state highways. Those mobile homes with dimensions exceeding the maximum limits are known as oversized vehicles and transporters must obtain permits to move them over the highways. Because nearly all mobile homes exceed the maximum dimensions, state permit

arrangements have significant impact on the economics of the mobile home industry.

The maximum dimensions for vehicles with a permit also vary from state to state. They range as shown in table 19.1. Those mobile homes with dimensions exceeding these limits may not travel the highways. Height limitations are generally based upon overpass clearances. Most mobile homes are not troubled by height regulations. Weight limitations similarly do not usually present problems. Length limitations, however, are more constraining because the maximum limits vary so widely. For example, although about one-half of the states set a maximum combined length of 85 feet, several states allow 95 feet and New Mexico allows 101 feet. Throughout the United States as the length of mobile homes has increased, the length of the trucks hauling them has decreased in order to comply with maximum combined length restrictions. Thus 70-foot mobile homes are sometimes hauled by trucks measuring 5 feet in length.

The most severe constraint for a mobile home is the width restriction because the width of the mobile home is absolutely limited by the width allowed on the highway. A maximum width of 12 feet is allowed in all states. But as recently as 1975 only thirty-nine states allowed 14-foot-wide mobile homes, and a PMHI survey of mobile home manufacturing company presidents in that year showed that manufacturers generally did not like 14-wides because of the commercial limitations. They could not be sold in states that prohibited transportation of 14-wides; and in those states that limited transportation to a maximum width of 14 feet, architectural amenities, such as overhanging roofs, had to be sacrificed to meet width restrictions. By 1977 all states except Hawaii and California allowed 14-wide movements.

Permits

Permits are issued by each state to allow the transportation of oversized vehicles on state highways, subject to special restrictions.

Table 19.1.
Maximum Dimension Ranges for Vehicles without and with Permits, 1977

Dimension	Vehicles without Permits	Vehicles with Permits
Mobile home length	33'–60'[a]	67'6"–85'[d]
Combined length	50'–75'[b]	85'–101'[e]
Width	8'–8'6"[c]	12'–16'[a]
Height	12'6"–14'	13'6"–15'[a]

a. Some states no limit.
b. 2 states no limit.
c. Alabama allows 12' w.
d. Most states no limit.
e. Many states no limit.

Because all states except Alabama set maximum widths ranging between 8 feet and 8 feet 6 inches, virtually all mobile homes are classified as oversized and therefore require special permits. A permit must be obtained from each state the mobile home will travel through. Sometimes application must be made to an additional agency of the state, such as the highway authority, if the mobile home is to be transported on a special route. Thus at least one permit is always required from each state and sometimes more are needed. In forty-eight states the permit application may be made by mail or telegraph. In six states the permit application must be made by mail or in person. Five states allow permits to be obtained at ports of entry. Two states allow the mobile home carrier to proceed without permit to the nearest office where the permit can be obtained.

Permit issuance procedures vary from state to state but are generally discretionary. The permits often specify route restrictions, equipment requirements, and a bond or proof of insurance or financial responsibility. Twenty-eight states now issue extended permits to licensed manufacturers, dealers, and mobile home transporters for the movement of several mobile homes. More often, however, a separate permit must be obtained for each mobile home transported. The duration of the single-trip permit varies from state to state. Single-trip permits that do specify duration range from one to fifteen days. Twenty-six states do not specify a standard amount of time but may specify on the individual permits.

Traffic Regulations

When transporting an oversized mobile home through differents states, the carrier must comply not only with the regulations imposed by each state on all normal-sized vehicles but also with the many traffic regulations imposed on oversized vehicles. The different regulations of each state the mobile home passes through must be followed. To transport an oversized mobile home, even with a permit, most states require flagmen, pilot cars, or both. Flagmen are frequently required at bridges and blind curves. Twenty-six states require one escort vehicle following or preceding the mobile home under certain conditions. Nineteen states require two escorts (front and rear) under certain conditions. Only six states do not require any escort at all.

The transportation of a mobile home is almost universally limited to daylight hours during weekdays. Travel is usually restricted on legal holidays and frequently on the days preceding and following such holidays. Many cities, especially those using an interstate highway as an expressway, restrict movement of mobile homes during rush hours.

Permits will frequently state a specific route that must be followed. In several states mobile homes may not use the interstate

Figure 19.1.
A traffic regulation sign for mobile home transporters only.

highways. In other states mobile homes may not use highways that carry a heavy load of public traffic. A few states prohibit all oversized mobile homes unless the final delivery is within the state. To handle such cases, transporters sometimes obtain a permit by claiming the mobile is to be delivered to a site just within the far borders of the state. On reaching that point, the transporter continues on out of the state without a permit, at the risk of a heavy fine.

State equipment requirements are equally complex. In most states all trailers, including mobile homes, are required to have assorted rear and side clearance lights or reflectors, flares or other warning devices, electrical or mechanical turn signals, and brake lights that can be seen from behind the trailer. Mobile homes may be required to have brakes on a specified number of axles or to use specific types of tow hitches. Most states require wide load signs and warning flags. Radio communication between escorts and hauler is often required.

The complexity of this system is obvious. For example, suppose a manufacturer is delivering a mobile home through four states. Assume that one state requires brakes on two axles and the others require brakes on only one axle. The transporter must install the extra set of brakes at the outset or else be prepared to stop and install them when entering the more restrictive state. Cost and inconvenience result as transporters comply with the most stringent state requirements.

At the same time, transporters are severely hampered by redundant state regulations. If a carrier moves through four states, each of which requires different wording, lettering, or coloring of wide load signs (as many states do), the carrier must bring a different sign for each state and must stop to switch signs before crossing state lines. As can be seen, equipment requirements force interstate transporters to expend a large amount of unnecessary labor in complying with inconsistent regulations. In addition, to change signs, replace warning flags, or reposition lights, the transporter must carry not only the equipment but also the correct tools—including a stepladder to reach signs. Even if laws are not strictly enforced, noncompliant carriers always run the risk of being caught.

B. Emerging Trends

Dimension Limitations

The trend in dimension limitations has been toward the longer and wider mobile home units. Use of longer and wider units may be the result of consumer demand or industry pressure, but certainly the increased number of superhighways and the increased number of highway safety devices have influenced the trend; public safety and convenience are no longer as adversely affected by the oversized units as they were in the past. Tables 19.2 and 19.3 document the emerging trends in state highway regulation of normal and oversized vehicles. (Our discussions and tabulations do not include Hawaii because there are so few mobile homes in this state that its regulatory system is not developed.)

Comparisons of the 1977 situation with that of 1972 show that in no state has the legal load length, combination length, or width for normal-sized vehicles decreased. Three states have abolished regulations concerning legal load length. Six states have increased the legal combination length by 5 to 15 feet. Vermont and Wyoming have both raised width limitations to 8 feet 6 inches. Height limitations, based as they are on overpass constrictions, have not changed significantly.

The dimension limitations for oversized vehicles have shown great advances over the past few years. Eight states have raised load lengths by 2 to 20 feet; nineteen states have

raised the combination length by 5 to 20 feet. The crucial width regulation has shown great change: eighteen states have increased their limits by up to 2 feet and six states now have no restrictions. Table 19.4 compares the restrictions of 14-wides in 1972 and 1977—a relatively short period in which 14-wide movement has evolved into a nationwide, common practice.

Three basic systems for granting oversize permits exist in the United States today: the individual permit system, the extended time system, and the per-trip system. The individual permit system, which requires a separate permit for each one-way trip, is the most common; but other systems have become more widespread in recent years. Table 19.5 shows the recent changes in permit regulations. Single-trip permits are available from every state, usually costing $5 to $10. Each permit may be used only once. As can be imagined, large manufacturers must obtain many of them each year.

A more feasible practice is the extended time permit, which allows individual mobile home transporters to ship all oversized units for a prescribed length of time. The cost varies from nothing to $500; the time period varies from one month to one year to open ended with no specified limit. States may offer more than one extended time permit. Idaho, for example, offers the transporter a choice of one month for $25 or one year for $75. Use of extended time permits is less cumbersome and more economical than use of individual permits. As a result this system has become increasingly widespread over the past few years. In 1972 it was available in seventeen states; by 1977 it was available in twenty-eight states.

States using the per-trip system charge the transporter for the number of units shipped rather than for the number of days or months used. Most states using this system require

Permits

Table 19.2.
Comparison of Ranges,
1977/1972

Regulatory Category	Combination Length	Mobile Home Length	Mobile Home Width	Maximum Height
Normal size:				
1977 variation	50'–75'	35'–60'[a]	8'–8'6"	12'6"–14'
Number of exceptions	2	1	1	1
1972 variation	50'–75'	35'–60'[a]	8–8'6"	12'6"–14'
Number of exceptions	2	1	1	2
Oversize:				
1977 variation	85'–95'–R	70'–80'–R	14'–16'–R	13'6"–14'
Number of exceptions	2	3	1	4
1972 variation	75'–85'–[a]	55–70'–[a]	12'–16'	12'6"–14'[a]
Number of exceptions	2	0	4	3

a. More than five states do not specify.
R = More than five states have no restrictions.

Source: Compiled between 1972 and 1977 by PMHI from information provided by state regulatory agencies and industry sources.

Table 19.3.
Comparison of
Dimension Limitations,
1977/1972

	1977								1972							
	Legal Size without Permit				Oversize Permits				Legal Size without Permit				Oversize Permits			
State	Comb L	MH L	W	HT	Comb L	MH L	W	HT	Comb L	MH L	W	HT	Comb L	MH L	W	HT
Alabama	75	N	12	13'6"	85	NR	14	13'6"	75	N	12	13'6"	N	N	N	N
Alaska	70	N	8	13'6"	N	N	16	N	60	40	8	13'6"	80	N	14	N
Arizona	65	40	8	13	85	70	14	13'6"	65	40	8	13'6"	75	65	NLB	N
Arkansas	60	N	8	13'6"	NR	NR	14	13'6"	60	N	8	13'6"	N	N	14	N
California	60	40	8	13'6"	85	70	12	13'6"	60	40	8	13'6"	85	65	12	13'6"
Colorado	65	N	8	13'6"	NR	80	14	13'6"	65	35	8	13'6"	N	N	14	N
Connecticut	55	N	8'6"	13'6"	85	NR	14	13'6"	55	N	8'6"	13'6"	75	N	12L	13'6"
Delaware	55	N	8	13'6"	NR	NR	NR	13'6"	55	N	8	13'6"	N	N	14	13'6"
Florida	55	40	8	13'6"	NR	NR	14	13'6"	55	40	8	13'6"	N	N	12	N
Georgia	55	N	8	13'6"	85	70	14	13'6"	55	N	8	13'6"	75	55	12	13'6"
Hawaii	—	—	—	—	—	—	—	—	—	—	—	—	—	—	—	—
Idaho	65	N	8	14	85	NR	14	14	60	N	8	14'0"	75	60	14	14
Illinois	60	42	8	13'6"	85	NR	14	13'6"	60	42	8	13'6"	70	N	12	N
Indiana	60	N	8	13'6"	85	70	14	13'6"	60	N	8	13'6"	80	68	14	13'6"
Iowa	60	48	8	13'6"	85	67'6"	14'5"	13'6"	60	48	8	13'6"	80	68	14	13'6"
Kansas	65	N	8	13'6"	95	80	14	14	55	N	8	13'6"	85	N	14	N
Kentucky	55	N	8	13'6"	85	70	14	13'6"	55	N	8	13'6"	75	N	14	N
Louisiana	65	N	8	13'6"	95	NR	14	13'6"	65	N	8	13'6"	85	N	14	13'6"
Maine	56'6"	N	8'6"	13'6"	NR	NR	14'6"	14	56'6"	N	8'6"	13'6"	N	N	N	N
Maryland	55	N	8	13'6"	NR	NR	14	13'6"	55	N	8	13'6"	N	N	14	N
Massachusetts	N	33	8	13'6"	NR	NR	14	NR	N	33'	8	13'6"	N	N	12'LB	N
Michigan	60	45	8'4"	12'6"	85	70	14	15	60	45	8'4"	12'6"	85	65	14	15
Minnesota	55	40	8	13'6"	85	70	14'6"	13'6"	55	40	8	13'6"	85	68	14'6"	13'6"
Mississippi	55	N	8	13'6"	85	NR	14	13'6"	55	N	8	13'6"	75	N	12	N
Missouri	55	N	8	13'6"	85	NR	14	13'6"	55	40	8	13'6"	85	70	12'4"	varies
Montana	60	60	8	13'6"	NR	NR	14	13'6"	60	60	8	13'6"	N	N	16	N
Nebraska	65	40	8	13'6"	95	NR	14	13'6"	65	40	8	13'6"	85	N	14	13'6"
Nevada	70	N	8	14'	85	NR	14	14	70	N	8	varies	70	N	14	varies
New Hampshire	55	N	8	13'6"	NR	NR	NR	13'6"	55	N	8	13'6"	N	N	12	N
New Jersey	50	35	8	13'6"	NR	NR	14	13'6"	50	35	8	13'6"	N	N	12	N
New Mexico	65		8'6"	13'6"	101	85	14	13'6"	65	N	8'6"	13'6"	80	65	14	N
New York	55	35	8	13'6"	NR	NR	14	13'6"	55	35	8	13'6"	N	N	12	N
North Carolina	55	35	8	13'6"	85	70	14	13'6"	55	35	8	13'6"	80	N	12	13'6"
North Dakota	N	60	8	12'6"	NR	80	16	13'6"	N	60	8	12'6"	N	70	14	12'6"
Ohio	65	40	8	13'6"	85	70	14	13'6"	65	40	8	13'6"	85	70	14	13'6"
Oklahoma	65	N	8	N	NR	NR	14	13'6"	55	N	8	13'6"	N	N	14	N
Oregon	50	35	8	13'6"	85	NR	14	13'6"	50	35	8	N	85	N	14	N
Pennsylvania	55	N	8	13'6"	NR	NR	14	13'6"	55	N	8	13'6"	N	N	12	N
Rhode Island	55	40	8'6"	13'6"	NR	NR	NR	13'6"	55	40	8'6"	13'6"	N	55	14	N
South Carolina	60	N	8	13'6"	85	70	14	13'6"	60	N	8	13'6"	75	N	12	N
South Dakota	65	35	8	13'6"	NR	NR	NR	13'6"	65	35	8	13'6"	N	N	14	N
Tennessee	69	N	8	13'6"	NR	NR	14	13'6"	55	N	8	13'6"	N	N	12	13'6"
Texas	55	N	8	13'6"	95	NR	NR	13'6"	55	N	8	13'6"	95	N	16	N
Utah	60	45	8	14	85	NR	14	14	60	45	8	14	80	N	14	N
Vermont	55	55	8'6"	13'6"	NR	NR	14	13'6"	55	55	8	13'6"	varies	N	14	N
Virginia	55	N	8	13'6"	85	70	14	13'6"	55	N	8	13'6"	75	N	12	N
Washington	65	45	8	13'6"	85	NR	14	13'6"	60	40	8	13'6"	85	N	14	N
West Virginia	50	35	8	12'6"	85	70	14	13'6"	50	35	8	12'6"	75	N	14	12'6"
Wisconsin	60	45	8	13'6"	85	70	14	13'6"	60	45	8	13'6"	85	70	12	N
Wyoming	75	N	8'6"	14	NR	NR	NR	NR	75	N	8	14	N	N	N	N

Note: N = nothing specified. NR = no restrictions.

Source: Compiled between 1972 and 1977 by PMHI from information provided by state regulatory agencies and industry sources.

Table 19.4.
Comparison of
14-Wide Regulations,
1977/1972

State	Date Permitted	Travel Times	Restrictions 1977	1972
Alabama	1971	+	1 esc. when comb. >75' for interstate travel.	NS
Alaska	**	*	NS	Single trip permits only, 3 escorts required.
Arizona	1973	*	1 esc. on interstate; 2 on 2–lane hwys.	Special permit required, movement on lowboy.
Arkansas	1971	*	≥12'w commercial haulers only. Tandem axles with brakes; 2 esc. on 2–lane hwys. 1 for all comb. >75' on 2–1anes.	≥12'w commercial haulers only. Tandem axles with brakes.
California	N	*	NA	NA
Colorado	1970	*	1 esc. on all hwys west of I–25.	Restricted days of travel.
Connecticut	1973	*	Special permit over approved rt. 2 escorts, special/ equipment req. Restricted travel times.	NA
Delaware	1973	*	NE	Special permit, lowboy.
Florida	++	*	NS	NA
Georgia	++	*	NS	NA
Idaho	1970	NS	Commercial haulers only; 1 escort on all hwys, 2 escorts on some roads, none on Interstates.	NS
Illinois	1973	*	2 escorts required.	NA
Indiana	1971	*	1 escort required.	Special permit, police escort.
Iowa	**	*	Maximum distance 50 miles. 1 escort required.	Lowboy. Maximum distance 50 miles.
Kansas	1969	—	Special permit over approved route. 2 escorts, 1 on Kansas Turnpike.	Special permit over approved route. 2 escorts.
Kentucky	1972	*	Single trip permit, commercial haulers only. "Reasonable" distances. 1 esc. on Interstates, 2 on 2-lane hwys.	Special permit, "reasonable" distances on 2 lanes. 1 escort on 4 lanes, 2 on 2.
Louisiana	1969	*	1 escort.	1 escort.
Maine	**	*	Restricted times of travel; 2 escorts.	No movement on turnpikes.
Maryland	1973	*	>10'w on lowboy; 1 escort.	NA
Massachusetts	++	*	2 escorts	NA
Michigan	1971	*	1 escort.	NA
Minnesota	1969	*	Approved routes; NE.	Approved routes.
Mississippi	++	*	2 escorts.	NA
Missouri	1973	*	2 on 2–lane hwys; 1 on multi-lanes.	NA
Montana	**	*	Routes as per permit; 1 escort, none on Interstate.	NS
Nebraska	1970	*	≥12'w single trip permit; 1 escort.	1 escort.
Nevada	1972	*	Special equipment; 2 escorts.	Special equipment.
New Hampshire	1970	*	Approval of undercarriage; Review, 2 escorts required.	Special permit.
New Jersey	++	*	NE	NA

Table 19.4. (Continued)

State	Date Permitted	Travel Times	Restrictions 1977	1972
New Mexico	**	+	Certified escort, 1 escort.	Police escort.
New York	1972	*	1 escort.	NA
North Carolina	++	*	NS	NA
North Dakota	1969	*	Commercial haulers only; NE.	Commercial haulers only.
Ohio	1970	*	Single trip permit, commercial haulers only; 1 escort.	No movement on turnpikes. Single trip permit, special equipment required, 1 escort.
Oklahoma	1969	*	Escort requirements vary: 2 escorts, 1 on 4-lane hwys; 1 esc. for comb. > 80', 2 esc. for comb. > 100'.	No movement on turnpikes. 1 escort on 4 lanes, 2 on 2.
Oregon	1970	*	Certain routes. Test run; 2 escorts: none on Interstates.	Special permit over approved routes. Test run.
Pennsylvania	++	*	1 escort.	NA
Rhode Island	1972	*	2 escorts.	2 escorts required.
South Carolina	++	*	NS	NA
South Dakota	1969	*	NE	Special equipment required.
Tennesee	++	*	NS	NA
Texas	**	+	1 escort on certain routes.	NS
Utah	1970	+	No movement on freeways or interstate highways; 1 escort.	Special equipment required.
Vermont	1970	NS	Police escort required.	NS
Virginia	++	*	NS	NA
Washington	1970	*	2 escorts, except 1 on Interstate.	Single trip permit over approved route. Special equipment required. Inspection by issuer required.
West Virginia	1971	*	Special equipment, approved route, 2 escorts required on 2–lanes, 1 on Interstate.	Special equipment, approved route.
Wisconsin	**	*	Single trip permit only, NE.	Single trip permit only.
Wyoming	**	+	1 on Interstate, 2 on all others.	Approved routes, specal equipment. 1 escort on 4 lanes, 2 on 2.
Hawaii	—	—	—	—

NE = No escort required.
N = Not permitted.
NA = Not applicable.
NS = None specified.
* Restricted weekend movement; no movement during hours of darkness.
+ No movement during hours of darkness.
** Prior to 1969.
++ After 1974.
Source: Compiled between 1972 and 1977 by PMHI from information provided by state regulatory agencies and industry sources.

Table 19.5.
Comparison of Permit
Regulations, 1977/1972

State	1977 Single Cost (Dollars)	1977 Single Duration (Days)	1977 Multiple Cost (Dollars)	1977 Multiple Duration (Months)	1972 Single Cost (Dollars)	1972 Single Duration (Days)	1972 Multiple Cost (Dollars)	1972 Multiple Duration (Months)
Alabama	$C	NS	$100	12	$0	N		
Alaska	10 to 50*	NS	25	1	0	N	$0	6
Arizona	5	varies	NA	NA	5	N		
Arkansas	25	NS	NA	NA	5	N		
California	3	NS	30	12	3	N	30	12
Colorado	5	15	NA	NA	5	15		
Connecticut	0	NS	NA	NA	0	N		
Delaware	5	NS	NA	NA	5	N		
Florida	5	5	20	12	5	3*	20	12
Georgia	10 to 50*	4	100	12	10	4	100	12
Idaho	3 to 5*	NS	25 or 75	1 or 12	3–5*	30		
Illinois	7 to 17*	5	22.50 to 40*	3	7–17*	5	22.50–40*	3
Indiana	10+	3 to 15*	10 or 25/trip	12	10+	15	10/trip++	varies
Iowa	5	NS	10	12	5	N	10	12
Kansas	5	NS	NA	NA	5	N		
Kentucky	10	10	40	12	5	10	20	12
Louisiana	8+	1	NA	NA	6	1		
Maine	varies	varies	NS	NS		N		
Maryland	15	NS	NA	NA	10	N		
Massachusetts	0	14	NA	NA	0	N		
Michigan	2	NS	NA	NA	0	N		
Minnesota	5	NS	NA	NA	5	N		
Mississippi	0	5	0++	6	0	5	0	6
Missouri	5	5	5	12	4	3		
Montana	6	NS	NA	NA	6	N		
Nebraska	5 to 10*	10	25	3	2–10*	90	100	12
Nevada	7	NS	25	12	0	N		
New Hampshire	5	5	NA	NA	5	5		
New Jersey	10*	1	NA	NA	5	N		
New Mexico	5	NS	10 to 20**	NA	2.50	N		
New York	11	8	10 or 75/tow	1 or 12	7	N		
North Carolina	0	10	5	NS	0	3/10	5	
North Dakota	5	NS	5	NS	5	N	5+5/trip*	12
Ohio	2+	5	6	NS	2+	N	6	12
Oklahoma	5	NS	25	25 trips	5	N		
Oregon	3	NS	3	12	N	N		
Pennsylvania	5 to 10*	NS	NA	NA	5*	N		
Rhode Island	0	NS	NA	NA	0	N		
South Carolina	5	14	5/trip	open ended	5	14	varies	open end
South Dakota	10*+	NS	500	6	5	N	500	6
Tennessee	5 to 25	NS	300	12	0	N		
Texas	5	10	NA	NA	5	10		
Utah	3	96 hours	15 or 25	3 or 12	3	4	15–25	3–12
Vermont	10	14	NA	NA	10	14		
Virginia	6	NS	5+1/trip	NS	6	N		
Washington	5	NS	150	12	5	N		
West Virginia	15–20*	5	1+1/trip	NS	15–20	5		
Wisconsin	1	NS	NA	NA	0	N		
Wyoming	5*	NS	NA	NA	5–25*	N		
Hawaii	—	—	—	—	—	—	—	—

* Varies by size and/or mileage.
** Varies with number of trips.
+ Extra cost for extension and/or change.
++ Special rates/extended permits for dealers, manufacturers, haulers only.
NS = Not specified.
NA = Not available.

Source: Compiled between 1972 and 1977 by PMHI from information provided by state regulatory agencies and industry sources.

either the posting of a surety bond (for example, Oklahoma) or the payment of an initial fee (for example, Virginia) before the service is made available to a transporter. The per-trip system is a relatively recent development.

Traffic Regulations

Outside of permits and dimension regulations, other areas in highway regulation have not, by and large, shown any definite advances. Changes have occurred in many states from 1972 to 1977, of course, but as table 19.6 shows no unifying trends have emerged. In the area of equipment requirements, more states are requiring two-way radio communication between escorting and hauling vehicles. In the area of escort requirements, many states are now mapping out escort requirements route by route.

C. Highway Regulation and Industry Performance

A Case Study

Some highway regulations hamper the economic performance of the mobile home industry more than others. PMHI has analyzed the effects of regulations to determine their usefulness, both to the industry and to the general public. Examination of a case study will illustrate the economic impact of highway regulation on the industry as well as indicating compliance costs and the extent of regulatory necessity.

From our exhaustive state-by-state survey of highway regulation, we have constructed a typical case of interstate mobile home transport. A cost analysis based on this case study lays the foundation for the reader to understand an alternate regulatory approach that we are proposing. The mobile home manufacturer, dealer, buyer, and transporter in this case study are fictitious and designed only as an analytical tool.

We decided on a typical transport distance of three hundred and fifty miles based on a survey conducted by Lorimer, Chiodo, and Associates.[1] The survey determined that 56 percent of a typical manufacturer's market (the dealerships that distribute the mobile homes) is located within two hundred and fifty miles of the manufacturing plant and that 44 percent is located within two hundred and fifty to five hundred miles of the plant. 83 percent of a typical dealer's market is located within two hundred and fifty to five hundred miles of the manufacturer's plant. Therefore, for the purposes of this study we used a trip of three hundred and fifty miles from manufacturer to dealer to consumer.

The PMHI Dealer Survey determined that most units are shipped to dealers in the same or an adjacent state. Some manufacturers do shipments to distant states but few mobile homes move through more than three states. Therefore a case study of a trip through two states was chosen as a typical situation. We chose Oklahoma and Kansas as two states with typical mobile home distribution and typical highway regulations.

The South Central region of the United States as a whole is perhaps the most typical in terms of distribution. The New England states contain almost no mobile homes, while the South Atlantic states contain unusually large numbers of mobile homes. Furthermore, Oklahoma and Kansas use some of the most common and representative state highway controls over mobile home transportation.

The fictitious manufacturer is defined as having an annual production of nine hundred units per year. Based on the PMHI Manufacturer Survey, this can be said to represent a fairly typical firm size.

Mobile home transporters may be private individuals, commercial hauling companies, or mobile home manufacturers who operate their own fleets. Because approximately 80 percent of those manufacturers surveyed by PMHI operate their own fleets, for the purpose of the case study we have assumed that the manufacturer uses its own fleet. Finally, we have chosen to discuss a 14-wide unit as most representative because sales of 14-wides have for some time outranked sales of all other mobile home types.

We begin the trip with a manufacturer located in Bristow, Oklahoma. A 14-wide mobile home unit has been ordered for delivery by a dealer whose lot is located in Salina, Kansas, approximately 300 miles away. The dealer expects to deliver the unit to a mobile home park in Concordia, 50 miles farther. The total distance is 350 miles. The transporter must comply with Oklahoma regulations for the first 165 miles and with Kansas regulations for the remaining 185 miles.

The transporter must start by obtaining permits from both states before moving the mobile home unit. It is possible to purchase individual permits at $5 each, but with the posting of a $5000 surety bond, the transporter can obtain Oklahoma Application Books containing twenty-five applications for $25. To obtain a permit, the applicant fills out and sends in the application form and then calls the permit office in Oklahoma City to complete the application. Kansas permits are available on an individual basis only at $5 per permit. Kansas permits are available by mail, phone, or in person, but 14-wides must have the approval of the Special Permit Department for designated routes.

The mobile home must have a current license plate and the driver must have a current chauffeur's license. In Kansas the driver must carry evidence that the mobile home and the truck hauling it are insured in the amounts of $100,000/$300,000/$25,000. In Oklahoma the minimum insurance requirements are $5000/$10,000/$5000. Kansas has complete license reciprocity with Oklahoma. Oklahoma has prorated reciprocity with Kansas.

Table 19.6.
Comparison of
Equipment Require-
ments, 1977/1972

State	1977 Wide Load Signs	Flags on Unit	Warning Lights on MH	Brakes	2–Way Radio	1972 Wide Load Signs	Flags on Unit	Warning Lights on MH	Brakes on MH
Alabama	N	6	N	N	Yes	N	N	N	N
Alaska	*	Yes	*	N	Yes	Yes	N	N	N
Arizona	Yes	Yes	N	Yes	Yes	—	N	N	N
Arkansas	N	4	N	>10′w	Yes	—	N	N	>10′w
California	Yes	NR	N	Yes	Yes	Yes	N	N	>10′w
Colorado	>10′w	6	N	>3000 lbs	Yes	>10′w	N	N	
Connecticut	>10′w	Yes	*>12′w	Yes	>12′w	>10′w	Yes	N	Yes
Delaware	Yes	NR	>10′w	Yes	N	N	Yes	N	Yes
Florida	>10′w	NR	N	Yes	N	>10′w	Yes	N	N
Georgia	>8′w	>8′w	N	Yes	Yes	N	Yes	N	N
Idaho	Yes	4	+	Yes	Yes	Yes	Yes	Yes	Yes
Illinois	>10′w	Yes	*>14′w	Yes	N	>10′w	Yes	N	N
Indiana	+	6	*	Yes	Yes	Yes	Yes	N	N
Iowa	>8′w	Yes	>25 mph	N	N	Yes	Yes	N	N
Kansas	*,10′4″w	Yes	Yes	Yes	N	Yes	Yes	>14′w	Yes
Kentucky	N	Yes	>14′w	>14′w	N	N	Yes	>14′w	>14′w
Louisiana	>10′w	NR	N	Yes	N	>10′w	N	N	Yes
Maine	>11′6″w	Yes	*	Yes	>13′6″w	>11′6″w	Yes	N	N
Maryland	>12′w	NR	N	N	N	>12′w	N	N	N
Massachusetts	N	NR	N	N	N	N	N	N	N
Michigan	Yes	Yes	>14′w,*	>2 axles	N	Yes	Yes	14′w	>2 axles
Minnesota	>8′w	>8′w	N	>12′w	N	Yes	Yes	N	>12′w
Mississippi	N	>10′w	N	N	Yes	N	>10′w	N	N
Missouri	>10′4″w	Yes	N	Yes	N	Yes	Yes	N	N
Montana	>9′w	NR	>10′w,*	>3000 lbs	N	>9′w	Yes	>10′w	Yes
Nebraska	Yes	Yes	Yes	Yes	N	>10′w	>10′w	N	>10′w
Nevada	Yes	Yes	>10′w,*	N	>12′w	Yes	>10′w	>12′w	N
New Hampshire	>10′w	>10′w	N	Yes	N	>10′w	>10′w	N	>10′w
New Jersey	Yes	Yes	N	N	N	Yes	Yes	N	N
New Mexico	Yes	Yes	>10′w,*	N	Yes	>10′w	Yes	>10′w	N
New York	≥12′w	>10′w	≥12′w	N	N	>12′w	>10′w	>12′w	N
North Carolina	>10′w	>10′w	N	Yes	N	>10′w	Yes	N	Yes
North Dakota	≥10′w	>10′w	N	N	N	Yes	Yes	N	N
Ohio	Yes	Yes	≥12′w,*	Yes	N	Yes	Yes	>14′w	Yes
Oklahoma	12′w	*12′w	N	Yes	Yes	>12′w	Yes	N	N
Oregon	Yes	Yes	Yes, **	Yes	Yes	Yes	Yes	Yes	Yes
Pennsylvania	Yes	Yes	N	Yes	N	Yes	Yes	N	N
Rhode Island	N	N	N	N	N	N	N	N	N
South Carolina	Yes	Yes	N	Yes	N	>12′w	>12′w	>12′w	Yes
South Dakota	Yes	Yes	>12′6″	Yes	N	Yes	Yes	>12′4″w	Yes
Tennessee	>10′w	>10′w	*	N	Yes	>10′w	>10′w	N	N
Texas	N	N	N	Yes	N	N	N	N	N
Utah	>10′w	>10′o	*,>20′o,5mph	Yes	N	>10′w	Yes	Yes	>12′w
Vermont	>8′w+	Yes	*	Yes	N	Yes	Yes	N	N
Virginia	N	>10′4″w	N	N	N	N	>10′4″w	N	N
Washington	≥12′w	≥12′w	≥12′w,*	≥12′w	≥12′w	>12′w	>12′w	>12′w	>12′w
West Virginia	Yes	Yes	Yes	Yes	N	Yes	Yes	N	N
Wisconsin	>8′w	Yes	>8′w	Yes	N	Yes	Yes	N	N
Wyoming	Yes	≥1′o, 25mph*	*	N	N	Yes	Yes	N	N
Hawaii	—	—	—	—	—	—	—	—	—

N = Nothing specified.
* = On escort vehicle.
** = On escort if motorcycle.
+ = Varies, or as per permit.
NR = No regulation.

Source: Compiled between 1972 and 1977 by PMHI from information provided by state regulatory agencies and industry sources.

In general, mobile home transporters may either use their own escort vehicles or hire escorts from a commercial escort service. Either way, escorts are expensive. A self-escort costs an estimated $.14 per mile while escorting and $.10 per mile while returning to plant or meeting a load. A commercial escort usually costs $.34 to $.40 per mile with a one hundred-mile minimum.[2]

All vehicles used to escort oversized mobile homes in Oklahoma must be registered and certified (the filing fee is $25). Operators must file evidence of insurance in the proper amount. All escorts must bear a current identification device ($3 a year). The actual escort vehicle must be a car or pickup weighing at least 3000 pounds. Two outside rear view mirrors, a fire extinguisher (2.5 pound CO_2 or equivalent), a minimum of three emergency reflectors and fuses, and a two-way radio capable of maintaining communication with the towing vehicle and second escort vehicle (if any) are part of the required safety harness. One escort is required on all four-lane highways, and two escorts are needed on all other highways.

Vehicles used to escort mobile homes through Kansas must meet slightly different requirements. Front escorts must have regulation wide load signs mounted above the front bumper and red flags on the rear corners; on rear escorts the installation is reversed. A flashing amber light at least 6 inches in diameter must be mounted on vehicles escorting 14-wide units. All 14-wide units transported on the Kansas Turnpike must be protected by one escort vehicle; two escorts are required on all other highways.

Both Oklahoma and Kansas have fairly specific equipment requirements regarding the mobile home itself. In Oklahoma 16-inch-square red flags must be placed on each corner and along the sides of the mobile home. "Caution Wide and Long Load" signs in red and white, at least 48 inches by 22 inches with letters 4 inches high must be placed on the front of the towing vehicle, the front of the escort vehicle, and the rear of the mobile home unit. All drawbar connections, safety hitches, safety chains, and brakes on the towing vehicle and the mobile home unit must comply with specific statutes.

When the mobile home enters Kansas, a few changes must be made. The same red flags and wide load signs are specified, but they must be moved. Red flags must be placed on the towing vehicle and the escort cars as well as the mobile home unit. The sign on the front of the towing vehicle must be placed on the cab, and an identical sign must be placed on the rear of a second escort vehicle. In addition each escort vehicle must have a flashing amber light on its roof. When the unit reaches the port of entry, it must stop and make these changes.

There are two possible routes from the manufacturing plant in Bristow to the junc-

tion of Interstate 35 just outside Oklahoma City (approximately 65 miles). The super-highway, Interstate 44, also known as the Turner Turnpike, is closed to all mobile homes 12 feet wide and over, so the 14-wide manufacturer must use the through highway US 66. This route requires two escort vehicles, one front and one rear; on Interstate 44 only one would be necessary. From this point the mobile home merges onto Interstate 35, a controlled access divided highway. The lead escort vehicle may return to the plant because only the rear escort is needed for the next 154 miles.

At the Kansas state line, Interstate 35 becomes the Kansas Turnpike, a toll highway. After stopping at the port of entry, changing equipment, and paying a toll, the mobile home unit proceeds with a rear escort forty-five miles to Wichita. The unit leaves the turnpike and takes Interstate 235 and is accompanied by two escort vehicles around Wichita along the controlled access divided highway Interstate 235 to the junction of US 81 (approximately fifteen miles). From Wichita to Newton (approximately twenty miles) US 81 is a divided highway; from Newton to MacPherson (approximately thirty miles) it is a principal through highway. The driver of the lead escort vehicle must stop all oncoming traffic at the far end of all bridges and culverts less than 28 feet wide until the mobile home can cross. The rear escort must keep traffic from passing the mobile home while it crosses. After MacPherson the unit takes Interstate 35W, a controlled access divided highway, twenty-five miles to the dealer lot in Salina.

The dealer takes over from the manufacturer and sells the unit. Delivery must be made to a mobile home park in Concordia, fifty miles away. The dealer's transporter takes US 81, a principal through highway, directly to the park. Two escorts are required for the entire trip to Concordia.

As the case study illustrates, the average mobile home delivery process is fraught with inefficiency, duplicated efforts, and unnecessary costs. We may define unnecessary cost as an expense, estimated in dollars and cents, resulting from the imposition of highway rules, regulations, or procedures that can be eliminated or significantly reduced without adversely affecting safety or state control of the highways. Our case study enables us to demonstrate which costs are necessary and which are unnecessary. We are using this cost analysis as an aid for the reader to understand policy alternatives that we see for achieving a new unified highway regulatory system for mobile homes.

Information Costs

One of the industry's greatest unnecessary expenses is the cost involved in keeping abreast of the highway regulations of each pertinent state. As it stands, various states have different regulations for mobile home transporters; if these regulations were standardized in every state, manufacturers and dealers could save a great deal of time and money and ultimately the savings could be passed on to consumers. At present transporters must tediously review separate regulations for each state every time a mobile home is moved. This often includes different equipment requirements, route restrictions, escort requirements, and travel hours. Even partial standardization of these factors would reduce costs. Detailed cost estimates of the case study show that the typical transporter could save $7.54 per unit shipped. Given the typical output of nine hundred units per year, this means a total savings of $6786 from streamlined information gathering.

Permit Costs

Use of permits is a reasonable way for states to control highway use. The permit process allows the state to ensure that responsible transporters are using the highways and in compliance with state regulations and procedures. Individual states, however, often exert their control in a costly, cumbersome, and inefficient manner. Under the present system the transporter must be familiar with the permit procedures of each jurisdiction traversed and must constantly keep abreast of any changes. The transporter must usually apply for a separate permit for each mobile home shipped. The fictitious mobile home manufacturer produces pproximately nine hundred units per year, so this means nine hundred separate applications—an unnecessary waste of work hours for both the state and the manufacturer.

A more efficient system has already been pursued by several states through use of extended or blanket permits usable for a prescribed length of time. The transporter may move any number of mobile homes during the period covered by the permit. This eliminates the cost of clerical labor and administrative materials involved in applying for nine hundred permits as well as the actual cost of nine hundred permits. States using the blanket permit system need process only one or two applications per manufacturer each year rather than the average of nine hundred applications per manufacturer each year. More states ought to consider the extended permit system. Even if $50 were charged to cover administrative costs, both the state and the transporter would benefit— the transporter saving the cost of nine hundred permits a year and the state saving the cost of processing nine hundred permits a year. Furthermore, the state does not relinquish any significant degree of control or highway safety with the blanket permit procedure. It need not grant permits for transportation not serving the public interest; it need not grant permits without proof of

insurance; and it need not, in fact, grant any permit under the new system it would not have granted under the old.

A cost analysis of the case study demonstrates savings under the blanket permit system: The manufacturer saves $5.07 in the application process and $6.71 for the actual permits for each mobile home shipped. This means a total savings of $10,602 for nine hundred units shipped. Obviously, under a fixed rate blanket permit system the large manufacturers, which ship more than nine hundred units per year, tend to benefit more than the smaller manufacturers, which ship fewer than nine hundred units per year. The state could control this by charging flexible rather than fixed rates. At the end of each designated permit period the manufacturer would specify the number of units shipped during that time and be charged accordingly.

Equipment Requirements

The great lack of uniformity of traffic regulations state to state is a major producer of unnecessary costs. Traffic regulation itself is a necessary cost, essential to the safe movement of traffic on the highways. Good safety regulations increase the likelihood of safe deliveries and are therefore conducive to improved economic performance. The state-to-state diversity of regulations, however, results in unnecessary expenditures. Overall continuity of safety regulation should be sought by states.

Major confusion stems from chaotic equipment requirements. On the surface they are basically similar from state to state, but the details may vary widely. As mentioned before, most states require a safety harness— flashers, lights, flags, oversized load signs— but different states require radically different size, color, or placement of this harness. There is no evidence to conclude that a red flashing light used in one state becomes any less safe when used in another; none to conclude that the black and yellow "Wide Load" sign on the roof of the towing vehicle required by one state is any safer than the black and white "Oversized Load" sign on the front bumper required by another state. These changes result in unnecessary costs: initial purchase costs, blue-collar labor costs, and white-collar labor costs. The transporter must purchase a different harness for each state, the drivers must change the harness at each state border, and the administrative staff must continuously compile and update information on state safety harnesses. Greater uniformity in safety regulations could significantly reduce these costs. The transporter could purchase one harness per hauling vehicle and install it at the beginning of a trip without changing it or having to research state codes.

The case study is a good example. In the same geographic area, over the same type of terrain, carrying the same load, on the same road, on the same day, Kansas and Oklahoma require different harnesses. If these two states had identical harnesses, transporters would save the initial cost of the second harness and the labor required to change the harness at the border. Typically, the savings would be $4.24 per trip.

Escort Requirements

State regulations concerning escort vehicles are nearly as varied as those concerning safety equipment. In some cases the variations are justified: One escort may suffice in flat, open country, but two escorts may be necessary in mountainous or forested areas where visibility is limited. On most highways, however, only one escort is needed for safety because the mobile home only travels in the daylight hours and can be seen easily. Although some research groups have argued that escorts may be a safety hazard rather than a safety aid, when the drivers are untrained (as they usually are) and when communication between escort and hauler is broken, we feel that escorts definitely improve highway safety when drivers are properly trained.[3] If the area is hilly, the road is poor, or the mobile home is wider than the road, two escort vehicles do not represent an unreasonable cost for the added safety factor. The unreasonable cost arises when more escorts are required than are needed for safety.

In the case study two escorts are required by law on three superhighways—the controlled access divided highways Interstate 235 and Interstate 35W, and the divided highway US 81. Unless there is severe traffic congestion on these roads two escorts are clearly unnecessary. A lead escort is extraneous when the traffic passing the unit in the opposite direction is separated from the unit by a highway divider. Later in the case study trip two escorts may be necessary. In this case the manufacturer can send its own escort ahead to await the mobile home unit or hire one from an escort service. A manufacturer using its own vehicle would save $41.71 per unit over the present system; a manufacturer hiring escorts to save sending and return costs would save $39.90.

Route Restrictions

Regulatory policies concerning travel times are very similar among states. Mobile homes may usually travel from dawn to dusk on weekdays except during rush hours around metropolitan areas. These regulations are necessary for the safety of the highway users and for the facilitation of traffic flow. Any additional expense to mobile home transporters resulting from these regulations are necessary costs. States should retain control over time considerations in their traffic areas.

Route restrictions, however, should in many cases be reevaluated. Almost all states have some route restrictions—some necessary, some not. A small number of states prohibit mobile homes on the interstate highways. Other states restrict mobile homes to certain routes, often secondary state highways or even county highways. Most states require the route to be specified on the oversize permit.

Mobile homes are transported most efficiently over the superhighways. The mobile home is generally not as much a safety hazard or a traffic impediment on a superhighway as it is on a two-lane state or county road, where the mobile home usually takes up well over half of the road surface, obstructing traffic in both directions and presenting a serious danger at blind curves even with an escort. In addition, these secondary routes are a source of expense for mobile home transporters. The routes are usually circuitous, adding mileage, driver time, route planning time, gas costs, and wear and tear on hauling and escort vehicles. Regulations restricting mobile homes from the superhighways are not necessary (except in special hazardous road situations) because they are not conducive to commerce, and they do pose an unreasonable cost burden on the industry.[4]

Interstate 44 in the case study was closed to 12-wide and wider mobile homes. The manufacturer was forced to use US 66, a through highway. Although the distance was essentially the same (not always the case), the manufacturer still loses money. US 66 requires two escorts but I-44 requires only one. This represents an unnecessary $10.61 per trip for escort vehicles alone. In addition the unit could not average as fast a speed. This represents additional driving time. If the unit averages 10 mph slower over the sixty-five miles, two hours of truck and escort driver time will be added, an unnecessary cost of $44.57 per trip. A longer detour route would mean additional time and additional gas and escort expenses. Additional wear and tear on the vehicles might also be considered. Consistent access to superhighways would save manufacturers time and money. PMHI proposes that mobile home transporters be allowed greater freedom of route choice for the safety and convenience of all concerned. Mobile home transporters should certainly not be allowed to use every highway in every state. Some routes may be so narrow or so congested at all hours of the day that mobile homes would necessarily be prohibited. State reevaluations of route restrictions for mobile homes could greatly facilitate mobile home movement and thus enhance the industry's ability to deliver.

Cost Summary

Under the proposed system the case study manufacturer that supplies its own escort vehicles would save

$7.54 per unit in information costs
$11.78 per unit in permit costs

$4.24 per unit in equipment requirements
$41.71 per unit in escort requirements
$44.57 per unit in route restrictions.

This is a total of $109.84 per unit. A manufacturer who ships the nine hundred units per year would save $98,856 per year.

The case study manufacturer that hires a commercial escort service would save equal amounts in information costs and permit costs, but saves

nothing in equipment requirements
$39.90 per unit in escort costs
$28.16 in route restrictions.

This is a total of $87.38 per unit. A manufacturer who ships the typical nine hundred units per year would save $78,642 per year.

These figures are at best rough estimates, and they are definitely low because quite a few expenses had to be neglected (for example, insurance for escort vehicles, breakdown procedures, extra costs due to added mileage necessary to comply with route restrictions). Thus, PMHI feels that the estimated savings are realistic.

D. Policy Alternatives

State regulation of mobile home highway movement takes three major forms: dimension limitations, permit requirements, and traffic regulations specific to oversized vehicles. Although these controls are designed in the interests of public safety and convenience, they often do not serve that purpose.

Because nearly all mobile homes exceed the maximum width dimensions, transporters must obtain permits to move them. Single-trip permits may be used only once each. A more feasible practice is the extended permit, which allows a manufacturer to move all mobile homes under a single permit for periods of up to one year. This system is far less cumbersome and far more economical—to the manufacturer, to the state, and, finally, to the public, either as consumers or as taxpayers. PMHI found that a "typical" manufacturer could save an estimated $7.54 per unit with the extended permit. We recommend this system.

In addition to regulations for all traffic, mobile home transporters must comply with specific regulations for oversized loads. These regulations include extra equipment requirements (lowboys, tandem axles, and so forth) and safety equipment requirements (caution signs, red flags, flares, and so forth); escort requirements; and route restrictions.

At present the system is ineffective and costly. Regulations vary widely from state to state, often arbitrarily. A transporter must comply with the regulations of each state entered, perhaps changing equipment at each border, because one state may require black and yellow signs and another, black and white. PMHI estimated that manufacturers (and ultimately consumers) could save $11.78 per unit in equipment if the system were simply standardized. Safety would not

be jeopardized—there is no evidence that any one state's safety equipment is safer than any other's.

Most states require more escort vehicles than are actually necessary for safety. We propose that only one escort be used on all divided highways and two only where roads are very narrow, curvey, or otherwise unsuited to mobile home use. With these minimized requirements a manufacturer could save an estimated $41.71 per unit.

Route restrictions cost manufacturers millions of dollars a year. We suggest that most mobile homes can be transported most efficiently and safely on the larger highways, yet many states restrict their use. A typical transporter could save an estimated $44.57 per unit if all divided highways in the area could be used.

The total estimated savings for a 14-wide unit is at least $109.84. This means that highway regulation adds an unnecessary cost of about 1.4 percent to FOB factory price that could easily be reduced significantly or eliminated completely if the system were as effective as it could be. The states are, of course, attempting to act in the best interests of the public. We feel that standardization of regulations, the granting of extended permits, and the requirement of fewer escort vehicles will not jeopardize public safety or convenience but will, in fact, contribute to it.

It is useful to move back to one of the key questions of this study: "What explains the unique cost advantage that the mobile home industry enjoys over the traditional home-building industry?" The explanation by now should be obvious. It is the industry's uniquely comprehensive exploitation of advantages and efficiencies in most areas of the total system that the industry proper and its larger economic-political environment represent. The industry's cost advantage stems from the overall, aggregate effect of literally hundreds of minor savings achieved in hundreds of different parts of this system. Viewed with this realization, the unnecessary price increase of 1.4 percent suddenly assumes importance. If the industry and the public alike would tolerate cost increases of this magnitude in all parts of the system, the 1.4 percent would be multiplied by a factor of one hundred or two hundred and the industry's cost edge would be eliminated.

The challenge is clear. Unnecessary costs of this magnitude must not be accepted, not in the realm of highway regulation or in any other area. Streamlining the operation of the highway regulatory system implies a joint task for the mobile home industry and government. The industry needs to maintain its competitive position; government needs to keep alive the only resource for least-cost housing. The mobile home industry has a long tradition of reshaping its regulatory environment; the initiative should come from it.

Notes to Chapter 19

1. Lorimer, Chiodo, and Associates, "Automated Total Housing Systems in the U.S., 1970, as Applied to the State of Minnesota," Minneapolis, Minnesota.

2. W.D. Glauz, B.M. Hutchisone, D.R. Kobett, *Economic Evaluation of Mobile and Modular Housing Shipments by Highway*, Volume 1, April 1974, prepared for the U.S. Department of Transportation and the U.S. Department of Housing and Urban Development.

3. Ibid.

4. PMHI Survey of mobile home transporting firms, 1977.

Tomorrow

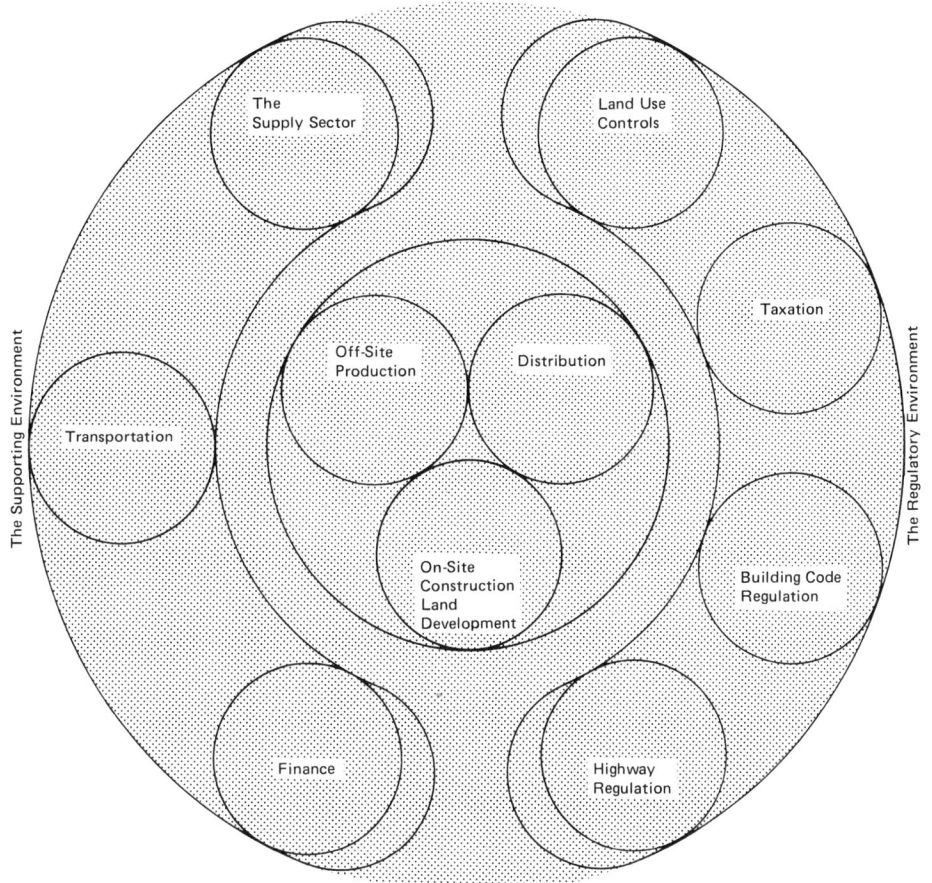

The Supply Sector

Land Use Controls

The Supporting Environment

The Regulatory Environment

Transportation

Off-Site Production

Distribution

Taxation

On-Site Construction Land Development

Building Code Regulation

Finance

Highway Regulation

The mobile home unit has remained a single-family detached dwelling, being limited from any fuller range of housing applications by the negative image of transient shelter that it presents to the general public. This has encouraged zoning regulations that isolate it from established communities. On the other hand, its vehicular design has exempted the mobile home from the regulatory constraints governing traditional housing, thus allowing it to gain ascendancy. Now that the mobile home is firmly established as primary housing, the industry can work toward integration of its product within the residential fabric.

At the same time, the ever-diminishing supply of land for residential development makes the cost of land available to the mobile home park developer more and more prohibitive. The on-site residential construction industry has dealt with the problem of rising land costs in the past two decades by switching from a clear reliance on the single-family, detached house to an increased use of higher-density forms of single-family housing. In the same way higher-density solutions for mobile home developments seem inevitable.

At a time when the need for new housing is increasing while the availability of the many resources required for that housing is decreasing, the mobile home industry can make an important contribution to the solution of the housing crisis. The degree to which it does so will depend upon improved response to the present market and expansion into new markets. As the nature and volume of demand changes, as the external constraints of regulation and finance lessen, and as the supply of land diminishes, there will be an increased opportunity and necessity for architectural innovation in mobile home design.

The mobile home industry thus has two routes for architectural innovation if it wants to participate fully in meeting future market demands. The first is to improve the design quality of the "single" detached mobile home structure. The immediate need is a design of the present product that more clearly communicates the feeling of a "home" and that more strongly fosters the associations of stability, permanence, and integration with a larger residential setting. Similarly, the industry must better adapt its products to nonresidential uses. The industry must perceive the mobile home even more rigorously as a permanent structure, not as a trailer. The ability to grow out of its constricted, boxlike shape and respond flexibly to diverse residential as well as nonresidential needs over time, as can conventional building, is imperative for greater product acceptance and continued future marketing success. When performance more closely resembles that of traditional shelter, its mortgaging, zoning, and taxing can better approximate those of the builder's structure, thereby opening up more residential land for its placement.

The second route is to push the industry's "systems" approach—its well-developed, innovative, and highly efficient approach to shelter delivery—into a wider range of residential as well as nonresidential applications. With the use of movable three-dimensional factory-finished building "components" in higher-density applications, demand from diverse market groups can be met.

The first route—calling for only modest product innovation—can enable the mobile home industry to expand into new markets. One possibility is to innovate in the application of its present product, or upgraded versions of it, for low- to medium-density developments. Examples of this are quality permanent subdivisions, cluster developments, specialty residential applications (like relocation and emergency housing), and nonresidential uses (like banks and showrooms).

Innovative applications of the present product have already been initiated. Industry sales are showing an increasing trend toward doublewides, which are frequently put on permanent foundations. The output of sectionals built on the same assembly line as doublewides is also growing.

The escalation in the price of housing reinforces the magnitude of need for lower-cost, permanent shelter. Innovative prototype developments have pointed to the great possibilities in the use of low- to medium-density groupings of mobile homes as an answer to this need. Higher-density groupings, such as clusters of mobile home units, maximize land use. Despite the extra development and contingency costs involved with prototyping, these projects were still competitive with conventional construction: Successes can be cited in university housing especially, as well as in low-density urban housing, resort housing, and ski lodges.

The use of mobile homes as temporary, short-term housing is recognized but not fully developed in the specialty housing field. Mobile homes designed specifically for temporary occupancy can aid in easing the housing shortages in many cities. For example, tracts of land currently undeveloped or set aside for a designated purpose at a future date could be conditionally assigned to mobile home park development for a limited amount of time, either until urban expansion increases the value of the land to support economically more intensive land uses or until the time to initiate original development plans arrives. In either case the mobile home occupants would realize in advance that their dependence on this type of shelter was temporary and that they will need to relocate after a specified period of time—an arrangement not conflicting with the housing needs of certain population segments such as students or armed forces personnel. In this way much land that remains unutilized for extended periods of time could be constructively activated for temporary residential use.

Singlewides have been extensively used as emergency housing to accommodate the victims of natural disasters. However, the units as they now exist are not designed to meet the highly specific requirements of these people. The industry can capture a larger share of this segment of the specialty housing market if it undertakes a program of designing units specifically for these needs.

With other minor design adjustments of the present product, the industry can also increase its penetration of the nonresidential market. Mobile homes already serve a wide variety of commercial and institutional needs, even though often in a somewhat haphazard manner. Construction field offices, branch banks, general offices, or small restaurants are but a few examples of the many commercial applications. "Little" city halls, libraries, laboratories, ambulant health care units, or churches are examples of the wide range of institutional uses. However, in many cases these units are produced on a custom-order basis in response to client initiative. The industry's flexibility should enable it to produce units specially adapted to suit an even greater percentage of the nonresidential market and aggressively to develop these markets.

The second route for expanding the markets for mobile homes is to design and produce units different from those currently available. Incorporated into this altered product must be design features that would enable the industry to penetrate some of the primary medium- to high-density markets that the other sectors of the building industry now control. The opening up of new market possibilities comes with a new consideration of the mobile home unit as a building "component" rather than a product for use solely as a single-story, detached structure. Modular and dimensional coordination can make a full multimarket repertoire of uses possible for a set of standardized, interchangeable building "components."

The greatest market as yet untouched by the mobile home industry is that of medium- to high-density urban housing. Urban governments have explored the use of mobile homes as relocation and temporary housing and inroads have been made in major cities with "traditional" code-conforming units for low-cost town houses. However, little attention has been paid to the vast potential market for permanent developments and infill housing.

In a reaction to the wholesale elimination of viable neighborhoods brought on by urban renewal programs in the 1960s, attention has turned to the virtues of these areas. The rehabilitation of row houses and the selective demolition of only the unsound and substandard houses shows a return to lower-density urban residential areas. As a result there arises a vast market for infill housing —small numbers of units to fit within existing urban frameworks—that remains to be supplied. The cost advantages that high-volume merchant builders enjoy come primarily from a rationalized and efficiently scheduled on-site process, which is fully dependent upon large-scale suburban or urban subdivision development. No low-cost system is available for on-site production of dispersed urban houses. Infill housing, then, could easily become a captive market for the mobile home industry, which can efficiently produce building "components" for on-site assembly in collaboration with traditional builders.

Another primary market as yet untapped by the mobile home industry is that of higher-density multifamily housing. As land costs have risen, single-family housing has diminished from close to 90 percent of the starts in the mid-1950s to only an approximate 70 percent of the starts in the late 1970s. Prototype projects have shown that the mobile home industry is capable of producing apartments of comparable quality and amenity to much of the rental and condominium developments underway today.

Similarly, there is great potential in the high-density nonresidential market. Industrial and commercial establishments as well as institutions can benefit from the mobile home industry's distinct advantage: a factory production-oriented housing delivery system supplying units year round on a guaranteed-date, fixed-price basis, which would mean shortened project time. Multistory structures serving as laboratories, offices, hotels, or schools are examples indicating the scope of this market.

What remains as important is not the particular unit the mobile home industry is presently producing but instead, the industry's unequaled production and delivery expertise, which could establish it as a major supplier of multifamily and single-family housing as well as nonresidential structures. The industry's success as a low-cost shelter producer has derived to a great extent from its ability to supply efficiently a product and service package that is responsive to its present market and that is moulded to "fit" constraints as well as opportunities presented by the industry's supporting and regulatory environments. Similarly, the industry can evolve a new generation of products designed for a perfect response to new market characteristics. A move into these new markets, with new products and new approaches to development, will require the industry to make both internal and external adjustments. Increasingly substantial changes in its production system, distribution system, park system, as well as its supporting and regulatory environments need to be made—and can be made—if the industry decides to expand from its present markets to related and finally to new markets.

B. The Product Tomorrow

The following discussion offers a wide variety of innovative schemes calling for either modifications of the present mobile home product or for the use of the mobile home building component within higher-density developments. Many innovations have already been successfully demonstrated. The modular housing industry is producing units that can expand on the site by using "fold-out" and "pullout" room sections as well as hinged roofs; the manufactured building industry is stacking volumetric components solidly and in checkerboard configuration; and the on-site building industry is employing high-rise suspension structures to support large new office buildings.

The introduction of novel structural systems and materials will achieve greater freedom in architectural and engineering design. In addition, these new techniques can help transform units into building components for larger systems without sacrificing manufacturing efficiency.

The present mobile home structure of glue-nailed plywood with aluminum siding on a framework of wood members on a steel chassis is engineered to act in its entirety as a structural box beam, a design principle more efficient than conventional wood-frame construction. However, new structural systems are available that can go beyond the advantage of the current system. These methods vary in adaptability to current manufacturing practice, but many of them can be introduced without fundamental changes in the plant.

Metal stud systems with their variability in placement of small openings and their use of many small-sized members are applicable to mobile home construction; the system was widely used in the past in trailer coach construction. Metals are lightweight, ductile, capable of any shape, and as strong as wood in tension and compression. A fastening method comparable to welding and gule-nailing that could take temperature change equally well will have to be developed.

The post and beam system, for which steel is the most likely material, not only is structurally very efficient but also permits highly flexible planning within the mobile home unit. Such design flexibility, combined with the high strength of steel, increases the possibility of adapting the mobile home unit to many different kinds of use, from singlewides to stacked configurations. Post and beam steel systems have already been manufactured in mobile home chassis plants for stacked unit construction.

The full height diagonal wall truss system potentially increases earthquake resistance, transport racking resistance, and ability to cantilever. It is similar to the present mobile home in functioning as a box beam but offers larger openings, fewer joints, and less need for strapping, thereby permitting large expansions of glass and variety in window placement.

In stressed-skin construction, lightweight exterior walls provide structural support, racking resistance, and limited moment connections. The stressed-skin structure is extremely efficient and requires no technical innovation because it is already used to some extent in mobile home and trailer design. A related concept is the structural sandwich panel of exterior and interior sheathing around an insulating core, involving reduced manufacturing time and great structural economy. Such panels can be manufactured from both metal and wood. They need no additional structure.

Building components can also be constructed of plastic or concrete as monolithic volumetric components, which would involve limited jointing and finishing, but with the trade-offs of more substantial capital investment, production inflexibility, greater labor skills, and higher tolerance requirements. Smaller-scaled monolithic building components, however, seem a viable proposal for the future.

The application of new structural systems in the construction of mobile home building components will often require the utilization of alternative building materials that are becoming increasingly available. The industry is already experimenting with new structural applications of wood and metals; concrete and plastics are promising substitute structural materials.

For example, wood can be used in the wall-height diagonal truss system, allowing potentially increased structural efficiency. A plywood stressed-skin panel system, using prefinished exterior grade plywood glue-nailed to studs, can replace aluminum siding with equal strength. A plywood vaulted roof running either across the mobile home or along its length can replace the present bowstring truss system while still acting as a sidewall positioner.

Metal framing systems can replace wood framing if steel or aluminum becomes less expensive. Stud systems exist, but they use metals to less advantage than do post and beam systems. Steel is currently used in the chassis framing, so there is a ready link for the post and beam system. Metal stressed skin also makes very economical use of materials, combining structure and sheathing. However, thermal performance is poor in all-metal stressed-skin systems, and there is less choice of opening sizes than with stud systems. Metals permit finer tolerances and better quality control then wood.

As sufficiently lightweight and fast-setting versions of concrete are developed, this material may become highly desirable. With further research and development concrete that incorporates radically reduced curing times, increased strength, insulation, fireproofing, and finish can be expected to be available. As a wet, controlled process, concrete would be especially amenable to future applications in more automated plants.

Tests employing plastics as substitutes for conventional structural systems in moulded or wound monolithic building elements have been conducted, expanding the role of plastics from coverings and finishes to major building materials. Plastic membranes and stiff sheets to replace glazing have also been developed. Fire and deterioration problems are still present, but plastics do offer lightweight and workable materials for building.

New finish materials are also available to the mobile home industry. They can increase the ease of maintenance, reduce costs in some cases, and, above all, take the mobile home into the architectural realm of the conventional house and beyond, into nonresidential building.

Exterior grade plywood can provide durability, strength, and stiffness comparable to the aluminum now used. Texture 1–11 prefinished panels are now extensively used for combination siding and sheathing in on-site housing. Hardboard sidings with an extremely durable finish and with a variety of appearances are made in large sheets for easy application; these can be manufactured for mobile home industry use. Suppliers to the industry are working on a range of exterior finishes that simulate the clapboards, shakes, or stucco of traditional construction. Aluminum sidings are manufactured in a variety of textures, colors, and finishes. Synthetic, sprayed-on finishes that have been successfully used on the mobile home roof can be used for sidewall finish. Solid vinyl exterior wall coverings are being merchandised, most commonly imitating wood boards or shakes. But although a variety of finish possibilities is highly desirable, imitation of "natural" materials not only weakens architectural design but also creates an impression of artificiality and "cheapness."

Material substitution in combination with a wider range of architectural elements can begin to alter the standardized look of different brands of mobile homes. For example, anodized aluminum can eliminate the metallic shine on aluminum windows, and glass can be used extensively to strengthen architectural expression. Manufacturers' demonstrated ability to use varied picture windows at the end of the mobile home can be carried through to other windows as well; prototype designs have explored the use of bay windows; floor-to-ceiling picture-and-awning window combinations; tall, narrow windows; and sliding glass doors.

The increased use of prefinished sheetrock for the interior walls would introduce a more alterable finish. Vinyl wall coverings can resist damage and aging, be washed, and be purchased in an endless variety of textures and colors; and lighter stains on plywood panels can increase the feeling of interior spaciousness.

Finally, the relatively low fire resistance of the mobile home structure would be improved by increased use of fire-resistant materials: fire-treated framing members, gypsum sheathing or nailing strips, fire-retardant treated plywood, asbestos cement or lightweight concrete. Decreased use of highly combustible thin interior paneling would make the unregulated parts of the home more fire safe. Even greater attention to the matter of fire safety now can help the industry anticipate future issues arising out of product innovation.

If the industry wishes to compete with the conventional housing market, it must place even greater emphasis on overcoming the box shape of units that has been dictated by highway regulation. Horizontal and vertical expansion of the mobile home unit is possible today and is achieved by the use of factory-installed foldouts, pullouts, pop-ups, and fold-ups traveling within the mobile home.

As an example, the foldout terrace is an especially simple form of horizontal expansion. It can travel folded up in a shallow recess, protecting a large window opening and providing in-transit stability to the unit. Another possibility, the car-towed addition, is an easily "reversible" miniunit measuring up to 8 feet × 32 feet. Also, by making a dividable chassis, the total allowable length of the unit can be broken into lesser lengths to form a variety of plans—doublewide, L-, H-, O-, T-, Z-shaped, or offset along a spine.

Hinging is currently familiar to the mobile home manufacturers in their foldout assemblies, but it has applications for vertical expansion as well. For example, a hinging roof that spans up to a stacked mobile unit can create a two-story living room. Units that travel as singlewides and hinge on-site into L-shaped or doublewide units have been detailed. Other examples of vertical expansion are the pop-up, a largely finished element that telescopes up, having traveled nested on the home, and the fold-up.

With the many available expansion options, the potentials of the innovated mobile home unit are endless. Furthermore, units that allow changes and additions over the entire lifespan of the mobile home can be designed. For example, families intending to settle with their homes could purchase an original "starter package" with all the necessary mechanical, electrical, and plumbing lines needed for long tenure already installed. With room layout no longer determined by a singular 14 foot × 70 foot chassis shape, the house could grow according to a family's specific needs. Owner modification could be helped by providing the buyer with an instruction book indicating places where changes could be made without threatening the structural stability or mechanical/electrical systems of the units. Original unit design can anticipate owner modification without requiring major design changes. This process offers a more responsive growth system than conventional building methods.

The ability to revert the site-modified mobile home to its original truckable shape has several advantages. Owners may easily trade in the home for a new one, selling the older unit without leaving their park site. Or they may take their home with them. Mobile home dwellers do not often use this potential because the units are increasingly difficult to move. However, park residents surveyed often considered the possibility of moving the unit an advantage over conventional homes and apartments. The desire to preserve reversibility, especially for resale, often discourages owners from making changes such as add-ons, which might tie the unit to its site. Expansions designed so they can be easily reversed might become more popular if their reversibility were emphasized.

It can be concluded that the movement of the mobile home industry into wider markets depends heavily on the architectural quality of its product. It will have to be demonstrated that the mobile home building component can provide both residential and nonresidential shelter equal or superior to that of the traditional building industry—this is one of the most important prerequisites for gaining acceptance by the general public, government, labor, and financial and consumer groups traditionally opposed to the mobile home.

Attempts at building industrialization characteristically have focused on the technological aspects of innovative architectural design and have paid less attention to their economic and political feasibility. Although the following discussion of innovative schemes intentionally highlights architectural and technical implications, it must be understood that successful implementation depends on the development of a comprehensive shelter production and delivery system, synthesizing and integrating architectural design with the production, distribution, development, and supporting and public regulatory functions. What has been included here is an indication of PMHI's assessment of architectural quality achievable by the mobile home industry. Instances of technical superiority have been pointed to with the assumption that they may be integrated with a high level of design. The full range of possible uses for the mobile home components can be broken down into the six categories below. These are termed "families" of architectural configurations, referring not to the functions of a building (such as a vacation home or relocatable classroom) but rather to their major architectural characteristic. These categories are as follows:

Family A: Singlewide:
A detached, single-story structure (usually dwelling) formed from one truck-towed mobile home unit. This unit may be expanded horizontally or vertically or added to with separately purchased accessories, add-on rooms, or car-towed units.

Family B: Doublewide and triplewide:
A detached, single-story structure (usually dwelling) formed from two or more mobile home units joined together. This unit may be expanded horizontally or vertically or added to with separately purchased accessories, add-on rooms, or car-towed units.

Family C: Cluster:
A group of attached, single-story structures (usually dwellings) formed from mobile home units. If properly designed and sited, these units may be expanded horizontally or vertically or added to with separately purchased accessories, add-on rooms, or car-towed units.

Family D: Low-rise stacked:
Mobile home building components stacked to form two- to four-story structures, usually serving residential needs either as multifamily or single-family detached units. The component mobile home units can also be designed to serve additional markets as singlewides, doublewides, triplewides, and clustered units interchangeably.

Family E: High-rise stacked:
Building components of increased strength, stacked beyond the four-floor walkup height, can make residential (multifamily) as well as nonresidential structures. Elevator and vertical services can be provided independent of the building components.

Family F: Megastructure:
Mobile home building components supported within a separately built
superstructure, from two stories to high-rise. If designed properly, addition
and expansion options are possible. Elevator and vertical services can be
provided independent of the components. If properly designed, the building
components may also serve interchangeably as singlewides, doublewides,
triplewides, clustered, and low-rise stacked units.

On the basis of architectural and engineering analysis of likely architectural
configurations for the final assembly, various types of individual building components are designed with different dimensions and varying architectural and
engineering characteristics. A virtually unlimited number of final-assembly
configurations can be constructed from different combinations of any number
of types of building components. Systematic design as well as modular and
dimensional coordination ensure a coherent, comprehensive system of a large
but limited number of compatible building components. While the components are highly standardized and interchangeable, mass produced and marketed by catalog, the architect using this system can achieve an almost unlimited variety of architectural expression and configuration.

The examples shown under the discussion of each family range from mobile-
home-industry-produced structures all the way to buildings designed for or
built by on-site construction firms. All examples not directly generated by the
mobile home industry have been chosen by PMHI engineers from hundreds of
candidate projects through a thorough evaluation process; all selected examples can be produced at lower than on-site-only costs by the mobile home
industry alone or in collaboration with on-site builders. Projects that either
have been designed for and/or with, or have been produced by the mobile
home industry are presented with the label "example." Projects not designed
specifically for the mobile home industry but determined by PMHI engineers
as produceable by that industry are presented as "PMHI simulations."

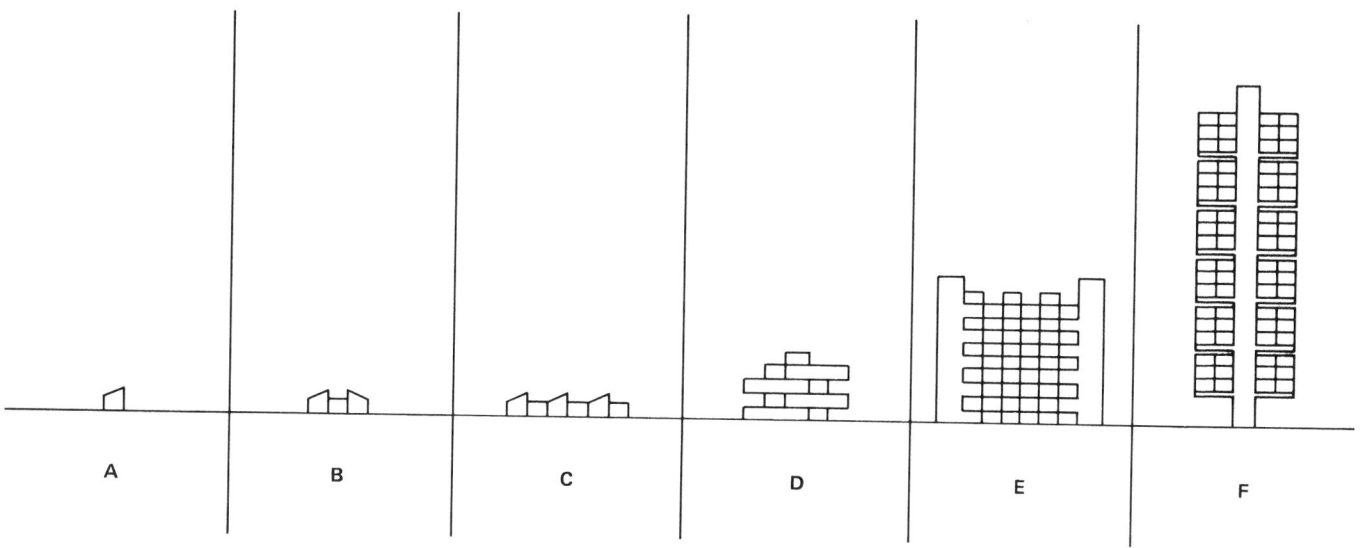

Figure 20.1

Family A:
Singlewide

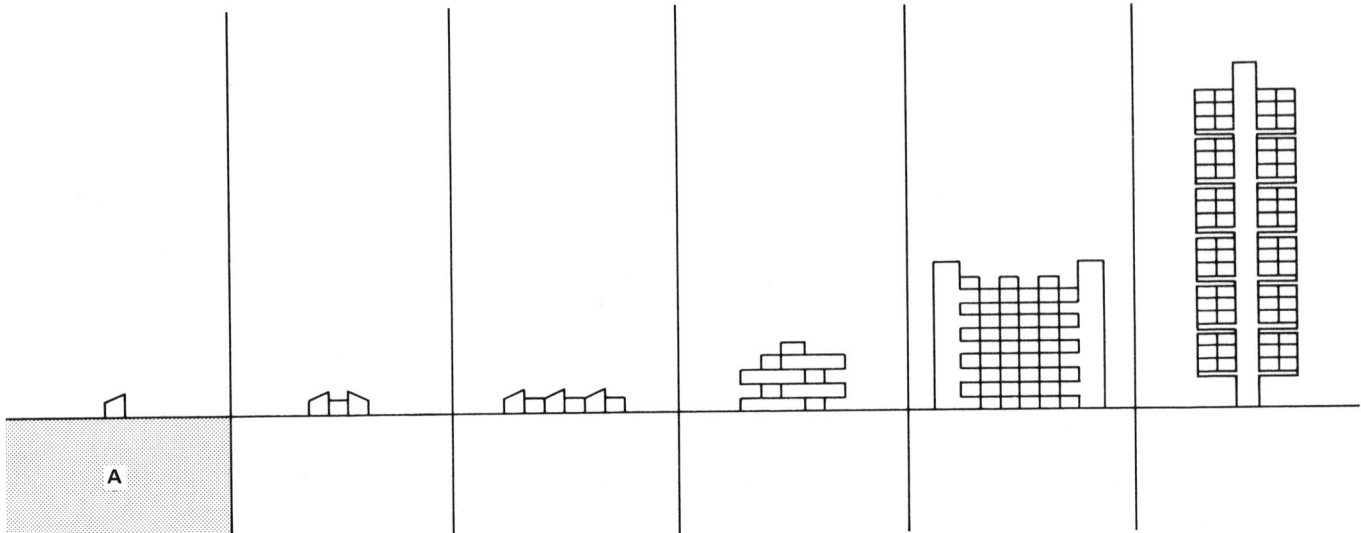

Tomorrow

Although the singlewide can increasingly serve nonresidential functions, its main role will continue to be in residential markets. Desirable modes of innovation therefore relate primarily to the making of a mobile home with the true qualities of a house—sheltering appearance, defined entries and outdoor spaces, adequate activity and storage areas, alterable finishes—rather than with the applied visual imagery of a house.

A better response to the needs of dwelling, as opposed to the needs of transport, must be built into the mobile home. Such architectural changes as new and varied shapes, distinct foyers, higher ceilings, larger windows, indirect lighting, natural materials, and congenial wall colors will transform the single-wide from an overgrown trailer into a true house. These improved amenities, along with foldout terraces, larger glass areas, and more storage space, can make the units more livable. Site planning that creates clear "front door" and "backyard" areas for every home can be achieved at present park densities. Opportunities for personal expression must also be considered; ability to modify the unit to respond to changing needs would be desirable.

The 14-foot-wide basic unit has become nationally accepted, although for transport and highway regulation reasons 12-wides still remain important in certain areas. Unit length can be expected to remain at an average of 60 to 70 feet, with some units reaching 80 feet. Room heights, presently lower than in conventional homes, can be varied by new roof structures, clerestory windows, pitched shed roofs, or a raised overall ceiling height. Fuller use of the 13 foot 6 inch height limit imposed by highway regulation is possible with units without attached wheels that ride on a low-boy carrier. Fullest use may come with hinged pitched roof sections like those used in sectional house construction. Horizontal expansion through pullouts, foldouts, and add-ons can increase the ultimate size and create a less boxlike shape. This will further enable design to focus on activity zoning and the relation of the unit to the outdoors. Unless the unit is embellished by additions or is assembled from a number of smaller components, the long, narrow shape will always be a strong element in its appearance. Accessories such as screens, fences, awnings, sunshades, walks, decks, pavers, and carports are already used to individualize mobile home units. One alternative to accessories is the concept of "options." Manufacturers now offer model choice to meet consumer demand even though provisions for choice reduces production efficiency. Industry cooperation could produce option packages at reasonable cost, manufactured either by mobile home plants or by suppliers or manufacturing operations specializing in such packages.

Availability of a wide range of finishes, roof shapes, expansion options, and integrated accessory packages would significantly improve singlewides' response to demand for housing. Functional constraints of the trailer shape would be eliminated and increased variety and richness of appearance would result. The costs of expanded site preparation would be readily absorbed by the home's increased overall value.

A. Singlewide

Horizontal expansion
Foldout
Pullout
Add on

Vertical expansion
Foldup
Popup

Horizontal and vertical expansion

Segmented unit

Example A1
Configuration:
Singlewide, simple
unit

Design: Pemtom, Inc.

- Designed for mobile home industry
- Designed with mobile home industry
- Produced in mobile home plant
  Could be produced by mobile home
  industry

Figure 20.2

Example A2

Configuration:
Singlewide, foldout
horizontal expansion

Duane A. Kell, Craig
E. Rafferty, M.Arch
A.S. Thesis (Supervi-
sor Eduardo F.
Catalano, with Waclaw
P. Zalewski), M.I.T.

- Designed for mobile home industry
- Designed with mobile home industry
  Produced in mobile home plant
- Could be produced by mobile home
  industry

Figure 20.3

Figure 20.4

Figure 20.5

Figure 20.6

Figure 20.7

Example A3
Configuration:
Singlewide, pullout
horizontal expansion

Architect: Barry A.
Berkus

- Designed for mobile home industry
- Designed with mobile home industry
- Produced in mobile home plant
  Could be produced by mobile home
  industry

Figure 20.8

Example A4
Configuration:
Singlewide, pullout
horizontal expansion
and vertical expan-
sion

Architect: The Archi-
tects Collaborative
Inc.

- Designed for mobile home industry
- Designed with mobile home industry
  Produced in mobile home plant
- Could be produced by mobile home
  industry

Figure 20.9

Example A5

Configuration:
Singlewide, seg-
mented

Design: Goldsworthy
Engineering, Inc.

- Designed for mobile home industry
  Designed with mobile home industry
  Produced in mobile home plant
- Could be produced by mobile home
  industry

Figure 20.10

The Product

Family B:
Doublewide
Triplewide

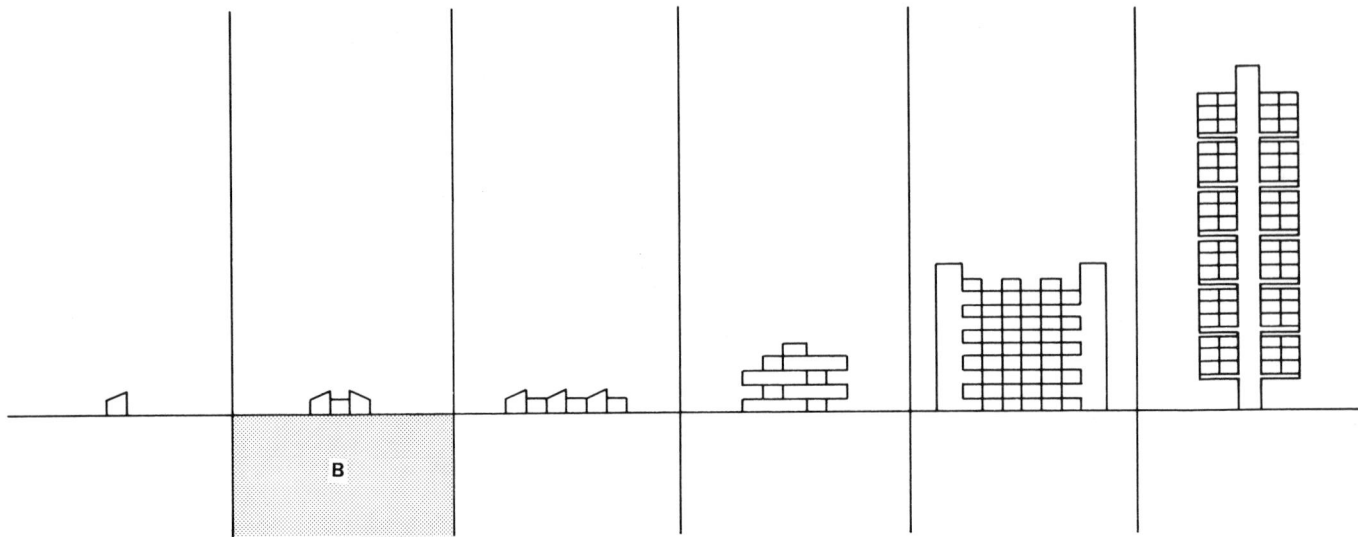

The doublewide and triplewide take the mobile home further into the realm of the traditional single-family house. The same amount of space and the same amenities become available at reduced cost. The doublewide and triplewide need not imitate the appearance of conventional contractor housing. They can take "L," atrium, and many other configurations, and by incorporating the features available in singlewides, from foldouts and add-ons to new finishes, they can achieve an immense variety of design possibilities.

Room dimensions need no longer be determined by the 12- or 14-foot width limitations. Innovative structural systems, such as post and beam, or diagonal truss systems allow the greatest freedom in opening the space between joined units and can make it easier to take advantage of the larger space possibilities. However, even the present mobile home structural system is capable of permitting wide plan flexibility in the doublewide and triplewide.

Doublewides and triplewides can be designed to grow from a singlewide "starter package." The actual design of a doublewide house, however, may vary greatly from the singlewide. Placing units parallel to each other is only one of many possibilities. Units may be arranged in "L," "T," "C," "H," or "Z" patterns, using boxes of the full 45- to 70-foot length or any shorter boxes transported on a divided chassis. Two units may be set apart and linked by a car-towed unit or a wide site-built bridge.

These configurations make possible differentiated interior zones and a wider variety of room uses than are now found in the doublewide. Bedrooms may be zoned into separate groups for age group privacy. Noisy hobby and play rooms may be set apart. Interior courts can create special outdoor rooms. And many of the potential configurations provide outdoor zones, permitting high-density park development.

The total floor area provided by doublewides and triplewides approaches or is equivalent to that of site-built single-family housing. The increased size of these dwellings makes room available for the special family needs that are limited or impossible in a singlewide. The house can contain ample strorage space; a well-defined entry area is no longer difficult to provide; the kitchen can be substantial; indoor play space becomes possible; and defined spaces for an office, den, guest, or game room can be included.

A doublewide or triplewide is more difficult to relocate than a singlewide; more fieldwork is required to disconnect and reconnect the units and more truck tows are needed. As the likelihood of relocation decreases, owner modifications and expansions can.be expected to increase.

Because doublewides are made of more durable materials and are admitted more readily into residential zones, the use of permanent foundations will increase. Thus it can be expected that the doublewides will still be built on chassis, but the running gear will be removable and reusable. The high cost of towing may make doublewides with foldouts more popular than triplewides.

B. Doublewide. Triplewide (Multiple-unit)

Perpendicular configuration:
"H," "C," or "Z"
Horizontal expansion
Vertical expansion
Horizontal and vertical expansion

Parallel configuration: flush or staggered
Horizontal expansion
Vertical expansion
Horizontal and vertical expansion

Perpendicular and parallel configuration
Horizontal expansion
Vertical expansion
Horizontal and vertical expansion

Example B1
Configuration:
Detached multiple-unit, parallel, flush, two units

Design: Vindale Corporation

- Designed for mobile home industry
- Designed with mobile home industry
- Produced in mobile home plant
  Could be produced by mobile home industry

Figure 20.11

Example B2
Configuration:
Detached multiple-
unit, parallel, stag-
gered, two units

Architect: Walter
Brown

- Designed for mobile home industry
- Designed with mobile home industry
- Produced in mobile home plant
  Could be produced by mobile home
  industry

Figure 20.12

Figure 20.13

Figure 20.14

The Product

Example B3
Configuration:
Detached multiple-
unit, parallel, stag-
gered, two units

Architect: Barry A.
Berkus

● Designed for mobile home industry
● Designed with mobile home industry
● Produced in mobile home plant
Could be produced by mobile home
industry

Figure 20.15

Tomorrow

Figure 20.16

Figure 20.17

Figure 20.18 ,

Figure 20.19

Figure 20.20

Example B4
Configuration:
Detached multiple-
unit, perpendicular
second parallel, three
units

Design: Vindale
Corporation

- Designed for mobile home industry
- Designed with mobile home industry
- Produced in mobile home plant
  Could be produced by mobile home
  industry

Figure 20.21

The Product

Family C:
Cluster

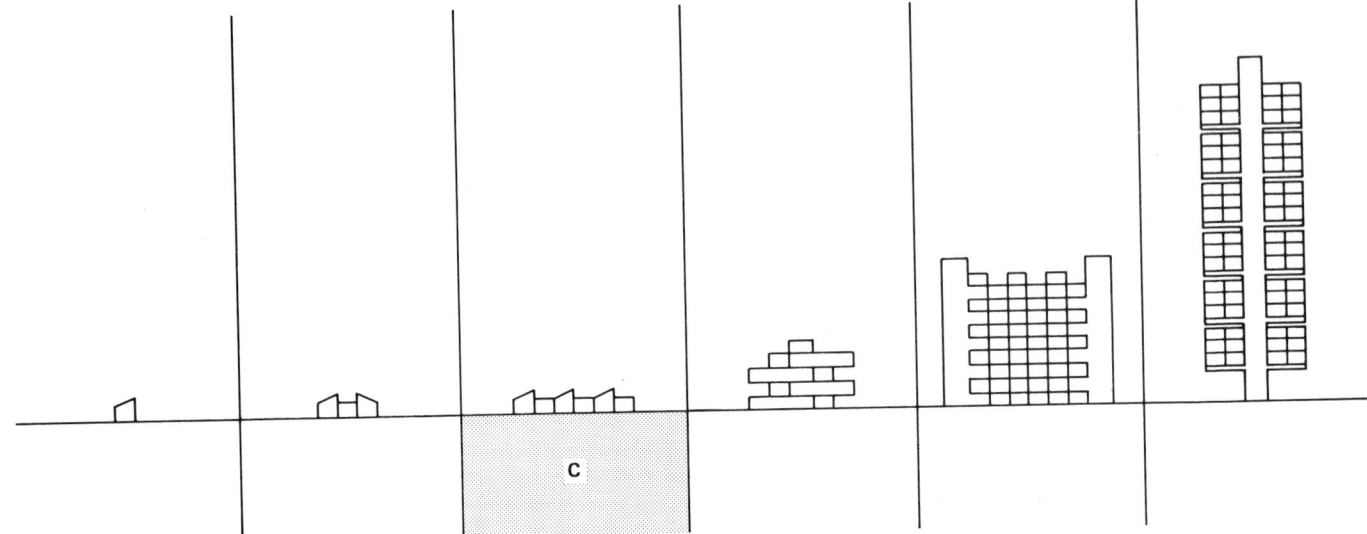

Tomorrow

Single-story high-density clusters are highly practical with no major change in the existing product. This holds true for nonresidential as well as residential applications, although housing is the most promising use for this configuration. The rising cost of land has caused many home builders to move into multi-family development, and the mobile home manufacturers and park developers need be no exception. Clustering of dwellings can greatly increase privacy at high densities, providing individual yards, clearly defined front entry areas, and large outdoor open areas. The unit walls define the space boundaries between dwellings, permitting very high standards of indoor and outdoor amenity at densities of ten and even fourteen doublewide dwellings per acre.

It is often the design of the park as much as of the mobile homes within it that bothers a municipality. By the use of clustered mobile homes designed to provide full amenities to the units while forming pleasant open green spaces, better land use and more attractive park development can be achieved. Clustering has received far too little attention from the industry and designers alike. Investigations of its possibilities could contribute greatly to the broadened acceptance of mobile homes.

A vast number of cluster configurations is possible. They divide into two main groups: perpendicular and parallel. The perpendicular configurations have the advantage of using the units to create private outdoor zones for dwellings. They provide ample yards and most of the atmosphere and amenities of single-family homes at much higher densities. The parallel configuration is more economical of space, can be staggered to create distinct private outdoor zones for each dwelling, and is more efficient in heat retention. The character of a dwelling in parallel configuration is more similar to a garden apartment than to a single-family house. Parallel configurations are also best for most nonresidential uses.

Expansion and combinations of units of varying size can increase the potential for plan variation. Plan variation should take into account the possibility for adaptability to a wide variety of potential sites and configurations.

With the exception of fireproofing needs, the construction of the mobile home unit suited to clustering need not be different from the singlewide, doublewide, or triplewide units. The same holds true for both structural and nonstructural materials. There is, however, a great need for standards of fire safety between dwellings. The present Federal Mobile Home Construction and Safety Standards make no provision for the fire walls necessary between clustered units. Until the federal code can be modified to cover factory-installed fire walls as integral components of the unit, site-built fire walls will be needed for clusters where local codes require them. Incorporating fire walls in-plant within a unit can be done in a number of ways. For example, a 1 1/2-inch fiberglass-reinforced gypsum wallboard between units can provide a two-hour rating yet is light enough to be part of the unit. Proprietary systems that provide this two-hour rating are available and have been used. Wood treatments have also been devised for construction that allows noncombustible materials both for framing and specially graded plywoods.

Site-built walls requiring minimal labor are the other alternative. Precast concrete panels less than 4 inches thick can be easily placed between dwellings or the exterior walls of the mobile home units themselves can become formwork for on-site pouring of concrete fire walls in a narrow gap left between units. Such innovations can significantly reduce the high cost of on-site masonry construction. Fire walls can be extended beyond the unit to become an architectural and planning asset. Configurations that reduce the length of the walls adjoining one another in a cluster can cut the need for fire walls by as much as 75 percent.

C. Cluster

Perpendicular configuration: Singlewide or doublewide
Linear sequence
   Straight-line
   Staggered
Circular sequence
   Outward-oriented (cross)
   Inward-oriented (atrium)

Parallel configuration
Straight-line sequence
   Flush
   Separated
   Articulated
Staggered sequence
   Alternating
   Stepped
   Articulated

Perpendicular and parallel configuration

Erection C

Figure 20.22

Tomorrow

**PMHI
Simulation C1**
Configuration:
Cluster, perpendicular

Design: Electro-
Mechanical Corporation

Designed for mobile home industry
Designed with mobile home industry
Produced in mobile home plant
● Could be produced by mobile home
industry

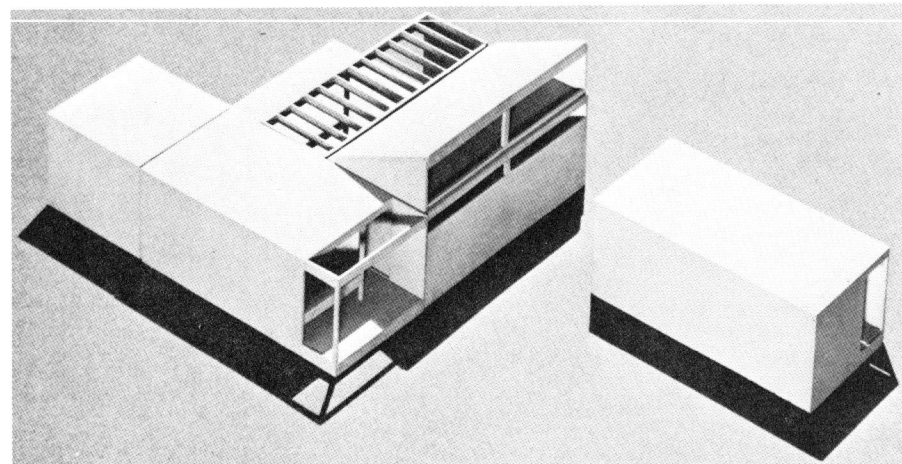

Figure 20.23

**PMHI
Simulation C2**
Configuration:
Cluster, parallel
(interwoven with
two- and three-story
structures)

Architect: The Archi-
tects Collaborative Inc.

Designed for mobile home industry
Designed with mobile home industry
Produced in mobile home plant
● Could be produced by mobile home
industry

Figure 20.24

The Product

PMHI
Simulation C3
Configuration:
Cluster, parallel

Architect: The Archi-
tects Collaborative Inc.

Designed for mobile home industry
Designed with mobile home industry
Produced in mobile home plant
● Could be produced by mobile home
industry

Figure 20.25

Figure 20.26

Figure 20.27

Figure 20.28

The Product

**PMHI
Simulation C4**
Configuration:
Cluster, parallel
(on sloped site)

Ho-Ling, Teng, M.
Arch. Thesis (Super-
visor Jan Lubicz-Nycz,
with Waclaw p.
Zalewski), M.I.T.

Designed for mobile home industry
Designed with mobile home industry
Produced in mobile home plant
● Could be produced by mobile home
industry

Figure 20.29

**PMHI
Simulation C5**
Configuration:
Cluster, parallel (on
sloped site)

Lawrence S. Gordon,
M.Arch. Thesis
(Supervisor Jan
Lubicz-Nycz, with
Kevin Lynch), M.I.T.

Designed for mobile home industry
Designed with mobile home industry
Produced in mobile home plant
● Could be produced by mobile home
industry

Figure 20.30

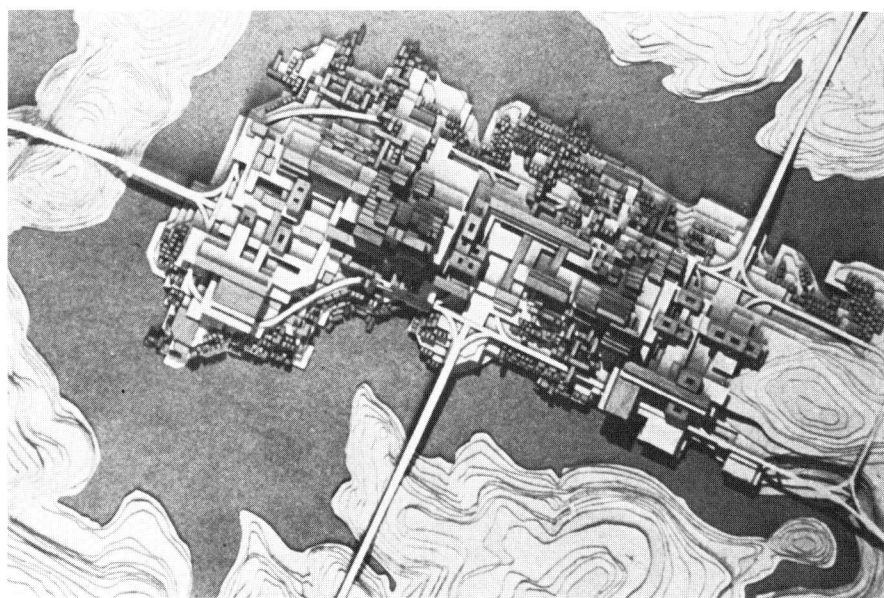

Figure 20.31

**PMHI
Simulation C6**
Configuration:
Cluster, perpendic-
ular, and parallel
(interwoven with
structures of more
than one story)

Architect: The
Architects Collabora-
tive Inc.

Designed for mobile home industry
Designed with mobile home industry
Produced in mobile home plant
● Could be produced by mobile home industry

Figure 20.32

Figure 20.33

Figure 20.34

**MHI
Simulation C7**
(Configuration:
Cluster, perpendic-
ular, and parallel
interwoven with
two- and three-story
structures)

Design: Pantek
Corporation

Designed for mobile home industry
Designed with mobile home industry
Produced in mobile home plant
● Could be produced by mobile home
industry

Figure 20.35

Family D:
Low-rise
Stacked

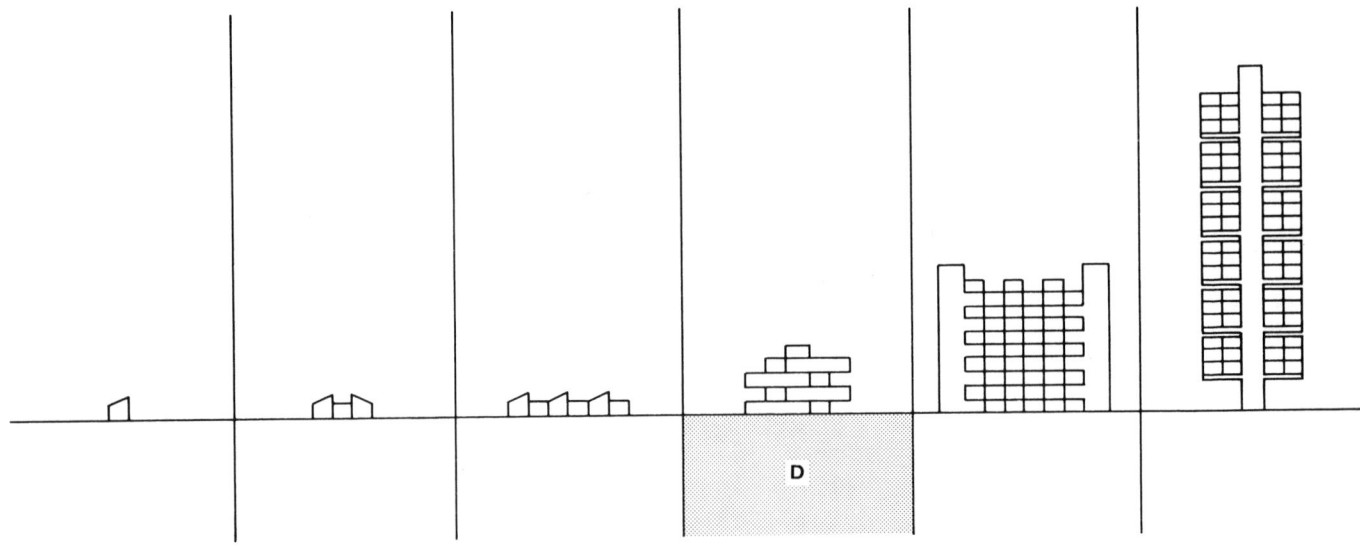

Tomorrow

Immense advantages in land use efficiency are to be gained from stacking building components. The stacked unit will enable the industry to enter urban and suburban markets for residential (for example, town house and apartment units) as well as nonresidential structures, markets permanently closed to the present unit. To gain these advantages, the industry must sacrifice some of the unit's economies in materials use, as well as its classification as a mobile home. Reversibility is gone, site work is increased. However, not last as a result of the efficiencies in manufacturing, costs can still remain substantially below the equivalent cost for conventional low-rise density housing.

The mobile home ceases to be an independent entity in the stacked configuration. It is no longer a "mobile home" but has become a component of a larger building. Although units can be designed for multiple use in other families, they must be able to work as a group in the larger stacked configuration.

The standard mobile home is not designed to support structurally additional units. There are two ways of increasing structural capability within the existing production system: Today's typical units with 2 x 4s on 16-inch centers can be stacked more than three stories if larger structural members are added at critical load points to form a hybrid frame; and site-built fire walls can be used to support building components.

With a greater degree of change, manufacturers could build stackable components that utilize innovations in either materials or structure. The use of metals seems a likely move. Metal stud or post and beam systems could stack to three stories. Steel structures offer greater strength, are extremely efficient, and permit a wide variety of infill materials and design variations—they can be seen as an extension of chassis fabrication. Metal stressed-skin systems offer greater volumetric structural economy in the use of materials yet when stacked require redundant material and limit plan flexibility.

Boxes of lightweight concrete could be practical in stacking because they offer high inherent sound- and fireproofing performance, good insulation properties, ease of running utilities, simplified fabrication and a high degree of factory finish. To stack only a few stories avoids the complex and expensive reinforcing problems that have plagued high-rise, heavy concrete box projects; and the materials saving of checkerboard stacking could be considerable. However, in this country, lightweight concrete is still in its infancy and requires concentrated research and development before it becomes a serious contender to conventional framed mobile home units.

As discussed previously in connection with clusters, there are means available to incorporate fire protection within the manufactured unit. The problem, especially for multiplant manufacturers, is that greater interstate uniformity in fire code regulation will be necessary before any design decisions about these integral walls can be made. Another problem, and major distinguishing characteristic of the low-rise stacked units, is the need for fire stairs and a second means of egress from each dwelling unit. Compliance with local regulations on these matters will be necessary, for local control will always remain strong. However, the industry could work out alternative model solutions to these fire protection problems designed to meet most local code requirements.

A number of approaches to utility connections are possible. One is to build a multistory utility core with all "wet" kitchen and bath elements within it or hooking into it. This core is fabricated in the factory along with the apartment units, then transported in a horizontal position, and finally tilted up on the site. Another approach is to fabricate "wet" components and "dry" components, being careful to locate the utility sections in close vertical proximity. Then special vertical runs for supply and waste can be incorporated into stair runs or special chases.

Because a stacked residential project cannot be designed as an aggregation of mobile homes, an anatomy with no corresponding physiology—mechanical systems, water supply, sanitary wastes, storm drains and gutters, vent stacks, electrical wires, louvers, exhaust fans, chimneys—must be carefully worked out in advance.

A corresponding need in low-rise stacked buildings is for the vertical circulation of people and goods. Inclusion of prefabricated public stairs and corridors within the components could be costly, owing to the close tolerances required when fitting parts together at the site. A probable solution is to build circulation cores—perhaps even an upended mobile home—or to field-apply the circulation on the exterior.

The most radical design opportunity derives from the box beam structure and the expansion capability inherent in the mobile home. Much of current apartment construction is strangled by cost constraints and is stripped of anything not required to keep it standing. Because of the cellular nature of the building components used in low-rise stacking, great facade articulation and cantilevers are possible; carports, terraces, and balconies add little cost. Variety in materials, window design, interior layout, and unit size are possible within any particular apartment development. Expansion options can produce even more variation in apartment appearance and layout, far surpassing that of bearing wall construction.

Four basic types of configuration are possible: perpendicular, parallel, checkerboard, and upended. In parallel stacking, the easiest type, units are flush, set back, or cantilevered; but they remain on the same axis. All interior spaces are within the boxes, prefinished. This pattern is comparatively uneconomical of materials and transport, but it reduces field labor. Stacking of building components at right angles in plan is structurally more complex but permits greater design variety. This configuration invites cantilevering and opens the possibilities of multiple exposures, cross-ventilation, zoned floor plans, and private outdoor areas. In checkerboard stacking boxes alternate with voids. The open spaces can be left that way or they can be site-finished. Pullouts, foldouts, or prefinished panels can reduce the need for site work, making this possibly the most economical form of stacking. Vertical units can find immediate use as stair towers and kitchen-bathroom units, but entire apartments could be made from upended building components.

D. Low-rise Stacked

Perpendicular configuration
Singlewide
Doublewide

Parallel configuration
Solid stacking
   Flush
   Alternating
Checkerboard stacking
   Linear
   Staggered
Vertical stacking with vertical infill

Perpendicular and parallel configuration

Upended components

Erection D

Figure 20.36

The Product

**PMHI
Simulation D1**
Configuration:
Low-rise stacked,
perpendicular

Architect: Philleo
Engineering and
Architectural Service

Designed for mobile home industry
Designed with mobile home industry
Produced in mobile home plant
● Could be produced by mobile home
industry

Figure 20.37

Figure 20.38

Tomorrow

Figure 20.39

Figure 20.40

PMHI
Simulation D2
Configuration:
Low-rise stacked,
perpendicular

Architect: Arthur
Klipfel

Designed for mobile home industry
Designed with mobile home industry
Produced in mobile home plant
● Could be produced by mobile home
   industry

Figure 20.41

Figure 20.42

Tomorrow

Example D3
Configuration:
Low-rise stacked,
parallel

Architect: Conklin &
Rossant

- Designed for mobile home industry
- Designed with mobile home industry
- Produced in mobile home plant (proto-
  types)
- Could be produced by mobile home
  industry

Figure 20.43

**PMHI
Simulation D4**
Configuration:
Low-rise stacked,
parallel

Lawrence S. Gordon,
M.Arch. Thesis
(Supervisor Jan
Lubicz-Nycz, with
Kevin Lynch), M.I.T.

Designed for mobile home industry
Designed with mobile home industry
Produced in mobile home plant
- Could be produced by mobile home
  industry

Figure 20.44

The Product

**PMHI
Simulation D5**
Configuration:
Low-rise stacked,
parallel

Architect: The
Architects Collabor-
ative Inc.

Designed for mobile home industry
Designed with mobile home industry
Produced in mobile home plant
● Could be produced by mobile home
  industry

Figure 20.45

Figure 20.46

Figure 20.47

Figure 20.48

Example D6
Configuration:
Low-rise stacked,
parallel

Architect: Tiffany
Armstrong

- Designed for mobile home industry
- Designed with mobile home industry
- Produced in mobile home plant
  Could be produced by mobile home
  industry

Figure 20.49

**PMHI
Simulation D7**
Configuration:
Low-rise stacked,
perpendicular, and
parallel

Architect: Insta-
Buildings, Inc.

Designed for mobile home industry
Designed with mobile home industry
Produced in mobile home plant
- Could be produced by mobile home
  industry

Figure 20.50

Figure 20.51

Example D8

Configuration:
Low-rise stacked,
perpendicular, and
parallel

Architect: Paul
Rudolph

- Designed for mobile home industry
- Designed with mobile home industry
- Produced in mobile home plant
  Could be produced by mobile home
  industry

Figure 20.52

Figure 20.53

Figure 20.54

PMHI
Simulation D9
Configuration:
Low-rise stacked,
perpendicular, and
parallel

Architect: Moshe
Safdie

Designed for mobile home industry
Designed with mobile home industry
Produced in mobile home plant
● Could be produced by mobile home
   industry

Figure 20.55

Figure 20.56

Tomorrow

PMHI
Simulation D10
Configuration:
Low-rise stacked,
upended components

Architect: Barry A.
Berkus

Designed for mobile home industry
Designed with mobile home industry
Produced in mobile home plant
● Could be produced by mobile home
industry

Figure 20.57

The Product

Figure 20.58

Figure 20.59

**PMHI
Simulation D11**
Configuration:
Low-rise stacked,
upended components
(combined with
low-rise, stacked,
parallel)

Architect: Tiffany
Armstrong

Designed for mobile home industry
Designed with mobile home industry
Produced in mobile home plant
● Could be produced by mobile home
industry

Figure 20.60

Figure 20.61

453   The Product

Family E:
High-rise
Stacked

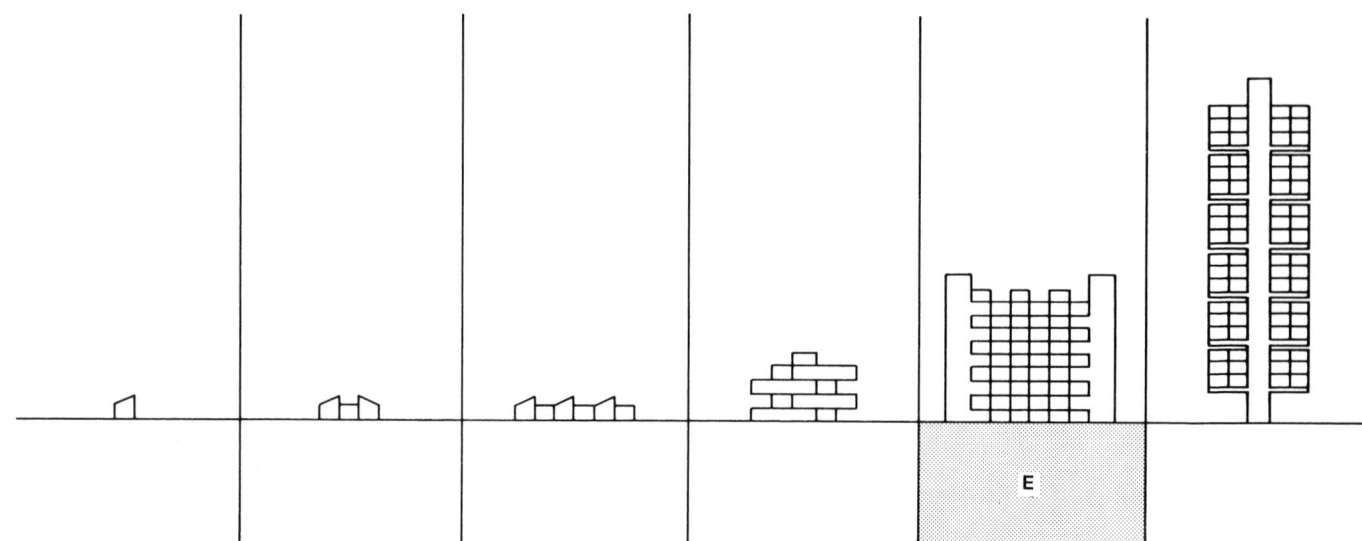

Tomorrow

In order for components to be stacked higher than four stories, some fundamental structural and resultant manufacturing changes would be necessary. This is the only family that would require such major changes. The potential market for cellular high-rise construction is great and the technical feasibility has been explored in many projects. The mobile home industry could choose to diversify into this kind of construction by recognizing that the past successes were primarily due to wise management rather than sophisticated technology. High-rise stacking offers the industry a chance to develop more sophisticated materials and methods that may find application both in this and other Families of construction. For example, development work has been done on volumetric metal units that stack from four to six stories and concrete has been used up to twenty-one stories. Whatever the structural solution, the high-rise stacked mobile home building component would offer a completely prefinished system that would radically cut on-site and development work.

Industrialized components are already strongly influencing the architectural expression of much high-rise construction, so the appearance of high-rise stacked buildings will not be considered "shocking" or "unacceptable" by the consumer. High-rise stacked construction, inherently nontraditional, would offer the possibility of exploring the genuine esthetics of box unit construction. The ability of the box to cantilever and cross-stack makes "exotic" designs possible. In the more economical checkerboard system, voids and lesser cantilevers might still add richness to a facade. Stacking of boxes implies a deeply modulated exterior rather than the sheer curtain wall or load-bearing wall.

The design of the boxes is critical in such a situation. Further, in view of the temptation to produce identical large-scale building components by automated processes, unit and process designs that make feasible variations in layouts, openings, and materials are important. The advantage of stacking is that the resulting buildings need not appear identical, for they are assemblies of many different components.

The structural materials of the standard mobile home, of course, are not adequate. Steel or, concrete become necessary. However, fire protection of structural elements in a high-rise building requires a three-hour fire rating, in contrast to the one-hour rating of single-family dwellings. Steel calls for careful fire protection. Lightweight concrete boxes are a very attractive potential alternative to steel because they solve the fireproofing problem and provide an excellent sound barrier.

Checkerboard stacking or stacking in combination with panels can yield great increases in efficiency, especially for concrete. Transportation is cut in half, as is heavy crane time on-site.

The need to standardize the box units comes into conflict with the need for boxes of varying strength for the lower and upper parts of a high-rise building. In order to avoid sharp limits on potential building height, boxes of varying strength become necessary. However, only a few different strength graduations are required for all but the tallest structures. In a highly efficient material, such as steel, a certain amount of structural redundancy (upper-story units being overstructured to match lower supporting units) may be acceptable in return for standardization of elements. Conventional steel construction makes this compromise by using some extra steel for the sake of standardization and ease of fabrication. Wind resistance, also a difficulty with high buildings, can generally be solved by the use of elevator towers and utility cores as shear walls.

A potential advantage of this building method is in the flexibility of interior layouts. Mechanical cores and access are fixed, but there is no premium to placing identical units throughout an entire building, as is the case today with apartment design. An assembly line for stackable components has the same capability for interior variations as the assembly line for mobile home models. With perpendicular and checkerboard stacking there is the opportunity for creation of voids for terraces or small-scale additions.

As in the case of the low-rise stacked building, there are four basic box configurations. Perpendicular stacking, parallel stacking, and upending boxes all lead to some duplication of structural elements. This means higher costs for materials and transportation. The increased weight requires some over-structuring of the lower boxes. On the other hand, these configurations permit complete factory finishing of boxes, an advantage that can often override this structural redundancy. Where this is not the case, checkerboard stacking can be a more economical solution.

E. High-rise Stacked

Perpendicular
Singlewide
Doublewide

Parallel configuration
Solid stacking
   Flush
   Alternating
Checkerboard stacking
   Linear
   Staggered
Vertical stacking with vertical infill

Upended components

Erection E

Figure 20.62

    The Product

PMHI
Simulation E1
Configuration:
High-rise stacked,
perpendicular

Architect: The Archi-
tects Collaborative
Inc.

Designed for mobile home industry
Designed with mobile home industry
Produced in mobile home plant
● Could be produced by mobile home
industry

Figure 20.63

Figure 20.64

Tomorrow

**PMHI
Simulation E2**
Configuration:
High-rise stacked,
perpendicular

Herbert G. Zeller, M.
Arch. Thesis (Super-
visor Jan Lubicz-
Nycz), M.I.T.

Designed for mobile home industry
Designed with mobile home industry
Produced in mobile home plant
● Could be produced by mobile home
industry

Figure 20.65

**PMHI
Simulation E3**
Configuration:
High-rise stacked,
perpendicular

Architect: Moshe
Safdie

Designed for mobile home industry
Designed with mobile home industry
Produced in mobile home plant
● Could be produced by mobile home
industry

Figure 20.66

Charles C. Wong,
M. Arch. Thesis (Super-
visor Jan Lubicz-
Nycz), M.I.T.

Designed for mobile home industry
Designed with mobile home industry
Produced in mobile home plant
● Could be produced by mobile home
industry

Figure 20.67

Figure 20.68

PMHI
Simulation E5
Configuration:
High-rise stacked,
parallel

Architect: The Archi-
tects Collaborative
Inc.

Designed for mobile home industry
Designed with mobile home industry
Produced in mobile home plant
● Could be produced by mobile home
industry

Figure 20.69

Figure 20.70

Figure 20.71

PMHI
Simulation E6
Configuration:
High-rise stacked,
parallel

Architect: Travers/
Johnson

Designed for mobile home industry
Designed with mobile home industry
Produced in mobile home plant
● Could be produced by mobile home
industry

Figure 20.72

PMHI
Simulation E7
Configuration:
High-rise stacked,
parallel (checker-
board)

Design: Shelley
Engineering Corpora-
tion

Designed for mobile home industry
Designed with mobile home industry
Produced in mobile home plant
● Could be produced by mobile home
industry

Figure 20.73

**PMHI
Simulation E8**
Configuration:
High-rise stacked,
parallel (checker-
board)

Architect: Moshe
Safdie

Designed for mobile home industry
Designed with mobile home industry
Produced in mobile home plant
● Could be produced by mobile home
industry

Figure 20.74

Figure 20.75

Tomorrow

PMHI
Simulation E9
Configuration:
High-rise stacked,
upended components

Architect: The Archi-
tects Collaborative
Inc.

Designed for mobile home industry
Designed with mobile home industry
Produced in mobile home plant
● Could be produced by mobile home
industry

Figure 20.76

The Product

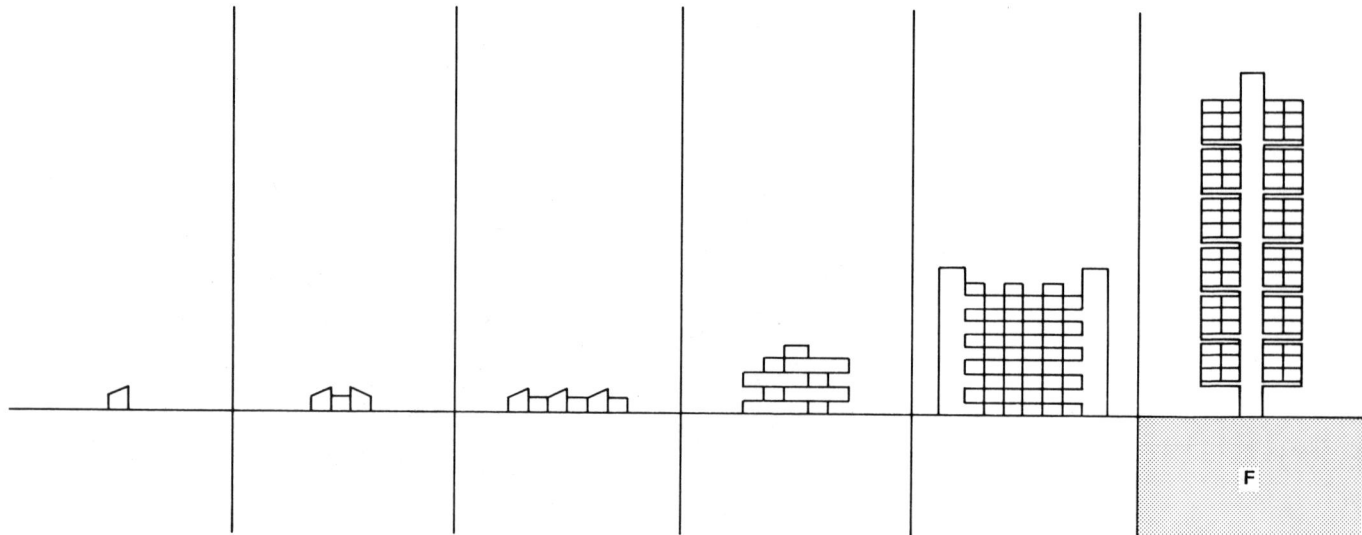

The megastructure concept supposes two distinct "systems" of construction—the supporting structure and the light "infill" mobile home building component—which may be engineered to work together structurally. The megastructure may take many forms, of which high-rise is one important possibility. A new flexibility of space planning becomes possible, as in office buildings. Multiple uses within a building and a wide range of residential layouts can now occur, for the particular function of a space no longer determines the size of the structural bay.

The mobile home building components within the megastructure have been looked at either as elements of a larger building or as independent components within a supporting structure. This latter notion has prompted proposals ranging from "plug-in-city" to mobile home parking garages. The economy of a permanent crane raising and lowering units is very questionable. The structural inefficiency of such proposals argues against them also because it necessitates about a 30 percent increase in support members.

The more promising approach introduces economy and efficiency into the conventional building process by utilizing the building components as integral parts of the total structure. The reduced costs of on-site labor and the shortened construction time that apply to other Families would pertain to the megastructure also.

The "infill" components and the supporting structure are largely independent. The components need not be very strong. The standard mobile home could be acceptable within a larger support structure so long as fire could not spread from one dwelling to another. No fundamental changes from the materials used in Families A through D would be necessary. There is the need, however, for a high degree of quality control and workmanship because the rate of repair must not be any greater than that of conventional high-rise construction. And it is clear that the appearance of the units used as components within the megastructure would depart from that of today's mobile home.

Three basic megastructure types are possible: frame, cantilever, and suspension. In the first, a frame of steel or concrete would support boxes that would probably be stacked two or three stories within the structural "cage." This megastructure is most similar to conventional high-rise apartment construction but uses fewer structural members. The second possible type of structure is a tower with "branches" extending out from a central core. Mobile home units would be supported on these arms, probably stacked for greatest efficiency. The third system would support the boxes on cables hung from a central core tower. Similar suspension systems, though seemingly extreme, are already in use for high-rise office construction. The suspension system is potentially very economical in its use of materials.

The hybrid building could be designed to match the architecture of conventional high-rise buildings or the components could be expressed as visual elements contrasting with the supporting structure. Very "exotic" structures become possible, but this is an option, not a requirement.

Existing megastructures, such as unused factories or warehouses, can also be reused to support, for example, mobile home housing. The resulting building can have architectural as well as economic significance if the units and the renovation are well designed.

There is also a new freedom of interior layout possibilities with such a system, a particularly important advantage for residential applications. Although the individual components are structurally the same, they may be assembled into an endless variety of dwelling types. Perhaps the greatest constraint to high-density housing design today is the economic necessity of exploring the efficiencies resulting from repetition of identical dwelling units, thus limiting income and age mix within a development. The megastructure is freed from these restrictions because the components and not the dwelling units are standardized; thus apartments of differing sizes, layouts, and amenities are possible. The megastructure makes possible multiuse buildings in which large site-finished spaces are combined with the smaller rooms of mobile home units. Hotels might make special use of this quality.

The idea of the reversibility of a megastructure development still holds the imagination of many designers, and indeed it does have advantages. The possibility of replacing a worn-out component and of maintaining each component separately has great appeal; the durability of every material that goes into today's monolithic high-rise construction contributes to the high initial cost that must be amortized and necessitates expensive repairs, disrupting building service as outdated or low-quality items wear out. The dream of a solution to this problem adds to the appeal of the megastructure concept. Such reversibility, although possible, is not so easy as to permit a megastructure whose infill components are in a constant state of flux, as has been proposed in some schemes. Removing components and replacing them is complex and expensive enough to be limited only to rare replacements due to severe damage or to major renovations for new uses or increased operating efficiency. But reversibility, even with such constraints, gives the megastructure a special long-term advantage over the conventional building. The megastructure itself can potentially be made of reversible elements, possibly a nonmonolithic precast system, also amenable to partial or total replacement over a long period of time.

Post-and-beam frame
Supports at every floor
Stacked components

Cantilever structure
Supports at every floor
Stacked components

Suspension structure
Supports for every component
Grouped components

Existing structure

rection F

Figure 20.77

The Product

PMHI
Simulation F1
Configuration:
Megastructure,
post-and-beam
frame, supports at
every floor

Architect: Kirk-
Wallace-McKinley

Designed for mobile home industry
Designed with mobile home industry
Produced in mobile home plant
● Could be produced by mobile home
industry

Figure 20.78

Figure 20.79

PMHI
Simulation F2
Configuration:
Megastructure,
post-and-beam
frame, stacked com-
ponents

Alexander P. Bailey et
al., M.Arch. Thesis
(Supervisor Jan
Lubicz-Nycz, with
Waclaw P. Zalewski),
M.I.T.

Designed for mobile home industry
Designed with mobile home industry
Produced in mobile home plant
● Could be produced by mobile home
industry

Figure 20.80

Figure 20.81

Figure 20.82

The Product

**PMHI
Simulation F3**
Configuration:
Megastructure,
cantilever, stacked
components

Richard G. Henriquez,
M.Arch. Thesis
(Supervisor Jan
Lubicz-Nycz, with
Waclaw P. Zalewski),
M.I.T.

Designed for mobile home industry
Designed with mobile home industry
Produced in mobile home plant
● Could be produced by mobile home
industry

Figure 20.83

Tomorrow

**PMHI
Simulation F4**
Configuration:
Megastructure,
cantilever, supports
at every floor

Ho-Ling Teng,
M.Arch. Thesis
(Supervisor Jan
Lubicz-Nycz, with
Waclaw P. Zalewski),
M.I.T.

Designed for mobile home industry
Designed with mobile home industry
Produced in mobile home plant
● Could be produced by mobile home
industry

Figure 20.84

Figure 20.85

The Product

Example F5

Configuration:
Megastructure,
suspension structure,
supports for every
component

Francis A. Bulbulian,
Joel H. Goodman,
M.Arch. Thesis
(Supervisor Eduardo
F. Catalano, with
Waclaw P. Zalewski),
M.I.T.

- Designed for mobile home industry
- Designed with mobile home industry
  Produced in mobile home plant
- Could be produced by mobile home
  industry

Figure 20.86

Figure 20.87

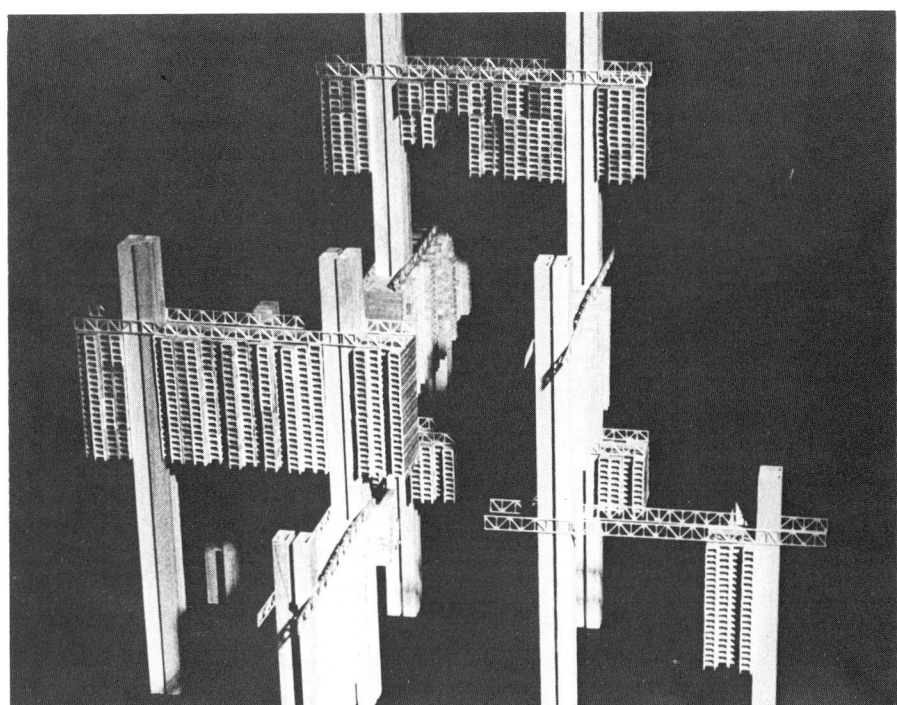

Figure 20.88

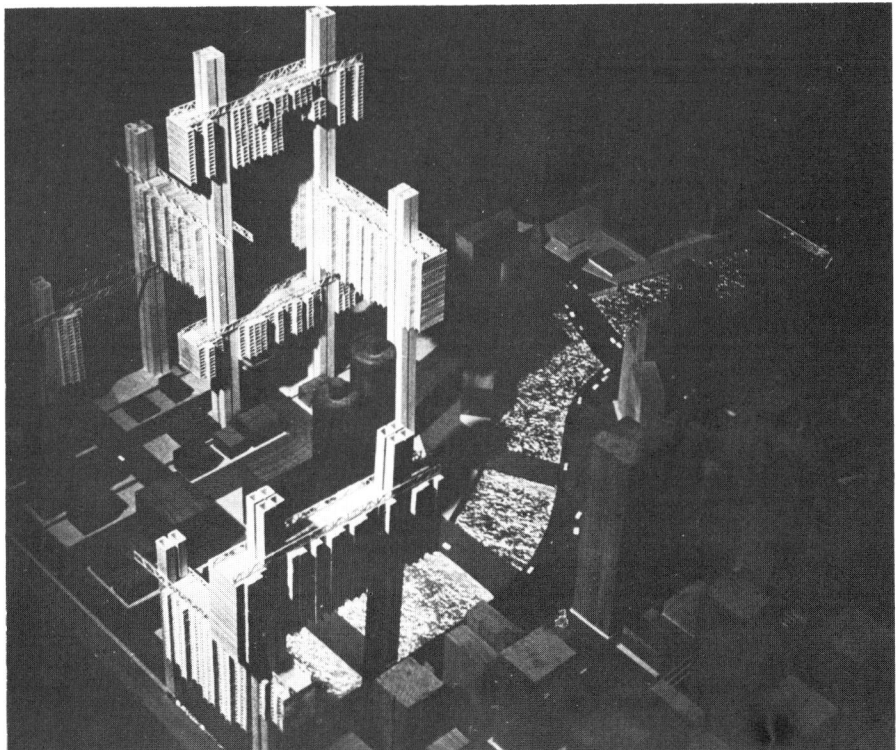

Figure 20.89

PMHI
Simulation F6
Configuration:
Megastructure,
suspension structure,
supports for every
component

David K. Hyun, Keun
S. Lee, M.Arch.
Thesis (Supervisor
Eduardo F. Catalano),
M.I.T.

Designed for mobile home industry
Designed with mobile home industry
Produced in mobile home plant
● Could be produced by mobile home
industry

Figure 20.90

Figure 20.91

Figure 20.92

PMHI
Simulation F7
Configuration:
Megastructure,
suspension structure,
supports for every
component

Architect: Moshe
Safdie

Designed for mobile home industry
Designed with mobile home industry
Produced in mobile home plant
● Could be produced by mobile home
industry

Figure 20.93

Tomorrow

Figure 20.94

C. Implications of Potential Product Innovation

Performance improvement of the mobile home industry is dependent on increasing the industry's capability to respond to future demand for a large variety of shelter types. If the mobile home industry is to develop the capacity to respond to markets that can be served by the architectural configurations described in the discussion of Families A through F, it must initiate many substantial changes in its own structure and operation as well as in its supporting and regulatory environments. The following pages identify and describe important changes that will be necessary if the industry is to develop the capability successfully to produce and market the wide range of shelter types in the form of the architectural configurations described here.

Needed Changes

Production

The mobile home production process is well suited to adapt to the production requirements of new products. Today's plants already turn out a range of modified products, including singlewides, expandables, add-on rooms, special-use buildings, doublewides, and sectional houses for placement on permanent foundations. The mobile home production process has continually instituted important innovations in housing production such as substitution of new materials, reliance on un- or semiskilled labor, and use of mechanized materials-handling equipment. The result is a highly flexible production process that can effectively adapt to change.

Because of this flexibility, many necessary innovations will require no significant change in the manufacturing process. Purchasing of alternative materials, from windows and interior wall coverings to sheathing and roof components, will initially pose inventory problems but will not alter the assembly work on the line. For example, addition of a fire wall to adapt units to clustering may easily be accomplished by purchasing prefabricated fire-retardant sheathing materials and by incorporating this extra material during wall assembly.

In the interest of serving wider markets, there are some potential innovations that do lead to considerable alterations of the present production process. For example, the increased efficiency of a steel post and beam system, especially for use in multistory construction, might justify the increased investment in equipment and retraining of labor. Conceivably, large producers might introduce the wet processes of lightweight concrete precasting which not only would open new markets but subassembly operations for construction tasks such as insulating, finishing, fireproofing, and wiring would be facilitated or eliminated. Investment in automated machinery could make sense for steel-frame, stressed-skin, or lightweight concrete systems involving fewer parts and fewer tasks, for these systems open up the possibility of multistory applications.

Although the present mobile home production process depends upon semi- or unskilled labor, an increase in job training and job security will become increasingly necessary to achieve high tolerances and quality control required for stacking and connecting utilities in higher-density applications.

Distribution

The function of dealers who continue to sell to the present mobile home market need not change significantly as industry response widens. However, substantial product innovation, with the implied expansion into new markets, will significantly alter the function of participating dealerships. Dealers may act primarily as brokers between manufacturers and developers.

The production of a building component designed for interchangeable use both as the traditional mobile home and for cluster and low-rise stack applications will reduce market risk. When this product is ordered as a "mobile" home, it is equipped with running gears and distributed in the traditional fashion. At the same time, prospective developers can inspect these units in the inventory on the dealer's lot, knowing that the same unit can be ordered (through the dealer) for factory-direct-to-site delivery without the running gears.

Finally, many dealers may decide to become developers and discontinue traditional mobile home distribution altogether. The dealership mode of mobile home distribution becomes untenable for developments of families other than singlewides and doublewides because of the absence of construction and development skills. Distribution of units for subdivisions, apartments, or planned unit developments (PUDs) will take place within an integrated system of planning, financing, land development, construction, erection, marketing, management, and maintenance. The need can be seen for a distribution/development system beyond the scope of the present dealerships.

The mobile home subdivision is presently the closest analogue of this latter future development mode: There, specially designed, high-quality units are placed, landscaped, and sold by the dealer/developer. This function demands expertise like that of apartment developers in the fields of construction and building management.

Park Development
As the industry moves toward new, higher-density markets, there will be an increasing necessity for the specialized park developer to move into the role of the more versatile general developer. The typical site for the purchased mobile home is the mobile home park offering residential services, recreational facilities, parking, utilities hookups, and a home site or "pad"—the equivalent of the foundation and basement of a site-built house. As developments using mobile home building "components" enter the multifamily, higher-density range, the need will arise for land improvement operations to include the construction of more substantial foundations. This new work requires drawing on the knowledge of both engineers and contractors much more than occurs now.

The work in the field for the erection of mobile home building components in stacked configurations or megastructures is more akin to apartment construction than to the placing and anchoring of a mobile home. It is in this realm of development rather than in production that the innovated product varies most significantly from today's product. Scheduling the delivery of the building components is very important. The foundations must be engineered to carry substantial loads, and the problem of fire protection must be solved either by in-plant fabricated fire walls attached to the unit or by fire walls built by the contractor along with the foundation. The lightness of the mobile home units will keep lifting equipment small and simple. Once stacked and in place, connections of the structure and utilities must be made to tie the building together, and all the joints must be sealed.

It is evident that this process involves the expertise of a contractor to do both the construction work and the project administration. Because skilled field labor becomes necessary, possible union resistance to factory-made units may have to be countered. Local union involvement in the building process can make this possible.

The apartments in higher-density structures must be marketed and financed conventionally because they no longer qualify as mobile homes. Unless turned over to institutional, cooperative, condominium, or other joint ownerships, the developer must market, manage, and maintain the complex as a whole. Already the park developer typically assembles the land package, arranges purchase and construction financing, obtains a survey and a layout design, constructs the "pad" for the anchorage of the mobile home, and undertakes all the land improvements, including clearing, grading, laying utility lines, installing sanitary and storm drainage, landscaping, and paving parking areas, sidewalks, and curbs. The park owner, often the original developer, then performs all the maintenance and management functions.

The rewards of using mobile home building components are great. The mobile home production system offers low cost, convenience, speed, and, perhaps most important, savings in total project time: On-site work can begin simultaneously with factory fabrication of the building components. As a result of preproduction code approval and in-plant inspection of the building components (the rule today with the new federal mobile home code or state-wide factory-built housing codes), the need for on-site inspection can be sharply reduced. The paperwork and development administration for a housing authority or institution decrease dramatically in time and complexity and the threat of costly delays is also cut. Project time is shorter, so occupancy is sooner, increasing revenues as relocation expenses and interim financing charges decrease or cease. The final building reflects the guaranteed work-manship of both factory production and on-site development.

The developer can then pass along the advantages accruing from this ap-proach to the consumer. Skilled labor has been more efficiently used to pro-duce more shelter and building materials have been employed with less waste. The developer can site the buildings in a manner that responds to the partic-ular climate and topography of the locale, and the buyer is offered the ameni-ties and choices of plans featured in quality developments.

The Supporting Environment

The mobile home industry is highly dependent upon its interactions with its supporting environment: the supply sector, the transportation system, and the financial sector. As the mobile home industry expands into new markets with innovated products and processes, it will become necessary to synchro-nize the innovations with changes in its relationship with these supporting functions.

The many industries comprising the supply sector presently provide manu-facturers with a number of services, including the warehousing of component supplies and research oriented toward improvements in production efficiency. This assistance has enabled the mobile home industry to remain flexible in many respects. However, dependence upon suppliers can often limit the manufacturer's perspectives and inhibit the development of new processes.

There are many ways to alleviate the problem of manufacturers' dependence upon suppliers. Increased standardization of many of the basic supplies will not only allow a greater variety of units to be produced at reduced costs but will also permit manufacturers to focus on more general changes in mobile home design, thus speeding new product development. This would be made possible by opening up more direct lines of communications between sup-pliers and manufacturers, thereby facilitating exchanges of needs and ideas and reducing the risks suppliers assume when developing specialized products for manufacturers.

Once a unit has been assembled and purchased, there is the task of deliver-ing it to the developer's or the consumer's desired site location. Improved industry response to its present markets will require continued expansion and adaptation of the present transportation system. However, expansion into new markets through major architectural innovations will require exploration of new modes of transportation. For example, no mode is now economically developed for transporting many units to one site on a tightly controlled schedule, so systems of transporting mobile home units or building components via special trains should be investigated further, along with techniques that integrate such systems with the continued use of highway transportation. If used consistently, water transport coupled with crane helicopters for large components could be economical and would virtually eliminate size restrictions of individual com-ponents. Such developments could allow much wider distribution of new products at lower costs.

The financial sector's influence is present in all stages of mobile home production, delivery, sales, and site location. Financial support is generally required by the major actors in this process—the manufacturer, dealer, park developer, and consumer. The manufacturer needs funds for plant construction and expansion as well as for operation. The dealer must build and furnish the sales lot along with paying for the mobile homes received from manufacturers. The park developer needs funds for purchase, development, and maintenance of the park. The consumer often needs loans to pay the full price of the mobile home and, if the lot is purchased, the site price.

Because of the pervasive influence of the finance sector, some basic changes will be necessary to enable full implementation of beneficial product innovation. Manufacturers may increase plant and firm capitalization and size to be able to invest more in research and development. Dealers developing large-scale projects may need to find funding sources to augment those currently available to them. Although not strictly necessary, substitution of lower-cost mortgage financing for the present high-cost chattel financing will become feasible as the new permanent uses of more durable mobile home building components eliminate lender uneasiness about mobility and depreciation. Mobile home park developers will find increased use of traditional real estate finance methods helpful as their developments become more ambitious. On the other hand, lenders' conservative caution will initially militate against provision of funds for moves into markets implied by Families D through F. Initial projects must be undertaken by financially strong and sophisticated groups because only once significant or at least reasonable returns on investment have been proven will lenders' reluctance cease.

The Regulatory Environment

The mobile home industry is publicly governed by land use controls, taxation, building code regulation, and highway regulation. This environment, without significant changes, may be a major deterrent to product innovation.

The land use control system is primarily designed to regulate land development within a community. If mobile home units continue to be excluded from residential districts or restricted to commercial or industrial districts, as is typically the case today, no major product innovation will be possible. In order for higher-density mobile home construction to be feasible, the land use control system must recognize mobile homes as a viable alternative to the conventional housing stock and thereby make provision for mobile homes in the currently "protected" single-family residential district and make provision for mobile homes in the high-density residential districts of urban areas. If it is to produce a total living environment equal to and compatible with that produced by the on-site building industry, the mobile home industry must not be discriminated against in the choice and quality of land available.

The system of taxation a community applies to mobile homes strongly affects the industry's ability to produce the mobile home of tomorrow. The long-standing practice of most communities to tax mobile homes by methods other than realty tax has led to the widespread allegation that mobile home owners do not pay their fair share of taxes. These methods of taxation have historically reinforced the negative attitudes of property owners and stimulated discriminatory land use controls. As the personalty tax and other nonrealty forms of taxation for mobile homes phase out, the use of real property taxation should prove a vital stimulant for product innovation. Then the mobile home will become a truly integral part of the housing stock; it can go on a permanent foundation; and it can be designed like traditional housing.

The Federal Mobile Home Construction and Safety Standards, based on the mobile home industry's self-policing code ANSI A119.1, has been tailored to the specific needs and the specific product of today's manufacturing system but has not been adapted to the needs and product of tomorrow's system. It does not address the particular needs of higher-density residential buildings. It does not treat those structures made of attached dwelling units (capable of firespread, of shared structures and services, and of structural action as a whole building); those made of both mobile home building components and separate ancillary spaces (commonly the corridors, stairs, elevators, maintenance areas, utility chases, and so forth); or those completed in the field rather than in the factory (thus involving foundation and structural conditions that can vary from site to site and require on-site inspection even though factory-produced components are used). The federal code is subject to continuous modification and can ultimately be amended to cover and permit such innovations as clustered or stacked configurations, but as it stands today it does not allow for major innovations.

Each state's highway regulations govern the movement of oversized loads, such as mobile home units, over the highway. The highway regulation system today is highly fragmented, each state specifying its own dimension limitations, permit requirements, and oversize traffic regulations. This system's lack of standardization from state to state has been one of the major deterrents of architectural innovation today and will continue so tomorrow. Furthermore, state highway regulation has not yet considered the particular needs of higher-density mobile home construction. Many states make no provision for shipment by convoy (an economic necessity if large numbers of units are to be shipped from one plant to one site over one route). Many states restrict the shipment of oversized units within populous areas (to be economically feasible, higher-density structures must be located in or near populous areas). The highway regulation system of tomorrow must treat these topics if major innovations are to be economically feasible, and it can do so without endangering public safety or convenience.

Cost Implications

This section addresses the problem of costs involved in the innovations to the families of mobile homes discussed in this chapter. Once such innovations have gained the acceptance of the regulatory environment and of labor and once the combined off-site/on-site building process has progressed from the development, prototyping, and "run-in" stages to smooth operation, many cost advantages to using factory-built mobile home units as building components rather than using exclusively conventional on-site construction will arise. In the analysis that follows, major development costs have been divided into two groups: those costs not affected and those costs affected by the use of mobile home building components. A comparison of the costs of development for the off-site/on-site building process and the traditional on-site-only process shows why costs will or will not be affected and, in qualitative terms, how much. A comparison among the families of mobile home developments discusses the relative importance of the affected and unaffected cost areas to each family and analyzes the potentials of each in order to show the overall effect of mobile home component use.

The use of mobile home building components could result in significant savings, but the mobile home manufacturer and the potential developer, to whom this part is primarily addressed, must realize that costs that cannot be affected by the use of mobile home building components are substantial. Three such cost areas are the overall administration of the development process, the acquisition and preparation of the building site (excluding excavation and foundation work), and the on-site construction of non-factory-produced items. Three cost areas that will be affected by the use of mobile home building components are off-site production, excavation and foundation work, and on-site construction.

Development Costs Not Affected by the Use of Mobile Home Building Components
Certain development costs will not be affected by the use of mobile home

units as building components. These costs in most cases arise from the nature of development: There must be administration; there must be a building site; and all elements of the building must be either assembled or constructed on-site.

Whether or not factory-produced building components are used, the costs of certain aspects of development administration cannot be reduced. Personnel must be hired; management must be set up. The building site must be mapped, surveyed, and so on. Interim financing must be arranged for; building permits, and so on, obtained; legal fees paid. The overall building must be designed; the components must be ordered; and the park or site must be landscaped. This is all basic development work not affected by the use of mobile home building components.

For any development land must be acquired—either leased or bought—and must be prepared for construction. Depending on the location—urban, suburban, or rural—buildings may have to be demolished and the land cleared and graded. Roads, curbs, sidewalks, and parking facilities must be provided. Utility lines, drainage systems, and sewers or septic systems must be installed. Landscaping must be done. These are all costs related to the building site rather than the building and as such cannot be affected by new building techniques using mobile home building components.

Although the mobile home building components are produced off-site, a certain amount of on-site construction is necessary. The amount of on-site construction necessary increases as one progresses from Family A to Family F. Staircases and elevator shafts must be constructed. Fire walls must be built between adjoining units of Family C. Stringent fire rating requirements for Families D, E, and F necessitate the construction of special fire barriers between the units. Electric and plumbing cores must be installed in Families E and F. Units must be joined, stacked, or inserted in the megastructure, which must be built on-site. All this must be done on-site and is thus not affected by the use of mobile home building components.

Although a quantitative analysis of the percentage of total costs represented by these factors is extremely difficult and beyond the scope of this book, PMHI estimates that about half of the total development cost is a direct result of factors not affected by the use of mobile home building components.

Development Costs Affected by the Use of Mobile Home Building Components
Although many aspects of development cannot be affected by the use of mobile home building components, many others can. Use of the mobile home unit as a building component not only can reduce the cost of construction of the dwelling unit, but some of its special features can also reduce the costs of other aspects of development.

Building Component Production
Use of the mobile home building component results in savings over conventional on-site construction in both time and money. A mobile home building component can be completely finished in the factory in significantly less time than an equal amount of on-site construction can be finished. The finished product includes all the rough carpentry (decking, framing, sheathing, subflooring, and so forth); the finished carpentry (woodtrim, cabinets, countertops, paneling); insulation; roofing; siding; doors, windows, and frames; wallboard; tile and flooring; and interior and exterior painting. The plumbing and heating systems and the electrical wiring for the basic unit are completely installed. When the mobile home building component leaves the factory, it is complete.

The cost of constructing the basic dwelling unit will be substantially reduced when mobile home units are used. The materials used in mobile home building component production are inexpensive relative to those used in on-site construction and can be assembled by unskilled labor. This is especially true for Families A, B, and C. Families D and F will require somewhat more expensive materials and perhaps a greater amount of skilled labor than A, B, and C, but the cost savings should be substantial. Family E, on the other hand, will require substantially more expensive materials and substantially more skilled labor to meet the more demanding structural and fire rating requirements and will probably incur minimal savings.

The completion and the transportation to the site of the mobile home building component takes less time than the on-site construction of a traditional unit. The actual transportation cost of the component will be higher than the cost of transportation of the raw materials for the traditional unit because of size, but this cost should be more than balanced by the savings in production costs.

Excavation and Foundation Costs

Conventional on-site building entails a great amount of excavation and foundation work. Most single-family conventional homes have basements, but single-family mobile homes do not (the advantages or disadvantages of basements are not under discussion here, merely the higher or lower cost of them). The heavy weight of conventional building construction necessitates a larger amount of foundation work than the relatively lightweight mobile home building components. In the more innovative Families D, E, and F, this weight advantage could have a cumulative effect and result in some cost reductions—if lightweight means of providing adequate fire protection can be found. It is also likely that despite the increased structural support necessary—especially in Family E—the weight advantage will remain.

Construction Time

Great savings in overall construction time may result from the use of mobile home building components. Table 20.1 depicts this. Conventional on-site building requires that all site preparation—foundations, land development, and so forth—be done before actual construction can begin, but off-site production of the mobile home building components and site preparation can be done concurrently.

Because of this savings in time, costs due to the time-related aspects of construction work are greatly diminished. Construction site services and equipment and all site administration work (such as security, lighting, signs) are required for substantially shorter times. Carrying charges on interim financing will decrease as the time carried decreases. Labor savings due to the shorter total construction time should be considerable.

Perhaps the most substantial savings, however, will come from increased revenue—the time saved in the construction effort is time gained in revenue produced. Residential rental units, for example, can begin renting considerably sooner with mobile home building components than with conventional on-site building, thus increasing revenue. The loss of revenue for on-site building could be large.

Summary

This qualitative comparison, mobile home to on-site construction, of the cost factors involved in the development process shows the validity of the innovative techniques discussed. Cost savings appear in nearly every phase of development, from project administration to on-site construction. To get an overall view of savings in development, however, the relative importance of cost items must be analyzed—a large cost reduction in one area may be less significant than a minor cost reductiuon in another.

The expected effects of mobile home building component construction are depicted qualitatively in table 20.2. The table indicates the relative savings family to family over conventional construction.

Table 20.1
The Time Element

Activity	Activity Sequence			
	Start			Completion
On-Site Only Construction	Land Acquisition	Land Development	On-Site Construction	
Mobile Home Building Components and On-Site Construction		Off-Site Production		
	Land Acquisition	Land Development	On-Site Construction	
				Time Savings

Table 20.2
Expected Effect of
Mobile Home Building
Component Use on
Development Cost

	Family					
	A	B	C	D	E	F
Development Administration:						
Time Affected	—	—	—	—	—	—
Not Time Affected	0	0	0	0	0	0
Construction Time:						
MH component	—	—	—	—	—	—
Total project	—	—	—	—	—	—
Construction Cost:						
MH component	—	—	—	—	—	—
Total project	—	—	—	—	—	—
General Conditions	0	0	0	0	0	0
Land Acquisition	0	0	0	0	0	0
Land Development	0	0	0	0	0	0
On-Site Construction	—	—	—	—	—	—
Excavation/Foundation	—	—	—	—	—	—
Transport Costs	+	+	+	+	+	+

— Great decrease expected.
— Some decrease expected.
0 No change expected.
+ Some Increase expected.

Table 20.3
Expected Savings over
Conventional On-Site
Building: Total Effect

Family	A	B	C	D	E	F
Total Savings[a]	10	9.5	8.5	6	2.5	4.5

a. Ranked on a scale from 1 to 10, where 1 represents "no savings," 3 stands for "low savings," and 10 for "high savings."

The cost of production of the units used as building components in the different families will vary considerably as the basic requirements for each family vary. As more and more stringent specifications must be met, higher and higher production costs will be entailed. Savings over on-site equivalents will be significant in Families A, B, and C, where only a few changes are necessary; somewhat less for Families D and F, where somewhat more changes are necessary; and very low for Family E, where a great deal of change is necessary.

Different families of mobile home units will require different amounts of on-site construction—setup, and joining, and foundation and excavation work. Although on-site construction is, in each family, less for construction with mobile building components than for conventional on-site construction, more on-site construction is required as progress is made from Family A to Family F, and therefore less savings can be made through the use of mobile home building components in the later families.

As in conventional housing, different families of housing have different land requirements. Families A, B, and C will require large amounts of land per unit but will be located where the price is relatively low; Families D, E, and F will require small amounts of high-cost land. The cost of land development will vary significantly. Families A, B, and C will require a great deal more land development than Families D, E, and F; therefore D, E, and F will incur greater savings.

PMHI's best estimates of the relative importance of these cost factors indicate that the overall savings over conventional construction will vary from family to family as indicated in table 20.3. Further analysis of the quantitative effects of using mobile home building components on development costs can meaningfully be undertaken if it is based upon implementation of specific projects.

Toward an Architecturally and Socially More Responsive Industry

The mobile home industry can make an even greater contribution toward providing affordable shelter for all Americans. Just as standardization of lumber milling made good housing available to growing numbers of people in the last century, so too can the mobile home raise the standard of living today. The demand for decent housing and lower-cost nonresidential shelter is ever-present and the mobile home industry seems uniquely capable of meeting it.

Mobile homes are America's fundamental (and uniquely successful) form of industrialized shelter. Failures of other forms in the past can be ascribed not to any technological shortcoming but rather to a misunderstanding of, and lack of responsiveness to, the complexity of the shelter delivery system. By contrast, the mobile home industry has already shown its ability to deal with this complexity that previously spelled disaster by devising a new, total approach to shelter delivery: a careful integration of the production, distribution, and land development functions with the crucially significant economic support functions and the all-important regulatory functions.

Although the mobile home industry has gained eminence as a primary producer of shelter, the trailer image and the frequent restriction of its product to parks have kept it from showing an equal contribution to the quality of life. This chapter has outlined avenues for the industry to make the last, yet crucial, step toward maturing into a producer of low-cost environments of outstanding architectural and social quality. Before it can take this final step, however, the industry must first deal with a more basic and crucial issue: it must define its identity within the building sector. The following chapter explores this challenge for the mobile home industry.

Chapter 21

The Building
Sector and
the Mobile
Home Industry
Tomorrow

By the year 2000, the mobile home industry will either be alive and thriving or it will be dead. The industry is now at the crossroads, and the behavior of its members today will determine whether the industry will continue to prosper with the same meteoric growth that has characterized its last twenty-five years, or whether it will wither and stagnate to become absorbed finally into one homogeneous building industry that would represent a full-circle journey from the single building sector of a century ago.

In order to understand the precipice upon which the mobile home industry now stands, it is important to trace the development of two major trends which have in large part set the stage for the probable future of the mobile home industry: the industry's interaction with other subsystems of the building sector, and major trends in building technology.

The first trend, the mobile home industry's increasing interdependence on the other segments of the building industry, is clearly illustrated in the evolution of today's building sector and its three primary components: the on-site (traditional) building industry, the manufactured building industry, and the mobile home industry. At the turn of the last century, there was only one homogeneous building industry, the on-site industry. By 1930, the manufactured building industry had begun to emerge as a distinct entity, stimulated by architects, engineers, and others of vision from the on-site industry who sought more efficient and cost-effective ways to produce shelter by standardizing and mechanizing on-site building operations and transferring them to off-site factory locations. At this time, the mobile home industry was not yet visible to the other two segments, and there was no interaction among the three groups. The mobile home sector was just beginning to take on the formation of an industry, and was producing shelter of a type and by methods totally different from any that had been tried before.

By 1950, all three components had evolved into separate industries. There was increasing interaction between the manufactured and on-site building industries because the manufactured building producers needed the expertise of the on-site builders for the setup, marketing, and financing of their factory-produced systems; as more on-site builders became builder-dealers for the building manufacturers, these two groups slowly but inexorably grew closer together. The mobile home industry had grown rapidly and was beginning to attract attention from people both within and without the building industry.

Now, as we enter the 1980s, the mobile home industry has matured into a sizable business, and there is pronounced interaction among the three components. The close relationship between the on-site and manufactured elements continues, but now the mobile home industry has begun to interlock with and become more similar to the building manufacturers as well. This relationship has developed for several reasons: the products of the two groups now are similar in appearance; many large corporations have mobile home and manufactured building divisions existing beneath the same corporate umbrella; and many communities, while outlawing mobile homes through restrictive zoning ordinances, accept traditional-looking manufactured housing units which adhere to factory-built housing codes, thus prompting mobile home manufacturers to build units that conform to codes which were not designed for their product.

A pattern of interaction has also evolved between the mobile home industry and the on-site building industry: the mobile home industry has recognized that its effective demand is determined by the availability of developed land, while many on-site builders have used their expertise in land development to become mobile home park developers. In addition, many mobile home manufacturers are often tempted to bypass their own distributors to make large-scale deals directly with on-site builders developing mobile home communities. Thus, by 1980 all three components, while still independent, have by extensive interaction blurred the distinctions between them.

The interaction of the three subsystems, however, is to the benefit of none, for this seemingly imminent move toward merger has come about by accident. Whereas a carefully planned design aimed at using the best of each subsystem to form a new entity greater than the sum of its parts could have led to a stronger industry able to further effectively the interests of its three components, the haphazard way in which the subsystems have drifted into this present marriage of convenience has resulted in a blurring of their traditionally unique roles within the building sector, producing an "industrial identity crisis" which could have especially dangerous ramifications for the mobile home industry. The evolutionary interactive process has of course yielded some advantages; for example, builders have injected their know-how into the manufactured building industry as builder-dealers and into the mobile home industry as park developers. However, whatever benefits have accrued are outweighed by the disadvantages, inefficiencies, and duplications that have also occurred. And even the advantages have attendant penalties: having lost much of their identities, the mobile home and manufactured building industries are now moving without much discernible enthusiasm toward a future threatened by loss of even more of their historical business advantages. Thus, effectively dealing with the identity crisis engendered by the increasing interaction of the building sector's three subsystems poses the greatest challenge for the mobile home industry in the 1980s: at stake today is nothing less than the industry's survival tomorrow.

The second major development influencing the future of the mobile home industry involves the technology of building. Examination of the mobile home industry and the other subsystems of the building sector from a technological perspective requires a review of one of the major trends in building technology: to an ever greater extent, basic building operations are being mechanized and/or shifted to off-site factory locations. Since this process is commonly referred to in the trade as "industrialization of building" the same phrase is pragmatically used here, even though this term is one of the most flexible and imprecise in the building vocabulary, applied to a wide spectrum of meanings ranging from narrow technological definitions to broad concepts in architectural theory.

The significance of the trend toward greater industrialization is evidenced by the fact that it is already a way of life in the entire building sector: other components besides mobile home producers are making use of industrialized techniques to varying degrees (although none can yet match the mobile home industry's efficiencies). From a technological perspective, these other subsystems of the building sector can be further broken out as follows: within the on-site building industry, there are stick builders, high-rise producers, and production builders; within the manufactured building industry, there are packaged home manufacturers and modular home manufacturers. In each of these segments, firms range from large, multiplant national and international operations to small, local, one-plant companies, and all but stick builders and high-rise producers have industrialized their operations.[1]

Production builders, who are track builders producing about one million homes and apartment units per year, use industrial production set-ups at their construction locations. Most build their structures at job sites using roof trusses, wall panels, floor trusses, or other components which are made for them by component manufacturers. Most production builders use subcontractors (for carpentry, plumbing, electrical, and other work) to finish their buildings on site. Some production builders use mechanized production methods or even assembly-line setups for component fabrication right on job sites; in favorable climates such operations can be carried out in the open, they may be done in simple shops, or at times they even involve sophisticated company-owned on-site component factories that can often be relocated. Production builders always sell their housing units directly to the consumer.

More closely resembling the general public's image of industrialized shelter producers are the packaged home manufacturers (also known as "prefabricated" or "panelized" home manufacturers or simply as "home manufacturers'"), who produce approximately 300,000 housing units per year. For the various models they offer, they manufacture many or most of the components (such as floor trusses, exterior wall and interior partition panels, roof trusses, cabinets, windows, doors), and in some cases they also preassemble one or all of the mechanical systems (heating, plumbing, electrical). Their home or apartment packages are always produced in off-site factories and then transported to the site for assembly. These manufacturers sell their packages through a network of builder-dealers who handle on-site erection and final marketing to the consumer.

Epitomizing the popular image of industrial mass production of shelter are the modular home manufacturers (also referred to as "sectional home manufacturers"), who produce some 100,000 units per year. Units are always manufactured in off-site factories, usually on an assembly-line basis quite similar to that used by mobile home manufacturers. Completely finished three-dimensional sections (including the mechanical systems) of one or more rooms are factory-assembled and then shipped by truck, railroad, or barge to the job site, where they are joined with one or more such sections to form single-family homes (similar to doublewide mobile homes) or occasionally apartments. The primary difference between modular and mobile homes is that modulars are usually built to state-wide factory-built housing codes and placed on permanent foundations. Modular homes are also sold primarily through builder-dealers, although in some instances a smaller company may sell its homes directly to the consumer.

These brief profiles of building producers other than mobile home manufacturers who have also industrialized their operations provide a first impression of the impact of industrialization on the building sector. But the importance of this process is even more dramatically evidenced by statistics showing the extent to which the building sector is already relying on it. Although industrialization in the building sector as a whole cannot yet be statistically measured, the impact of industrialization on the housing industry can be gauged and thus give an indication of the order of magnitude within the larger sector.

Industry sources estimate that in 1977, industrialized housing accounted for 1.8 million housing units produced by over 3,000 companies in some 6,000 locations or factories.[2] Including mobile homes but not pure stick-built units or high-rise apartments, this figure represents about 80 percent of all U.S. housing production for the year. Table 21.1 gives a more detailed comparative statistical profile of the various industrialized housing producers.

The most striking fact revealed here is that the mobile home industry is not dominating the scene, in terms of either share of total industrialized housing

Table 21. 1
1977 Profile of
Industrialized/
Manufactured
Housing Producers

Type of Housing Producer	Firms	Factories/ Locations	Housing Units Produced
Production builders	2,000	4,500	1,100,000
Packaged home manufacturers	670	810	300,000
Modular home manufacturers	225	275	135,000
Mobile home manufacturers	220	480	266,000
Totals	3,115	6,065	1,800,000

Source: *Automation in Housing/Systems Building News* (estimates).

production or number of firms or plants. In fact, the table clearly shows that production builders account for the lion's share of industrialized housing production. It is true, of course, that the extent to which the different segments rely on industrialization varies greatly; the mobile home manufacturer's product is almost completely finished in the factory, while the production builder's unit might use only a few industrialized components. Nevertheless, it is important to note the growing technological homogeneity within the housing industry, for it is yet another factor contributing to the identity crisis gripping the mobile home industry; since the technologies of the modular and packaged home producers are becoming so similar to those of the mobile home manufacturers, the mobile home industry no longer has the unique technological leadership that has been one of its identifying characteristics.

Not only does industrialized housing already account for about 80 percent of U.S. housing production but, even more relevant, the extent of industrialization is steadily increasing (see table 21.2). (Although there are some aberrations in this progression, particularly during the last recession, tracing the pattern back to the 1950s would show a clear upward trend.) However, the rising incidence of industrialization in the housing industry at large is clearly occurring at the expense of the mobile home industry: table 21.2 shows that the mobile home industry's share of total housing production decreased from 22 percent in 1969 to 12 percent in 1977, while the other industrialized producers' share has grown from less than 50 percent to close to 70 percent over the same period.

These statistics again reinforce the thesis that the mobile home industry is in the throes of an identity crisis: not only is it losing significance in total industrialized housing production, but its dominance among industrialized producers is slipping as well. Technologically, the industry no longer shows any significant differences from other industrialized segments. Gone are the days when it stood apart from the crowd of industrialized producers; now it is in danger of losing itself in that group. Mobile home manufacturers, dealers, and park developers and operators are confused by this new and increasing presence

Table 21.2
Industrialized/Manufactured Housing Producers' Share of Total Housing Production: 1969-1977

		1969	1970	1971	1972	1973	1974	1975	1976	1977
Total housing production (including mobile homes)	(1)	1,913,000	1,870,000	2,582,000	2,955,000	2,624,000	1,681,000	1,384,000	1,794,000	2,255,000
Production builders	(2)	725,000	850,000	1,050,000	1,350,000	1,150,000	500,000	490,000	790,000	1,100,000
Packaged home manufacturers	(3)	200,000	250,000	315,000	390,000	350,000	275,000	280,000	250,000	300,000
Modular home manufacturers	(4)	10,000	20,000	58,000	90,000	120,000	82,000	90,000	105,000	135,000
Mobile home manufacturers	(5)	413,000	401,000	497,000	576,000	567,000	329,000	213,000	246,000	266,000
Totals for (2) through (4) as % of total housing production		49%	60%	55%	62%	62%	51%	62%	64%	68%
Mobile home production (5) as % of total housing production[a]		22%	21%	19%	20%	22%	20%	15%	14%	12%
Totals for (2) through (5) as % of total housing production[a]		71%	81%	74%	81%	83%	71%	78%	78%	80%

[a]All percentages rounded.

Sources: (1) and (5), U.S. Department of Commerce, Bureau of the Census; Elrick and Lavidge, Inc. (all figures rounded).
(2) through (4), *Automation in Housing/Systems Building News* (estimates).

of operations that are so technologically similar to their own. In responding to this threat to their traditional identity, they are divided on whether to branch out into technologically related fields or to concentrate on their own specialty. This basic conflict within the industry itself leads to further fragmentation, which only compounds the problem.

The technological aspect of the mobile home industry's identity crisis is further exacerbated by a danger brewing within the building sector in general: industrialization as it evolves and as it is perceived can spell disaster. There is nothing wrong with the concept of industrialization per se. However, substantial risk lies in the fact that many believers in the concept consider and rely on it as an important end in itself. This narrow and shortsighted fascination has already tempted many to neglect the much more important business functions of the shelter delivery process, such as financing, marketing, or monitoring public regulatory initiatives. Such an attitude can only result in a continuing emphasis on this relatively unimportant aspect of technology at the expense of other functions of greater economic and business potential. The leaders who will steer the building sector's future are beginning to be blinded by the myth of industrialization, and it is all too possible that the further evolution of an entire industry will be misdirected through reliance on an intuitively based, irrelevant model.

The weakening of the mobile home industry's identity as a culmination of the business and technology trends discussed unfortunately coincides with other unsettling recent developments. The shakeout of the 1973–1975 recession, which decimated the ranks of the mobile home firms, has left the survivors reeling and confused, lacking the energy and enthusiasm to chart a coherent course for the industry tomorrow. Adding to the uncertainty about the future is the industry's inability to come to grips with the question of why other components of the housing industry have rebounded more sharply from the last recession (as table 21.2 clearly shows). There are indeed logical reasons for the other segments' more rapid recovery, given the more capital-intensive nature of the mobile home industry and the difficulty of re-entry, which is not as great a problem in other components, but the mobile home industry's failure to assess the damage objectively and move more consistently toward a recovery is yet another sign of the disarry in its ranks. As it continues to lag behind the other housing producers, which have by now become so similar to itself, the mobile home industry becomes even more discouraged and listless, and finds it all the more difficult to retain a discrete identity.

Thus, the mobile home industry is currently in a precarious position in terms of its own development as well as that of the building sector at large: after a proud fifty-year history as a maverick infusing new life and ideas into the housing industry, it must now deal with the fact that is has unnecessarily allowed its singularity to be severely compromised. Its uniqueness, which has been the cornerstone of its identity, has historically sparked the drive of the mobile home industry, and the loss of much of that energy augurs badly for it and for the larger building sector that it has inspired.

Not only have the business and technological trends within the building sector combined to induce an identity crisis in the mobile home industry, but they have also proved to be undesirable in themselves. In terms of business organization, the interaction of the three subsystems represents an inefficient and ineffective mesh that has masked the need for synergism through a design based on intelligent and imaginative planning. In terms of technology, the widespread obsession with industrialization has led to the neglect of the more important business functions. Thus, without a farsighted, shrewd initiative from its midst to spur the building sector, the current misguided trends look as if they will inevitably lead to a bleak future.

But must this necessarily happen ? Not if the mobile home industry shakes itself out of its present torpor to recognize and grasp its historic chance of taking a leading role as a catalyst in the development of the building sector. It must not by its inactivity passively allow current trends to shape the industry of tomorrow, but must rather pioneer a new, viable alternative strategically designed to parlay its own strengths and those of the other subsystems into a larger, better, stronger industry. The mobile home industry can best accomplish this ambitious goal by remembering and using what has always been its real trump card: its unique, if largely unconscious, method of perceiving and structuring to its advantage its operations (production, distribution, park system), its supporting industries (supply, finance, transportation), and its regulatory environment (land use controls, taxation, building code and highway regulation). It is this different way of thinking about a total building concept which explains the industry's efficiencies and thus its competitive edge, and which the mobile home industry must continue to employ as the chief contributor to its success.

The industry can go in one of two directions: it can continue to drift on the same course it has followed recently and lose its drive and uniqueness until it becomes swallowed by the other segments of the building industry, or it can break out of its current lethargy to regain the identity and enthusiasm that has made it the world's most efficient producer of shelter and go on to new heights. The remainder of this chapter is devoted to a more detailed description of each of these scenarios, which we characterize as *stagnation* and *growth*.

A. Scenario: Stagnation

In twenty years, the increasing interaction among the three components of the building sector will lead to total absorption of the mobile home and manufactured building elements into the on-site building sphere. All three groups will combine into one relatively homogeneous building industry that ironically resembles the basic industry of a hundred years ago. Several factors will contribute to the inevitability of this merger. The structures of the mobile home and manufactured building industries will come to resemble each other because of the increased similarity of their products and operations as well as interindustry mergers and acquisitions. The mobile home industry will have lost ground because of its passive, reactive attitude of recent years, while the manufactured building industry will have gained an advantage by adapting the pioneering cost-efficient technologies of the mobile home industry. Both of these components in turn will be relatively weak compared to the on-site building industry. The on-site industry, like the manufactured building group, will have applied to its own operations many of the technologies of the mobile home industry to become more competitive in an area that had long been the mobile home industry's exclusive purview. In addition, the on-site industry of the year 2000 will retain a distinct advantage in its superior political organization, while the mobile home industry will not have significantly increased its political clout in proportion to its growing importance.

How has the mobile home industry allowed itself to be placed in such a precarious position, facing extinction within the next two decades? A brief look at the attitude of the industry as it evolved from the beginning of the century through the 1970s provides the needed perspective. In its early years, the industry existed in a legal vacuum: since it was breaking ground in a totally new area, it was subject to few controls or regulations, and had little competition or resistance to its unique product. Mobile home manufacturers correctly assessed the business opportunity open to them, and shrewdly exploited this legal vacuum. By 1950, the mobile home industry had become more visible, and it faced increasing resistance on several fronts. The on-site building industry noticed the competition the industry posed and fought it in such areas as finance and public regulation; labor unions began to direct organizing drives against the historically nonunion mobile home industry; and the government (local, state, and federal) began to impose regulatory burdens. Thus, the industry was quickly put on the defensive; instead of being free to experiment with its innovative techniques, it was now forced into a position of countering the challenges of its opponents.

Although the 1950s and 1960s represented a period of spectacular growth and prosperity for the mobile home industry, this very growth was engendering a potential problem that the industry failed to foresee and adequately prepare for: lulled by its success, it did not recognize the need to create new markets in time to augment its initial market before it showed the first signs of saturation in the 1970s. Ironically, the incredibly rapid growth of the industry, especially in the 1960s when it became the pet of Wall Street, helped to foster its reactive posture. Many of its leaders seem to have lost interest in the further development of the unique overall approach to building that they were originally committed to. Rather than formulate and implement a coherent strategy concerning its present and future role in the general building sector, the mobile home industry went off on tangents. By the 1970s, reaction had become disproportionately important to the industry; since it was constantly losing ground in the area of governmental regulation, much of its energy was being channeled into responding to the increasing number of new standards and requirements contemplated by federal and state governments, most typically in the area of consumer legislation.

If these dangerous attitudes on the part of the mobile home industry continue over the next twenty years, the inevitable outcome will be the industry's demise. Because of its decline in innovative energy, its reliance on an excessively reactive posture, and the imminent saturation of its current market, the industry will soon be overwhelmed by the pace of development and evolution in the rest of the building industry; it will be forced to cope with unfamiliar practices in the on-site building industry, increasing government regulatory action, and more competition in areas that were previously its exclusive domain.

The course that the mobile home industry now seems destined to take in the next twenty years can also be indicated by an examination of major trends in each of its systems, which when taken together yield a composite picture of the state of the industry today and tomorrow. In the production system, the trend is toward a product which looks more like traditional housing. While this is a desirable development for marketing purposes, its negative aspects far outweigh the positive points. To an increasing extent, the mobile home's look of traditional housing is being achieved by using specifications for structural and mechanical systems similar to provisions in traditional codes—codes that are based on the vagaries and inaccuracies inherent in on-site construction methods which make quality control difficult. Thus, because the mobile home industry is beginning to conform to standards that are unnecessarily high considering the controlled conditions of factory production, it is sacrificing some of its unique efficiency. With such an emphasis on resemblance to traditional housing, various types of units (mobile homes and sectionals), custom-constructed to different codes and uses, are often manufactured in the same plant, often in uneconomically mixed production runs. The industry is thus prostituting its production process to respond to markets that are too diverse and in many cases not lucrative enough to be compatible with efficient and profitable operation.

Dealers are the focal point of the major trend within the distribution system. Many dealers are currently torn between their intuitive (and wise) inclination to continue specializing in distributing and selling mobile homes and the temptation to move into modular housing distribution. Rather than definitely deciding on only one specialization, or at least cautiously pacing entry into modular housing, many hastily try to do both. However, most dealers are spreading themselves too thin in attempting to do justice to mobile home distribution while at the same time assuming the additional tasks of financing, land development, and on-site setup that resemble the function of the builder-dealers in the manufactured building industry. These are two separate distribution channels requiring different sets of skills, and few dealers can effortlessly make the transition without seriously jeopardizing one or both operations in the process. Dealers trying to do both lose their specialty, thus decreasing the efficiency of the mobile home distribution system and making it more expensive. Even more serious is the fact that without a clear sense of direction, the most crucial challenge for the system, to identify and activate new markets, is forgotten.

Within the mobile home park system, the mobile home community has also undergone a great many changes as it has taken on the design characteristics of a traditional residential subdivision. Although this development has positive ramifications in terms of marketing as well as overcoming regulatory objections, it is dangerous in its cost element: because of ever-rising standards, the cost of developing the site (as important a component of the industry's product as the mobile home itself) is steadily increasing, to the point where it is beginning to exceed the cost of the actual mobile home unit. This trend represents an unfortunate departure from the industry's tradition (broken only in the 1970s) of increasing quality while keeping constant or even reducing costs.

The most pronounced trends in the supporting environment are in the area of financing. Like the on-site building industry, the mobile home industry is pressing for more governmental assistance, but it is not fully realizing the penalties entailed. Excessive reliance on artificial public-sector subsidization might become a habit which would strangle entrepreneurial creativity, and have a long-term negative impact on the industry's cost performance. (Even more dangerous, withdrawal of this artificial support could result in a sudden drop in demand from which the industry might not be able to recover.) Paralleling this development is the growing disparity between recent rapid unit price increases of mobile homes and the traditionally conservative financing terms available to mobile home purchasers. Although a mobile home is far less expensive than a comparable conventional home, the existing financing structure has always entailed surprisingly high monthly payments for mobile home owners. While mobile home prices have risen greatly in the 1970s, there has been little attendant liberalization of retail financing terms for mobile home buyers; this has made monthly payments disproportionately even higher. These trends in financing tend to reduce the economic viability and hence the desirability of mobile home living.

Significant changes are also taking place in the important regulatory environment. Within the area of land use controls, the fact that mobile homes are being recognized and treated more like traditional housing is positive in itself, but a substantial price is being paid as the mobile home industry shies away from building low-cost housing. Since low-cost housing invites a negative fiscal zoning response from local communities, the industry is unconsciously moving toward producing more medium- and high-cost units (such as sectionals) to attract higher-income consumers who are more acceptable to the host community. In the taxation area, there is also a tendency to treat mobile homes more like traditional housing. Again, beneficial though this is, it does lead to increased occupancy costs; this continually erodes the industry's traditional stronghold in low-income markets and tempts it to depend more on high- and medium-income markets.

All of these trends reflect two underlying themes: the mobile home industry is striving to develop a product similar in appearance to traditional housing, and it is (largely unconsciously) beginning to abandon the realm of low-cost housing. Inevitable conclusions about the future of the mobile home industry can be drawn from these developments. By the end of this century, it will be able to rival the on-site industry in terms of product quality, but at the same time it will have lost much of its cost advantage, thereby forfeiting its competitive edge and increasing its business risk from the on-site builder. As the industry comes to resemble the manufactured building industry, it directly competes against both on-site producers and building manufacturers in markets which have been their historic strongholds, while needlessly retreating from the low-cost housing market it has traditionally dominated and in which the other two segments cannot compete.

Unfortunately, by the year 2000 these developments could well lead to the disappearance of the mobile home industry as a distinct entity if the mobile home and manufactured building sectors are absorbed into the on-site sphere to form one homogeneous building industry. However, this scenario by no means represents the optimal future for the building industry. In such an industry, the industrialized building segments, clearly overshadowed politically and economically by the on-site sector, would no longer contribute innovative energy and momentum. Although the new industry would be more efficient in general because of the influence of the industrialized segments, many of the efficiencies that led to the mobile home industry's unique success would be lost in the transition. Thus, this new industry would not be able to produce shelter at as low a cost as it could, and would forfeit tremendous business and unusual social opportunities. A significant business opportunity would be lost because the new industry, lacking efficient operations and reduced costs, would have to confine itself to delivering the American dream of the single-family home to a very small segment of the population, thus ignoring the large market of approximately two-thirds of all U.S. families that simply cannot afford a median-price new home. A building industry not as efficient as it could be results in an obvious social loss: all segments of the American population would have to pay more for shelter, and home ownership would eventually be limited to a fortunate few.

For the mobile home industry, such a scenario would represent foregone opportunity and promise. The mobile home industry, the most innovative and vigorously resourceful building industry in history, will have failed to live up to its potential to evolve as the catalyst of a new building sector combining greater social effectiveness with undiluted economic efficiency. But if the mobile home industry does lose its identity in one larger building industry, it has only itself to blame. If the mobile home industry is to get back on the growth track that signals its survival, it must overcome its current inertia and recapture the energy of its younger days; it must resume its pioneering position as the farsighted experimenter, the daring innovator; it must take the lead in shaping policy, in establishing new markets, in setting coherent objectives for its orchestrated growth within the larger building sector. In short, the mobile home industry must act—or die.

B. Scenario: Growth

An optimal future for the mobile home industry and for the building sector as a whole can be accomplished by collaboration between the mobile home and on-site building industries. The marriage of these two subsystems can create a new industry capable of mass producing low-cost shelter with the same quality as on-site-built structures for a wide spectrum of markets, including medium- and high-density urban areas. Housing can efficiently be built in the factories of the mobile home manufacturers, taken to sites, and then installed and finished by the on-site builders, to the profit and benefit of both. Mobile home manufacturers and on-site builders must go beyond the traditional rivalry that has led to so much unnecessary infighting over the years to see the enormous business opportunity that lies in the pooling of their expertise. The ideal solution is a combination of the best elements of each industry: the factory builders should concentrate on building shelter in their factories, and the on-site builders should focus on assembling and developing land, securing financing, dealing with the complex system of local politics, and cutting through the maze of local public regulations.

This scenario is predicated on one of our major findings, that the mobile home industry can replace its traditional material, wood, with alternative materials such as steel, aluminum, and even lightweight concrete without having to sacrifice its efficiency and cost performance. With these new materials, the industry can devise a modular system of dimensionally coordinated, standardized, three-dimensional building components that can even be assembled into high-density medium- and high-rise configurations. The interchangeable catalogued building components, designed to be extremely compact for transportation purposes yet also capable of being expanded on the site, would be mass produced in mobile home factories with complete interior (but not exterior) finish. The builder, although participating in shaping and implementing the broad framework for the coalition, would basically operate independent of the manufacturer, tackling a wide range of complex tasks only he or she can perform. For example, the developer of any sizable project may have to take up to three years merely to procure as many as 120 different approvals before getting a building permit. Once the site has been developed, the builder would use the components ordered from the manufacturer's stock to assemble and set up the units. Then, in order to make the structure more marketable, the builder would finish the exterior with indigenous local materials and add such finishing touches that the completed structure never looks as though it came out of a factory.

In essence, the mobile home industry would become a major supplier to the traditional homebuilder. However, this in no way implies that the mobile home industry would become dominated by the on-site sector. Rather, this is a scenario of synergism, in which the mobile home industry must foster its unique identity for the benefit of the collaborative effort. For the industry's value in this partnership lies in those very qualities that have made it the wunderkind of the housing industry. It must remain strong and discrete so that it can act as catalyst for the new industry, injecting vitality with its innovative thinking and shaping coherent growth objectives around its total building concept.

We believe that such a collaborative scenario is eminently realistic, for it is in the best interest of the traditional on-site builders, small and large, to join with the mobile home industry. In the past 20 years, traditional builders have been continually retreating from low-cost markets because they simply cannot build that cheaply. Builders realize that each purchase of a mobile home means the potentially lost purchase of a traditional home. A major factor that will nudge traditional builders into the arms of the mobile home industry is the steadily rising costs of materials, labor, and especially land. These increasing costs are encouraging the construction of apartment dwellings at the expense of single-family homes. Not only does each single-family unit cost more to build, but it also has a higher profit margin. Thus, in simplified terms, each substitution of an apartment for a single-unit dwelling reduces the total dollar volume of residential construction as well as profit margins for the homebuilder. Therefore it is obviously in the best interest of the traditional builder to provide as many single-family homes as possible—an interest which, fortunately for the builder, is matched by the American consumer's deeply rooted preference for this type of housing as well as the government's willingness to support this important constituency with generous subsidies of construction and occupancy costs. Although this will not reduce the cost of land, the most effective way for traditional builders to keep the cost of a single unit low is to ally themselves with mobile home manufacturers.

Collaboration with the mobile home industry may be the only way for traditional builders to protect the higher-priced, higher-profit market for single-family units (and related forms such as townhouses), for the situation in America today is dangerously close to duplicating the disastrous European experience. Whereas owner-occupied housing used to be prevalent on the European housing scene, this has now become a luxury, and rental dwellings in multi-unit structures are the general mode of housing. If the housing industry is to keep dollar and profit volume as high as possible, it must tip the new-housing product mix in favor of the single-family unit without reducing total annual effective demand for new housing. The business danger for the homebuilding industry arises when people begin to accept apartment dwelling as the norm, for then potential buyers eliminate the possibility of a single-family home. This country could then become a nation of renters instead of homeowners; this would be to the detriment of the builders, for it could result in less pressure on the government to provide subsidies for single-family housing or tax deductions for mortgage interest payments. If this attitude is allowed to continue for too long, it becomes permanently entrenched in public thinking. It Is too late to reverse the situation in Europe, but there is still time for the homebuilding industry to stop the business potential of our housing market from deteriorating to such an extent.

Thus, just as it is to the benefit of the mobile home industry to team up with the on-site building industry in order to continue its growth, it is equally advantageous for the on-site builder to work with mobile home manufacturers in order to keep building costs manageable and markets open. One of the major advantages of such a coalition is the ability to activate new markets of significant size. At the end of the 1970s, the median sales price for a single-family on-site built home was over $60,000, up 150 percent from about $24,000 at the beginning of that decade; given ever-increasing building costs as well as the recent product mix shift back to the single-family dwelling, this price will continue to rise. However, we estimate that strategically coordinated collaboration between the mobile home and on-site industries could reduce sales prices to $48,000 and less. This would activate a giant new market. At $60,000, less than one-third of all U.S. families can afford a single-family home; at $48,000, approximately 8 million more families could afford such dwellings. This could eventually mean an annual production level higher than the previous production record of close to three million units in 1972. Such unprecedented market volume would not only represent a business opportunity beyond the wildest dreams of either sector, but would also aid in economic expansion; since housing starts contribute strongly to economic growth, such an increase in effective production levels would have a significant impact on the U.S. economy.

While the mobile home industry would be the guiding force in spearheading further penetration and expansion of its territory, the low-cost market, at the other end of the spectrum a new building industry could deliver housing for medium- and even high-income groups as well. During the off-season, employees of mobile home concerns could be kept on the payroll producing more elaborate models for spring delivery to the builder; not only would this help the mobile home industry fight its ever-troublesome seasonality, but it would also be unusually profitable, since higher lines have higher profit margins. The mobile home industry would be indispensable to the builder in exploiting these more expensive markets for several reasons. Allied with the mobile home manufacturer, the builder can promise faster, guaranteed-date, guaranteed-price delivery, which means less interest paid on construction financing and a quicker return on investment; the builder could deliver housing for higher-income groups at a price lower than that prevalent in the on-site market; and the product would be better because of the mobile home industry's superior in-plant quality control. The business potential of an industry with a sound base in low-cost shelter is obvious: given this capability, higher-price, higher-quality markets can also be touched at will. On the other hand, an industry specializing in higher-cost shelter cannot easily (and perhaps not at all) serve the low-cost market as well.

In the new building sector we envision, the mobile home industry would assume the crucial role of catalyst. But before it can take on this responsibility, it must strengthen its own position on several fronts. Its role in a building coalition must be based on a realistic power analysis. The mobile home industry is presently not capable of competing successfully with the major existing building interests, especially traditional builders and labor. Thus, it has two alternatives: either it exploits only those markets that the home builders and other strong political interests have already abandoned or cannot reach, or it goes beyond this and works with those interests to explore new markets that will (and can) exist solely because the mobile home industry is the only factor through which they can be stimulated. The main characteristic of these new markets is that they match the main strength of the mobile home industry: low cost. Other important political interests with whom the industry must come to terms include building materials suppliers, public officials, and legislators. The only way for the industry to survive in this environment is to implement an "all win" strategy. Rather than compete with interests that are stronger than itself, the mobile home industry must create an alliance in which there are incentives for each major force. It can then use the strong political power of these allies to topple barriers to the opening of new markets that it alone cannot presently overcome. For example, if labor and home building lobbies ally themselves with local politicians sensitive to their needs, "no growth" opposition can be obliterated, red tape in building departments can be cut, and zoning for low- and middle-income housing is more likely to be obtained. When the new coalition has successfully moved into the new markets, it can strategically call on its newly created clients (such as low-income groups and minorities) to strengthen its political clout. The ability to deliver housing to such groups without public subsidy can also make the difference in obtaining support from local politicians.

To prepare itself for its place in the building industry of tomorrow, the mobile home industry today must work to enhance its present advantages as well as to overcome its major weaknesses. It must extend its efficiencies, which are threatened by increasing government interference; it must maintain its low-cost characteristics; it must actively maneuver to preserve the legal vacuum in which it has operated so profitably. Instead of competing with interests stronger than itself, the mobile home industry must continue to cultivate its present market as well as strive to carve out specialty niches that it alone can serve (such as emergency shelter, temporary housing for energy exploration). In addition, the mobile home industry must work unceasingly to maintain its identity. Proprietary industry-specific skills must be protected so that the industry always remains in a favorable bargaining position; it must always be able to offer its special skill—delivery of low-cost, factory-built shelter—in exchange for the skills that are unique to on-site builders.

One of the major weaknesses that currently hampers the mobile home industry is the fact that it is not yet marketing-oriented. It must become a market leader, must discover and develop rich new markets, must create demand for the types of shelter that it is especially well equipped to handle. Its current market is showing the first signs of saturation. Even worse, the industry can no longer take for granted what has long been its most effective (and free) marketing aid: that construction as well as occupancy costs for traditional housing will continue to rise at present rates and tempt actual and prospective homeowners to switch to mobile homes. Although on-site builders have not yet launched a concerted effort to make their construction costs more competitive with those of the mobile home industry, they may do so sooner or later. Ever-rising occupancy costs must not be assumed either: for example, the unexpected tax revolt of the late 1970s markedly weakened demand for mobile homes in some regions; when it appeared that property taxes would be reduced, many prospective mobile home buyers felt that they could afford to keep their homes. And it is conceivable that increases in other occupancy cost components may also be less rapid than in the past. The point of course is not that the industry's current market must become saturated, but rather that it may; the need for new markets, therefore, is dictated as much by business caution as by the concern for continued growth. A similarly important marketing objective for the industry must be to identify and penetrate new markets that can be used to offset its seasonality of demand. One possibility is for the industry to work with energy companies that need shelter at exploration sites. Since these firms are aware of their needs well in advance, mobile home manufacturers might make floating delivery date contracts with them, allowing the manufacturers to put these units on line whenever normal demand slackens.

Another industry shortfall is the lack of both corporate planning on the firm level and long-range planning on the regional, state, and national association level. The industry must identify its goals for tomorrow and then isolate specific objectives in order to shape individual actions and daily responses more shrewdly. The industry also suffers from its lack of political strength, and it must develop a more sophisticated organization as well as more effective lobbying tactics. Its political involvement has largely been limited to merely reacting to unpopular legislation, when it should be concentrating on establishing a constructive political image that will allow it to shape and initiate policy. The industry should play up housing as a "motherhood" issue that is of utmost concern to the population and thus to its governmental representatives. The industry will need significant political clout if it is to deal effectively with the danger that the added expense caused by government intervention poses for its cost performance. Ever-expanding governmental intervention in its affairs is slowing the mobile home industry just as it hampers all industry. While no figures exist on the cost impact this has on the mobile home industry, it is clearly significant: the private sector spends at least an estimated $70 billion per year to meet requirements of federal regulations alone (the annual cost to the private and public sectors of merely filling out federal forms is estimated at an annual $100 billion), and the cost of regulations mandated by all levels of government has been approximated as $130 billion per year.[3] As a part of the proposed coalition, the mobile home industry will be more exposed to on-site work and will become even more vulnerable to public regulation; for example, it has been estimated that unnecessary government regulations (in areas such as environmental controls, zoning requirements, building codes, energy conservation requirements, and regulation of settlement and financing costs) add about 20 percent to the cost of a median-priced new site-built single-family home.

Our growth scenario is eminently feasible. The mobile home industry came out of the last recession stronger and trimmer; the companies that have survived are tough and lean, and the industry, although not yet highly sophisticated, is on the threshold of becoming a mature business. Thus, the industry is now able to move in the only direction that offers growth and profitability, and the significant business potential inherent in this scenario leaves little doubt that the traditional home-building industry would follow. Our scenario is also imminently achievable—the development of this new industry could begin immediately and bear fruit as soon as two to three years from now.

A collaborative effort between the mobile home and on-site building industries is logical. There is no reason for the factory builder to acquire the expertise that the on-site developer took centuries to evolve to a very high level, just as it makes no sense for the traditional builder to duplicate the efforts of the shelter manufacturer by trying to adopt its technologies. It is counterproductive for the two industries to compete against each other when by joining forces they can vastly increase their total market. Thus, collaboration is obviously the only "all win" strategy that will eventually lead to the best of all possible building worlds.

Why can the mobile home industry deliver low-cost, quality shelter when no other building industry here or abroad can do so ? The answer lies in the fact that over the years the industry has created an entire new national industrial structure uniquely tailored to its specific needs. This achievement proves the validity and promise of the general strategy for the development of the building sector that I introduced in the first chapter: the sector can improve its performance only if it creates a comprehensive nationwide shelter delivery system by restructuring and integrating its own organization as well as its business and political environments.

As we have pointed out throughout this book, the mobile home industry has become the world's most efficient building industry because it has thoroughly understood and strategically manipulated virtually all of the important functions that operate in or affect the larger building industry. It is not important that much of its approach has not been specifically plotted and that the system it built is in no way perfect; what is important is that its approach has been the right one. Instead of concentrating solely on technology, a common bias in the building community, the mobile home industry has given equal weight to all phases of the production and delivery process. The fruit of the industry's labors is a comprehensive nationwide system, a total production—distribution—land development network effectively synchronized with its supporting and regulatory environments. It is this orchestrated manipulation of the entire shelter delivery system that the other segments of the building industry here and abroad must master if they aspire to match the mobile home industry's success.

In order to depict graphically the right and wrong ways to go about developing a building industry, we have fashioned "failure" and "success" models which show how (and how not) to evolve the interrelationships between the various functions within the shelter delivery system. Our "failure" model (figure 22.1) illustrates an approach that desperately overemphasizes a very few areas at the expense of others. Damaging though this approach is, it continues to be the typical style of many who believe that technology is the answer. As shown in our "success" model (figure 22.2), simultaneous efforts must be undertaken in all directions. The building industry, which is governed by many well-established institutions, looks askance at any swift and major changes; thus, any revolutionary actions are doomed. Movement into any one direction must therefore be gradual, with the wisest action being slow and methodical movement into all. Iconoclastic and energetic development in only a few directions while neglecting others is doomed to failure, for many of the steps that must be taken necessitate changes in other areas; for example, attack on restrictive land use controls must include revision of the taxation structure.

This book has focused on the mobile home industry as a role model for any other industry attempting to improve its performance. But since the mobile home industry's secret is neither its product nor its production process, other industries cannot simply duplicate it in hopes of matching its success. The mobile home industry's system is specifically suited to its own needs, and other industries face the long and arduous task of developing systems that will work in their own particular situations. Our purpose here is not to give detailed instructions, but rather to outline the basic policy recommendations implied in my general strategy for the development of the building sector. The following delineation of the basic strategy is illustrated with examples of the ways in which the mobile home industry has accomplished its evolution into a total system, for it is a working model of how the strategy can be applied.

Any building industry attempting to evolve a total shelter delivery system must predicate its efforts on the realization that such a system must be both national and comprehensive. The industry per se must be the starting point for structuring any system. All functions of the basic shelter production and delivery process—

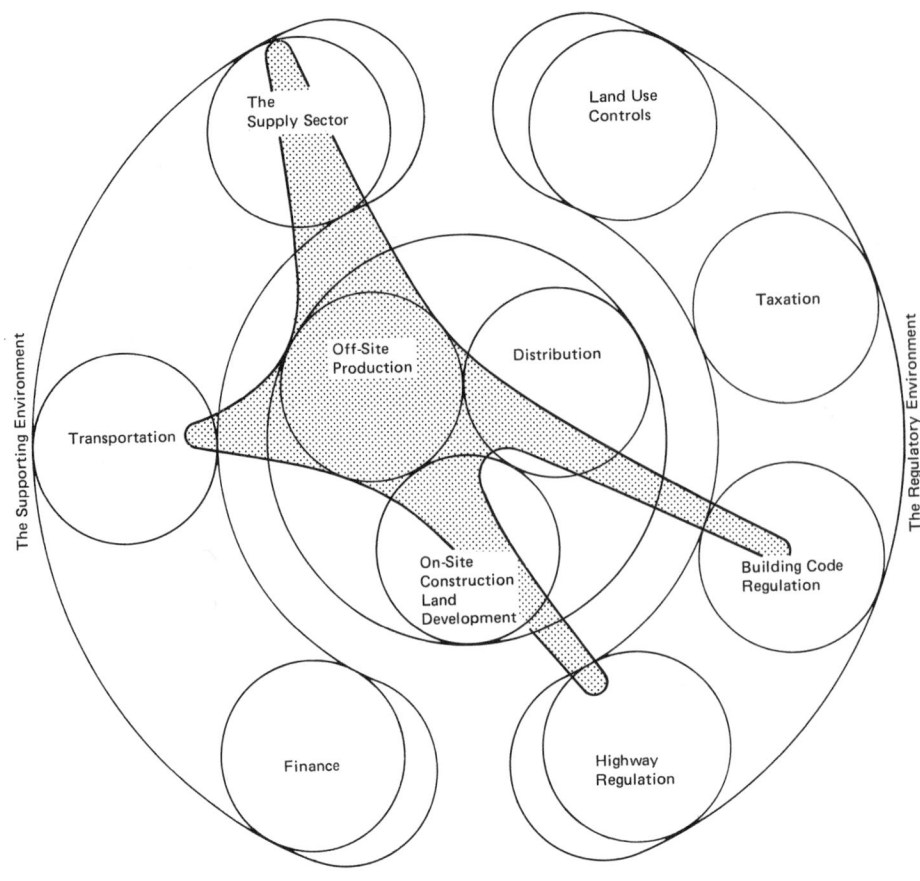

Figure 22.1
Failure model

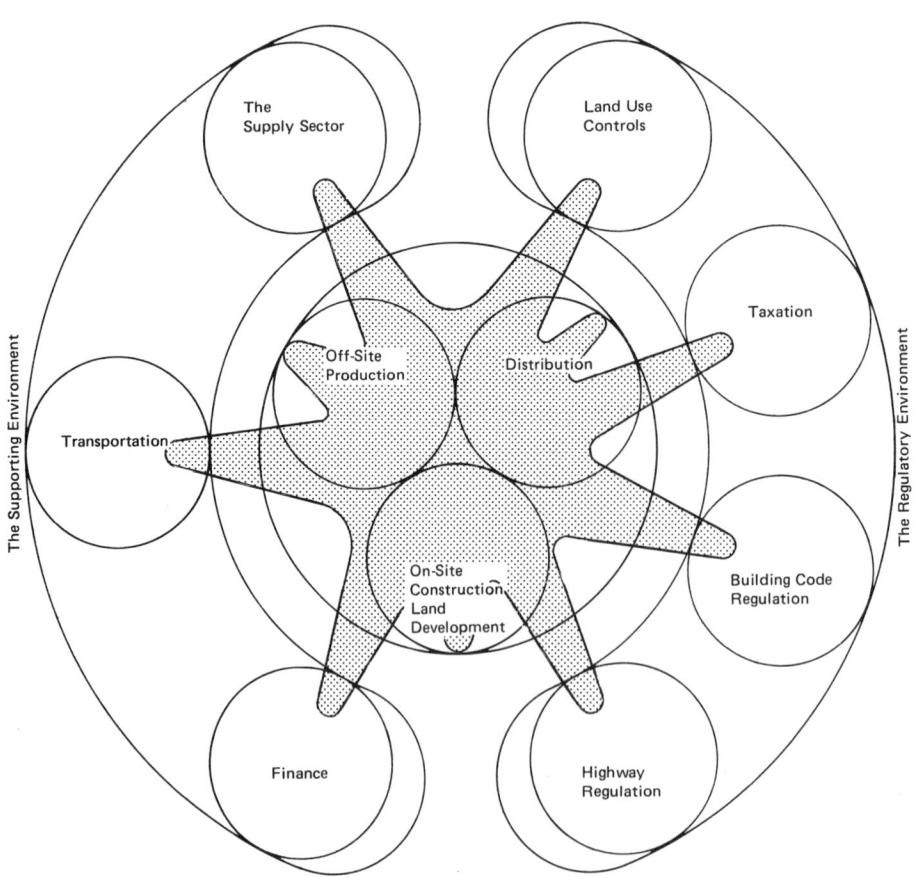

Figure 22.2
Success model

Tomorrow

production, distribution, and land development—must be organized and developed simultaneously. If any of these functions do not currently exist, they must be created. If one function is significantly less mature than the others, it must be brought up to par. The three functions must then be integrated so that the entire process runs smoothly and efficiently. While this may sound simplistic, the importance of this first step is readily apparent for the on-site building industry: in Europe and many developing countries, the vertical process is often top-heavy at the production phase while one or both of the downstream functions are embryonic at best or in some cases do not even exist.

The effective manner in which the mobile home industry has organized production, distribution, and land development provides a striking contrast to the way other building segments regard these functions. The mobile home industry's production system is well designed to respond to its market. Its industrial organization (such as plant distribution, which is constantly adjusted as the market changes) represents an optimal response to demand characteristics. Similarly, its technology, geared to the vagaries of local and seasonal demand, is neither automated nor capital-intensive. Other building sector subsystems have failed to see the intelligence of this approach. In some European countries and in Japan, the highly automated facilities that have been established reveal more of an obsession with high technology than rational business sense. Too many people in the building industries here and abroad continue to see advanced technology as the ultimate panacea, when the significant level of investment involved is simply not justified by the nature of this business. The most common misapprehension shared by building industries in all countries is that the production function is *the* process phase to be emphasized, when it is actually no more important than many of the other functions in the larger system.

Unlike many other building industries, the mobile home industry understands the importance of a shrewdly organized and wide-ranging distribution system; while other segments have essentially ignored this function, the mobile home industry knows that it would be extinct without it. The mobile home industry has based its distribution system on strong convictions about the significance of marketing: the sales function is the most important one; sales must be carefully synchronized with production; the product ideally should be sold before it is produced; and distribution and marketing must determine the product. The industry thus built a network that serves as a reliable piepline connecting the centralized production function with local demand, shielding production from seasonal fluctuations, and divesting the manufacturer of the responsibility for the local tasks of the dealer and the park developer. Compare this logically implemented approach with one of the classic failure stories in the building sector: the bankruptcies of Lustron Corporation and Alside Homes Corporation in the 1950s and 1960s. These two companies represented the largest-scale attempts ever made in the U.S. to introduce automated mass production into housing. After investing tens of millions of dollars to design their steel- and aluminum-based housing systems and put in place production capacities of about 30,000 housing units per year per plant each, these companies realized after production had begun that they had neglected to develop any kind of viable distribution system. At that point it was too late: there was no market for their products, and soon there were no Lustron and Alside Homes. Although this is an extreme example, the problem is a common one in the building industry: throughout the world, it is standard operating procedure for an inventor to patent an innovation, solve the technological problems, even persuade investors to underwrite startup of production, and then begin to worry about marketing the product, when in fact the distribution system should have been developed in conjunction with the other facets of the operation.

For any building industry, demand depends on availability of developed land for placement of the product. At an early stage in its development the mobile home industry realized that no mechanism existed to assure this final outlet for its product, so it built its own market: it became the parent of the park system, and persuaded the financial sector to bankroll this new system and local government to accept it. As soon as the park system became self-sustaining, the mobile home industry withdrew and let it take care of itself. This was a much wiser course to take than the downstream integration into land development that used to be favored by many building manufacturers; the mobile home industry thus avoided spreading managerial and financial resources too thin while still achieving the land-supply mechanism. This tactic is without precedent in the building industry; the other extreme, a common approach taken by the on-site building industries in many countries, is to leave land appropriation decisions to the government. This attitude robs the industry of initiative and control, for it loses time and opportunity waiting for new towns or major new developments to be approved by notoriously slow and tortuous governmental procedures. In fact, in most countries there are groups that demand that govern-ment aggregate demand and guarantee it to business; ironically, this government guarantee is often alleged to be a prerequisite for innovation by industry.

As a building industry organizes and synchronizes its basic shelter production and delivery system, it must simultaneously tackle the equally important task of shaping its supporting environment. Any missing sectors must be created, the workings of the entire environment must be finely adjusted so that it is func-tioning as a whole entity with maximum efficiency, and the supporting environ-ment, the regulatory environment, and the industry itself must be harmoniously integrated. The attention that the mobile home industry has devoted to its sup-porting environment is unusual, for neglect of this sector is a mistake common to the building industries in most countries, which have rarely entertained the possibility that this system can indeed be manipulated.

For a mass-production industry, synchronization of the production and supply functions can be as important as securing suppliers. The mobile home industry's recognition of this fact prompted it to shape a supply sector uniquely responsive to its needs. The industry stimulated the emergence of supplying industries, persuaded suppliers to provide an unusually wide range of mobile home–specific services, convinced suppliers to go beyond this function and become financiers for the mobile home industry, and smoothly synchronized the functions of the industry and its suppliers. These efforts have resulted in the unusually productive relationship between the mobile home industry and its suppliers that remains an important determinant of the industry's success.

Influencing the finance system has been a demanding task for the mobile home industry. Originally, it was very difficult if not impossible for the industry to obtain financing for its various operations because manufacturers, dealers, and park developers had no established business reputation. And consumers could rarely get financing since it was feared that they were bad credit risks who would disappear with their newly purchased "mobile" homes. In the 1940s the mobile home industry, largely through its national association, began to remedy this impossible situation by educating lenders to the fact that these businesses were not only good risks but also profitable, and that consumer financing could be unusually lucrative. These decades of effort have paid off, for the mobile home industry today has a workable (though still not optimal) financing system within its supporting environment.

Conscious of the fact that transportation is the vital link in the mobile home production and delivery process, the mobile home industry has encouraged the formation of a national industry which serves as its transportation system. The existence of such an industry is particularly beneficial for small manufacturers: since they do not need to maintain their own fleets, manufacturers can increase their financial flexibility and better cope with the seasonality of demand because their fixed costs are reduced. The transportation system also adds an important service function to the product package for consumers who wish ever to relocate their units.

In addition to organizing its shelter production and delivery process and shaping its supporting environment, a building industry attempting to structure a comprehensive national industrial system must at the same time be cultivating its regulatory environment. The on-site building industries in most countries have accepted as a given the existing regulatory structures; this fatalism has blinded them to the fact that public regulation must be regarded and managed like any other function as a target of business planning. If necessary, an industry should work to supply any missing component in the regulatory environment, as the mobile home industry did when it lobbied for state governments to adopt its construction code in order to ensure minimum industry standards. An industry must be bold in striving to eliminate or weaken all debilitating regulations, and it must integrate its own structure and its supporting environment in such a fashion that they can accommodate any necessary regulatory burden with the least impact on efficient operation.

The mobile home industry has made major strides in shaping its regulatory environment to its best advantage. In the area of land use controls, a substantial effort has involved improving the public's perception of mobile homes and their residents in order to break down the exclusionary zoning practices that represent one of the industry's primary business problems. The mobile home park system was created not only to provide an effective marketing outlet for the product, but also to help overcome the restrictive zoning policies aimed at excluding low-income groups. By self-policing park developers and operators and nurturing greater professionalism in these functions, the mobile home industry's national association attempted to encourage high-quality parks that would enhance the image of mobile home living. This effort dovetailed with the positive public relations campaign waged over the past few decades by the national association and many state and regional groups. On the other hand, the building manufacturers and on-site builders have retreated from the low-cost housing arena because of the problems associated with negative zoning and have thereby sacrificed a tremendous market. When these industries did serve the low-cost market in the 1940s and 1950s, they found that low-cost housing attempts are almost sure to be penalized by restrictive zoning, while zoning for higher-income housing is easily obtained. Although they vigorously fight "limited growth" and other obstacles to higher-income housing, these two groups have basically accepted the status quo in low-cost housing, with the perverse result that since World War II public regulation has forced two industries that could produce lower-cost shelter to lean more and more toward the higher end of the market.

Shrewd exploitation of its unique taxation situation has also allowed the mobile home industry to manipulate its regulatory environment advantageously. Initially, the industry made good use of the vacuum that resulted when no one thought of taxing mobile homes, and then benefited from the fact that when the states eventually did tax units they used a different and usually less expensive method than that employed for conventional housing. The industry deliberately maintained its product design so that buyers could take advantage of the mobile home's definition as a vehicle for taxation purposes. The taxation definition of a mobile home as "nonhousing" also enabled the industry to retain several other advantages: it was thus still exempt from the local building codes in force for traditional housing, and trade unions did not yet realize that the mobile home industry was actually producing housing. These factors allowed the industry to standardize and mass-produce its product nationwide and to rely on un- or semi-skilled nonunion labor. In essence, the mobile home industry strategically developed its shelter production and delivery system around a tax loophole.

While the industry understands the impact of taxation on its operations, home builders surprisingly do little to fight the ever-rising burden of property taxes on traditional home owners. This could pose a very serious threat to their market if such a taxation burden encourages prospective conventional home buyers to switch to mobile homes or to decide against home ownership in general.

The mobile home industry's response to building code regulation practices which were strangling its efficiency was novel and inspired: it devised its own system and persuaded regulatory authorities to adopt it. Once mobile homes became widely considered as housing, they were often subjected to the stringent local building codes that regulated traditional builders, which forced the industry to build to specifications and methods totally foreign to its own unique process. This placed mobile home manufacturers in an untenable position: if they built to the codes they would lose their competitive edge, and if they did not buyers would not be allowed to site and occupy their units. The mobile home industry, however, foresaw this danger and in the late 1940s set out to develop its own building code. The industry enlisted prestigious national organizations to develop the code while it prepared the regulatory environment: it persuaded most states to adopt and enforce its standard, and also set up an internal self-policing mechanism by operating its own in-plant inspection system. Although this effort took about twenty years, the resulting code, ANSI A119.1, was so sound that in the mid-1970s the U.S. Department of Housing and Urban Development essentially adopted it as the basis for the federal mobile home construction and safety standards. The mobile home industry found a radical but workable solution to its building code problems, but the manufactured and on-site building industries continue to suffer from theirs. For decades building manufacturers either accepted uneconomical mixed runs by producing to different local codes or they built to the highest standard, which permitted more efficient production but resulted in a hopelessly over-engineered product. Although the uniform factory-built housing statutes preempting local codes that many states adopted in the 1970s solved most of the building manufacturer's code problems in those states, this was primarily due to federal and state government initiative rather than industry machinations. On-site builders still put up with a maze of local building codes which raise construction costs because of red tape and delays. This industry has concentrated its energies on fighting the existing system, rather than looking for original alternatives, as the mobile home industry did.

In the area of highway regulation, the mobile home industry again worked to adjust the system to its needs. In the 1940s, when most states did not allow transportation of units wider than 6 or 8 feet, the mobile home industry realized the design constraints inherent in such dimensions: it simply could not offer a product that could compete with traditional housing in terms of either size or good functional layout. It thus began a concerted lobbying campaign to change the dimensional limitations, and over the decades has persuaded state legislatures to expand the maximum width allowance from 6 feet to the present 16 feet, which translates into a gain in floor space from about 100 square feet to approximately 1000 square feet. Lobbying efforts have also been directed toward interstate standardization of dimension limitations, special permits, and traffic regulations concerning the transportation of mobile homes, for the current morass of different requirements in each state is costly and chaotic for the industry. The mobile home industry refused to accept limitations which threatened its competitive advantage, but building industries in other countries have not been so bold in attempting to solve their own problems in this area. In Europe and Japan, for example, manufacturers of three-dimensional building components accept the prevailing general width limit of 2.50 meters (approximately 8 feet), with damaging results: any larger structure must be assembled from many more building components than would be necessary if 12- or 14-wide components could be used. Despite the economic inefficiencies of these dimensional limitations, manufacturers in these countries have made no attempts to restructure the highway regulatory systems to their greater advantage.

The practical implications of my general strategy for the development of the building sector should be clear from this example of how the mobile home industry has successfully melded its shelter production and delivery process and its supporting and regulatory environments into one integrated cohesive system. Any building industry here or abroad attempting to restructure its own system for optimal performance must mount a comprehensive attack, simultaneously developing all facets of its operation. It is equally imperative to remember that the system that results be a national one. Although the markets for shelter are basically regional because the demand side is clearly regional or even local, many characteristics of the supply side are national in scale; for example, many firms in the building industry and its supporting industries are national operations, as are many institutions in the regulatory environment.

In countries with market economies, the rebuilding of the building sector into a comprehensive nationwide system would most effectively and appropriately be undertaken by private initiative. This initiative would most logically be designed and spearheaded by trade associations and other organizations representing the major interests in and affiliated with the sector, in conjunction with major national corporations in the industry and its business environment. A supportive but passive stance would be government's most effective role in such an endeavor.

Once the system has been built by private initiative, it must develop political clout; this is as important for its performance as for its industrial organization, since the building sector is competing with many other industries for scarce resources. A notable example of an industry which has understood this principle is

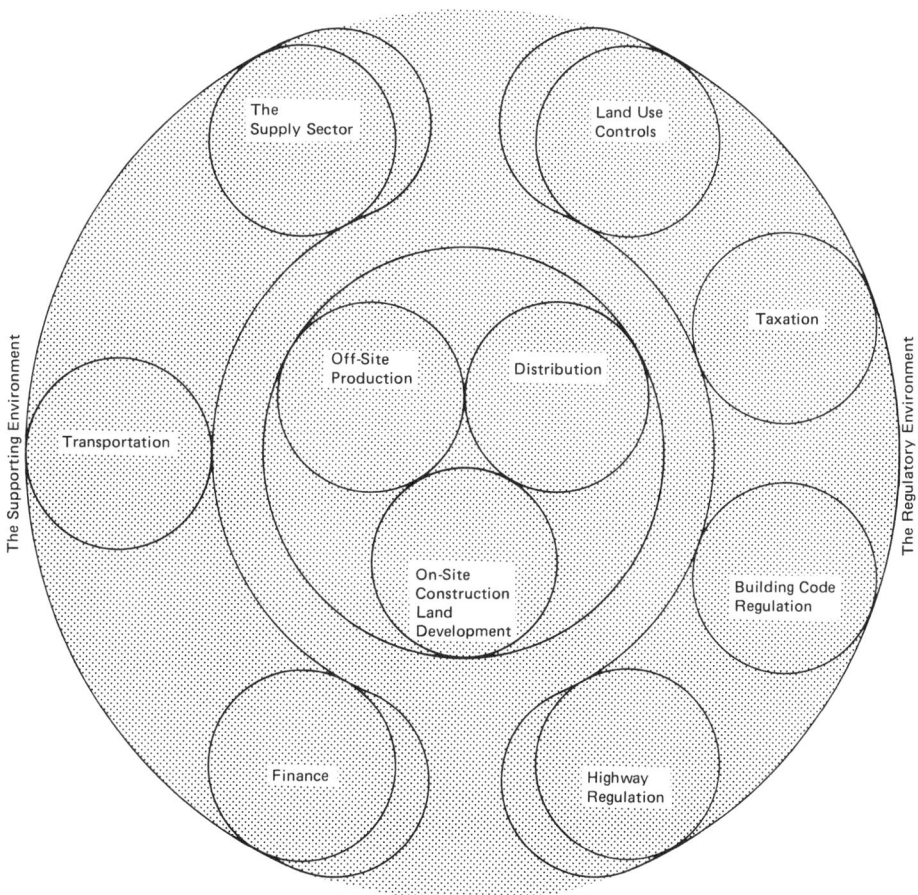

Figure 22.3.
Development of the building sector: Comprehensive restructuring of the total environment

America's traditional housing industry, which owes much of its business success to its superb political organization and strength. However, this need for political weight is not recognized in most countries, and many building industries remain somewhat naive giants in a highly political economy.

This book has examined the mobile home industry in light of my thesis that only a comprehensive attack on all fronts can yield success. Our conclusions can help other subsystems of the U.S. housing industry as well as building industries abroad to achieve a level of economic efficiency similar to that of the mobile home industry. As figure 22.3 illustrates, only a comprehensive rebuilding of the building sector can create an economically more efficient and socially more responsive building industry of tomorrow.

2.1 Architect: The Architects Collaborative Inc. Photographer: Bob Harvey

3.1 Author's archives
3.2 Courtesy of Moduline International, Inc.
3.7 Architect: The Architects Collaborative Inc. Photographer: Phokion Karas
3.8 Architect: Moshe Safdie
3.9 Architect: The Architects Collaborative Inc. Photographer: Phokion Karas

4.1 Courtesy of Schult Mobile Home Corporation
4.2 Courtesy of Schult Mobile Home Corporation
4.3, 4.4 Author's archives
4.5 Courtesy of Liberty Homes, Inc.
4.6 Courtesy of Barry A. Berkus, AIA
4.7 Courtesy of L.C.S. Homes, Inc.
4.8 Courtesy of American Plywood Association
4.9 Courtesy of Barry A. Berkus, AIA
4.10, 4.11 Courtesy of L.C.S. Homes, Inc.

5.1 Source: Liberty Homes, Inc.
5.2–5.5 Photos: Arthur D. Bernhardt
5.6 Courtesy of Zimmer Homes Corporation
5.7 Courtesy of Manufactured Housing Institute
5.9, 5.10 Author's archives
5.11–5.16 Photos: Arthur D. Bernhardt
5.17 Courtesy of Manufactured Housing Institute
5.18–5.24 Photos: Arthur D. Bernhardt
5.25 Courtesy of Barry A. Berkus, AIA
5.26–5.33 Photos: Arthur D. Bernhardt
5.34–5.35 Photos: DMH Company

8.1–8.3 Courtesy of *Mobile-Modular Housing Dealer*

10.1 Author's archives
10.2 Courtesy of Manufactured Housing Institute
10.3 Courtesy of *Mobile-Modular Housing Dealer*
10.4 Courtesy of *Mobile Home Merchandiser*
10.5 Author's archives
10.6 Courtesy of Oak Forest Mobile Estates

11.1 Author's archives
11.2 Courtesy of Oak Forest Mobile Estates
11.3 Author's archives
11.4 Source: Douglas M. Ruth/H.W. Behrend
11.5 Source: H. W. Behrend Associates
11.6 Source: Herbert Behrend
11.7 Source: H. W. Behrend Associates/ANSI A119.3-1977
11.8 Source: H. W. Behrend
11.9 Author's archives
11.10 Courtesy of *Mobile-Modular Housing Dealer*
11.11–11.14 Courtesy of Oak Forest Mobile Estates

12.1 Source: PMHI

13.1 Source: *Automation in Housing/Systems Building News* (some PMHI modifications)

14.1 Courtesy of National Trailer Convoy, Inc.
14.2 Courtesy of Sikorsky Aircraft Division of United Technologies Corporation

16.1, 16.2 Source: 50-state PMHI Survey

17.1 PMHI National Surveys, 1977
17.2 PMHI National Surveys, 1969–1977

19.1 Author's archives

20.2 Courtesy of American Plywood Association
20.3–20.7 Duane A. Kell, Craig E. Rafferty, M.Arch.A.S. Thesis (Supervisor Eduardo F. Catalano, with Waclaw P. Zalewski), M.I.T.
20.8 Architect: Barry A. Berkus, AIA
20.9 Architect: The Architects Collaborative Inc.
20.10 Courtesy of Goldsworthy Engineering, Inc.
20.11 Courtesy of Vindale Corporation
20.12–20.14 Courtesy of American Plywood Association
20.15–20.20 Architect: Barry A. Berkus, AIA
20.21 Courtesy of Vindale Corporation
20.22 Courtesy of Insta-Buildings, Inc. (U.S. Pat. No. 3,461,633; Canadian Pat. No. 938,895)
20.23 Courtesy of U.S. Department of Housing and Urban Development/Electro-Mechanical Corporation
20.24–20.28 Architect: The Architects Collaborative Inc. Photographer: Phokion Karas
20.29 Ho-Ling Teng, M.Arch. Thesis (Supervisor Jan Lubicz-Nycz, with Waclaw P. Zalewski), M.I.T.
20.30, 20.31 Lawrence S. Gordon, M.Arch. Thesis (Supervisor Jan Lubicz-Nycz, with Kevin Lynch), M.I.T.
20.32–20.34 Architect: The Architects Collaborative Inc. Photographer: Phokion Karas
20.35 Courtesy of U.S. Department of Housing and Urban Development/Pantek Corporation
20.36–20.42 Courtesy of American Plywood Association
20.43 Architect: Conklin & Rossant
20.44 Lawrence S. Gordon, M.Arch. Thesis (Supervisor Jan Lubicz-Nycz, with Kevin Lynch), M.I.T.
20.45–20.48 Architect: The Architects Collaborative Inc. Photographer: Wayne Soverns, Jr.
20.49 Courtesy of American Plywood Association
20.50–20.51 Courtesy of Insta-Buildings, Inc. (U.S. Pat. No. 3,461,633; Canadian Pat. No. 938,895)
20.52–20.54 Courtesy of American Plywood Association/Architect: Paul Rudolph
20.55–20.56 Architect: Moshe Safdie
20.57–20.59 Architect: Barry A. Berkus, AIA
20.60–20.61 Courtesy of Hercoform
20.62 Courtesy of *Concrete Products*
20.63, 20.64 Architect: The Architects Collaborative Inc. Photographer: David Hirsch
20.65 Herbert G. Zeller, M.Arch. Thesis (Supervisor Jan Lubicz-Nycz), M.I.T.
20.66 Architect: Moshe Safdie
20.67, 20.68 Charles C. Wong, M.Arch. Thesis (Supervisor Jan Lubicz-Nycz), M.I.T.
20.69–20.71 Architect: The Architects Collaborative Inc. Photographer: Wayne Soverns, Jr.
20.72 Architect: Travers/Johnson
20.73 Courtesy of U.S. Department of Housing and Urban Development/Shelley Engineering Corporation
20.74–20.75 Architect: Moshe Safdie
20.76 Architect: The Architects Collaborative Inc. Photographer: Phokion Karas
20.77 Courtesy of *Concrete Products*
20.78, 20.79 Architect: Kirk-Wallace-McKinley
20.80–20.82 Alexander P. Bailey et al.,

M.Arch. Thesis (Supervisor Jan Lubicz-Nycz, with Waclaw P. Zalewski), M.I.T.

20.83 Richard G. Henriquez, M.Arch. Thesis (Supervisor Jan Lubicz-Nycz, with Waclaw P. Zalewski), M.I.T.

20.84–20.85 Ho-Ling Teng, M.Arch. Thesis (Supervisor Jan Lubicz-Nycz, with Waclaw P. Zalewski), M.I.T.

20.86–20.89 Francis A. Bulbulian, Joel H. Goodman, M.Arch. Thesis (Supervisor Eduardo F. Catalano, with Waclaw P. Zalewski), M.I.T.

20.90–20.92 David K. Hyun, Keun S. Lee, M.Arch. Thesis (Supervisor Eduardo F. Catalano), M.I.T.

20.93, 20.94 Architect: Moshe Safdie

Index

highway regulations in, 392, 393, 395, 397
land use controls in, 332, 334
location of mobile homes in, 217
number of mobile homes in, 209
quality levels in, 235, 237
taxation of mobile homes in, 358, 368

Jackson, Sen. Henry, 351
James v. Valtierra, 349
Joiners and Carpenters, 83
Joint ventures, for park financing, 321–322
Judy-Berner Blue Book, 365

Kansas
highway regulations in, 392, 393, 395, 396, 397, 398
land use controls in, 332, 334, 451
location of mobile homes in, 217
mobile home production volume in, 44
number of mobile homes in, 209
quality levels in, 235, 237
taxation of mobile homes in, 358, 368
Kennedy Park Homes Association v. City of Lackawanna, 349
Kentucky
highway regulations in, 392, 393, 395, 397
land use controls in, 332, 334, 451
location of mobile homes in, 217
number of mobile homes in, 209
quality levels in, 234, 237
taxation of mobile homes in, 358, 368
Kitchens, costs of, 138, 148
Korean War, and mobile home production, 30

Labor
and assembly point mode, 108, 109
vs. automation, 111
and average pay, 81
consumption, 124, 125
costs of, 138, 144
direct costs, 136, 137
in mobile home industry, 15, 22–23, 78–83
model costs for, 59, 60
productivity measures for, 90, 91
and quality control, 129
regional statistics for, 79
and seasonality, 93
unionization, 57, 82–83
and wage structure, 80
Land
costs of, 267
and future of mobile home industry, 503–504
Land development, of park owners, 224
Landscaping, in mobile home parks, 243, 250, *256*
Land use controls, 20–21, 66, 213, 218
complete exclusions, 331
constructive exclusions, 337–338
and conventional housing, 352
frontage consents, 337
historical perspective on, 329–331
impact on industry performance, 344–347
limits on numbers, 336
linear probability model for, 343
and local preferences, 338–344
policy alternatives for, 262
restriction of mobile homes to parks, 331–334
and taxation methods, 367
time limits, 336
Lavoie v. Bigwood, 346
Leasing, of mobile home units, 178, 324
Leasing agreements, 233, 299
Lenders, and park developers, 325. *See also* Financing

Lending institutions, 301
Liability
of dealer, 189–190
of manufacturer, 189
Licensing, of dealerships, 192
Lighting, mobile home building code standards for, 381
Linear probability model, for land use controls, 343
Linoleum, 101. *See also* Floor system
Loading conditions, 98
Loans
FHA-insured, 321
government insurance programs for, 312, 313
mobile home, 310
term, 303
Location, mobile home
park vs. non-park, 215, 216
on private property, 371
and taxation, 372
Location, park, 245–246
and community facilities, 248
and land use controls, 346
Lorimer, Chiodo, and Associates, 396
Lot organization, 172–173
Lots
in mobile home parks, 249
new mobile homes displayed at, 173
and park density, 270
Louisiana
highway regulations in, 392, 393, 395, 397
land use controls in, 332, 334
large retailers in, 160
location of mobile homes in, 217
number of mobile homes in, 209
quality levels in, 234, 237
taxation of mobile homes in, 358, 368
Low-line, price structure for, 145. *See also* Product
Low-rise stacked units, 411, *438*–453
parallel configurations, *445–448*
perpendicular configurations, *442–444*
perpendicular and parallel configurations, *448–450*
upended components for, *451–453*

Maine
highway regulations in, 392, 393, 395, 397
land use controls in, 332, 334, 350
location of mobile homes in, 217
number of mobile homes in, 209
quality levels in, 234, 237
taxation of mobile homes in, 358, 368
Maintenance, 188–189
Management. *See also* Firms
inventory, 128
park, 257–262 (*see also* Parks)
and plant organization, 127–130
of production, 124–130
and recession, 88
and unionization, 83
Managers, park
background of, 153
characteristics of, 257–259
and dealers, 262
principal types of, 259
responsibilities of, 260
Manufactured building industry, 9. *See also* Building sector
Manufactured Housing Institute (MHI), 17, 170, 377
Dealer Relations Committee, 175
design criteria for mobile homes, 250
Land Development Committee of, 218
mobile home definition of, 373

and park system, 205
Research Center of, 282, 289
Manufacturers of mobile homes
cost regressions for, 141
dealership representation of, 175
and finance sector, 299–304
inventories of, 17
leverage factors for, 303
liability of, 189
models of, 95
modular home, 489
parks developed by, 322
PMHI model of, *302*
relations with dealers, 174–175
remedial actions of, 385
research and development of, 282
return-on-investment (ROI) figures for, 304
and suppliers, 18
vs. transporters, 297
transport system of, 295
Manufacturing firms, mobile homes. *See also* Firms
entry into market, 35–36
sector of origin of, 35
size characteristics of, 35–36
Manufacturing process
architectural design, 95–98
cost analysis of, 135–144
and facilities engineering, 128
mobile home construction, 100
Market, mobile home, 31
advertising in, 184
in future, 406–407
industry control of, 13
preowned homes in, 169
and price policies, 180
product differentiation in, 68
profile of, 182–184
regional shares in, 42
trailer coach, 29
used units in, 171, 179
Marketing, in supply sector, 284–285
Marketing research, 182–185
Markup
computation of, 316
dealer, 180, 307
retail, 315
Maryland
highway regulations in, 392, 393, 395, 397
land use controls in, 332, 334
location of mobile homes in, 217
number of mobile homes in, 209
quality levels in, 234, 237
taxation of mobile homes in, 358, 368
Massachusetts
highway regulations in, 392, 393, 395, 397
land use controls in, 332, 334, 339, 350, 351
location of mobile homes in, 217
number of mobile homes in, 209
quality levels in, 234, 237
taxation of mobile homes in, 358, 368
Mass production, 107. *See also* Assembly line
Material-handling equipment, 111
Materials, 23
costs, 136, 137, 138
metal, 119, 120
model costs of, 59, 60
Mechanical service systems, 104–106, 118. *See also* Service systems
Mechanization, 79
Medium-line, price structure for, 145. *See also* Product
Megastructure, 412, *466–479*
cantilever configuration, *472–473*
post-and-beam frame, *470–471*
suspension structure, *474–478*

Metal, in mobile home construction, 119,
120
Metal stud systems, 408
Michigan
  highway regulations in, 392, 393, 395, 397
  land use controls in, 332, 334
  location of mobile homes in, 217
  mobile home production volume in, 44
  number of mobile homes in, 209
  quality levels in, 235, 237
  taxation of mobile homes in, 359, 368
Mid-Atlantic states
  location of mobile homes in, 216
  new mobile home parks in, 218
  park system revenues in, 229, 231
  quality levels in, 234, 237
  Woodall-rated parks in, 219, 221
Migrant laborers, 30
Military bases
  and mobile homes, 365
  trailer parks on, 30
"Minimum Property Standards for Mobile
  Home Courts," 334
Minnesota
  highway regulations in, 392, 393, 395, 397
  land use controls in, 332, 334, 339, 351
  location of mobile homes in, 217
  number of mobile homes in, 209
  quality levels in, 235, 237
  taxation of mobile homes in, 359, 368
Minority groups, and zoning restrictions, 349
Mississippi
  highway regulations in, 392, 393, 395, 397
  land use controls in, 332, 334
  large retailers in, 160
  location of mobile homes in, 217
  number of mobile homes in, 209
  quality levels in, 234, 237
  taxation of mobile homes in, 359, 368
Missouri
  highway regulations in, 392, 393, 395, 397
  land use controls in, 332, 334
  location of mobile homes in, 217
  number of mobile homes in, 209
  quality levels in, 235, 237
  taxation of mobile homes in, 359, 368
Mixed line method, of production scheduling,
  129
Mixed system, of taxation, 362
Mobile home building code, 382. See also
  Building code; Federal Mobile Home
  Construction and Safety Standards
  enforcement of, 382
  evolution of, 377–380
  technical regulation of, 380–382
Mobile home industry
  architectural innovation in, 405–407
  barriers to entry to, 93
  capacity utilization in, 73, 76
  concentration of, 47–50
  cost performance, 141
  defined, 13
  diversification in, 52–57
  dominance of larger units in, 38
  economies of scale in, 57–67
  failure in, *504*
  financial sector in, 19
  financial structure of, *300*
  functional systems of, 13
  growth in, 38, 84–90, 200–201
  identity crisis of, 493
  impact of land use controls on, 344–347
  impact of taxation on, 371–373
  interactions of, *16*
  major problems of, 190
  optimal future for, 497–501

organization of, 505
origin of, 31, 34–35, 93
performance of, 22, 34
potential of, ix, 9, 23–25, 130–134
potential product capabilities of, *11, 24, 25*
production trends in, 36–42
and realty tax, 375
regulatory environment for, 19–22, 483–484
  (see also Regulations)
seasonality in, 72 (see also Seasonality)
service companies in, 307
stagnation in, 494
structure of, *14*, 42–83
success of, 488, *504*
supply sector of, 17–18 (see also Supply
  sector)
supporting environment for, 10, 17–19, 480
transition of, 191
transportation system in, 18–19, 291–298
wage structure in, 80–82
Mobile home lots, 172–173. See also Lots
Mobile Home Manufacturers Association, 30
*Mobile Home Owners Protective Association
  v. Town of Chatham,* 334
Mobile home paper, 312
Mobile Home and Park Directory, 218
Mobile home park industry, 205
Mobile home park operators, 369–370
Mobile home parks. See Park system
Mobile Home and Recreational Vehicle Dealer,
  189
Mobile homes
  ANSI standards for, 21
  commercial classification for, 336
  communities of, *239* (see also Communities)
  construction of, 100–106
  controls on, 331–335
  defined, 13, 387 n.7, 387 n.8
  design objectives of, 95
  dimensions of, 22
  disadvantages of, 30
  doublewide (or multisection), *14, 33, 36* (see
    also Doublewides)
  economic life of, 310
  8-wide, *32*
  18-wide, 42
  evolution of, *32–33*
  expandable 10-wide, *33*
  fire resistance of, 410
  14-wide, 42
  geographical distribution of, 207–211
  hauling of, 292
  history of, 29
  inventory of, 207–213
  legal definition of, 374
  movement of, 291
  national distribution of, 212
  official definition of, 355
  in park system, 213–215
  per-square-foot comparisons, 148
  pipe connections for, *254*
  possibilities for, 411
  preowned, 169, 194
  sales form for, 146, 147
  vs. single-unit housing, 37
  single-wide (or single-section), *14*
  structural box design of, 98
  10-wide, 31
  "tin-can" appearance of, 69
  trends in, 47
  12-wide, *33*
  used, 179, 194
  various uses of, 406–407
Mobile homes vs. conventional, 106–107
  cost advantages of, 401
  and family income, 241

Mobile/Manufactured Housing Merchandiser,
  284
Mobile/Modular Housing Dealer Annual
  Directory, 69, 170, 189
Model parks, 190, 191. See also Park system
Models
  variations in costs for, 141
  yearly changes in, 127
Modular home, 13, 491
Modular housing industry, diseconomies in,
  18–19
"Mom and Pop" tradition, 222, 232
Monopoly, 67, 346
Montana
  highway regulations in, 392, 393, 395, 397
  land use controls in, 332, 334
  location of mobile houses in, 217
  number of mobile homes in, 209
  quality levels in, 235, 237
  taxation of mobile homes in, 359, 368
Mortgages, 313, 314, 321
Moss, Frank, 378
Motor vehicles, taxation of, 363
Mountain states
  land use controls in, 332, 334
  location of mobile homes in, 216
  park system ROE in, 231
  quality levels in, 235, 237
  quality of parks in, 238
  Woodall-rated parks in, 219, 221
Multilot chains, 172
Multiple units
  parallel, flush, *422*
  parallel, staggered, *423, 424–425*
  perpendicular and parallel, *427*
Municipal revenues, and land use controls,
  340, 342

Nader, Ralph, 378
National Association of Home Builders, 192
National Conference of States on Building
  Codes and Standards (NCSBCS), 378, 385,
  387
National Electrical Code, 379
National Fire Protection Association (NFPA),
  377, 379
National Gypsum, 133, 285
*National Land & Investment Co. v. Easttown
  Township Board of Adjustment,* 349
National Mobile Home Advisory Council,
  378
National Mobile Home Construction and
  Safety Standards Act, 368, 373, 374, 382
Nebraska
  highway regulations in, 392, 393, 395, 397
  land use controls in, 332, 334
  location of mobile homes in, 217
  number of mobile homes in, 210
  quality levels in, 235, 237
  taxation of mobile homes in, 359, 368
Nectow v. City of Cambridge, 329
Nevada
  highway regulations in, 392, 393, 395, 397
  land use controls in, 332, 334
  location of mobile homes in, 217
  number of mobile homes in, 210
  quality levels in, 235, 237
  taxation of mobile homes in, 359, 368
New England
  land use controls in, 332, 334
  location of mobile homes in, 216
  mobile homes in, 396
  new mobile homes in, 218
  park rentals in, 230
  park system ROE in, 231
  quality levels in, 234, 237